Criminal Law

Criminal Law

An Introduction to Key Concepts and Cases

Henry F. Fradella, J.D., Ph.D.

OXFORD
UNIVERSITY PRESS

OXFORD
UNIVERSITY PRESS

Oxford University Press is a department of the University of Oxford. It furthers the University's objective of excellence in research, scholarship, and education by publishing worldwide. Oxford is a registered trade mark of Oxford University Press in the UK and certain other countries.

Published in the United States of America by Oxford University Press
198 Madison Avenue, New York, NY 10016, United States of America.

Library of Congress Control Number: 2022903689
ISBN 978–0–19–068247–7

9 8 7 6 5 4 3 2 1
Printed by Marquis, Canada

Contents

Preface

When I started teaching criminal law to advanced undergraduate students roughly thirty years ago, I was dismayed to learn that I had two choices. My first option was to adopt a criminal law casebook that was published primarily for the law school market. My second option was to adopt a criminal law textbook specifically written for use at the undergraduate level. I found both options to be less than satisfactory.

THE CASEBOOK APPROACH

Casebooks are designed to present students with a range of edited judicial opinions relevant to each topic. This typically translates into somewhere between three and six cases per topic, resulting in most criminal law casebooks ranging from between 650 and 1,200 pages. As a result, these books are too long and too expensive. But more importantly, I rejected the casebook approach because casebooks lack sufficient pedagogy for students. To be sure, learning how to read a case is an important skill that I want my students to develop. But casebooks are filled with too many edited judicial opinions that are often presented without any context. Law students routinely have trouble making sense of these cases because they were not written for a novice audience; judicial opinions are written by judges for lawyers and other judges. Thus, casebooks throw beginning learners into the deep end of the pool, often without any resources to help those learners succeed.[1] Consider the following critique of law school casebooks by legal research and writing instructor Sam Jacobson:

> First, casebooks do not establish an adequate foundation for learning when they lack textual explanation and guidance. Modern textbooks generally begin each section by highlighting what the learner should extract from the section and by providing valuable context for the discussion. They end by summarizing the main ideas of the section and listing questions that the learner should be able to answer after having read the material. In between, they guide the reader with the use of various organizational cues, including introductory paragraphs, headings, thesis sentences, and transitions. Casebooks, on the other hand, typically include none of this information. . . . [M]ost casebooks only include notes after each case or group of cases. Those notes sometimes include information that would have been more helpful had it preceded the cases, but more often the notes refer the reader to materials outside the casebook or pose questions that can be answered only with additional research.

Second, casebooks present information inconsistent with the way most students learn. The vast majority of people are top-to-bottom learners; that is, they need to know why they are reading something before the details of what they are reading make sense. Without an overview or contextual information, students do not know what details are important or why they are important. However, with an overview and contextual information, the details have something to which they can stick. Think of the overview and contextual information as being conceptual velcro. Casebooks are missing the velcro. They present information from bottom-to-top, although most often the top is missing unless a helpful note is included after the case. Instead, casebooks by their nature are a compilation of details, the details from many cases. The burden is on the learner to determine how the details fit together, usually through the process of outlining. . . .

Third, casebooks do not present material efficiently. At times, inefficiency in presentation may serve a valid pedagogical purpose, such as to advance critical thinking skills. Most often, though, what is inefficient is also ineffective. Course materials are most effective when they lead to deep learning. Deep learning occurs when learners have a new experience (for example, reading new material), reflect on it, draw conclusions from it, and apply it to new situations. . . . If a case includes a useful statement of policy, discuss the policy rather than include the entire case. If the test for evaluating a matter has changed over time, summarize the relevant historical information rather than include the earlier cases. If cases provide interesting factual variations, create hypotheticals rather than include all the cases. The cases provided in a casebook should not inspire a parody of a lightbulb joke:

Question: How many cases does it take to cover a topic?

Answer: Nine. Four to establish the test that existed when the authors were in law school. One to establish the current test, what it means, and what policy supports it. And four to explain why the decision was wrong or why the decision would have been wrong if the facts had been different.[2]

In short, law school cases are far too challenging and unnecessarily complicated. So, I went with my second option: a traditional criminal law textbook.

THE TEXTBOOK APPROACH

On the plus side, criminal law textbooks are rich in pedagogy designed to facilitate learning not only through textual explanation, but also through an organizational structure that includes "introductory paragraphs, headings, thesis sentences, and transitions."[3] But their advantages pretty much stop there.

Oversimplification

Most criminal law textbooks grossly oversimply the law by presenting the "black letter law" (the rules) concerning major crimes and defenses. Textbooks rarely present any corresponding exploration of the grey areas that most cases occupy beyond the basic rules of law.

In addition to watering down the criminal law, most of the textbooks do not present edited judicial opinions of sufficient length, if at all. This, in turn, means that students are not presented with the opportunity for developing the critical thinking skills associated with reading a case. In other words, students do not get to hone their deductive, inductive, and analogical reasoning skills by dissecting a case into its critical components and extrapolating the complexities of legal reasoning beyond the simple "black letter" rules. Sure, there are one or two exceptions to this general shortcoming, but even those few books that included edited cases often reduced them to a single page or two. In other words, the cases are often distilled to such a degree that the critical thinking benefits of reasoning from the cases is diminished so significantly as to be of little value.

Broader Learning Goals

Another shortcoming of the approach taken in most criminal law textbooks concerns the focus on "the law." But what "the law" is today may not be "the law" tomorrow. After all, law evolves through both legislative and judicial actions. I want my students to gain an understanding of how and why criminal law evolved into its current status. To do so, I think it is important for the study of criminal law to be grounded in a historical framework. Put differently, I want my students to understand how select crimes were defined at common law and how those definitions—sometimes from hundreds of years ago—might still affect how a crime is defined today.

On a related note, I think it is very important that the study of law be grounded in the liberal arts tradition.[4] Unlike law schools that are designed to mint legal professionals, college degrees are supposed to represent more than professional or paraprofessional training. Many criminal justice programs fail in this regard because they emphasize the vocational over the academic.[5] As a result, criminal justice programs are often not respected by other academic disciplines at four-year colleges and universities.[6] Indeed, the discipline has been criticized even from within as lacking "theoretical integrity and coherence."[7]

Partially to address these shortcomings, and partially because I believe deeply in the value of the liberal arts,[8] I believe that the study of criminal law should be grounded in the humanities and social sciences—particularly history, philosophy, and sociology. To my dismay, most criminal law textbooks fail in this regard.

GROWING FRUSTRATION AND A SOLUTION

The first few semesters that I taught criminal law, I tried several undergraduate textbooks. I found a few that were pretty good, but none that met all the goals I had for teaching the course in a manner that promoted learning beyond the most basic subject matter. In other words, I found most criminal law textbooks to be appropriate for lower-division instruction, but completely inadequate for challenging students in upper-division undergraduate or graduate coursework. So, I switched to a law school casebook for one year; it was an unmitigated disaster for all of the reasons Sam Jacobson identified and as previously mentioned.

As my frustration grew, I decided to create a hybrid—a cross between a criminal law casebook and textbook. I taught with my own book for nearly a decade. Not only were my students learning the "black letter" criminal law, but they also learned the nuances of applying the law to complicated fact patterns. Thus, they were developing critical thinking skills that would serve them well whether they went on to law school, a career in law enforcement, or any other career that demands reasoning abilities beyond the regurgitation of rote memorization. Additionally, their understanding of the criminal law was grounded in history; my students understood where the law came from why it evolved into its present form. Moreover, they understood the shortcomings of the law—especially with regard to the law's role in perpetuating systemic disparities on the bases of race, ethnicity, sex and gender, and sexual orientation. In other words, my students could *critique* the law using both philosophical, historical, and empirical arguments. Perhaps best of all, my students reported to me on course evaluations that they valued my approach to teaching the course and the corresponding learning they felt it facilitated. But that approach only served my students. With the publication of this book by Oxford University Press, other instructors and their students can now avail themselves of what I call a "hybrid approach" to teaching and learning about criminal law.

A HYBRID APPROACH

Criminal Law: An Introduction to Key Concepts and Cases offer a unique hybrid approach to learning criminal law. Most textbooks grossly oversimply the law by presenting the "black letter law" for major and defenses, but they rarely present any corresponding exploration of the gray areas that exist beyond the basic rules of law. Conversely, casebooks present numerous edited judicial opinions, often with any context. They are quite long and very expensive. *Criminal Law* takes the best from each of these approaches by merging textual pedagogy and case analyses into a coherent framework that includes legal history, social context, and public policy. *Criminal Law* takes a historical approach by presenting the law as it evolved at common law (from the English heritage through the mid-twentieth century in the United States), and then comparing and contrasting the common law with the modern statutory approach to crimes set forth in the American Law Institute's highly influential Model Penal Code (which forms the basis of contemporary statutory criminal law in more than forty US states). After providing such comparative pedagogy for each crime or defense, *Criminal Law* presents an edited case or two (unlike the three to six edited cases per topic in most casebooks) that allows the reader to compare and contrast how the "black letter law" plays out in the real world. After each case, a series of questions challenge students to engage in critical thinking about the case and its implications as precedent. Finally, chapters contain a number of additional pedagogical features that focus on public policy concerns and statutory interpretation skills using penal laws from a variety of US states.

I believe this hybrid approach offers the best of both worlds for teaching and learning criminal law. Moreover, by grounding criminal law in the liberal arts tradition, this book fosters creative intellect. "A creative mind is one that interrogates the world around it, posing questions of order and meaning, that never accepts common knowledge without reflection, that can initiate a search for answers to its own questions, and that can communicate lucidly its questing and discovery."[9]

Henry F. Fradella
Arizona State University

1

Introduction to Criminal Law and Punishment

LEARNING OBJECTIVES

1. Describe the different ways in which society seeks to control deviant behaviors.
2. Discuss the sources and functions of law.
3. Identify key milestones in the historical development of criminal law.
4. Compare and contrast the major philosophical justifications for criminal punishment.
5. Analyze how the principles of culpability, legality, and proportionality limit criminal punishment.
6. Evaluate the relationship between law and morality as it applies to the criminalization and punishment of deviant behaviors.

Outline

INTRODUCTION

This book is devoted to the body of law that defines select deviant behaviors as criminal offenses against the state. Our exploration of criminal law will primarily focus on the elements of various criminal offenses and the applicable defenses to such crimes. In the first two chapters, we will also explore the limits the US Constitution places on the creation of criminal laws and the punishments associated with violations of those laws.

One of the key features of this book is the integration of real criminal cases. By exploring the written decisions of judges, you will see that the law is rarely black or white, but rather is nuanced into various shades of gray. Applying the rules of law to the facts of particular cases helps to facilitate a deeper understanding of the complexities of criminal law. In doing so, you should develop the ability to reason through the logic (and, perhaps, illogic) of the criminal law as you encounter it in the future as a professional in the justice system.

DEVIANCE AND SOCIAL CONTROL

Deviance and crime are widely misunderstood concepts. **Deviance** refers to any departure from behaviors that are typical, acceptable, or expected.[1] By contrast, a **crime** is "an intentional act [or omission] in violation of the criminal law . . . committed without defense or excuse, and penalized by the state as a felony or misdemeanor."[2] As Figure 1.1 illustrates, crime is a subset of deviant behaviors.

For instance, shoplifting is a crime because it is prohibited under criminal law, but it is also an example of deviance, because it is viewed as an unacceptable behavior. In contrast, failing to hold a door open for the person immediately behind you could be viewed as deviant because it violates an expected behavior, even though such a failure of courtesy is not criminal.

Throughout life, we look to social norms to tell us what to do and not do. **Norms** that tell us what we ought to do—get an education, respect our elders, obey the law—are *prescriptive norms*. Norms that tell us what we ought not to do—commit crimes, lie, drop out of high school—are *proscriptive norms*. Norms vary across both situation and time.[3] For example, language that you use with friends may be inappropriate to use at home with your family. Similarly, behaviors that are considered perfectly acceptable by today's standards, such as men wearing earrings, would have been taboo to many of our grandparents or great-grandparents.

Norms also vary across cultures. For example, belching at the dinner table is considered rude in many Western cultures, but is considered to be a compliment to the host or cook in some African and Asian countries.[4] Even within a given culture, there may be subcultures that have their own set of norms that differ from those of the larger society. Subcultures may exist based on race, ethnicity, religion, sexual orientation, occupation, and even hobbies. For example, in certain ethnic subcultures, wine is routinely served with dinner, even to family members under the legal drinking age. It is important to note that the deviant norms and behaviors of subcultures may or may not be criminal. For example, nuns may be deviant in terms of how they act and dress, but are likely law-abiding citizens.

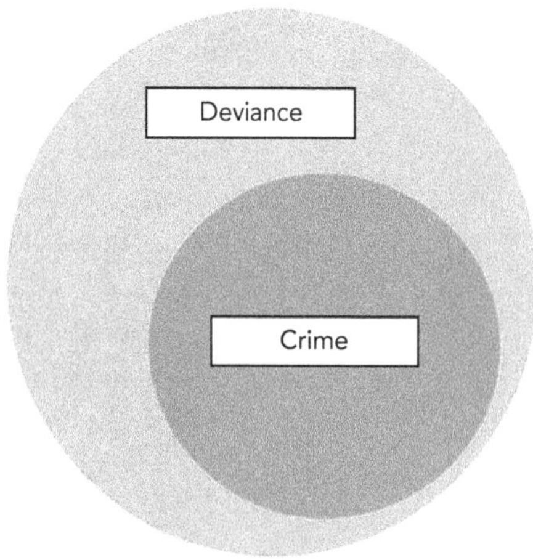

FIGURE 1.1
Crime and Deviance

The processes by which society controls behavior at the individual and group levels are known as **social controls.**[5] Today, the term tends to be used more narrowly to refer to the mechanisms by which deviant behaviors are controlled, both informally and formally.

Informal social controls are the tools used to control behavior in everyday social life—"within families, friendships, neighborhoods, organizations, and groups of all kinds."[6] They are both *internal* (often referred to as "self-control") and *external* (often referred to as "relational controls"). Virtually any type of positive or negative reaction from others constitutes informal social control. Positive reactions—such as praise, a smile, tangible rewards, and emotional support—encourage and positively reinforce desired behaviors. In contrast, negative reactions—such as ridicule, gossip, corporal punishment, shaming, ostracism, and even something as simple as a disapproving look—discourage and punish undesired behaviors.

Formal social controls are those mechanisms exercised by government to control human behavior. Law is the most obvious form of formal social control, but it is not the only instrument of formal social control.[7] For example, welfare agencies and medicine also exert control over those who deviate from societal norms.[8] These need not be "bad" people; for instance, people who are poor or mentally ill are deviant because their behavior runs counter to social expectations, sometimes through no fault of their own.

The criminal justice system represents the ultimate form of formal social control because through the power to arrest, hold trials, and punish, the government seeks to regulate behavior. Nevertheless, the criminal justice system increasingly bridges formal and informal social control with policies such as community policing, community courts, and victim-offender reconciliation programs, all of which involve the criminal justice system collaborating with community partners to promote the same desired behaviors.[9]

Styles of Social Control

Donald Black, a leading scholar of law and society, argued that law is used as a tool of formal social control in four related yet distinct ways, as summarized in Table 1.1.[10]

In societies where informal social control is strong and effective in controlling behavior, there is less need to rely on law to do so. Conversely, in societies lacking strong and consistent systems of informal social control, it becomes necessary to have a greater reliance on law to control behavior.

All four styles of formal social control listed in Table 1.1 are important for the functioning of the US justice system. However, the therapeutic style of social control is intertwined with both the public health and criminal justice systems because of the role that medicine—especially psychiatry and psychology—plays in defining and treating deviant behavior. One of the most comprehensive treatments of medicine as an institution of social control is Peter Conrad and Joseph Schneider's book *Deviance and Medicalization: From Badness to Sickness*. In their work, Conrad and Schneider trace the history of how "moral-criminal definitions of deviance

Table 1.1 Styles of Social Control

Style of Social Control	Summary of Style
Penal	Views the violator of a social norm, which has been codified into criminal law, as an offender who is deserving of official condemnation and punishment through the criminal justice system. Four main justifications are proffered for using criminal law as a tool of formal social control: retribution, deterrence, rehabilitation, and incapacitation.
Compensatory	Focuses on providing restitution to the victim of an act. In other words, it attempts to compensate a wronged or aggrieved person in a way that restores them as closely as possible to the *status quo ante*—the way they were before the deviant person wronged them. This is typically accomplished via the civil justice system when the victim sues the rule-breaker and is financially compensated for injuries or losses. Restitution may also be ordered as part of a criminal sentence.
Therapeutic	Views the deviant person as someone who needs help to become nondeviant. This is often accomplished via science and medicine, especially psychology and psychiatry.
Conciliatory	Attempts to create and preserve social harmony via dispute resolution, or mediation. This style allows both sides to express their displeasures or concerns and work toward a compromise that not only removes the irritants in a relationship, but may also produce some semblance of social harmony.

[changed] to medical ones."[11] By labeling something a disease, the moral blame is shifted away from the individual, who comes to be viewed as "sick" and in need of treatment, instead of being viewed as "bad" and in need of punishment. For example, the excessive consumption of alcohol was once considered sinful and immoral, requiring punishment. Through the process of medicalization, such behavior is now understood as the disease of alcoholism, which requires treatment. Similarly, in the past, an unruly, unfocused child was thought to need discipline. Today, however, such behaviors may be symptoms of a condition called attention-deficit/hyperactivity disorder (ADHD), which may be treated instead of punished. Defining a deviant behavior as an illness, or a symptom of an illness, and then providing medical intervention to treat the illness, is what Conrad and Schneider refer to as the medicalization of deviance.

Medicalization of deviance can occur by redefining behavior previously labeled as criminal, as a medical issue. In the criminal justice system, some medical conditions might allow criminal offenders to offer an excuse in defense of certain crimes, such as insanity or diminished capacity. Medicalization might even remove some behaviors from the reach of the criminal law. Consider the following case.

Lawrence ROBINSON

v.

The State of CALIFORNIA.

370 U.S. 660 (1962).

A California statute makes it a criminal offense for a person to "be addicted to the use of narcotics." This appeal draws into question the constitutionality of that provision of the state law, as construed by the California courts in the present case.

* * *

This statute . . . is not one which punishes a person for the use of narcotics, for their purchase, sale or possession, or for antisocial or disorderly behavior resulting from their administration. It is not a law which even purports to provide or require medical treatment. Rather, we deal with a statute which makes the "status" of narcotic addiction a criminal offense, for which the offender may be prosecuted "at any time before he reforms." California has said that a person can be continuously guilty of this offense, whether or not he has ever used or possessed any narcotics within the State, and whether or not he has been guilty of any antisocial behavior there.

It is unlikely that any State at this moment in history would attempt to make it a criminal offense for a person to be mentally ill, or a leper, or to be afflicted with a venereal disease. A State might determine that the general health and welfare require that the victims of these and other human afflictions be dealt with by compulsory treatment, involving quarantine, confinement, or sequestration. But, in the light of contemporary human knowledge, a law which made a criminal offense of such a disease would doubtless be universally thought to be an infliction of cruel and unusual punishment in violation of the Eighth and Fourteenth Amendments.

We cannot but consider the statute before us as of the same category. In this Court, counsel for the State recognized that narcotic addiction is an illness. Indeed, it is apparently an illness which may be contracted innocently or involuntarily. We hold that a state law which imprisons a person thus afflicted as a criminal, even though he has never touched any narcotic drug within the State or been guilty of any irregular behavior there, inflicts a cruel and unusual punishment in violation of the Fourteenth Amendment. To be sure, imprisonment for ninety days is not, in the abstract, a punishment which is either cruel or unusual. But the question cannot be considered in the abstract. Even one day in prison would be a cruel and unusual punishment for the "crime" of having a common cold.

We are not unmindful that the vicious evils of the narcotics traffic have occasioned the grave concern of government. There are, as we have said, countless fronts on which those evils may be legitimately attacked. We deal in this case only with an individual provision of a particularized local law as it has so far been interpreted by the California courts.

Reversed.

Questions

1. Do you agree with the majority opinion in this case? Why or why not?
2. Since 1962, the state of medical knowledge has deepened our understanding of addiction as a disease. Yet since then, the United States has incarcerated hundreds of thousands of people for drug offenses.[12] Critique the approach to using penal social controls to control drug use and abuse. How might a public health approach to drug abuse using therapeutic social controls work?

SOURCES AND FUNCTIONS OF LAW

Defining law is no easy task.[13] One of the most influential definitions of law comes from the sociologist Max Weber, who conceptualized **law** as a rule of conduct that is "externally guaranteed by the probability that coercion (physical or psychological), to bring about conformity or avenge violation, will be applied by a staff of people holding themselves especially ready for that purpose."[14] Weber's definition of law has since been modified into three distinct elements:

1. explicit rules of conduct,
2. planned use of sanctions to support the rules, and
3. designated officials to interpret and enforce the rules, and often to make them.[15]

Much of US law has its roots in English **common law**, which first appeared in England in the eleventh century and grew in a manner that promoted one set of "common" laws throughout the country.[16] As the common law developed, judges were called upon to interpret the law as it existed in prior cases and then apply it in each case that came before them. The method of reasoning they used, based in logical and analytic reasoning, is still used in the courts of England and the United States today. The decisions handed down by judges add to the prior body of judge-made law and subsequently serve as **precedent** to guide the resolution of future disputes. Other sources of law appear in Table 1.2.

Table 1.2 Sources of Law

Constitutional Law	The body of law set forth in the constitution of a government that determines the structure of government and the powers that may and may not be exercised by that government.
Common Law	The body of law handed down in judicial decisions based on logical analysis and precedent.
Statutory Law	Laws enacted by a legislative body, such as the US Congress, a state assembly, a county government, and a local city or municipal council.
Administrative Law	Regulations issued by administrative agencies that carry the force of law by an act of a legislative body.

In addition to its social control function, law also serves other important purposes, including:

- coordinating for the collective advantage of society (e.g., laws regulating radio and television broadcasting);
- promoting governmental operations (e.g., tax and election laws);
- promoting public health, safety, and welfare (e.g., building and sanitation codes);
- remedying social problems (e.g., discrimination laws);
- settling disputes; and
- promoting social change.[17]

Categories of Law

Law may be categorized in many ways. In terms of content, it may be substantive or procedural. **Substantive law** sets forth legal prescriptions and proscriptions—the rules of what one must do, may do, and may not do. **Procedural law** sets forth the mechanisms through which substantive laws are administered. Homicide statutes are examples of substantive law. The rules regulating trial procedure and the way in which evidence may be introduced in a homicide trial are examples of procedural laws.

Another way of categorizing law is the distinction between civil and criminal law. **Criminal law**, also referred to as *penal law*, defines conduct that is criminally punishable by the government as a wrong committed against society as a whole. In contrast, wrongs committed against an individual, called *torts*, are the realm of civil law. However, civil law encompasses more than just torts; it includes many areas that regulate the relationships between individuals, such as business law (e.g., corporate and contract law); family law (e.g., marriage, divorce, child custody); and property/estate law (e.g., the law of wills, trusts, and inheritance; landlord/tenant relations), just to name a few.

A BRIEF HISTORY OF CRIMINAL LAW

The earliest known written set of laws is the Code of Ur-Namma (sometimes called Ur-Nammu) from around 2100 BCE.[18] This ancient Sumerian code set forth its laws in an "if–then" manner—*if* a man committed the act of kidnapping, *then* the code specified that he was to be imprisoned and pay a fine in silver. The code used monetary fines as the predominant form of punishment, even for crimes that inflicted bodily injury. Only crimes viewed as most serious by ancient Sumerian society—murder, robbery, adultery, and rape—were punishable by death.[19]

The Babylonian Code of Hammurabi was written approximately 300 years after the Code of Ur-Namma.[20] Hammurabi's Code focused more extensively on retribution, a philosophy grounded in notions of inflicting on offenders the same pains they delivered to their victims. Retributive punishment is often interpreted as embodying the principle of ***lex talionis***—"an eye for an eye, a tooth for a tooth"—as stated in Hammurabi's Code.[21] Retribution is also infused in Hebrew law, although it is expressed as representing a covenant under which God would not act capriciously so long as followers "held up their end of the bargain by adhering to a prescribed ethical tract."[22] Thus, scholars who study biblical law usually do not interpret the expressions of *lex talionis* as advocating revenge. Instead, the principle represents "a measured and proportionate response to punishable conduct by a member of the community . . . [rather than] the unbridled and unchecked vengeance that had earlier prevailed."[23]

Criminal Law in Ancient Greece and Rome

Ancient Greeks conceptualized law as divinely inspired, but not divinely given.[24] Moreover, they saw obedience to the law as part of one's civic duty and, above all, as rational behavior necessary for the orderly control of the universe.

In roughly 594 BCE, Greece was transforming into a more democratic society. The city-state of Athens led the development of a system of criminal law and procedures, including the creation of a system to prosecute specific acts before public courts comprised of citizens (excluding women and slaves) who served in large numbers (often in excess of 500) on juries that decided both guilt and punishment.[25] There was no public prosecutor; any Athenian citizen could initiate proceedings. Many acts that we think of today as crimes, such as homicide and rape, were not viewed as crimes in Ancient Greece.[26]

Some Greek punishments focused on restitution; other punishments were quite harsh, including death, imprisonment, fines, and exile/banishment from the city (a punishment often tantamount to death, as chances for survival were low when completely separated from the community and its resources). The Greeks also used the deprivation of civil rights as a form of punishment, including the rights to vote, to serve as a juror, to speak in the public forum, or to have a proper burial.[27]

In Ancient Rome, the *Lex Duodecim Tabularum*—Law of the Twelve Tables—marginally separated criminal law from other forms of law. However, the punishments for a number of acts that we think of as crimes today were often civil in nature. For example, thefts, assaults, and robberies were treated as civil property violations. As such, the remedies for these offenses were monetary compensation.[28] By the time of the Emperor Justinian, a clearer division between civil wrongs and true crimes had evolved. Crimes included "treason, adultery, assassination, parricide, kidnapping, and extortion, among others."[29] Most crimes were punishable by death or exile. Other common criminal punishments included flogging, enslavement, and imprisonment.[30]

Criminal Law in Early Christendom

As Christianity spread throughout Europe during the Middle Ages, the view that law represented the "will of God" took hold.[31] Moreover, as the power of the Catholic Church grew, interpretations of God's law as expressed in ecclesiastical (religious) law blended with secular (nonreligious) law, such that the distinction between the two became almost impossible to discern. Criminal law trials became searches for the "truth" of God's will in a particular case. Perhaps the best examples of this belief were trial by combat and trial by ordeal.

Trial by combat was essentially a judicially sanctioned duel in which the parties in a dispute (frequently over land) fought, often until the victor slayed his opponent. In trial by ordeal, the accused was subjected to a painful experience, such as being made to hold a scalding or burning object, and the verdict would depend on the degree of injury—which reflected God's intervention. The judge, often a religious official, would wait for three days to see if the wound had healed, and, if it did, the accused was cleared. In cases where this seventy-two-hour delay seemed too long for the crowd to wait, trial by water was employed. The accused who floated was guilty. If the accused sank, it was a sign of innocence, even though it might have had other consequences, such as drowning.[32]

From English Common Law to Modern Penal Laws

By the time Henry II ruled England in the mid- to late twelfth century, English common law began to develop. Under this approach, crimes were no longer private matters but instead were viewed as offenses against the Crown.[33]

In 1215, King John agreed to the Magna Carta, a charter of rights that stated "No free man shall be taken, imprisoned, disseised, outlawed, banished, or in any way destroyed . . . except by the lawful judgment of his peers and by the law of the land."[34] The next clause went on to state: "To no one will We sell . . . deny or delay right of justice." Originally, these protections were meant for noblemen, but they quickly came to apply to all citizens.[35]

At the time of its founding, criminal law in the United States rested largely on how crimes and defenses were fashioned in England from the period of Henry II to the time of the American Revolution.[36] In time, those concepts matured such that modern criminal laws are a mixture of common-law traditions and a series of statutory changes.* The most significant changes to criminal law in the United States occurred from the mid-1960s through the mid-1980s as a result of the American Law Institute (ALI) publishing the **Model Penal Code (MPC)** in 1962 and updating it in 1981.

The ALI is a think tank devoted to simplifying and harmonizing the common law across the fifty states to lead to more consistency among states. Comprising of judges, lawyers, and scholars from a variety of disciplines, the ALI researches and writes "model" sets of laws governing probate codes (the law of wills, trusts, and estates), foreign relations, unfair competition, property, torts, contracts, employment law, and criminal law. Although none of these model laws is the actual law of any particular state, they are highly influential. For example, the MPC has served as the basis for replacing or updating the criminal laws of more than two-thirds of all US states.[37] Accordingly, this book will emphasize the MPC definitions of crimes and criminal defenses.

IMPOSING PUNISHMENT

Punishment is a form of deprivation imposed on a person. There are many possible deprivations, including freedom, which is deprived by sending a person to prison; bodily integrity, which may be deprived through corporal punishment; money, which may be deprived through fines; and life, which may be deprived by the death penalty.

In 1958, criminologist Gresham Sykes wrote what is considered one of the most important studies of prison life.[38] Based on his observations, Sykes reported that prison inmates suffer five deprivations by virtue of being behind bars: liberty, goods and services that would be available in the outside world, heterosexual relationships, individual autonomy or decision-making, and personal security. Today, Sykes's observations still hold true as accurate descriptors of prison life.

* A complete history of the evolution of English common law to its maturation in the United States is beyond the scope of this book. Nonetheless, one this book's key features is comparing crimes as they existed at common law to the way those crimes are statutorily defined today.

Legal philosopher H. L. A. Hart noted that true criminal punishment must meet the following criteria:

1. must involve pain or other consequences normally considered to be unpleasant;
2. must be for an offense against legal rules;
3. must be of an actual or supposed offender for his offense;
4. must be intentionally administered by human beings other than the offender; and
5. must be imposed and administered by an authority constituted by a legal system against which the offense is committed.[39]

Hart's second and fifth criteria differentiate criminal punishment from other sanctions involving similar deprivations. For instance, deprivation of liberty occurs when a judge imposes a prison term for an offender who committed an armed robbery, and when a parent grounds a child for not cleaning his room. Only the former would be considered criminal punishment because it is a deprivation in response to a violation of criminal law imposed by a judge within the legal system.

Opinions vary widely on what types of punishments are acceptable. These views may be based on factors including political ideology, finances, religious beliefs and values, and advances in science (e.g., the latest behavioral modification techniques), to name a few. For instance, in the United States, the death penalty is used for a small number of offenses (treason and murders that meet designated criteria) in some jurisdictions, but not others. In other countries, the death penalty has been abolished and is viewed as an abuse of a government's power. Views on acceptable punishments also vary with the "mood" of society at a particular point in time as shaped by politics—especially the people who control the executive and legislative branches of government, and even by current events ranging from mass shootings to terrorist attacks.

Punishment and the Social Contract

Much of the theoretical underpinnings of modern theories of punishment are based on what is known as the **Classical School of Criminology**, primarily founded upon the work of philosophers Jeremy Bentham and Cesare Beccaria.[40] Bentham argued that people exercise their free will based on a *hedonistic calculus* in which rational beings seek to maximize pleasure and minimize pain. If in the course of an action the potential pleasure outweighs the potential pain, Bentham argued that the person would likely engage in the act. Conversely, if the potential pain outweighed the potential pleasure, a rational person would not engage in the act.

In eighteenth-century Europe, the criminal justice system was characterized by a focus on the value of social order over procedure, even at the expense of rights. Bentham and Beccaria were concerned that criminal punishments seemed incompatible with people rationally giving up freedom to become part of a social order in which torture and arbitrariness were the rule. As reformists, they believed the state should play a highly limited role and should be "accorded only that power necessary to protect individuals' rights and liberties . . . based on a consensus between rational citizens."[41]

The consensus upon which the classical school is based is referred to as the **social contract**—a concept formulated to explain the legitimacy of the state, the exercise of its civil and criminal regulatory power, and the source of political obligation.[42] Social contract theory begins with humans in what philosophers Thomas Hobbes and John Locke called the *State of Nature*.[43] In this state, all humans are equal and have complete autonomy; no person has authority over another person.[44] The State of Nature is a chaotic environment in which every person is out to protect himself or herself without any rules for doing so. In the State of Nature, people need to meet their basic needs—food, water, shelter, and sleep—and when two people want the same thing and cannot use or enjoy it at the same time, "they become enemies; and . . . endeavour to destroy or subdue each other."[45]

Given this violence and the need for self-preservation, some form of cooperation is necessary. Social contract theorists posit that humankind opted to relinquish some of their autonomy in exchange for the stability and peace provided by government. Each person has an obligation to obey the rules set forth by the state. Correspondingly, the state has an obligation to protect its citizens by honoring their freedoms and protecting their interests.

The role of law in this social contract is utilitarian—to "promote the greatest happiness shared among the greatest number."[46] Not only, then, should law represent the wishes of the majority, but it should also ensure compliance with that consensus via punishment.[47] Punishing those who violate the law avoids descent back into the State of Nature in two ways. First, it builds consensus about right and wrong, which influences the socialization process and the development of internal/self-control.[48] Second, punishment represents coercive, external social control and its use is therefore justified to maintain the social order.[49] When someone violates the social contract, it is the institution of government—not any aggrieved citizen—that has the unique authority to punish those who do not obey its laws.[50]

Justifying Punishment

In exercising the power to punish, the US criminal justice system relies on five common justifications, or goals, of punishment: retribution, deterrence, rehabilitation, incapacitation, and restitution. The popularity of each justification has varied over time.

RETRIBUTION

The justification of **retribution** is grounded in the notion that offenders deserve to be punished. There are three competing views of retribution. The first is *revenge*. As previously mentioned, this view of retribution has its roots in ancient legal codes, like the Code of Hammurabi, that posited that if a victim were wronged, then punishment should be designed to "get even" by imposing the same hardship, with its associated pains, onto the offender.

The second view of retribution is *just deserts.* This, too, is a payback, but with less emphasis on individual revenge and one-for-one correspondence between crime and punishment. This view asserts that the offender should be punished not only because he or she committed a bad act against an individual but also because all criminal acts are offenses against society as a whole. The resulting punishment should be proportional to the crime; that is, the punishment should be equally severe to the offender as the offender's criminal act was to the victim.[51]

The third view of retribution is *expiation*, which refers to atonement through suffering.[52] Expiation is based on the idea that crime causes pain to the victim, so the only way for the criminal to repent and learn his or her lesson is through experiencing his or her own pain.

DETERRENCE

To deter means to discourage someone from doing something. For a punishment to deter, it should convince people not to commit crime. This is usually accomplished through fear of punishment. If a person understands what punishment would likely occur if he or she were caught committing a crime, then that person might choose not to act, and would thus be deterred from committing the crime.

There are two types of deterrence: general and specific. **General deterrence** is intended to deter all people from committing crime by making an example out of others who have. The idea is that as members of the public see punishments meted out, they will decide not to commit crime out of fear of being punished themselves. General deterrence theory suggests that every time a person is punished—whether sentenced to prison, jail, probation, or other sanctions—it serves as a reminder to the rest of society that similar crimes will also be punished. Consider the example of laws prohibiting text messaging while driving. One goal of the law is to discourage people from texting while driving out of fear that they will be punished for doing so. Knowing that another person actually received a punishment, such as a fine (not just that it is hypothetically possible to receive one), can also encourage others to avoid the behavior.

Specific deterrence, sometimes referred to as individual or special deterrence, is not targeted at the general public. Rather, it is designed to discourage or prevent an individual offender from committing any additional crimes beyond those for which he or she has already been punished. Specific deterrence occurs if an offender decides that the punishment he or she already experienced was unpleasant and something to avoid in the future. To avoid future punishment, the offender would live a law-abiding lifestyle and thus be deterred from future criminal activity. For instance, if an individual were fined for texting while driving, and as a result decided not to text while driving again, specific deterrence would have occurred.

FACTORS THAT IMPACT DETERRENCE In order for deterrence to be effective, Beccaria believed that three things are necessary. The first is that the punishment should *swiftly* follow the crime. Sometimes referred to as celerity, the timing of punishment is important because the more distance there is between the criminal act and the punishment, the less likely an offender is to associate the punishment with the crime. Second, the punishment should be *certain*. This factor is concerned with whether an offender believes that he or she will be caught and punished. If an offender believes that he or she can commit a crime without being caught, then concerns about potential punishments become moot. Third, the punishment must be *severe*, but nonetheless proportional to the harm caused by the crime (much like just deserts). Although Beccaria was an advocate for deterrence, he strongly believed that there are limits to the severity of punishment. When punishments are too severe, they can actually be counterproductive to deterrence; for instance, an offender may perceive the criminal justice system as lacking legitimacy and therefore not feel compelled to abide by its laws. Overly harsh punishments can also increase the likelihood that an offender will resort to violence in order to avoid being caught.

There is great debate over the effectiveness of deterrence.[53] First, deterrence assumes that people think rationally, but this is not always the case. Rational thinking can be clouded by a variety of factors, such as mental illness. For instance, a person with schizophrenia suffering from delusions (fixed, false beliefs) that he or she is under personal attack may not be deterred from committing harm against another person because they strongly believe that their actions are in self-defense (for further discussion, see Chapter 15).

It is also important to realize not all decisions are made on a rational basis; in fact, much of human behavior may be motivated by irrational factors. Behaviorists believe that behavior is produced through a combination of both punishments for negative behavior and rewards for good behavior, suggesting that punishment, or the threat of punishment, by itself is insufficient to produce change; a system of rewards is also necessary.[54] Others argue that criminal behavior is a function of genetic makeup and cannot be controlled via threat of punishment.[55] At a more basic level, sometimes individuals just do not think carefully about actions and their consequences. Therefore, deterrence theory's reliance on rationality as the primary basis for human behavior is likely misplaced.

Second, punishment is usually not swift; it may take years before a criminal case goes to trial, particularly for complicated legal cases involving murder or other serious crimes. Punishment is also not always certain. There is just no way to predict if an offender will be caught and punishment enforced, let alone how punishment will be administered. Many crimes are not reported to the police, and, of those that are reported, most are never cleared or solved. Additionally, offenders are not always aware of the punishments. Although ignorance of the law generally does not constitute a criminal defense (see Chapter 13), a person must know the potential punishment in order to enter into the calculus of pleasure versus pain that can lead to deterrence.

Lastly, punishment is not always proportional despite the fact that the Eighth Amendment limits the criminal sanction by prohibiting punishment that is excessive in relation to the crime committed, at least under certain circumstances, as will be explored later in this chapter.

REHABILITATION

Rehabilitation is an attempt to correct an offender's behavior to make it conform to the norms of society. The rehabilitative perspective views the proper aim of the criminal justice system to be reforming criminal offenders so that they can become part of the general social order.[56] Indeed, the very notion of criminal corrections connotes "correcting" the criminal wrongdoer.

To be effective, the focus of rehabilitation must be specific to the offender. Treatment may occur through therapy, vocational or work-release programs, or educational training, to mention just a few.

Rehabilitation as justification for imposing criminal punishment fell out of favor with legislators and much of the public in the 1980s when the "get tough on crime" attitude became prevalent. During this time, states moved away from rehabilitation and toward incapacitation as a guiding philosophy. This was due, in part, to a landmark study by sociologist Robert Martinson that concluded, "with few and isolated exceptions, the rehabilitative efforts that have been reported so far have had no appreciable effect on recidivism."[57] Summarized as "nothing works," politicians and the public quickly accepted this result.

At the same time, correctional experts began a research program focused on rehabilitation. A follow-up study by Martinson found that rehabilitation still held promise—especially when it occurs in the community (i.e., outside prisons).[58] Evaluation research produced additional evidence showing that rehabilitation could in fact be effective if rehabilitative efforts were properly designed.[59] Keys to successful rehabilitative programming include identifying the behaviors or factors that were most amenable to treatment, designing programs that specifically target those behaviors and patterns, and then determining which programs were most appropriate for which offenders.[60] As a result, rehabilitation has made a bit of a resurgence.[61] Additionally, rehabilitative efforts have been justified as cost-saving correctional alternatives because offenders who can be rehabilitated do not incur costs for long-term incarceration.[62] As states experience budget woes and prison overcrowding, interest in rehabilitation programs has grown—especially for offenders with mental health or substance abuse problems who can be treated in the community at a significant cost savings over prison-based rehabilitative programs.[63]

INCAPACITATION

Incapacitation is a form of punishment that removes or reduces an offender's ability to commit criminal activities. The most common form of incapacitation is imprisonment. Under this justification of punishment, a person who is confined in prison will be unable to commit crimes against society. The key word here is "society." Crimes can and do occur in a prison setting; for the most part, those crimes are committed by inmates against other inmates or staff members, such as physical assaults, thefts, robberies, and so forth. Even in prison, inmates can be physically separated from other inmates, which would render it more difficult to commit criminal activities in the prison setting.

Incapacitation has been a principal goal of the US criminal justice system since the 1980s. As a result, the use of prisons as a form of punishment expanded dramatically (see Figure 1.2). The notion of prisons as a place for rehabilitation or deterrence is unimportant to the philosophy of incapacitation.

Incapacitation is not limited to confinement in a prison. It can be argued that the death penalty is a form of incapacitation because execution certainly prevents an offender from committing another crime. In earlier times, banishment was a popular method of incapacitation in which offenders were expelled from their towns and told never to return, with the threat of execution if they did.

Incapacitation can also include removing the instrumentalities of the crime—that is, the tools or capabilities that made the crime possible in the first place. For instance, some offenders convicted of driving under the influence (DUI) must forfeit their driver's licenses (and in some cases, their cars), which could render them unable to commit another DUI offense. Likewise, some sex offenders undergo chemical castration, which is meant to reduce or remove their physical ability to commit a sexual offense.

RESTITUTION

Restitution is a justification for punishment that requires the offender to pay back the victim—whether an individual, family, or society—for the harm caused by the offender's criminal behavior. More often than not, restitution involves some type of financial payback. It can also involve community service, which can symbolically provide restitution by requiring the offender to do something that betters the community harmed by the offense.

Restitution has largely become part of the larger framework of **restorative justice**, which goes beyond a mere personal financial settlement by seeking restoration of the health of the community while focusing on the needs of both the victim and the offender. For restorative justice to be effective, the offender must play an active role in the healing process by taking responsibility for his or her actions. By accepting and repaying the harm caused by his or her actions, the offender may be "restored" to society.

Restorative justice includes a variety of strategies, such as mediation and apologies between victim and offender, and its purpose is to resolve low-level criminal complaints, such as harassment and assault.[64] In cases when both parties agree to participate, mediation can provide several advantages over a traditional criminal proceeding: the opportunity to communicate face to face, enabling disputants to see each other as human beings rather than abstract opponents, and identifying common ground that can lead to conflict resolution.[65]

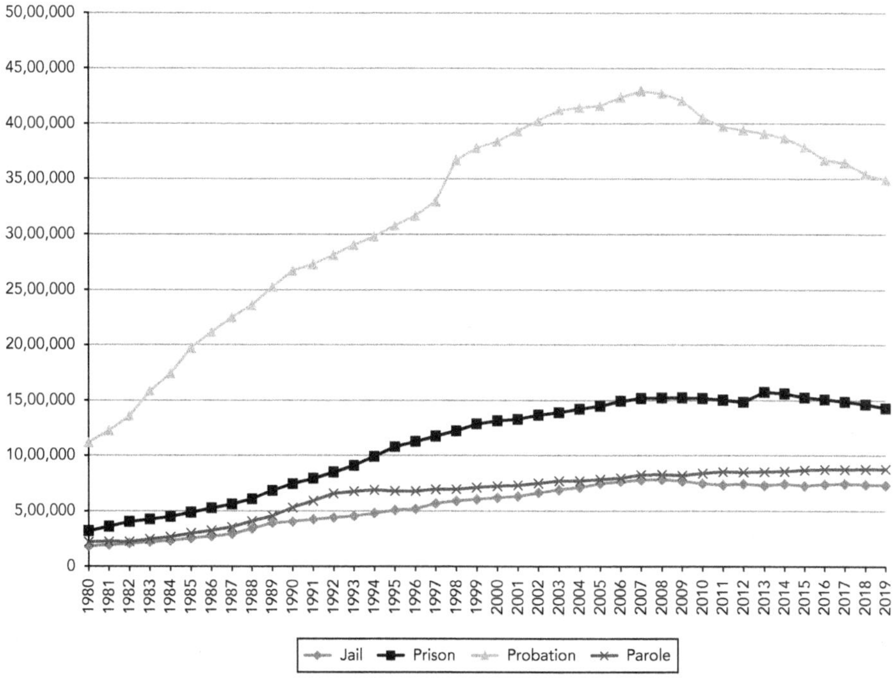

FIGURE 1.2

US Population under Correctional Supervision

Source: SOURCEBOOK OF CRIMINAL JUSTICE STATISTICS, ADULTS ON PROBATION, IN JAIL, OR PRISON, AND ON PAROLE, UNITED STATES 1980–2011 [Table 6.1] (2012), https://www.albany.edu/sourcebook/pdf/t612011.pdf; DANIELLE KAEBLE & MARY COWHIG, BUREAU OF JUST. STATISTICS, CORRECTIONAL POPULATION OF THE UNITED STATES, 2016 (2018), https://www.bjs.gov/content/pub/pdf/cpus16.pdf; LAURA M. MARUSCHAK & TODD D. MINTON, BUREAU OF JUST. STATISTICS, CORRECTIONAL POPULATION OF THE UNITED STATES, 2017–2018 (2020), https://www.bjs.gov/content/pub/pdf/cpus1718.pdf.

LIMITING PUNISHMENT

There are three philosophical principles that limit punishment under the criminal law: culpability, legality, and proportionality. Collectively, these principles underlie several important provisions in the US Constitution.

Culpability

A great deal of Western political philosophy argues that human beings are and should be autonomous. In American jurisprudence, the notion of **autonomy** stems largely from the Enlightenment writings of John Locke.[66] To Locke, "liberty was freedom from restraint, and the exercise of coercive power by the sovereign was always suspect."[67] Political theorist Isaiah Berlin summarized autonomy as the notion that "there ought to exist a certain minimum area of personal freedom which must on no account be violated."[68] Thomas Jefferson expressed this viewpoint in The Declaration of Independence when he declared "life, liberty, and the pursuit of happiness" to be "inalienable rights."[69]

Much of Anglo-American jurisprudence is in accord with the philosophical views that, as autonomous beings, humans exercise their autonomy as rational creatures of free will.[70] Thus, the law generally assumes not only that people *should* be free to control their own decisions, but also that they *are*, in actuality, free to decide how to act, and that they do so in a rational, self-interested manner.[71]

Given the law's assumptions about human nature and conduct, criminal law usually requires some level of **culpability**, or blameworthiness for wrongdoing, as a prerequisite to criminal punishment.[72] Thus, the criminal law generally does not seek to punish those who are without fault for their conduct. Accordingly, the law does not seek to criminally punish involuntary acts (see Chapter 3), acts committed under duress (see Chapter 13), or even the deliberate actions of those who are not culpable due to youthful age or severe mental illness (see Chapter 14).

MALA IN SE AND *MALA PROHIBITA* CRIMES

Crimes like murder, rape, arson, and theft are referred to as ***mala in se*** because they are evil (morally wrong) unto themselves. In contrast, ***mala prohibita*** offenses are not necessarily acts that are inherently bad, but rather are "statutorily-created, regulatory-type offenses with no common law counterpart," such as gambling, criminal speeding, and drug use.[73] The distinction between *mala in se* and *mala prohibita* crimes is not always easy or clear-cut as illustrated by crimes such as insider trading, selling alcohol or cigarettes to minors, and prostitution.[74] Nonetheless, *mala prohibita* offenses can present challenges when considering issues relating to culpability.[75]

In the 1952 case of *Morissette v. United States*, the US Supreme Court explained that criminal intent must be an element of all *mala in se* crimes in order to establish culpability, but such intent may not be required for a narrow class of *mala prohibita* offenses.[76] The defendant in *Morissette* trespassed onto government property even though there were signs that read, "Danger—Keep Out—Bombing Range."[77] While hunting on the property, he came across spent bomb casings, many of which were old and rusted. Believing the casings to have been abandoned property, he gathered three tons of casings and sold them for scrap. He was subsequently charged with the theft of the casings. The Court carefully explained that *mala prohibita* offenses designed to promote public health, safety, or welfare may be criminally punished without any evidence of culpability—meaning the actor possessed no criminal intent.[78] In contrast, *mala in se* crimes, like stealing, "stir a sense of insecurity in the whole community and arouse public demand for retribution."[79] Accordingly, given the comparatively harsh punishments associated with such crimes, proof of culpability vis-à-vis criminal intent is constitutionally required.[80]

Legality

The Latin phrase *nullum crimen sine lege, nulla poena sine lege* expresses there can be no crime without a law that defines it, and there can be no punishment without a law that allows it.[81] The **legality** principle maintains no one can be punished for an act that is not expressly designated a criminal act by a penal code. A police officer cannot make up a law on the spot and arrest a person for it, nor may a court make up a law and then punish a person for it. The principle of legality's emphasis on notice is central to notions of fairness and, therefore, a number of implications stem from it.

Article I of the US Constitution contains two different clauses that prohibit Congress and the states from enacting any ***ex post facto* law**, a law passed "after the fact." The prohibition on *ex post facto* laws is a direct result of this maxim concerned with fair notice before imposing criminal punishment.[82] The US Supreme Court has interpreted the ban on *ex post facto* laws as follows:

> [A]ny statute which punishes as a crime an act previously committed, which was innocent when done, which makes more burdensome the punishment for a crime, after its commission, or which deprives one charged with crime of any defense available according to law at the time when the act was committed, is prohibited as *ex post facto*.[83]

The principle of legality also requires that there are rules for statutory construction. Criminal statutes are to be construed according to their plain meaning.[84] Thus, when criminal statutes are not clear, most states will construe them using common sense and the statutory intent of the lawmakers when they enacted the law.[85] However, to ensure compliance with the underlying principles of legality, some states mandate that courts strictly construe their criminal laws "so that only that conduct which is clearly and manifestly within the statutory terms is subject to punitive sanctions."[86]

Under the Due Process Clauses of the Fifth and Fourteenth Amendments, laws that fail to give citizens fair notice of what conduct will be deemed criminal may be struck down as unconstitutionally vague. The declaration of a law as being void for **vagueness** occurs when a criminal law is written in such a way that people "of common intelligence must necessarily guess at its meaning and differ as to its application."[87] This is important because it prevents the need to guess at the meaning of the law. It also prevents police officers and judges from making up the meaning of law—and from applying made-up meanings unfairly and unequally.

Criminal statutes may also violate due process by being overbroad. **Overbreadth** occurs when a law "sweep[s] unnecessarily broadly and thereby invade[s] the area of protected freedoms."[88] In other words, a law must be precise enough to give fair warning to people regarding what they are not allowed to do (so as not to be unconstitutionally vague) while simultaneously making it clear to people that they will not run afoul the law by engaging in conduct that is constitutionally protected.

Proportionality

The Eighth Amendment reads, "Excessive bail shall not be required, nor excessive fines imposed, nor cruel and unusual punishment inflicted." This single sentence raises many important issues and debates surrounding the principle of **proportionality**, the idea that the punishment should "fit the crime."

PROPORTIONALITY AND EXCESSIVE FINES

Fines are financial penalties that are imposed after the accused has been found guilty of a crime. The law often provides an upper limit that a fine may not exceed. For instance, a state criminal code might specify that the maximum fine for a low-level misdemeanor is $250 while the maximum fine for a serious felony is up to $100,000. Generally, judges impose whatever fines they believe are appropriate within the legal limit. Fines are usually applied for minor offenses, such as traffic violations and some misdemeanors, and less frequently applied for more serious felony offenses.

Although the Eighth Amendment's prohibition against excessive fines applies to both the federal and state governments, its prohibitions remain unclear.[89] What does excessive really mean? The "You Make the Public Policy Call" feature in Box 1.1 explores this question.

PROPORTIONALITY AND CRUEL AND UNUSUAL PUNISHMENT

What constitutes a cruel and unusual punishment? You will probably agree that capital punishment (the death penalty) for motor vehicle theft is too extreme, but what is it that would make this hypothetical punishment cruel and unusual?

Punishments may be unconstitutional when they are grossly excessive in relation to the crime committed. In *Weems v. United States*, the Supreme Court first signaled that the principle of proportionality was a part of Eighth Amendment jurisprudence.[90] The defendant in *Weems* was convicted of falsifying a cash book for a small amount of money and was sentenced to a fine and fifteen years of imprisonment in shackles at the ankles and hands while being forced to perform hard labor. The Court sided with Mr. Weems, finding his sentence was disproportionately lengthy in light of the offense he committed and, further, that it was cruel and unusual because of its harsh and oppressive nature. Decades later, however, in *Rummel v. Estelle*, the Court explained that it was not the length of Weems's incarceration, but rather the "unique nature" of the punishment that was cruel and unusual.[91] Today, the *Weems* decision is generally understood as banning inhumane punishment.

What kinds of punishments are inhumane and unacceptable? The first Supreme Court case to explore this issue was *Wilkerson v. Utah*, which upheld executions by firing squad, but prohibited burning, disemboweling, and drawing and quartering.[92] The Court stated, "Difficulty would attend the efforts to define with exactness . . . cruel and unusual punishments; but it is safe to affirm that punishments of torture . . . and all others in the same line of unnecessary cruelty, are forbidden."[93]

In *Gregg v. Georgia*, the Supreme Court made it clear "that excessiveness alone, without regard to the barbaric nature of the punishment, was sufficient to invalidate a sentence."[94] A year later, the Court decided *Coker v. Georgia*, which held that the death penalty for

BOX 1.1

YOU MAKE THE PUBLIC POLICY CALL

Should the US Criminal Justice System Make Greater Use of Day Fines?

In many European countries, fines are utilized more frequently as punishments than in the United States, even for serious and violent criminal offenses. One problem with fines is determining the proper amount: fines that are too high may go unpaid by offenders, and fines that are too low may diminish the seriousness of an offense. One solution, common in European countries but not in the United States, is the day fine. Day fines allow judges to assign a fine that is proportional to an offender's daily income. The government assigns a number of fine units based on the severity of each offense. Using motor vehicle theft as an example, assume that it is worth 30 fine units. Next, the government determines the value of each fine unit. Let's assume that each fine unit is valued as half of an offender's daily income. If an offender who makes \$80 per day commits motor vehicle theft, that offender's fine would be:

\$80 / 2 = \$40 (the value of the fine unit)
\$40 × 30 fine units = \$1,200 fine

If an offender makes \$1,000 per day, that offender's fine would be:

\$1,000 / 2 = \$500 (the value of the fine unit)
\$500 × 30 fine units = \$15,000 fine

Therefore, day fines vary based on an offender's income. In one case, a wealthy driver in Finland who was going 25 miles per hour over the posted speed limit received a \$204,000 penalty.[131]

- What arguments can you make for and against day fines?
- What philosophies of punishment do day fines illustrate?
- If day fines were utilized in the United States, would they violate the Eighth Amendment?

the crime of rape constituted cruel and unusual punishment in light of the disproportionate nature of the offense to the punishment, again signaling that the excessiveness of a sentence was sufficient to render a criminal sanction unconstitutional.[95] Yet the *Rummel* Court dismissed both of these decisions as being "'of limited assistance' in deciding the constitutionality of terms of imprisonment" because they involved sentences of death, not imprisonment.[96]

The dismissive approach the Supreme Court took in *Rummel* toward the principle of proportionality was further solidified in *Hutto v. Davis*.[97] The defendant was sentenced to forty years imprisonment and a fine of $20,000 for possession with intent to distribute nine ounces of marijuana. In upholding the sentence, the Court reiterated that the cases requiring an Eighth Amendment proportionality analysis were limited to death penalty cases, while any "assessment of the excessiveness of a prison term was inherently subjective and therefore 'purely a matter of legislative prerogative.'"[98]

The Supreme Court breathed new life into the principle of proportionality when it decided *Solem v. Helm*.[99] The defendant had been convicted of forging a check, a felony under applicable state law that carried a maximum penalty of five years of incarceration and a $5,000 fine. However, the defendant already had three prior felony convictions, so he was sentenced to life in prison without the possibility of parole. In vacating the defendant's sentence as being excessive, the Court set forth three factors to guide courts when wrestling with questions of proportionality:

1. the proportionality between the severity of the crime and the severity of the sentence;
2. the proportionality of the sentence imposed in other jurisdictions for the crime at issue in a case; and
3. the proportionality of the sentence imposed in the jurisdiction at issue in the given case on other criminals who commit similar or more series crimes.[100]

When weighing these factors, the *Solem* Court noted, "There are generally accepted criteria for comparing the severity of different crimes."[101] These criteria reflect back to utilitarian ideals such as the "harm caused or threatened to the victim or society" and the relative culpability of the defendant in terms of his/her level of criminal intent.[102]

The *Hutto* and *Solem* decisions sent "a mixed and confusing message with respect to . . . the requirement of proportional sentencing."[103] This confusion led the Court to conclude that the Eighth Amendment contains no proportionality guarantee, at least with respect to the length of incarceration, in *Harmelin v. Michigan*.[104] Convicted of possessing 672 grams of cocaine and sentenced to a mandatory term of life in prison without possibility of parole, the defendant argued that this sentence violated the Eighth Amendment because it was so disproportionate to his offense that it constituted cruel and unusual punishment. In support of this argument, he pointed out that some states treated possession of the same amount of cocaine as a relatively minor offense punishable by only six months in jail.[105] Conversely, other states did not impose mandatory life sentences without possibility of parole even for murder. Nonetheless, the Court rejected his arguments, largely because the principles of federalism allow states great latitude to define crimes and their associated punishments.

Since *Harmelin*, most proportionality-based appeals have failed. For instance, *Ewing v. California* upheld California's "three strikes" sentencing scheme.[106] The defendant was sentenced to life in prison for shoplifting three golf clubs valued at approximately $1,200 because he had several prior misdemeanor and felony convictions, including one for robbery and three for residential burglary, which served as the triggering crimes for application of the three strikes rule. The Court found Ewing's life sentence was not unconstitutionally disproportionate to the theft, but rather that it reflected "a rational legislative judgment, entitled to deference, that offenders who have committed serious or violent felonies and who continue to commit felonies must be incapacitated."[107]

The decisions in *Harmelin* and *Ewing* strongly suggest that the principle of proportionality has little relevance today when examining the severity of a lengthy prison sentence. As the following case illustrates, however, proportionality does play a role when it comes to capital punishment.

Patrick KENNEDY, Petitioner,

v.

LOUISIANA, Respondent.

554 U.S. 407 (2008).

Patrick Kennedy . . . was charged by the State of Louisiana with the aggravated rape of his then-8-year-old stepdaughter. [He] was convicted and sentenced to death under a state statute authorizing capital punishment for the rape of a child under 12 years of age.[108]

* * *

The Court explained in *Atkins* [*v. Virginia*][109] and *Roper v. Simmons*,[110] that the Eighth Amendment's protection against excessive or cruel and unusual punishments flows from the basic "precept of justice that punishment for [a] crime should be graduated and proportioned to [the] offense."[111] Whether this requirement has been fulfilled is determined not by the standards that prevailed when the Eighth Amendment was adopted in 1791, but by the norms that "currently prevail."[112] The Amendment "draw[s] its meaning from the evolving standards of decency that mark the progress of a maturing society."[113]

* * *

[W]e held in *Roper* and *Atkins* that the execution of juveniles and mentally retarded persons are punishments violative of the Eighth Amendment because the offender had a diminished personal responsibility for the crime. The Court further has held that the death penalty can be disproportionate to the crime itself where the crime did not result, or was not intended to result, in death of the victim. In *Coker*, for instance, the Court held it would be unconstitutional to execute an offender who had raped an adult woman.[114] And in *Enmund v. Florida*, the Court overturned the capital sentence of a defendant who aided and abetted a robbery during which a murder was committed but did not himself kill, attempt to kill, or intend that a killing would take place.[115]

* * *

Thirty-seven jurisdictions . . . have the death penalty . . . only six of [which] authorize the death penalty for rape of a child. Though our review of national consensus is not confined to tallying the number of states with applicable death penalty legislation, it is of significance that, in 45 jurisdictions, petitioner could not be executed for child rape of any kind.

* * *

[N]o individual has been executed for the rape of an adult or child since 1964, and no execution for any other nonhomicide offense has been conducted since 1963. . . . [We therefore] conclude there is a national consensus against capital punishment for the crime of child rape.

* * *

It must be acknowledged that there are moral grounds to question a rule barring capital punishment for a crime against an individual that did not result in death. These facts illustrate the point. Here the victim's fright, the sense of betrayal, and the nature of her injuries caused more prolonged physical and mental suffering than, say, a sudden killing by an unseen assassin. The attack was not just on her but on her childhood. . . . Rape has a permanent psychological, emotional, and sometimes physical impact on the child. We cannot dismiss the years of long anguish that must be endured by the victim of child rape. It does not follow, though, that capital punishment is a proportionate penalty for the crime . . . Evolving standards of decency that mark the progress of a maturing society counsel us to be most hesitant before interpreting the Eighth Amendment to allow the extension of the death penalty, a hesitation that has special force where no life was taken in the commission of the crime. . . .

* * *

Our concern here is limited to crimes against individual persons. We do not address, for example, crimes defining and punishing treason, espionage, terrorism, and drug kingpin activity, which are offenses against the State. As it relates to crimes against individuals, though, the death penalty should not be expanded to instances where the victim's life was not taken. . . .

* * *

Justice ALITO, dissenting:

The Court today holds that the Eighth Amendment categorically prohibits the imposition of the death penalty for the crime of raping a child. This is so, according to the Court, no matter how young the child, no matter how many times the child is raped, no matter how many children the perpetrator rapes, no matter how sadistic the crime, no matter how much physical or psychological trauma is inflicted, and no matter how heinous the perpetrator's prior criminal record may be. . . .

In assessing current norms, the Court relies primarily on the fact that only 6 of the 50 States now have statutes that permit the death penalty for this offense. But this statistic is a highly unreliable indicator of the views of state lawmakers and their constituents [because the] Court's decision in *Coker v. Georgia* has stunted legislative consideration of the question whether the death penalty for the targeted offense of raping a young child is consistent with prevailing standards of decency. . . . In just the past few years, despite the shadow cast by *Coker*, five States have enacted targeted capital child-rape laws. If, as the Court seems to think, our society is "[e]volving" toward ever higher "standards of decency," these enactments might represent the beginning of a new evolutionary line.

* * *

With respect to the question of moral depravity, is it really true that every person who is convicted of capital murder and sentenced to death is more morally depraved than every child rapist? Consider the following two cases. In the first, a defendant robs a convenience store and watches as his accomplice shoots the store owner. The defendant acts recklessly, but was not the triggerman and did not intend the killing.[116] In the second case, a previously convicted child rapist kidnaps, repeatedly rapes, and tortures multiple child victims. Is it clear that the first defendant is more morally depraved than the second?

* * *

With respect to the question of the harm caused by the rape of child in relation to the harm caused by murder, it is certainly true that the loss of human life represents a unique harm, but that does not explain why other grievous harms are insufficient to permit a death sentence. And the Court does not take the position that no harm other than the loss of life is sufficient. The Court takes pains to limit its holding to "crimes against individual persons" and to exclude "offenses against the State," a category that the Court stretches—without explanation—to include "drug kingpin activity." But the Court makes no effort to explain why the harm caused by such crimes is necessarily greater than the harm caused by the rape of young children. . . .

* * *

Questions

1. Describe how each of the five justifications for punishment apply (or do not apply) to using the death penalty to punish the crime of raping a child.
2. Is execution so unique a criminal punishment that the Eighth Amendment should guarantee proportionality of punishment in its imposition, but not in the imposition of other criminal sanctions? Why or why not?

WHAT TO PUNISH?

Lawmakers frequently struggle with questions about whether certain conduct should be regulated by the criminal law or the civil law via compensatory, restorative, or therapeutic social controls. However, there is no magic formula to discerning how undesirable behavior should be formally regulated when informal social controls fail.

Critics argue that lawmakers have created too many crimes, resulting in too much punishment, which, in turn, can produce even greater injustices than the commission of the conduct originally criminalized.[117] Consider the fact that it is a federal crime for retailers and distributors of mattresses to remove tags explaining flammability warnings. Does this really need to be a crime? Might civil fine penalties be sufficient to make sure mattress tags remain on beds until the consumer decides whether to remove them? The process of creating more and more crimes, especially those that are not traditionally morally blameworthy, is referred to as **overcriminalization.**[118]

Ideally, common sense, economics, and evidence-based public policies would guide decisions regarding what conduct is criminalized. Nevertheless, this ideal does not work in reality, largely because of the politics of lawmaking.[119]

Once a criminal law is enacted, it is extraordinarily difficult to get it repealed. Few legislators vote to repeal crimes for fear of being accused of being "soft on crime" when they run for reelection.[120] This is especially the case when legislators have adopted laws that are widely perceived as popular because they address some "moral panic" created by the intense media attention accompanying the commission of high-profile crimes.[121] A moral panic describes "a condition, episode, person, or group of persons which emerge to become defined as a threat to societal values and interests."[122] When the media present an issue as a social problem, policy makers often respond with crime control strategies that address the moral panic surrounding the issue, rather than creating policies that are based upon empirical data and analysis to address the root causes of the issue itself.[123]

The Hart-Devlin Debate on the Legislation of Morality

Legislative responses to moral panics often concern conduct that most people would agree is "bad." However, that term is descriptive of conduct that necessarily depends upon some normative beliefs about what is wrong or immoral. Take, for example, the commandment "Thou shalt not kill." Most of us would agree it is wrong to kill another human being in cold blood. But what about in war, or self-defense? Morality clearly plays a big role in deciding what ought to be illegal.[124]

The degree to which the criminal law ought to be related to conceptualizations of morality is the central focus of what scholars have termed the **Hart-Devlin debate.**[125] Philosopher H. L. A. Hart asked us to consider three questions:

1. Does society have the right to pass judgment at all on matters of morals? In other words, should there be a public morality? Or are morals a matter for private judgment?
2. If society has a right to pass judgment, does it also have the right to use law to enforce it?
3. If so, should society use law in all cases, or only in some, and if only in some, on what principles should it be distinguished?[126]

Lord Patrick Devlin, who was a legal moralist because he believed law and morality ought to be closely linked, responded to Hart's three questions as follows:

1. Without such a thing as public morality . . . "without shared ideas on politics, morals, and ethics," no society can ever exist.[127]
2. Accordingly, society is entitled, by means of its laws, to protect itself from dangers. Just as society may punish treason to protect itself, it should protect violation of common morality to prevent societal decay.
3. Nothing should be punished by the law that does not lie "beyond the limits of tolerance."[128]

Hart, as a legal pragmatist, maintained that Devlin's notion of criminalizing that which lies "beyond the limits of tolerance" invites relativistic answers, which are vulnerable to charges of hypocrisy. Accordingly, such laws would be self-defeating in that they cause people to lose respect for the law, which breeds cynicism and indifference, resulting in both increased violations of law and discriminatory enforcement of law. Given these problems, Hart advocated that society only concern itself with breaches of morality when the resultant harm affects someone other than the actor.[129]

Another problem with criminalizing conduct that lies "beyond the limits of tolerance" is the fact that people have very different tolerance levels. For instance, norms that are acceptable in Los Angeles and New York might not play well in other parts of the United States. Geography aside, religious conservatives and social liberals typically differ over what behavior should be tolerated. It is no different in Congress or on the US Supreme Court, as representatives and justices clearly have very different viewpoints when it comes to the law. If we use morality as a baseline to set the prescriptions and proscriptions of law, then the question becomes, "whose morality?" Hart seeks to avoid this question, to the extent possible, by pragmatically divorcing law and morality up to the point that one's conduct causes harm to another.

Hart's reference to harm as the gauge by which the criminal law ought to be set is based upon the **harm principle**, a notion asserting that if no harm is caused to another's autonomy, then the law ought not to interfere with the conduct, even if the conduct is undesirable in the eyes of most people.[130] For an opportunity to apply the principles underlying the Hart-Devlin debate to a series of current and former criminal offenses with moral underpinnings, see the "You Make the Public Policy Call" feature in Box 1.2.

BOX 1.2

YOU MAKE THE PUBLIC POLICY CALL

The Hart-Devlin Debate: Choose a Side

In the United States, there have been a number of laws criminalizing acts that were widely deemed to be immoral that have been invalidated on privacy and/or equal protection grounds. The following is a list of acts that either are illegal today or were illegal at one point in our nation's history.

- Recreational use of marijuana
- Drinking alcoholic beverages by persons over the age of twenty-one (Prohibition)
- Drinking alcoholic beverages by persons under the age of twenty-one
- Fornication (sex between two unmarried persons)
- Adultery (sex when one or more of the participants is married to a nonparticipant)
- Interracial marriage
- Prostitution
- Speeding in excess of twenty-five miles per hour over the speed limit

1. What is the appropriate role for morality in shaping the proscriptions of the criminal law? In other words, with whom do you side more—Hart or Devlin?
2. Are there reasons other than morality that might justify the criminalization of any of these behaviors? If so, what do you think would be an appropriate punishment for each offense for a first-time offender? For a repeat offender?
3. Are there current criminal offenses that you think should be repealed or invalidated because they violate one or more of the principles limiting criminal punishment? Explain your reasoning.

CONCLUSION

Learning Objectives	Summaries
1. Describe the different ways in which society seeks to control deviant behaviors.	Society seeks to control deviant behaviors by enforcing social norms both informally and formally. Informal social controls involve socializing people to control their own behaviors by exercising self-control. When self-control is not enough, family, friends, and other important figures in people's lives use external, relational controls to positively reinforce desired behaviors and negatively reinforce or punish undesirable ones. When informal social controls fail, direct, formal social control—such as social welfare agencies, medicine, and law—utilizes penal, compensatory, therapeutic, and conciliatory means to control deviant behaviors.
2. Discuss the sources and functions of law.	Law is set forth in constitutions, judicial decisions, statutes and ordinances, and administrative regulations. All of these sources of law seek to achieve one or more important social functions, such as coordinating for the collective advantage of society; promoting governmental operations; promoting public health, safety, and welfare; remedying social problems; resolving disputes; or facilitating social change.
3. Identify key milestones in the historical development of criminal law.	The earliest written criminal codes, such as the Codes of Ur-Namma and Hammurabi, set forth proscribed acts and the associated penalties. Societies in Ancient Greece and Rome similarly provided notice of crimes and punishments, but added procedural processes that formed the basis of many criminal procedures today. In England, as religious influence gave way to state authority, key procedural justice rights came to be guaranteed to those accused of crimes, especially under the Magna Carta and English common law. Although the elements of crimes and defenses in the United States mirrored those of English common law for much of the nation's history, the Model Penal Code revolutionized statutory criminal law and continues to influence the criminal laws of more than two-thirds of US states.
4. Compare and contrast the major philosophical justifications for criminal punishment.	Punishment is typically justified in one of five ways: 1. Retribution is premised upon the idea that wrongdoers deserve to be punished either for the sake of revenge, just deserts, or expiation. 2. Deterrence seeks to discourage crime by using the threat of punishment to generally deter people from criminal wrongdoing in order to avoid punishment. Deterrence also seeks to specifically deter criminal offenders by making their punishment so unpleasant that they refrain from future criminal offending so as to avoid more punishment. 3. Rehabilitation, which attempts to correct an offender's behavior to make it conform to the norms of society. 4. Incapacitation removes or reduces an offender's ability to commit crimes either by incarceration, death, or the removal of the instrumentalities of the crime. 5. Restitution requires an offender to "restore" the victim to the way they were before the offender's criminal behavior, via financial compensation, community service, mediation, or other forms of conflict resolution.

Learning Objectives	Summaries
5. Analyze how the principles of culpability, legality, and proportionality limit criminal punishment.	Culpability posits that only people who are morally blameworthy deserve punishment. The criminal law generally does not seek to punish those who are without fault for their conduct, including involuntary acts, acts committed under duress, or the deliberate actions of those who are of youthful age or severely mentally ill. Legality posits that no one can be punished for an act that is not a crime. This principle underlies the constitutional ban on *ex post facto* laws and underpins contemporary due process notions concerning the narrow interpretation of the criminal law's scope and the vagueness and overbreadth doctrines. Proportionality limits punishment by making it "fit the crime." This is partially achieved when legislative bodies define crimes as either violations, misdemeanors, or felonies, and by the legislative differentiation of degrees of criminal wrongdoing and the authorized associated punishments. Proportionality is also served by judges who impose more severe criminal sentences on those who commit more severe crimes. It is also achieved by the constitutional limitation on cruel and unusual punishment, which bans torture and places limits on capital punishment.
6. Evaluate the relationship between law and morality as it applies to the criminalization and punishment of deviant behaviors.	Legal moralists, like Lord Patrick Devlin, argued that the law ought to be used to enforce widely shared public morals by criminalizing conduct that lies beyond the limits of social tolerance. Legal pragmatists, like H. L. A. Hart, argued that that approach leads to overcriminalization, hypocrisy, cynicism and indifference toward law, and even discriminatory enforcement of the law. To prevent such outcomes, Hart argued that criminal law should not be used to enforce morality, but to prevent harm to others.

KEY TERMS

autonomy
Classical School of Criminology
common law
crime
criminal law
culpability
deviance
ex post facto law
formal social control
general deterrence
harm principle
incapacitation
informal social control
law
legality
lex talionis
mala in se crimes
mala prohibita crimes
Model Penal Code (MPC)
norms
overbreadth
overcriminalization
precedent
procedural law
proportionality
punishment
rehabilitation
restitution
restorative justice
retribution
social contract
social control
specific deterrence
substantive law
vagueness

2

Constitutional Restraints on Criminalization

LEARNING OBJECTIVES

1. Describe how the First Amendment prohibits the criminalization of certain types of conduct relating to the freedom of religion.

2. Assess how valid time, place, and manner regulations may constitutionally limit the First Amendment rights to free speech and peaceable assembly.

3. Differentiate the types of speech that do not receive First Amendment protection.

4. Discuss what limits the Second Amendment places on the regulation of firearms.

5. Differentiate between the crime control and due process models of the criminal justice system.

6. Compare and contrast the various standards of review that courts use to analyze the constitutionality of criminal laws that infringe on due process and equal protection rights.

7. Analyze the constitutional limits of using the criminal law to enforce morality.

Outline

INTRODUCTION

The US Constitution secures a number of rights for citizens and other persons within the borders of the country. **Rights** are powers, privileges, immunities, or protected interests that are due to a person by nature of the legal guarantee.[1] Some constitutional rights are so central to US notions of liberty and justice that they are considered fundamental rights, such as the freedom of religion, the freedom of speech, the freedom to travel, the right to access the courts, and the right to vote.[2] There are also a select group of rights not explicitly provided for in the text of the Constitution, but are strongly implied therein, and thus are considered fundamental, like the right to marry and the right to privacy.[3]

Since the founding of the Republic, the federal government and those of the states have attempted (sometimes successfully, sometimes unsuccessfully) to regulate various types of conduct using the criminal law. However, the power to regulate behavior is not unrestricted: the US Constitution places limits on what behaviors may be criminalized. This chapter explores those limits.

THE FIRST AMENDMENT

The First Amendment to the US Constitution states: "Congress shall make no law respecting an establishment of religion, or prohibiting the free exercise thereof; or abridging the freedom of speech, or of the press; or the right of the people peaceably to assemble, and to petition the Government for a redress of grievances." This amendment provides several protections that place limits on the power of government to criminalize religious practices, speech, and the ability to assemble and demonstrate peacefully.

Freedom of Religion

The first part of the First Amendment is known as the **Establishment Clause** because it prevents local, state, and the federal governments from enacting any law that establishes an official religion, or favoring one religion over another (or over none at all). For example, laws that criminalized failure to attend weekly religious services or failure to tithe (donate money to a religious organization) would be unconstitutional exercises of the state's police power in light of the Establishment Clause's protections. Similarly, laws that require public school students to say a nonsectarian prayer, read from the bible, or start the day with a moment of silent meditation or voluntary prayer violate the Establishment Clause.[4] The Supreme Court has interpreted this amendment as providing a "wall of separation between church and state."[5]

In *Lemon v. Kurtzman*, the Supreme Court established a three-part test to determine whether a statute or governmental practice is permissible under the Establishment Clause:

1. it must have a secular purpose,
2. its principal or primary purpose must be one that neither advances nor inhibits religion, and
3. it must not foster an excessive government entanglement with religion.[6]

Applying this test in the *Lemon* case, the Court held that states cannot supplement or reimburse parochial schools for teachers' salaries and textbooks. On the other hand, states may provide free bus transportation to children attending church or parochial schools if transportation is also furnished to children in the public schools.[7] A state may not require that the Ten Commandments be posted in public school classrooms because such a requirement does not have a secular purpose.[8] However, a public university must fund an evangelical student newspaper if it funds other, secular student activities.[9]

The second part of the First Amendment, known as the **Free Exercise Clause**, also protects people's rights to act on or exercise their beliefs (or to believe nothing at all). For instance, the Supreme Court struck down a local ordinance that prohibited the ritual killing of animals (such as "chickens, pigeons, doves, ducks, guinea pigs, goats, sheep, and turtles," some of which are cooked and then consumed after sacrifice) because it infringed upon the religious beliefs of a group that practices animal sacrifice.[10] However, as with other constitutional rights, the freedom to act on religious beliefs is not absolute. With few exceptions, no one may violate otherwise valid laws in the name of freely practicing religion. For instance, laws criminalizing polygamy are valid even if one's religion condones having multiple spouses.[11] In addition, some governmental restraint on the free exercise of religious beliefs is also permissible in settings where people's rights are already curtailed to some extent, such as in the military or in correctional settings.[12]

Free Speech and Peaceable Assembly

The free speech protections of the First Amendment generally allow people to speak or write about any topic. People may exercise these liberties alone or in groups to share their ideas with others—so long as they do so peacefully. Nevertheless, like other constitutional rights, the rights to free speech and assembly are not absolute. Public authorities may impose reasonable limitations designed to prevent fire, health hazards, obstruction and occupation of public buildings, or traffic obstruction.

In light of the First Amendment, it is quite rare for a law to ban any type of protected speech or expression. Recall from Chapter 1, however, that criminal statutes may by being either too vague or overbroad. Vagueness and overbreadth challenges are most common in cases involving the regulation of symbolic speech.

SYMBOLIC SPEECH

Many judicial decisions have made it clear that "speech" goes beyond oral communication. Free speech encompasses nonverbal communication that includes both artistic expression and **symbolic speech**—conduct that expresses an idea or opinion. Wearing buttons or clothing with political slogans, displaying a sign while picketing, or burning a flag as a mode of expression are examples of symbolic speech.[13] Even hate speech, like burning a cross, may receive some First Amendment protection as symbolic speech depending on the circumstances under which such an act occurs.[14] These cases make clear that when conduct is the functional equivalent of speech, it gets significant First Amendment protection.

TIME, PLACE, AND MANNER RESTRICTIONS

Although neither state, local, nor the federal government may constitutionally ban the content of speech it may find objectionable, governmental entities are entitled to regulate the time, place, and manner of speech—including protests and symbolic speech—in a content-neutral way for the good of society. For example, employees who are striking have a right to express themselves in the form of picketing, but they may not block traffic, block access to or egress from a building, or otherwise interfere with the rights of others in the immediate vicinity.[15]

In *United States v. O'Brien*, the Supreme Court established a four-part test to determine if a law is a valid governmental **time, place, and manner regulation** of speech.[16] The case held that such regulations are permissible if:

1. the regulation furthers an important or substantial governmental interest;
2. the governmental interest served by the regulation is unrelated to the suppression of free expression;
3. the regulation is narrowly tailored to serve the government's interest such that the restriction on free speech is not greater than is necessary to achieve the governmental interest; and
4. the regulation still leaves open ample, alternative means for people to communicate their message.

The *O'Brien* case is a good example of a valid manner regulation on free speech. The Court upheld a federal law that criminalized the destruction of Selective Service Certificates (draft cards). The defendant had symbolically communicated his dissatisfaction with the Vietnam War by burning his draft card. However, he had other ways of expressing his opinions that did not involve the destruction of a piece of property issued by the government that was a necessary part of the government's ability to regulate the operation of the Selective Service System. Accordingly, the manner in which the defendant's speech occurred could be constitutionally regulated. Similarly, though people are free to make speeches on public streets, they may be prevented from doing so in a manner that disturbs the peace, such as using an amplifier or a bullhorn in a hospital zone or a residential neighborhood. Laws designed to protect against **disturbing the peace** may be offenses on their own, or may be subsumed in broader **disorderly conduct** statutes, such as this one from Wisconsin:

> Whoever, in a public or private place, engages in violent, abusive, indecent, profane, boisterous, unreasonably loud or otherwise disorderly conduct under circumstances in which the conduct tends to cause or provoke a disturbance is guilty of a Class B misdemeanor.[17]

In most US jurisdictions, criminal liability for this offense does not depend on whether the conduct was intended to purposefully disturb the peace; one can do so recklessly—meaning with a conscious disregard for whether others will be disturbed. Note, however, that in spite of the inclusion of terms like "indecent" and "profane," using swear words or raising one's middle finger would be constitutionally protected free speech.[18] Offensive speech may only be criminally punished if it invites an immediate violent response during a face-to-face confrontation.[19]

An example of a valid regulation on the time of speech would be restrictions on political protests. Organizers may want to hold a demonstration in a large city to gain attention to their cause, and they have a right to, but not whenever they choose. For example, no one has the right to "insist upon a street meeting in the middle of Times Square at the rush hour as a form of freedom of speech."[20] Thus, the time of a demonstration can be prescribed, but not its content. Even groups espousing distasteful, unpopular, or offensive messages have the right to speak their minds. For example, *National Socialist Party of America v. Village of Skokie* upheld the right of a neo-Nazi group to parade down the streets in a predominantly Jewish neighborhood.[21] However, the group had to obtain valid permits and conduct their demonstration at a time when authorities could maintain order.[22]

Additionally, there are valid governmental interests in setting limits on where free speech rights may be exercised. Public locations like parks, sidewalks, and streets are particularly well-suited for holding rallies, demonstrations, parades, and the like. As such, they are called **traditional public forums**. Governments may not prevent people from expressing their rights to free speech and peaceable assembly in these public venues. However, even within a traditional public forum, governmental entities may constitutionally limit the places and manners in which certain types of free speech activities may be exercised. In *Frisby v. Schultz*, for example, abortion opponents peacefully picketed outside the home of a physician who performed abortions.[23] In response to neighborhood complaints, the town passed an ordinance banning "picketing before or about the residence or dwelling of any individual" in the town.[24] The Court upheld the ordinance because it was narrowly tailored to serve a significant government purpose: protecting residential privacy by banning picketing that targets a particular residence. The ordinance did not ban protestors from entering residential neighborhoods, going door to door to distribute literature, nor prevent them from contacting residents through the mail or by telephone, thereby leaving open ample alternative channels of communication.[25]

In contrast to traditional public forums, governments are given greater authority to regulate **limited public forums**— areas that a government often opens up for civic discourse, like the grounds of capitol buildings, courthouses, state fairs, and public universities. However, people who enter such forums who then disturb or disrupt the proceedings may be prosecuted for disorderly conduct.

Governments are given the most latitude in regulating free speech and expression in **nonpublic forums**—places like airports, correctional institutions, military bases, and private property. Picketing on private, nonresidential property has been upheld, but only where the property is open to the public and the picketing relates to the business being conducted on the property. Therefore, the First Amendment would not protect the distribution of antiwar handbills on the premises of a privately owned shopping center, but it would protect peaceful anti-abortion demonstrations outside healthcare facilities that provide abortion services so long as such protests did not block access to or egress from the facility.[26]

Speech Beyond First Amendment Protection

The protections afforded by the First Amendment do not extend to all forms of expression. There are a number of categories of speech that the Supreme Court has specifically identified as being of such little value to the core principles underlying the First Amendment that they receive no constitutional protection.

DEFAMATION

Defamation is false, public statement of fact (not opinion) that injures or damages a person's reputation. Defamation may be in writing, in which case it is called *libel*, or it may be spoken, which is called *slander*. While anyone can be defamed, public figures, like celebrities and politicians, must prove a higher standard in court to collect civil damages for injury to their reputations from an act of libel or slander.[27]

WORDS THAT INCITE IMMINENT LAWLESSNESS

The First Amendment does not protect highly inflammatory remarks that invite an imminent breach of peace. For many years, courts used the clear and present danger test to determine if speech fell outside the realm of First Amendment protection. "The question . . . is whether the words used are used in such circumstances and are of such a nature as to create a clear and present danger that they will bring about the substantive evils that Congress has a right to prevent. It is a question of proximity and degree."[28]

Under the clear and present danger test, yelling the word "fire" in a crowded theater is not protected free speech because it would immediately threaten the safety of the people in the theater.[29] However, the Supreme Court later expanded the clear and present danger test to include words that had a "tendency" to cause lawlessness, as illustrated by *Whitney v. California*.[30] *Whitney* upheld the conviction of a woman under California's Criminal Syndicalism Act for helping to establish the Communist Labor Party, a group that California alleged was devoted to teaching the violent overthrow of government. In so ruling, the Court expanded the clear and present danger test to allow the punishment of speech that was "inimical to the public welfare," or "tend[ed] to incite crime, disturb the public peace, or endanger the foundations of organized government and threaten its overthrow."[31] This expansive view of speech that lies beyond the protections of the First Amendment—the "tendency" to cause lawlessness—was abandoned by the Supreme Court in *Brandenburg v. Ohio* and replaced with the test used today.[32]

Brandenburg was a Ku Klux Klan leader in rural Ohio who invited a television reporter to a rally. The reporter attended and filmed the rally, capturing images of men in hoods, some with firearms, burning a cross and making speeches advocating "revengeance" against racial and religious minorities and their supporters. As a result, Brandenburg was charged and convicted of violating Ohio's Criminal Syndicalism Statute for "advocat[ing] . . . the duty, necessity, or propriety of crime, sabotage, violence, or unlawful methods of terrorism as a means of accomplishing . . . reform" and for "voluntarily assembl[ing] with any society, group, or . . . persons formed to teach or advocate the doctrines of criminal syndicalism."[33] The Supreme Court reversed his conviction because the statute did not distinguish "mere advocacy" from "incitement to imminent lawless action."[34] *Brandenburg* asserted that government cannot punish speech, no matter how inflammatory, unless the speech is directed to incite or is likely to incite **imminent lawless action**. Thus, governments are free to criminalize actions like inciting a riot since riots are, by their very nature, breaches of peace that are likely to incite imminent lawless action.[35]

FIGHTING WORDS AND THREATS

Fighting words and threats are subtypes of speech that fall outside the realm of First Amendment protection given their propensity to incite imminent lawless action. The fighting words doctrine was first announced by the Supreme Court in *Chaplinsky v. New Hampshire*.[36] Chaplinsky was a Jehovah's Witness arrested for calling a town marshal "a God-damned racketeer" and "a damned Fascist" in response to the marshal's attempts to stop Chaplinsky from preaching on a public sidewalk. The Court upheld the conviction because Chaplinsky used **fighting words**—words that by their very utterance are "likely to provoke the average person to retaliation, and thereby cause a breach of the peace."[37]

Like fighting words, **threats** of violence do not communicate a constitutionally protected idea; they are designed to terrorize people with fear of imminent personal injury.[38] Threats against public officials, like the president of the United States, are taken particularly seriously.[39] Threats need not be made in person to be criminal. Threats that are made via the US mail, telephone, or even over the internet can subject the person making the threats to criminal prosecution and punishment.[40] Even if no direct threat is made, someone using email or a telephone in a manner that reasonably causes someone else to be "seriously alarmed, annoyed or harassed" may be guilty of **harassment**.[41]

Distinguishing between conduct that is constitutionally protected free speech and that which crosses the line into the realm of fighting words, threats, or disturbing the peace is not always easy, especially when dealing with hate speech.[42] However, when hate speech is combined with conduct such as threats or behaviors that disturb the peace, they might well constitute fighting words. For example, *People v. Rokicki* upheld a sentencing enhancement for disturbing the peace when the defendant's conduct was motivated by hate.[43] The defendant made a scene in a pizzeria when he yelled at an employee for 10 minutes, hurling antigay slurs and repeatedly pounding his fist against a counter. In affirming his conviction with a hate crime sentencing enhancement, the court stated:

> In this case, defendant is not being punished merely because he holds an unpopular view on homosexuality or because he expressed those views loudly or in a passionate manner. Defendant was charged with hate crime because he allowed those beliefs to motivate unreasonable conduct. Defendant remains free to believe what he will regarding people who are homosexual, but he may not force his opinions on others by shouting, pounding on a counter, and disrupting a lawful business. Defendant's conduct exceeded the bounds of spirited debate, and the First Amendment does not give him the right to harass or terrorize anyone.[44]

OBSCENITY

In evaluating the free speech rights of adults, the US Supreme Court has held that sexually explicit expression, which is indecent or profane, is protected by the First Amendment, but obscene materials are not.[45] However, just because indecent speech is constitutionally protected does not mean it cannot be regulated under valid time, place, and manner restrictions. For example, the Federal Communications Commission (FCC) is empowered to keep indecent speech off free, public airwaves, primarily to protect children.[46] However, the FCC has little to no power to regulate indecent materials transmitted on pay-cable television or satellite radio. The crime of obscenity is covered in more detail in Chapter 9.

Freedom of the Press

The First Amendment generally forbids censorship or other restraints on speech or expression by the media, whether in print or in broadcasting (e.g., radio, television, and movies). Thus, for example, a school board's dismissal of a teacher who had protested school board activities in a letter to the editor of the local newspaper was held to infringe on the teacher's First Amendment rights in the absence of evidence that the teacher's activity caused significant disruption or interference with the delivery of educational services.[47] And a state court order, issued in anticipation of the trial of an accused mass murderer, restraining the press and broadcast media from reporting any confessions or incriminating statements made by the defendant or from reporting other facts "strongly implicative" of the defendant, was similarly struck down.[48]

Like with free speech, there are limits to the First Amendment's protection of the press. Neither defamation nor obscenity receives First Amendment protection. Similarly, limits on the media's dissemination of information may be permitted if it concerns a matter of national security, such as the location of troops and their combat plans.[49]

The burgeoning development of computers and the internet are providing unique First Amendment challenges to the courts. For example, in *United States v. American Library Association, Inc.*, the Supreme Court ruled that libraries can be required to use software filters to prevent children from accessing pornography on all computers or be denied federal financial assistance for internet access.[50] The Court found that the filters did not violate the First Amendment rights of library users, because the filters can be shut off on request.

THE SECOND AMENDMENT

The Second Amendment to the US Constitution states, "A well-regulated militia, being necessary to the security of a free state, the right of the people to keep and bear arms, shall not be infringed." In *District of Columbia v. Heller*, the US Supreme Court interpreted the Second Amendment as protecting "an individual right to possess a firearm unconnected with service in a militia, and to use that arm for traditionally lawful purposes, such as self-defense within the home."[51] In 2010, the Court applied the same ruling in *McDonald v. City of Chicago*, and invalidated a Chicago ordinance that banned handgun possession by almost all private citizens.[52]

The Second Amendment places substantive limits on laws regulating firearms. Laws banning the possession of handguns by law-abiding citizens are presumed to be unconstitutional since they interfere with the "the core lawful purpose of self-defense."[53] On the other hand, like other constitutional rights, the right to bear arms is not unlimited. The Second Amendment does not imply a right to possess weapons suitable for warfare, rather than self-defense, such as bazookas, bombs, grenades, tanks, or biological, chemical, or nuclear weapons. But what about other types of guns?

The *Heller* Court specifically endorsed the legality of certain gun control regulations, such as bans on firearm possession by convicted felons and people with serious mental illnesses, bans on carrying firearms "in sensitive places such as schools and government buildings," bans on carrying concealed weapons, and regulations limiting the conditions and qualifications on the commercial sale of firearms.[54] However, the constitutionality of a range of gun-related laws has yet to be decided by the US Supreme Court, from laws criminalizing the possession of unregistered handguns to limiting firearm registrations to those persons who pass a series of qualifications in the same way that drivers are licensed, to bans on semiautomatic weapons. To date, most lower courts that have considered matters like these have upheld the authority of states and municipalities to regulate firearms in these ways.[55] Until the US Supreme Court offers definitive resolutions on the particulars of firearm restrictions, the scope of the right to bear arms will undoubtedly continue to cause public debate (see Box 2.1, "You Make the Public Policy Call").

DUE PROCESS UNDER THE FIFTH AND FOURTEENTH AMENDMENTS

Due process is the cornerstone of American law, as it provides basic protections against the states and the federal government from enacting arbitrary or unreasonable legislation or other measures that would violate peoples' rights. Due process is guaranteed through two clauses in the US Constitution, located in the Fifth and Fourteenth Amendments. The Fifth Amendment restrains the power of the federal government, and the Fourteenth Amendment restrains the power of the state governments. The Due Process Clause of the Fourteenth Amendment is responsible for making nearly all of the criminal procedural rights guaranteed in the Bill of Rights (see Table 2.1) applicable to the states. Both clauses prohibit deprivations of life, liberty, or property without fundamentally fair processes. In other words, due process prohibits "governmental conduct that offends the community's sense of justice, decency and fair play."[56]

The due process clauses protect against the arbitrary use of government power in two related, yet distinct ways: procedurally and substantively. **Procedural due process** concerns the fairness of the processes used when applying the law. Procedural due process is grounded in the idea that fair procedures are the best guarantees for fair outcomes. Moreover, if everyone is treated fairly, then it is easier for people to accept outcomes with which they disagree.[57] The Fourth, Fifth, Sixth, Eighth, and Fourteenth Amendments to the US Constitution contain procedural mandates that attempt to ensure procedural justice.[58] In contrast, **substantive due process** protects against governmental infringement of important constitutional rights. Indeed, due process has

BOX 2.1

YOU MAKE THE PUBLIC POLICY CALL

What Should Be the Contours of the Second Amendment?

As you learned, First Amendment rights, like all other constitutional rights, are limited, not absolute. Courts have not yet crystalized the limits of Second Amendment rights, although it is clear that they are not absolute. For example, in *United States v. Hayes*,[113] the Supreme Court affirmed the use of a federal law barring people convicted of domestic violence crimes from owning guns. In the coming years, the courts will undoubtedly clarify the contours of the Second Amendment as they review the constitutionality of a wide range of gun control laws in the wake of *Heller* and *McDonald*, such as those prohibiting the carrying of concealed weapons, requiring the registration of firearms, and limiting the sale of certain types of firearms for other than military use. To date, most—but not all—lower court decisions have upheld a range of regulations on firearms, including:

- Limiting the "open carry" of guns in public[114]
- Requiring gun licensing[115]
- Requiring a minimum age for "concealed carry" licenses[116]
- Restricting possession of firearms in certain locations[117]
- prohibiting the issuance of gun licenses to those with misdemeanor assault convictions[118]
- Barring the possession of silencers and short-barreled shotguns[119]
- Prohibiting the possession of firearms by individuals who have been involuntarily committed to a mental institution[120]
- Requiring a waiting period before the purchase of a firearm[121]

1. For each of these restrictions, explain what public policy goals you think legislatures were trying to achieve.
2. Which, if any, of these regulations do you think would be constitutional under the Second Amendment? Explain your reasoning.

been interpreted as the basis for providing substantive rights not explicitly guaranteed in the Constitution, thus imposing limits on governmental interference with individual liberties.[59] To be valid, governmental restrictions placed on these liberties must be reasonable and consistent with justice and fair play. Courts have applied this type of

Table 2.1 Summary of Procedural Justice Rights in the Fourth through Eighth Amendments of the US Constitution

Amendment	Rights Guaranteed
Fourth Amendment	• The right to be free from unreasonable searches and seizures • The requirement that no search or arrest warrants be issued without probable cause having been established under oath
Fifth Amendment	• The right to a grand jury indictment in federal cases • The right to be free from double jeopardy (protection "against a second prosecution for the same offense after acquittal, against a second prosecution for the same offense after conviction, and against multiple punishments for the same offense"*) • The right to be protected against being compelled to incriminate oneself • The right to due process of law • The right to be justly compensated if the government seizes one's property
Sixth Amendment	• The right to a speedy and public trial • The right to a trial by an impartial jury • The right to confront witnesses against the accused via cross-examination • The right to compel witnesses to testify on one's behalf • The right to effective assistance of counsel in most criminal prosecutions
Seventh Amendment	• The right to a jury trial in certain civil cases • The right not to have courts overturn certain factual findings by juries
Eighth Amendment	• The right to be free from the imposition of excessive bail • The right to be free from the imposition of excessive fines • The right not to be subjected to cruel and unusual punishment

* Roberts v. Maine, 48 F.3d 1287, 1291 (1st Cir. 1995); *see also* Justices of Boston Municipal Court v. Lydon, 466 U.S. 294, 306–07 (1984).

analysis to subjects as varied as railroads and public utilities, marriage, and the refusal of medical treatment.[60]

Crime Control and Due Process

In *The Limits of the Criminal Sanction*, criminologist Herbert Packer described two models of the criminal justice process.[61] The **crime control model** can be viewed as assembly line justice. Its focus is to move the offender through the criminal justice process as quickly and efficiently as possible. The idea is to arrest, try, convict, and punish offenders with ease and finality. For example, traffic court judges sometimes minimize the time it takes to adjudicate cases by asking if the defendants would be willing to plead guilty in exchange for a reduced fine, the minimum court costs, and perhaps even the reduction or dismissal of driving points. The people who agree are then pronounced "guilty" and sentenced. The violator benefits because he or she receives a lighter punishment. The judge benefits by having cleared the courtroom in a timely manner. Thus, the system functions quickly and efficiently, though not with attention to individual details.

The crime control model assumes guilt and the need for quick and effective punishment. Under this philosophy, the belief is that if accused persons were not guilty, they would not have been arrested in the first place. Furthermore, the prosecutor, the judge, and often the defense attorney believe the accused is guilty. Proponents of the crime control model recognize the possibility that some of those accused of criminal activity are in fact not guilty. However, punishing a few innocent people is viewed as an acceptable price to pay for controlling crime rapidly and efficiently.

In contrast, the **due process model** focuses on the rights of the accused. This model assumes that the accused is innocent until proven guilty, that a person's freedom is paramount and that there must be conclusive evidence OF guilt supported by valid and reliable information before a person can be punished. This is only determined when both sides—the prosecution and the defense—have the opportunity to argue their cases while contesting the case put forth by the opposing side. If the crime control model is assembly line justice, the due process model is obstacle course justice. In other words, there are numerous steps to go through to assure that only the guilty are punished. If at any point there is reasonable doubt that the offender is guilty, then he or she should be freed.

The due process model advocates formal decision-making procedures. Accused persons should have the right to have their day in court. For example, if you wished to contest a traffic ticket in court, you would be able to do so without fear of reprisal. If you were found guilty, the judge should not impose additional fines, court costs, or driving points just because you decided to have your case heard rather than proceeding through the assembly line process.

Although Packer's two models conflict with each other, elements from both work simultaneously throughout the criminal justice process. Striking the balance between crime control, on one hand, and constitutional rights and liberties, on the other, is a constant tension in our system of justice. Nevertheless, honoring the due process rights of the accused is not just a question of philosophy; it is so important to the concepts of liberty and justice that it is mandated in two provisions of the US Constitution.

Due Process Standards of Review

When courts analyze the constitutionality of a law under guarantees of due process, they apply different levels of scrutiny—called **standards of review**—depending upon the right the law is alleged to burden.

If a fundamental right is burdened by a law, the courts will apply strict scrutiny. **Strict scrutiny** is the most exacting level of judicial review. The formal test for strict scrutiny is whether a law is narrowly tailored to achieve to achieve a compelling governmental interest. If the government does not have a compelling reason to justify a law's interference with a fundamental right, then the law will be declared unconstitutional. Moreover, even if the government has a compelling interest, if there are other ways of achieving that interest without burdening the fundamental right, then the law will fail strict scrutiny review for not being narrowly tailored.

If a right other than a fundamental right is burdened by law (e.g., some other constitutionally protected right or liberty interest that is not "fundamental"), then the rational basis test is applied to assess the constitutionality of the law. The **rational basis test** asks if a law is rationally related to a legitimate governmental interest. This standard of review presumes the constitutional validity of all laws that do not burden any fundamental rights. People challenging a law on rational basis grounds bear the difficult burden of proving that there is no rational basis for the challenged law's existence, or alternatively, that the law bears no reasonable relationship to any legitimate governmental interest.

EQUAL PROTECTION UNDER THE FIFTH AND FOURTEENTH AMENDMENTS

The Due Process Clause of the Fifth Amendment has been interpreted as also guaranteeing the equal protection of law—the notion that similarly situated people should be treated in a similar manner.[62] The Fifth Amendment does not mention equal protection per se; it is specified in the Equal Protection Clause of the Fourteenth Amendment. These two concepts are associated with each other and sometimes overlap. "[Due process] tends to secure equality of law in the sense that it makes a required minimum of protection for every one's right of life, liberty and property, which the Congress or the legislature may not withhold."[63]

For example, in *Bolling v. Sharpe,* the Court held that segregation of pupils in the public schools of the District of Columbia violated the Due Process Clause:

> The Fifth Amendment, which is applicable in the District of Columbia, does not contain an equal protection clause as does the Fourteenth Amendment which applies only to the states. But the concepts of equal protection and due process, both stemming from our American ideal of fairness, are not mutually exclusive. The "equal protection of the laws" is a more explicit safeguard of prohibited unfairness than "due process of law," and, therefore, we do not imply that the two are always interchangeable phrases. But, as this Court has recognized, discrimination may be so unjustifiable as to be violative of due process.[64]

In addition to guaranteeing due process, the Fourteenth Amendment also prohibits states from denying the equal protection of laws to all persons and the Fifth Amendment makes this guarantee applicable to the federal government. The **Equal Protection Clause** prevents the government from making unreasonable, arbitrary distinctions between different persons as to their rights and privileges. If a law applies evenly to all people and does not discriminate in any way, the mandates of equal protection are satisfied. It should be noted that while the government may not discriminate based on characteristics like race, ethnicity, and religion, if people are not similarly situated, then the law could treat them differently.[65] Consider, for example, that the law may deprive people convicted of certain felony offenses of a variety of rights and privileges that are available to other people who are not similarly situated (those without felony convictions), such as voting rights, the right to lawfully possess a firearm, and the ability to be licensed in certain professions.

Equal Protection Standards of Review

Analyzing a classification in the law that treats different classes of people differently is a multi-step process. First, a court must examine the type of distinction that the law makes in order to determine the standard of review to be applied in the case. Next, the court must determine if the distinction affects groups of people who are similarly situated with respect to their circumstances and conditions under the law. If the groups are not similarly situated, then the constitutional line of inquiry ends. Only if the groups are found to be similarly situated do courts have to analyze the classification at issue under the relevant standard of review.

Plyler v. Doe explained that courts are to evaluate equal protection claims according to three levels of scrutiny: strict scrutiny, intermediate or heightened scrutiny, and rational basis review.[66] Which standard of review is applied in any particular case depends on the nature of the law being challenged.

STRICT SCRUTINY FOR LAWS BURDENING FUNDAMENTAL RIGHTS

Just as strict scrutiny is used in the due process context when laws burden a fundamental right, strict scrutiny is also used in the equal protection realm when a law makes distinctions among people with regard to a fundamental right. Strict scrutiny is the most exacting level of judicial review used in evaluating laws under the Equal Protection Clause. The formal test for strict scrutiny is whether a law is narrowly tailored to achieve to achieve a compelling governmental interest. If the government does not have a compelling reason for treating similarly situated people differently under the law, then the law will be declared unconstitutional. Even if the government does have a compelling interest in treating similarly situated people in a dissimilar manner, if there are other ways of achieving its goal(s) without burdening the right to equal protection, then the law will fail strict scrutiny review for not being narrowly tailored.

Take for example the case of *McIntyre v. Ohio Elections Commission.*[67] In *McIntyre,* a woman distributed leaflets at a school board meeting in opposition to an upcoming referendum on a proposed school tax levy. The handbills were factually accurate and were signed "Concerned Parents and Tax Payers." A school district official who supported the tax proposal advised the woman that Ohio election laws did not allow unsigned leaflets to be distributed, yet the woman continued to hand them out. She was subsequently charged with violating the election code and was fined $100. She challenged the law on equal protection grounds since it treated similarly situated people—those who wish to comment on the political process anonymously and those who were willing to identify themselves—in a patently different manner by criminalizing the speech of the former group while allowing the speech of the latter group.

Reversing the conviction in *McIntyre,* the Supreme Court applied strict scrutiny because the law limited political expression, a fundamental right under the First Amendment's guarantee of free speech and expression. Ohio defended the law by arguing that it served two compelling governmental interests: "preventing fraudulent and libelous statements and its interest in providing the electorate with relevant information."[68] The Court held that the ban on anonymous speech related to elections was not narrowly tailored to achieve either of these interests because it reached the kind of free political expression prevented in this very case—free speech that presents "neither a substantial risk of libel nor any potential appearance of corrupt advantage."[69]

> Under our Constitution, anonymous pamphleteering is not a pernicious, fraudulent practice, but an honorable tradition of advocacy and of dissent. Anonymity is a shield from the tyranny of the majority . . . The State may, and does, punish fraud directly. But it cannot seek to punish fraud indirectly by indiscriminately outlawing a category of speech, based on its content, with no necessary relationship to the danger sought to be prevented.[70]

STRICT SCRUTINY FOR LAWS USING SUSPECT CLASSIFICATIONS

Laws often draw distinctions between groups of people, such as those older or younger than a certain age, or those with or without a felony conviction on their criminal records. However, sometimes laws draw distinctions between groups of people based on factors that are inherently suspect when evaluating equality under the law, known as **suspect classifications.**[71]

Although the US Supreme Court "has not provided a coherent explanation for precisely what factors trigger heightened scrutiny," most courts typically analyze a combination of the following factors when determining whether a group constitutes a suspect class for equal protection purposes:[72]

1. Has the group historically been discriminated against, and/or has the group been subjected to prejudice, hostility, and/or stigma?[73]
2. Does the group possess an immutable and/or highly visible trait that causes members of the group to experience prejudice, hostility, or stigma?[74]
3. Is the group a discrete and insular minority such that they are often powerless to protect themselves from discrimination via the normal political processes?[75]
4. Is the distinguishing characteristic of the group something that does not inhibit its members from contributing meaningfully to society?[76]

Applying these factors, the US Supreme Court has declared that distinctions made between groups of people based on race, religion, or national origin are all suspect classifications.[77] Some lower courts have held that sexual orientation constitutes a suspect classification, but so far, the Supreme Court has avoided making any such ruling.[78] Similarly, the Court has yet to determine if the physically disabled or mentally disabled constitute suspect classes.[79]

Suspect classifications are reviewed using strict scrutiny. Thus, courts will presume laws that treat suspect classes differently than others are unconstitutional unless the government can prove that the differential treatment is narrowly tailored to achieve a compelling governmental interest. Using such strict scrutiny, courts have struck down racial segregation in public schools and other public places, and laws that prohibit the sale or use of property to certain races or minority groups.[80]

INTERMEDIATE SCRUTINY FOR LAWS USING QUASI-SUSPECT CLASSIFICATIONS

Intermediate scrutiny, sometimes referred to as heightened scrutiny, asks if the governmental classification at issue in a case is substantially related to achieving an important governmental interest. This intermediate level of judicial scrutiny is used only when a law makes a distinction using what the US Supreme Court has held to be a **quasi-suspect classification.** Biological sex and legitimacy at birth are the only classifications that the Supreme Court has determined to be quasi-suspect classifications.

In *Craig v. Boren*, two men challenged an Oklahoma statute that prohibited the sale of "non-intoxicating 3.2% alcoholic beer" to males under the age of twenty-one, but only prohibited such sales to females under the age of eighteen.[81] The men argued that the law unconstitutionally discriminated on the basis of sex by allowing eighteen- to twenty-one-year-old women access to beer that men in the same age group could not legally obtain. The state attempted to justify the distinction by arguing the age-based classification served the important governmental interest of enhancing traffic safety. In support of this assertion, the state presented statistical evidence that males in that age group were much more likely to be arrested both for public drunkenness and for driving under the influence. While accepting the enhancement of traffic safety as an important governmental interest, the Supreme Court rejected that the aged-based classification in the beer-sales law was substantially related to achieving the goal of increased traffic safety because a gender difference for these two crimes persists at all ages, not just between the ages of eighteen and twenty-one.[82]

The following case is another example in which a criminal defendant argued that a law that punished men, but not women, for the same conduct violated the Equal Protection Clause. However, the Supreme Court disagreed and upheld the gender classification.

MICHAEL M.

v.

SUPERIOR COURT of Sonoma County, California

450 U.S. 464 (1981).

The question presented in this case is whether California's "statutory rape" law... violates the Equal Protection Clause of the Fourteenth Amendment. [That law] defines unlawful sexual intercourse as "an act of sexual intercourse accomplished with a female not the wife of the perpetrator, where the female is under the age of [eighteen] years." The statute thus makes men alone criminally liable for the act of sexual intercourse.

* * *

[A] legislature may not "make overbroad generalizations based on sex which are entirely unrelated to any differences between men and women or which demean the ability or social status of the affected class."[83] But because the Equal Protection Clause does not "demand that a statute necessarily apply equally to all persons" or require "things which are different in fact to be treated in law as though they were the same."[84] This Court has consistently upheld statutes where the gender classification is not invidious, but rather realistically reflects the fact that the sexes are not similarly situated in certain circumstances. . . .[85]

Applying those principles to this case, the fact that the California Legislature criminalized the act of illicit sexual intercourse with a minor female is a sure indication of its intent or purpose to discourage that conduct. Precisely why the legislature desired that result is of course somewhat less clear. This Court has long recognized that "inquiries into congressional motives or purposes are a hazardous matter,"[86] and the search for the "actual" or "primary" purpose of a statute is likely to be elusive. . . . Here, for example, the individual legislators may have voted for the statute for a variety of reasons. Some legislators may have been concerned about preventing teenage pregnancies, others about protecting young females from physical injury or from the loss of chastity, and still others about promoting various religious and moral attitudes towards premarital sex.

The justification for the statute offered by the State, and accepted by the Supreme Court of California, is that the legislature sought to prevent illegitimate teenage pregnancies. That finding, of course, is entitled to great deference. . . .

We are satisfied not only that the prevention of illegitimate pregnancy is at least one of the purposes of the statute, but that the State has a strong interest in preventing such pregnancy. At the risk of stating the obvious, teenage pregnancies, which have increased dramatically over the last two decades,[87] have significant social, medical and economic consequences for both the mother and her child, and the State.[88] Of particular concern to the State is that approximately half of all teenage pregnancies end in abortion.[89] Of those children who are born, their illegitimacy makes them likely candidates to become wards of the State.

We need not be medical doctors to discern that young men and young women are not similarly situated with respect to the problems and the risks of sexual intercourse. Only women may become pregnant and they suffer disproportionately the profound physical, emotional and psychological consequences of sexual activity. The statute at issue here protects women from sexual intercourse at an age when those consequences are particularly severe.

The question thus boils down to whether a State may attack the problem of sexual intercourse and teenage pregnancy directly by prohibiting a male from having sexual intercourse with a minor female. . . . We hold that such a statute is sufficiently related to the State's objectives to pass constitutional muster.

Because virtually all of the significant harmful and inescapably identifiable consequences of teenage pregnancy fall on the young female, a legislature acts well within its authority when it elects to punish only the participant who, by nature, suffers few of the consequences of his conduct. It is hardly unreasonable for a legislature acting to protect minor females to exclude them from punishment. Moreover, the risk of pregnancy itself constitutes a substantial deterrence to young females. No similar natural sanctions deter males. A criminal sanction imposed solely on males thus serves to roughly "equalize" the deterrents on the sexes.

* * *

Justice BRENNAN, dissenting:

* * *

[E]ven assuming that prevention of teenage pregnancy is an important governmental objective . . . , California still has the burden of proving that there are fewer teenage pregnancies under its gender-based statutory rape law than there would be if the law were gender-neutral. To meet this burden, the State must show that because its statutory rape law punishes only males, and not females, it more effectively deters minor females from having sexual intercourse. . . .

The State has not produced such evidence in this case. Moreover, there are at least two serious flaws in the State's assertion that law enforcement problems created by a gender-neutral statutory rape law would make such a statute less effective than a gender-based statute in deterring sexual activity.

First, the experience of other jurisdictions, and California itself, belies the plurality's conclusion that a gender-neutral statutory rape law "may well be incapable of enforcement." There are now at least 37 States that have enacted gender-neutral statutory rape laws. California has introduced no evidence that those states have been handicapped by the enforcement problems the plurality finds so persuasive. . . .

The second flaw in the State's assertion is that even assuming that a gender-neutral statute would be more difficult to enforce, the State has still not shown that those enforcement problems would make such a statute less effective than a gender-based statute in deterring minor females from engaging in sexual intercourse. Common sense, however, suggests that a gender-neutral statutory rape law is potentially a greater deterrent of sexual activity than a gender-based law, for the simple reason that a gender-neutral law subjects both men and women to criminal sanctions and thus arguably has a deterrent effect on twice as many potential violators. . . .

* * *

Questions

1. Do you agree with the plurality or the dissent that the sexes are not similarly situated when it comes to the prevention of teen pregnancy and, thus, discrimination on the basis of gender as applied to statutory rape laws is not constitutionally impermissible? Explain your answer.
2. Today, many states impose statutory rape liability on males and females alike. When women are convicted of statutory rape, however, they tend to receive significantly more lenient sentences than when a male statutorily rapes a female. What, if anything, does this say about societal notions regarding statutory rape and sex between teenagers and people who are older than they are?

THE RATIONAL BASIS TEST FOR ALL OTHER CLASSIFICATIONS

Recall that the rational basis test asks if the governmental classification at issue is *rationally related to a legitimate governmental interest*. This standard of review presumes the constitutional validity of all types of distinctions made in laws that do not involve suspect or quasi-suspect classifications, and do not burden any fundamental rights. A person challenging a legislative classification that does not burden a fundamental right or a protected class bears the difficult burden of proving that there is no rational basis for the distinction in the law, or alternatively, that the law bears no reasonable relationship to any legitimate governmental interest. The "Case Study Extra" feature in Box 2.2 illustrates how the rational basis test is typically applied to criminal laws.

Using rational basis review, courts typically uphold the constitutionality of laws that make distinctions between groups, assuming that a fundamental right is not at issue and neither a suspect nor quasi-suspect classification is drawn. Indeed, rational basis review is so deferential that it has been called "minimal scrutiny in theory and virtually none in fact."[90] The US Supreme Court has upheld more than a hundred classifications under

BOX 2.2

CASE STUDY EXTRA

Recreational Marijuana for Some Teens, But Not Others?

In 1982, Alaska experimented with legalizing marijuana by allowing adults over the age of nineteen to possess less than four ounces of the drug. Possession of marijuana remained illegal for minors who could be charged through the juvenile justice system for violating the law. The law, however, criminalized possession of marijuana by eighteen-year-olds even though they were no longer minors. In *Allam v. State*, an eighteen-year-old who was caught possessing a small amount of marijuana challenged the validity of a state's possession law.[122] He argued that the law illegally discriminated on the basis of age since all adults in the state could possess small quantities of the drug except for those who were eighteen years of age. Because age is neither a suspect classification, nor a quasi-suspect classification, and because possession of marijuana is not a fundamental right, the court applied the rational basis test to review the constitutionality of the law. Applying that test, the court upheld the age-based classification finding that the state had two rational bases to discriminate against eighteen-year-olds. First, many eighteen-year-olds are in high school where they would be able to share marijuana with minors. Second, eighteen-year-olds are still relatively inexperienced drivers; giving them an extra year to mature before allowing them access to a drug was a rational legislative judgment.

1. Do you agree with the premise that age is neither a suspect, nor quasi-suspect classification? Why or why not?
2. Critique the two rational bases upon which the court upheld the law. Explain your agreement or disagreement with them.

rational basis review between 1971 and 2014; in contrast, it has invalidated only seventeen classifications.[91]

BALANCING DUE PROCESS, EQUAL PROTECTION, AND CRIME CONTROL

Now that you have learned about the standards of review that courts use to evaluate the constitutionality of laws under the Fifth and Fourteenth Amendments, let's return to the Hart-Devlin debate concerning the legislation of morality using so-called privacy cases as an example.

In *Bowers v. Hardwick*, the police had legally entered the home of the defendant, Michael Hardwick, to serve an unrelated warrant upon him.[92] When the police entered, they discovered him engaging in oral sex with another man, and arrested him. Hardwick was never prosecuted for the crime, but in fear of such prosecution, he brought suit claiming that Georgia's sodomy law violated his rights to privacy, due process, and freedoms of expression and association.[93]

The majority decision began with the following:

> This case does not require a judgment on whether laws against sodomy between consenting adults in general, or between homosexuals in particular, are wise or desirable. . . . The issue presented is whether the Federal Constitution confers a fundamental right upon homosexuals to engage in sodomy.[94]

The situation presented in *Bowers* was not covered by what had been (until then) generally thought of as sexual privacy cases:

1. *Griswold v. Connecticut*, which struck down an anti-contraceptive law as an "impermissible intrusion on the right of the association protecting the marital relationship, [the] enforcement of [which] threatens police intrusion into the marital bedroom";[95]
2. *Eisenstadt v. Baird*, which extended *Griswold*'s holding to unmarried persons on equal protection grounds;[96] and
3. *Roe v. Wade*, which held that the right to privacy guaranteed a woman's right to choose to have an abortion during the first trimester of pregnancy.[97]

Distinguishing these cases as dealing with the family, marriage, and procreation, the majority reasoned that homosexual sodomy did not concern any of these issues, and, therefore, was outside the realm of the constitutional right to privacy that these three key cases collectively represented.[98]

The *Bowers* majority then determined no fundamental right was at issue since sodomy was neither "deeply rooted in our Nation's history or tradition," nor "implicit in the concept of ordered liberty."[99] Accordingly, the justices applied the rational basis test. In so doing, the Court upheld the constitutionality of the Georgia sodomy statute as being rationally related to the legitimate governmental interest of regulating morality.[100] In short, the Court embraced Lord Patrick Devlin's views on the legislation of morality by endorsing the notion that "sodomy is immoral and unacceptable" when it refused to declare that purpose an insufficient rational basis upon which to criminalize the act.[101]

The majority opinion in *Bowers* was sharply criticized by the dissenting justices and many scholars for having framed the issues much too narrowly.[102] If the Court had framed the issue in the case as one of sexual privacy, it could easily have fit the facts into the line of precedent descending from *Griswold* and held the statute unconstitutional. This is especially true because *Griswold, Eisenstadt,* and *Roe* can be interpreted as guaranteeing that adults have a right "to engage in non-procreative sexual relations, even outside the traditional setting of marriage."[103]

The Supreme Court's decision in *Bowers* has also been criticized for defining fundamental rights as those "deeply rooted" in history. It is worth noting that the right to access contraceptives, as established in *Griswold,* and the right to choose to terminate a pregnancy, as established in *Roe,* were both found within the scope of the right to privacy despite the fact that neither right was "deeply rooted" in history and tradition.[104]

Seventeen years after the decision in *Bowers,* the Supreme Court changed its mind regarding the unconstitutionality of laws criminalizing acts of sodomy committed in private between consenting adults.

John Geddes LAWRENCE and Tyron GARNER, Petitioners,

v.

The State of TEXAS, Respondent.

539 U.S. 558 (2003).

* * *

In Houston, Texas, officers [lawfully] . . . entered an apartment where one of the petitioners, John Geddes Lawrence, resided. . . . The officers observed Lawrence and another man, Tyron Garner, engaging in a sexual act. The two petitioners were arrested, held in custody overnight, and charged and convicted before a Justice of the Peace. [They subsequently were unsuccessful in their attempts to have the statute invalidated and were each fined $200 and assessed court costs of $141.25.]

* * *

The Court began its substantive discussion in *Bowers* as follows: "The issue presented is whether the Federal Constitution confers a fundamental right upon homosexuals to engage in sodomy and hence invalidates the laws of the many States that still make such conduct illegal and have done so for a very long time."[105] That statement, we now conclude, discloses the Court's own failure to appreciate the extent of the liberty at stake. To say that the issue in *Bowers* was simply the right to engage in certain sexual conduct demeans the claim the individual put forward, just as it would demean a married couple were it to be said marriage is simply about the right to have sexual intercourse. The laws involved in *Bowers* and here are, to be sure, statutes that purport to do no more than prohibit a particular sexual act. Their penalties and purposes, though, have more far-reaching consequences, touching upon the most private human conduct, sexual behavior, and in the most private of places, the home. . . .

* * *

Two principal cases decided after *Bowers* cast its holding into even more doubt. In *Planned Parenthood of Southeastern Pa. v. Casey*,[106] the Court reaffirmed the substantive force of the liberty protected by the Due Process Clause. . . . In explaining the respect the Constitution demands for the autonomy of the person in making these choices, we stated . . . "choices central to personal dignity and autonomy, are central to the liberty protected by the Fourteenth Amendment."[107] . . . The decision in *Bowers* would deny them this right.

The second post-*Bowers* case of principal relevance is *Romer v. Evans*.[108] There the Court struck down class-based legislation directed at homosexuals as a violation of the Equal Protection Clause. *Romer* invalidated an amendment to Colorado's constitution which named as a solitary class persons who were homosexuals, lesbians, or bisexual either by "orientation, conduct, practices or relationships,"[109] and deprived them of protection under state anti-discrimination laws. We concluded that the provision was "born of animosity toward the class of persons affected" and further that it had no rational relation to a legitimate governmental purpose.[110]

* * *

The rationale of *Bowers* does not withstand careful analysis. . . . *Bowers* was not correct when it was decided, and it is not correct today. It ought not to remain binding precedent. *Bowers v. Hardwick* should be and now is overruled.

The present case does not involve minors. It does not involve persons who might be injured or coerced or who are situated in relationships where consent might not easily be refused. It does not involve public conduct or prostitution. It does not involve whether the government must give formal recognition to any relationship that homosexual persons seek to enter. The case does involve two adults who, with full and mutual consent from each other, engaged in sexual practices common to a homosexual lifestyle. The petitioners are entitled to respect for their private lives. The State cannot demean their existence or control their destiny by making their private sexual conduct a crime. Their right to liberty under the Due Process Clause gives them the full right to engage in their conduct without intervention of the government. "It is a promise of the Constitution that there is a realm of personal liberty which the government may not enter."[111] The Texas statute furthers no legitimate state interest which can justify its intrusion into the personal and private life of the individual. Had those who drew and ratified the Due Process Clauses of the Fifth Amendment or the Fourteenth Amendment known the components of liberty in its manifold possibilities, they might have been more specific. They did not presume to have this insight. They knew times can blind us to certain truths and later generations can see that laws once thought necessary and proper in fact serve only to oppress. As the Constitution endures, persons in every generation can invoke its principles in their own search for greater freedom.

* * *

Justice O'CONNOR, concurring:

* * *

The statute at issue here makes sodomy a crime only if a person "engages in deviate sexual intercourse with another individual of the same sex." Sodomy between opposite-sex partners, however, is not a crime in Texas. That is, Texas treats the same conduct differently based solely on the participants. . . . The Texas statute makes homosexuals unequal in the eyes of the law by making particular conduct—and only that conduct—subject to criminal sanction. . . .

* * *

A State can of course assign certain consequences to a violation of its criminal law. But the State cannot single out one identifiable class of citizens for punishment that does not apply to everyone else, with moral disapproval as the only asserted state interest for the law. The Texas sodomy statute subjects homosexuals to "a lifelong penalty and stigma. A legislative classification that threatens the creation of an underclass . . . cannot be reconciled with" the Equal Protection Clause.[112]

* * *

Justice SCALIA, dissenting:

* * *

The Texas statute undeniably seeks to further the belief of its citizens that certain forms of sexual behavior are "immoral and unacceptable"—the same interest furthered by criminal laws against fornication, bigamy, adultery, adult incest, bestiality, and obscenity. *Bowers* held that this was a legitimate state interest. The Court today reaches the opposite conclusion. . . . This effectively decrees the end of all morals legislation. If, as the Court asserts, the promotion of majoritarian sexual morality is not even a legitimate state interest, none of the above-mentioned laws can survive rational-basis review.

* * *

It is clear . . . that the Court has taken sides in the culture war, departing from its role of assuring, as neutral observer, that the democratic rules of engagement are observed. Many Americans do not want persons who openly engage in homosexual conduct as partners in their business, as scoutmasters for their children, as teachers in their children's schools, or as boarders in their home. They view this as protecting themselves and their families from a lifestyle that they believe to be immoral and destructive. The Court views it as "discrimination" which it is the function of our judgments to deter. . . .

Let me be clear that I have nothing against homosexuals, or any other group, promoting their agenda through normal democratic means. Social perceptions of sexual and other morality change over time, and every group has the right to persuade its fellow citizens that its view of such matters is the best. That homosexuals have achieved some success in that enterprise is attested to by the fact that Texas is one of the few remaining States that criminalize private, consensual homosexual acts. But persuading one's fellow citizens is one thing, and imposing one's views in absence of democratic majority will is something else. I would no more require a State to criminalize homosexual acts—or, for that matter, display any moral disapprobation of them—than I would forbid it to do so. What Texas has chosen to do is well within the range of traditional democratic action, and its hand should not be stayed through the invention of a brand-new "constitutional right" by a Court that is impatient of democratic change. . . .

Questions

1. In the context of sodomy laws, the alleged biblical condemnation of sodomy is often cited as the justification for morally condemning sodomy. What role should the separation of church and state play, if any, in determining whether the religious nature of the condemnation of sodomy ought to be codified into criminal law? Explain your answer.
2. In *Washington v. Glucksberg*, the Court, applying the rational basis test, held that substantive due process did not include the right to assisted suicide. Since *Lawrence* counsels against making moral arguments, why are the principles of privacy, autonomy, and self-determination construed under rational basis review in a manner that allows someone to be free from unwanted governmental regulation in the sexual realm, yet those same principles do not serve as rational bases for allowing assisted suicide?

CONCLUSION

Learning Objectives	Summaries
1. Describe how the First Amendment prohibits the criminalization of certain types of conduct relating to the freedom of religion.	The Establishment Clause prevents local, state, and the federal governments from enacting any law that establishes an official religion, or favoring one religion over another (or over none at all). The Free Exercise Clause protects people's rights to exercise their religious beliefs (or to believe nothing at all).

Learning Objectives	Summaries
2. Assess how valid time, place, and manner regulations may constitutionally limit the First Amendment rights to free speech and peaceable assembly.	A law may restrict the time, place, and manner of free speech and peaceable assembly if it (a) furthers an important or substantial governmental interest; (b) is unrelated to the suppression of free expression; (c) is narrowly tailored to serve the government's interest such that the restriction on free speech is not greater than is necessary to achieve the governmental interest; and (d) leaves open ample, alternative means for people to communicate their message.
3. Differentiate the types of speech that do not receive First Amendment protection.	Defamation, words that incite imminent lawlessness, fighting words, threats, harassment, and obscenity do not receive protection under the First Amendment.
4. Discuss what limits the Second Amendment places on the regulation of firearms.	The Second Amendment prohibits laws that ban the possession of handguns by law-abiding citizens. It does not protect the possession of weapons suitable for warfare, rather than self-defense, such as bazookas, bombs, grenades, tanks, or biological, chemical, or nuclear weapons. Nor does it prevent certain gun control regulations, such as bans on firearm possession by convicted felons and people with serious mental illnesses, bans on carrying firearms in certain places, or limits on carrying concealed weapons.
5. Differentiate between the crime control and due process models of the criminal justice system.	The crime control model concerns the suppression of crime and the swift punishment of offenders. Its focus is to move offenders through the criminal justice process as quickly and efficiently as possible (assembly line justice). The due process model concerns the rights of the accused. Its focus is to move offenders through the criminal justice process carefully to ensure that the guilty are punished and the innocent go free (obstacle course justice).
6. Compare and contrast the various standards of review that courts use to analyze the constitutionality of criminal laws that infringe on due process and equal protection rights.	Strict scrutiny is the most exacting level of judicial review in which courts examine whether a law is narrowly tailored to achieve a compelling governmental interest. It applies to due process and equal protection claims in which a fundamental right might be burdened. It also applies to equal protection claims involving a suspect classification, race, religion, or national origin. Intermediate scrutiny asks if a quasi-suspect classification, such as distinctions on the basis of biological sex and legitimacy at birth, is substantially related to achieving an important governmental interest. The rational basis test asks if a law is rationally related to a legitimate governmental interest. It presumes the constitutional validity of all laws that do not burden any fundamental rights and do not differentiate on the basis of any suspect or quasi-suspect classification.
7. Analyze the constitutional limits of using the criminal law to enforce morality.	The legislation of morality is constitutionally suspect. Laws may not infringe upon privacy rights protected by the Fifth and Fourteenth Amendments because morality alone (i.e., without additional reasons, such as the prevention of harm to others), does not constitute a rational basis for intruding upon the liberty and autonomy of adults engaged in consensual activity, in private, that other people might find morally objectionable.

KEY TERMS

crime control model
defamation
disorderly conduct
disturbing the peace
due process
due process model
Equal Protection Clause
Establishment Clause
fighting words
Free Exercise Clause
harassment
imminent lawless action
intermediate scrutiny
limited public forums
nonpublic forums
procedural due process
quasi-suspect classifications
rational basis test
rights
standards of review
strict scrutiny
substantive due process
suspect classifications
symbolic speech
threats
time, place, and manner regulation
traditional public forums

3

Starting Points

EVIDENCE, ACTS, AND OMISSIONS

LEARNING OBJECTIVES

1. Differentiate conclusive presumptions and rebuttable presumptions from inferences.
2. Identify the primary types of evidence.
3. Distinguish between the burden of production and the burden of persuasion.
4. Compare and contrast the quantum of evidence needed under each of the major burdens of persuasion.
5. Describe the requirements of establishing an *actus reus* by voluntary act.
6. Explain the ways in which an *actus reus* may be established by omission.
7. Discuss how the act of possession can constitute an *actus reus*.

Outline

INTRODUCTION

Recall from Chapter 1 that the principle of culpability seeks to limit the imposition of criminal punishment to those who are blameworthy. But establishing culpability requires either that those accused of crimes plead guilty by admitting their guilt in open court or, alternatively, that the prosecution prove the guilt of those accused of crimes at trials.

All criminal trials are governed by both rules of procedure and rules of evidence. This chapter summarize some of the key rules that not only form the bedrock of the criminal trial process, but also for proving that the acts of which a criminal defendant may be accused.

STARTING POINTS FOR CRIMINAL TRIALS: PRESUMPTIONS AND INFERENCES

One of the foundations of evidence law is that the trier-of-fact, which is typically a jury, but can be a judge in nonjury trial, must have an evidentiary starting place at the outset of a trial. In a criminal trial, that starting place usually involves presumptions. **Presumptions** are conclusions or deductions that the law requires the trier-of-fact to make in the absence of evidence to the contrary. There are two main types of presumptions. The first type is known as a **conclusive presumption**, or mandatory presumption. If the law makes the presumption conclusive, then the finder of fact must accept the fact as presumed regardless of the evidence presented. Very few mandatory presumptions exist today in the criminal law. However, one that remains relevant is the presumption of incapacity for a child under the age of seven to commit a crime. While it is theoretically possible for a six-year-old genius to plot and carry out a crime with criminal intent, the law conclusively presumes that a child under the age of seven is incapable of doing so. No evidence regarding the uniqueness of that particular child to show why the presumption should not be applied in a particular case would be admissible because the presumption is mandatory.

Conclusive presumptions played a larger role in the past than they do today. For example, at common law, it was conclusively presumed that a husband could not rape his wife. Today, nearly all US jurisdictions penal codes recognize marital rape as a crime. Another example of a conclusive presumption that is no longer relevant is the presumption of paternity. At common law, any child born to a married woman was conclusively presumed to be the child of that woman's husband. Evidence that the husband was infertile was inadmissible because the presumption was mandatory. Today, that presumption has either been abolished or converted to the second type of presumption, known as a rebuttable or permissive presumption.

Most presumptions today are **rebuttable presumptions**. That is, the trier-of-fact must presume a certain fact to be the case unless the presumption is overcome or rebutted by other evidence. Criminal trials start with two rebuttable presumptions: the presumption of sanity and the presumption of innocence. The **presumption of sanity** requires that all defendants be presumed sane unless sufficient evidence of their insanity is proven, usually by clear and convincing evidence. The **presumption of innocence** requires the trier-of-fact to accept that the defendant is innocent unless the prosecution meets its burden to prove that the defendant is guilty beyond a reasonable doubt.

In contrast, **inferences** are conclusions or deductions the trier-of-fact may reasonably make based on the facts which have been established by the evidence. But unlike presumptions, which the trier-of-fact is required accept, inferences are permissive. Put differently, jurors might draw a conclusion from evidence, but they might not. For instance, if a defendant's car were found parked a block away from a bank at the time someone robbed that bank, one could draw an inference that the accused committed the robbery. But such a conclusion would be quite a stretch from the mere fact that the defendant's car was near the bank. The defendant might have been a customer who was on the premises to conduct lawful banking business. Or perhaps the defendant was not in the bank at all, but was merely in the vicinity while patronizing another business. A reasonable juror would want far more evidence to support the inference that the defendant committed the bank robbery. Thus, a prosecutor will need to present an array of evidence to meet the burden of proof. In the next sections, we will examine the types of evidence prosecutors use to establish their cases.

Proving the Case with Evidence

Evidence consists of physical objects, testimony, or other things offered to prove or disprove the existence of a fact. Facts in criminal trials may be proven by direct evidence and by circumstantial evidence.

Direct evidence is first-hand evidence that does not require presumptions or inferences in order to establish a proposition of fact. The best example of direct evidence is eyewitness testimony. One need not draw any inference from a witness's testimony that she saw something. She either saw it or she did not. Of course, an eyewitness might be mistaken or might even be intentionally misleading. In fact, faulty eyewitness testimony is the leading cause of wrongful convictions in the United States.[1] Thus, just because evidence is direct evidence does not necessarily establish its truth.

Circumstantial evidence is indirect evidence. To reach a conclusion, the trier-of-fact would have to reason through circumstantial evidence and infer the existence of some fact in dispute. If circumstantial evidence is believed, it requires additional inferences or presumptions, and may require the fact finder to examine a chain of evidence in order to accept the fact at issue.

Circumstantial evidence is very important because in many criminal cases, the perpetrator of a crime does not leave a trail of direct evidence. Take, for example, a homicide investigation where a husband is thought to have killed his wife, but there is no direct evidence that he did it. The fact that the husband cannot account for his whereabouts during the time period the medical examiner has determined to be the time of death is circumstantial evidence of his guilt. Certainly, though, that fact alone would not be sufficient evidence to obtain a conviction. But if more circumstantial evidence were uncovered, the case would get stronger. Suppose that the husband stood to inherit a million dollars in life insurance proceeds upon her death. What if you also learned she was very unhappy in the marriage and planned to divorce the husband, thereby terminating his right to inherit her estate? As you can see, as circumstantial evidence amounts, it is possible to become more and more confident that these facts, if proven, go a long way toward confirming the husband's guilt. That is the significance of circumstantial evidence.

The distinction between direct and circumstantial evidence depends on the context of the question being examined. Suppose your fingerprints are found on a gun that forensic firearm testing reveals was the weapon used to kill a victim. Are your fingerprints direct or circumstantial evidence? It depends. They are direct evidence that you came in contact with the gun, but that does not mean you are the person who fired the weapon and killed the victim. Thus, your fingerprints are only circumstantial evidence of your being guilty of a homicide. An inference needs to resolve the question of your guilt.

Types of Evidence

Evidence can be classified as testimonial evidence, physical evidence, scientific evidence, and demonstrative evidence.

- **Testimonial evidence** is oral testimony given under oath by witnesses.
- **Physical evidence** (also referred to as real evidence) consists of tangible objects such as contracts, bank statements, or other documentary evidence; firearms; drug paraphernalia; clothing; and traces of objects that may be found at a crime or accident scene, such as fingerprints or trace amounts of drugs.
- The scientific examination of physical evidence (in a laboratory, for example) yields **scientific evidence**—the formal results of forensic investigatory techniques (often in documentary form) such as autopsy reports, firearm matches, and DNA analyses.
- **Demonstrative evidence** has no evidential value by itself. Rather, it serves as a visual or auditory aid to assist the fact finder in understanding the evidence. Charts, maps, videos, and courtroom demonstrations are forms of demonstrative evidence.

There is an evidentiary short-cut called **judicial notice** that excuses a party from the burden of having to prove certain facts through testimonial, physical, or other means when the matter is commonly known in the community. Thus, judicial notice does not involve evidence per se, but rather is a process that excuses a party from having to introduce evidence in order to prove something. In other words, judicial notice is the process whereby the trier-of-fact accepts certain facts as true without the necessity of formal proof. For example, a court would take judicial notice of the fact that Halloween falls on October 31 or that Christmas falls on December 25 without the requirement of having a calendar introduced into evidence. This would be appropriate because the dates of these holidays are within the common knowledge of the jury and the community at large. The meaning of certain words and phrases is another example of something which a court might take judicial notice of, such as "turning a trick" or "getting a fix."

Burdens of Proof

Simply put, the phrase "burden of proof" refers to an obligation to prove a claim. The concept of burden of proof encompasses two separate burdens, the burden of production and the burden of persuasion. If a party has the **burden of production** (often referred to as the burden of going forward), they must produce sufficient evidence to put facts in issue; put differently, there must be a enough evidence to allow a jury to consider a claim and form a reasonable verdict from it.[2] If the party with the burden of production introduces sufficient evidence to prove the basic elements of its case (called establishing a ***prima facie* case**), then the case may move forward for resolution by the trier-of-fact.[3] However, if insufficient evidence is introduced to establish a *prima facie* case, then the trier-of-fact will not even get a chance to deliberate any factual issues due to the insufficiency of evidence to establish a fact in issue.[4]

The **burden of persuasion** is the obligation of a party to prove certain facts to a certain level or quantum of proof—either beyond a reasonable doubt, by clear and convincing evidence, or by a preponderance of the evidence.[5] The burden of persuasion comes into play after all the evidence is produced, when it is time for the judge to decide the ultimate issue in a bench trial, or time to instruct the jury. The prosecution always bears the burden in persuading the trier-of-fact that the defendant committed each and every element of all crimes charged. In some circumstances, however, the defendant in a criminal trial bears the burden of persuasion to prove a certain defense, such as legal insanity at the time the offense was committed. When the defendant bears the burden of persuasion to prove a defense, it is called an **affirmative defense**. See Table 3.1 for a depiction of the various levels of proof used in evaluating whether the burden of persuasion has been met.

At the low end of the scale illustrated by Table 3.1, there is no proof. Just above that, there is what the law calls mere suspicion, which is a fancy way of expressing a hunch or the feeling of intuition. While intuitively knowing something is undoubtedly a skill that serves law enforcement officers well, mere suspicion is insufficient proof of any fact in a court of law.

The next level up from mere suspicion is **reasonable, articulable suspicion**. It differs from mere suspicion only slightly, but in an important way. Instead of just having a hunch, a person can articulate the reasons why he or she is suspicious. Moreover, the explanations

Table 3.1 Levels of Proof for Satisfying the Burden of Persuasion

0%--50%-- 100%

No Proof	Mere Suspicion	Reasonable Articulable Suspicion	Probable Cause	Preponderance of the Evidence	Clear and Convincing Evidence	Beyond a Reasonable Doubt	Beyond all Doubt
	A hunch or feeling of intuition; insufficient proof in any stage of the judicial process.	The ability to articulate reasons for suspicion in an objective manner.	Independent verifiable factual information that supports the conclusion that there is a "fair probability" that a crime occurred or a particular person was involved in a crime.	Proof that something is more likely than not.	Evidence that is highly and substantially more likely to be true than untrue.	Prosecution's burden to prove each element of a criminal offense.	Proof to an absolute certainty is not required in any phase of the judicial process in the United States.

offered as the bases for the suspicion are objectively reasonable. In other words, when explained to the next person, they also understand why a person would be suspicions under the circumstances as described. This level of proof is necessary for law enforcement personnel to conduct a "stop and frisk," a brief, limited, investigative detention.[6]

The next highest level of proof is called **probable cause.** Defining probable cause is no easy task. What differentiates it from reasonable, articulable suspicion is the existence of facts—independently verifiable factual information that supports the conclusion that there is a "fair probability" that a crime occurred or that a particular person was involved in a crime.[7] Probable cause is necessary to arrest a person, conduct a search, or seize evidence.

In most civil cases, the standard of proof is a **preponderance of the evidence,** which is commonly understood as proof that something is more likely than not. Thus, if a plaintiff is able to show the probability is more than 50 percent that a defendant did what is claimed, the judgment will be for the plaintiff. It is also the standard of proof used to establish the validity of waivers of constitutional rights, as well as the burden for proving that exceptions to the Exclusionary Rule apply.[8]

Clear and convincing evidence is a higher level of proof than the preponderance of the evidence standard, yet it falls short of proof beyond a reasonable doubt; in other words, it is evidence that is highly and substantially more likely to be true than untrue. It is the standard of proof in a handful of civil cases, such as those establishing defamation of character against a public figure.[9] It is also the level of proof to which a defendant in some criminal cases must establish an affirmative defense, such as insanity (see Chapter 14). If there is clear and convincing evidence, the trier-of-fact should be reasonably satisfied as to the existence of the fact, yet they may have some doubts.

Because a criminally accused defendant is presumed innocent until proven otherwise, the prosecution has the burden to prove all the elements of the crime(s) charged in its case **beyond a reasonable doubt**. If the prosecution fails to meet this burden of proof on any element, the defendant must be acquitted.[10] Reasonable doubt is a term requiring little interpretation, although various courts have attempted to formulate somewhat involved definitions that add little beyond its plain meaning. A specific definition for the beyond a reasonable doubt standard has not been adopted by the US Supreme Court, leading to some confusion amongst jurists and jurors alike. In fact, jury instructions explaining reasonable doubt are often the basis for appeal. It is sufficient to say that proof beyond a reasonable doubt requires that the guilt of the defendant be established to a reasonable, but not absolute or mathematical, certainty. Probability of guilt is not enough. In other words, to satisfy the beyond a reasonable doubt standard, the jury must be satisfied that the charges against the defendant are almost certainly true.

In *Victor v. Sandoval*, the US Supreme Court wrestled with the use of jury instructions that equated proof beyond a reasonable doubt as constituting proof "to a moral certainty."[11] Although the Court ultimately upheld a conviction based on a jury instruction that included that language, the Court noted that the term had lost its historical meaning as a synonym for proof beyond a reasonable doubt. The Court also upheld a definition of reasonable doubt as "an actual and substantial doubt arising from the evidence, from the facts or circumstances shown by the evidence, or from the lack of evidence."[12] Nonetheless, the Court cautioned that the term substantial doubt could be problematic. To clarify the concept, Justice Ginsburg's concurring opinion encouraged trial courts to instruct juries with the following definition of reasonable doubt as promulgated by the Federal Judicial Center:

> [T]he government has the burden of proving the defendant guilty beyond a reasonable doubt. Some of you may have served as jurors in civil cases, where you were told that it is only necessary to prove that a fact is more likely true than not true. In criminal cases, the government's proof must be more powerful than that. It must be beyond a reasonable doubt.
>
> Proof beyond a reasonable doubt is proof that leaves you firmly convinced of the defendant's guilt. There are very few things in this world that we know with absolute certainty, and in criminal cases the law does not require proof that overcomes every possible doubt. If, based on your consideration of the evidence, you are firmly convinced that the defendant is guilty of the crime charged, you must find

> him guilty. If on the other hand, you think there is a real possibility that he is not guilty, you must give him the benefit of the doubt and find him not guilty.[13]

Keep in mind that reasonable doubt is an inherently qualitative concept; it cannot be quantified, and any attempt to do so for a jury is likely to result in reversible error.[14]

OVERVIEW OF THE ELEMENTS OF CRIMES

Crimes generally consist of a combination of two or more of four established elements: *actus reus*, *mens rea*, attendant circumstances, and a result. Every crime, by definition, sets forth some physical act or conduct that is prohibited—the "thing" you are not allowed to do under the criminal law. Such proscribed conduct is called the ***actus reus*** (Latin for "evil act"). For example, taking the personal property of another person, coupled with the mental state of intent to steal, is the crime of theft. The *actus reus* is the actual taking of the property. As will be explored in more detail in this chapter, an *actus reus* must be the consequence of either a voluntary act (which can even be a state of knowing possession of something), or a qualifying omission.[15]

Most crimes, however, do not impose a criminal sanction for doing an *actus reus* unless it is coupled with some culpable state of mind referred to as the ***mens rea*** (Latin for "evil mind"). *Mens rea* is concerned with the level of intentionality with which the *actus reus* occurred. For example, was the *actus reus* committed purposefully, or was it done accidentally due to someone's negligence? Take the theft example again. If you accidentally take someone else's property, that is not the crime of theft. But if you purposely take it, then a theft may have occurred. The level of *mens rea* entertained by a person is often what differentiates an accident from a crime, or serious crimes from petty ones. Although this brief introduction to *mens rea* may seem straightforward, issues surrounding criminal intent are actually quite difficult—both conceptually and in terms of proof in practice. Accordingly, we explore *mens rea* in much greater details in Chapter 4. For now, keep in mind that a union of *actus reus* and *mens rea* forms the basic elements of most crimes. Put differently, the commission of a criminal act via a voluntary act or qualifying omission, when coupled with a specific level of criminal intent, is necessary to impose criminal liability for the overwhelming majority of offenses. Recall, however, from cases like *Morissette v. United States* (see Chapter 1) and *Michael M. v. Superior Court of Sonoma County* (see Chapter 2) that there is a narrow class of crimes that are exceptions to this general requirement of a union of *actus reus* and *mens rea*.[16] Offenses that are punished without regard to the actor's state of mind are referred to as crimes of **strict liability**. Strict liability crimes are covered in more detail in Chapter 4.

The third major component of crimes are **attendant circumstances**, those circumstances which must surround the occurrence of the *actus reus* for the crime to have occurred, or for it to be graded in a particular manner. For example, the crime of speeding cannot take place unless one is traveling on a public roadway. Hence, it is not a crime to race in the Indianapolis 500 because the attendant circumstance of the racetrack being a public roadway is not present.

Some crimes have a **result** element that requires the prosecution to prove that something actually occurred as a result of the commission of the *actus reus*. As stated previously, all crimes, save strict liability offenses, require some union of *actus reus* and *mens rea*, making both *actus reus* and *mens rea* necessary components of nearly all criminal offenses. The same cannot be said for the result component, or attendant circumstances, for that matter. Only certain crimes require that a particular result occur. All forms of homicide are good examples. One cannot be convicted of any type of homicide unless one's act caused a particular result, namely, the death of another human being. As we will explore in Chapter 4, proving causation of a particular result, however, can be a complicated task.

A VOLUNTARY ACT AS AN *ACTUS REUS*

A **voluntary act** is a bodily movement performed consciously and as a result of effort and determination.[17] For example, punching someone is a voluntary act that would qualify as the *actus reus* for the crime of battery. Similarly, shooting someone is a voluntary act that would qualify as the *actus reus* for a homicide if the victim died. Even speaking certain prohibited words may be a voluntary act upon which a criminal prosecution may be based, as in the crime of a criminal solicitation (see Chapter 5), or in the use of fighting words which incite violence (see Chapters 2 and 12).

In contrast, an involuntary act, defined as any bodily movement that is not a product of the effort or determination of the actor (whether conscious or habitual), does not qualify as an *actus reus* for criminal law purposes.[18] In other words, acts that are not a product of volition, such as acts that are a product of automatism (e.g., innate reflexes, spasms, spontaneous convulsions, and other muscular actions that occur without the conscious control of the mind) are not considered to be voluntary acts, and thus, are not crimes.[19] The "Case Study Extra" feature in Box 3.1 compares and contrasts two cases the reach different conclusions about the voluntariness of acts that may have been a function of police action.

An act is not considered involuntary merely because (a) the actor does not remember it; (b) the actor could not control his or her impulses; (c) the act was unintentional or its consequences were unforeseen; or (d) it was habitual.[20] Similarly, because voluntariness presupposes consciousness, any act that occurs while the actor is unconscious does not qualify as an *actus reus* so long as the unconscious state was not self-induced.[21] While this is a seemingly clear rule, there are situations in which a defendant may be held criminally liable even though the action immediately causing the harm was clearly involuntary. Consider the following case.

BOX 3.1

CASE STUDY EXTRA

What Constitutes a Voluntary versus Involuntary Act?

Martin v. State, an influential case decided by the Alabama Court of Appeals in 1944, wrestled with the seemingly straightforward question of whether the defendant was guilty of a public drunkenness charge.[53] A statute in effect at that time provided, "Any person who, while intoxicated or drunk, appears in any public place where one or more persons are present, . . . and manifests a drunken condition by boisterous or indecent conduct, or loud and profane discourse, shall, on conviction, be fined."[54]

Police arrested the defendant, Martin, at his home and took him onto the highway, where he "manifested a drunken condition by using loud and profane language."[55] He was convicted and appealed, arguing that he had not committed a voluntary act constituting the *actus reus* of the offense. The appellate court agreed, reasoning that "an accusation of drunkenness in a designated public place cannot be established by proof that the accused, while in an intoxicated condition, was involuntarily and forcibly carried to that place by the arresting officer."[56]

In 2010, Tommy Gastello relied on the *Martin* case to argue that his conviction for knowingly bringing methamphetamine into a jail was unjust because he had them on his person when he was arrested.[57] Specifically, Gastello maintained that because he was not present in the jail by choice, the fact that he had illicit drugs on his person when he was arrested for being under the influence of a controlled substance did not constitute a voluntary act sufficient to establish *actus reus*.[58] After being convicted, Gastello successfully appealed. The court noted that Gastello had been "arrested for being under the influence of a controlled substance during a traffic stop, transported by patrol car to jail, and escorted inside by the arresting officer to undergo the booking process."[59] The court described the defendant's role as being one of pure "passivity and omission" for having submitted "to the lawful authority of the police."[60] Citing the *Martin* case, the intermediate appeals court ruled that "someone who is brought into jail in such an involuntary and submissive state does not 'bring' drugs inside . . . even if he previously secreted them on his person and knows he possesses them when he enters the facility."[61]

The state then appealed the reversal of Gastello's conviction. The Supreme Court of California reinstated it, disagreeing with the intermediate appeals court because Gastello knew that he had the drugs on him when he was booked into the jail. "The critical fact is that an arrestee has the opportunity to decide whether to purge himself of hidden drugs before entering jail, or whether to bring them inside and commit a new crime."[62] Moreover, Gastello was specifically wanted by the arresting officer that he would be committing another crime if he brought drugs into the jail with him; yet Gastello failed to disclose he had the drugs on him.

- Critique the outcome in the *Martin* case.
- Do you agree with the way in which the court in *Gastello* differentiated *Martin* in order to conclude that the defendant had, in fact, committed a voluntary act? Explain your reasoning.

The PEOPLE of the State of New York, Appellant-Respondent,
v.
Emil DECINA, Respondent-Appellant.
138 N.E.2d 799 (N.Y. 1956).

* * *

A group of six schoolgirls were walking north on the easterly sidewalk of Delaware Avenue, two in front and four slightly in the rear, when defendant's car struck them from behind. One of the girls escaped injury by jumping against the wall of the viaduct. Three of the children, 6 to 12 years old, were found dead on arrival by the medical examiner, and a fourth child, 7 years old, died in a hospital two days later as a result of injuries sustained in the accident.

After striking the children, defendant's car continued on the easterly sidewalk, and then swerved back onto Delaware Avenue once more. It continued in a northerly direction, passing under a second viaduct before it again veered to the right and remounted the easterly curb, striking and breaking a metal lamppost. With its horn blowing steadily apparently because defendant was stooped over the steering wheel the car proceeded on the sidewalk until it finally crashed through a 7¼-inch brick wall of a grocery store, injuring at least one customer and causing considerable property damage.

When the car came to a halt in the store, with its horn still blowing, several fires had been ignited. Defendant was stooped over in the car and was "bobbing a little." To one witness he appeared dazed, to another unconscious, lying back with his hands off the wheel. Various people present shouted to defendant to turn off the ignition of his car, and "within a matter of seconds the horn stopped blowing and the car did shut off."

Defendant was pulled out of the car by a number of bystanders and laid down on the sidewalk. To a policeman who came on the scene shortly he appeared "injured, dazed"; another witness said that "he looked as though he was knocked out, and his arm seemed to be bleeding." An injured customer in the store, after receiving first aid, pressed defendant for an explanation of the accident and he told her: "I blacked out from the bridge."

* * *

From the police station defendant was taken to the [hospital where] . . . Defendant then proceeded to relate to Dr. Wechter his past medical history, namely, that at the age of 7 he was struck by an auto and suffered a marked loss of hearing. In 1946 he was treated in this same hospital for an illness during which he had some convulsions. Several burr holes were made in his skull and a brain abscess was drained. Following this operation defendant had no convulsions from 1946 through 1950. In 1950 he had four convulsions, caused by scar tissue on the brain. From 1950 to 1954 he experienced about 10 or 20 seizures a year, in which his right hand would jump although he remained fully conscious. In 1954, he had 4 or 5 generalized seizures with loss of consciousness, the last being in September, 1954, a few months before the accident. Thereafter he had more hospitalization, a spinal tap, consultation with a neurologist, and took medication daily to help prevent seizures. On the basis of this medical history, Dr. Wechter made a diagnosis of Jacksonian epilepsy, and was of the opinion that defendant had a seizure at the time of the accident . . . and had knowledge of his susceptibility to such attacks.

Defendant was indicted and charged with violating section 1053-a of the Penal Law. That section provides that any person who operates or drives any vehicle of any kind in a reckless or culpable negligent manner, whereby a human being is killed, is guilty of criminal negligence in the operation of a vehicle resulting in death. . . . [Liability under the statute is proper when] conduct manifests a "disregard of the consequences which may ensue from the act, and indifference to the rights of others. . . ."

. . . [T]his defendant knew he was subject to epileptic attacks and seizures that might strike at any time. He also knew that a moving motor vehicle uncontrolled on public highway is a highly dangerous instrumentality capable of unrestrained destruction. With this knowledge, and without anyone accompanying him, he deliberately took a chance by making a conscious choice of a course of action, in disregard of the consequences which he knew might follow from his conscious act, and which in this case did ensue. . . .

. . . To have a sudden sleeping spell, an unexpected heart or other disabling attack, without any prior knowledge or warning thereof, is an altogether different situation . . . and there is simply no basis for comparing such cases with the flagrant disregard manifested here.

* * *

Accordingly, the order of the Appellate Division should be affirmed.

Questions

1. What is the *actus reus* at issue in *Decina*?
2. As the case makes clear, acts that someone commits while unconscious are not voluntary acts that will qualify as an *actus reus* so long as the unconscious state was not

self-induced. Why do you think there is an exception for unconscious states that are self-induced? Given the general requirement of consciousness, how do you think the criminal law would deal with an act committed while the actor was sleepwalking?[22]

3. Given the requirement of a conscious, voluntary act, how could the court have deemed a qualifying *actus reus* to have occurred in *Decina* since he was not conscious at the time the car went out of control and killed the children?

AN OMISSION AS AN *ACTUS REUS*

A person's failure to perform an act of which he or she is physically capable, known as an **omission**, can qualify as an *actus reus* in limited circumstances.[23] Liability for the commission of an offense may not be based on an omission unaccompanied by any other action unless: (a) the omission is expressly made sufficient by the law defining the offense (such as the failure to pay income taxes or the failure to yield when traffic laws require it); or (b) a duty to perform the omitted act is otherwise imposed by law. The "imposed by law" part of the previous sentence is important because only legal duties to act—not moral ones—can serve as the basis of an omission qualifying as an *actus reus*.[24]

Establishing a Legal Duty to Act

Legal duties to act normally come about in one of five ways: by relationship, statute, contract, voluntary assumption of care, and creation of peril. Each duty will be explored in turn.

BY RELATIONSHIP

The first way a legal duty to act may be imposed is by the nature of a special relationship.[25] For instance, a parent owes a legal duty to care for his or her child; spouses owe a legal duty to care for each other; and a physician owes a legal duty to care for his or her patient. Failure to live up to the duties imposed by the nature of a special relationship can be an omission that qualifies as an *actus reus* for criminal law purposes. Explores this concept in greater detail in the "You Make the Public Policy Call" feature in Box 3.2.

BY STATUTE

The second way a legal duty to act might be imposed is by statute.[26] Failure to pay income taxes on earned income or the failure of a male to register with the Selective Service upon his eighteenth birthday are classic examples of statutory duties to act, the breach of which qualifies as an *actus reus* by omission. Another example is that certain social service providers, especially teachers, healthcare personnel, and social workers, all have a statutorily imposed duty to report suspected child abuse or neglect.[27] There

BOX 3.2

YOU MAKE THE PUBLIC POLICY CALL

A Deadly Day at the Beach

Suppose that a married couple bring their two children to a secluded beach where there is no lifeguard on duty. While the mother takes one child for a walk, the father was supposed to be watching the other child. But he became so engrossed reading a book that he failed to notice that his ten-year-old daughter had gone into the ocean and was drowning.

1. Assuming that the young girl died, would there be criminal liability for the father?
2. What if the father could not swim?
3. What about the mother? Should she have any criminal liability for her daughter's death? Are there any additional facts you would need to determine whether her leaving her daughter with her husband should qualify as an *actus reus*? Explain your reasoning.

are laws in most US jurisdictions that require a driver to stop and render aid at the scene of an accident in which he or she was involved. Failing to do so can be deemed an *actus reus* by omission.

A handful of US jurisdictions have enacted **mandatory Good Samaritan laws.**[28] Minnesota, Vermont, Rhode Island, Wisconsin, and some municipalities have all criminalized the failure to come to the aid of another person if such aid can be rendered safely.[29] Other states, like Massachusetts and Hawaii, have mandatory Good Samaritan laws that are applicable only to failing to give aid to a victim of certain types of crimes; in Massachusetts, specifically, if someone knows that another person is a victim of aggravated rape, rape, murder, manslaughter or armed robbery and is at the scene of the crime, he or she must report the crime to law enforcement as soon as is reasonable without putting themselves or others in danger.[30] Most European countries require people to aid one another as well.[31] Even in states that do not require Good Samaritan aid to be rendered, most states make it a crime to refuse to obey the lawful order of a police officer who commands a bystander to assist them.[32]

As an aside, when one who acts to help someone does so out of a moral duty, as opposed to a legal one, he or she may be subject to a civil suit if they act negligently in assisting the person in need. To prevent this, every US jurisdiction has enacted a civil Good Samaritan law that absolves bystanders from civil liability when they help persons in need.[33] These are different from criminal Good Samaritan Law which, as described in the preceding paragraph, require someone to render aid to someone in need when they are capable of doing so without harm to themselves.

Before leaving the category of statutory duty to act, it should be noted that in the past, the common-law crime of **misprison of felony** made it so that "[o]ne was liable for misprison of felony if he failed to report a felony that he knew of and had reasonable opportunity to disclose without harm."[34] Today, however, there is no such legal duty to disclose a felony to authorities in the United States. Thus, if people simply keep their mouths shut about crimes they know occurred, doing so will not normally subject them to criminal liability absent some other legal duty to act. However, as we will discuss in Chapter 6, any affirmative act of concealing a crime can subject a person to complicity or accessory liability and/or obstruction of justice charges.[35]

BY CONTRACT

The third way a legal duty to act is imposed is by contract.[36] People take on contractual obligations all the time. Contractual obligations require one of the parties to act when they otherwise may not have had a duty to act. For example, a babysitter contractually agrees to act to protect the child under his or her care.[37] Similarly, a lifeguard contractually agrees to act when witnessing a drowning.[38] In contrast, a civilian on the beach, even if an Olympic gold medalist swimmer, has no legal duty to act to save the life of that same drowning victim. Similarly, a police officer contractually agrees to act when witnessing a felony in progress, while the ordinary citizen normally has no such legal duty to act.

BY VOLUNTARY ASSUMPTION OF CARE

The fourth way in which a legal obligation to act can be imposed is when someone voluntarily assumes care of another person.[39] Such a voluntary assumption of care creates a legal duty "to complete the assistance and to guard against any harm coming to the imperiled person."[40] Thus, if one were to allow a sick friend to move into his or her house, and the person did not call for medical help when the sick friend needed it, that person would have breached a legal duty to act and could be held criminally responsible for whatever happened to the sick friend. It used to be that to trigger the legal duty to act, the voluntary assumption of care had to be to the exclusion of others, meaning other people could not effectively render aid to the person. But it appears this requirement has been omitted by courts in recent years.

BY CREATION OF PERIL

The fifth and final way in which a legal duty to act arises is when someone causes another person to be in danger.[41] A failure to help someone in danger qualifies as an *actus reus* by omission for criminal law purposes.

Establishing Liability by Omission

Any one of the previously described methods that impose a legal duty to act is sufficient to constitute an *actus reus* via omission. It is not unusual, however, for two or more of these methods to be present simultaneously. Take babysitting, for example. When one agrees to act as a babysitter, that person has contractually undertaken a legal duty to protect the children in his or her care. The babysitter has also voluntarily assumed care of the child to the exclusion of others (usually, the parents or legal guardians). A babysitter's failure to act can give rise to criminal sanctions under both of these theories.

As with many of the rules of law presented in this book, it is all too easy to say there is no legal duty to act unless one of the five criteria are met. The application of legal principles to the complexities of the real world, however, often leaves room for argument. Consider the following case.

STATE of Connecticut
v.
Santos MIRANDA
715 A.2d 680 (Conn. 1998).

* * *

The defendant commenced living with his girlfriend and her two children in an apartment in September, 1992. On January 27, 1993, the defendant was twenty-one years old, his girlfriend was sixteen, her son was two, and her daughter, the victim in this case, born on September 21, 1992, was four months old. Although he was not the biological father of either child, the defendant took care of them and considered himself to be their stepfather. He represented himself as such to the people at Meriden Veteran's Memorial Hospital where, on January 27, 1993, the victim was taken for treatment of her injuries following a 911 call by the defendant that the child was choking on milk. Upon examination at the hospital, it was determined that the victim had multiple rib fractures that were approximately two to three weeks old, two skull fractures that were approximately seven to ten days old, a brachial plexus injury to her left arm, a rectal tear that was actively "oozing blood" and bilateral subconjunctival nasal hemorrhages. On the basis of extensive medical evidence, the trial court determined that the injuries had been sustained on three or more occasions and that none of the injuries had been the result of an accident, a fall, events that took place at the time of the child's birth, cardiopulmonary resuscitation, a blocked air passageway or the child choking on milk. Rather, the trial court found that the injuries, many of which created a risk of death, had been caused by great and deliberate force.

The trial court further found in accordance with the medical evidence that, as a result of the nature of these injuries, at the time they were sustained the victim would have screamed inconsolably, and that her injuries would have caused noticeable physical deformities, such as swelling, bruising and poor mobility, and finally, that her intake of food would have been reduced. The court also determined that anyone who saw the child would have had to notice these injuries, the consequent deformities and her reactions. Indeed, the trial court found that the defendant had been aware of the various bruises on her right cheek and the subconjunctival nasal hemorrhages, as well as the swelling of the child's head, that he knew she had suffered a rectal tear, as well as rib fractures posteriorly on the left and right sides, and that he was aware that there existed a substantial and unjustifiable risk that the child was exposed to conduct that created a risk of death. The trial court concluded that despite this knowledge, the defendant "failed to act to help or aid [the child] by promptly notifying authorities of her injuries, taking her for medical care, removing her from her circumstances and guarding her from future abuses. . . ."

The trial court concluded that the defendant had a legal duty to protect the health and well-being of the child based on the undisputed facts that he had established a familial relationship with the child's mother and her two children, that he had voluntarily assumed responsibility for the care and welfare of both children, and that he considered himself the victim's stepfather. On the basis of these circumstances, the trial court found the defendant guilty.

* * *

It is undisputed that parents have a duty to provide food, shelter and medical aid for their children and to protect them from harm. . . . Additionally, " '[t]he commonly understood general obligations of parenthood entail these minimum attributes: (1) express love and affection for the child; (2) express personal concern over the health, education and general well-being of the child; (3) the duty to supply the necessary food, clothing, and medical care; (4) the duty to provide an adequate domicile; and (5) the duty to furnish social and religious guidance. . . .' "[42]

In addition to biological and adoptive parents and legal guardians, there may be other adults who establish familial relationships with and assume responsibility for the care of a child, thereby creating a legal duty to protect that child from harm. . . .[43]

* * *

We conclude . . . that, in accordance with the trial court findings, when the defendant, who considered himself the victim's parent, established a familial relationship with the victim's mother and her children and assumed the role of a father, he assumed, under the common law, the same legal duty to protect the victim from the abuse as if he were, in fact, the victim's guardian. Under these circumstances, to require the defendant as a matter of law to take affirmative action to prevent harm to the victim or be criminally responsible imposes a reasonable duty. . . .

[W]e recognize the continuing demographic trend reflecting a significant increase in nontraditional alternative family arrangements. Consequently, more and more children will be living with or may depend upon adults who do not qualify as a natural or adoptive parent. The attachment by children to the adults who care for them does not, however, depend exclusively upon whether the caregiver is the natural or adoptive parent or another person who has assumed the caretaker role. Children become attached to people who care for them, and this attachment is "rooted inevitably in the infant's inability to ensure his own survival."[44] To distinguish among children in deciding which ones are entitled to protection based upon whether their adult caregivers have chosen to have their relationships officially recognized hardly advances the public policy of protecting children from abuse.

Questions

1. The majority opinion spent considerable time explaining the imposition of a legal duty to act on Mr. Miranda, even though he was not the biological or adoptive parent of the child in this case. How far should such logic be extended?
2. As discussed by the court, babysitters were included in the class of persons having a legal duty to act on behalf of a child. But often, babysitters are teenagers—sometimes the older siblings or cousins of the children entrusted to the sitter, and sometimes having no familial relationship at all. To what standard of care should a teenager be held if he or she fails to act?
3. As stated by the court, parents owe explicit duties to their minor children. But what should the law do with parents who are financially unable to provide basic needs, such as food, clothing, and shelter for their children? Does a fair reading of the *Miranda* opinion support a case for criminal liability for child neglect of parents who live in extreme poverty?
4. The court included references to parental duties to "express love and affection for the child" and "the duty to furnish social and religious guidance." Are these appropriate responsibilities for the law to place on parents? Why or why not? What are the potential consequences of the latter responsibility for parents who are atheists?

POSSESSION AS AN *ACTUS REUS*

There are a number of laws that criminalize the possession of contraband. Although we often think of contraband as being certain types of weapons, illicit drugs, drug paraphernalia, counterfeit or fraudulent documents, or even obscene materials, in reality, crimes of possession are more extensive. Consider, for instance, that it is illegal to possess taximeter accelerating devices in New York, spearfishing equipment in Florida, and undersized catfish in Louisiana.[45]

As you now know, an *actus reus* requires either an affirmative, voluntary act or an omission when there is a legal duty to act. But crimes of possession do not fit into either category. Thus, at common law, possession did not constitute a criminal offense on the theory that the state of being in possession of something was not an act.[46] But once statutory laws began to be enacted, laws barring possession of different types of contraband emerged.[47]

Statutes banning possession of contraband typically target two types of harms. First, possession of some types of contraband is criminalized not because the possession of the items is harmful in and of itself, but rather because its possession is likely a precursor to other crimes. Possession of burglar's tools is a good example, as illustrated by *People v. Ocasio*.[48] The defendant in that case was arrested shortly after midnight outside a discount merchandise store that was closed on account of the late hour. "When arrested, he was found to be in possession of a screwdriver, channel lock pliers, and two flashlights," also while wearing gloves and a ski mask.[49] He was convicted of attempted burglary and possession of burglar's tools. The reason for criminalizing the possession of such instruments is precisely because they provide the means to commit burglaries. Their possession can be thought of as preparation to commit a more serious crime. By criminalizing the possession of such tools, the law seeks to accomplish a type of preventative strategy that helps to reduce the subsequent harm that would be attendant to the commission of a target offense.

The second reason for criminalizing possession of contraband has to do with convenience. Illicit drugs provide an example. "[I]t is often easier to detect, and prove, possession than use."[50]

The *actus reus* for crimes of possession is being in possession of the contraband in question. But there are different ways that possession can be conceptualized. The Model Penal Code provides that "[p]ossession is an act, within the meaning of this Section, if the possessor knowingly procured or received the thing possessed or was aware of his control thereof for a sufficient period to have been able to terminate his possession."[51] This definition encompasses two distinct types of possession. First, actual possession involves knowing what one has on one's person or under one's physical control. In contrast, constructive possession is knowing that something is stored in a location under someone's "dominion and control."[52] The "Case Study Extra" feature in Box 3.3 explore these concepts in more detail.

BOX 3.3

CASE STUDY EXTRA

Did the Defendant Unlawfully Possess Contraband?

The question of whether someone illegally possessed contraband often turns on whether the prosecution can introduce sufficient evidence to allow the trier-of-fact to infer that the accused had actual or constructive knowledge that they physically possessed or exercised dominion and control over items that the law prohibits. Consider the following cases and explain whether you agree or disagree with the outcomes.

- The defendants, who were commercial fishermen, were arrested for being in possession of undersized crawfish, a violation of Florida law.[63] They argued that although they were in physical possession of undersized crawfish, merely holding the crawfish to measure them in an attempt to determine if they were of legal size was merely "superficial possession" that should not be sufficient to support a criminal prosecution.[64] The court agreed.
- The defendant offered to give a drunken acquaintance a ride home.[65] After dropping the passenger off, the defendant and his wife then picked up her cousin who, upon getting into the back seat of the defendant's car, found a rifle that had belonged to their previous passenger. The defendant checked to make sure it was not loaded and then proceeded to drive home. He was then stopped by the police who discovered the weapon. In challenging his conviction for unlawful possession of the firearm, the defendant argued that the rifle was in his control for only a "brief interlude" because he had not yet been able to terminate his possession of the rifle that its rightful owner had left in his car.[66] The court concurred, reasoning that a grace period was necessary "to separate illegal possession from temporary control incidental to the lawful purpose of terminating possession."[67]
- The police stopped the defendant for driving recklessly while she had two passengers in the car she had rented.[68] When the police smelled marijuana coming from the car, they searched the vehicle and found not only a bag of marijuana in the back seat, but also a gallon sized zip-lock bag containing a pound of marijuana, a baggie containing crack cocaine, and two digital scales. The defendant denied the drugs were hers, claiming that they must have belonged to one of her passengers. On appeal for her convictions for possession of controlled substances with intent to sell and possession of drug paraphernalia, the court ruled that she either knew or should have known about the presence of the marijuana in the car from its smell.[69] Nonetheless, the appeals court determined that the prosecution failed to show that she had exercised sufficient "dominion and control" over the contraband that was found lodged between

the driver's seat and the console of the car, mainly because she was not the sole occupant of the vehicle.[70]

- Police officers obtained a search warrant to search the defendant's home because they had observed her daughter and her son engaged in drug transactions outside the house.[71] When police searched the house, they found marijuana and narcotics in the master bedroom, some of which were near the defendant's insurance card. Additionally, mail addressed to the defendant was found on the bed. A trial court dismissed the case against the defendant, finding that the state failed to establish her dominion and control over the contraband. But an appellate court ruled that because the defendant owned the home and resided in the master bedroom alone, an inference could be made that she did exercise dominion and control over the contraband and, therefore, that the dismissal of the charges had been in error.[72]

Do you agree with the outcome in these cases? Or do you see valid reasons why the acts of possession should not have constituted a criminal offense under the particular facts of each case?

CONCLUSION

Learning Objectives	Summaries
1. Differentiate conclusive presumptions and rebuttable presumptions from inferences.	Presumptions are conclusions the law requires the trier-of-fact to make in the absence of evidence to the contrary. Conclusive presumptions must be accepted as true in spite of evidence to the contrary, whereas rebuttable presumptions must be accepted as true until sufficient evidence is introduced to prove the presumption is not true. Inferences, by contrast, are reasonable conclusions that may be drawn after evaluating all of the evidence, but are not required.
2. Identify the primary types of evidence.	Testimonial evidence is oral testimony given under oath by witnesses. Physical evidence consists of tangible objects with evidentiary value. Scientific evidence is the results of scientific analyses of physical evidence. Demonstrative evidence serves as a visual or auditory aid to facilitate the understanding of other evidence. Finally, judicial notice is a short-cut that excuses a party from the burden of having to prove certain commonly known facts.
3. Distinguish between the burden of production and the burden of persuasion.	The burden of production involves presenting a prima facie case—sufficient evidence to warrant a jury deliberating a claim and forming a reasonable verdict with respect to that claim. The burden of persuasion concerns the proof needed to sustain a particular outcome under the law.

Learning Objectives	Summaries
4. Compare and contrast the quantum of evidence needed under each of the major burdens of persuasion.	Mere suspicion, a hunch or an instinct, does not meet any judicial standard of proof. Reasonable, articulable suspicion involves the ability to articulate one's reasons for suspicion in an objective manner. It is differentiated from probable cause by the existence of independent verifiable factual information that supports the conclusion that there is a fair probability that a crime occurred or a particular person was involved in a crime. Preponderance of the evidence means proof that something is more likely than not. Clear and convincing evidence means that is highly and substantially more likely to be true than untrue. Proof beyond a reasonable doubt requires evidence that leaves one firmly convinced of the existence of a fact, such as a defendant's guilt.
5. Describe the requirements of establishing an *actus reus* by voluntary act.	A voluntary act is a bodily movement performed consciously and as a result of effort and determination.
6. Explain the ways in which an *actus reus* may be established by omission.	A failure to act gives rise to criminal liability when there was breach of duty to act as function of a qualifying relationship, a statute, a contract, the voluntary assumption of care, or the creation of peril.
7. Discuss how the act of possession can constitute an *actus reus.*	The possession of contraband—items that are prohibited by law—constitutes an *actus reus* if the accused had either actual or constructive knowledge of the possession.

KEY TERMS

actus reus
affirmative defense
attendant circumstances
beyond a reasonable doubt
burden of persuasion
burden of production
circumstantial evidence
clear and convincing evidence
conclusive presumption
demonstrative evidence
direct evidence
evidence
inferences
judicial notice
mandatory Good Samaritan laws
mens rea
misprison of felony
omission
physical evidence
preponderance of the evidence
presumption of innocence
presumption of sanity
presumptions
prima facie case
probable cause
reasonable, articulable suspicion
rebuttable presumptions
result
scientific evidence
strict liability
testimonial evidence
voluntary act

4

Intent and Causation

LEARNING OBJECTIVES

1. Compare and contrast the common law's use of general intent, specific intent, and malice as levels of *mens rea*.

2. Differentiate the Model Penal Code's use of purpose, knowledge, recklessness, and negligence as levels of *mens rea*.

3. Distinguish between strict liability and vicarious liability and the circumstances under which they may attach to criminal offenses.

4. Apply the concept of transferred intent to determine criminal liability.

5. Evaluate how cause-in-fact and proximate cause limit criminal liability for crimes with result elements.

Outline

INTRODUCTION

Most crimes require not only that some prohibited act occurs, but also that the *actus reus* be accompanied by some culpable level of intentionality. Recall from the previous chapter that the mental state that must exist at the time of the commission of an *actus reus* is referred to as ***mens rea***—Latin for "the guilty mind." The term refers to the defendant's level of intentionality with respect to having done the *actus reus*.

At the outset, it is important to note that *mens rea* "operates as a tricky issue of proof in many cases and when dealing with many statutes. Was a defendant *malicious* or *negligent* when she committed homicide? Did a defendant *know* that she was transporting heroin in her car, or was she merely *reckless*?"[1] In this chapter, we will parse out such terms.

COMMON-LAW LEVELS OF *MENS REA*

At common law, crimes were either crimes of general intent, crimes of specific intent, or crimes of malice. We will explore each of these levels of intentionality in turn—and not just because of their historical importance. Even today, there are many criminal laws that continue to use these terms despite the Model Penal Code's rejection of the common law's approach to *mens rea*.[2]

Specific Intent

In **specific intent** crimes, "it must be shown that the defendant had actual intent to do the proscribed action."[3] In other words, specific intent meant that the actor formed a goal, aim, or objective to engage in specific conduct and cause a particular result. For example, assume you decided that you wanted to kill someone. You took a gun, aimed it at the person you intended to kill, and then pulled the trigger causing a bullet to strike and kill your intended victim; you have clearly acted with specific intent to kill. Similarly, if you took and carried away the personal property of another person, say a wallet, and you did so with the intent to permanently deprive the rightful owner of the wallet, then you would have acted with the specific intent to steal.

It is quite rare that we have direct evidence of the defendant's state of mind at the time of the commission or attempted commission of a crime. Sometimes, a person declares his or her intent ahead of time. Other times, a person subsequently confesses what his or her level of intent was at the time they committed a crime. When either of these situations arise, we have direct evidence of *mens rea*. But more often than not, we have no direct evidence of intentionality, meaning that *mens rea* must usually be inferred from the facts and circumstances surrounding the defendant's conduct. Doing so, however, is not always easy. Consider the following case.

John THACKER
v.
COMMONWEALTH of Virginia
114 S.E. 504 (Va. 1922).

The accused, in company with two other young men, . . . was attending a church festival in Alleghany County, at which all three became intoxicated. They left the church between 10 and 11 o'clock at night, and walked down the county road about 1½ miles, when they came to a sharp curve. Located in this curve was a tent in which . . . Mrs. J. A. Ratrie, her husband, four children, and a servant were camping. . . . [While waiting for her husband to return, Mrs. Ratrie] placed a lighted lamp on a trunk by the head of her bed. After 11 o'clock she was awakened by the shots of a pistol and loud talking in the road nearby, and heard a man say, "I am going to shoot that Goddamned light out;" and another voice said, "Don't shoot the light out." The accused and his friends then appeared at the back of the tent, where the flaps of the tent were open, and said they were from Bath County and had lost their way, and asked Mrs. Ratrie if she could take care of them all night. She informed them she was camping for the summer, and had no room for them. One of the three thanked her, and they turned away, but after passing around the tent the accused used some vulgar language and did some cursing and singing. When they got back in the road, the accused said again he was going to shoot the light out, and fired three shots, two of which went through the tent, one [barely missing Mrs. Ratrie and her baby], who was sleeping with her. The accused did not know Mrs. Ratrie, and had never seen her before. He testified he did not know any of the parties in the tent, and had no ill will against either of them; that he simply shot at the light, without any intent to harm Mrs. Ratrie or anyone else; that he would not have shot had he been sober, and regretted his action.

* * *

An attempt to commit a crime is composed of two elements: (1) The intent to commit it; and (2) a direct, ineffectual act done towards its commission. The act must reach far enough towards the accomplishment of the desired result to amount to the commencement of the consummation.[4]

* * *

When a statute makes an offense to consist of an act combined with a particular intent, that intent is just as necessary to be proved as the act itself, and must be found as a matter of fact before a conviction can be had; and no intent in law or mere legal presumption, differing from the intent in fact, can be allowed to supply the place of the latter. . . .

> To do an act from general malevolence is not an attempt to commit a crime, because there is no specific intent, though the act according to its consequences may amount to a substantive crime. To do an act with intent to commit one crime cannot be an attempt to commit another crime, though it might result in such other crime. To set fire to a house and burn a human being who is in

it, but not to the offender's knowledge, would be murder, though the intent was to burn the house only; but to attempt to set fire to the house under such circumstances would be an attempt to commit arson only and not an attempt to murder. A man actuated by general malevolence may commit murder, though there is no actual intention to kill; to be guilty of an attempt to murder there must be a specific intent to kill.

* * *

The application of the foregoing principles to the facts of the instant case shows clearly, as we think, that the judgment complained of is erroneous. While it might possibly be said that the firing of the shot into the head of Mrs. Ratrie's bed was an act done towards the commission of the offense charged, the evidence falls far short of proving that it was fired with the intent to murder her. However averse we may be to disturb the verdict of the jury, our obligation to the law compels us to do so. The judgment complained of will be reversed, the verdict of the jury set aside, and the case remanded for a new trial therein, if the commonwealth shall be so advised.

Questions

1. Thacker testified that he had no intent to kill Mrs. Ratrie, only an intent to shoot out the light in her tent. But the jury apparently thought that specific intent to kill could be inferred from Thacker's conduct and convicted him accordingly. Yet the court reversed Thacker's conviction on appeal. Is the self-serving testimony of a defendant sufficient to create reasonable doubt as to the *mens rea* element of a specific intent crime? Explain your reasoning.
2. Assume that Thacker shot at Mrs. Ratrie with the intention of killing her. Further assume the bullet hit and killed her. Thacker would have acted with specific intent to kill her and could be convicted of murder accordingly. In fact, as explained in Chapter 7, such an intentional killing constitutes murder in the first degree in most states today. But what if Thacker had no intent to kill, but his shot nonetheless resulted in someone's death? In other words, assuming Thacker was shooting at the light without any intent to harm anyone else, what if the bullet had struck and killed Mrs. Ratrie? What level of intent would you assess him to have acted with under such circumstances? As you will learn in Chapter 7, shooting at a light in a tent likely constitutes grossly reckless conduct manifesting an extreme indifference to the value of human life. At common law, unintentionally causing a death under such circumstances would have been called depraved heart murder. Today, it constitutes murder in the second degree in many states.

General Intent

In contrast to specific intent, the level of common-law *mens rea* known as **general intent** requires the prosecution to prove that the offender committed the prohibited act volitionally or deliberately, as opposed to accidentally.[5] In other words, the defendant need only have entertained a generally blameworthy state of mind needs at the time he or she committed the *actus reus*.[6] Thus, for conviction of a general intent crime, the defendant only needed to know, in general terms, that the conduct in which he or she was engaged might be illegal. This is so even if the actor does not foresee the result that the conduct may produce. *State v. Rocker* illustrates this principle well.[7]

The defendants in *Rocker* were charged with "creating a common nuisance" by having sunbathed in the nude on a public beach. Because the crime only required general intent, the issue in the case was not whether the defendants intended to expose themselves to others, but rather whether they exposed themselves in a manner that was likely to be observed by others. The defendants argued they had no such intent because they had been sunbathing on a beach that was "isolated by a hill and a ledge, away from the view of the public road and adjoining beaches."[8] Nonetheless, the court upheld their convictions because the beach was a public one that fisherman often accessed.

As the *Rocker* case illustrates, indecent exposure is typically a general intent crime. But the location in which the alleged exposure takes place would be relevant to the actor's intent. Consider the varying outcomes in two Minnesota cases. In *State v. Peery*,[9] the defendant was convicted of indecent exposure after several young women saw him naked through his dormitory window because he had accidentally neglected to draw the shades. Importantly, he had not signaled or called to the women or otherwise attempted to direct their attention to himself. In overturning his conviction, the court reasoned that carelessness in forgetting to close shades did not constitute sufficient *mens rea*. By contrast, in *State v. Stevenson*,[10] the defendant's conviction for indecent exposure was upheld on appeal because he was caught masturbating in his truck, which was parked facing a playground. The court reasoned that given the public location, there was a reasonable "likelihood that the conduct would be witnessed by others" and, from that fact, his general intent to be observed could be inferred.[11] From these and similar cases, the Minnesota Supreme Court stated in 2019 that the prosecution need only prove "that the openly lewd exposure was volitional, as opposed to accidental" and that "the nature and location of the exposure that impacts the certainty of the observation."[12] The Statutory Analysis Exercise in Box 4.1 further explores the nuances of differentiating general from specific intent at common law.

Malice

At common law, there was another category of *mens rea* that was a hybrid of general intent and specific intent known as **malice**.[13] Malice was difficult and somewhat vague concept. It was not taken in the old sense of wickedness or evil. It can refer to states of mind that encompass both specific and general intent. For example, if one acts with specific intent (i.e., purpose to cause a result, such as specific intent to kill), the one can also be said to have acted maliciously. But a lack of specific intent did not necessarily mean that a person did not act with malice. One can act with general intent and still be acting maliciously if one consciously disregards a known risk that a particular harm might occur.[14] As one court phrased it, malice was "a state of mind showing a heart that is without regard for the life and safety of others."[15] Say, for example, you were to load a revolver with a single bullet and then play Russian Roulette with a friend. If the friend pulled the trigger and died, it cannot be said that you acted with specific intent to kill your friend. However, even without such specific intent, you nonetheless acted with malice because you disregarded a substantial and unjustifiable risk to human by playing the game. You knew, in general terms, that having put

BOX 4.1

STATUTORY ANALYSIS EXERCISE

Is Stalking a General or Specific Crime?

Prior to 2001, Louisiana defined the crime of stalking as the "willful, malicious, and repeated following or harassing of another person with the intent to place that person in fear of death or bodily injury."[78] In 2001, however, the crime was amended, deleting the language requiring an offender to act "with the intent to place that person in fear of death or bodily injury." The law was amended again in 2005 to remove the requirement that the offender's actions be "willful" and "malicious."

The anti-stalking statute now reads: "Stalking is the intentional and repeated following or harassing of another person that would cause a reasonable person to feel alarmed or to suffer emotional distress." The statute further defines the term *harassing* as "the repeated pattern of verbal communications or nonverbal behavior without invitation which includes but is not limited to making telephone calls, transmitting electronic mail, sending messages via a third party, or sending letters or pictures."[79]

1. Explain whether the version of the stalking law as it existed prior to 2001 required specific or general intent.
2. Explain whether the version of the stalking law as has existed since 2001 requires specific or general intent.

For a judicial analysis of these statutory changes and their effect on whether stalking is now considered to be a crime of general or specific intent under Louisiana law, see *State v. Terrio*.[80]

a bullet in the revolver and subsequently played Russian Roulette could have caused your death or the death of your friend. That generalized knowledge would have been sufficient *mens rea* to convict you of the malicious killing of another. The following case illustrates the application of common-law malice as the *mens rea* for a contemporary crime.

PEOPLE of the State of Michigan

v.

James E. HENDERSON, Jr. and Matthew P. Mercier.

765 N.W.2d 619 (Mich. App. 2009).

Between January 1, 2007, and March 20, 2007, defendant James Edward Henderson, Jr., owned most, if not all, of the 69 horses that were on the Turn Three Ranch located in Grass Lake Township. Defendant Matthew Patrick Mercier was the primary caretaker of the horses, while Henderson primarily paid the bills associated with the horses and the horse farm. On March 13, 2007, when some of the horses were found outside the farm, as had happened several times in the past, Jackson County Animal Control was contacted. After animal control conducted a limited inspection of the farm, a detailed investigation followed. Thereafter, the farm was seized. Three felony charges of animal torture and one misdemeanor charge of failing to provide adequate care to the horses were filed against both defendants.

Extensive testimony regarding the general condition of the land, barn, buildings, fences, horse shelters, hay, water tanks, and the horses was presented at the preliminary examination. Three horses were the subject of the felony charges: Ice, . . . Moose, . . . and Lucky Seven. . . Ice had a severely infected leg wound caused by having wire embedded in her leg for three weeks or more. Moose was severely emaciated and heavily infested with parasites. Lucky Seven was severely emaciated, had severe lice, was rendered significantly lame by an extremely painful degenerative arthritic condition, and was ultimately euthanized. The testimony also included that many, if not all, of the horses at the farm had lice, worms, parasites, hair loss, and long hooves. Many were significantly underweight. There was also testimony that there was inadequate food, water, shelter, and veterinary care, as well as unsanitary conditions. At the conclusion of the seven-day preliminary examination, [the judge found probable cause for the defendants to stand trial on felony] charges. . . .

First, the prosecution argues that, in light of the evidence, the district court did not abuse its discretion by finding probable cause to believe that defendants "willfully, maliciously and without just cause or excuse" tortured three horses in violation of MCL 750.50b(2). Specifically, the prosecution argues that the circuit court misread *People v. Fennell,*[16] and ignored *People v. Iehl,*[17] which require only a showing of probable cause that defendants acted with conscious disregard of the known risks, and not that they acted with an intent to cause harm. We agree.

* * *

In *Fennell*, the defendant threw a firecracker into a horse stable, causing the stable to burn to the ground and killing 19 horses. The defendant was convicted of 19 counts of willfully and maliciously torturing or killing animals. . . . The defendant in *Fennell* argued on appeal that the trial court erred by refusing to instruct the jury that the prosecution was required to show that he specifically intended to kill or torture the horses. [The Court rejected that interpretation when it ruled that the statute] required a showing of general malice. . . . Then the *Fennell* Court . . . adopted a definition of malice from *Iehl*, [and held]:

> Malice has been described [as an] essential element in a conviction for animal cruelty. . . . In *People v. Iehl*, this Court held that the element of malice . . . "requires only that the jury find that defendant 1) committed the act, 2) while knowing it to be wrong, 3) without just cause or excuse, and 4) did it intentionally or 5) with a conscious disregard of known risks to the property of another." Considered as a whole, we find that the trial court's instructions properly conveyed the element of malice to the jury.
>
> . . . [T]he *Fennell* court clearly recognized that malice can be established by showing that the defendant acted either intentionally or with conscious disregard of known risks. . . . Therefore, . . . [t]he prosecution need not prove that defendants intended to harm the animals.

The testimony in this case was extensive. There was a plethora of evidence regarding (1) the poor, unsanitary, or hazardous conditions of the land, barn, horse stalls, buildings, fences, and horse shelters, (2) the lack of quality hay or food for the horses for a lengthy period, and (3) the lack of quality water for the horses, including evidence that the horses were likely drinking from a county drainage ditch that was contaminated with *E. coli*. . . . There was also abundant evidence regarding the condition of the horses. . . .

***

Here, . . . the evidence established probable cause to believe that defendants willfully failed to seek necessary veterinary care and treatment for these three horses, despite defendants' extensive experience with horses, the longstanding and obvious nature of the horses' problems, and defendants' knowledge that the horses were not healthy, in conscious disregard of the known risk that they would continue to decline in health to the point of having to be euthanized and that without just cause or excuse, defendants caused them to suffer "torture," which the district court defined as "severe physical or mental pain, agony or anguish." Dr. Hammer testified that these three horses were "tortured," i.e., suffered severe physical or mental pain, agony, or anguish. And Dr. Marteniuk testified that Lucky Seven suffered torture, i.e., agony of body or mind, as a result of his condition. The testimony was consistent-the abhorrent conditions at the farm, as well as the unhealthy conditions of the horses, existed for several months.

***

In summary, there was significant evidence of Henderson's involvement in this farm, as well as the longstanding nature of the poor condition of both the farm and the horses. He was the primary source of funding for the farm and for the care, including veterinary care, of the horses. Caring for and feeding the horses was costly. He was seen at the farm during the relevant months. Circumstantial evidence and reasonable inferences from the evidence establish probable cause to believe that Henderson willfully failed to seek necessary veterinary care and treatment for these three horses, despite his extensive experience with horses, the longstanding and obvious nature of the horses' problems, and his knowledge that the horses were in unhealthy conditions, in conscious disregard of the known risk that they would continue to decline in health to the point of having to be euthanized, and that without just cause or excuse, he caused them to suffer "torture," which the district court defined as "severe physical or mental pain, agony or anguish." . . . Accordingly, the district court properly . . . [concluded that whether] . . . defendants did not intend to violate MCL 750.50b(2) or that they did not intend to cause these three horses to suffer torture is of no consequence. . . .

Questions

1. Supposed that instead of Henderson having been actively involved in running the farm as he was, he had, instead, been a passive investor who never visited the farm. Do you think under such circumstances that he could be said to have acted maliciously? Why or why not?
2. Given the evidence of the condition of the stable and the horses housed there, under which definition of malice do you think Mercier acted—with intent or with conscious disregard for the consequences? Why? Would your answer change if Mercier had not only been the primary caretaker of the horses but also part owner? Why or why not?

MENS REA UNDER THE MODEL PENAL CODE

The common-law levels of *mens rea* are often confusing, to say the least. In fact, one commentator called the common law of *mens rea* an " 'amorphous quagmire,' reflected by 'a thin surface of general terminology denoting wrongfulness.' "[18] Accordingly, many US jurisdictions abandoned the common-law classifications of *mens rea* adopted those established by the American Law Institute in its influential Model Penal Code. The Code set forth four levels of *mens rea*: purpose, knowledge, recklessness, and negligence.[19]

Purpose

Under the Model Penal Code, the highest/most culpable degree of *mens rea* is called **purpose.** When someone acts purposefully, the actor possesses specific intent—a conscious objective or desire—to engage in proscribed conduct or, alternatively, to specifically cause a particular result. This is, perhaps, the easiest of the levels of *mens rea* to understand and is well illustrated by returning to the same example given for common-law specific intent to kill. If you, with the purpose (i.e., specific intent) of killing someone, were to raise a loaded gun, aim the gun at the intended victim, pull the trigger, and thereby kills your intended victim, you have acted "purposefully" under the Model Penal Code's definition of *mens rea.*

Knowledge

Also known as *scienter,* the *mens rea* level of **knowledge** requires that the actor act knowingly—meaning acting with a conscious "awareness" or "belief"—that he or she is engaging in proscribed conduct, and further that the actor knows, believes, or is aware of practical certainty that the result achieved would occur by engaging in the conduct.[20] It is key level of *mens rea* when the *actus reus* involves the state of possession.

Knowledge includes both **actual knowledge**—what one actually, subjectively knows—and **constructive knowledge.** The doctrine of constructive knowledge imputes knowledge to someone who has "willfully blind" to facts or the high probability of the existence of circumstances by "turning the other cheek" and consciously ignoring information that would have given the ordinary, reasonable prudent person knowledge. In other words, one cannot be deliberate ignorant of what is transpiring and thereby avoid knowledge that one should have had.

In *Wetzler v. State,*[21] for example, the defendant used his pickup truck to tow a padlocked U-Haul trailer.

> [He] told the Sheriff that he had been given $400 to come to Sarasota, rent a U-Haul trailer and leave it hooked to his truck. He told the Sheriff that for a period of time the truck and trailer were out of his possession. The rig was taken, brought back, and he was supposed to have received another $400 when he got back to Atlanta, Georgia. Appellant told the Sheriff that he knew it was a "shady deal" by the way "they wanted to do things by being secret."[22]

Because of the way the arrangement had been structured, the defendant did not actually know that the trailer contained 164 potted, growing marijuana plants. Nonetheless, in upholding his conviction on the grounds that he had constructive knowledge of the contents of the trailer, the court quoted *United States v. Jewell* to emphasize the willful blindness doctrine: "[I]f a party has his suspicion aroused but then deliberately omits to make further enquiries, because he wishes to remain in ignorance, he is deemed to have knowledge."[23]

Recklessness

The Model Penal Code provides that recklessness is the *mens rea* for any material element of a criminal offense unless a statute specifically provides a different level of *mens rea.*[24] When one acts recklessly, the actor is actually aware of a risk that his or her conduct could cause a particular result, but consciously disregards that known risk and acts anyway. Key to criminal **recklessness** is that the defendant actually (subjectively in his or her own mind) be aware of a substantial and unjustifiable risk, but then act anyway with disregard for the risk he or she perceived.[25] In other words, the reckless actor just doesn't care. Recall that the defendants in *People v. Henderson* were deemed to have acted maliciously, under the language of the common law. But using Model Penal Code terminology, at minimum, they acted with recklessness for having consciously disregarded the condition of the horses under their care.

The criminal law has held onto a common-law *mens rea* concept that has resulted in the recognition and use of different levels of recklessness: regular or mere recklessness as described in the preceding paragraph, and gross recklessness. *Gross recklessness* involves something more than a conscious disregard of a substantial and unjustifiable risk. The risk must be so great that the conscious disregard of it rises to the level of manifesting an "extreme indifference to the value of human life."[26] The difference between the two is difficult to define because it is really only a matter of degree. Since reasonable people might differ over what is reckless conduct as opposed to grossly reckless conduct, this is often a question of fact to be resolved by a jury.[27] But in some cases, gross recklessness is clear. Consider, for example, the second question after the *Thacker* case. If his shots had caused someone's death, even without the purpose to kill or knowledge that someone would die, Thacker's firing of a gun at a light inside a tent would unquestionably constitute grossly reckless conduct because it clearly manifests an extreme indifference to the human lives inside the tent.

Negligence

Negligence is similar to recklessness with the exception that with negligence, the actor is not aware of a risk (and hence could not have consciously disregarded it), but the actor should have been aware of the risk. In other words, using an objective standard, the ordinary, reasonable prudent person in the same circumstances as the actor would have perceived the risk that the criminally negligent defendant failed to perceive. But the failure to perceive any risk will not suffice for the imposition of liability under the criminal negligence standard. The failure to become aware of the risk must involve some gross deviation from the conduct that a reasonable person would observe in the situation, rather than mere inadvertence, which is the realm of civil negligence under tort law. And, if the gross deviation involved an inherent risk to human life, then the conduct is not just negligent, but grossly negligent. *Gross negligence* occurs when a person is not aware of high degree of risk to human life, but he or she should have been—such as when acting negligently with an inherently dangerous instrument like a gun.[28]

As previously stated, the lines between grossly reckless conduct, reckless conduct, criminally negligent conduct, and grossly criminally negligent conduct are largely a matter of degree. Consider the "Case Study Extra" presented in Box 4.2.

The distinctions between the general-intent levels of *mens rea* are further complicated by the fact that criminal negligence is often confused with civil negligence, although the two are distinct. Civil negligence is really nothing more than mere careless. Although such carelessness is sufficient to impose civil liability, it is insufficient to impose criminal liability. Criminal negligence is aimed at morally culpable behavior, not mere inadvertence. Criminal negligence must involve some "gross deviation"[29] from the conduct that a reasonable person would observe in the situation—a deviation substantial enough to establish some moral blameworthiness on the part of the defendant.[30] *State v. Pittera*[31] illustrates this distinction. The defendant in that case was convicted of criminally negligent homicide for killing someone swimming in lake on which the defendant was operating a boat. It was undisputed that the defendant was operating the boat at an excessive speed while dangerously close to the shoreline. The court affirmed his conviction because he failed to perceive how his conduct posed a substantial and unjustifiable risk of death or serious harm to swimmers in the water.

STRICT LIABILITY: CRIMES WITHOUT *MENS REA*

Nearly all crimes require a union of *actus reus* and *mens rea*. But there are a small yet growing number of criminal offenses that do not follow this rule.[32] These crimes are called **strict liability** offenses (sometimes referred to as "absolute liability" crimes). When a crime carries strict liability, a person can be convicted of the crime for having engaged in the proscribed act (the *actus reus*) even though there was no accompanying criminal intent. Thus, a person acting without any *mens rea* whatsoever may nonetheless be convicted of a strict liability crime.

Interestingly, the Model Penal Code does not recognize strict liability as a level of *mens rea*. Rather, the Code specifically rejected the use of strict liability for all crimes (misdemeanors and felonies alike), and recognized the applicability of strict liability only in the limited context of quasi-criminal violations that are exclusively penalized by fine or "other civil penalty."[33] In spite of the American Law Institute's push to ban strict liability for criminal offenses, the use of strict liability for crimes "has continued to gain momentum."[34]

Recall from *Morissette v. United States*[35] (in Chapter 1) that applying strict liability to *mala in se* crimes—those criminal acts proscribed at common law that are innately evil (such as rape, murder, and theft)—is prohibited by the constitutional guarantees of due process. Rather, strict liability has historically attached only to a small number of

BOX 4.2

CASE STUDY EXTRA

An Omissions Leads to Three Deaths by Carbon Monoxide Poisoning

The defendant in *State v. Brooks*[81] owned a home in Vermont that had a driveway heated by a gas-powered boiler to melt snow and ice. One day, members of the household became ill from carbon monoxide leaking from that heating system. A repair company explained to the defendant that the system was not safe to operate until significant repairs were made. Nonetheless, the defendant did not have the system fixed. He subsequently placed the home on the market and instructed his real estate agent to demonstrate the driveway heating system to prospective buyers. The defendant never mentioned the system's faulty condition to the people who ultimately purchased the home. The new owners subsequently turned on the driveway heater one night when it was snowing. They, and their four-year-old daughter, died of carbon monoxide poisoning that night.

The defendant was charged and convicted of three counts of involuntary manslaughter, a form of homicide premised on reckless conduct. Brooks argued that he was not reckless, but rather negligent. But because he actually knew that the driveway hearing system had not been repaired and because he failed to disclose the problems with the system to the home's new owners, he actions were, in fact, reckless. He consciously disregard the substantial and unjustifiable risk of serious injury or death from carbon monoxide attendant to the operation of the faulty heater system. Note that the *actus reus* in the case was an omission—a failure to disclose the defective state of the heater system.

1. The critical difference between recklessness and criminal negligence is whether the defendant subjectively perceived and then consciously disregarded a substantial and unjustifiable risk, or whether the defendant failed to perceive that risk. Do you think Brooks was merely negligent or was he reckless? Why?
2. Although not an issue in the case, there is an argument to be made that Brooks committed murder in the second degree. Whether someone is liable for murder in the second degree or involuntary manslaughter depends on whether the jury finds a defendant's conduct to be reckless using the ordinary recklessness standard, or "grossly reckless" such that the nature of the reckless conduct manifests an extreme indifference to the value of human life. Do you think there was sufficient evidence to have held Brooks liable for murder in the second degree? How do you differentiate between acts that are "reckless" and "grossly reckless"?

statutorily *mala prohibita* crimes (crimes that are not innately "evil" unto themselves). But distinguishing between *mala in se* and *mala prohibita* crimes often proves to be an insufficient basis for determining when strict liability should be applied. Consider the US Supreme Court's 2015 decision in *Elonis v. United States*.[36]

The defendant in *Elonis* wrote rap lyrics and posted them on Facebook. Many these posts used "crude, degrading, and violent material about his soon-to-be ex-wife."[37] Some of the lyrics he posted online evoked imagery so violence that they caused his wife to fear for her life. He was convicted of violating a federal law that makes it a crime to transmit "in interstate or foreign commerce any communication containing any threat to kidnap any person or any threat to injure the person of another."[38] The statute was silent about any *mens rea* requirement. Relying on *Morissette*,[39] the Court reasoned that a defendant must generally "know the facts that make his conduct fit the definition of the offense."[40] In other words, the Court rejected the notion that the crime carried strict liability. But it is unclear whether its decision to do so was because transmitting threats online is *malum in se*. Moreover, the Court did not specify what the *mens rea* requirement would be moving forward. The Court was clear that transmitting any communication either for the express purpose of making a threat, or with knowledge that it would be viewed as a threatening would be sufficient. The Court was also clear that negligence would not be sufficient to impose liability under the statute because that would mean criminal liability might attach when communications are understood as threatening by a reasonable person without regard to the subjective intent of the person making the communication. "Such a 'reasonable person' standard is a familiar feature of civil liability in tort law, but is inconsistent with 'the conventional requirement for criminal conduct—awareness of some wrongdoing.' "[41] Yet the Court refused to specify whether a recklessness would suffice. Despite that open question, the *Elonis* decision suggests that the Supreme Court clearly wants to limit criminal liability by requiring that federal crimes be interpreted as requiring moral blameworthiness that involves as least some level of subjective intentionality. With that in mind, the following framework provides a guide to the permissible uses of strict liability in the criminal law.

Public Health, Safety, and Welfare Offenses

There are a narrow class of regulatory offenses that were "designed out of necessity at the time of the industrial revolution to 'impos[e] more stringent duties on those connected with particular industries, trades, properties, or activities that affect public health, safety or welfare.' "[42]

> Traditional public welfare offenses include: (1) illegal sales or transport of intoxicating liquor; (2) sales of impure or adulterated food; (3) sales of misbranded articles; (4) violations of anti-narcotics acts; (5) criminal nuisances; (6) violations of traffic regulations; (7) violations of motor-vehicle laws; and (8) violations of

> general police regulations passed for safety, health, or well-being of the community. Although seemingly disparate offenses with different objectives, they share a common characteristic: each affects the lives and health of those in the community.[43]

Because strict liability usually attached to such public health, safety, and welfare offenses, a person may be convicted of such an offense without ever having entertained any *mens rea*. Consider a bartender's liability for selling alcoholic beverages to someone under the legal drinking age. There are circumstances in which a bartender, knowing that a patron was underage, might decide to sell alcohol to the minor nonetheless. Clearly, such a disregard for the law evidences the bartender's *mens rea*. Accordingly, under the traditional criminal law model requiring a union of *actus reus* and *mens rea*, the bartender could be properly convicted under such circumstances. But what if the patron produced identification to establish that he or she was over the legal drinking age, but in actuality, the patron was underage? Assuming that the false identification looked genuine, the bartender would have lived up to his or her duty of care in checking the ID to ensure the patron was old enough to be lawfully served alcoholic drinks. Accordingly, the bartender was not even negligent. Yet even without any *mens rea* whatsoever, the bartender could nonetheless be convicted of selling alcohol to a minor because the bartender did, in fact, sell alcohol to someone who has not yet reached the legal drinking age. The crime is complete by having done the *actus reus* without any regard to the bartender's lack of any mental or moral culpability.

In *Commonwealth v. Olshefski*,[44] the defendant was cited for driving a truck in excess of the maximum capacity permitted by Pennsylvania's vehicle code. But the defendant had proof that he had gone to a licensed weighmaster and received a weigh bill showing that the truck was loaded within the lawful weight limits. His good faith efforts to comply with the law, however, did not matter. Because the *malum prohibitum* offense carried strict liability, his lack of *mens rea* was irrelevant. His conviction was therefore affirmed. Compare this outcome to the one in *People v. Stuart*.[45]

The PEOPLE of the State of California, Plaintiff and Respondent,

v.

Stephen STUART, Defendant and Appellant.

302 P.2d 5 (Cal. 1956).

Defendant was licensed as a pharmacist by this state in 1946 and has practiced here since that time. . . . On July 16, 1954, he filled a prescription for Irvin Sills. It had been written by Dr. D.M. Goldstein for Sills' eight-day-old child. It called for "Sodium phenobarbital, grains eight. Sodium citrate, drams three. Simple syrup, ounces two. Aqua peppermint, ounces one. Aqua distillate QS, ounces four." Defendant assembled the necessary drugs to fill the prescription.... Sills returned home, put a teaspoonful of the prescription in the baby's milk, and gave it to the baby. The baby died a few hours later.

* * *

An analysis made by the staff of the head toxicologist for the Los Angeles County Coroner of the contents of the bottle given to Sills disclosed that it contained 1.33 drams of sodium citrate and 1.23 of sodium nitrite....

There is nothing in the record to indicate that the contents of the bottle labeled sodium citrate could have been identified as containing sodium nitrite without laboratory analysis. There was testimony that at first glance sodium citrate and sodium nitrite are identical in appearance, that in form either may consist of small colorless crystals or white crystalline powder, that the granulation of the crystals may vary with the manufacturer, and that there may be a slight difference in color between the two....

No evidence whatever was introduced that would justify an inference that defendant knew or should have known that the bottle labeled sodium citrate contained sodium nitrite. On the contrary, the undisputed evidence shows conclusively that defendant was morally entirely innocent and that only because of a reasonable mistake or unavoidable accident was the prescription filled with a substance containing sodium nitrite.... The question is thus presented whether a person can be convicted of manslaughter or a violation of section 380 of the Penal Code in the absence of any evidence of criminal intent or criminal negligence.

The answer to this question as it relates to the conviction of manslaughter depends on whether or not defendant committed an "unlawful act" within the meaning of section 192 of the Penal Code when he filled the prescription. The Attorney General contends that even if he had no criminal intent and was not criminally negligent, defendant violated section 26280 of the Health and Safety Code and therefore committed an unlawful act within the meaning of section 192 of the Penal Code.

Section 26280 of the Health and Safety Code provides: "The manufacture, production, preparation, compounding, packing, selling, offering for sale, advertising or keeping for sale within the State of California ... of any drug or device which is adulterated or misbranded is prohibited." In view of the analyses of the contents of the prescription bottle and the bottle labeled sodium citrate and defendant's stipulation, there can be no doubt that he prepared, compounded, and sold an adulterated and misbranded drug.

Because of the great danger to the public health and safety that the preparation, compounding, or sale of adulterated or misbranded drugs entails, the public interest in demanding that those who prepare, compound, or sell drugs make certain that they are not adulterated or misbranded, and the belief that although an occasional nonculpable offender may be punished, it is necessary to incur that risk by imposing strict liability to prevent the escape of great numbers of culpable offenders, public welfare statutes like section 26280 are not ordinarily governed by section 20 of the Penal Code and therefore call for the sanctions imposed even though the prohibited acts are committed without criminal intent or criminal negligence.[46]

It does not follow, however, that such acts, committed without criminal intent or criminal negligence, are unlawful acts within the meaning of section 192 of the Penal Code, for it is settled that this section is governed by section 20 of the Penal Code. Thus, in *People v. Penny*,[47] we held that "there was nothing to show that the Legislature intended to except section 192 of the Penal Code from the operation of section 20 of the same code" and that the phrase "without due caution and circumspection" in section 192 was therefore the equivalent of criminal negligence. Since section 20 also applies to the phrase "unlawful act," the act in question must be committed with criminal intent or criminal negligence to be an unlawful act within the meaning of section 192. By virtue of its application to both phrases, section 20 precludes the incongruity of imposing on the morally innocent the same penalty, PEN. CODE § 193, appropriate only for the culpable. Words such as "unlawful act, not amounting to felony" have been included in most definitions of manslaughter since the time of Blackstone . . . and even since the time of Lord Hale, "unlawful act" as it pertains to manslaughter had been interpreted as meaning an act that aside from its unlawfulness was of such a dangerous nature as to justify a conviction of manslaughter if done intentionally or without due caution.[48] To be an unlawful act within the meaning of section 192, therefore, the act in question must be dangerous to human life or safety and meet the conditions of section 20. . . .

It follows, therefore, that only if defendant had intentionally or through criminal negligence prepared, compounded, or sold an adulterated or misbranded drug, would his violation of section 26280 of the Health and Safety Code be an unlawful act within the meaning of section 192 of the Penal Code. Thus, in *People v. Penny*, in discussing section 7415 of the Business and Professions Code, which prohibits the use by licensed cosmetologists of a solution of more than 10% phenol on a human being, we said that had the defendant been a licensed cosmetologist, she would have been guilty of violating section 7415 and therefore of an unlawful act within the meaning of section 192 of the Penal Code. The defendant in that case knew that she was using such a solution. The intentional or criminally negligent use of such a solution on a human being by a licensed cosmetologist in violation of section 7415 of the Business and Professions Code would clearly meet the conditions of section 20 of the Penal Code and would therefore be an unlawful act within the meaning of section 192. When, as in this case, however, the defendant did not know, and could not reasonably be expected to know, that the sodium citrate bottle contained nitrite, those conditions are not met and there is therefore lacking the culpability necessary to make the act an unlawful act within the meaning of section 192.

* * *

The judgment and order are reversed.

Questions

1. Mr. Stuart was convicted of unlawful act manslaughter. It is a catch-all type of homicide that holds one liable for any death one causes during the commission of an unlawful act, even though the death was not intended. In this case, the predicate unlawful act was the strict liability offense of selling the adulterated or misbranded drug. Do you think that the sale of such a drug should subject a nonculpable pharmacist to criminal sanctions? Why? Why do you think the California legislature provides for such a penalty, even in the absence of negligence?
2. The court in *Stuart* determined that the strict liability offense of selling an adulterated or mislabeled drug was not an unlawful act within the meaning of the unlawful act manslaughter statute. Why? Do you agree with the court's analysis, separate and apart from the result?

The Legal Regulation of Morality

Morals legislation may be thought of as a specific subtype of public welfare offense.[49] Recall from Chapter 2 that in order to preserve the integrity of society's well-being, a number of offenses that were considered immoral were criminalized without regard to *mens rea,* such as bans on statutory rape, obscenity, gambling, and public intoxication.[50] Statutory rape is the quintessential example of a strict liability crime regulation immoral conduct.

> At its most basic, statutory rape is the carnal knowledge of a person who is deemed underage as proscribed by statute and who is therefore presumed to be incapable of consenting to sexual activity. The crime serves to protect its underage victims from a host of dangers, including pregnancy, venereal disease, and the vulnerability to physical and psychological harm as a result of the lack of mature judgment. Unlike rape, the crime of statutory rape acknowledges that the actions by the victim may appear to be consensual. Although evidence at trial may demonstrate that the victim engaged in the sexual activity voluntarily, the victim is presumed to lack the capacity to consent because of the victim's age. Noted one court, "the state has long recognized an obligation to protect its children from others and from themselves." The essence of the crime, then, is not the victim's lack of consent but the state's responsibility to protect those who, because of youth and lack of maturity, are unable to protect themselves from an imprudent decision to engage in the sexual activity.[51]

Traditionally, statutory rape laws criminalized sexual contact with an underage female. Today, however, the great majority of US states have made their statutory rape law gender-neutral, thereby recognizing that both underage persons, regardless of sex, may be statutorily raped.[52] However, strict liability still attaches to the crime in more than half of all US states.[53] Therefore, it would not be a defense to statutory rape in the majority of US jurisdictions that the defendant honestly and reasonably believed that the person with whom he or she had sex was over the age of consent. In such a case, the defendant's *mens rea* would be irrelevant because if the *actus reus* took place (i.e., sex with a minor), that alone would be sufficient to impose criminal liability for statutory rape under the strict liability approach to the crime. This would be true even if the victim lied about being over the age of consent. It would still be true even if the victim produced false identification "proving" that he or she was over the age of consent.

Elements Not Central to the Criminality of an Act

As discussed earlier in this chapter, *mens rea* is usually applied either to the conduct element of an offense (the *actus reus*) or the result element of an offense.[54] In contrast, the prosecution need not prove any *mens rea* with respect to elements of a crime that are not central to the criminality of proscribed act, such as certain attendant circumstances elements or elements regarding jurisdiction.

ATTENDANT CIRCUMSTANCES

When attendant circumstances are not central to the criminality of an act, strict liability often attaches to those circumstances. For example, assume that a jurisdiction makes it a felony for anyone other than a licensed pharmacist to "purposefully or knowingly distribute, sell, or dispense any controlled and dangerous substances." Further assume that a person is arrested and charged with violating this statute when an undercover police officer witnesses him selling cocaine. The *actus reus* of the crime would be the sale or distribution of the cocaine—a controlled and dangerous substance. Such a drug transaction was purposeful, so the *mens rea* of the statute would be satisfied and the defendant could be properly convicted. But what if the drug deal had taken place within a "school zone"—defined by statute in that jurisdiction as being within 1000 feet of a school—and the defendant did not know there was a school nearby? The defendant could nonetheless be properly convicted of distributing drugs within a school zone, and could be sentenced to a longer period of incarceration accordingly. The fact that the defendant did not know that he was selling drugs within a school zone would be irrelevant because the location of the sale is not central to the criminality of the act. The intentional sale of cocaine is what is central to the criminality of the act (i.e., the union of *actus reus* and *mens rea*). The fact that the defendant was unaware of the existence of the attendant circumstance of being within a school zone would be irrelevant because strict liability can be attached so that attendant circumstance since it is not central to the criminality of the act.[55]

JURISDICTION

Along the same line of reasoning, elements regarding jurisdiction often carry strict liability. Thus, a defendant need not know that crossing state lines makes something a federal offense which might carry a stiffer penalty than if it had just been committed in one state. *United States v. Feola*[56] is a good example of how strict liability may be applied to attendant circumstances that are not central to the criminality of an act, as well as to attendant circumstances that establish jurisdiction. The defendants in *Feola* had arranged to sell heroin to buyers who, unbeknownst to the defendants, were actually federal law enforcement officers.

> The group planned to palm off on the purchasers, for a substantial sum, a form of sugar in place of heroin and, should that ruse fail, simply to surprise their unwitting buyers and relieve them of the cash they had brought along for payment. The plan failed when one agent, his suspicions being aroused, drew his revolver in time to counter an assault upon another agent from the rear. Instead of enjoying the rich benefits of a successful swindle, Feola and his associates found themselves charged, to their undoubted surprise, with conspiring to assault, and with assaulting, federal officers.[57]

The defendants argued that because they did not know that their victims were federal officers, they could not be convicted of either assaulting federal officers or conspiring to assault federal officers. Central to the criminality of the defendant's actions was their agreement, supported by specific intent, to commit assaults in furtherance of their fraudulent narcotics scheme. The status of their victims as federal officers was an attendant circumstance that established federal jurisdiction over such assaults. Because such an attendant circumstance is not central to the criminality of the act, the status of the federal officers was held to be an attendant circumstances to which strict liability attached.

This interpretation poses no risk of unfairness to defendants. It is no snare for the unsuspecting. Although the perpetrator of a narcotics "rip-off," such as the one involved here, may be surprised to find that his intended victim is a federal officer in civilian apparel, he nonetheless knows from the very outset that his planned course of conduct is wrongful. The situation is not one where legitimate conduct becomes unlawful solely because of the identity of the individual or agency affected. In a case of this kind the offender takes his victim as he finds him. The concept of criminal intent does not extend so far as to require that the actor understand not only the nature of his act but also its consequence for the choice of a judicial forum.[58] Accordingly, the US Supreme Court affirmed the *Feola* defendants' convictions for both the substantive crime of assaulting federal officers and the conspiracy charge as well.

VICARIOUS LIABILITY

Vicarious liability holds someone other than the person who actually committed the *actus reus* of a crime liable for the criminal act. While vicarious criminal liability is the rare exception to the rule in the United States that criminal liability requires a union of *actus reus* and *mens rea*, it can be imposed when there is some legal relationship, and it is deemed socially desirable, for another person to be held criminally responsible for the criminal acts of another. Examples of vicarious criminal liability include holding the president of a corporation criminally liable for toxic dumping by those in his or her employ;[59] holding a parent liable for having negligently entrusted a vehicle to an underage child; and holding a parent liable for the criminal acts of their children. For example:

> An ordinance for Fairburn, Alabama, provides that parents of repeated curfew violators may be jailed for sixty days and fined $500. Ordinances enacted in Madison Heights and Roseville in Michigan go even further, providing for jails terms of up to ninety days and a fine of up to $500 for the parent of any child who, within a twelve month period, commits two or more criminal acts, or four moving traffic violations. A parent whose child violates the curfew laws in Holly, Michigan, may be jailed for one year and fined $500.[60]

The doctrine of vicarious liability has been extended into the criminal realm for acts of hazing.[61] Perhaps the most notable of these cases involved an incident at the Massachusetts Institute of Technology in 1997. In the fall semester of that year, Phi Gamma Delta hosted an "'Animal House Night' initiation party for its new pledges."[62] During that party, pledges were "instructed" to drink a significant amount of alcohol. One of the new pledges, freshman Scot Krueger, became ill. He complained of nausea and eventually lost consciousness.[63] Two fraternity members carried Krueger to a bedroom where they left him lying on his stomach. When checked on approximately ten minutes later, he was covered in vomit and could not be awoken. An ambulance was called, but by the time emergency medical personnel arrived, his "face had turned blue and he was choking on his own vomit."[64] He was taken to the hospital in a coma where he died two days later. His blood alcohol content was .401, more than five-times the limit for legal intoxication in the state.[65]

> The Boston Police immediately launched a criminal investigation. In September of 1998, a Suffolk County grand jury indicted the fraternity on one count of misdemeanor hazing and another count of criminal manslaughter under Massachusetts law. This indictment marked the first time ever in the history of the United States that a fraternity was charged with the criminal death of an individual.

* * *

> A day after the indictment against the fraternity was filed, the Phi Gamma Delta chapter at MIT officially disbanded. When the court date arrived, no one showed up in defense of the fraternity. A warrant was later issued against the fraternity and "filed away" in case the Phi Gamma Delta fraternity ever tries to reorganize at MIT. A spokesman for the Krueger family opined that "[t]he criminal justice system has failed."[66]

In 2007, Rider University officials (including the dean of students and the university's director of Greek Life) and students (including a residence director and housemaster of the Phi Kappa Tau fraternity, as well as the fraternity chapter president) were criminally charged in New Jersey in connection with the alcohol-poisoning death of a student, Gary DeVercelly, during a night a heavy drinking at an on-campus fraternity house. DeVercelly's blood alcohol content was .426, more than five times the legal limit. Although the charges against the university officials were eventually dropped, the criminal charges against the fraternity president led to a guilty plea on hazing charges in exchange for a term of probation and community service and a civil settlement of $150,000; the residence director and other fraternity members were fined and sentenced to community service as part of diversion program that allowed them to escape formal criminal liability.[67] DeVercelly's parents filed a civil wrongful death lawsuit against Rider University and the fraternity for $75 million. It was settled for an undisclosed amount, in addition to a number of policy changes at the university concerning alcohol at Greek-life and other social events, hazing, and a "Good Samaritan policy that encourages students to seek help first for medically compromised students without fear of campus repercussions."[68] Answer the questions in the "You Make the Public Policy Call" feature in Box 4.3.

TRANSFERRED INTENT

Suppose that you were to shoot at some someone, with the purpose (i.e., specific intent) to kill that person, but due to poor aim, you wind up killing the person sitting next to your intended victim instead. Do you think you could avoid a charge of premeditated murder by arguing that there was not a concurrence of *actus reus* and *mens rea* for the killing that occurred since you did not intent to kill the person whom you did? That would be a rather absurd outcome, would it not? The common law solved this problem by creating the legal fiction of **transferred intent**.[69]

Under the doctrine of transferred intent, the *mens rea* entertained with respect to doing a particular *actus reus* with the intent of causing result *A* can be used to satisfy the *mens rea* requirement of having actually caused result *B*, so long as the same type of intended harm occurred. Thus, to follow up the hypothetical used in the preceding paragraph, the specific intent to kill you entertained while trying to shoot and kill your intended victim

BOX 4.3

YOU MAKE THE PUBLIC POLICY CALL

Vicarious Liability and Serving Alcohol

Suppose that a fraternity or sorority sponsored an off-campus party at the home of one its members at which the members of the organization "chipped in" to buy kegs of beer. Further suppose that the beer is provided to guests at the party, some of whom are members of the organization and some of whom are not, some of whom are of legal drinking age, and some of whom are not. Finally, presume one of the underage guests leaves the party, gets into a car accident while driving under the influence, and kills the driver of the other car who was not at fault for the accident. It is clear that the driver would face both driving under the influence charges and some nonintentional homicide charge such as involuntary manslaughter. What, if anything, though, should happen to the hosts of the party who provided the alcohol to the driver? Why? Should the affiliated college or university have any liability, civil or criminal, for this act?[82]

Consider the following summary of the normal rules of vicarious liability in civil tort law:

> Parents may incur liability when they negligently entrust their child with an instrumentality (such as a gun or car) which, because of the child's immaturity or lack of experience, may become a source of danger to others. . . . A parent may also be held responsible for failure to exercise reasonable control over the child when the parent knows, or should know, that injury to another is a probable consequence. . . . Finally, when parents know of the child's wrongdoing and consent to it, direct it or sanction it, they may be held liable.[83]

1. What would you do to parents who give their underage child permission to host a party at which alcohol will be served? What if one of the underage guests in attendance at the party leaves and is involved in a fatal accident while driving under the influence; should the parents be held vicariously liable for the death? Why or why not? Be sure to include a discussion of the parents' level of *mens rea*, if any, in your analysis.
2. Should it make a difference if both the hosts and the guests at a party at which alcohol is served are all over the legal drinking age? The court in *Kelly v. Gwinnell*[84] held such a social host civilly liable because the host directly served the guest and continued to do so even after the guest was visibly intoxicated. Should criminal charges be filed against such a host if the intoxicated person then drives and kills someone? What if the intoxicated person gets violent at the party and commits a criminal assault and battery on another guest? What if the intoxicated guest rapes another guest? Where should the law draw the line for the imposition of criminal vicarious liability?

3. In *Commonwealth v. Koczwara*,[85] the owner of a store was fined $500 and sentenced to three months in jail for the actions of an employee who sold liquor to a minor. The Pennsylvania Supreme Court upheld his conviction and fine, but found that imprisonment under such facts deprived the defendant of due process. Do you agree with the outcome of the case? Why or why not? Should this logic be extended to the owners of bars and restaurants whose employees serve alcohol to underage patrons? What purpose is served by having such a policy?

would transfer to be the *mens rea* for the result you actually caused, the death of the person who was sitting next to your intended victim.

There are two limitations on the application of the doctrine of transferred intent that cannot be overemphasized. The first concerns a limitation on transferring different levels on intentionality; the second concerns a limitation on the type of harm.

Limits on the Level of *Mens Rea* Transferred

The doctrine of transferred intent can only be used to transfer the *mens rea* for one crime to another if the crime to which the *mens rea* is being transferred carries the same level of *mens rea* as the original crime, or some lower level of *mens rea*. Accordingly, *mens rea* cannot be transferred to impose criminal liability for a crime that carries a higher degree of mental fault than the defendant actually entertained when doing the *actus reus*. For example, if someone acts purposefully, there is no problem transferring that level of *mens rea* to any other crime since it is the highest level of mental culpability recognized by the criminal law. In contrast, though, if someone acted recklessly in doing an *actus reus*, the doctrine of transferred intent could not be used to impose criminal liability for any crime that carried purpose or knowledge as the requisite *mens rea*. Recklessness could only be transferred as the *mens rea* for other crimes that require the same level of *mens rea*—recklessness—or a lower level of *mens rea*, namely negligence. *Smith v. State* illustrates this point.

Danny Smith, the defendant, made several disparaging remarks about Leonard Thomas. The next time the two saw each other, Thomas charged at Smith. Thomas's brother, Clarence, tried to restrain him from attacking Smith. But Smith, who claimed he feared Leonard Thomas was armed with a gun, fired one round from a 20-gauge shotgun at him. Pellets hit both Thomas brothers. Smith was charged with two counts aggravated assault, one for having harms each of the brothers. Smith successfully argued that he shot at Leonard Thomas in self-defense and was therefore acquitted of that assault. But he was convicted of the assault on Clarence Thomas. In reserving his conviction on appeal, the court reasoned that the doctrine of transferred intent could not be used because Smith had been charged with a specific intent crime—aggravated assault requires proof of purpose as its *mens rea* element. But Smith has no specific intent to unlawfully injure Clarence Thomas. Rather, his intent was to defend himself against the unlawful attack by Leonard Thomas. Because the actions were justified under the law of self-defense (see Chapter 15), he had no criminal intent that could be transferred from shooting at Leonard, but injuring Clarence. Moreover, although a fair argument could be made that Smith was reckless by firing his shotgun in a manner that injured an innocent third party, recklessness is a lower level of *mens rea* than purpose. Thus, it could not be transferred to satisfy the higher level of *mens rea* required for an aggravated assault conviction. As you will learn in Chapter 10, if Davis had been charged with battery, which is general intent crime for which recklessness suffices, then he could have lawfully been convicted of that crime for having recklessly discharged his shotgun.

Limits on the Types of Harm for Which *Mens Rea* May Be Transferred

The second limitation on the doctrine of transferred into involves the type of harm actually caused. The doctrine can be applied only situations where the same harm as was intended actually occurred, but on an unintended victim.[70] For example, in *State v. Bryant*,[71] the defendant was convicted of resisting arrest, assault and battery on a law enforcement officer, and of malicious damage to property, among other charges. The key events occurs when the defendant struggled to avoid being arrested. During the struggle, he slammed the officer against the patrol car, causing damage to the car. It was clear to the appeals court that the defendant intended to resist arrest and, in doing so, he assaulted and battered the office trying to make the arrest. But the court determined that the defendant did not intend to cause damage to the patrol car when he threw the officer against it. Rather, the damage to the patrol car was an unintended harm. Because the doctrine of transferred intent is limited to situations of the same type of harm intended, the intent to assault and batter the police officer could not be transferred to satisfy the *mens rea* for the damage to the police car. The first involves harm to a person, whereas the second involves harm to property. Because these types of harms are different, the doctrine of transferred intent could not be used to hold the defendant responsible for the damage to the vehicle.

CAUSATION OF RESULT

When a crime requires a particular result, such as the death of a human being for any homicide liability to attach, it is not enough for the prosecution to prove the elements of *actus reus* and *mens rea*. The prosecution must also prove that the defendant's *actus reus*, performed with the requisite *mens rea*, caused the required result.[72] The doctrine of causation applicable in criminal law requires two distinct types of causation: cause-in-fact and proximate cause.

Cause-in-Fact

Cause-in-fact is what we normally think of as "causing": if person does some act that directly brings about a particular result, then the person is said to have caused the result. To determine cause-in-fact, ask yourself, "Would the result have occurred 'but for' the defendant's conduct?" If so, the conduct is not cause-in-fact of the result since it would have occurred anyway. In contrast, though, if the answer to the question is "no," then conduct is the cause-in-fact of the result since the result would not have occurred but for the act.[73]

Proximate Cause

The law requires more than the line of direct causation embodied in cause-in-fact analysis to impose criminal liability. The law also requires what is known as **proximate cause.** Proximate cause is concerned with whether there were other causes that contributed to the result. If there were no other causes contributing to the result other than the defendant's *actus reus*, then proximate cause is established and liability can be imposed. But if there were factors other than the defendant's *actus reus* that contributed to the end result, then a careful proximate cause analysis must be undertaken. Consider the following hypothetical:

> There plainly are cases, however, in which we would not say that the shooter caused the victim's death, even though the shooting was a "but for" cause of that death. For example, assume that the shooter, fully intending to kill, shot at the victim but missed. To escape further assault, the intended victim fled in an airplane which then crashed, killing him. To be sure, by engaging in a voluntary act—squeezing the trigger of the gun—with intent to kill the victim, the shooter is guilty of attempted murder or assault with intent to kill, but we would not think of her as guilty of murder. If, however, "but for" causation were sufficient to establish the cause of a harm, we must conclude that the shooter's act of firing the gun caused the victim's death, and thus that she is guilty of murder. The purpose of proximate cause analysis is to avoid such unfair results. It seeks to align causation principles applied in cause-and-result crimes with everyday commonsense concepts of causation, in short, to draw a sensible and predictable line between cause and condition, even in complex cases involving numerous necessary conditions.[74]

When there are factors other than the defendant's *actus reus* contributing to the result, criminal liability may only be imposed if the contributing factor was foreseeable given the original act setting the chain of events into motion. A cause that is sufficiently foreseeable or sufficiently related to the defendant's conduct so as to make it fair to hold the defendant responsible for the result is called a **dependent, intervening cause**. Accordingly, a dependent, intervening cause "is one that is a natural and foreseeable result of the defendant's acts, and will not absolve the defendant of criminal liability."[75]

On the other hand, a cause that is sufficiently independent of the defendant's conduct so as to make it unfair to hold the defendant responsible for the result is deemed to be an **independent, supervening cause** that breaks the chain of causation.[76] Thus, an independent, supervening cause will absolve a defendant of criminal liability. For a contributing causal factor to be deemed an independent, supervening cause, it has to be rather extraordinary and/or abnormal such that its very occurrence requires that the defendant not be held liable for the end result.

Whether a contributing cause is deemed a dependent, intervening cause or an independent, supervening cause is generally considered a question of fact for a jury to determine at trial. The determination, however, is not always easy. Consider the classic hypothetical of medical malpractice that is committed by a physician treating the victim of an aggravated assault.

> Negligent medical treatment may constitute a dependent, intervening act. Generally, if the defendant wounds a victim in a manner that is either very dangerous or "calculated to destroy life," the negligence, mistake, or lack of skill by a physician or surgeon that contributes to the victim's death is not a defense to a charge of homicide. Mere negligence in the treating of the wound, even if it is the sole cause of death, is not a defense because it is a foreseeable intervening cause.[77]

However, if the treating physician intentionally did some act that caused the death of an aggravated assault victim that the physician was treating, that deliberate act would not be reasonably foreseeable and would therefore be classified as an independent, supervening cause that relieved the perpetrator of the initial assault of any homicide liability. The "Case Study Extra" feature in Box 4.4 presents an example of how proximate causation may be established when the victim of a crime responds by committing suicide.

BOX 4.4

CASE STUDY EXTRA

When Are Unintended Deaths after Criminal Victimizations Reasonably Foreseeable?

In *Stephenson v. State,*[86] a man abducted a woman her home and forced her to travel with him. He beat her and tried to rape her. During her period of captivity, the victim had access to some poison that she took in an attempt to commit suicide. When she became seriously ill, her captor offered to take her to the hospital. She declined, so he decided to return her to her home. During that trip, she cried out in pain for help, but her captor did nothing. Upon her return home, she received medical treatment, but one of her wounds became infected. She grew worse, unable to eat and sleep. She died twenty-seven days later as a result of a combination of shock, exhaustion, complications from the infected wound, and the lingering effects of the poison.

The victim's abductor was charged with murder, among other crimes. His defense centered on the argument that there was insufficient causation to impose any homicide liability on him. Specifically, he argued that his victim's voluntary consumption of poison in a failed suicide attempt was an independent, supervening cause that broke the chain of causation from his crimes (i.e., kidnapping, assault, and attempted rape) to her death. Thus, he asserted that her own acts—not his—were the proximate cause of her death.

The defendant was convicted at trial. An appellate court affirmed his conviction reasoning that whether his actions toward the victim naturally and probably resulted in rendering the victim so emotionally upset that attempted to commit suicide was a question of fact for the jury. The court agreed with the jury's assessment that the acts he committed could be reasonably viewed as directly causing her to become suicidal, and that her acts, in turn, were both dependent upon his crimes and reasonably foreseeable in light of them.

1. Conduct your own proximate cause evaluation of the victim's death in this case. If you were a judge ruling on an appeal by the defendant, how would you rule and why?
2. Assume that a defendant unlawfully stabbed another person. The victim is transported a hospital for treatment and dies, and autopsy reveals the victim died from medical malpractice suffered at the hands of the emergency room staff treating the victim, not from the stab wounds themselves. What should the outcome of the case be? Why?

CONCLUSION

Learning Objectives	Summaries
1. Compare and contrast the common law's use of general intent, specific intent, and malice as levels of *mens rea*.	Specific intent requires that an actor form a goal, aim, or objective to engage in specific conduct and cause a particular result. General intent requires than an actor commit a prohibited act volitionally, as opposed to accidentally, even if the actor did not intend to cause a particular result. Malice captures two types of situation, either when person acts with specific intent or when an actor consciously disregards a known risk that a particular harm might occur.
2. Differentiate the Model Penal Code's use of purpose, knowledge, recklessness, and negligence as levels of *mens rea*.	Purpose refers to when someone possesses a conscious objective or desire to engage in proscribed conduct or, alternatively, to cause a particular result. Knowledge refers to when someone acts with an awareness or belief that he or she is engaging in proscribed conduct, and further that the actor knows, believes, or is aware of practical certainty that the result achieved would occur by engaging in the conduct. Recklessness involves conduct by an actor who is aware of a substantial and unjustifiable risk that his or her conduct could cause a particular result, but consciously disregards that known risk and acts anyway. Negligence involves engaging in conduct that the actor is not aware poses a substantial and unjustifiable risk, but the actor should have been aware of the risk because a reasonable person in the same circumstances would have perceived the risk that the criminally negligent defendant failed to perceive.
3. Explain the circumstances under which strict liability and vicarious liability may attach to criminal offenses.	Strict liability involves the criminal punishment of a person who engages in proscribed conduct (*actus reus*) regardless of whether any *mens rea* was entertained. It typically attached to *mala prohibita* offenses regulating either public health, safety, and welfare or public morality. Strict liability also attaches to attendant circumstances that are not central to the criminality of an act, such jurisdictional issues. Vicarious liability holds someone other than the person who actually committed a *actus reus* of a crime liable for the act. It may be applied when there is some legal relationship between the actors (such as parents and children) or when there is some other socially desirable reason for holding someone criminally responsible for the acts of another person (such as social hosts).
4. Apply the concept of transferred intent to determine criminal liability.	The doctrine of transferred intent allows the *mens rea* entertained with respect to doing a particular *actus reus* tied to causing a particular result to be used to satisfy the *mens rea* requirement of having actually caused a different result than the one intended, so long as the same type of harm occurred and the same or lesser degree of intentionality is applicable.

Learning Objectives	Summaries
5. Evaluate how cause-in-fact and proximate cause limit criminal liability for crimes with result elements.	Cause-in-fact involves analyzing if an act brings about a particular result: that is, Would the result have occurred "but for" the defendant's conduct? But establishing cause-in-fact only establishes criminal liability if there are no other contributing causes. If there are other causes, then proximate cause must be established by evaluating whether the other causes were dependent, intervening causes—those that are reasonably foreseeable in light of the defendant's actions such that it is far to hold the defiant responsible for them, or independent, supervening causes—those contributing cases that were not reasonably foreseeable in light of the defendant's actions and, therefore, should absolve a defendant of liability for the ultimate result.

KEY TERMS

actual knowledge
cause-in-fact
constructive knowledge
dependent, intervening cause
general intent
independent, supervening cause
knowledge
malice
mens rea
negligence
proximate cause
purpose
recklessness
specific intent
strict liability
transferred intent
vicarious liability

5

Solicitation, Facilitation, and Attempt

LEARNING OBJECTIVES

1. Explain the crime of solicitation

2. Differentiate the crime of facilitation from other inchoate offenses.

3. Compare and contrast the *mens rea* approaches for attempt liability under the common law and the Model Penal Code.

4. Evaluate the *actus reus* element for the crime of attempt to determine criminal liability for that crime as distinct from solicitation.

5. Explain the defenses that may exonerate liability for the crimes of solicitation and attempt.

Outline

INTRODUCTION

Inchoate crimes involve various types of activities leading up to the commission of another crimes. In other words, they are not completed criminal offenses in the way that most crimes are, but rather concern steps that might be taken along the way to committing some substantive target or object crimes that an actor anticipates doing in the future.[1] This means that inchoate offenses punish early stages of criminal activity—acts of preparation that occur before someone has an opportunity to consummate the crimes that are planned.[2]

> Like a completed offense, an inchoate offense requires both a *mens rea* and an *actus reus*. Unlike the *actus reus* in a completed offense, however, the proscribed act in an anticipatory crime is not prohibited because of its harmful effect, but because it demonstrates a firm purpose on the part of an individual to act in furtherance of a criminal intent. The *mens rea* for inchoate crimes, therefore, is the specific intent to commit a particular completed offense, or target or object crime.[3]

With the exception of the crime of attempt, which can be committed alone, the other inchoate crimes involve the actual or feigned participation of two or more people. In 43 BCE, the Latin writer Publilius Syrus said, "To help the guilty is to share his crime."[4] This sentiment underlies criminal **complicity theory**—the tool by which one is made legally accountable for the criminal acts of another.[5] The most frequent ways in which complicity theory operates is by imposing liability on the nonprincipal actor as a solicitor, a facilitator, an accomplice, an accessory, or co-conspirator. This chapter explores the first two of these ways that one may be held criminally responsible for target offenses that may not ever be completed, along with the crime of attempt. This chapter also explores obstruction of justice and related offenses that have replaced after-the-fact accomplice liability. The accomplice and accessory liability, along with crimes related to obstruction of justice, and the crime conspiracy are explored in Chapter 6.

SOLICITATION

Solicitation, as the word connotes, involves "asking." In contrast to solicitations for sales of goods or services, a criminal solicitation concerns asking, persuading, or otherwise enticing another person to commit a criminal offense that the solicitor specific intends the other person to commit.[6]

The *actus reus* for the crime of solicitation is the actual "asking," but the term is broadly defined. Asking need not be an explicit question. It does not even have to involve words, as a solicitation can be accomplished with gestures. What is key to understanding the *actus reus* of solicitation is that the solicitor is attempting to get another person to commit a specific crime.[7]

The *mens rea* for solicitation is purpose or specific intent;[8] and, the crime has an interesting result element in most US jurisdictions. The person being solicited must reject the solicitation.[9] In other words, the person being asked to commit a crime must decline the solicitor's request to do so. If, however, the person being solicited accepts or agrees to the solicitation, then the crime of solicitation "evaporates" into the more serious crime of conspiracy (Chapter 6).[10] "Thus, solicitation can be viewed as an attempt to conspire."[11]

There is an attendant circumstance requirement for the crime of solicitation that varies significantly by jurisdiction concerning the crime solicited. At common law, it was only a crime to solicit someone to commit a felony or a misdemeanor that tended to "breach the peace" either by obstructing justice or otherwise injuring the public health, safety, or welfare.[12] The Model Penal Code, in contrast, punishes solicitation to commit any crime.[13] Some US states follow the common-law rule and criminalize solicitation to commit felonies and a handful of misdemeanors that constitute breaches of the peace;[14] other states follow the Model Penal Code's approach of having a general solicitation statute that criminalizes all solicitations to commit any criminal offense;[15] and still other states reject both approaches and criminalize solicitation to commit only specific, enumerated offenses.[16] The federal government follows the last approach of enumerating specific offenses:

> Whoever, with intent that another person engage in conduct constituting a felony that has as an element the use, attempted use, or threatened use of physical force against property or against the person of another in violation of the laws of the United States, and under circumstances highly corroborative of that intent, solicits, commands, induces, or otherwise endeavors to persuade such other person to engage in such conduct, shall be imprisoned not more than one-half the maximum term of imprisonment or . . . fined not more than one-half of the maximum fine prescribed for the punishment of the crime solicited, or both; or if the crime solicited is punishable by life imprisonment or death, shall be imprisoned for not more than twenty years.[17]

It should be emphasized that in most US jurisdictions, a mere solicitation—unaccompanied by some acts moving directly toward the commission of the intended crime—does not qualify as a substantial step constituting the *actus reus* element for the crime of attempt. More simply put, merely soliciting someone one to commit a crime does not constitute a criminal attempt to commit the object crime in most states, as we will explore in more detail later in this chapter.

What if a person being solicited to commit a crime does not hear or receive the solicitation? Box 5.1, containing the "Case Study Extra" feature, explores this question.

Defenses to Solicitation

After a solicitation was made with the requisite specific intent, the common law did not recognize any *abandonment* (sometimes referred to *renunciation* or *withdrawal*) as a criminal defense. But the Model Penal Code[18] and about half of all US states do recognize such a defense so long as the withdrawal of the solicitation is complete, effective, and

BOX 5.1

CASE STUDY EXTRA

Can One Be Liable for Solicitations That Are Never Received?

In *State v. Lee*,[57] correctional officers intercepted a letter that the defendant had written while he was in jail to an acquaintance who was incarcerated at juvenile detention facility. The letter outlined the defendant's plans to commit two robberies upon his release from jail:

> I wrote about two weeks ago. I guess you didn't get it. So, I'll tell you again. The job I got set up will get us some guns. On the other page is a picture of the place. And then I want to go to Washington. Okay.

Because jail personnel seized the letter, the intended recipient never received it.

The defendant was charged with solicitation to commit robbery, but he argued that because the letters containing the solicitation were never received by the intended recipient, he did not commit the crime of solicitation, but only the crime of attempted solicitation. That is the approach that the common law would have taken.[58] But the Model Penal Code specifically provides that solicitation may be based on an incomplete communication.[59] However, not all states follow this approach. Because Oregon had not adopted that specific provision of the Model Penal Code, the court in *State v. Lee* reversed the defendant's solicitation conviction, holding the correct conviction would be for attempt to solicit.

1. Which do you prefer—the common-law approach that a solicitation must be received in order for criminal liability to be imposed for the crime of solicitation, or the Model Penal Code approach? Why do you think the drafters of the Model Penal Code decided such receipt was not necessary?
2. The defendant in *State v. Lee* was adjudged to have committed the crime of attempted solicitation. Since solicitation boils down to asking someone else to commit a crime with the intent that the person solicited do so, what do you believe the logic behind attempted solicitation to be? Does such a crime make sense?

voluntary.[19] Accordingly, the solicitor must prevent the crime solicited from occurring. Some jurisdictions require not only that the solicitor notify the person solicited that the crime should not be carried out, but also require the solicitor to notify law enforcement or make similar efforts to ensure the crime does not occur.[20]

Similarly, *true legal impossibility* is a defense to solicitation. Thus, if a defendant encourages behavior that is, in fact, not a crime, a criminal solicitation has not occurred. This is true both at common law and under the Model Penal Code.

Finally, *factual impossibility* is never a defense to the crime of solicitation. For example, it would not be a defense to an otherwise criminal solicitation that the person solicited is factually incapable of committing the particular offense, such as soliciting the rightful owner of property to "steal" property that rightfully belongs to him or her.

FACILITATION

Solicitation and facilitation are often confused, perhaps because the two crimes both sound alike and may occur together. But they are separate and distinct criminal offenses. The crime of **facilitation** occurs when someone knowingly provides another person with either the means or the opportunity to commit a crime. Providing the means or opportunity for the commission of a crime (such as providing a weapon or drawing a map) is, therefore, the *actus reus* for the crime of facilitation.

Unlike the other inchoate offenses that require purpose as their respective levels of *mens rea*, the *mens rea* for the crime of facilitation is knowledge. That means that in order for liability to be imposed for facilitating a crime, a defendant must have had actual or constructive knowledge that the person to whom they are providing the means and opportunity to commit a crime is actually planning to commit the target offense. Without such knowledge that the other person plans to commit a crime, giving someone something that subsequently might be used during the commission of crime does not give rise to criminal liability for facilitation.

States vary in their approaches to the crime of facilitation. Most jurisdictions follow the Model Penal Code approach by considering facilitation to be a form of aiding and abetting, thereby transforming a criminal facilitator into an accomplice.[21] Other jurisdictions maintain a separate offense for knowing facilitation;[22] hence, this book addresses the crime as its own offense.

Some that maintain facilitation as its own offense apply it to all crimes,[23] while others states limit the crime to the facilitation of only felonies.[24] A handful of states do not impose any criminal liability for knowing facilitation, but rather punish purposeful assistance as the basis of accomplice liability.[25] Even in the jurisdictions that have a knowing facilitation statute, the laws differ with regard to whether the target offense must actually occur if facilitator liability is to be imposed.[26]

ATTEMPT

Attempt is the easiest of the inchoate offenses to conceptualize, because all of us know what it means in our everyday lives to try to do something unsuccessfully. The same meaning of attempt applies in the criminal law setting. If a person, acting with the specific intent (i.e., purpose) of committing a crime, tries to commit the crime, but fails, then a criminal attempt has occurred. If, on the other hand, one tries to commit a crime and succeeds, then attempt merges into the target offense. In other words, a person generally cannot be convicted for both an attempt and the actual commission of the offense attempted.[27] For example, suppose person *X* decides to kill person *Y* and goes so far as to lie in wait with a gun and fires upon the intended victim. If the bullet misses *Y*, then person *X* attempted to kill *Y* and is, therefore, guilty of the inchoate crime of attempted murder. If, on the other hand, the bullet strikes and kills person *Y*, then *X* is not guilty of attempted murder, but rather is guilty of the substantive crime of murder.

> The principal purpose behind punishing an attempt . . . is to provide a basis for law-enforcement officers to intervene before an individual can commit a completed offense. A secondary function is to punish those who have carried out their criminal scheme but have failed to effect the harmful result due to the intervention of external physical circumstances, including on-the-spot prevention.[28]

The crime of attempt generally has three elements. The *mens rea* is the specific intent/purpose to commit a criminal offense (often referred to as the "target crime"); the *actus reus* is the taking of certain qualifying steps toward the commission of the target crime; and the result element is a failure to consummate the target crime.[29]

Mens Rea for Attempt

No matter what the *mens rea* level is for a target offense, any attempt to commit a target crime necessarily involves specific intent or purpose. This makes perfect logical sense insofar as it is impossible to try to do something accidently. If one is trying to do something, by definition, his or her efforts to bring about the desired result are a product of purposeful actions. Thus, the *mens rea* for the crime of attempt is always purpose. The rule that one must have purpose to commit the target crime to satisfy the *mens rea* requirement for the crime of attempt does not tell us, however, to what the purpose requirement attaches. The common law differed in its treatment of this issue from the way in which the Model Penal Code treats the issue.

COMMON-LAW APPROACH

At common law, a defendant had to have the specific intent to engage in *all* the elements of the crime in order to be guilty of the crime of attempt, even those elements such as attendant circumstance which may have carried strict liability. Recall the case of *Thacker v. Commonwealth* from Chapter 4.[30] In that case, the defendant, while intoxicated, shot a bullet into a woman's tent. According to him, he wanted to knock out a light she had inside the tent. His conviction for attempted murder was reversed on appeal because the prosecution did not prove he had specific intent to kill the woman. The result in the case demonstrates the *mens rea* requirement that purpose must go to all elements of the crime. Surely Thacker purposefully shot the gun while aiming at the tent. But that is the conduct element of the offense. To be guilty of attempted murder, he would have also had to have the purpose of causing the woman's death—the result element of the target offense. Without such intent, there is no attempted murder.

But what if the bullet had struck and killed the woman in the tent? Thacker could then have been convicted of some form of homicide even though he had no intent to kill. This lack of intent to kill would be immaterial to the homicide charges if she had died, since neither murder in the second degree nor involuntary manslaughter requires purpose as its requisite level of *mens rea*. The crime of attempt, however, does require purpose. Thus, as the *Thacker* case illustrates, the *mens rea* for the crime of attempt is always purpose even if the target offense carries some lower level of *mens rea*.

The crime of statutory rape provides another good example of how *mens rea* for attempt differs from that of the target crime. Recall that statutory rape at common law was a strict liability crime. Accordingly, if a twenty-one-year-old male had sexual intercourse with a seventeen-year-old female whom he mistaken believed was nineteen, and the age of consent were eighteen in that jurisdiction, then the male would be guilty of statutory rape. The fact that he was mistaken about the young woman's age would be of no consequence. Why? Because despite having no *mens rea* to commit the crime of statutory rape, he would nonetheless be guilty since *mens rea* is irrelevant to the crime because strict liability attaches to the attendant circumstance of the victim's age. But what if he had been caught with the young woman before any sexual activity took place? Could he be successfully prosecuted for attempted statutory rape? At common law, the answer to this question would clearly have been "no." Why? Because he did not know that she was underage. According, he had no specific intent to commit the crime of statutory rape. Without such *mens rea*, he could not be convicted of the crime of attempt. Thus, at common law, there was quite a difference in the way *mens rea* worked with respect to attendant circumstances. As the statutory rape example nicely illustrates, even if strict liability attached to attendant circumstances for the target offense, one still needed specific intent with respect to those same attendant circumstances to be guilty of an attempt to commit the target offense. This incongruity in the way *mens rea* was treated with respect to attendant circumstances for attempt and for target crimes was one of the major changes made to the law of attempt by the Model Penal Code.

MODEL PENAL CODE APPROACH

In contrast to the common law, the Model Penal Code requires the *mens rea* of purpose only with respect to the conduct element of the target crime *or* the result element of the target crime. *Mens rea* is not necessary with respect to attendant circumstances. Rather, the *mens rea* requirement for attendant circumstances is the same for the crime of attempt as that which is required for the object offense. This means that if the target crime's level of requisite *mens rea* is recklessness, negligence, or even strict liability respect to any attendant circumstances, the same would apply to the attempt to commit that crime. Let us consider the statutory a rape example again, but this time, we will apply the Model Penal Code rather than the common law.

The facts of the hypothetical situation remain the same. A twenty-one-year-old male is caught just before he has sexual contact with a seventeen-year-old female whom he mistakenly believes was nineteen. The age of consent in this jurisdiction is eighteen. Because no sexual contact took place, he cannot be convicted of statutory rape because there was no *actus reus* to support such a conviction. But could he be successfully prosecuted for attempted statutory rape? As previously stated, the answer would be a resounding "no" at common law because he had no specific intent to commit the target crime of statutory rape since he mistakenly believed the young woman was of legal age. By contrast, the Model Penal Code requires either purpose to engage in proscribed conduct or purpose to cause a particular result; *mens rea* is not required with respect to attendant circumstances.[31] In this hypothetical, therefore, the young man certainly had the specific intent to engage in the conduct element of the offense, namely engaging in sexual contact with the young woman. The fact that he had no *mens rea* with respect to the other elements of statutory rape would be irrelevant; if strict liability applies to the attendant circumstance of the victim's age for the target crime (which it does for the crime of statutory rape), then the same rule or strict liability would apply to the attendant circumstance of the victim's age for the crime of attempt to commit statutory rape. Indeed, this very fact pattern transpired in *Commonwealth v. Dunne*.[32] In affirming the defendant's conviction for attempted statutory rape under Massachusetts law (modeled after the Model Penal Code approach), the court wrote:

> The fact that the defendant was ignorant of the age of [the victim] or that he did not intend the intercourse to be with a [person] of nonage would not prevent his act from constituting [statutory] rape if completed, or an attempt, if it failed. . . . Indeed, it would be incongruous for us to posit one rule for the completed act and another for the attempt. . . . This is simply a matter of common sense, for the policies underlying the rules in both cases are identical. The Legislature's

BOX 5.2

YOU MAKE THE PUBLIC POLICY CALL

Variations on the *Mens Rea* for Attempt

Suppose you had the specific intent to kill someone. In order to carry out your intended plan, you fire a loaded gun at your intended victim. The bullet, however, only grazes the skin of your intended victim, leaving the victim alive and in need of only a few stitches. You committed the crime of aggravated battery because you caused physical injury to a person using a deadly weapon. Your intent, however, was to kill that person. If charged with both attempted murder and aggravated battery, what should the outcome of your case be and why?

intention was "to put upon everyone the burden of finding out whether his contemplated act is prohibited, and of refraining from it if it is."[33]

The "You Make the Public Policy Call" feature contained in Box 5.2 further explores the *mens rea* for the crime of attempt.

Actus Reus for Attempt

The *actus reus* for attempt consists of the steps taken toward trying to complete the target offense. But both the common law and the Model Penal Code require more than acts of mere preparation. For there to be criminal liability for the crime of attempt, a defendant must take sufficient steps toward committing the target crime such that the justice system has confidence in surmising that the actor was, in fact, purposefully trying to complete a particular target offense.[34]

THE COMMON-LAW PROXIMITY TEST

The common law required defendants to have come "dangerously close" to committing the target crimes in order to be convicted of attempt. This test, often referred to as the **proximity test**, examines how much further a defendant have left to go before actually committing the target crime.[35] If there were so few steps left such that the defendant had already come dangerously close to committing the target crime, then the common-law proximity test was satisfied and the defendant could, therefore, be convicted of attempt. The following case illustrates the common law's approach to the *actus reus* for the crime of attempt.

The PEOPLE of the State of New York

v.

Charles RIZZO, et al.

158 N.E. 888 (N.Y. 1927).

Charles Rizzo, the defendant-appellant, with three others, . . . planned to rob one Charles Rao of a payroll valued at about $1,200 which he was to carry from the bank for the United Lathing Company. These defendants, two of whom had firearms, started out in an automobile, looking for Rao or the man who had the payroll on that day. Rizzo claimed to be able to identify the man, and was to point him out to the others, who were to do the actual holding up. The four rode about in their car looking for Rao. They went to the bank from which he was supposed to get the money and to various buildings being constructed by the United Lathing Company. At last they came to One Hundred and Eightieth Street and Morris Park Avenue. By this time, they were watched and followed by two police officers. As Rizzo jumped out of the car and ran into the building, all four were arrested. . . .

Does this constitute the crime of an attempt to commit robbery in the first degree? The Penal Law prescribes: "An act, done with intent to commit a crime, and tending but failing to effect its commission, is an attempt to commit that crime." The word "tending" is very indefinite. It is perfectly evident that there will arise differences of opinion as to whether an act in a given case is one tending to commit a crime. "Tending" means to exert activity in a particular direction. Any act in preparation to commit a crime may be said to have a tendency towards its accomplishment. The procuring of the automobile, searching the streets looking for the desired victim, were in reality acts tending toward the commission of the proposed crime. The law, however, had recognized that many acts in the way of preparation are too remote to constitute the crime of attempt. The line has been drawn between those acts which are remote and those which are proximate and near to the consummation. The law must be practical, and therefore considers those acts only as tending to the commission of the crime which are so near to its accomplishment that in all reasonable probability the crime itself would have been committed, but for timely interference. . . . The act or acts must come or advance very near to the accomplishment of the intended crime.

* * *

Rao was not found; the defendants were still looking for him; no attempt to rob him could be made, at least until he came in sight. . . . There was no man there with the payroll for the United Lathing Company whom these defendants could rob. . . . In a word, these defendants had planned to commit a crime, and were looking around the city for an opportunity to commit it, but the opportunity fortunately never came. . . .

For these reasons, the judgment of conviction of this defendant appellant must be reversed and a new trial granted.

THE MODEL PENAL CODE SUBSTANTIAL STEPS TEST

As illustrated by the *Rizzo* case, one of the major drawbacks of the common law's proximity test is that it tied the hands of law enforcement from preventing crime before a dangerous situation was created. The proximity test emphasized physical and temporal closeness to completing criminal acts "with insufficient regard to the dangerousness of the actor's personality, as demonstrated only partially by the dangerousness of his actions."[36] The Model Penal Code approach made it easier for law enforcement to act before dangerous situation were at hand by looking not at how much further a defendant had left to go before completing a target offense, but rather looking at how far a defendant has already gone. Under this more lenient approach, a defendant no longer had to come "dangerously close" to committing the intended offense. So long as a defendant takes **substantial steps** that strongly corroborated his or her *mens rea* of purposely committing the target substantive offense, then liability for the crime of attempt can be imposed.

Just as with the common-law approach, mere preparation does not constitute sufficient and substantial steps to qualify as the *actus reus* of the crime of attempt under the Model Penal Code. What steps go beyond mere preparation and into the realm of being substantial enough to corroborate *mens rea* is a question of fact for a jury to decide. The following case illustrates the difficulty courts have when trying to determine when the threshold of preparation has been crossed over into the realm of sufficient substantial steps.

Roger Matthew WALTERS, Petitioner-Appellant,

v.

Manfred MAASS, Superintendent, Respondent-Appellee.

45 F.3d 1355 (9th Cir. 1995).

Roger Matthew Walters . . . challeng[es] his conviction and sentence for attempted rape, attempted sodomy, and attempted kidnapping of a thirteen-year-old girl.

Walters first contends that he was denied a fair trial when the state court admitted evidence that in 1981, he approached another thirteen-year-old girl with the ploy of searching for a nonexistent white German shepherd, offered her $20, and then kidnapped her, took her to his trailer, and forcibly raped and sodomized her. Walters used the same German shepherd ploy in this case to try to lure the thirteen-year-old victim into his truck. The state court admitted the prior bad acts evidence as proof of intent.

The Oregon court did not err by admitting evidence of Walters' 1981 convictions. Walters' use of the German shepherd ploy in 1981 was relevant to show his intent in using the same ploy in 1987. Moreover, the prior act was not too remote in time.

* * *

Under Oregon law, conviction for attempt requires proof beyond a reasonable doubt that the defendant "intentionally engaged in conduct which constitutes a substantial step toward commission of the crime."[37] To constitute a substantial step toward the commission of a crime, the defendant's conduct must (1) "advance the criminal purpose charged, and (2) provide some verification of the existence of that purpose."[38] Mere preparation is insufficient to constitute a substantial step.[39]

The difference between making preparations and taking a substantial step toward the commission of a crime is one of degree.[40] In evaluating whether conduct constitutes a substantial step, we have stated that although behavior need not be incompatible with innocence to be punishable as an attempt, "it must be necessary to the consummation of the crime and be of such a nature that a reasonable observer, viewing it in context[,] could conclude beyond a reasonable doubt that it was undertaken in accordance with a design" to commit the particular crime charged.[41] Moreover, a substantial step must entail "an overt act adapted to, approximating, and which in the ordinary and likely course of things will result in, the commission of the particular crime."[42]

* * *

Certainly Walters' intent is manifested by (1) evidence regarding his use of the German shepherd ruse in 1981 to kidnap, rape, and sodomize another thirteen-year-old girl, (2) his persistent attempts to lure the victim into his truck using the same ruse, (3) his actions in following the victim home, (4) his strange speech patterns when he talked to the victim's mother, and (5) his statements to the police officer. In addition, Walters' attempt to entice the victim into his truck clearly advances the criminal purpose of first-degree kidnapping and strongly corroborates the existence of his purpose to commit that crime. Thus, we agree . . . that this conduct constitutes a substantial step toward the commission of the crime of first-degree kidnapping, and we do not disturb Walters' conviction for attempted first-degree kidnapping.

The more troubling question is whether Walters' attempt to entice the victim into his truck constitutes a substantial step toward the commission of the crimes of rape and sodomy when the only evidence of intent to rape and sodomize is Walters' 1981 conviction for kidnapping, raping, and sodomizing another thirteen-year-old girl. If in 1981, Walters had committed other crimes (for example, breaking the victim's arm and stealing her wallet), it would be difficult to conclude now that enticement into the truck constituted a substantial step toward the commission of those crimes. At some point, the link between the enticement and the charged crimes becomes too attenuated: we cannot say that the enticement strongly corroborates any intent to commit those crimes such that a reasonable observer, viewing it, in context, could conclude beyond a reasonable doubt that it was undertaken in accordance with a design to commit the crimes.

The only step Walters took toward the commission of the charged crimes was his attempt to entice the victim into his truck. It may be that this act to some extent corroborates Walters' intent to commit some sexual assault, but we cannot agree that it *strongly* corroborates his intent to commit those crimes. Moreover, attempting to entice the victim into a truck does not, in the ordinary and likely course of events, result in the crimes of rape and sodomy.

* * *

Questions

1. The *Rizzo* court found insufficient evidence to convict the defendants of attempted bank robbery using the common-law proximity test. What effect, if any, on the outcome of the case do you think it would have made if the Model Penal Code's substantial steps test had been in effect at that time? Explain your reasoning.
2. In the *Maass* case, the court had no problem determining that Mr. Maass's actions were strongly corroborative of his intent to kidnap the girl, and therefore found sufficient evidence to uphold his conviction for attempted kidnapping. Do you agree? Why or why not? Would your opinion differ if you did not know about his previous crimes regarding the same *modus operandi* (i.e., using the German Shepherd as a lure)?
3. When does mere preparation turn into substantial steps? The jury convicted Mr. Maass attempted statutory rape and attempted sodomy. Presumably, therefore, the jury was satisfied that his act of enticing the girl to his truck went beyond mere preparation and was strongly corroborative of his intent to commit both target crimes, but the court disagreed. Do you think the acts described as "enticing" in the *Maass* case were acts of mere preparation or were they substantial steps sufficient to impose criminal liability for attempt? Why?

SOLICITATIONS AS SUBSTANTIAL STEPS?

In most circumstances, a solicitation to commit a crime—without more—does not constitute a substantial step toward the commission of a target crime. Thus, by merely soliciting the commission of a crime—even when accompanied by a bribe or other offer of money—one does not automatically become liable for attempt to commit that crime.[43] But Model Penal Code Section 5.01(2)(g) contain an exception to this general rule. It provides that solicitation of a wholly "innocent agent" can constitute a substantial step for attempt liability so long as the act is strongly corroborative of an actor's criminal purpose.

Consider the example crafted by Professor Glanville Williams in which an actor, *D*, tells another person, *E*, "to set fire to a haystack, and gives him a match to do it."

> If, as *D* knows, *E* (mistakenly) believes that it is *D*'s stack and that the act is lawful, *E* is an innocent agent, and *D* is guilty of attempted arson. *D*, in instructing *E*, does the last thing that he intends in order to effect his criminal purpose. (It would be the same if he only used words and did not give *E* a match.)[44]

As you might imagine, circumstances in which a truly "innocent agent" is solicited to do an act that he or she is wholly unaware would constitute the commission of a crime are quite rare. Thus, the general rule is that solicitations normally constitute insufficient steps to qualify as the *actus reus* for a criminal attempt. But as the "Statutory Analysis Exercise" in Box. 5.3 illustrates, this distinction is not always as clear-cut as it seems.

BOX 5.3

STATUTORY ANALYSIS EXERCISE

Was a Murder-for-Hire Plan a Solicitation or an Attempt?

In *State v. Daniel B.*,[60] the defendant and his wife were engaged in a bitter divorce. At times, the defendant was violent, resulting in courts issues orders of protection (sometimes referred to as "restraining orders") for him to stay away from his wife and their three-year-old son. The defendant met with old friend and complained that his wife was "getting the house, the kids . . . and she was trying to get some money" in the divorce.[61] He asked if his friend "knew anybody that could murder" his wife for him, stating that "he had been thinking about it for two years, and he made up his mind. . . . He needs it done."[62] The friend notified the police who, in turn, arranged for an undercover officer to pretend to be a hit man. The fake hit man met with the defendant and agreed on a plan to murder the defendant's wife in a staged carjacking in exchange for $10,000. The defendant showed the fake hit man a photograph of his wife and gave him a handwritten note containing his wife's full name, home address, place of employment, and work schedule. He was arrested and convicted of attempted murder.

The Connecticut statute criminalizing attempt is based on the Model Penal Code. It provides, in relevant part that:

> (a) (2) [a] person is guilty of an attempt to commit a crime if, acting with the kind of mental state required for commission of the crime, he . . . intentionally does or omits to do anything which, under the circumstances as he believes them to be, is an act or omission constituting a substantial step in a course of conduct planned to culminate in his commission of the crime. . . .
>
> (b) [c]onduct shall not be held to constitute a substantial step . . . unless it is strongly corroborative of the actor's criminal purpose."[63]

Relying on this statute, courts reversed a conviction for attempted murder in *State v. O'Neil*,[64] in which the defendant had mailed a letter asking someone to kill a witness, reasoning the act constitute a solicitation, not an attempt. The defendant in *Daniel B.* relied on this case as precedent, arguing he had not taken substantial steps toward the commission of the crime because he had not yet paid any money to the fake hit man and, therefore, he was guilty of solicitation to commit murder, not attempted murder. His argument was bolstered by a Missouri Supreme Court decision requiring proof that "something beyond conversation has occurred"—something like "making a cash payment, delivering a weapon, visiting a crime scene, waiting for a victim, etc." must accompany a conversation to evidence the *mens rea* for attempt of purpose, and bring "the planned crime closer to fruition."[65]

1. If you were a judge on the Supreme Court of Connecticut, how would you have ruled in the appeal? Why?
2. Given the fake hit man in this case was an undercover police officer, why do you think the courts were not applying the "innocent agent" exception to the general rule that solicitations cannot constitute attempts?

Defenses to Attempt

"A multitude of reasons and circumstances can lead to the failure of a defendant to consummate a substantive crime. The impossibility doctrine in attempt law considers a distinct type of failure—those that stem from some mistake on a defendant's part as to a crime's attendant circumstances."[45] This section discussed the varying approaches to the defense of impossibility for the crime of attempt. It should be noted, however, that many US jurisdictions have statutorily abolished the defense of impossibility.[46] Thus, the law in your state may or may not recognize this defense.

FACTUAL IMPOSSIBILITY

Suppose that, with the specific intent to kill, you walked into a bedroom in which you believed your intended victim to be sleeping. You then fired at the bed believing your victim to be in it. As the fates would have it, however, your victim was not in the bed that night. Your bullet merely pierced some pillows and bedding. Are you guilty of attempted murder? Both the common law and the Model Penal Code would answer this question in the affirmative and hold you liable for attempted murder. Circumstances being what they were (i.e., the bed was empty), rather than what you believed them to be (i.e., that your intended victim was in the bed) caused it to be factually impossible for you to have killed your intended victim. But **factual impossibility** is not a defense to the crime of attempt under either the common law or the Model Penal Code.[47]

The classic example of the "unlucky pickpocket" is an excellent example of factual impossibility. If a pickpocket picked a pocket that has nothing in it to steal (and, therefore, no theft could actually occur), would the pickpocket be liable for attempted theft? Since the pickpocket tried and failed (because the pocket from which he attempted to steal was empty), it was factually impossible for him to succeed in his attempt. But since factual impossibility is not a defense, the pickpocket would have criminal responsibility for his attempt.

In both of these examples, the aims of the actors were both crimes: murder in the first hypothetical; theft in the second. The impossibility of succeeding with their respective turned not on the law, but rather on the facts and circumstances of the case. Hence, the impossibility at issue is factual, not legal impossibility. But what if the law itself made it impossible for an actor to succeed in his or her criminal attempt? Such situations are covered by the defense of legal impossibility.

LEGAL IMPOSSIBILITY

Can someone be legally convicted of attempting to do something that was, in actuality, not a crime? At first blush, the question seems silly. Why would we punish trying but failing to do something that is not illegal? Well, if phrased that way, the obvious answer to the question should be a resounding no. Neither the common law nor the Model Penal Code impose any criminal liability for attempting to that which is perfectly legal. The law would say there is a **true legal impossibility** to be guilty of the crime of attempt under such circumstances. True legal impossibility is a defense in all US jurisdictions.[48] But when if an actor engages in conduct that he or she believes to be illegal, but is not actually prohibited by law? The common law and the Model Penal Code answered this question differently using a defense that is often referred to as **hybrid legal impossibility**.

At common law, if one attempted to do an act that he believed was illegal, but turned out not to be illegal, there was no criminal attempt. In other words, regardless of the actor's guilty state of mind, if one did not try and fail to do an act that was actually illegal, there was no liability for criminal attempt. Thus, at common law, legal impossibility was a bona-fide defense to the crime of attempt. Consider, for example, a group of friends who decide to play poker for money in one of their homes. Assume the house at which this fictional poker game takes place was in Las Vegas, Nevada. The poker players all believe that they are committing the criminal offense of gambling because they are playing poker in a private home, rather than at a state-licensed casino. Thus, they had the *mens rea* of purpose to commit the crime of illegal gambling. Suppose, however, that there were no laws in Nevada that made such a private poker game illegal. Thus, the group—specifically intending to commit a crime—did nothing illegal. Their criminal intent notwithstanding, they would not be guilty of any crime under the common-law approach because what they did was not actually illegal.[49]

The Model Penal Code sought to eliminate the defense of impossibility in virtually all situations. While it is still a requirement that the result intended or desired by the actor constitute a crime (otherwise there would be true legal impossibility), the Model Penal Code shifted the focus to the defendant's *mens rea*. Accordingly, attempt liability is now judged not on the external circumstances of what the law actually is, but rather on whether the defendant's intent warrants criminal sanctioning. The Model Penal Code holds that there is no defense if, under the attendant circumstances, a crime was factually or legally impossible of commission, "if such crime could have been committed had the attendant circumstances been as such person believed them to be."

> From this viewpoint, the only relevant consideration is the actor's subjective perception of the attendant circumstances, and not the objective reality of those circumstances. Fortunately, this approach rarely results in an anomalous outcome. Usually, a person's subjective intent is reflected in a dangerous act, thus allowing a conviction for the attempted crime . . . .[50]

For example, in the gambling example, a group of friends thought they illegally gambling but were not, in fact, breaking any law. The common law would not allow a conviction for attempted illegal gambling under such circumstances despite their specific intent to commit such a crime. However, under the Model Penal Code approach, if the circumstances were as they believed them to be (i.e., if such a home poker game were, in fact, illegal), then they would have committed a crime. Their *mens rea* with respect to their conduct (i.e., gambling) and attendant circumstance (i.e., believing their conduct to be illegal) would determine their criminal liability. The actual attendant circumstances of their conduct not being illegal would not exonerate them the way such circumstances would have exonerated the group under the common law. The "Statutory Analysis Exercise" in Box 5.4 explores the concept of hybrid legal impossibility in more detail.

ABANDONMENT

At common law, one could not abandon, withdraw from, or renounce his or her criminal attempt and assert that as a defense to the crime after the actor had already come "dangerously close" to effectuating the target crime.[51] Accordingly, once the elements of the crime of attempt had occurred, there was no defense to the crime for not having followed to completion of one's criminal intentions. Many US jurisdictions continue to follow this common-law rule with respect to the crime of attempt.

In contrast to the common-law approach, the Model Penal Code recognizes the defense of **abandonment** (sometimes referred to as the defense of *renunciation* or *withdrawal*). The rationale for the Model Penal Code approach hinges on the fact that the target offense must have been prevented from the abandonment. If it was, then excusing the defendant from attempt liability is seen as good public policy that benefits society at large because the availability of the defense encourages would-be criminals to stop their attempts, thereby reducing the risk of crime.[52]

For the defense to be successfully asserted, the Model Penal Code requires that three criteria be met. The abandonment must be (a) effective, (b) complete, and (c) voluntary.[53] If all three requirements are not met, a defendant cannot successfully assert the defense of abandonment.

BOX 5.4

STATUTORY ANALYSIS EXERCISE

The Confusing Nature of Hybrid Legal Impossibility

Evaluating Inchoate Liability for Internet Crimes Against Children in *People v. Thousand*, an undercover sheriff's deputy pretended to be an underage female in various internet chat rooms.[66] While logged in using the fake screen "Bekka," the defendant struck up conversion with the officer. The defendant identified himself as being twenty-three, whereas Bekka reported that "she" was fourteen. Over several days, conversations between the two became sexually explicit. At one point, the defendant sent Bekka of photograph of male genitalia and then invite her to his apartment, detailing the sexual things he would do to her, including engaging in sexual intercourse. When Bekka replied that she wanted to do the things the defendant had detailed, he warned Bekka that they had to be careful, because he could go to jail. He even told her to lie about her age to his roommates if they were home. They made plans to meet at a local McDonald's and then go back to his place. When he showed up at the designated time, he was arrested and charged with solicitation to commit sexual conduct with a minor and attempted distribution of obscene material to a minor.

The Michigan Penal Code provides, in relevant part:

> a person who solicits another person to commit a felony [other than murder], or who solicits another person to do or omit to do an act which if completed would constitute a felony [other than murder], is punishable [by up to five years in prison].[67]

Another provision states,

> Any person who shall attempt to commit an offense prohibited by law, and in such attempt shall do any act towards the commission of such offense, but shall fail in the perpetration, or shall be intercepted or prevented in the execution of the same, when no express provision is made by law for the punishment of such attempt, shall be punished.[68]

The defendant argued that the existence of a child victim was an essential element of the solicitation and attempt charges. The trial court agreed with him and dismissed the case, reasoning that it was legally impossible for defendant to have committed the charged offenses. Because those decisions were upheld by an appellate court, the prosecution appealed to the Supreme Court of Michigan.

Courts have recognized a defense of legal impossibility or have stated that it would exist if [a defendant] receives . . . unstolen property believing it was stolen; tries to pick the pocket of a stone image of a human; offers a bribe to a "juror" who is not a juror; tries to hunt deer out of season by shooting a stuffed animal; shoots a corpse believing that it is alive; or shoots at a tree stump believing that it is a human.

Notice that each of the mistakes in these cases affected the legal status of some aspect of the defendant's conduct. The status of property as "stolen" is necessary to commit the crime of "receiving stolen property with knowledge it is stolen"—i.e., a person legally is incapable of committing this offense if the property is not stolen. The status of a person as a "juror" is legally necessary to commit the offense of bribing a juror. The status of a victim as a "human being" (rather than as a corpse, tree stump, or statue) legally is necessary to commit the crime of murder or to "take and carry away the personal property of another." Finally, putting a bullet into a stuffed deer can never constitute the crime of hunting out of season.

On the other hand, in each example of hybrid legal impossibility [a defendant] was mistaken about a fact: whether property was stolen, whether a person was a juror, whether the victims were human or whether the victim was an animal subject to being hunted out of season.[69]

1. Assume you were a judge on the Michigan Supreme Court. For the purposes of this question only, further assume that Michigan does not recognize the defense of hybrid legal impossibility, in much the same way that the Model Penal Code does not. Based on your reading of the statutes, would you uphold the dismissal of the attempt charge or order it reinstated? Why?
2. For the purposes of this question only, assume that Michigan followed the common-law approach to the defense of impossibility. How would you rule on the appeal of the attempt charge? Why?
3. With regard to the solicitation charge, put aside the issue of impossibility for the moment. Instead, analyze whether the defendant solicited the commission of crime. To do so, keep in mind that although it would be a felony for a twenty-three-year-old to engage in sexual activity with a fourteen-year-old, the converse is not true. The underage person is the victim in a statutory rape, not an offender.

By effective, the Model Penal Code requires that the actor stop his or her criminal attempt at the target crime. Thus, the target crime cannot occur. However, abandoning an attempt out of frustration after one has done everything possible to attempt the crime is not an effective abandonment. Similarly, if the actor has put in motion forces that he is powerless to stop, then the attempt has been completed and cannot be effectively abandoned.[54]

Secondly, the defendant's renunciation of his or her criminal intent must be complete. That is to say that the defendant must totally abandon all intent to commit the target crime, not just postpone it to a later time or "to transfer the criminal effort to another but similar objective or victim."[55]

And finally, the abandonment must be voluntary. It must out of the defendant's own remorse or feeling that he or she should not be doing the crime, not due to the circumstances surrounding the attempt. In the words of the Model Penal Code, an abandonment is not voluntary "if it is motivated, in whole or in part, by circumstances . . . that increase the probability of detection or apprehension or that make more difficult the accomplishment of the criminal purpose."[56]

CONCLUSION

Learning Objectives	Summaries
1. Explain the crime of solicitation	Solicitation involves asking or otherwise enticing someone to commit an offense with the purpose that the other person will engage in the crime. At common law, it was only a crime to solicit the commission of a felony or breach of the peace. The Model Penal Code criminalizes all criminal solicitations.
2. Differentiate the crime of facilitation from other inchoate offenses.	Facilitation occurs when someone knowingly provides another person with either the means or the opportunity to commit a crime. Unlike other inchoate offense that require purpose as their *mens rea*, facilitation requires knowledge.
3. Compare and contrast the *mens rea* approaches for attempt liability under the common law and the Model Penal Code.	The *mens rea* for attempt liability is always specific intent/purpose. But at common law, the intent had to apply to all elements of the target crime. Under the Model Penal Code, however, purpose may attach to either the conduct element or the result element of the target crime; there need not be any *mens rea* with respect to attendant circumstances for attempt liability if the target crime does not require *mens rea* with respect to attendant circumstances.
4. Evaluate the *actus reus* element for the crime of attempt to determine criminal liability for that crime as distinct from solicitation.	The *actus reus* for attempt is trying, but failing, to commit a target crime. At common law, the actor had to come dangerously close to committing the target crime. But under the Model Penal Code, taking substantial steps toward the commission of the target crime is sufficient to establish liability, provided that the steps taken strongly corroborate criminal intent. As a rule, solicitation does not constitute a substantial step to establish the *actus reus* for attempt liability, although an exception allows for such liability when the actor solicits an innocent agent to commit an offense they do not know is criminal.

Learning Objectives	Summaries
5. Explain the defenses that may exonerate liability for the crimes of solicitation and attempt.	Factual impossibility is never a defense to any inchoate crime. Although legal impossibility may be a defense, it is highly unlikely that it will succeed since most claims of impossibility involve a hybrid of mistakes of facts and of law that do not negate *mens rea*. At common law, one could not abandon a solicitation or an attempt. The former was complete once the actor asked someone to commit and crime with the purpose the other person did so. The latter was complete once the actor came dangerously close to the commission of a target crime. But to facilitate renunciation of criminal plans, the Model Penal Code recognizes abandonment as a defense to the crimes of solicitation and attempt so long as they involve complete, effective, and voluntary withdrawals.

KEY TERMS

attempt
complicity theory
facilitation
inchoate crimes
proximity test
substantial steps
solicitation

6

Aiding and Abetting, Obstructing Justice, and Conspiracy

Outline

LEARNING OBJECTIVES

1. Analyze the scope of criminal liability for accomplices.
2. Compare and contrast liability for being an accessory after the fact with obstruction of justice liability.
3. Describe various ways that someone may be held criminally liability for interference with the orderly administration of justice.
4. Define the elements of a criminal conspiracy.
5. Explain the ways in which the *mens rea* for conspiracy liability may be established.
6. Differentiate wheel and chain/ladder conspiracies.
7. Explain the defenses that may exonerate liability for the crimes of aiding and abetting and conspiracy.

INTRODUCTION

Recall from Chapter 5 that complicity theory is the tool by which a person is made legally accountable for the criminal acts of another.[1] In this chapter, we explore the ways in which complicity theory operates to impose criminal liability on people who aid in the planning and execution of crimes, as well as those who try to help offenders get away with their crimes after the fact.

AIDING AND ABETTING: ACCOMPLICE LIABILITY

An **accomplice** (sometimes called an *accessory before-the-fact*) is a person, other than a peace officer acting in his or her official capacity within the scope of his or her authority and in the line of duty, who actually helps or attempts to help someone else with the specific intent (purpose) to promote or facilitate the commission of an offense.[2] An **accessory** is a person who provides aid after the commission of a crime with the specific intent (purpose) to help someone evade detection, arrest, or punishment. Unlike the crime of conspiracy (which, as will be explained later in this chapter, is an offense that punishes forming a crime-related agreement), accomplice and accessorial liability requires that someone give some aid to the **principal**—the one primarily responsible for committing the crime. At the outset, there are three significant limitations on accomplice liability that should be noted.

First, while the common law made very clear distinctions between principals, accomplices, and accessories, many jurisdictions—including the federal government—have abolished these terms and hold all participants equally liable for the completed offenses.[3] It is notable, however, that although distinctions in *liability* may have been abolished, the underlying concepts of complicity theory that define the substantive act of aiding and abetting that gives rise to this liability remain important.[4]

Second, a person cannot be an accomplice or an accessory just because he or she knew about a crime or was innocently present during the commission of a crime. "There must be some additional evidence that the person intended to aid in the commission of the underlying crime, and then aided or attempted to aid."[5]

Third, those who are victims of a crime or who take part in a crime that by its definition "takes two to tango" are not held liable under any theory of complicity.[6] In other words, there is no accomplice liability for those who are incident to an offense; one who is a necessarily party to an offense by definition may not be held an as accessory to the crime. For example, an underage person who is the victim of a statutory rape cannot be charged as an accessory to the statutory rape, even if the person "aided and abetted" the crime by encouraging someone older to have sex with the underage person.[7]

Elements for Accomplice Liability

Aiding and abetting is the traditional way in which the *actus reus* for accomplice liability is described. The quantity or quality of the aid offered is not measured, nor is its success. Any form of giving aid, however minimal, can satisfy the *actus reus* requirement.[8] The aid given does not even need to be effective. For example, if person *A* gives person *B* a gun to commit a murder, and person *B* winds up killing the intended victim with person *B*'s own knife, *A* is still an accomplice to the homicide since actual aid was given by *A*, even though it was not effective aid.

Similarly, the aid given need not be affirmative aid, such as actually assisting the principal carry out the crime, for the *actus reus* requirement to be satisfied. Simply giving moral support, advice, or counsel can suffice.[9] It can even be an omission when there is a legal duty to act. For example, a police officer who "turns the other cheek" while witnessing a fellow officer use unlawful force on a suspect becomes an accomplice to the principal officer's assault and battery of the suspect. But absent the rare situation where an omission constitutes an *actus reus* due to a legal duty to act, accomplice liability requires that some aid must be given. Mere presence at the scene of a crime—without more (such as a prior agreement with the principal to be at the scene to provide a false eyewitness account of what transpired, or to just provide moral support)—is insufficient to qualify as the *actus reus* for accomplice liability. This makes perfect logical sense, otherwise simply being at the wrong place at the wrong time could make anyone an accomplice. Consider the classic case of *Hicks v. United States*, decided by the US Supreme Court in 1893.[10]

John Hicks was indicted with Stand Rowe for murdering Andrew Colvard. Both men attended a party at the home of Rowe's brother. After a night of dancing and heavy drinking, a several people departed the party on horseback. The Court summarized what happened next as follows:

> As Colvard and Hicks approached the point where Stand Rowe was sitting on his horse, Stand Rowe rode out into the road and halted. . . . [W]itnesses . . . saw Stand Rowe twice raise his rifle and aim it at Colvard, and twice he lowered it. They heard Colvard say, "I am a friend to both of you." They saw and heard the defendant, Hicks, laugh aloud when Rowe directed his rifle towards Colvard. . . . They heard Hicks say to Colvard, "Take off your hat, and die like a man." They saw Stand Rowe raise his rifle for the third time point it at Colvard, and fire it. . . . They saw Colvard fall from his horse. They went to where he was lying in the road, and found him dead. They saw Stand Rowe and John Hicks ride off together after the shooting.[11]

Hicks denied that his statement Colvard, "take off your hate and die like a man" was intended to encouraged Rowe to shoot Colvard. In fact, Hicks testified that he made the comment in desperation, fearing that Rowe would shoot both him and Colvard.[12] He also testified that he rode off with Rowe after the shooting because he feared for his life.

The Court took care to say that Hicks's mere presence at the time and place of the shooting would not make Hicks guilty of any crime.[13] The Court also explained that if his presence had been prearranged as part of a conspiratorial agreement whereby he agreed to be present to lend support to Colvard to kill Rowe, then Hicks would be liable for Colvard's death. But without any proof of such an agreement, Hicks could not be held liable for Colvard's death on conspiracy grounds.[14] The Court acknowledged that if Hicks were present at the scene and, while there, "he aided, abetted, or advised, or encouraged the shooting,"[15] then he would be guilty of Rowe's murder as an accomplice, so long as his "acts or words of encouragement and abetting" had occurred "with the intention of encouraging and abetting Rowe."[16] The Court ruled that because the trial judge had not properly instructed the jury to consider Hicks's intent in making the words, his conviction needed to be overturned, even if his words actually had the effect of encouraging Rowe to shot Colvard. That effect is not relevant unless the words were said with intent of bringing about the killing:

> [Hicks's] words may have been used for a different purpose, and yet have had the actual effect of inciting Rowe to commit the murderous act. Hicks, indeed, testified that the expressions used by him were intended to dissuade Rowe from shooting. But the jury were left to find Hicks guilty as a principal because the effect of his words may have had the result of encouraging Rowe to shoot, regardless of Hicks' intention.[17]

As previously stated, the *mens rea* required to hold someone liable as an accomplice is purpose. That means the accomplice must have offered some aid, however minimal and regardless of its effectiveness, with the specific intent that the aid offered would facilitate the principal's commission of the target crime.[18] Indifference to the outcome is not enough, as the following case illustrates.

The STATE of Washington, Respondent,

v.

Bruce W. GLADSTONE, Appellant.

474 P.2d 274 (Wash. 1970).

A jury found defendant Bruce Gladstone guilty of aiding and abetting one Robert Kent in the unlawful sale of marijuana.... He appeals....

Gladstone's guilt as an aider and abettor in this case rests solely on evidence of a conversation between him and one Douglas MacArthur Thompson concerning the possible purchase of marijuana from one Robert Kent.... When asked by Thompson—an agent of the police—where marijuana could be bought, the defendant did no more than name Kent as an individual who might be willing to sell some and draw a sketch of his location. There was no evidence whatever that the defendant had any association, understanding, agreement or arrangement, direct or indirect, tacit or express with Kent to aid or persuade him in any way in the sale of marijuana.... The two officers then took Thompson to Kent's residence where marijuana was purchased....

***

If all reasonable inferences favorable to the state are accorded the evidence, it does not, in our opinion, establish the commission of the crime charged. That vital element—a nexus between the accused and the party whom he is charged with aiding and abetting in the commission of a crime—is missing. The record contains no evidence whatever that Gladstone had any communication by word, gesture or sign, before or after he drew the map, from which it could be inferred that he counseled, encouraged, hired, commanded, induced or procured Kent to sell marijuana to Douglas Thompson as charged, or took any steps to further the commission of the crime charged. He was not charged with aiding and abetting Thompson in the purchase of marijuana, but with Kent's sale of it.

***

This court has recognized the necessity of proof of a nexus between aider and abettor and other principals to sustain a conviction. In *State v. Hinkley*,[19] amplifying the term "abet," we said: "Although the word 'aid' does not imply guilty knowledge or felonious intent, the word 'abet' includes knowledge of the wrongful purpose of the perpetrator, as well as counsel and encouragement in the crime...." It would be a dangerous precedent indeed to hold that mere communications to the effect that another might or probably would commit a criminal offense amount to an aiding and abetting of the offense should it ultimately be committed.

There being no evidence whatever that the defendant ever communicated to Kent the idea that he would in any way aid him in the sale of any marijuana, or said anything to Kent to encourage or induce him or direct him to do so, or counseled Kent in the sale of marijuana, or did anything more than describe Kent to another person as an individual who might sell some marijuana, or would derive any benefit, consideration or reward from such a sale, there was no proof of an aiding and abetting, and the conviction should, therefore, be reversed as a matter of law. Remanded with directions to dismiss.

Questions

1. The defendant in the case testified that he "did not know that Kent used marijuana or kept it for sale to other people." If that is the case, then why would he send Thompson to Kent's house when he knew that Thompson was seeking to purchase marijuana? His own testimony is that Thompson asked him about Kent by name, but Thompson testified that he never asked Gladstone about Kent by name, but rather that he asked Gladstone if he knew of anyone who had pot to sell and that Gladstone then referred

him to Kent. Given these disputed facts, the trial court found Gladstone guilty. Why do you think the appellate court reversed?

2. As the court noted, Gladstone "was not charged with aiding and abetting Thompson in the purchase of marijuana, but with Kent's sale of it." Evaluate whether the outcome would have been different if Gladstone had been charged with aiding and abetting Thompson's purchase.
3. Do you think that Gladstone should have any criminal liability as a facilitator, rather than as an accessory who purposefully aided and abetted? Explain your response.

Generally speaking, *mens rea* applies to aiding the conduct element of the target offense. In other words, one who aids a principal in committing an *actus reus* for another crime is an accomplice to that crime. There need not be any *mens rea* with respect to either the result elements or the attendant circumstance elements of a crime for accomplice liability to be imposed. For example, suppose *X* aids and abets his friend *Y* into having sexual intercourse with a person under the age of consent, but did so without knowing that person was not of age. As you learned in Chapter 4, *Y* is guilty of statutory rape because it is a strict liability crime. But is *X* guilty as an accomplice for aiding and abetting statutory rape? Yes, because he purposely aided and abetted the conduct element of the offense (i.e., encouraged the sexual intercourse). Since strict liability attaches to the attendant circumstance of the victim's age for the principal, it also attaches to the same attendant circumstance for the accomplice.[20]

Scope of Accomplice Liability

A person who satisfies all the requirements for being an accomplice is an accomplice to all offenses committed by the principal that are the probable consequences of the offense aided. In other words, an accomplice is liable for all of the acts committed by the principal that are reasonably foreseeable in light of the aid given. Thus, so long as the accomplice purposefully aided and abetted the conduct element of the principal's crime, the fact that a result occurred other than the one envisioned by the accomplice is not relevant so long as it was reasonably foreseeable. Consider, for example, if two people engage in a high-speed drag race with each other. Suppose that one driver loses control of his car and crashes into the car of an innocent third party, who is killed along with passengers. Certainly, the person whose car crashed into the victim's would be liable for some form of homicide—probably vehicular manslaughter or criminal negligent homicide. But what about the driver of the other car that was involved in the drag race? Should that driver also be held criminally liable for the victim's death? An appellate court in New York answered that question in the affirmative in *People v. Abbott*, a case presenting such facts.[21] The court reasoned as follows:

> A "drag race" involves two or more drivers engaged in a contest of speed with the use of their automobiles. When this activity occurs on a public highway there is an inherent danger of increasing the death-dealing potential of the automobile. The significance of this conduct should be apparent to anyone who shares the community's general sense of right and wrong. It necessarily evinces a failure to perceive a substantial and unjustifiable risk, constituting a gross deviation from the standard of care that a reasonable person would observe in the situation and it is sufficient to sustain the conviction for criminally negligent homicide.
>
> While [the accomplice] did not personally control [the principal's] vehicle which struck and killed the three victims, it could reasonably be found that he intentionally aided . . . in the unlawful use of the vehicle by participating in a high-speed race, weaving in and out of traffic, and thus shared . . . culpability.[22]

The "You Make the Public Policy Call" feature in Box 6.1 presents another scenario for you to consider the scope of accomplice liability for unintended consequences.

Guilt and Grading Difference Between Principal and Accomplice

At common law, accomplice liability was *derivative*, meaning that the guilt of the accessory was predicated on the guilt of the principal.[23] But this rule periodically resulted in a windfall for an accomplice when the principal was acquitted on grounds not related to the criminality of the accessory, such as the insanity of the principal or if the principal died before trial. The Model Penal Code rectified this quirk of the common law by severing the derivative nature of an accomplice's liability and holding the accomplice liable based on his or her own actions and *mens rea* independent of those of the principal.[24] Most US jurisdictions have adopted the Model Penal Code approach.

Because the guilt of the accomplice was derivative at common law, an accomplice could not be held liable for any felony more serious than those actually committed by the principal, even if the accomplice's level of *mens rea* was higher than that of the principal (this rule did not apply to misdemeanors). For example, if someone killed another in the heat of passion upon a legally adequate provocation, that person would not be guilty of murder, but of voluntary manslaughter (see Chapter 7). But if the person was purposefully aided and abetted in the killing, the accomplice aided and abetted a murder. The common law would not have allowed the accomplice to be convicted of the more severe crime. The Model Penal Code, in contrast, would allow the different convictions, judging principal and accomplice on each person's level of culpability independent from the other.

BOX 6.1

YOU MAKE THE PUBLIC POLICY CALL

Accessorial Liability for Driving Under the Influence

Suppose that *X* gives *Y* his car keys, knowing *Y* is drunk, and *Y* is subsequently in a car accident that kills an innocent third party. *Y* would be liable for driving under the influence and for the homicide, mostly likely for involuntary manslaughter or vehicular homicide.

- Is *X* an accessory to *Y*'s drunk driving? If so, why? If not, then might there be some other form of inchoate liability that could be used to hold *X* accountable for giving *Y* the car keys with the knowledge that Y was drunk?
- Should *X* be held criminally liable as an accomplice to *Y*'s homicide? Explain your answer considering the court's reasoning in *Abbott*.

Abandonment as a Defense

Both the common law and Model Penal Code recognize the defense of **abandonment** for aiding and abetting.[25] At common law, any abandonment of aiding and abetting an offense must be complete, effective, and voluntary.[26] But in order to be deemed both *effective* and *complete* after one has given aid to another with the intention that a crime be committed, the accomplice must take three steps under the common-law approach. First, the accomplice must inform the principal that the offense should not be committed. Second, the accomplice must do everything possible to render all prior aid ineffective. And third, the accomplice must accomplish this before it is too late to prevent the offense.[27]

The Model Penal Code requirements for satisfying the *effective* and *complete* elements of the defense are even more stringent. The same three criteria the common law required must be satisfied, but in rendering all prior aid ineffective, the Model Penal Code imposes a duty on the accomplice to either (a) give timely warning to law enforcement authorities; or (b) otherwise make a "proper effort" to prevent the commission of the offense, a standard which is not clarified by the Code.[28]

AIDING AFTER THE COMMISSION OF A CRIME

At common law, people who provided assistance to others with the intent to help them escape justice were known as *accessories after the fact*. Although some states retain this approach, such activities in many US states are now subsumed under the definition of a broad crime known as obstruction of justice.

The common law defined an **accessory after the fact** as any person who harbored, concealed, or otherwise aided an offender, knowing or having reasonable grounds to believe (i.e., no willful blindness allowed) the offender had committed a felony.[29] Further, the aid given with such knowledge had to be given with the specific intent that the offender avoid or escape arrest, trial, or punishment. Under this definition, if one did not actually or constructively know someone had committed a felony, harboring or concealing that person would not have made the person providing the aid an accessory after the fact because such a person would have lacked the necessary *mens rea*. See the "Statutory Analysis Exercise" feature in Box 6.2 for an example of how such liability might attach.

The common law made an exception to the accessory after-the-fact rule for spouses stemming from the old common-law theory of marital unity (i.e., that the two were one).[30] A spouse aiding a husband or a wife did not have choose between breaking the marital unity and being an accessory after the fact for helping the spouse.[31]

In the minority of US states that retain an accessory after-the-fact statutory framework, the spousal exemption has been abandoned in many jurisdictions. Thus, spouses who purposefully provide assistance to help their husbands or wives subvert the reach of the criminal justice system may be held criminally liable for doing so.[32] Not all states, however, subscribe to this point of view; some retain a variation on the old common-law rules.

> [I]n fourteen states, the prosecution of family members for harboring fugitives is not an option, regardless of the nature of the crime or the extent of the family member's involvement. These states typically exempt spouses, parents, grandparents, children, grandchildren, and siblings from prosecution for providing assistance to an offender after the commission of a crime "with the intent that the offender avoids or escapes detection, arrest, trial, or punishment."[33] An additional four states reduce liability for an immediate family member but do not exempt them from prosecution entirely.[34]

Under the Model Penal Code and majority view taken in most US jurisdictions today, the specific category of being an accessory after the fact has been abolished.[35] Accordingly, many US jurisdictions treat such behavior as obstruction of justice, which can apply to all types of crimes, not just felonies.

OBSTRUCTION OF JUSTICE AND RELATED CRIMES

"**Obstruction of justice** is any 'interference with the orderly administration of law and justice,' and can be made up of 'a medley of crimes' "[36] that obstruct, impair, or pervert "the administration of law or other governmental function."[37] Obstruction of justice encompasses not only the common-law definition of being an accessory after the fact

BOX 6.2

STATUTORY ANALYSIS EXERCISE

When Might Helping One's Adult Child Become a Crime?

Sheriff's deputies went to Ruby Young's home in Mississippi to arrest her son, Jason Roberson, on a warrant for failing to appear in court on felony charges related to his possession of marijuana with the intent to distribute it illegally. Young reported that Roberson was not home and consented to a search of her home to confirm she was telling the truth. Before departing, deputies warned Young that she would be charged with "harboring" if she allowed Roberson to stay with her.

Approximately six months later, Young moved into a trailer home. After receiving a tip that Roberson was staying in his mother, deputies went to the trailer and saw Roberson's car parked outside. They knocked and announced themselves, but no one answered the door. But because the windows were open, they could hear people moving around in trailer and whispering. After obtaining a warrant, the deputies entered the trailer where they found Young, Roberson, and Roberson's girlfriend. Young was conscious and communicative.

Young was arrested and charged with being an accessory after the fact. At her trial, she testified that she had been under the influence of narcotic medication due to a recent back surgery and, therefore, was not aware that Roberson was in her trailer until the deputies apprehended him. Young also stated the medication caused her to fail to hear the officers knocking for some time. She was convicted and appealed.

The statute under which Young was convicted provided, in relevant part, that "[e]very person who shall be convicted of having concealed, received, or relieved any felon, or having aided or assisted any felon, knowing that the person had committed a felony, with intent to enable the felon to escape or to avoid arrest, trial, conviction or punishment after the commission of the felony, on conviction thereof shall be imprisoned . . ." for between one and twenty years, pending on the underlying felony.

1. Based on the statutory language and your understanding of the requirements for accessory after-the-fact liability, what should the result in this appeal be?[119] Why?
2. Florida's after-the-fact statute reads as follows:

   Any person not standing in the relation of husband or wife, parent or grandparent, child or grandchild, brother or sister, by consanguinity or affinity to the offender, who maintains or assists the principal or an accessory before the fact, or gives the offender any other aid, knowing that the offender had committed a crime and such crime was a third degree felony, or had been an accessory thereto before the fact, with the intent that the offender avoids or escapes detection, arrest, trial, or punishment, is an accessory after the fact.[120]

If this case had occurred in Florida, rather than Mississippi, would your answer be different? Why?

(sometimes referred to as "harboring" or "concealing"), but also a broad array of other acts that hinder the apprehension or prosecution of a criminal offender, including providing weapons, moneys, transportations, disguises; concealing or destructing evidence of the crime; tampering with a witness, informant, document; warning some of impending apprehension; or volunteering false information to a law enforcement officer investigating a crime.[38] As a rule, however, obstruction of justice statutes typically do not include resisting arrest or fleeing from law enforcement. As discussed later in this chapter, those acts usually constitute their own distinct criminal offenses.

The Model Penal Code provides that obstruction of justice constitutes a felony of the third degree "if the conduct which the actor knows has been charged or is liable to be charged against the person aided would constitute a felony of the first or second degree. Otherwise it is a misdemeanor."[39]

The Model Penal Code does not exempt spouses or family members from criminal liability for obstruction of justice. A majority of US jurisdictions are in accord with this principle. However, a handful of state have retained some variation the common-law spousal exemption for accessories after the fact in their obstruction of justice statutes either by excluding spouses from liability,[40] or by mitigating their responsibility such that their obstruction of justice to aided a spouse is punishable only as a low-level felony or misdemeanor.[41] A handful of states have even expanded the spousal mitigation factor to include parent-child relationships.[42]

Given the rather broad nature of the conduct that may qualify as the *actus reus* for the crime of obstruction of justice, it should come as no surprise that applying the particularized statutory definitions to facts of particular cases is often challenging. For example, in both *Commonwealth v. Neckerauer*[43] and *State v. D'Addario*,[44] the highest courts in Pennsylvania and New Jersey, respectively, overturned obstruction of justice convictions for people who had provided false information to police investigating crimes. In both cases, the courts were applying statutes that defined the offense using the Model Penal Code's language prohibiting the "volunteering" of false information to law enforcement.[45] The courts both reasoned that the meaning of the word "volunteer" connotes taking the initiative in giving false information, rather than failing to answer questions honestly. The drafters of the Model Penal Code explained their reasoning for differentiating volunteering false information and giving false answers to police-initiated inquiries as follows was to prevent inviting abusive charges by police against persons interviewed in the course of investigating crimes.[46]

The PEOPLE of the State of Michigan, Appellee

v.

Christopher MEISSNER, Appellant.

812 N.W.2d 37, 47 (Mich. Ct. App. 2011)

On November 28, 2009, Candace Worthington appeared at the Waterford police station, visibly shaken and upset. She reported that defendant, with whom she had a relationship, had broken her door and had sent her threatening text messages. She showed a police officer the text messages, which included "You trying to die?" and "now you will reap the repercussions," as well as defendant's pointed message in response to Worthington's telling him that she had gone to the police: "I am going to beat the s**t out of you." Worthington described to the police several experiences she had with defendant over the prior months, including one in which defendant had destroyed her phone, another in which he pushed her down the stairs, and another in which he put her in a chokehold. Worthington wrote a statement recounting the threatening text messages, the prior physical injuries, and the other information she had given to the police.

Worthington's statement also described an incident that had occurred just that morning when Worthington had been awakened by a crashing noise and saw defendant in her bedroom. Defendant pushed her shoulder, asked for a cigarette, tossed coins at her, and then left. The prosecutor subsequently charged defendant with home invasion, obstruction of justice, and domestic violence.

By the time of trial in May 2010, Worthington was pregnant with defendant's child. When the prosecutor called her to testify, Worthington recast and recharacterized many of the facts from her November statements. She testified that when she went to the police in November, she was enraged because defendant was having a relationship with another woman. She further testified that because of her anger she had embellished and exaggerated the facts in her statement. For example, she testified that although defendant was living with her, she had told the police he was not living with her. She also testified that the text messages she had shown the police were out of context. She attempted to justify the text message that said, "You trying to die?" by explaining that the message was his response to her text message informing him that she would be walking home from a bar late at night. . . . At the close of the prosecutor's direct examination, Worthington testified that defendant had never beaten her and had never threatened her.

* * *

Obstruction of justice is a common-law charge that can be prosecuted under MCL 750.505 and "is generally understood as an interference with the orderly administration of justice."[47] Obstruction of justice is considered a category of offenses; a common example is witness coercion.... Coercion involves an attempt to dissuade a witness from testifying, and "words alone may be sufficient to constitute the crime."[48]

The prosecution presented evidence that defendant sent several harassing text messages to Worthington. At least one of the text messages explicitly referred to a police investigation, while the other text messages implied police involvement in the dispute. For example, the investigating officer testified that some of the text messages stated:

"You made grave mistake and now you will reap the repercussions."
"If you really did that, then I am going to beat the s**t out of you."
"How did I f**k you? Whatever. I'll be there in a bit. If you really called the cops, you will really get beat bad."

A reasonable jury could find that these messages constituted obstruction of justice. Defendant sent the messages to Worthington shortly after breaking into her apartment and assaulting her. The messages made it clear that he would harm Worthington if she made a statement to police. By sending the text messages to Worthington, defendant "willfully and corruptly hampered, obstructed, and interfered with a proper and legitimate criminal investigation."[49]

Questions

1. Assume you were Meissner's defense attorney representing him in a subsequent appeal. How might you attack his conviction on *mens rea* grounds? What about on causation of result grounds?
2. Even though Michigan has a statutory provision prohibiting making inducements or promises to witnesses, as well as threating or intimidating witnesses,[50] the defendant in *Meissner* was charged under a statute that states, "Any person who shall commit any indictable offense at the common law, for the punishment of which no provision is expressly made by any statute of this state, shall be guilty of a felony."[51] Do you think the principle of fair notice (Chapter 1) and due process (Chapter 2) are both satisfied when someone is prosecuted for witness coercion under such a catch-all provision? Explain your reasoning.

Obstruction of Justice as a Sentencing Enhancement

Under the US Sentencing Guidelines, persons convicted of any crime may have their sentences enhanced (i.e., extended) because they engaged in one or more types of conduct that were intended to obstruct the administration of justice. Consider the following commentary from the Sentencing Commission:

3. Covered Conduct Generally. Obstructive conduct can vary widely in nature, degree of planning, and seriousness....
4. Examples of Covered Conduct. The following is a non-exhaustive list of examples of the types of conduct to which this enhancement applies:

   (A) threatening, intimidating, or otherwise unlawfully influencing a co-defendant, witness, or juror, directly or indirectly, or attempting to do so;
   (B) committing, suborning, or attempting to suborn perjury, including during the course of a civil proceeding if such perjury pertains to conduct that forms the basis of the offense of conviction;
   (C) producing or attempting to produce a false, altered, or counterfeit document or record during an official investigation or judicial proceeding;
   (D) destroying or concealing or directing or procuring another person to destroy or conceal evidence that is material to an official investigation or judicial proceeding (e.g., shredding a document or destroying ledgers upon learning that an official investigation has commenced or is about to commence), or attempting to do so; however, if such conduct occurred contemporaneously with arrest (e.g., attempting to swallow or throw away a controlled substance), it shall not, standing alone, be sufficient to warrant an adjustment for obstruction unless it resulted in a material hindrance to the official investigation or prosecution of the instant offense or the sentencing of the offender;
   (E) escaping or attempting to escape from custody before trial or sentencing; or willfully failing to appear, as ordered, for a judicial proceeding;
   (F) providing materially false information to a judge or magistrate judge;
   (G) providing a materially false statement to a law enforcement officer that significantly obstructed or impeded the official investigation or prosecution of the instant offense;
   (H) providing materially false information to a probation officer in respect to a presentence or other investigation for the court;
   (I) other conduct prohibited by obstruction of justice provisions under Title 18, United States Code;52
   (J) failing to comply with a restraining order or injunction . . . ;53
   (K) threatening the victim of the offense in an attempt to prevent the victim from reporting the conduct constituting the offense of conviction.

This adjustment also applies to any other obstructive conduct in respect to the official investigation, prosecution, or sentencing of the instant offense where there is a separate count of conviction for such conduct.[54]

Because many of these acts also constitute distinct criminal offenses, we will explore them in more detail.[55]

Perjury, False Swearing, and Unsworn Falsifications

The crime of **perjury**, which is usually a felony, occurs when a person makes a false, material statement under oath or equivalent affirmation in in any official proceeding (or swearing or affirming the truth of a statement previously made), when the person either knows or does not believe the material statement to be true.[56] If the statement is not "material," then the crime of perjury has not occurred; however, the lesser crime of **false swearing** has instead been committed.[57] Whether a statement is material involves a judgment call that presents a question of fact for a jury. As a rule, a statement is material when, if believed, would tend to influence or affect the issue under determination.[58]

A person commits the crime of making **unsworn falsifications**, a crime that is typically a misdemeanor, if "with purpose to mislead a public servant in performing his official function, he: (a) makes any written false statement which he does not believe to be true; or (b) purposely creates a false impression in a written application for any pecuniary or other benefit, by omitting information necessary to prevent statements therein from being misleading."[59]

It is important to keep in mind that with respect to all three offenses relating to falsehoods that interfere with the orderly administration of justice, the false or misleading statement serves as the *actus reus*, but that alone is not sufficient for conviction because these are not strict liability offenses. The prosecution must also prove *mens rea*, namely that the person knowingly provided false information, rather than having done so "as a result of confusion, mistake, or faulty memory."[60] Thus, "consciousness of wrongdoing" is key to the commission of these crimes.[61]

In *United States v. Dunnigan*, the defendant was charges with a variety of drug offenses related to her alleged distribution of cocaine.[62] At her trial, the prosecution called a series of witnesses who testified about her involvement in the drug trade. The defendant took the stand in her own defense and denied any such involvement. Two rebuttal witnesses then testified that the defendant had sold crack to them. After a jury convicted her, the judge imposed an enhanced sentence, under § 3C1.1 of the US Sentencing Guidelines, because the defendant "defendant willfully impeded or obstructed, or attempted to impede or obstruct, the administration of justice during the investigation or prosecution of the instant offense."[63] The US Supreme Court upheld the sentencing enhancement, reasoning that perjury at trial constituted obstruction of justice.[64] Although subsequent decisions of the Court have limited the scope of *Dunnigan*, its core holding remains "good law" insofar as it illustrates how perjury can not only be prosecuted as its own criminal offense, but also may serve as the basis of sentencing enhancements for obstruction of justice.[65]

Witness Tampering

Anyone who "attempts to induce or otherwise cause a witness or informant to: (a) testify or inform falsely; or (b) withhold any testimony, information, document or thing; or (c) elude legal process summoning him to testify or supply evidence; or (d) absent himself from any proceeding or investigation to which he has been legally summoned" is guilty of **witness tampering.**[66] Witness tampering may be classified as a misdemeanor under some circumstances, but it usually constitutes a felony when accomplished by force, deception, threats, or bribes.[67]

Tampering with Evidence

Altering, destroying, concealing, or removing any evidence concerning with the intent "to impair its verity or availability" in an official proceeding or investigation commits the offense of **tampering with evidence.**[68] This crime is typically classified as a misdemeanor; however, if the evidence tampering involved changing or altering public records in order to injure or defraud, then such conduct is typically punished as a felony.[69]

Resisting Arrest

A person commits the misdemeanor offense of **resisting arrest** when, "for the purpose of preventing a public servant from effecting a lawful arrest or discharging any other duty, the person creates a substantial risk of bodily injury to the public servant or anyone else, or employs means justifying or requiring substantial force to overcome the resistance."[70] Of course, other crimes may also be committed during resistance of an arrest, such as assault on an officer of the law in the line a duty, a felony which can carry a long prison sentence.

Eluding/Unlawful Flight

Trying to outrun a law enforcement directive to "stop," "halt," or "freeze," or failing to pull over while operating a motor vehicle when signaled to do so, constitutes the crime of **eluding**, which is also referred to as **unlawful flight** in some jurisdictions. In some states, this crime is a felony that is punishable by a lengthy prison sentence.

There is one more thing to keep in mind about the crime of eluding. Many people delight in the vicarious thrill of watching high-speed police chases in movies and on television. In reality, however, failing to pull over when law enforcement officers activate lights or sirens can have serious consequences. Certainly, the person attempting to flee the police, the officers who engage in pursuit of a fleeing vehicle, and innocent third parties can all be seriously injured in an accident. But if someone were to die, some states would punish that unintentional death as a felony murder, a serious type of homicide that will be explored in more detail in Chapter 7.[71]

Escape

If a person unlawfully removes himself/herself from "official detention" (i.e., while under arrest or incarcerated), or fails to return to official detention following temporary leave granted for a specific purpose or limited period, then the person is guilty of the crime of **escape.**[72] The crime of escape is usually a felony, the level of which depends on the type of escape effectuated by the escaping person. Helping someone escape from official detention similarly constitutes the crime of escape using the usual rules of accessorial liability.[73] Moreover, public officials who recklessly allow a detainee to escape may face criminal liability for their recklessness.[74]

Additional Offenses

Table 6.1 summarizes select additional offenses that interfere with the administration of justice.

Table 6.1 Additional Offenses Related to Obstruction of Justice

False Alarms	Causing a false alarm of fire or other emergency to be transmitted to any official or volunteer emergency agency that serves to combat danger to life or property typically constitutes a misdemeanor.[*]
Falsely Incriminating Another	The crime of false incrimination occurs when someone implicated another person in a crime knowing that the person implicated was not connected to the offense is typically punished as a misdemeanor.[†]
Filing a False Police Report	Reporting an offense or incident to law enforcement authorities knowing that it did not occur usually constitutes a misdemeanor.[‡]
Impersonating a Public Servant	"A person commits a misdemeanor if he falsely pretends to hold a position in the public service with purpose to induce another to submit to such pretended official authority or otherwise to act in reliance upon that pretense to his prejudice."[§]
Failure to Appear	The crime of failure to appear (sometimes known as "bail jumping") is committed when a person who has been released either on bail or on his/her own recognizance on the condition that s/he will subsequently appear at a specified time and place, but who fails to appear at that time and place. It may be a felony or a misdemeanor depending on the nature of the underlying charges.[‖]

[*] Model Penal Code § 241.4.
[†] Model Penal Code § 241.5(a).
[‡] Model Penal Code § 241.5(b).
[§] Model Penal Code § 241.9.
[‖] Model Penal Code § 242.8.

CONSPIRACY

Conspiracy is a rather odd crime because it punishes what boils down to a mental offense. A **conspiracy** is nothing more than an agreement—a meeting of the minds—with wrongful intent. The object of the agreement must be either the commission of an unlawful act or the commission of a lawful act by illegal means. If two or more people make such an agreement, a criminal conspiracy has occurred.[75] Note that the unlawful act upon which the parties agree in a criminal conspiracy must be a crime in some jurisdictions[76] (i.e., an offense defined in the penal code for which a criminal punishment is authorized), while in others, the unlawful act may be any act prohibited by the law, such as civil wrongs that are sanctioned through fines, civil forfeiture, or other civil remedies.[77]

Although conspiracy is an inchoate offense that falls within the ambit of complicity theory, conspiracy differs from accomplice liability in that an agreement must be formed for conspiratorial liability; aiding and abetting, in contrast, does not require proof of any agreement.[78] The US Supreme Court has repeatedly described criminal conspiracy as "a distinct evil" that "poses a 'threat to the public' over and above the threat of the commission of the relevant substantive crime—both because the 'combination in crime makes more likely the commission of other crimes' and because it 'decreases the probability that the individuals involved will depart from their path of criminality.' "[79]

Actus Reus for Conspiracy

At both common law and under modern penal statutes, the *actus reus* for the crime of conspiracy is making an agreement, and all of the details of a conspiracy need not be known for liability to be imposed. It is sufficient that was a meeting of the minds with the requisite criminal intent. In other words, for criminal liability to attach, the conspirators need only have reached an agreement on the "essential nature of the plan, not necessarily on the details of their criminal scheme."[80] Moreover, the agreement need not be express; it may be implied. In other words, evidence, like a nod of head that tends "to show a mutual, implied understanding will suffice" as proof of the *actus reus* for conspiracy.[81]

The crime of conspiracy has historically been concerned with addressing the added dangers posed by two or more people acting in criminal concert. Thus, at common law, for a conspiracy to occur, there had to be a bona-fide agreement between two or more people. This was known as a **bilateral conspiracy**. Although some US jurisdictions still hold on to this common-law view that a conspiracy necessarily "takes two to tango," most US states have adopted the Model Penal Code's view that criminal liability may be founded upon a **unilateral conspiracy**.[82] This approach allows a conviction for a conspiracy if one party thinks there is an agreement between two more people, even though the other party (or parties) did not actually agree, but rather feigned agreement—a situation that frequently occurs when undercover law enforcement officers enter into an agreement with a person who actually entertains criminal intent. Recall the murder-for-hire case explored in Box 5.3. Had the defendant been charged with conspiracy to commit murder, it would have been no defense that there was no bilateral agreement because the hit man turned out to be an undercover law enforcement officer.

Mens Rea for Conspiracy

Technically, the *mens rea* for the crime of conspiracy is purpose—a specific intent to further a criminal enterprise.[83] Thus, conviction of the crime of conspiracy requires proof that the defendant voluntarily made or joined an agreement with the purpose (i.e., specific intent) of furthering the agreement's target offense(s).[84] But proving such intent can be difficult.

Proof by direct evidence, of course, is the best way of proving a conspiracy. But since "secrecy and concealment are essential features of a successful conspiracy"[85] (after, all, criminal conspirators rarely write down their plans and sign them in the form of a contract), direct evidence of a conspiracy "may be hard to come by."[86] One of the more frequent means of proving a conspiracy by direct evidence is through the testimony of a co-conspirator. Since the US Supreme Court's decision in *Caminetti v. United States*,[87] the federal system and some US states allow a conspiracy conviction to be based solely on the uncorroborated testimony of a conspirator.[88] This methods of proving a conspiracy, however, may be unreliable, especially if one co-conspirator has been granted immunity or a favorable plea bargain in exchange for his or her testimony against other co-conspirators.[89] Accordingly, some states prohibit conspiracy convictions based solely on the uncorroborated testimony of a conspirator, instead requiring some corroborating evidence to sustain a conviction.[90]

Because direct evidence of the formation of a criminal conspiracy is often unavailable, the law allows the *mens rea* of intent to agree to a conspiracy to be proven using hearsay evidence and, under some circumstances, intent to agree may be inferred from conduct.

USING HEARSAY TO PROVE A CONSPIRACY

Hearsay is a complicated part of the law of evidence which is beyond the scope of this book.[91] For our purposes, however, you should know that the rules of evidence generally disallow out-of-court statements to be used as substantive proof of a fact in issue at a trial. There are, however, both exemptions and exceptions to the hearsay rule. One of these exemptions to the usual ban on hearsay applies to the crime of conspiracy so that damaging statements made by a co-conspirator may be admissible against other co-conspirators.[92]

There is an important limitation on Rule 801(d)(2)(E)'s hearsay exemption that should be noted. Its applicability is limited to those statements made *before* the consummation of the offense that is the target of the conspiracy.[93] The rationale for this limitation rests, in large part, on the fact that a conspiracy is presumed to include, as part of its nature, an agreement to avoid detection because, once the crime is committed, the participants presumably do not want to get caught. Thus, one might erroneously infer that a new conspiracy is formed to cover up the existence of the original conspiracy and the crimes committed pursuant to it. If this were the case, anything ever said pertaining to the crime between co-conspirators would be admissible hearsay. But since there is no separate or subsidiary conspiracy to prevent detection and punishment, the hearsay exception ends when the target crimes of the conspiracy are completed.

INFERRING INTENT FROM CONDUCT

" 'A defendant's mere presence at the scene of a criminal act or association with conspirators does not constitute intentional participation in the conspiracy,' even if the defendant had knowledge of the conspiracy."[94] However, in narrow circumstances, courts have allowed the intent to further a conspiracy to be inferred from conduct that circumstantially proves that the defendant knew of a conspiracy and voluntarily participated in some aspect of it by having done something (even an act or service that might otherwise be perfectly legal) that had the effect of furthering the conspiracy.

The Model Penal Code does not allow any inference of intent to further the objectives of a conspiracy from conduct evidencing knowledge of a conspiracy because the level of culpability for conspiracy is technically purpose.[95] In contrast, as illustrated by of *People v. Lauria,*[96] the common law allowed inferences of intent for felonies and for misdemeanors in which the accused had some special interest associated with the offense.

In *Lauria,* the defendant operated a telephone answering service. He knew that some people used his service to procure "call girl" prostitution services. He was subsequently charged and convicted of conspiracy to commit prostitution. His conviction was ultimately set aside because the court ruled his intent to further prostitution could not be inferred from the defendant having furnished the lawful services of his telephone answering service. The court had three primary reasons for this conclusion. First, running a message service is qualitatively different from distributing dangerous products. In reaching this conclusion, the court compared two leading US Supreme Court cases, *United States v. Falcone*[97] and *Direct Sales Co. v. United States.*[98] *Falcone* absolved the sellers of large quantities of sugar, yeast, and cans from participation in a moonshining conspiracy among distillers who bought from them because the products were otherwise innocuous. *Direct Sales,* by contrast, upheld the conviction of drug wholesaler for conspiracy to violate the federal narcotic laws by selling drugs in large quantities to a codefendant physician who was supplying them to addicts. In *Lauria,* the court clearly thought that telephone answering and messaging services at issue were more similar to the products in *Falcone* than those in *Direct Sales.* Second, the defendant had no stake in the outcome of the prostitution ventures. For example, he did not charge a higher rate to those using his answering services for prostitution reasons than he did to any other client.[99] Nor did he derive a grossly disproportionate amount of his income from the clients using his answering service for prostitution reasons compared to those using it legitimate ends. And third, the defendant furnished otherwise lawful services, not those lacking any legitimate use such as the manufacturer of loaded dice or marked cards for sale to casinos.[100]

Lauria stands for the proposition that if intent to join a conspiracy cannot be established by direct evidence, it may be inferred, but only if there is some special interest in the activity or the crime itself is aggravated nature. Although decided in 1967, some states still follow the approach accounted in *Lauria*; other states adopted the Model Penal Code Approach and still others formulated their own approaches to the issue of inferring criminal intent to join a conspiracy from conduct, especially when the facts suggest willful blindness/deliberate ignorance of the existence of a conspiracy as the "Case Study Extra" feature in Box 6.3 illustrates.[101]

Overt Act Requirement

An **overt act** is an act performed in the furtherance of a conspiratorial objective. The overt act requirement for conspiracy liability is usually satisfied by any act, whether legal or illegal, so long as it evidences the conspiratorial agreement, "such as picking a lock, standing as a lookout or lying in wait, taking a trip, making a telephone call, or mailing a letter."[102] The overt act does not need to be a substantial act that approaches the substantive crime as is required for conviction of attempt.

At common law, a conviction for conspiracy generally did not require an overt act; the crime was complete upon formation of the agreement and no act in furtherance of the conspiracy was necessary to sustain a conviction.[103] The Model Penal Code requires an overt act for a conspiracy conviction if the substantive crime is a minor offense (i.e., a misdemeanor or a felony in the third degree),[104] but does not require an overt act if the conspiracy is to commit a felony of the first or second degree. Today, many states have rejected both the common law and the Model Penal Code approaches and instead require proof of an overt act in further of the conspiracy as an element of all conspiracies regardless of whether the target offense(s) are felonies or misdemeanors.[105]

Limitations on Parties to a Conspiracy Under Wharton's Rule

Because conspiracy punishes the act of agreeing with criminal intent, it is a separate crime from the target offense. Accordingly, conspiracy is generally charged and punished as a separate and distinct offense from the substantive target crime or its attempted commission. This means one may be convicted of conspiracy to commit crime *X* as well as crime *X* (presuming the object crime is committed) or the attempt to commit crime *X* (if the conspirators try, but fail, to commit the target offense). There is, however, a narrow common-law exception to the general rule that a conspiracy and its target offense do not merge into one crime known as **Wharton's Rule**. Although the Model Penal Code does

BOX 6.3

CASE STUDY EXTRA

How Might Intent to Joint a Conspiracy Be Inferred?

United States v. Fuchs[121] involved prosecutions of several people in connection with two internet-based pharmacies owned and operated by defendant Clayton Fuchs, a licensed pharmacist. Customers throughout the United States requested prescriptions online. The pharmacy then paid a physician $40 to approve each prescription requested and then filled the prescription and shipped it to the requesting web-based customer. Among other charges, defendant Lemons, a pharmacist employed by Fuchs, was convicted of conspiracy "to dispense and possess with intent to dispense hydrocodone, a Schedule III controlled substance, not in the usual course of professional practice." On appeal, argued that he was not a member of the pharmacy's "inner circle"; that he did not share in the pharmacy's profits but rather was paid a salary; and that he was thus nothing more than a conscientious, yet unwitting, pharmacist working in a "climate of activity that reeks of something foul."

> Testimony from various witnesses established that during [the relevant] period the pharmacy dispensed over 1,000 prescriptions monthly for controlled substances; a very large percentage of the pharmacy's total prescriptions was for hydrocodone and other controlled substances; the prescriptions were initiated by orders sent to the pharmacy via its web site; the pharmacy's customers were located throughout the United States; the pharmacy completed the prescription forms and forwarded them to physicians for approval and signature; Dr. Thompson was the approving physician for nearly all these prescriptions; Dr. Thompson was not paid by the customers, but rather was paid per each prescription filled by the pharmacy; the dosage for most prescriptions was standardized rather than tailored for each patient; the pharmacy's prices for drugs were exceedingly higher than average; and the pharmacy did not accept insurance. Dr. Thompson testified that the circumstances at the pharmacy were such that it should have been obvious to anyone working there that he did not have a valid physician/patient relationship with the customers for whom he was approving prescriptions for controlled substances. And Humphreys testified that Lemons expressed to him some concern about the pharmacy's legality. A rational jury could have found from this circumstantial evidence that Lemons knew of an agreement to unlawfully distribute controlled substances.

Additionally, Lemons' participation in the conspiracy is evidenced by his untruthfulness to [an] inspector [who] testified that Lemons was the first person he spoke with when he arrived at [the pharmacy] for [an] inspection. When [the inspector] noticed the high volume of unusual drugs being dispensed, he asked Lemons about the pharmacy's customer base. Instead of acknowledging that the Internet was the source of the vast majority of [its] customers, Lemons responded that the pharmacy's customers came from the neighborhood and a rehab center in the same shopping center. Were Lemons merely an unwitting pharmacist working in a "climate of activity that reeks of something foul," as he purports to have been, he presumably would have had no reason to lie about the customer base. The jury could have inferred from this that Lemons was aware of the conspiracy and lied in order to conceal it.[122]

1. Do you agree with the court that Lemons had knowledge of the conspiracy and specific intent/purpose to further its ends? Why or why not?
2. Compare and contrast Lemons's involvement in this case to those of the defendant in *Falcone, Direct Sales*, and *Lauria*. Which case is most analogous to his?

not recognize Wharton's Rule, many US jurisdictions still apply the rule to limit conspiracy liability under state law.

Simply put, Wharton's Rule precludes a conviction for conspiracy to commit an offense which, but its very nature, requires a "concert of action" between as part of the substantive offense.[106] The crimes of dueling, bribery, adultery, and drag-racing are all good examples of offenses to which Wharton's Rule would apply because all of these offenses necessarily require a concert of action between two people for the substantive offenses to take place. After all, one cannot duel oneself or commit adultery alone.

Wharton's Rule, however, does not apply if the crime could have been committed by one person. *United States v. Brenson* is a good example of this principle.[107] In that case, the court held that Wharton's Rule did not apply to a conspiracy to obstruct justice because a person could commit that offense without acting in concert with another person, such as when one person, acting alone, destroys evidence.

Additionally, under what is sometimes termed the "third-party exception" to Wharton's Rule, the rule does not apply "if the number of actual conspirators exceeds the number required to commit the substantive offense."[108] In other words, once someone else participates beyond the minimum required number for the target crime to take place, the rationale for the Wharton Rule is inapplicable and, therefore, Wharton's Rule will not bar convictions for both conspiracy to commit the target crime and either the actual crime itself or its attempt. For example, if a petty criminal successfully bribed a police officer to avoid arrest, Wharton's Rule would prevent a conviction for conspiracy to commit bribery since the concert of action between the offender and the police officer is "part and parcel" of the crime of bribery. In contrast, if a group of petty criminals bribed several officers to ignore their criminal activities, then Wharton's Rule would not apply, and the whole group could be convicted of conspiracy to commit bribery as well as the actual crime of bribery.

Distinguishing the Number and Types of Conspiracies

One of the more difficult issues surrounding the crime of conspiracy is the type of conspiracy that has been formed. In a simple conspiracy, and handful of people agree to do something illegal and then carry out their plan together. For example, if two men conspire to rob a bank, then there is a singular conspiracy to commit bank robbery. If three or four people had been a part of this simple conspiracy, the result would still be that there is one singular conspiracy to commit bank robbery; the only thing that has changed in the number of co-conspirators.

But what if two, three, or four people conspired to commit three separate crimes, say bank robbery, murder, and sexual assault? How many conspiracies are there? According to the Supreme Court's decision in *Braverman v. United States*,[109] the answer is just one conspiracy, even though the singular conspiracy has three target offenses. *Braverman* held that when two or more people enter into a conspiracy to commit several crimes, there is only one conspiracy, not several conspiracies. The rationale behind this rule is that conspiracy punishes the act of forming an illicit agreement; the criminal acts which are the objects of that agreement are, of course, punished separately.

Some conspiracies can be quite large and may involve many people who do not even know the identities of the other people who are a part of the conspiracy. The extent of the knowledge each person has and the degree of interdependence they have on each other will determine the type of conspiracy that is deemed to exist. The type, in turn, can help answer the question of whether there are multiple conspiracies or one, large conspiracy. The resolution of this issue is important because, in any given conspiracy, each co-conspirator is potentially criminally liable for the acts of the co-conspirators. Thus, the more people that can be connected to a large conspiracy, the more charges can be brought against each defendant. This serves several important goals in terms of the administration of the criminal justice system. First, it often gives prosecutors the ability to try many defendants together in a single trial, rather than relitigating the same evidence over and over again in multiple trials. Second, the more charges that can be made to "stick" against each co-conspirator, the longer the potential sentence terms might be, thereby increasing public safety via incapacitation of criminal conspirators. And third, plea bargaining agreements for the minor players in a conspiracy often allow for the dropping of many charges against such defendants in exchange for cooperation in prosecuting the central figures in large criminal conspiracies. While the fairness of such practices is open to debate from both an ethical and legal standpoint, traditional wisdom holds that letting the little fish off lighter to catch the big fish is a worthwhile venture. Moreover, as co-conspirators in a single, large conspiracy, the hearsay rule is not applicable with respect to any one co-conspirator's testimony with respect to what another co-conspirator said.[110]

WHEEL CONSPIRACY

In a **wheel conspiracy**, there is generally one person (or a small group of people) in the "hub" or center of the wheel. A number of different and unrelated persons (or groups) form separate agreements with those in the hub. When this occurs, there is not one large conspiracy, but several smaller conspiracies between the people in the hub or center of the wheel and the people at the end of each spoke. An organized crime hypothetical provides an excellent example of this type of conspiracy. In the center or hub would be the leader of the organized crime syndicate. Those in the hub might enter into several illegal ventures with separate groups of people: a prostitution ring in Dallas; a drug import and distribution business in Miami; fixed gambling operations in a casino in Las Vegas; a construction contracting company in New York who obtains its contracts illegally; and so on. The people at the end of each spoke of the wheel have conspired with those at the hub, but not necessarily with any of the people who are at the end of a different spoke. Each spoke would represent a separate conspiracy from the other unless there were a way to connect the spokes to form a true wheel.

In order to connect the spokes in a wheel conspiracy, it must be shown that there is not only knowledge of the criminal enterprise at the end of another spoke, but some form of interdependence between those at the end of each spoke to be connected. Thus, when a group of people are related to each other only through their mutual agreements with those in the hub, proof of knowledge of a comprehensive conspiracy is necessary to treat it as one, large. Without such proof, the agreements remain separate, smaller conspiracies. In the organized crime example, the success of the illegal gambling operation in Las Vegas presumably has nothing to do with the success of the contracting venture in New York. Connecting the two spokes to form a larger conspiracy, therefore, would be difficult.

Kotteakos v. United States[111] is the seminal case in distinguishing wheel conspiracies from wheel conspiracies with connected spokes. *Kotteakos* involved multiple conspiracies to defraud the Federal Housing Administration. The key figure, Brown, arranged with thirty-two people to submit false loan applications. None of the applicants had any connection with the others, although each had a relationship with Brown. The government, however, charged all the applicants with participation in a single conspiracy Brown at the hub of a wheel, and the various applicants were the spokes. Because those at the end of each spoke had only conspired with Brown, and not each other, and further because the success of one was not dependent on the success of others, the Court ruled that this was a series of separate conspiracies between Brown and each of the applicants, not one large conspiracy, as depicted in Figure 6.1.

CHAIN/LADDER CONSPIRACY

In contrast, the other major type of conspiracy is known as the **chain** or **ladder conspiracy**. Each person in the chain is a link whereby one agrees with another who in turn agrees with another, and so on and so on. It is possible for lots of small conspiracies to exist this way, but it is more likely that persons in the chain are interdependent on each other, making for one big conspiracy. Drug conspiracies frequently operate in this way, as depicted in Figure 6.2.

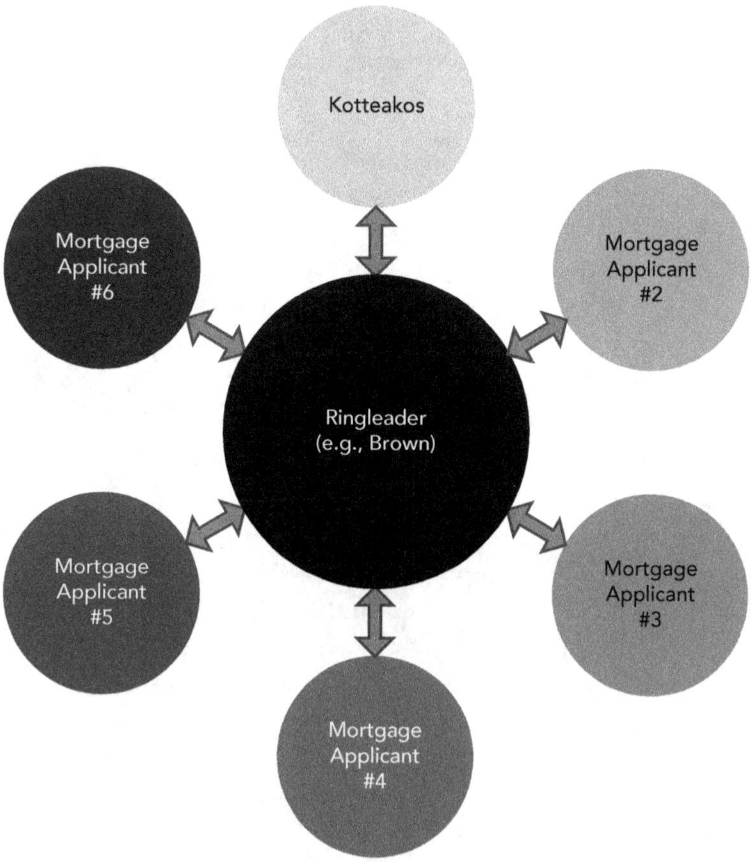

FIGURE 6.1
Wheel Conspiracy

Each person in the chain is dependent upon everyone else in the chain in order for the entire conspiracy to be successful. When this occurs, one large conspiracy is formed, not a number of smaller conspiracies.

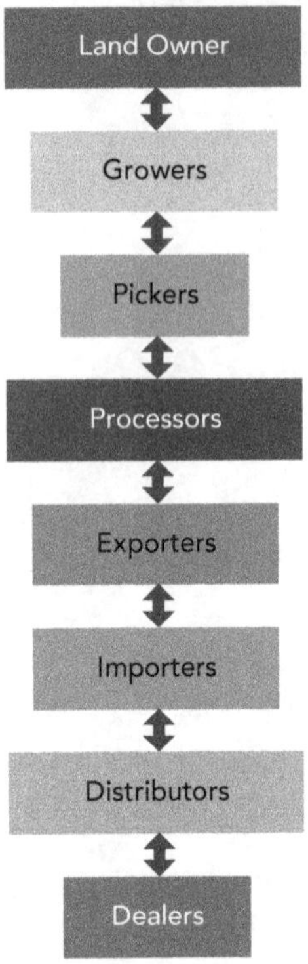

FIGURE 6.2
Chain Drug Conspiracy

Scope of a Conspiracy

Under the normal rules of complicity, all co-conspirators are liable for any offenses that are explicitly agreed to as part of the conspiracy. But what of those offenses that occur that were not specifically agreed to as a part of the original conspiracy? The common law and the Model Penal Code take very different approaches to answering this question.

The Model Penal Code examines the relative individual culpability of each co-conspirator.[112] That is to say that each person will be judged based on his or her own level of *mens rea* with respect to crimes that were not a part of the conspiracy. Only a minority of US jurisdictions, however, have adopted the Model Penal Code approach to the scope of a conspiracy. The criminal law of many states and the federal government continue to follow the common law.

The common law's approach to discerning the scope of a conspiracy is known as the **Pinkerton Rule**. The name of the rule is derived from the following case.

Walter and Daniel PINKERTON, et al.

v.

UNITED STATES of America.

328 U.S. 640 (1946).

Walter and Daniel Pinkerton are brothers who live a short distance from each other on Daniel's farm. They were indicted for violations of the Internal Revenue Code. The indictment contained ten substantive counts and one conspiracy count. The jury found Walter guilty on nine of the substantive counts and on the conspiracy count. It found Daniel guilty on six of the substantive counts and on the conspiracy count. . . .

* * *

It is contended that there was insufficient evidence to implicate Daniel in the conspiracy. But we think there was enough evidence for submission of the issue to the jury.

There is, however, no evidence to show that Daniel participated directly in the commission of the substantive offenses on which his conviction has been sustained, although there was evidence to show that these substantive offenses were in fact committed by Walter in furtherance of the unlawful agreement or conspiracy existing between the brothers. The question was submitted to the jury on the theory that each petitioner could be found guilty of the substantive offenses, if it were found at the time those offenses were committed petitioners were parties to an unlawful conspiracy and the substantive offenses charged were in fact committed in furtherance of it.

* * *

. . . We have here a continuous conspiracy. There is here no evidence of the affirmative action on the part of Daniel which is necessary to establish his withdrawal from it. Having joined in an unlawful scheme, having constituted agents for its performance, scheme and agency to be continuous until full fruition be secured, until he does some act to disavow or defeat the purpose, he is in no situation to claim the delay of the law. As the offense has not been terminated or accomplished, he is still offending. . . . And so long as the partnership in crime continues, the partners act for each other in carrying it forward.

It is settled that "an overt act of one partner may be the act of all without any new agreement specifically directed to that act."[113] Motive or intent may be proved by the acts or declarations of some of the conspirators in furtherance of the common objective. A scheme to use the mails to defraud, which is joined in by more than one person, is a conspiracy. Yet all members are responsible, though only one did the mailing. . . .

A different case would arise if the substantive offense committed by one of the conspirators was not in fact done in furtherance of the conspiracy, did not fall within the scope of the unlawful project, or was merely a part of the ramifications of the plan which could not be reasonably foreseen as a necessary or natural consequence of the unlawful agreement. But as we read this record, that is not this case.

Affirmed.

Mr. Justice RUTLEDGE, dissenting in part.

The judgment concerning Daniel Pinkerton should be reversed. In my opinion, it is without precedent here and is a dangerous precedent to establish. Daniel and Walter, who were brothers living near each other, were charged in several counts with substantive offenses, and then a conspiracy count was added naming those offenses as overt acts. The proof showed that Walter alone committed the substantive crimes. There was none to establish that Daniel participated in them, aided and abetted Walter in committing them, or knew that he had done so. Daniel in fact was in the penitentiary, under sentence for other crimes, when some of Walter's crimes were done.

There was evidence, however, to show that over several years Daniel and Walter had confederated to commit similar crimes concerned with unlawful possession, transportation, and dealing in whiskey, in fraud of the federal revenues. On this evidence both were convicted of conspiracy. . . .

* * *

The court's theory seems to be that Daniel and Walter became general partners in crime by virtue of their agreement and because of that agreement without more on his part Daniel became criminally responsible as a principal for everything Walter did thereafter in the nature of a criminal offense of the general sort the agreement contemplated, so long as there was not clear evidence that Daniel had withdrawn from or revoked the agreement. Whether or not his commitment to the penitentiary had that effect, the result is a vicarious criminal responsibility as broad as, or broader than, the vicarious civil liability of a partner for acts done by a co-partner in the course of the firm's business.

* * *

Questions

1. As should be evident from a reading of *Pinkerton*, co-conspirators are criminally liable for all acts of other co-conspirators if, and only if, those acts are both (a) reasonably foreseeable in light of the conspiracy; and (b) in furtherance of the conspiracy. But any test that speaks to reasonable foreseeability invites ambiguity. For example, suppose two co-conspirators plan a burglary of a house with the intent to steal various items from the house. Further suppose that one of the thieves has a history of sexual assault that is known to the other. On the night of the planned burglary, it turns out that someone is home in the house and, although not planned, the person with a history of sexual assault rapes the woman who is home. Is that reasonably foreseeable? Why or why not?
2. Assuming, for the sake of argument, that the sexual assault scenario described in question #1 were deemed to be reasonably foreseeable, would the other co-conspirator have criminal liability for the rape under *Pinkerton*? Why or why not? Separate and apart from conspiratorial liability, would the co-conspirator have any other type of liability for the sexual assault, say, perhaps, as an accomplice? Explain your answer.
3. Suppose a group of three or four people plan to rob a bank and then carry out their plan. Part of their agreement is that, although they would arm themselves, their weapons would not be loaded. In other words, they only carry the guns to scare people in the bank into compliance. They all specifically agree that if anything went wrong, they would surrender, rather than use any actual force, as they sincerely do not want anyone to be hurt, as their true objective is to get money. In spite of this specific agreement, one of the co-conspirators brings with him a loaded weapon and uses it during the robbery to kill an armed security guard. What should the liability of the other co-conspirators be in a *Pinkerton* jurisdiction? In a non-*Pinkerton* jurisdiction? Explain your answers.

Grading for Conspiracy

The common law treated conspiracy as a misdemeanor, even if the target offense of the conspiracy was a felony.[114] Today, however, many criminal codes tend to tie the punishment for the crime of conspiracy to the underlying target offense. Maryland, for example, provides that: "The punishment of a person who is convicted of conspiracy may not exceed the maximum punishment for the crime that the person conspired to commit."[115] Rhode Island does the same, but adds a limitation that regardless of the underlying target offense, punishment for conspiracy "shall not exceed ten years."[116] The law of most states is in accord with Rhode Island's approach insofar as conspiracy to commit a felony is usually punished less severely that the commission of the target crime itself.

Defenses to Conspiracy

At common law, most (but not all) courts did not recognize either factual or legal impossibility as a defense to a criminal conspiracy. The Model Penal Code retained this ban on the defense by not recognizing a defense of factual or hybrid legal impossibility in conspiracy cases.[117] Abandonment, however, may be a defense, although states take different approaches it depending on whether the follow the common-law approach or the one taken by the Model Penal Code.

Once a conspiracy was formed, the common law did not recognize abandonment or withdrawal as a defense to the charge of conspiracy. In other words, after a conspiratorial agreement was formed, if the defendants abandoned their efforts to complete the target offence(s), they would still have criminal liability for the crime of conspiracy.

Under the Model Penal Code, abandonment may be a limited defense to the crime of conspiracy.[118] As with most of the other inchoate offenses under the Model Penal Code, one can successfully withdraw from a conspiracy if the abandonment is complete, effective, and voluntary. In other to be deemed effective, though, it is not enough that a conspirator renounces his or her criminal purpose. The actor must take affirmative steps to thwart the successful completion of the conspiratorial objectives. This usually requires the person withdrawing from the conspiracy to notify the authorities of the plan. If the conspiracy goes in spite of the withdrawing person's efforts to thwart the success of the conspiracy, then abandonment will not be a valid defense since it was not effective.

CONCLUSION

Learning Objectives	Summaries
1. Analyze the scope of criminal liability for accomplices.	Someone becomes an accessory by purposefully aiding and abetting a principal's commission of a crime. The aid can be minimal and need not even be effective. Accomplices are liable for the crimes they aid a principal to commit, as well as other crimes that are the probable consequences of the offense aided. Accomplices may avoid criminal liability by completely, effectively, and voluntarily withdrawing any aid offered before it is too late to prevent the offense.

Learning Objectives	Summaries
2. Compare and contrast liability for being an accessory after the fact with obstruction of justice liability.	An accessory after the fact is any person who harbors, conceals, or otherwise aids an offender, knowing or having reasonable grounds to believe the offender had committed a felony. Spouses and select family members may be exempt from accessorial liability in some states. Many jurisdictions have abandoned accessory after-the-fact liability and replaced it with the broader crime of obstruction of justice which involves obstructing, impairing, or otherwise interfering with the orderly administration of law, justice, or other governmental functions.
3. Describe various ways that someone may be held criminally liability for interference with the orderly administration of justice.	A number of acts that obstruct justice may be statutorily defined as their own crimes. Examples include perjury, false swearing, making unsworn falsifications, tampering with witnesses or evidence, resisting arrest, eluding/unlawful flight, escaping from official custody, causing a false alarm, falsely incriminating another person, filing a false police report, impersonating a public servant, and failing to appear in court.
4. Define the elements of a criminal conspiracy.	An actor commits the crime of conspiracy when he or she enters into an agreement with another person with the purpose to commit an unlawful act or, alternatively, to commit a lawful act by illegal means. The agreement need not be express; it may be implied. And although the common law required a true bilateral agreement, the Model Penal Code imposes conspiracy liability for unilateral conspiracies if the actor believes a bilateral agreement was actually formed. In some jurisdictions, there must also be an overt act performed in the furtherance of a conspiratorial objective.
5. Explain the ways in which the *mens rea* for conspiracy liability may be established.	Specific intent to join a conspiracy may be proven by direct evidence, by the hearsay testimony of a co-conspirator, or by inference if there is some special interest in the activity or the crime itself is aggravated nature.
6. Differentiate wheel and chain/ladder conspiracies.	A wheel conspiracy involves a person or a small group of people at the hub of an enterprise in which they form a series of separate agreements with other persons or groups. Proof of knowledge of a comprehensive conspiracy and some interdependence among the groups is necessary to treat it as one, large conspiracy. By contrast, a chain/ladder conspiracy exists when one person agrees with another who, in turn, agrees with yet another, and so on. Because the success of the whole criminal venture is likely dependent on each persons in the chain being interdependent on the others, a chain/ladder conspiracy usually constitutes one, large conspiracy.
7. Explain the defenses that may exonerate liability for aiding and abetting and conspiratorial liability.	Factual impossibility is never a defense to any inchoate crime. Although legal impossibility may be a defense, it is highly unlikely that it will succeed since most claims of impossibility involve a hybrid of mistakes of facts and of law that do not negate *mens rea*. At common law, one could abandon being an accomplice, but not being a co-conspirator. A conspiracy was complete upon the formation of an agreement with the requisite criminal intent. But to facilitate renunciation of criminal plans, both the common law and the Model Penal Code recognize abandonment as a defense to aiding and abetting. The Model Penal Code also recognized abandonment as a defense to conspiracy, so long as they involve complete, effective, and voluntary withdrawals.

KEY TERMS

abandonment
accessory
accessory after the fact
accomplice
aiding and abetting
bilateral conspiracy
chain/ladder conspiracy
conspiracy
eluding
escape
failure to appear
false swearing
hybrid legal impossibility
obstruction of justice
overt act
perjury
Pinkerton Rule
principal
resisting arrest
tampering with evidence
unilateral conspiracy
unlawful flight
unsworn falsifications
Wharton's Rule
wheel conspiracy
witness tampering

7

Homicide

Outline

LEARNING OBJECTIVES

1. Define the corpus delicti of all forms of criminal homicide.
2. Differentiate between the different types of murder.
3. Distinguish between the different types of manslaughter and criminally negligent homicide.
4. Explain how the law attempts to deter suicide and assisted suicide.
5. Summarize the Model Penal Code's attempts at reforming common-law approaches to homicides.

INTRODUCTION

The term **homicide** refers to the unlawful killing of a human being—referred to as a *person* in some homicide statutes. This definition, however, is deceiving simple, as reasonable people often differ over what it means "to kill" unlawfully, as well as who counts as a "human being." Before turning to an in-depth examination of the various forms of homicide (which are primarily differentiated from each other by the defendant's *mens rea*), we begin by exploring these preliminary concepts within the context of *corpus delicti* since its elements are common to all forms of homicide.

CORPUS DELICTI

Corpus delicti is Latin for "the body (or substance) of the crime."[1] *Corpus delicti* has two component elements in homicide cases: (1) the death of a human being, and (2) the criminal agency of another person as the cause of that death.[2] Both of these elements must be proved beyond a reasonable doubt.[3]

Killing: Causing the Death of a Human Being

Killing means to cause a premature end to another human's life. If life is at all shortened—even by a few seconds—then a killing has taken place. This element of the killing of a human being is a common element to all forms of criminal homicide. But how do we know when someone is dead?

At common law, death was defined as the cessation of heart and respiratory functions.[4] But today, we know that the heart is not the body's most vital organ, especially since (1) it can be transplanted, and (2) it can be kept functioning by artificial means, such as a respirator.[5] The brain is now considered to be the body's most important organ. Thus, under modern law, **brain death** is the standard for determining death. It is defined as the total cessation of brain functioning as manifested by the absence of spontaneous movement, respiration, all brainstem reflexes.[6]

> Several criminal defendants charged with murder have argued that they should be absolved of the crime because while they may have injured a victim by rendering him brain dead, the removal of the victim from life support was the actual cause of death. While it is true that many brain-dead patients indefinitely retain cardiopulmonary functioning with the assistance of life support, courts have uniformly dismissed such arguments. In fact, such an argument has never been successful.[7]

Time Limitations on Determinations of Killing

At common law, if the victim of an attack died within one year and one day of the attack, the person responsible for the attack on the victim could be held liable for the death; but if the victim of an attack lived for more than one year and one day, then no homicide was deemed to have taken place.[8] The rationale underlying the **year-and-a-day rule** posited that unless death occurred within this time period, either the injury could not be not the cause of death or, alternatively, that whether the injury were the cause of death could not be discerned beyond a reasonable doubt.[9]

The US Supreme Court has commented that the year-and-a-day rule "is widely viewed as an outdated relic of the common law."[10]

> The jury may now rely on the testimony of expert witnesses and need not decide issues on the basis of their own individual knowledge. Furthermore, since great advances have been made in scientific crime detection and scientific medicine, the doubt that a mortal blow is the cause of death, when death ensues a year and a day after the blow, has been largely removed. Consequently, a period of a year and a day after which death is conclusively presumed to result from natural causes is no longer realistic.[11]

Accordingly, "the year-and-a-day rule has been legislatively or judicially abolished in the vast majority of jurisdictions recently to have addressed the issue."[12] The Model Penal Code is in accord with this modern view, as it contains no mention of any time limitation.[13]

In spite of the Model Penal Code's abolition of a fixed time period for homicide liability, a number of US jurisdictions continue to follow the year-and-a-day rule.[14] Still other jurisdictions have modified it; California, for example, statutorily adopted a "three years and a day" rule in 1969.[15] In 1996, however, California changed this rule to a rebuttable presumption:

> To make the killing either murder or manslaughter, it is not requisite that the party die within three years and a day after the stroke received or the cause of death administered. If death occurs beyond the time of three years and a day, there shall be a rebuttable presumption that the killing was not criminal. The prosecution shall bear the burden of overcoming this presumption . . . .[16]

In the jurisdictions that do not have any time limitation, the usual rules of causation need to be applied. Thus, the relevant question becomes whether the defendant's act was both the cause-in-fact and proximate cause of the victim's death, even if the death occurred several years later. This can present difficult questions about whether other factors were dependent, intervening causes of death over the passage of time, or alternatively whether they were independent, supervening causes. Consider *Commonwealth v. Casanova*[17] in which someone was shot and paralyzed from the neck down. This, in turn, compromised his ability to breathe normally. The person who shot the victim was convicted of aggravated assault, among other crimes. Over the years that followed, the victim's condition worsened such that could no longer breathe without a ventilator. He eventually developed a respiratory syndrome associated with long-term ventilator use and died. Despite that he passed away six years after the shooting, the defendant was subsequently indicted for the victim's murder. In refusing the dismiss the indictment, the Supreme Judicial Court of Massachusetts reasoned that advancements in medicine "can now sustain the critically afflicted for months and even years beyond what might have been imagined only decades ago."[18] Similarly, forensic pathology now allows cause of death determinations "with greater accuracy than was possible in earlier times and thus causation, even in complex cases, is a less difficult problem in modern-day prosecutions."[19]

Defining a Human Being for Homicide Purposes

It should be self-evident from the definition that a human being must be the victim of a killing for homicide liability to attach. Accordingly, as much as one might love one's pet, if someone killed the family dog, no homicide would be deemed to have taken place.

The common law did not punish the killing of a fetus *in utero*; a child had to be "born alive" and then killed in order for a homicide to have taken place.[20] The common law's **born alive rule** remains the law in several US jurisdictions today.[21] However, a seemingly ever-growing number of states have enacted fetal homicide laws.

More than three-quarters of US states have abandoned the common law's born alive rule.[22] Some of these states have adopted legislation either includes a fetus within the protection of their general homicide statutes while others have enacted a special feticide statute. Of these thirty-eight states with fetal homicide laws, twenty-three apply at any state of gestation; in other words, from the moment of fertilization onward.[23] The majority of the remaining fetal statutes become applicable only after a fetus is viable.

Criminal Agency as the Cause of Death

Corpus delicti requires proof that a criminal defendant unlawfully caused the death of another person. Such proof may come in many forms. Direct evidence, such as the testimony of an eyewitness who saw the defendant kill the victim, is preferred by prosecutors and jurors alike, even though eyewitness testimony is notoriously unreliable.[24] But direct evidence is not available in many cases. The prosecution must therefore prove *corpus delicti* using circumstantial evidence—no easy task since there is no presumption of *corpus delicti* in homicide cases; it must be proven beyond of a reasonable doubt.

Historically, when a suspected homicide victim's body was discovered, a thorough criminal investigation by law enforcement officers could assemble sufficient circumstantial evidence to prove *corpus delicti*. Police efforts were often aided by medical science—usually through forensic pathology and forensic toxicology. Autopsies and their accompanying post-mortem tests on a dead body typically allow medical examiners to draw conclusions on the causes of a person's death to a reasonable degree of scientific certainty. When that is the case, *corpus delicti* may be circumstantially proven by the testimony of such experts and through the introduction into evidence of their scientific reports (e.g., an autopsy report and a death certificate).[25]

In recent years, criminal investigation work by police has increasingly integrated other branches of forensic science to help prove *corpus delicti*.[26] Paradoxically, the public's fascination with all things forensic has made it more difficult for prosecutors to obtain criminal convictions based on circumstantial evidence.[27] Television shows have collective planted "heightened and unrealistic expectations of how conclusively forensic evidence can determine a defendant's innocence or guilt" in the minds of jurors—a phenomenon called the **CSI effect.**[28] For example:

> In Arizona, a man charged with a burglary in Tempe was acquitted, even though a witness testified about seeing the defendant dragging a stereo from the store, and burglary tools were in his car when he was arrested. The Arizona Republic reported jurors said the police should have found the man's fingerprints inside the store.[29]

Given how difficult the CSI effect can make it to prove *corpus delicti* when there is a dead body in light of the high expectations jurors bring to their deliberations, it should come as no surprise that proving *corpus delicti* when there is no body can be extremely difficult. But even without a body, good investigation work by police can still prove *corpus delicti* via circumstantial evidence.

When the victim's body has not been found, the prosecution may introduce evidence of matters such as the defendant's history of violence toward the victim and statements that he would kill the victim, or the defendant's conduct during the period around the time the crime was committed. The state may also present evidence of the victim's character, habits, traits, and relationships to negate theories of suicide, natural death, accidental death, justifiable or excusable homicide, or continuing life in absentia, as part of the circumstantial evidence tending to prove the *corpus delicti*.[30]

But the reality is that bodiless homicide cases "based entirely on circumstantial evidence are few and far between."[31] One might think that a confession might be one type of evidence that could help overcome the significant evidentiary hurdles that exist in bodiless homicide cases. But a rule of evidence commonly referred to as the ***corpus delicti* rule** restricts the use of uncorroborated confessions as evidence in homicide cases because "[c]onfessions can be notoriously unreliable and extra-judicial confessions doubly so."[32]

People v. Lipskey is one of the leading cases in which a defendant was convicted without a body having been discovered.[33] What makes the *Lipskey* case somewhat unique is that the part of the corroboration for the defendant's confession came in the form of a poem. In that case, the victim, Mary Robinson, was a prostitute who worked out of several hotels in Rochester, New York. When Robinson did not return home one evening, her sister and brother-in-law went looking for her. They checked two of the hotels Mary typically frequented, as well an apartment that the three of them shared. Although Robinson was not in the apartment, her glasses, the clothing she wore, and the purse she carried were all found there. Lipskey came to the attention of police when his girlfriend found some of Robinson's personal items in their apartment, including Robinson's wire frame glasses and a red plaid wallet containing an identification card, as well as some family pictures. When she asked Lipskey about the articles, he told her that they likely belonged to a former tenant who had must have abandoned the items.

Lipskey moved to Utah, where was arrested for aggravated assault. During a meeting with a psychiatric social worker, he admitted that he had murdered a prostitute in Rochester whom he identified as Mary Robinson. Although Robinson's body was never recovered, Lipskey was indicted for her murder. The prosecution presented Robinson's belonging that Lispkey's prior girlfriend had found in their Rochester apartment. They also called two witnesses who testified that Lipskey had told them he had murdered someone. Finally, the prosecution introduced a poem that police discovered in Lipskey's apartment, which read:

> To crush out a life with a hand or a heel;
> To be carelessly senseless and not even feel;
> To treat one as nothing and not even real;
> To be as a jackal, a thief who did steal.
> I was such a man, and it's a part of me now.
> I was such a fool and can't even tell how I did such a thing.
> Now, it weighs on my brow and I think of the peace such an act won't allow.
> But still I live on and remember it well.
> Yet still I must live to remember the hell.
> I can never let go of the body that fell, and it tears me to pieces where my thoughts on this dwell.
> I can never be free of this feeling inside.
> I will never be able to successfully hide.
> And there is no way to share the tears that I've cried.
> So I now live for two; by my hand one has died.

The jury convicted Lipskey, but the trial court judge set aside the conviction on the grounds that *corpus delicti* had not been proven. On appeal, New York's highest court clarified that *corpus delicti* may be established by circumstantial evidence, including a confession that is corroborated by other evidence. The court reasoned that Lipskey's statement to the social worker in Utah was sufficiently corroborated by the discovery of Robinson's personal items in Lipskey's former apartment within a week after her disappearance; his statements to two co-workers in Utah; and the poem found in his Utah apartment. For a more recent example of how the *corpus delicti* rule works, see the "Case Study Extra" feature in Box 7.1.

BOX 7.1

CASE STUDY EXTRA

Applying the *Corpus Delicti* Rule

In *State v. Leniart*,[129] the victim, who was then fifteen years old, snuck out of her parents' home to meet her friend PJ, also a teenager, so that they could smoke marijuana, drink alcohol, and have sex. Both the victim and PJ were picked up by the defendant, age thirty-three, who then drove to a secluded, wooded location in his truck. At one point, the defendant pulled PJ aside, explained he was in a cult, said he wanted "to do" the victim, and that he "wanted a body for the altar."[130] PJ and the defendant subsequently sexually assaulted the victim. The defendant then drove PJ back to the neighborhood in which he lived and dropped him off close to his home. The victim remained in the defendant's truck and was never seen again.

Four people testified at the defendant's murder trial that he had confessed to them. One of these witnesses testified that the defendant claimed to have strangled the victim and disposed of her body by placing it in a lobster trap and dropping them into the mud at the bottom of the Thames River. Importantly, the defendant was a lobster fisherman at the time.[131] A jury convicted the defendant. He appealed, arguing that the *corpus delicti* rule operated in such a way as to prevent his uncorroborated statements from forming the factual basis for his murder conviction. In affirming his conviction, the Supreme Court of Connecticut reasoned as follows:

> The fifteen-year-old victim disappeared suddenly and without warning. . . . She left home that night without taking any money, clothing, or personal belongings, despite the fact that nearly $1,000 was available in the house. . . . [S]he enjoyed her family, friends, life, and routines . . . and had no desire to run away from home or to commit suicide.
>
> At the time of trial, she had been missing for more than thirteen years, without having made any known contact with family or friends, and a nationwide search had failed to locate her or to flag any use of her social security number. . . . In addition, . . . [PJ] testified that both he and the defendant had raped the victim on the evening in question, and that he had left the victim alone in the defendant's company. That testimony, if credited, established that the defendant already had assaulted the victim that night and that he had both the motive and the opportunity to kill her.[132]

1. Assess the strength of the circumstantial evidence of Leniart's guilt. Do you think it rises to the level of proof beyond a reasonable doubt?

2. How much circumstantial evidence (and what types of it) do you think is necessary before *corpus delicti* can be deemed proven beyond a reasonable doubt? Give specific examples.[133]
3. In light of the modern-day CSI effect, do you think the trial court verdict in *Lipsky* or *Leniart* would be different today? Why or why not?

MURDER

Murder is defined as the commission of a homicide with **malice aforethought**.[34] Malice aforethought is typically construed to mean the premeditated killing of another human being, but it is actually a much broader term. Malice aforethought is the presence of *mens rea*, which includes both specific intent and general intent, combined with the absence of legally adequate justification, excuse, or circumstances that can mitigate an intentional killing to the level of manslaughter.[35] Blackstone described the term malice aforethought as "not so properly spite or malevolence . . . as any evil design in general . . . ."[36] Thus, "malice in this connection is not limited in its meaning to hatred, ill will, or malevolence, but denotes a wicked and corrupt disregard of the lives and safety of others—a failure to appreciate social duty."[37]

The broad definition of malice aforethought included intentional murders, as well as those murders that were not specifically intended. Specific intent to kill murders were based *express malice*—what "we would now call . . . purpose or knowledge in the language of the Model Penal Code."[38] Unintentional murders, in contrast, were based on implied malice that could occur in one of two ways: (1) nondeliberate killings caused as a result of purposeful, cruel act that was not provoked (e.g., the intent to cause some serious bodily harm);[39] and (2) "those that were based on a level of recklessness displaying a 'depraved heart.' "[40]

The common law generally classified express malice killings as murders in the first degree, while classifying implied malice killings as murders in the second degree or felony murders (depending upon the underlying intentional act).[41] Many US jurisdictions retain these classifications today, while others have followed the Model Penal Code's elimination of degrees and differentiate only between murder and manslaughter rather than levels of murder.[42]

Murder in the Second Degree

Murder in the second degree is a broad type of homicide. It is defined in several different ways depending on the jurisdiction. The three most common definitions of murder in the second degree mirror its common-law definitions.

SPECIFIC INTENT TO KILL WITHOUT PREMEDITATION

Murder in the second degree can be founded upon a specific intent to kill that was formed and acted upon without premeditation or deliberation.[43] Thus, it is not the absence or presence of the *mens rea* of purpose (i.e., the specific intent to kill) that differentiates murder in the first degree from murder in the second degree; rather, it is the presence or absence of some aggravating factor—of which premeditation is just one—that causes an intentional killing to be deemed a murder the first degree. Conversely, the existence of some mitigating factor, such as serious but nonlegally adequate provocation or an unreasonable belief in justification that causes an intentional killing to be deemed a murder the second degree.[44]

INTENT TO CAUSE SERIOUS BODILY HARM

The second way in which a conviction for murder in the second degree may be obtained is upon of showing of specific intent or purpose to do serious bodily harm.[45] Thus, if a defendant has no actual intent to kill, but intends to seriously hurt someone—say, for example, the defendant beats the victim severely and the victim dies from the beating—the perpetrator is guilty of murder in the second degree. The malice the defendant entertained when specifically intended to inflict serious bodily harm is sufficient to impose second-degree murder liability (using the theory of implied malice) even though there was no specific intent to kill.

DEPRAVED HEART MURDER

The third common manner in which a conviction for murder in the second degree may be obtained is known as **depraved heart murder**. Under this formulation, the defendant neither entertained specific intent to kill nor specific intent to inflict serious bodily harm. Instead, the defendant acted with such gross recklessness as to manifest an extreme indifference to the value of human life.[46] Note that unlike the other two ways in which a murder in the second degree may occur, depraved heart murder does not require either purpose or knowledge as the requisite *mens rea*. Rather, a person acting with general intent—gross recklessness—may be properly be convicted of murder in the second degree, as the following case illustrates.

Kinte Leeon BROWN, Appellant,
v.
COMMONWEALTH of Kentucky, Appellee.
975 S.W.2d 922 (Ky. 1998).

Appellant [Kinte Brown] and several others were at a friend's house watching television. Dwayne Cardine took Appellant's pager from him and, after making a "playfully insulting remark," returned it upon request. Thereafter, Appellant reached under a couch and pulled out a .38 caliber handgun. Appellant placed the barrel of the gun at or near Cardine's head. According to Appellant and several witnesses, Appellant used his thumb to pull back the hammer of the gun. He was in the process of lowering the hammer when the gun discharged, striking Cardine in the head and causing his death. Appellant was subsequently charged with the intentional or wanton murder of Cardine.

At trial, Appellant testified that he had held the gun near Cardine's head but that the shooting was an accident. Appellant stated that he did not know whether the gun was loaded, but did concede that he was aware of some problem with the gun. The jury was instructed on wanton murder, second-degree manslaughter, and reckless homicide. Appellant objected to the wanton murder instruction on the grounds that the Commonwealth had not proven the element of extreme indifference to human life. The jury subsequently convicted him of wanton murder and recommended a sentence of twenty years imprisonment....

* * *

Wanton murder is distinguished from second-degree (involuntary) manslaughter ... which also punishes "wantonly caus[ing] the death of another person," by the additional element described in the phrase "under circumstances manifesting extreme indifference to human life...."

Appellant is correct in his observation that extreme indifference to human life is not a phrase capable of precise definition, and the drafter of the Model Penal Code and the Kentucky Penal Code admitted as much.

> [Wantonness] ... presupposes an awareness of the creation of substantial homicidal risk, a risk too great to be deemed justifiable by any valid purpose that the actor's conduct serves. Since risk, however, is a matter of degree and the motives for risk creation may be infinite in variation, some formula is needed to identify the case where [wantonness] should be assimilated to [intention]. The conception that the draft employs is that of extreme indifference to the value of human life. . . . Whether recklessness is so extreme that it demonstrates similar indifference is not a question that, in our view, can be further clarified; it must be left directly to the trier of the facts. If recklessness exists but is not so extreme, the homicide is manslaughter. . . .[47]

[A]ttempting to emphasize that only the highest levels of unjustifiable homicidal risk should render an actor eligible for a murder conviction, the drafters of [our laws] provided illustrations of conduct sufficient to support findings of extreme indifference: "Typical of conduct contemplated for inclusion in 'wanton' murder is shooting into a crowd, an occupied building or an occupied automobile; placing a time bomb in a public place; or derailing a speeding locomotive."

Setting this conduct apart from behavior that would not warrant an unintentional murder conviction are the following characteristics: (i) homicidal risk that is exceptionally high; (ii) circumstances known to the actor that clearly show awareness of the magnitude of the risk; and (iii) minimal or non-existent social utility in the conduct. Such conduct plainly reflects more than mere awareness and conscious disregard of a substantial and unjustifiable risk of death. It manifests a high disregard for life and evinces what the common law chose to call a depravity of mind or heart. . . .

* * *

Appellant's conduct in this case clearly justified his conviction for wanton murder. The conviction and sentence of the Jefferson Circuit Court is affirmed.

Questions

1. Where should the line be drawn between grossly reckless conduct, sufficient for a murder in the second degree conviction, as compared to regular reckless conduct that does not rise to the level of manifesting an extreme indifference to the value of human life, and therefore only be sufficient to impose liability for involuntary manslaughter? Would playing Russian Roulette qualify? Why or why not?[48]
2. If a car accident occurred in which someone were killed as a result of the driver's operating the motor vehicle under the influence of alcohol with a blood alcohol concentration of 0.08 percent (which is the legal limit in most US states), what level of homicide liability should be imposed? Why? Would your response change if the person were driving at two or three times the legal limit?[49]

Murder in the First Degree

As previously stated, the key factor in distinguishing a murder in the first degree from another type of intentional killing is the existence of *express malice*.[50] Express malice is usually interpreted to mean that some aggravating factor occurred. **Premeditation**—a deliberate "design to take life"—is the most common of these aggravating factors.[51] But premeditation is not the only aggravating factor. The manner of killing or the status of the victim might also constitute an aggravating factor that elevates what would otherwise have been a murder in the second degree up to a murder in the first degree.[52] New York, for instance, defines murder in the first degree as the purposeful killing under any of a number of specifically enumerated circumstances, including if:

- the victim was a police, court, probation, parole, or institutional corrections officer who was killed in the line of duty; a firefighter, emergency medical technician, ambulance driver, paramedic, physician or registered nurse who was involved in a first-response team; a judge; or a witness to a crime (or the immediate family member of such a witness) for the purposes of preventing the witness from testifying in any criminal proceeding or in retribution for such testimony;

- the perpetrator was an inmate in a state correctional institution; or had previously been convicted of murder; or
- the killing was part of a murder-for-hire scheme; part of serial murder plan; part of a plan involving the "intentional and depraved" infliction of torture; or an act of terrorism.[53]

Statutory variations aside, the definition of murder in the first degree in most states includes a provision regarding premeditation. Yet there is considerable disagreement on what constitutes premeditation or how long a defendant must entertain premeditation before a conviction for murder in the first degree is permissible. The majority approach to this issue follows the common-law rule that premeditation need not exist for any substantial period of time.[54] Under this approach, if intent to kill is formed, reflected upon even momentarily, and then acted upon, the killing would be premeditated. Thus, premeditation excludes actions which were taken so spontaneously that there was no time to think.[55] But if the killing is not "the instant effect of impulse, if there is hesitation or doubt to overcome, a choice made as the result of thought, however short the struggle between the intention and the act, it is sufficient to characterize the crime as deliberate and premeditated murder."[56]

In contrast, a minority of jurisdictions define deliberate premeditation as having had time for measured, unhurried thinking. The leading case using this approach is *People v. Anderson*, a case decided by the California Supreme Court in 1969.[57]

> The jury had convicted Anderson of first-degree murder and fixed the penalty at death. Evidently, the jury concluded that infliction of sixty stab wounds on a ten-year-old child, during the course of activity that involved tearing off her clothes, tearing her panties, and chasing her throughout the house while she bled profusely enough to leave footprints from one room to the next and blood in nearly every part of the house, was sufficient to show a deliberate and premeditated killing.[58]

But the state high court reduced Anderson's conviction to murder in the second based upon a determination that the defendant had not premeditated the killing. Quite the contrary, the court asserted that the defendant's actions did not evidence "careful thought and weighing of considerations."[59] Instead, the court construed the more than sixty stab wounds as evidence of a "frenzied killing" that "resulted from a 'random,' 'violent,' and 'indiscriminate' attack, 'rather than from deliberately placed wounds inflicted according to a preconceived design.' "[60]

Regardless of which approach is used, determining if a defendant acted with premeditation and deliberation must usually "be established by circumstantial evidence, because both are processes of the mind not ordinarily susceptible to proof by direct evidence."[61] But doing so is often a difficult task for jurors and even judges who review the records of criminal trials on appeal, as illustrated by the following case.

Thomas GREEN, Plaintiff in Error,

v.

STATE of Tennessee, Defendant in Error.

450 S.W.2d 27 (Tenn. Ct. Crim. App. 1969).

* * *

The deceased, Morris Snow, age 21 and three other young men (Sylvester Hill, Tommy Lee Billups, and Larry Code) were at Velma's Tea Room in Chattanooga in the early morning hours of January 19, 1968. There was some disagreement between Snow and the defendant. Billups says that the defendant and two other people came to Snow's table and the defendant argued with him, telling Snow: "My brother killed a man the other night, and you're going to mess around here and get killed, too." After this the defendant and Snow shook hands and the defendant said to forget it. He then returned to his table in another part of the room and the deceased, Snow, sat at his table with his three friends and was drinking a bottle of beer.

A short time later, estimated by the witnesses from four to twenty minutes, the defendant returned to the table where Snow was seated and told him to go home, to which Snow replied that he was grown and didn't have to go home. The defendant asked the deceased to repeat himself and he again said he was grown. All of the witnesses agree that the defendant pulled a pistol and shot the deceased while he was seated at the table with his hands on it. The defendant fired several shots, one striking the deceased back of the left ear and another back of the left shoulder. The second shot was fired after Snow had fallen to the floor. The defendant and one of his friends ran out of the building....

Of course, to support a verdict finding a defendant guilty of murder in the first degree, there must be an evidentiary basis for a conclusion that the killing was willful, deliberate, malicious and premeditated, unless effected by poison or lying in wait or in the perpetration of one of the felonies named in the defining statute, in which cases the specified circumstances make it otherwise unnecessary to prove deliberation and premeditation....

Here the defendant had had an argument, during which he threatened to kill the deceased. After some minutes and time to become cool, he returned and shot the deceased. The jury was well warranted in concluding the killing came from deliberation and premeditation. It is not necessary that the design or intention to kill should have been conceived or have pre-existed in the mind any definite time anterior to its execution. It is sufficient if it preceded the assault, however short the interval, and the length of time is not the essence of this constituent of the offense. The design may be conceived and deliberately formed in an instant. Hence it is not material that the interval of premeditation was brief. . . .

* * *

Judge Galbreath, dissenting:

* * *

What is the proof in the record that proves premeditation? There is none. On the contrary, there is undisputed proof from which it may plainly be inferred that an instant before the shooting there was no plan in the mind of the defendant to kill the victim. Green walked up to the table at which the victim was seated and said simply, "Go home." It is submitted for logical consideration that these actions and words mitigate against a previously designed plan to kill. If the defendant had acceded to the imperious request to go home, nothing appears in the record to suggest that he would not be alive today. Of course, he had every right not to go home, and for the defendant to become angry enough to kill him for not obeying his dictatorial order he should be subjected to such punishment as the law provides for taking the life of another under such circumstances. He should not, in my judgment, be subjected to the same punishment reserved for the felon who carefully plans to insure his child's life and then kills it to collect money. Or the depraved killer who lies in wait to slay his victim from ambush. Or the bandit who kills his robbery victim to conceal his guilt of that crime. These are more serious matters than the rash, impulsive, stupid, impetuous act described in the record before us.

* * *

Premeditation may, of course, be inferred from the acts and words of the killer. Nowhere in the record from the point the defendant shook hands with the deceased and told him to forget an argument they had concluded does anything at all appear to indicate the defendant's state of mind. If he had stood up and announced, "I am going over and kill Snow"; or if he had taken his pistol out and walked over to Snow's table in a threatening way, these facts would justify the jury in concluding a previously formulated design to kill had taken shape. Instead of such actions or words the circumstances prove without dispute that the defendant walked over and did something that completely dispels the notion that he planned to kill; he told the deceased to leave! Should we go further and infer that the defendant had planned to kill the deceased even if the victim had said, "yes, sir, I am going home," and had left? Just as in any other case involving circumstantial evidence (and this case as far as proof of premeditation goes, rests completely on such proof) every reasonable hypothesis save that tending to prove guilt must be excluded by the jury before they can find the necessary element to have been proved beyond a reasonable doubt. The defendant did not indicate by word or deed that he had determined to kill the deceased if his order had been obeyed. It was his almost infantile, petulant reaction to the deceased's perfectly valid reaction to his demand that triggered the anger that resulted in this hot blooded, second-degree murder.

Questions

1. As should be evident from the case, Tennessee follows the majority approach to premeditation, holding that it need not exist for any appreciable period of time. The dissent makes a strong argument, however, there was no premeditation in the case. With whom do you side—the majority or the dissent? Why?[62]
2. Do you agree that the manner of killing in this case demonstrates premeditation, or can it alternatively be explained as a killing in the heat of the moment? What if Green had strangled the victim?[63]
3. Usually, juries want to know the motive for a killing. Motive, however, is not an element of any criminal homicide, but rather is only circumstantial evidence of guilt. Why do you think it is so important to show a motive? What is its relationship, if any, to premeditation?

Felony Murder

When someone is killed during the commission or attempt to commit a felony that, by its nature, poses an inherent risk to human life, then the killing, even if unintentional, is deemed to be a type of murder called **felony murder**. The *mens rea* the defendant had to commit the underlying felony transfers to satisfy the *mens rea* for felony murder. It is important to note that some jurisdictions have a statutory offense called "felony murder," while other states have merged the definition of felony murder into one of the other types of murder definitions.[64] For example, some states consider any qualifying felony murder one of the aggravating circumstances sufficient to elevate an unintentional homicide to murder in the first degree.

LIMITED TO INHERENTLY DANGEROUS FELONIES

Given the harshness of the felony murder doctrine—especially since it was created at a time when all felonies were punishable by death, the common law developed a number of limitations on it. First, the underlying felony generally has to be one that is "inherently dangerous," such as burglary, arson, robbery, sexual assault, and kidnaping. Today, some jurisdictions have very broad felony murder statutes, adding crimes like escape, drug trafficking, aggravated child abuse, and unlawful flight/eluding police. But in the states that do not enumerate qualifying felonies and instead apply the "inherently dangerous" test, determining what felony is not always a clear-cut task. For example, in *State v. Noren*, the defendant was convicted of felony murder for having struck someone on the head three times with his closed fist during a robbery. The victim was extremely drunk at the time of the robbery; indeed, his blood alcohol concentration was.38%. The blows caused the victim to lose consciousness and to become comatose. The victim died while in the coma, partially because he suffered from a preexisting respiratory disease that impeded the removal of mucus from his lungs—something the defendant did not know about.

> We agree that generally death is not the natural and probable result of a blow with a hand. . . . Our inquiry is not complete, however, because the particular traits of the victim also must be considered. Conduct that is unlikely to cause the death of a healthy adult may be dangerous to others. . . . Only special attributes that the defendant was aware of may be considered. . . . Conduct does not become inherently dangerous on the basis of latent danger. . . .
>
> Applying the inherently dangerous test to this case, we conclude that sufficient evidence supports . . . conviction. Although [the victim's] respiratory disease was irrelevant to the issue of inherent danger, his extreme intoxication was a factor that distinguished him from a healthy adult. Striking an intoxicated person exposes him to familiar risks that a sober person would not face. He may fall and fatally strike his head. He also may asphyxiate from vomit while unconscious. . . . [T]he jury could consider such possibilities when determining whether [the defendant's] conduct was inherently dangerous.

The "You Make the Public Policy Call" feature in Box 7.2 considers another complex question concerning what constitutes an inherently dangerous felony.

TIMING LIMITATIONS

Another limitation on felony murder liability is that of timing. Whatever act the defendant did to cause the death of another had to have occurred during the commission or attempt to commit an inherently dangerous felony, or during immediate flight therefrom. As with the determination of what constitutes an inherently dangerous felony, what constitutes a killing "during" either the attempt or actual commission of a crime, or "immediate flight therefrom" leaves some room for argumentation, as the following case illustrates.

BOX 7.2

YOU MAKE THE PUBLIC POLICY CALL

Is Unlawful Flight an Inherently Dangerous Felony?

Recall from Chapter 6 that when a person willfully attempts to flee or elude a pursuing law enforcement vehicle that is being driven with its lights or siren activated, that person commits the crime of unlawful flight. In *People v. Schmies*,[134] the defendant, whose license has been suspended, was driving a motorcycle on a freeway at speeds exceeding 90 miles per hour. When a California Highway Patrol Officer tried to pull over the driver, the motorcycle operator accelerated and then existed the freeway in an attempt to loose the officer in pursuit. The driver drove through red lights, stop signs, and over double yellow lines to weave around cars, sometimes at speeds approaching 100 miles an hour. The officer chased the motorcycle driver despite the fact that there was a formal policy prohibiting officers from engaging in high speed pursuits. At one point, the officer hit the car of a bystander, killing its driver.

1. What should the homicide liability of the motorcycle driver be? Why?
2. Should the law enforcement officer have any homicide liability? Explain your answer, including a discussion of public policy concerns that such chases raise.

STATE of Tennessee, Appellee,

v.

Donald C. LEE, Appellant.

969 S.W.2d 414 (Tenn. Ct. Crim. App. 1997).

The appellant [Donald C. Lee] entered the Super-X drug store in Knoxville. He forced the pharmacist to open the safe and give him all [the] narcotics. A witness saw him leaving the pharmacy in a white truck. The driver of the white truck let the appellant out in an adjacent parking lot. The police immediately apprehended the driver. He informed the police that the appellant left in a brown Ford containing one passenger. Approximately 25 minutes later the appellant was spotted by the police and a high-speed chase ensued. In an effort to get away, the appellant struck the side of the police car. He erratically cut in front of other motorists. He slammed on his brakes causing the police car to slam into the rear of his car. The appellant eventually swerved into the oncoming lane of traffic and struck a Jeep. The appellant's passenger and the driver of the Jeep were killed in the head-on collision.

In his first issue the appellant contends that the evidence was insufficient to support a conviction for felony murder. He argues that the killing of the victim did not occur during the perpetration of the robbery. He claims that he had successfully completed the robbery and made a successful getaway when the police chase ensued....

* * *

The appellant's contention is simply that the robbery had been completed when he collided with the Jeep causing the death of its driver. We note that the protraction of events over time and distance accentuate the problem of determining whether the underlying felony had reached completion before the death occurred. However, other jurisdictions have held that a person is engaged in the commission or perpetration of a robbery while the criminal is trying to escape with the property taken in such robbery.[65]

Factors to be considered in determining whether there has been a break in the chain of circumstances include the relationship between the underlying felony and the homicide in point of time, place, and causation. One commentator suggests that in the case of flight, the most important consideration is whether the fleeing felon has reached a "place of temporary safety."[66] We also note that the determination of whether the act of escape or flight is a continuous part of the accomplished crime or whether the defendant has reached a place of temporary safety is a question for the trier of fact.[67]

In this case the appellant was spotted by a police officer approximately 25 minutes after the robbery occurred.... Nothing in the record indicates that the appellant had reached a place of temporary safety. The homicide was clearly a result of the high-speed chase necessitated by the appellant's attempt to flee the area of the crime. It is a legitimate and logical assumption that one who plans a robbery and carries it out has also planned to escape from the scene of the crime. His flight is an integral part of the crime....

* * *

Accordingly, we affirm the judgment of the trial court.

Questions

1. Why do you think nearly all US jurisdictions limit felony murder liability to those deaths that occur during the commission of a qualifying felony or immediate flight therefrom? What do you think about this limitation? Why?
2. How do we know when immediate flight from the scene of a felony is over? Critique the logic of immediate flight ends upon reaching a temporary place of safety.

LIMITATIONS ON VICTIMS

Some jurisdictions limit the application of the felony murder rule to when innocent, third parties are killed.[68] Thus, in jurisdictions with this limitation, if an accomplice or co-conspirator dies during the actual or attempted commission of an inherently dangerous felony, then no felony murder will be deemed to have taken place.

LIMITED TO KILLINGS IN FURTHERANCE OF THE UNDERLYING FELONY

If one is being charged with felony murder due to the actions of an accomplice and/or co-conspirator, some states require that the killing be "in furtherance of" the felony before liability for felony murder can be imputed via complicity theory. This effectively eliminates complicity liability for felony murder for any homicide that occurs outside the common plan of the felony.[69]

MERGER RULE

The **merger rule** provides that manslaughter cannot be merged to serve as the underlying/qualifying felony in felony murder. The reason for this is simple. If manslaughter qualified as one of the inherently dangerous felonies that triggered the application of the felony murder rule, then no one would ever escape liability for murder since even manslaughter killings—those without malice—would then trigger the application of the felony murder rule. Accordingly, the merger rule prohibits manslaughter from ever qualifying as the underlying felony.[70]

MANSLAUGHTER

Manslaughter is defined as the killing of a human being without malice. There are three types of manslaughter: voluntary manslaughter, involuntary manslaughter, and unlawful act manslaughter.

Voluntary Manslaughter

Voluntary manslaughter is a type of homicide in which the defendant entertains specific intent to kill, but the intent is formed under special circumstances which the law recognizes as mitigating factors. Then common law recognized several situations in which someone might form intent to kill and suddenly act upon such intent, yet did not deserve to be punished for murder.

IMPERFECT SELF-DEFENSE

The first of three situations that mitigates what would otherwise be murder down to voluntary manslaughter is called **imperfect self-defense**. As discussed in more detail in Chapter 15, if one acts in self-defense, but is either mistaken about either the nature or existence of imminent harm, or mistaken about the reasonableness of the force used, he or she is not deprived of the defense. Such a mistake, if both honest and reasonable, can be a complete defense to homicide, assault, and/or battery. In contrast, when a defendant makes a subjectively honest but objectively unreasonable mistake, the common law would label the homicide as being one of voluntary manslaughter due to the doctrine of imperfect self-defense. Under this doctrine, an unreasonable mistake regarding the defendant's acting in self-defense that resulted in the death of another mitigates a charge of murder to manslaughter.[71]

LEGALLY ADEQUATE PROVOCATION

The second circumstance that mitigates what would otherwise be murder down to voluntary manslaughter is when the defendant was provoked into killing the victim and the provocation is deemed legally adequate. **Legally adequate provocation** is quite limited, such as when the defendant is the victim of some unlawful act. Mere words, no matter how offensive or insulting, never constitute legally adequate provocation.[72] In some jurisdictions, the criminal statutes enumerate the crimes which qualify as legally adequate provocation, often limiting them to battery, mutual combat, and the sudden discovery of adultery.[73] It should be noted that a legally valid marriage is required for adultery to qualify as legally adequate provocation; in the absence of a legally valid marriage, finding one's significant other cheating usually does not qualify for a voluntary manslaughter instruction.[74] Moreover, the law views the "sudden discovery" of adultery differently than being told by one's spouse that he or she has cheated. Accordingly, some courts refuse to allow a voluntary manslaughter instruction when a spouse confesses to infidelity.[75]

HEAT OF PASSION

The final circumstance under which murder may be mitigated to voluntary manslaughter is when the intent to kill is formed during the heat of passion due to the actions of the person killed. **Heat of passion** is defined as anything that would cause the ordinary, reasonable, prudent person to have formed the desire to kill on impulse, without reflection, under similar circumstances.[76] Although abusive, offensive, or insulting words, by themselves, do not give rise to a heat of passion claim, when such words are coupled with physically threatening or hostile actions, a heat of passion claim may be permissible.[77]

For a heat of passion instruction to be warranted, there must be both casual and temporal link between the actions of the victim and the killer. The victim must have caused the heat of passion to occur and the killer must have actually killed while enraged in the heat of passion. If, in contrast, someone other than the victim ignited the killer's passion, or, alternatively, if sufficient time had passed to allow the killer to "cool down," such a cooling off period nullifies a valid heat of passion argument, resulting in a killing being properly punished as a murder, not a voluntary manslaughter.[78]

EXTREME EMOTIONAL DISTURBANCE

The Model Penal Code does not differentiate between voluntary and involuntary manslaughter, per se. Rather, it provides that: "Criminal homicide constitutes manslaughter when it is recklessly committed"—unintentional killings the common law referred to as involuntary manslaughter.[79] In a similar yet distinct manner to the common law's recognition of voluntary manslaughter, the Model Penal Code recognizes that there are situations in which a person might form the intent to kill and act upon that intent, yet still does not deserve to be punished for murder. But the Model Penal Code's approach to such killings is more expansive than the common law's narrow approach to killings that occur in the heat of passion upon legally adequate provocation. Rather, the Model Penal Code uses a test for **extreme emotional disturbance** (EED) in recognition "that some intentional homicides may result from 'an understandable human response deserving of mercy.'"[80]

In advocating the EED test, the Model Penal Code drafters criticized the common-law approach to provocation because they thought it focused too heavily on the situations which might lead to murder under mitigating circumstances rather focusing on "the understandable human frailties of certain murderers."[81] Accordingly, the Model Penal Code's formulation of the EED defense "does not require that the actor's emotional distress arise from some injury, affront, or other provocative act perpetrated upon him by the deceased."[82]

In the jurisdictions that have adopted the Model Penal Code's EED test for voluntary manslaughter,[83] it is an affirmative defense in which the defense must prove: (1) an objective element requiring sufficient proof that there was a reasonable explanation or excuse for the extreme emotional disturbance; and (2) a subjective element requiring sufficient proof that the conduct was influenced by an extreme emotional disturbance at the time the alleged crime was committed.[84] The defense is limited to the homicide context; it is unavailable for other crimes such as assault or battery.[85]

The most common application of the extreme emotional disturbance test is in "near-miss insanity cases"—cases in which the defendant exhibits some mental illness, such as a personality disorder, that does not rise to the level of being a "mental disease or defect" that qualifies for asserting a full insanity defense (Chapter 14).[86] But as some critics have argued, the extreme emotional disturbance test has been used by some defendants to escape murder liability for killings that perpetuate outdated notions toward women, LGBTQ people, or persons from different cultures.[87] For example, in a study of reported EED cases over a fifteen-year period, Professor Victoria Nourse found that juries were permitted to consider EED evidence in many cases in which the victim had been killed by a former intimate partner because the victim left the relationship under circumstances devoid of evidence of adultery or infidelity.[88]

In *State v. Martinez*, the defendant's former boyfriend had seen her "dancing with another man," two weeks before the killing and the jury was instructed that it could return a manslaughter verdict based on EED. In *People v. Wood*, the

> defendant's theory was that the victim had "turned her back" on him after sex and the jury was instructed that it could return an EED manslaughter verdict.[89]

In another study on EED, the researchers concluded that the defense was far more likely to be successful in cases in which the defendant acted out of fear of harm than out of anger or rage.[90] Although the successful defendants in that study often suffered from some mental disorder that did not rise to the level of legal insanity, some of the cases in which EED was successfully asserted still evidence bias or prejudice, such as the case of "Defendant S1" in the study, a twenty-one-year-old male who had previously been sexually abused by a camp counselor and had been shot during a robbery within a year of the incident. While in the park, the victim approached the defendant and offered him money in exchange for sex. The defendant "became agitated, shouted invectives at the victim, and told him to leave."[91] He then left the park, had a beer, and then returned to the park whereupon the victim propositioned him again. A "scuffle ensured" which led the defendant to shoot and kill the victim. "The defense psychiatric examiner stated that the defendant was suffering from depression and was in a homosexual panic at the time of the incident. The prosecutor, who did not retain an expert, accepted a manslaughter conviction by plea."[92]

A similar version of this defense strategy has been deployed against transgender victims. In such a "trans panic" defense, the almost inevitably male defendant argues that he engaged in sexual relations believing the victim was a biological woman. Upon discovering the partner is transgender, the defendant argues he was provoked to an uncontrollable heat of passion to the point of killing. Critics of using EED in this manner note that even of this somehow constituted "sexual misrepresentation," panic defenses should not be permitted to form the basis of legally adequate provocation because the criminal law does not condone violent retribution for misrepresentations or deceits of any other kind.[93]

Involuntary Manslaughter

Involuntary manslaughter is the unintended killing of another human being. Accordingly, specific intent to kill never exists for this crime; rather, involuntary manslaughter punishes reckless or grossly negligent acts that unintentionally cause a victim's death.

RECKLESSNESS

There are at least three types of homicides in which the victim's death was unintentional: depraved heart murder, involuntary manslaughter, and criminally negligent homicide. The actor's *mens rea* differentiates between these three levels of homicide liability. As previously discussed, if the defendant acted so grossly recklessly such that the conduct manifests and extreme indifference to the value of human life, then the defendant can be held liable for murder in the second degree under the depraved heart murder rule. But if the person's acts were reckless (rather than grossly reckless), then the crime is involuntary manslaughter.[94] In other words, if the defendant consciously disregarded a known risk of death or serious bodily injury that did not rise to the level of an extreme disregard for the value of human life, then the *mens rea* requirement for involuntary manslaughter is satisfied as illustrated by the next case.

Consider two cases from Massachusetts. In *Commonwealth v. Twitchell*, a married couple were convicted of involuntary manslaughter in connection with their two-year-old son.[95] Their child suffered from a perforated bowel that could have been surgically corrected, but the Twitchells were practicing Christian Scientists who believed "in healing by spiritual treatment."[96] The court began its analysis of the case by quoting from a prior case that had upheld a manslaughter conviction of a parent who had "made no effort to obtain medical help, knowing that her child was gravely ill."[97] The court held that the failure to provide for the child's serious medical needs constitutes an *actus reus* by omission. That same logic might have applied to the Twitchells if had they not relied on a church publication that quoted a state law which provided, "A child shall not be deemed to be neglected or lack proper physical care for the sole reason that he is being provided remedial treatment by spiritual means alone in accordance with the tenets and practice of a recognized church or religious denomination by a duly accredited practitioner thereof."[98] The publication also relied heavily on a state attorney general's opinion that expressed the view that the law in question precluded criminal liability as a negligent parent for failing to provide medical care because of religious beliefs. The court ruled that the although the "spiritual treatment provision protects against criminal charges of neglect," it did not extend to the higher *mens rea* level of recklessness. Thus, when a parent consciously disregards a serious risk of death by failing to obtain proper medical care for a child in obvious need of it, a manslaughter conviction would be proper. Nonetheless, the court ordered a new trial for the Twitchells on the grounds they lacked proper notice and warning about the meaning of the spiritual healing provision in Massachusetts law since the state attorney general's had issued a flawed interpretation of the law.[99]

In *Commonwealth v. Welansky*,[100] the defendant operated a nightclub. He ordered his employees to block or lock all of the fire doors to the club so customers could not leave without paying. One night, a match ignited flammable decorations in the club, starting a fire. Many patrons were killed since they could not escape through the fire doors. The defendant's conviction for involuntary manslaughter was upheld on appeal because his conduct was deemed to be reckless in light of the substantial likelihood of resulting harm.

GROSS NEGLIGENCE

In addition to acts of criminal recklessness, acts of *gross negligence*—an objective standard—also qualify for involuntary manslaughter liability. As with recklessness and gross recklessness, the difference between negligence and gross negligence is one of degree, not one of kind. Gross negligence is present when actor fails to perceive a real and substantial risk to human life, but the ordinary, reasonable, prudent person would have perceived such a risk.[101] The classic example is when someone mishandles an inherently dangerous instrumentality, such as a gun or other deadly weapon, and, through such negligent handling, inadvertently kills another.[102] When such grossly negligent acts unintentionally causes the death of another human being, an involuntary manslaughter conviction is proper.[103]

Criminally Negligent Homicide

In contrast to acts of gross negligence, if someone is merely criminally negligent, then the requisite *mens rea* involuntary manslaughter is not met. Such acts are the realm of another homicide crime called **criminally negligent homicide**, a catch-all type of homicide offense does not exist in all US jurisdictions. A person commits criminally negligent homicide when he or she, acting with criminal negligence, causes the death of another person.[104] In this context, criminal negligence means something more than civil negligence, which is concerned with carelessness. In contrast, criminal negligence concerns situations in which a person "fails to perceive the substantial and unjustifiable risk that his or her conduct will cause another's death. Such failure to perceive must be a gross deviation from the standard of care that a reasonable person would observe."[105]

Vehicular Manslaughter

Involuntary manslaughter or criminally negligent homicide are often the crimes with which people are charged when someone dies in a car accident that involves conduct beyond mere carelessness. Of course, by definition, a car accident is just that—an accident; no intent to kill is present. But whether there will be homicide liability for a car accident depends upon the level of *mens rea* entertained by an at-fault driver. If the driver had been grossly reckless (e.g., drag racing), a conviction for murder in the second degree would be proper. If the driver had been reckless (e.g., excessively speeding, weaving, tail-gaiting, driving at night without headlights, driving while so tired that the operator fell asleep), then an involuntary manslaughter conviction would be proper. If the driver had been criminally negligent (e.g., running a red light that the driver did not see because he or she was not paying proper attention), then the law might deem that a criminal negligent homicide, although since a motor vehicle is an inherently dangerous instrumentality, such conduct might be deemed grossly negligent; but juries sometimes disagreed. Prosecutors often faced uphill battles equating motor vehicles to other deadline weapons when trying to convince "juries that someone who kills another with a motor vehicle is as criminally responsible as someone firing a gun or using a knife."[106]

Similarly, prosecutors using tradition homicide laws face daunting tasks when trying to convince a jury that a particular level of impairment should qualify for a particular level of homicide liability. For instance, juries might decide that lower levels of intoxication translate into lower levels of *mens rea* and higher levels of intoxication into higher level of *mens rea*. Is someone involved in a fatal car accident while "under the influence" but not "legally intoxicated" criminally negligent or reckless? Is someone driving with a blood alcohol concentration two or three times the legal limit grossly reckless? To address they gray areas, some states passed special laws to cover deaths that occur while driving called **vehicular manslaughter** (or vehicular homicide) laws. Although some statutes define vehicular homicide as the unintentional death of a human being caused by operating a vehicle or vessel in a reckless manner (simply a variation on involuntary manslaughter, which does not solve the ambiguities previously mentioned), other states passed vehicular manslaughter laws with driver impairment as an element of the offense.

Most vehicular homicide statutes limit the jury's role to determining the following:

- Whether the defendant was operating a motor vehicle on a public way while impaired by alcohol or other drugs;
- Whether the defendant's impairment was the proximate cause of the victim's death; and
- Whether the defendant was otherwise negligent or reckless in the operation of the motor vehicle beyond being impaired.

Juries in strict-liability jurisdictions need not determine the last factor. Some other jurisdictions hold that impaired driving alone is reckless or negligent enough and do not require a separate showing of the defendant's general intent mental state. In those jurisdictions that do require a separate showing, acts of recklessness or negligence are usually: driving on the wrong side of the road, driving at unsafe speeds, or ignoring traffic signals.[107]

Unlawful Act Manslaughter

Although this crime is disappearing today, approximately half of the states have an **unlawful act manslaughter** law (sometimes called misdemeanor manslaughter). These laws are similar to felony murder laws insofar as they impose homicide liability on an actor who unintentionally causes the death of another human being during the commission of an unlawful act. Recall that felony murder liability is predicated on the underlying act being an inherently dangerous felony. Those unlawful acts that do not qualify—namely misdemeanors and felonies that are not inherently dangerous—can be the basis of unlawful act manslaughter liability.[108] But because manslaughter—even unlawful act manslaughter—is considered to be a *malum in se* crime, the underlying unlawful act must not be one of strict liability for the doctrine of transferred intent to work as illustrated by *People v. Stuart*[109] (Chapter 4). Put differently, here must be some criminal *mens rea* for the underlying unlawful act, even if only criminal negligence.[110]

SUICIDE

Criminal law was developed at a time when medicine was not able to keep people alive via artificial means. As science has progressed, the criminal law has also had to adapt. Courts are hesitant to step into this arena, though, often finding it the realm of legislatures. With the exception a very small minority of jurisdictions, nearly all states have clung to the common-law tradition that suicide, assisted suicide, and active euthanasia are all criminal offenses.

At common law, **suicide**—the intentional killing of oneself—was a crime. Of course, if successful, the defendant was dead, so one might think it was a crime only in theory. But actually, the trial for the crime could go forward against the defendant *in absentia*. If convicted, the decedent's estate could be forfeited to the crown. The logic underlying such a law was that one of the King's taxpayers, who should be alive and paying taxes, no longer was. Suicide laws allowed the crown to collect monies from those who ended their own lives prematurely as a penalty for have "cheated" the crown out of the taxed that would have been paid until the decedent had died a natural death.[111]

Today, no US state has a statute criminalizing suicide;[112] however, it apparently "is still a common law crime in Virginia, Rhode Island, and, possibly, Illinois."[113] In contrast, nearly all US states criminally prohibit assisting someone commit suicide, even if such assistance is provided out of a sense of compassion to ease the suffering of a terminally ill person. Such conduct is often referred to as **euthanasia**, although for criminal and constitutional law purposes, that term needs to be differentiated into active and passive forms.

Passive euthanasia is legal in the United States. It is defined as the withdrawal of medical aid and/or treatment such that nature can take its course. Living wills and durable healthcare powers of attorney are documents designed to ensure that someone's constitutional right to refuse medical treatment is honored.[114] In contrast, *active euthanasia*, or mercy killing, is illegal in the United States. The rule is clear: one who intentionally kills another, even if their purpose is to end suffering, is guilty of murder. However, active euthanasia, when performed by a licensed physician under limited circumstances, has been legalized in a handful of US states. In 1994, Oregon enacted the "Oregon Death with Dignity Act," which permits physician-assisted suicide for terminally ill patients under a narrow and specific set of conditions.[115] In 2008, the state of Washington passed a virtually identical law.[116] Since that time, California, Vermont, and the District of Columbia enacted physician-assisted suicide laws,[117] and Montana has partially legalized the practice by judicial decision.[118] Colorado voters adopted such a law by referendum in 2016. In the forty-five other US states, physician-assisted suicide can be criminally prosecuted like any other form of active euthanasia.

Although there is a distinction made between actively killing and passively allowing someone to die, some critics have argued the difference is one that asserts form over substance. At least two US Circuit Courts of Appeals thought so when they declared there to be a constitutional right to commit suicide, one under a right to privacy analysis, the other under an equal protection analysis. The Michigan Supreme Court in *People v. Kevorkian* disagreed.[119] In 1997, the US Supreme Court resolved these conflicting rulings in *Washington v. Glucksberg*[120] and *Vacco v. Quill*[121] in which the Court held that neither then due process nor equal protection provides a constitutional right to commit suicide.

HOMICIDE UNDER THE MODEL PENAL CODE

The Model Penal Code "replaced the common law's multitude of homicide offenses" with a *mens rea* approach.[122] Section 210.1 defines "criminal homicide" as "purposely, knowingly, recklessly, or negligently caus[ing] the death of another human being."[123] The Code then defines three grades of homicide:

1. *murder* requires purpose, knowledge, or gross recklessness, thereby incorporating common-law murder in the first and second degrees, including depraved heart murder;[124]
2. *manslaughter* requires recklessness or an extreme emotional disturbance that mitigates an intentional killing, thereby incorporating common-law involuntary manslaughter and expanding common-law voluntary manslaughter beyond the narrow confines of a killing in the heat of passion upon legally adequate provocation;[125] and
3. criminally negligent homicide requires negligence.[126]

Note that the Model Penal Code does not reference *malice* nor does it differentiate between degrees of murder or manslaughter. Although a minority of US jurisdictions have adopted the Model Penal Code's approach to homicide, many have rejected this particular part of the Code and continue to use the common law's approach to distinguish between degrees of murder and manslaughter or some variation of them. Minnesota's statutory scheme provides a good example of this, as the "Statutory Analysis Exercise" contained in Box 7.3 illustrates.

The Model Penal Code also attempted to abolish strict liability felony murder. In lieu of it, the Model Penal Code includes felony murder within its definition of the crime of murder, but requires recklessness that evidences a depraved heart:

> Such recklessness and indifference are presumed if the actor is engaged or is an accomplice in the commission of, or an attempt to commit, or flight after committing or attempting to commit robbery, rape or deviate sexual intercourse by force or threat of force, arson, burglary, kidnapping or felonious escape.[127]

BOX 7.3

STATUTORY ANALYSIS EXERCISE

Which Acts Constitute Different Levels of Murder?

Minnesota law specifies three degrees of murder.

- Murder in the first degree encompasses premeditated killings; unintentional deaths during the commission or attempted commission of sexual assaults; intentional deaths caused during the commission or attempted commission of enumerated inherently dangerous felonies; intentional deaths a class of victims that include peace officers, judges, prosecutors, and victims of domestic abuse victims; and grossly reckless deaths that occur attendant to acts of terrorism.[135]
- Murder in the second degree encompasses intentional deaths committed without premeditation (mirroring the common law); intentional deaths committed during drive-by shootings; unintentional deaths caused during the commission or attempted commission of enumerated inherently dangerous felonies (somewhat mirroring common-law felony murder); and unintentional deaths caused as a result of intentionally inflicting or attempting to inflict bodily harm upon the victim (mirroring the common law).[136]
- Murder in the third degree encompasses unintentional deaths caused "by perpetrating an act eminently dangerous to others and evincing a depraved mind, without regard for human life" (mirroring common-law depraved heart murder); and unintentional deaths proximately caused by "unlawfully selling, giving away, bartering, delivering, exchanging, distributing, or administering" certain controlled substances.[137]

Based on these definitions, what degrees of murder would be appropriate under the following circumstances?

1. After drinking several alcoholic beverages, a person operates a snowmobile at nearly 60 miles per hour on a lake where people are ice fishing. While doing so, the person strikes and kills an eight-year-old child and injures the child's father.[138]
2. A defendant and his accomplice go to an apartment to rob the person living there. During the robbery, the defendant hands the accomplice a loaded pistol. Within minutes, the victim tackles the accomplice and the accomplice shoot and kills the victim as the victim tried to escape.[139]
3. By selling heroin to someone who then shoots up and dies of an overdose.[140]

4. A defendant drives to his attorney's office armed with a handgun. Upon arriving, he climbs a set of stairs, enters the office, asks a clerk a question, and dissatisfied with the response, shoots the clerk five times in the chest at close range. Before leaving, he then shoots the clerk three more times, leaving the clerk to bleed to death.[141]
5. The defendant kills a women who tried to blackmail him. He leaves the victim's body in her apartment along with the victim's fourteen-month-old baby. He returns to the apartment one or more times to remove evidence that might inculpate him and to feed the child. After the smell from the decomposition became too pungent, instead of feeding the child, putting her in the hallway, or leaving the door open, he decides to lock the apartment door with the child inside and not go back because of fear of arrest. The child dies of starvation. What level of homicide did he commit with regard to the baby?[142]

Some states, like Delaware, adopted an approach to felony murder that combines some facets of both the common law and the Model Penal Code. The Delaware Code provides that a person is guilty of murder in the second degree when, "[w]hile engaged in the commission of, or attempt to commit, or flight after committing or attempting to commit any felony, the person, with criminal negligence, causes the death of another person."[128] Note that this formulation follows the Model Penal Code's recommendation to eliminate strict liability felony murder, but rejects the Code's approach to the *mens rea* requirement for felony murder by presuming gross recklessness. Instead, Delaware imposes felony murder liability for any negligent killing during the commission of any felony.

In short, it is clear that homicide liability today depends the specific statutory language used in each state's criminal code. Although some statutory provisions concerning homicide offenses have been influenced by the Model Penal Code, the common law's long history of differentiating different types of murders and manslaughters is alive and well. Thus, it is important to be able to distinguish the various approaches to homicides. Table 7.1 presents a summary of the major forms of homicide under the common law, much of which remains viable today in many US states.

Table 7.1 Elements of the Major Homicide Offenses

Crime	*Actus Reus*	*Mens Rea*	Result	Attendant Circumstances
Murder in the First Degree	Any act or qualifying omission that kills another person	Malice aforethought—purpose or knowledge (i.e., specific intent to kill or specific intent to cause serious bodily harm)	Death of a human being	Any statutorily authorized aggravating factor, such as premeditation, a victim under a certain age, or a victim who was a law enforcement officer
Murder in the Second Degree	Any act or qualifying omission that kills another person	Malice aforethought—purpose or knowledge (i.e., specific intent to kill or specific intent to cause serious bodily harm)	Death of a human being	None
Depraved Heart Murder (another form of Murder in the Second Degree)	Any act or qualifying omission that kills another person	Gross recklessness (i.e., conscious disregard of a known risk of death or serious bodily harm of such severity that it manifests an extreme indifference to the value of human life)	Death of a human being	Conduct must manifest an extreme indifference to the value of human life
Voluntary Manslaughter	Any act or qualifying omission that kills another person	Purpose or Knowledge (i.e., specific intent to kill or cause serious bodily harm)	Death of a human being	Killing must have taken place in the heat of passion prompted by legally adequate provocation; under an extreme emotional disturbance; or under conditions constituting imperfect self-defense

Continued

Table 7.1 Continued

Crime	*Actus Reus*	*Mens Rea*	Result	Attendant Circumstances
Involuntary Manslaughter	Any act or qualifying omission that kills another person	Recklessness (i.e., conscious disregard of a known risk of death or serious bodily harm) or gross negligence (i.e., negligence with a deadly weapon)	Death of a human being	None
Felony Murder	Commission of a qualifying felony that kills another person	Whatever the *mens rea* is for the underlying felony (due to the doctrine of transferred intent)	Death of a human being	(1) Underlying felony must be inherently dangerous; (2) death must occur during the commission or attempted commission of the felony, or during immediate flight therefrom; (3) victim may be limited to innocent third parties; (4) killing may be limited to those in furtherance of the underlying felony
Unlawful Act Manslaughter	Commission of a qualifying unlawful act that kills another person	Whatever the *mens rea* is for the underlying unlawful act (due to the doctrine of transferred intent)	Death of a human being	(1) Underlying unlawful act must be a *malum in se* misdemeanor or a *malum in se* felony that is not inherently dangerous; (2) death must occur during the commission or attempted commission of the unlawful act, or during immediate flight therefrom
Criminally Negligent Homicide	Any act or qualifying omission that kills another person	Negligence (i.e., failure to perceive a risk of death or serious bodily harm that an ordinary, reasonable, prudent person would have perceived)	Death of a human being	None

Table 7.1 Continued

Crime	*Actus Reus*	*Mens Rea*	Result	Attendant Circumstances
Vehicular Manslaughter	Any act or qualifying omission that kills another person	Recklessness (i.e., conscious disregard of a known risk of death or serious bodily harm) or negligence (i.e., failure to perceive a risk of death or serious bodily harm that an ordinary, reasonable, prudent person would have perceived); in some jurisdictions, this is a strict liability offense (i.e., no *mens rea* need be proven)	Death of a human being	*Actus reus* must occurs as a result of the actor operating a motor vehicle either while impaired from alcohol or drugs or, in the absence of any impairment, from the reckless or criminally negligent operation of a motor vehicle
Suicide	Any act that kills oneself	Purpose or Knowledge (i.e., specific intent to kill or cause serious bodily harm)	Death of oneself	None
Assisting Suicide	Causing, aiding, or otherwise assisting another person to commit or attempt to commit suicide	Purpose or Knowledge (i.e., specific intent to cause another person to commit or attempt to commit suicide)	Death of the human being aided or assisted	None

CONCLUSION

Learning Objectives	Summaries
1. Define the *corpus delicti* of all forms of criminal homicide.	The *corpus delicti* of all homicide offenses involve proving that some unlawful act caused the death of a human being. Some corroboratory evidence beyond the statements of the accused is usually necessary to prove *corpus delicti*.
2. Differentiate between the different types of murder.	Murder involves killing with malice aforethought, which can take several forms: purposeful or knowingly killing with or without premeditation; unintentionally killing that results from purposeful or knowing actions that were intended to cause serious bodily harm but actually caused death; unintentional killing that result from grossly reckless conduct that manifests an extreme indifference to the value of human life; or unintentional deaths of innocent third parties that result from the natural and probable consequences of committing, attempting to commit, or immediately fleeing from the commission of an inherently dangerous felony.

Learning Objectives	Summaries
3. Distinguish between the different types of manslaughter and criminally negligent homicide.	Voluntary manslaughter is homicide in which an actor entertains specific intent to kill, but that intent is formed under mitigating circumstances, such as during acts of imperfect self-defense, acts committed in the heat of passion upon legally adequate provocation, or during an extreme emotional disturbance. Involuntary manslaughter occurs when reckless or grossly negligent acts unintentionally cause a victim's death. Vehicular manslaughter occurs when an unintentional death is caused by operating a vehicle or vessel in a reckless or negligent manner or while impaired.
4. Explain how the law attempts to deter suicide and assisted suicide.	Suicide is a killing oneself. It used to be a crime, but today is not in most jurisdictions. Assisting someone commit suicide, however, is a crime in most US states. One who intentionally kills another in act of active euthanasia, even if their purpose is to end suffering, is guilty of murder. By contrast, passive euthanasia—the refusal or withdrawal of medical aid and/or treatment—is legal in the United States.
5. Summarize the Model Penal Code's attempts at reforming common-law approaches to homicides.	The Model Penal Code streamlined homicide offenses using a *mens rea* approach. It defines homicide as "purposely, knowingly, recklessly, or negligently caus[ing] the death of another human being." Murder involves purpose, knowledge, or gross recklessness; manslaughter requires recklessness or an extreme emotional disturbance that mitigates an intentional killing; and criminally negligent homicide requires negligence. The Model Penal Code also replaced strict liability felony murder by requiring recklessness that evidences a depraved heart for felony murder liability.

KEY TERMS

born alive rule
brain death
corpus delicti
corpus delicti rule
criminally negligent homicide
CSI effect
depraved heart murder
euthanasia
extreme emotional disturbance
felony murder
heat of passion
imperfect self-defense
involuntary manslaughter
killing
legally adequate provocation
malice aforethought
manslaughter
merger rule
murder
premeditation
suicide
unlawful act manslaughter
vehicular manslaughter
voluntary manslaughter
year-and-a-day rule

8

Rape and Nonconsensual Sex Crimes

LEARNING OBJECTIVES

1. Define the *actus reus* and attendant circumstances of rape under the common law.

2. Discuss how the *actus reus* and attendant circumstances of rape evolved from their common-law definitions to their modern-day counterparts.

3. Analyze the varying approaches to the *mens rea* element for the crime of rape.

4. Discuss the varying degrees of sexual assault and sexual battery.

5. Differentiate child molestation from statutory rape.

6. Distinguish the ways in which the knowing transmission of a sexually transmitted infection may subject someone to criminal liability.

Outline

INTRODUCTION

According to the National Crime Victimization Survey administered by the US Department of Justice, approximately 300,000 rapes and sexual assaults of US residents age twelve or older occur each year, only about 35 percent of which are ever reported to the police.[1] To put that in context, a sexual assault occurs nearly every two minutes in the United States.

The US Centers for Disease Control and Prevention (CDC) reports that nearly 20 percent of US women and 1.7 percent of US men are raped in their lifetime.[2] These victimizations are not evenly distributed across sexual orientations and gender identities. "Approximately 1 in 8 lesbian women (13.1 percent), nearly half of bisexual women (46.1 percent), and 1 in 6 heterosexual women (17.4 percent) have been raped in their lifetime."[3] The distribution of male rapes across sexual orientations is too unreliable for the CDC to report, although the CDC reports that roughly "4 out of 10 gay men (40.2 percent), half of bisexual men (47.4 percent), and 1 in 5 heterosexual men (20.8 percent) in the United States have experienced sexual violence other than rape at some point in their lives."[4] And a shocking high 47 percent of all transgender people are sexually assaulted in their lifetimes, with transgender people of color representing the highest percentages of victims.[5]

Regardless of the sex or sexual orientation of the victim, it should be noted that statistics concerning sexual victimization underestimate the number of rapes that occur each year due to underreporting to the police, irregular reporting practices by police, and the methodological shortcomings of self-report survey data concerning sexual victimization.[6]

Sexual assaults represent a particularly traumatic type of criminal victimization.

> These crimes are devastating, extending beyond the initial victimization to such consequences as unwanted pregnancy, sexually transmitted infections, post-traumatic stress disorder, depression, flashbacks, sleep disorders, eating disorders, post-incident substance abuse, self-harm, and even suicide. The effects are often long lasting and can lead to health and work productivity issues for years. Using analyses from three different studies of the cost of crime, Heaton . . . estimated that the victim-related costs for nonlethal rape and sexual assault are between $150,000 and $283,626 per victim.[7]

Nonreporting rates by lesbian, gay, bisexual, transgender victims of sexual violence are particularly low because distrust of resources that are supposed to help victims, including police and personnel who work at hospitals, shelters, and crisis centers.[8]

This chapter explores the history of the offense of rape and its evolution into modern-day statutes governing sexual assaults and related crimes.

RAPE AT COMMON LAW

The common-law crime of **rape** was defined as "the unlawful carnal knowledge of a woman by a man who is not her husband, without her effective consent."[9] The terms used in this definition of rape require explication.

Necessary Parties

The common law's restrictive attendant circumstances for the crime of rape limited its reach such that "only a female could be the victim of a rape and only a male could be the perpetrator."[10] Moreover, the concept of marital rape was not recognized by the common law.[11] In his treatise *History of the Pleas of the Crown*, Sir Matthew Hale said: "A husband cannot be guilty of a rape committed by himself upon his lawful wife, for by their mutual matrimonial consent and contract the wife hath given up herself in this kind unto her husband, which she cannot retract."[12] In other words, by the nature of the marital contract as understood in an era when a wife was viewed as her husband's property, sexual intercourse between husband and wife was always lawful, even if the husband used force or violence to accomplish it.[13]

Vaginal Penetration

Over time, the *actus reus* element of *unlawful carnal knowledge* came to be defined as forcible penetration, however slight, of a woman's vagina by a man's penis.[14] The inclusion of the qualifier "however slight" meant that that penile penetration from the opening of the vulva to the cervix of the uterus was unnecessary. Rather, even partial penetration of the labia was sufficient to constitute the *actus reus* of rape.[15] Once a nonconsensual penile penetration of the vagina occurred, however slight, the *actus reus* for the crime of rape was complete; ejaculation was not necessary.[16]

Because the common law limited the definition of rape to a vaginal penetration by a penis, other types of nonconsensual sex, such as oral or anal penetrations, fell outside the definition of rape. But such acts were still criminally punished as other crimes, such as *forcible sodomy*.[17]

Without Effective Consent: Force and Resistance

Neither force nor threats of force were technically required as part of *actus reus* for the common-law crime of rape.[18] Rather, the law merely required that the penetration be without the effective consent of the victim. But proving nonconsent in the absence of force-induced physical injuries was nearly almost always difficult. In fact, women's allegations of rape were viewed with such suspicion that Hale, wrote: "Rape is . . . an accusation easily to be made and hard to be proved, and harder to be defended by the party accused, tho never so innocent."[19] As a result, the common law evolved over time such that, by the end of the 1600s, the nonconsent of the victim came to be interpreted as requiring proof of force as either part of the *actus reus* for rape or an attendant circumstance to the crime.[20]

Threats of force were included in the definition of "force" for the purposes of proving nonconsent, but "claims of threatened use of force were rarely persuasive."[21] This in turn gave rise to the common-law requirement that the victim of a rape needed to resist "to the utmost" to provide physical evidence of her nonconsent. The *resistance to the utmost* standard effectively required a woman to be physically brutalized while being sexually brutalized. Bishop explained the standard by quoting a nineteenth-century appellate judge as follows: "The resistance must be up to the point of being overpowered by actual force, or of inability, from loss of strength, longer to resist, or, from the number of persons attacking, resistance must be dangerous or absolutely useless, or there must be dread or fear of death."[22] As a result, medical evidence of forcible penetration, documented injuries caused by violence, or proof of venereal infection linked to the accused became the hallmarks of evidence proof of rape under the common law.[23] But nineteenth-century medicine was often complicit in protecting men by perpetuating the belief that "absent extraordinary force and violence, it was impossible to commit a rape upon a grown woman who had full possession of her faculties."[24]

The utmost resistance requirement almost always produced one of two unacceptable outcomes. Either the requirement proved to be "an invitation to danger of death or serious bodily harm" to the woman[25] or it provided a rapist with a defense to his crime. Consider the case of *Brown v. State*.[26] The victim in the case was a sixteen-year-old who was attacked by her neighbor. At trial, she testified: "I tried as hard as I could to get away. I was trying all the time to get away just as hard as I could. I was trying to get up; I pulled at the grass; I screamed as hard as I could, and he told me to shut up, and I didn't, and then he held his hand on my mouth until I was almost strangled."[27] Although the jury convicted the defendant, that conviction was overturned because the appellate court found that the victim had not resisted the attack to her utmost ability. In so ruling, the court reasoned that "[n]ot only must there be entire absence of mental consent or assent, but there must be the most vehement exercise of every physical means or faculty within the woman's power to resist the penetration of her person, and this must be shown to persist until the offense is consummated."[28]

It is important to note that rape was the only crime that "required the victim to resist physically in order to establish nonconsent."[29] In contrast, other crimes that included a lack of consent as an element, like robbery," did not require an examination of how the victim resisted. "It simply inquires whether the accused took something from another person by violence or intimidation."[30]

MODERN RAPE LAW

Starting in the 1960s, activists began to challenge much of the outdated reasoning behind the common-law definition of rape.[31] Regretfully, the drafters of the Model Penal Code failed to address their concerns, as the Code retains the notion that only a male could rape a female who is not his wife.[32] Indeed, the American Law Institute itself recognized that its provisions on rape are "outdated and no longer a reliable guide for legislatures and courts."[33] Nonetheless, advocacy efforts led to reform of rape laws in every US state by the mid-1980s.[34] Although a handful of states, continue to define rape using the common law's approach to the crime,[35] nearly all US jurisdictions changed the statutory definition of rape to some variation of "a sexual intercourse accomplished without the consent of the victim."[36] This change in terminology reflects several important developments in the law of rape.

Sexual Intercourse

By eliminating the phrase "unlawful carnal knowledge of a woman" and replacing it with the broader term of nonconsensual "sexual intercourse," legislatures expanded the definition of rape beyond nonconsensual vaginal penetrations. Thus, under most modern rape laws, any nonconsensual penetration of the vagina, mouth, or anus constitutes rape (although some states have separate offenses for acts of forcible sodomy).[37]

Moreover, in most states today, a nonconsensual penetration need not be by a penis to qualify as a rape. The crime now includes nonconsensual cunnilingus, fellatio, anal intercourse, digital penetration, or the insertion of a foreign object into the genital or anal opening of another person.[38] Importantly, because both males and females can commit such acts, this broader definition recognizes that any person, regardless the person's biological sex or gender expression, may be a perpetrator or a victim of rape.[39]

A few US jurisdictions, however, continue to define the crime of rape as the penetration of the vagina by a penis. Some of those jurisdictions have separate statutes to cover the forcible rape of a male by another male, or of a female by another female, called *homosexual rape* or *aggravated sodomy* laws.

Spousal Exemption

Many modern rape laws have eliminated, either wholly or in part, the spousal exemption to rape in recognition of the sad reality that spousal rapes do occur. Accordingly, a husband who sexually assaults his wife can now be criminally prosecuted for rape in most US jurisdictions.[40] But the approaches to marital rape taken by US states vary greatly, ranging from criminalizing "a narrower range of offenses if committed within marriage," to subjecting marital rape "to less serious sanctions," and/or creating "special procedural hurdles for marital rape prosecutions."[41] In sum, as one critic has put it, the "current state of the law represents a confusing mix of victory and defeat for the exemption's contemporary feminist critics."[42]

Nonconsent, Force, and Resistance

The requirement of resistance to the utmost has been eliminated in all US jurisdictions.[43]

Accordingly, under the modern law of rape, a victim no longer has to fight back to the utmost, thereby subjecting the victim to further brutalization. However, proof of the victim's lack of consent remains the key element in a rape prosecution.

Shifting the focus from the victim's level of resistance to the victim's lack of consent has not produced any uniform rules on what is required to prove rape. Some jurisdictions continue to require that the victim undertook "some resistance"—defined as whatever resistance is appropriate under the circumstances.[44] In sharp contrast, other some states do not require any resistance at all; simply saying "no" is technically sufficient.[45] But because forcible compulsion remains an element of rape in nearly all US jurisdictions,[46] the removal of any formal resistance requirement may be form over substance, producing an illusory removal of the resistance requirement.[47] Courts usually "insist on something more than the movements that are customary in sex. Thus, most jurisdictions, in effect, require 'reasonable' resistance."[48] A prosecutor interviewed by Horney and Spohn explained why this is: "Juries still expect some resistance or some explanation as to why there was none. This is especially true if it was a date gone sour; if we can't show some resistance in this case we're in a lot of trouble."[49] This approach, however, is flawed for the following reason:

> All intercourse, or at least all unwanted intercourse, can be thought of as forcible, because penetration requires some force. As Professor Robin West puts it, "unwanted, undesired penetration of a woman who has expressed a refusal, by a man who then ignores her refusal, is a violent act. It is a physical intrusion of one's body, it causes pain . . . ." Why doesn't that amount to "force"?[50]

Recognizing this, a few courts have held that the minimal force necessary to accomplish an act of sexual penetration is sufficient for rape liability, even in the absence of any resistance by the alleged victim.[51] But this represents the minority view. The "overwhelming majority of jurisdictions in this country continue to require proof of both force and lack of consent to support a rape conviction."[52] The following case illustrates how courts struggle with factual findings regarding lack of consent.

STATE of Connecticut
v.
Richard T. SMITH.
554 A.2d 713 (Conn. 1989).

* * *

[T]he victim, T, a twenty-six-year-old woman, and her girlfriend, A, a visitor from Idaho, went to a bar in West Haven. T was introduced by a friend to the defendant, who bought her a drink. The defendant invited her and A, together with a male acquaintance A had met at the bar, to dinner at a restaurant across the street. After dinner, the defendant having paid for T's share, the four left the restaurant. The defendant proposed that they all go to his apartment in West Haven. Because A's acquaintance had a motorcycle, the defendant gave them directions to the apartment so that they could ride there, while he and T walked.

After a twenty-minute walk, the defendant and T arrived at the apartment at about 10:00 p.m. A and her acquaintance were not there and never arrived at the apartment. When T and the defendant had entered the apartment, they sat on the couch in the living room to watch television. After a while the defendant put his arm around T and told her he wanted a kiss. She gave him a kiss. She testified that "He wouldn't back off. He wouldn't let go of me. So I said, look, I am not kidding. I really don't want to do anything. I don't know you and whatnot." The defendant still held onto T. She testified that he was "still right in my face wanting to kiss me. You know, saying so, saying that you don't think I paid for dinner for nothing, do you."

T testified that she was scared: "At first I didn't know what to do. I did spit in his face and he didn't even take it seriously. Then I tried kicking him off, which was to no avail. He was way too big for me." T described the defendant as "at least six foot two" and "at least two hundred pounds." She testified: "He told me he could make it hard on me or I could make it easy on myself, which I finally decided was probably my best bet." T understood that the defendant was determined to "have sex" with her and that either he would hurt her or she "was going to go along with it." At the point where T ceased resistance, she was "down on the couch" and the defendant was "on top of" her. T testified that she had informed the defendant that she had to pick up her daughter, had insulted him, and had told him that he was "a big man to have to force a woman." She testified, however, that after she decided to "give in," she tried to convince the defendant that she was not going to fight and "was going to go along with him and enjoy it."

The defendant removed T's clothing as she remained on the couch and led her into the bedroom. When she declined his request for oral sex, he did not insist upon it, but proceeded to engage in vaginal intercourse with her. After completion of the act, the defendant said that he knew the victim felt that she had been raped, but that she could not prove it and had really enjoyed herself. After they both had dressed, the defendant requested T's telephone number, but she gave him a number she concocted as a pretense. He also offered her some sherbet, which she accepted and ate while she waited for a cab that the defendant had called. T, however, placed her pink cigarette lighter underneath the couch, so that she would be able to prove she had been in the apartment. When the cab arrived, she left the apartment.

She told the cab driver to take her to the police station because she had been raped. At the station she gave her account of the event to the police. The defendant was arrested. The police found T's lighter under the couch in his living room, where T had informed them it was located.

* * *

The defendant . . . urges that we adopt a construction of § 53a-70 making the mental state of the defendant the touchstone for the resolution of the issue of consent when presented in a prosecution for first degree sexual assault. He refers to this mental state as . . . an awareness on the part of a man that he is forcing sex upon a woman against her will and that he intends to do so. . . .

The position advocated by the defendant that the requisite *mens rea* should be an element of the crime of sexual assault in the first degree is supported by a widely publicized decision of the British House of Lords in 1975, *Director of Public Prosecutions v. Morgan*.[53] A majority of the court held that a defendant cannot properly be convicted of rape if he in fact believed that the woman had consented, even though the basis for his belief may not have been reasonable. . . .

* * *

While the word "consent" is commonly regarded as referring to the state of mind of the complainant in a sexual assault case, it cannot be viewed as a wholly subjective concept. Although the actual state of mind of the actor in a criminal case may in many instances be the issue upon which culpability depends, a defendant is not chargeable with knowledge of the internal workings of the minds of others except to the extent that he should reasonably have gained such knowledge from his observations of their conduct. . . . [W]hether a complainant has consented to intercourse depends upon her manifestations of such consent as reasonably construed. If the conduct of the complainant under all the circumstances should reasonably be viewed as indicating consent to the act of intercourse, a defendant should not be found guilty because of some undisclosed mental reservation on the part of the complainant. Reasonable conduct ought not to be deemed criminal.

* * *

From our review of the evidence detailed previously, it is clear that the jury could properly have found beyond a reasonable doubt that T's words and actions could not reasonably be viewed to indicate her consent to intercourse with the defendant. According to her uncontradicted testimony, she expressly declined his advances, explaining that she did not know him and wanted to pick up her child. She spat in his face and "tried kicking him off." She "gave in" only after the defendant declared that "he could make it hard" for her if she continued to resist. This statement she could reasonably have regarded as a threat of physical injury. Only by entertaining the fantasy that "no" meant "yes," and that a display of distaste meant affection, could the defendant have believed that T's behavior toward him indicated consent. Such a distorted view of her conduct would not have been reasonable. . . .

* * *

Questions

1. Assume that this case had been tired under the common law. Do you think that victim's verbal actions along with her spitting at the defendant and her kicking him would have been sufficient to satisfy the resistance to the utmost requirement? Why or why not?
2. A minority of states allow nonconsent to be proven by the victim's testimony that he or she did not consent. But most states, as the *Smith* case illustrates, require a showing of some resistance to prove nonconsent. Which approach do you think is best? Why? In a jurisdiction that requires some resistance, how much is enough? Would you have upheld Smith's conviction if the victim had not spat on him or kicked him? Explain the reasoning underlying your response.

The defense in the *Smith* case tried to argue there was a genuine question about the victim's consent. As explained in Chapter 13, an honest and reasonable mistake of fact may constitute a defense to many crimes if the mistake negates *mens rea*. The "Statutory Analysis Exercise" in Box 8.1 explores this issue in more depth.

Other Attendant Circumstances Establishing Nonconsenting as a Matter of Law

Nearly all US states have modern rape or sexual assault laws that statutorily recognize at least three attendant circumstances that demonstrate the victim's lack of consent even in the absence of the use or threated use of force or any resistance thereto.

YOUTHFUL AGE

The youthful age of the victim is the most common of attendant circumstance establishing lack of effective consent as a matter of law. Depending on how young the victim may be, the crime may be deemed rape or child molestation (typically for prepubescent children) or statutory rape (for teenagers under the age of legal consent). Both offenses are discussed later in this chapter.

INCAPACITY

The incapacitation of the victim is another common attendant circumstance establishing nonconsent in most US states. Such incapacitation can be a function of the victim being asleep, being impaired by alcohol or drugs (either legal or illicit), or being cognitively impaired due to some mental condition that either prevents the victim from understanding the distinctively sexual nature of the conduct or impairs the victim's ability to understand or exercise the right to refuse to engage in the conduct with another.[54] Note that the Model Penal Code only recognizes intoxication as

BOX 8.1

STATUTORY ANALYSIS EXERCISE

Disentanging *Mens Rea* and Attendant Circumstances for the Crime of Rape

The *Smith* court cited the case *Director of Public Prosecutions v. Morgan*.[174] In that case, there were four defendants, all of whom were members of the Royal Air Force. One of them defendant invited the other three back to his home to have sexual intercourse with his wife. He explained to them that she would protest, but that it was all part of a fantasy he had agreed to provide for her. Thus, the men honestly believed that the wife wanted to have sex with them. They were subsequently charged with rape and acquitted on the basis that they had made honest, but unreasonable mistakes regarding the wife's consent based on her husband's lies. The case was widely criticized and led Parliament to change the law to require criminal recklessness as the *mens rea* for rape, requiring an honest and reasonable mistake to negate such *mens rea*. A majority of US states follow this same approach. But others do not. Consider the law in Massachusetts:

"Whoever has sexual intercourse . . . with a person and compels such person to submit by force and against [the person's] will, or compels such person to submit by threat of bodily injury, shall be punished by imprisonment."[175] Case law in Massachusetts establishes that although the prosecution must prove lack of consent, this statute does "not require that the defendant intend the intercourse be without consent."[176] In other words, lack of consent is an attendant circumstance in Massachusetts that does not require any *mens rea* whatsoever.

In *Commonwealth v. Lopez*, victim and the defendant went for a walk in the woods together.[177] She testified that the defendant pinned her down and raped her while she repeatedly told him "no," whereas the defendant testified that he thought the victim was a willing participant because she kissed him and never said "no."

1. What so you think the outcome of the case should be under the statute and case law in Box 8.1?
2. What approach regarding whether there was an honest and reasonable mistake regarding consent do you think is best—the majority approach that mirrors the one in England, or the approach Massachusetts and a minority of other US states take? Why?

vitiating consent if a man "has substantially impaired [a women's] power to appraise or control her conduct by administering or employing without her knowledge drugs, intoxicants or other means for the purpose of preventing resistance."[55] Most states, however, do not follow this approach. Indeed, in some states, if an actor either knows or should have known that someone is intoxicated, that suffices to establish that the victim was unable to grant effective legal consent.[56]

The flawed notion that victims are somehow responsible for someone sexually assaulting them after they have voluntarily consumed alcohol or drugs is, sadly, alive and well. Minnesota's statutory provision serves as an example: "'Mentally incapacitated' means that a person under the influence of alcohol, a narcotic, anesthetic, or any other substance, *administered to that person without the person's agreement*, lacks the judgment to give a reasoned consent to sexual contact or sexual penetration."[57] Due to this provision excluding voluntary intoxication as the basis of vitiating the ability to grant consent to sex, the Minnesota Supreme Court ruled that a twenty-four-year-old man could not be guilty of raping a twenty-year-old woman because she had consumed five shots of vodka and a prescription pill before blacking out and then awakening to find she was being sexually assaulted.[58]

DECEPTION

Some states criminalize sex as rape if consent was fraudulently induced by one of two types of deceptions: impersonation and phony medical "treatment."[59] As one might imagine, impersonation of a spouse or lover occurs infrequently; it requires sufficient similarity between the imposter and the victim's spouse or lover such that the victim consents to engaging in sexual intercourse honestly and reasonably believing that the sexual acts were being performed with his or her spouse or lover. False treatment ruses also involve fraud. In such schemes, the victim is intentionally deceived as to the nature of the act, such as when someone impersonates a physician by pretending to conduct a medical exam. Barring one of these types of frauds, most states do not otherwise criminalize sex induced by deception. Thus, the gullible should be wary in the face of false promises to marry, fake declarations of love, or untruthful representations of status ranging from being single or on birth control, to having been a war hero or an Olympic gold medalist.

There is one type of deception, whether affirmatively voiced as lie or passively made through nondisclosure, that rarely constitutes an attendant circumstance establishing nonconsent in a manner that would give rise to rape liability: failure to warn about one's known status as carrying a sexually transmitted infection (STI).[60] Instead, failure to disclose one's status as a known carrier of a potentially life-threatening STI can be prosecuted as assault, battery, reckless endangerment, and even under homicide statutes.[61] But more than thirty states have adopted separate statutory offenses to criminalize such conduct. These laws typically criminalize engaging in sexual conduct with another person (the *actus reus*) knowing (the *mens rea*) that one is positive for one or more enumerated STIs (attendant circumstance) without first disclosing his or her STI-positive status to other person prior to engaging in sexual conduct (attendant circumstance). These laws are discussed in more detail later in this chapter.

THE *MENS REA* FOR RAPE

As *State v. Smith*[62] illustrates, the *mens rea* for the crime of rape may be tied to the *actus reus* (a question of intent regarding the use of force or compulsion to achieve a sexual penetration), or the *mens rea* may be tied to the attendant circumstance that requires a lack of consent. But what level of *mens rea* did the court use in the case? The *Smith* court clearly rejected purpose or knowledge as the *mens rea* for rape, but did the court apply a recklessness or negligence standard? The difficult in answering this question illustrates one of the most confounding issues concerning the crime of rape.

Mens Rea for Rape at Common Law

At common law, the *mens rea* for rape was "general intent." This means that a defendant need not have entertained any specific intent to rape, but rather need only have acted with a general sense of morally blameworthiness.[63] At first blush, it might seem bizarre to think that a man might not know whether he was raping a woman and, therefore, could be without moral blame. But the restrictively narrow definition of rape under the common law made it virtually unnecessary to grapple with the question of *mens rea*.

In effect, the *mens rea* for rape was all but eliminated by the common law's focus on the victim's nonconsent as expressed through her utmost resistance. Thus, in sharp contrast to other crimes, the central issue at a rape trial rarely, if ever, concerned the man's criminal intent, but rather focused on the victim's response to his actions. In essence, proof of the woman's resistance established the necessary *mens rea* that the man acted with a morally blameworthy state of mind sufficient to satisfy the *mens rea* requirement for a rape conviction. The twofold legacy of this refocusing of responsibility from the defendant to the victim often created situations in which the victim of a rape was basically put on trial, rather than the accused rapist.[64] Not only would the woman be subjected to a grueling cross-examination about the amount of resistance she offered, but also to humiliating innuendo about her character, dress, demeanor, and sexual history in the hopes that such character assassination would lead the jury to entertain reasonable doubt with regard to whether she consented to sex.[65] Starting in the 1970s, some US jurisdictions began to enact **rape shield laws** designed to prevent the victim and his or her past sexual conduct from being put on trial, thereby attempting to focus attention at trial on the facts of the incident in question.[66] Today, rape shield laws have been adopted in some manner in federal criminal law,[67] the military,[68] and all US states.[69]

Generally speaking, rape shield laws prohibit the introduction of any evidence of the alleged victim's past sexual conduct. Most jurisdictions, however, recognize exceptions to this general bar and admit evidence of the alleged victim's past sexual conduct with the accused, reasoning the past sexual history between the accused and the accuser is highly relevant.[70] Similarly, most US jurisdictions allow evidence of the alleged victim's prior sexual conduct to refute physical or scientific evidence, such as the victim's virginity, the origin of semen found, the presence of disease or pregnancy, the source of injuries, and so on.[71] Some states also admit evidence of the alleged victim's prior sexual conduct when the defendant argues that the alleged victim consented to an act of prostitution or that the alleged victim had made an unsubstantiated charge of rape in the past.[72] Many states also include a catch-all exception to admit prior sexual conduct evidence when the trial judge agrees that it is relevant. Such an exception seemingly undermines the purpose underlying the existence of rape shield laws, but a failure to allow a defendant to introduce relevant, probative evidence at trial can violate the accused's Sixth Amendment rights to a fair trial or to conduct a reasonable cross-examination.[73] The "You Make the Public Policy Call" feature in Box 8.2 explores two other Sixth Amendment questions that rape shield laws raise—one concerning flirtatious behavior and another concerning social media posts.

Mens Rea for Rape Under Modern Law

The long-standing focus on the victim's resistance, rather than the defendant's intent, created such confusion with regard to the requisite *mens rea* for rape that many US states have yet to clarify this aspect of their criminal law even to this day. Indeed, very few modern rape statutes even mention any *mens rea* requirement,[74] and those few states that specify a level of criminal intent are not in agreement. Some states require knowledge;[75] others require purpose.[76] Some states have judicially applied a recklessness standard in accordance with the provisions of the Model Penal Code Section 2.02(3), which requires proof of at least recklessness in cases where a criminal statute fails to specify a *mens rea* requirement.[77] A handful of states appear to use negligence as the *mens rea* for rape.

In addition to the lack of consensus as to what level of *mens rea* is required to sustain a rape conviction, there is also no uniformity with regard to what element any level of *mens rea* may attach. Some jurisdictions require the *mens rea* to attach to the use of force—purposefully, knowingly, recklessly, or negligently using force to achieve penetration. For example, in *Reynolds v. State*,[78] the presence of a gun in plain view of the assailant's bed led the court to hold that the defendant "should have known" the gun would have intimidated the victim into compliance. Thus, the defendant's negligence was applied to the use of force element.[79] Other states, in contrast, apply the *mens rea* element to lack of consent issue—knowing or recklessly disregarding whether consent was given.

Finally, some jurisdictions appear to have adopted a strict liability approach to rape.[80] The states that use strict liability for rape apply it to the element of consent. In these jurisdictions, a defendant's honest and reasonable mistake with regard to whether the victim consented is not a defense to the crime.[81] This approach is quite rare. If one generalization can be made about the *mens rea* of rape, it is that some level of general intentionality is implicit in the crime, even when the statute "is silent on the subject."[82]

Sadly, confusion about the *mens rea* for rape is not the only problem that plagues this crime. As the case of *In re John Z.* illustrates, the timing of consent and the manner in which consent may be granted or withdrawn, also pose significant challenges.[83] In that case, the

BOX 8.2

YOU MAKE THE PUBLIC POLICY CALL

What Constitutes Prior Sexual Conduct?

At times, courts struggle with what constitutes the victim's "prior sexual conduct." Does flirtatious behavior count? In *State v. Garron* (2003), the New Jersey Supreme Court held that the victim's prior flirtations with the defendant should not have been excluded at his rape trial. These flirting incidents included suggestive comments, such as, "if your wife's never around let me know . . . I can take care of you."[178] Witnesses of the flirtation testified that they had seen the victim brush her breasts against the accused on one occasion and had seen her grab the defendant's buttocks and give him a passionate kiss on another occasion. But a significant amount of time had passed from these events to the time of date of the alleged rape; some had occurred months earlier while others had occurred more than six years in the past. Nonetheless, the high court ruled that all the excluded testimony of past flirting—most especially those that could be offered by the victim's former co-workers who were "disinterested witnesses"—should have been admitted into evidence to assure a fair trial for the defendant.[179]

1. Critics of the decision in *Garron* pointed out that past flirting—even flirting that indicates a willingness to have sex at one point in time—does not indicate a willingness to have at any point.[180] Do you think flirting behavior should be admitted into or excluded from evidence? Justify your position.
2. Defense teams typically investigate a wide range of prior conduct by victims, including on social media. Despite the purpose of rape shield laws to reduce victim-blaming, photos from Twitter, Facebook, Instagram, and the like might be used to call into question whether the complainant consented to sex by raising unstated issues about the victim's style of dress, flirtatiousness, and alcohol use.[181] Even purely textual posts can affect trial outcomes. Consider, for example, what happened to one victim who, after being assaulted, went home, looked up an article on consent that she recalled reason when she was younger. She posted it on Facebook "as a timely reminder" about consent.[182] In acquitting her attacker, the judge reasoned that "the fact that [she] did look up articles about consent when she was home leads me to think that there was some genuine confusion on her part as to whether or not she was consenting."[183] Critique this outcome. Do you think the rape shield laws should work to exclude to social media posts? Or would that raise Sixth Amendment concerns about a fair trial for the accused?

seventeen-year-old victim consumed alcohol at a party with some other teenagers. At one point, she went into the host's bedroom with another of his friends. The boys took turns kissing her. One sexually assaulted her while the other, the defendant in the case, was out of the room. He returned unclothed and, according to the victim's testimony,

> he lay down on the bed behind her and touched her shoulder with just enough pressure to make her move, a nudge. He asked her to lie down and she did. He began kissing her and she kissed him back. He rolled on top of her, inserted his penis in her and, although she resisted, he rolled her back over, pulling her on top of him. She was on top of him for four or five minutes, during which time she tried to get off, but he grabbed her waist and pulled her back down. He rolled her over and continued the sexual intercourse. [She] told him that she needed to go home, but he would not stop. He said, "just give me a minute," and she said, "no, I need to get home." He replied, "give me some time" and she repeated, "no, I have to go home." Defendant did not stop, "[h]e just stayed inside of me and kept like basically forcing it on me."[84]

In reviewing the defendant's liability, the Supreme Court of California assumed, for the sake of argument, that the sex began consensually. It cited the precedent of *People v. Roundtree* that held rape is committed when a victim withdraws consent during an act of sexual intercourse but is forced to complete the act.[85] Relying on that case, it upheld the finding of delinquency against the defendant. In doing so, the court reasoned that the victim had withdrawn consent and the defendant failed to stop the sex act within a "reasonable time." Courts in other states have taken issue with that language, holding in clearer terms that a defendant is not entitled to reasonable time to discontinue sexual intercourse when consent is withdrawn during the act and communicated to the defendant.[86]

The question of time notwithstanding, the dissent in *John Z.* took issue with the majority's conclusion that the victim had clearly communicated her withdrawal of consent:

> [Her] silent and ineffectual movements could easily be misinterpreted. And, none of her statements are unequivocal. While [she] may have felt these words clearly conveyed her unwillingness, they could reasonably be understood as requests for reassurance or demands for speed. And, [her] own testimony demonstrates that is precisely how John Z. interpreted what she said. . . . When asked if she had made it clear to John that she didn't want to have sex, [she] says "I thought I had," but she acknowledges she "never officially told him" she did not want to have sexual intercourse. When asked by the prosecutor on redirect why she told John "I got to go home," Laura answers: "Because I had to get home so my mom wouldn't suspect anything."[87]

The *John Z.* court did not meaningfully analyze the defendant's *mens rea* in the case. Did he know he was committing a rape, or did he honestly and reasonably believe that the sex was consensual? If it had been consensual, was he reckless or even negligent about the victim withdrawing consent? And what about the burden of persuasion in the case; do the facts establish proof beyond of reasonable doubt? The court's opinion leaves these questions unanswered. Nonetheless, the case and others like it illustrate the principle that the continuation of intercourse after consent has been withdrawn may constitute the crime of rape.[88] Whether a defendant reasonably understands that consent was withdrawn and nonetheless continues penetration by force or threats of force are questions of fact that must normally be decided by a jury.

GRADING OF RAPE OFFENSES

Whether termed rape or sexual assault or battery in the first degree, many US states differentiate the degree of the offense depending on the amount of force that was used. Tennessee law provides a good example by defining two degrees of rape in its criminal code. It defines "aggravated rape" as sexual penetrations accomplished by force or coercion using a weapon, causing bodily injury to the victim, or if the acted were aided and abetted by others.[89] Rape in its nonaggravated form involves sexual penetrations accomplished by force or coercion without the use of a weapon and not causing other bodily harm, or otherwise "accomplished without the consent of the victim" when the defendant "knows or has reason to know" the victim did not consent.[90]

RESPONDING TO RAPE

The trauma victims experience does not end when sexual assaults conclude. Medical exams to collect evidence are uncomfortable and can even be painful. Police investigations can be downright humiliating, especially if law enforcement officers either express skepticism or outright disbelief, or if they blame the victim. And prosecutors, defense attorneys, judges, and juries alike can all behave in ways that can cause victims to experience even more trauma.[91] In short, all phases of criminal justice responses to sexual assaults can compound the psychological distress that victims experience, ranging from guilt, anger, self-blame, irritability, a loss of self-esteem, and deep feelings of shame to serious bouts of depression and post-traumatic stress disorder that can affect both social, sexual, and psychological functioning.

To help reduce the secondary victimization that can occur after reporting sexual assault, many police departments have established special victims units in which personnel are trained to engage in trauma-informed interviewing. For example, the Forensic Experiential Trauma Interview (FETI) trains investigators "to move away from interrogation-type interviewing methods in order to get better information from trauma victims and to help victims feel more supported during interviews."[92]

> FETI training focuses more on the science of trauma and its impact on the brain's processing of memories in order to help trainees conduct more effective, empathetic, trauma-informed interviews. Traditional investigative interviews are geared toward gathering information like "who, what, where, when, how, and why." The brain gathers and organizes this type of information using higher-level neural processes, but these processes can shut down during traumatic events. FETI trainees learn a method of interviewing that allows victims to recall memories in a way that is more consistent with and sensitive to the way the brain processes traumatic events. FETI relies heavily on showing genuine empathy, privileging emotional reactions, evoking sensorial memories, and remaining patient. Using FETI, interviewers can gather more accurate and reliable information while making victims feel safer and more willing to participate in the investigative process.[93]

Lawmakers can also help sexual assault victims. In addition to statutory reforms to rape laws, they can strengthen systemic responses to the needs of victims. One of the most notable legislative efforts to do so occurred in 1994 when Congress enacted the Violence Against Women Act to change the criminal justice system's responses to acts of domestic violence and sex crimes.[94] It made orders of protection (i.e., "restraining orders") enforceable nationwide across state lines; extended immigration protections to those who would not otherwise qualify to remain in the United States if they left abusive partners; and funded a range of victim's services from shelters to rape crises centers and hotlines. The law was reauthorized in 2000, 2015, and 2013. Among other changes, the 2013 reauthorization extended the law's protections to same-sex couples, enhanced measures to prevent sex trafficking (see Chapter 9), gave Native American tribes the ability to prosecute sex offenses committed by non-Indians on tribal territories, created a right to bring a civil lawsuit for any sexual acts committed against those in federal custody, and provided funding to help with the DNA analysis of untested evidence collected from sexual assault victims. But the law expired when the US Senate refused to renew it in 2018 and 2019 largely due to objections by conservatives over provisions in the reauthorization bill concerning immigration and the protections it would afford to lesbian, gay, bisexual, and transgender victims.

SEXUAL ASSAULT AND SEXUAL BATTERY

Roughly half of US states continue to use the term "rape,"[95] while the other half have statutes that "replaced the word 'rape' with terms such as 'sexual assault,' 'sexual battery,' or 'criminal sexual conduct.'"[96] Such changes in terminology were made with two primary goals in mind: (1) "to shift the focus from the sexual aspect to the violent aspect of the crime"; and (2) to facilitate changes in the pervasive prejudices, preconceptions, and stigma concerning rape.[97]

Sexual Assault or Battery in the First Degree

Most of statutes differentiate various degrees of sexual assault or battery. The modern definition of rape—sexual penetration without the consent of the victim—is often, but not always, subsumed in the definition of **sexual assault** in the first degree[98] or **sexual battery** in the first degree.[99] Some US jurisdictions, however, differentiate between degrees of sexual assault or sexual battery based on the amount of force used or on the age of the victim. For example, if the amount of force used to perpetrate a rape resulted in severe physical injury to the victim, then the crime would be classified as a sexual assault in the first degree or an *aggravated sexual assault*. If the amount of force used to perpetrate a rape did not result in severe physical injury to the victim, then the crime would be classified as a sexual assault or battery in the second degree.

Other circumstances that might raise a sexual assault or battery to the level of being an aggravated sexual assault/sexual assault in the first degree would include those acts performed on a child under a certain age (e.g., thirteen or fourteen); those involving the actual or threatened use of a deadly weapon, or those that are committed during the commission or attempted commission of another felony; or those in which there are multiple attackers.

Other Levels of Sexual Assault or Battery

In contrast to statutes that differentiate first- or second-degree sexual assault or battery offenses by the level of force used to effect a sexual penetration, some US state laws enumerate second or lesser degrees of sexual assault or battery based on sexual contact that does not involve a penetration. For example, Alaska defines sexual assault in the second degree as the "sexual contact with another person without the consent of that person."[100] For the purposes of such statutes, "sexual contact" is typically defined broadly to include an "offensive touching" of an "intimate part" or "private part" of the body. The following provision in the US Uniform Code of Military Justice is typical of such statutes:

> The intentional touching, either directly or through the clothing, of the genitalia, anus, groin, breast, inner thigh, or buttocks of another person, or intentionally causing another person to touch, either directly or through the clothing, the genitalia, anus, groin, breast, inner thigh, or buttocks of any person, with an intent to abuse, humiliate, or degrade any person or to arouse or gratify the sexual desire of any person.[101]

It should be noted that statutory language in sexual assault laws, like the one quoted here from military law, is troublesome. Sexual assaults are typically crimes of violence and power,[102] and thus may not be crimes committed for sexual gratification. Proving the requisite statutory intent of sexual gratification may, therefore, be problematic in some cases.[103]

Some states have avoided the problem of motivation by enacting laws that omit any such references. Arizona, for example, has a statute that criminalized **sexual abuse**, defined as "intentionally or knowingly engaging in sexual contact [defined as any direct or indirect touching, fondling, or manipulating of any part of the genitals, anus, or female breast by any part of the body or by any object or causing a person to engage in such contact] with any person who is fifteen or more years of age without consent of that person or with any person who is under fifteen years of age if the sexual contact involves only the female breast."[104]

CHILD MOLESTATION

In many states, the age of the victim may be the factor that determines the degree of a rape or sexual assault, regardless of the level of force or violence that may have been used or threated. South Dakota, for example, defines rape in the first degree only as those perpetrated against a child less than thirteen years of age and designates second-, third-, and fourth-degree rapes based on other factors, such as whether an intoxicant was used or whether the victim was physically or mentally incapacitated such that valid consent could not be given.[105]

Other states, though, have created special statutory offenses that punishes a sexual act on a child under a particular age more severely than other forms of sexual assault. For example, Arizona's **child molestation** statute punishes sexual intercourse or sexual contact with a minor under the age fifteen as a class 2 felony.[106] Moreover, the state provides a sentencing enhancement if a sexual penetration occurred and the child victim was twelve years of age or younger such that a sentence of life imprisonment is mandated with the possibility of parole until after the perpetrator has served at least thirty-five years of the sentence.[107] Other states incorporate other factors, in addition to a child's age, to grade child molestation. Indiana, for example, differentiates degrees of child molestation based on the level of force used, whether a deadly weapon was used, whether the child sustained serious bodily injury, and whether an intoxicant was administered.[108]

STATUTORY RAPE

Statutory rape laws criminalize sex between adults and underage minors. Statutory rape differs from rape or sexual assault in that force or threats of force are absent; yet the sex cannot be labeled "consensual" due to the youthful age of the victim who is presumed to lack the legal capacity to consent to sexual activity.[109]

Common-Law Statutory Rape Laws

At common law, statutory rape was defined as the carnal knowledge of a female under the age of consent as set by statute.[110] The crime was first codified in English law in 1275, when the Statute of Westminster provided "[T]he King prohibiteth that none do ravish, nor take away by force, any Maiden within Age."[111] The age of consent was initially twelve years of age, but it was lowered to ten in 1576.[112] That same age of ten years was incorporated into early American laws, but rose to eighteen or even twenty-one during the 1800s. Today, all US jurisdictions continue to have criminal laws penalizing sexual conduct with someone under their specified age of consent.

STRICT LIABILITY

The common law applied strict liability to the age of consent; it was no defense to statutory rape that the defendant was mistaken about the age of the victim, even if the mistake had been both honest and reasonable. Accordingly, the only proof required for conviction was proof of the *actus reus* for statutory rape—the proscribed sexual activity with an underage person.[113]

THE ATTENDANT CIRCUMSTANCE OF FEMALE VICTIMIZATION

The common-law approach to statutory rape was gender-specific insofar as it criminalized a male engaging in sexual activity with an underage female, but not a female engaging in sexual activity with an underage male.[114] This gender disparity was due largely to antiquated concepts of females as "special property in need of protection."[115] Penalizing only the male for statutory rape would appear to raise equal protection concerns under the Fourteenth Amendment to the US Constitution. But recall from Chapter 2 that the Supreme Court upheld such laws in 1981 over an Equal Protection Clause challenge in *Michael M. v. Superior Court of Sonoma County, California*.[116]

Modern Statutory Rape Laws

Contemporary statutory rape laws vary so dramatically across the United States that one commentator said, "Rarely does one find a crime whose statutory schemes engender as much division of thought."[117] The major changes in the law of statutory rape concern the age of consent; the gender-neutrality of statutes; and the *mens rea* for the offense.

AGE OF CONSENT

As Figure 8.1 illustrates, approximately thirty states and the District of Columbia set the age of consent at sixteen; the remaining states set the age of consent at seventeen[118] or eighteen.[119] Some states, however, have created special statutory provisions that lowers the age of consent to as low as twelve when the act occurs between two teenagers close in age. These provisions are commonly referred to as **Romeo and Juliet age-gap provisions**.

For example, New Jersey adopted a variation of the Model Penal Code's approach to statutory rape[120] by setting the age of consent at sixteen, but allowing children as young as thirteen to lawfully consent to sex with a teenager who is not more than four years older (i.e., seventeen years old).[121] Other states have more complex Romeo and Juliet age-gap provisions, with different ages of consent applying for different ranges in the ages between the two actors, such as a two-year difference in ages for preteens; a three-year difference for mid-teens; and a four-year difference for late teens.[122]

GENDER-NEUTRAL STATUTORY RAPE LAWS

Since the decision in the *Michael M.* case,[123] nearly all US states have changed their statutory rape laws to be gender-neutral, "both in who may be the perpetrator and in who may be the victim."[124] Thus, in most US jurisdictions, both males and females may commit statutory rapes by engaging in sexual activity with either a male or female under the age of consent.

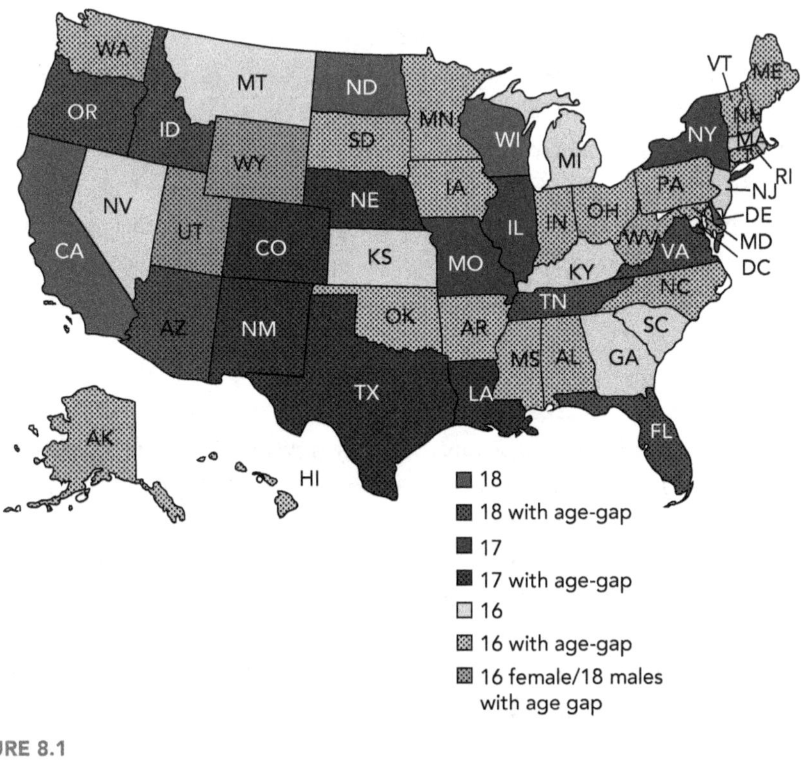

FIGURE 8.1

Age of Consent Laws in the United States

MENS REA FOR STATUTORY RAPE

The final significant change to statutory rape laws concerns the *mens rea* for the offense. The majority of US states continue to apply strict liability to the offense just as the common law did.[125] A handful of states, however, statutorily added a *mens rea* requirement to the crime concerning whether defendant knew or should have known that person with whom they engaged in sexual activity was under the age of consent.[126] In such states, defendant may assert a "mistake of fact" defense regarding the victim's age. This defense to the crime is limited to situations in which the defendant labored under an honest and reasonable mistake of fact regarding the age of the victim; as with all other mistakes of fact as explained in Chapter 13, a subjectively honest, but objectively unreasonable mistake will not suffice.

In still other US jurisdictions, the age of the victim determines whether strict liability will be imposed (e.g., for younger teens)[127] or whether the defendant may assert a mistake of fact defense (e.g., for older teenagers still under the age of consent or for when the age difference between the defendant and victim is less than two or three years).[128] Consider, for example, *People v. Paz*.[129] In that case, a convicted the twenty-eight-year-old defendant of, among other crimes, lewd or lascivious acts upon fourteen-year-old. The victim had told the defendant that she was sixteen years old. At the relevant time, California used a strict liability approach to lewd and lascivious acts performed on children under the age of fourteen (making such acts felonies), but recognized a mistake of age defense if the acts were performed on a teenager between the ages of sixteen and eighteen. Thus, the defendant maintained that the trial court judge should have instructed the jury to acquit the defendant if he honestly and reasonably believed the victim to be sixteen. But the court refused to allow a defense based on a mistake of the victim's age involving acts on teens who were fourteen and fifteen years old if the perpetrator was more than ten years older than the victim, largely because of explicit statutory changes to that effect. The court cited a prior case that had reasoned younger teenagers were in need of special protection that older teenagers do not need.[130]

Is There a Double Standard for Statutory Rape?

The adoption of gender-neutral statutory rape laws were designed to legislative overrule the *Michael M.* case (Chapter 2) by imposing criminal liability on males and females alike. Indeed, numerous cases have garnered media attention when female high school teachers took sexual advantage of their underage male students.[131] When these women are convicted of statutory rape, they tend to receive significantly more lenient sentences than male teachers who victimize underage female students. Numerous researchers in psychology have documented what these light sentences seem to intuitively tell us—namely that we appear to have a double-standard for what is acceptable intergenerational sex.[132] One of these researchers concluded that some people see "sexual interaction between a fifteen-year-old male and a thirty-five-year-old female [as] an acceptable means of providing sex education for boys."[133] But the double standards that exist in contemporary society may violate equal protection (see Chapter 2).

In *Commonwealth v. Bernardo B.*,[134] a fourteen-year-old boy entering the ninth grade was charged with the statutory rape of three female friends, two of whom were twelve years old and entering the seventh grade, one of whom just shy of her twelfth birthday and was entering the sixth grade. The charges stemmed from several incidents that occurred over the summer during games of "manhunt" and "truth or dare." The boy defended against the charges arguing that he was being selectively prosecuted on the basis of his gender, since none of the girls had been charged with statutory rape for the sex acts in which they had engaged with him. The high court of Massachusetts agreed with him because "the boy and the three complaining witnesses appeared to have engaged in 'mutually consensual acts of oral sex,'" and all four children were under the age of consent of sixteen in Massachusetts, where statutory rape a strict liability offense. Yet none of the girls were charged with the statutory rape of the boy.

KNOWING TRANSMISSION OF SEXUALLY TRANSMITTED DISEASES

Does someone who consents to sex assume the risk of exposure to treatable sexually transmitted infections (STIs) like chlamydia, gonorrhea, and syphilis? What about potentially life-threatening STIs, like hepatitis or HIV?

The Ryan White Comprehensive AIDS Resources Emergency Act of 1990 was an important piece of legislation enacted, in large part, to provide the states with federal funding for the prevention and treatment of HIV/AIDS.[135] At the time the Ryan White Act was initially enacted, the HIV/AIDS epidemic was relatively young. In fact, the first recognized cases of AIDS first came to light in 1981 and the virus that causes AIDS—the human immunodeficiency virus (HIV) was not discovered until 1983.[136] More importantly, in the 1980s, effective treatments for HIV had not yet been discovered.[137]

The Ryan White Act required states to certify that criminal laws were adequate to prosecute individuals who knowingly exposed another person to HIV. According to the US Centers for Disease Control and Prevention, this caused a number of states to implement "HIV-specific criminal exposure laws [that] impose criminal penalties on people living with HIV who know their HIV status and who potentially expose others to HIV."[138]

The Elements of the Offense

Of the roughly thirty-three states with criminal laws regulating people with HIV, approximately twenty-four states criminalize sexual activity by persons with HIV who do not disclose their STI-positive status to their sexual partners.[139] Such statutes are commonly referred to as **knowing transmission laws** and they typically contain three elements:

1. a *mens rea* requirement that the defendant must know he or she is HIV positive;
2. an *actus reus* requirement that an HIV-positive defendant engage in certain prohibited conduct; and
3. an attendant circumstance requirement that the defendant's sexual partner must not be aware of the defendant's HIV-positive status.[140]

The third element sets up an affirmative defense in which defendants can argue that they disclosed their seropositive status to their partner.[141] But some state's laws are so restrictive that they do not appear to leave room for a defense of consent after disclosure. Alabama's law, for example, criminalizes persons with any STI from engaging in "any act which will probably or likely transmit such disease to another person."[142]

Not all states limit their knowing transmissions laws to HIV. Some states include forms of hepatitis and classify the offense as a felony.[143] Other states have knowing transmission statutes targeting a full array of STIs that grade the severity of the crime dependent on the diagnosis, typically making the offense a misdemeanor if it involves chancroid, gonorrhea, genital herpes, syphilis, or chlamydia, and designating it a felony if it involves HIV or hepatitis.[144] Regardless of whether such statutes target HIV or STIs more broadly, most of the states with such laws require proof of nondisclosure as an element of the crime that the prosecution must prove beyond a reasonable doubt.

The "prohibited conduct" contained in the *actus reus* of the offense includes more than vaginal or anal sex in many states, often including oral sex; needle-sharing; engaging in acts of prostitution; biting, spitting, and throwing bodily fluids, especially in correctional institutions; and donating blood, tissue, or bodily fluids.[145] Four states also criminalize sharing sex objects/toys and one, Colorado, even bars an HIV-positive person from engaging in an act of mutual masturbation part of any prostitution arrangement.[146] Thus, many states fail to differentiate between high-risk (e.g., vaginal or anal intercourse), low-risk (e.g., oral sex), and negligible-risk behaviors (e.g., mutual masturbation). Consider, for instance, that "there are no documented cases of HIV transmission from spitting."[147] And few states take into account behaviors that significantly reduce the risk of transmission, such as condom use (a defense in only four states), antiretroviral therapy, or pre-exposure prophylaxis.[148] Nonetheless, most of the laws lump all such "prohibited conduct" together and classify the offenses as felonies, with 18 states imposing sentences up to 10 years, 7 states imposing sentences between 11 and 20 years, and 5 states imposing sentences of more than 20 years.[149]

Public Policy Concerns

The use of criminal law to regulate the sexual behavior of people with STIs was initially justified on two grounds: as means of deterring risky sexual behaviors and as a way of exacting retributive punishment on those who engaged in such behaviors.[150] When many states first adopted knowing transmission laws, HIV was widely considered to be a death sentence.[151] Today, there is still no cure for HIV and HIV can still lead to death if left untreated. But there are now treatments that have changed the prognosis for those infected with HIV into a treatable, chronic disease.[152] Yet knowing transmission laws ostensibly serve a public health goal. But research indicates that these laws do little to change the behaviors of people who are HIV positive.[153] Moreover, these laws may actually be damaging public health efforts by increasing "stigma towards persons living with HIV"; reducing "the likelihood of disclosure to sexual or needle-sharing partners" and the "frequency of HIV testing since knowledge of status is required for culpability" ' and perpetuating "inflammatory or ill-informed media coverage that may perpetuate misinformation regarding modes of HIV transmission."[154]

To prevent overinclusive criminalization that potentially rises to the levels of due process violations, several scholars have called for revising knowing transmission laws.[155] At minimum, they argue that safer sex practices "are so important and so relevant to the risk of transmission of HIV that the criminal law should distinguish between protected and unprotected sex in HIV exposure and nondisclosure cases."[156] Consider the following case.

Nick RHOADES, Appellant,

v.

STATE of Iowa, Appellee.

848 N.W.2d 22 (2014).

[Petitioner Nick Rhoades was diagnosed with HIV and receiving treatment that rendered his viral load nondetectable. He met A.P. on a social networking site. The two eventually engaged in sexual activity with each other. A.P. believed Rhoades to be HIV-negative, in part because Rhoades's online profile listed him as such. A.P. subsequently learned Rhoades was potentially HIV-positive. A.P. contacted the police and the State charged Rhoades with criminal transmission of HIV in violation of Iowa Code section 709C.1. Rhoades pled guilty to one count of criminal transmission of HIV and was sentenced to twenty-five years imprisonment with life parole. He then filed a petition to set aside his conviction arguing that his lawyer failed to provide effective assistance of counsel.]

* * *

[T]o establish the crime of criminal transmission of HIV the State must prove the following elements: (1) the defendant engaged in intimate contact with the victim, (2) at the time of intimate contact the defendant's HIV status was positive, (3) the defendant knew his HIV status was positive, and (4) at the time of the intimate contact, the victim did not know that the defendant had a positive HIV status. . . . In considering the definition of "intimate contact," we have previously [interpreted] the criminal transmission statute as requiring "that transmission of . . . HIV from the infected person to the exposed person was *possible* considering the circumstances."[157] Although there are multiple definitions of "possible," we have not previously elaborated on what "possible" means here. First, "possible" may mean something "that may or may not occur. . . ." Second, "possible" may mean "having an indicated potential by nature or circumstances. . . ." This definition considers the reality of a thing occurring, rather than a theoretical chance.

We find the second definition is more appropriate in the context of this criminal statute for at least two reasons. First, we recognize this statute requires expert medical testimony on the likelihood of transmission of HIV. Experts are not required to testify in absolutes when it comes to causation. . . . Second, and more importantly, we would not want to deprive a person of his or her liberty on the basis the defendant's actions caused something that can only theoretically occur. Causation must be reasonably possible under the facts and circumstances of the case to convict a person of criminal transmission of HIV. . . .

[During the plea hearing], the district court used technical language from the statute that was insufficient to establish a factual basis. The district court asked Rhoades if he had intimate contact with the victim. At most, we can surmise from Rhoades's affirmative response that he had some sort of sexual relations with the victim. . . . We find the district court's reference to intimate contact and Rhoades's acknowledgement he had intimate contact does not establish the necessary factual basis an exchange of bodily fluid took place or that Rhoades intentionally exposed A.P. to his bodily fluid in a manner that could result in the transmission of HIV. . . .

[T]estimony establishes A.P. received oral and anal intercourse from Rhoades. It also establishes Rhoades used a condom when performing anal sex. The . . . testimony [does] not establish any exposure of bodily fluids between Rhoades and A.P. . . . Nor [does] the testimony show the likelihood the sexual activity in this case could result in the transmission of HIV.

* * *

At the time of the plea, Rhoades's viral count was nondetectable, and there is a question of whether it was medically true a person with a nondetectable viral load could transmit HIV through contact with the person's blood, semen or vaginal fluid or whether transmission was merely theoretical. . . . Thus, there was not a sufficient factual basis for the district court to accept the plea. Therefore, trial counsel was ineffective for allowing the district court to accept the plea without a factual basis.

Questions

1. Does the current status of HIV treatments change the way you view knowing transmission laws? Why or why not?
2. Should use of a condom exempt someone from criminal prosecution even when that person fails to disclose his or her HIV-positive status? In the wake of the *Rhoades* case, Iowa replead its criminal law against the knowing transmission of HIV and replaced it with a statute establishing different punishments depending on whether the offender

intended to infect another person or acted recklessly. The revised law also added other diseases, including hepatitis and tuberculosis, and specifies that taking "practical means to prevent transmission" is a defense.[158] Should all states allow use of condoms or dental dams to be an affirmative defense in knowing transmission prosecutions?

3. Do modern HIV treatments undercut the logic of prosecuting people for attempted murder, aggravated assault, or other specific-intent crimes for having unprotected sex when they know they are HIV positive? Explain your reasoning.

Beyond Knowing Transmission Laws

Even in states without specific laws targeting the behavior of people with STIs, the criminal law can all be used to prosecute people who knowingly expose others to HIV and other serious STIs. Indeed, because a failure to disclose one's status as positive for potentially life-threatening STIs may vitiate consent to sex,[159] such actions may even constitute the crime of rape in jurisdictions that define rape in terms of the absence of consent, rather than by the use of force. But because rape by fraud is a tricky prosecutorial enterprise even more so than "regular" rape cases,[160] other criminal laws—such as reckless endangerment, aggravated assault, and even homicide and attempted homicide laws—are more commonly used to prosecute knowing exposure to STIs. For example, *State v. Neatherlin*[161] affirmed a conviction for assault with a deadly weapon in a case involving a defendant infected with the Hepatitis C virus who bit a woman and then said that he hoped she would die. But proving the *mens rea* associated with certain specific intent crimes can be tricky; the intent must often be inferred.

CONTROLLING SEX OFFENDERS WITH CIVIL LAW

In 1994, "Megan's Law"[162] was enacted by the New Jersey state legislature in the wake of the death of Megan Kanka, a seven-year-old girl who was raped and killed by a neighbor who had been released from prison after having twice been convicted of sex offenses with young girls.[163] The law established a system of registration to permit law enforcement officials to identify and alert the public of the release of those offenders who have committed predatory acts against children when necessary for the public safety. Since that time, all US states and the federal government have adopted some requirement that people convicted of certain sex crimes register as a sex offender. States vary in how they classify offenders and the ways in which they notify communities about the release of a sex offender. Most states, however, make information such as the offender's name, residence, and place of work via a telephone information system, publication in local newspapers, or most commonly, a website. The constitutionality of such registration and notification schemes has been fought in many courts, but they have generally been upheld.[164]

Given the wide variability in ways states approached sex offender registration and notification, the federal government has enacted a series of laws to tighten enforcement and bring uniformity to the ways in which sex offenders are monitored after their release from custody.[165] In 1997, Congress required states to implement procedures for identifying which sex offenders were **sexually violent predators** and to implement methods of tracking sex offenders across state lines.[166] Congress modified how states defined sexually violent predators just one year later in an attempt to bring uniformity to the classification.[167] In 2003, federal law mandates that each state create and maintain a publicly accessible web site on which sex offender information could be found.[168] And in 2006, Congress adopted the Adam Walsh Child Protection and Safety Act (AWA).[169]

In addition to creating the first federal involuntary civil commitment law (targeting "sexually dangerous persons"), and creating a national child abuse and neglect registry, the AWA substantially overhauled federal registration and community notification policy, in the process expressly repealing [a number of prior pieces of federal legislation concerning sex offender registration and notification in order to] establish a "comprehensive national system for the registration [of sex offenders and offenders against children]."[170]

The AWA creation of a federal involuntary civil commitment law for sexually dangerous persons was modeled, in large part, on legislation that had already been enacted in several states. Kansas pioneered this approach in 1994 when it enacted a "Sexually Violent Predator Act" which establishing procedures for the civil commitment of convicted sex offenders who, due to a "mental abnormality" or a "personality disorder," were likely to engage in "predatory acts of sexual violence" again.[171] In the landmark decision of *Kansas v. Hendricks*,[172] the US Supreme Court upheld the constitutionality of the Kansas statute. The Court's rationale rested primarily on the fact that such involuntary civil commitment to a mental hospital at the expiration of a term of criminal incarceration is not "punishment" (which would be barred by double jeopardy since a convicted sex offender would have already served a prison sentence), but rather is "treatment."

In its 2002 decision in *Kansas v. Crane*,[173] the Supreme Court again reviewed the Kansas statute for compliance with due process guarantees. The Supreme Court held that something more than a "mental abnormality" or a "personality disorder," coupled with a likelihood to engage in "predatory acts of sexual violence," is required for due process to be satisfied in the involuntary civil commitment of sexually dangerous persons; a significant impairment of the ability to control one's dangerous behavior is also required. Put differently, a person may not be involuntarily committed without proof that some mental disorder significantly impairs a person's volitional control of sexually violent impulses.

CONCLUSION

Learning Objectives	Summaries
1. Define the *actus reus* and attendant circumstances of rape under the common law.	The common-law crime of rape was defined as the unlawful carnal knowledge of a woman by a man who is not her husband, without her effective consent. The restrictive definition required the penetration of a vagina, however slight, by a penis, meaning that only a man could rape a woman. Moreover, because spouses were exempt, sexual assaults by a husband against his wife were not punishable as rapes. Finally, the prove lack of effective consent, a woman had to resist her attacker to the utmost.
2. Discuss how the *actus reus* and attendant circumstances of rape evolved from their common-law definitions to their modern-day counterparts.	Today, most US jurisdictions define rape as any form of sexual intercourse accomplished without the consent of the victim. Oral, anal, and vaginal penetrations are subsumed in the definition of sexual intercourse in most states. Additionally, most states now have gender-neutral laws recognizing that people of all sexes and gender identities can be perpetrators or victims of rape. The spousal exemption has been eliminated in many jurisdictions or, alternatively, rape of one's spouse is punished as a separate offense. Finally, although the common-law requirement of resistance to the upmost has been universally abolished, many states require evidence that a rape was accomplished using force or threats of force that were met with reasonable resistance under the circumstances. A minority of states, however, no longer require proof of any resistance and instead on a lack of consent.
3. Analyze the varying approaches to the *mens rea* element for the crime of rape.	Rape was a general intent crime at common, but it was unclear to which elements of the crime *mens rea* must attach. Even today, few statutes specify a *mens rea* requirement. Those that do vary from purpose, knowledge, recklessness, and negligence. But confusion remains about whether those varying levels of *mens rea* apply to the conduct (sexual intercourse) or attendant circumstances (using force or threats, without the victim's consent) elements of rape.
4. Discuss the varying degrees of sexual assault and sexual battery.	In that state that use such nomenclature, sexual assault or battery in the first degree is defined as rape, although the age of the victim, the degree of force use, or the injuries caused may also differentiate the grading of the offense. Lesser forms of sexual assault or battery typically involve nonconsensual sexual contact not involving penetration.
5. Differentiate child molestation from statutory rape.	Some states' rape laws grade the offense based on the age of the victim. But other states have created a separate offense of child molestation to punish sexual contact with a minor under a certain age. By contrast, statutory rape criminalizes nonforcible sex between adults and underage minors who have reached sexual maturity, but as teenagers, lack the ability to give effective legal consent. It is a strict liability offense in most states that although used to apply only to males who statutorily rapes females, is now mostly defined using gender-neutral terms.

Learning Objectives	Summaries
6. Distinguish the ways in which the knowing transmission of a sexually transmitted infection may subject someone to criminal liability.	Failure to disclose to a sexual partner that one has a sexually transmitted infection can result in criminal liability, presuming that such an actor knew of the infection. This can be its own offense or, in states lacking a knowing transmission law, may constitute rape, reckless endangerment, aggravated assault, and even attempted homicide.

KEY TERMS

child molestation
knowing transmission laws
rape
rape shield laws
Romeo and Juliet age-gap provisions
sexual abuse
sexual assault
sexual battery
sexually violent predators
statutory rape

9

Other Sex Crimes

LEARNING OBJECTIVES

1. Evaluate the ways in which *Lawrence v. Texas* limits laws criminalizing sodomy, fornication, adultery, and bigamy.

2. Define the crime of incest.

3. Differentiate between the various laws criminalizing sex offenses of a public nature.

4. Compare and contrast the crime of prostitution with related crimes that aid or abet the offense.

5. Explain the elements of the crime of obscenity.

6. Discuss the ways in which criminal laws attempt to protect children and teenagers from sexual exploitation.

Outline

INTRODUCTION

Chapter 2 traced a line of US Supreme Court cases dealing with the right to privacy under the Ninth and Fourteenth Amendments to the US Constitution established limits on the government's ability to regulate sexual conduct between consenting adults that occurs in private. One of these landmark cases, *Lawrence v. Texas*, invalided the criminalization of private, consensual acts of oral or anal sex between adults.[1] One paragraph in the *Lawrence* case contains the following three sentences that are of particular importance to the sex crimes discussed in this chapter: "The present case does not involve minors. It does not involve persons who might be injured or coerced or who are situated in relationships where consent might not easily be refused. It does not involve public conduct or prostitution . . . ."[2]

This chapter explores a range of laws criminally regulating sexual acts, many of which are consensual. We begin by exploring four crimes that, although still "in the books," are rarely prosecuted: sodomy, fornication, adultery, and bigamy. After exploring these crimes, the chapter then turns to examining sex crimes that continue to be enforced today.

SEX CRIMES THAT ARE PROSECUTED INFREQUENTLY

There are a number of sex offenses that are still on the books in the penal codes of many states. Yet, they are prosecuted infrequently for a number of reasons. Some simply occur infrequently. Others are commonplace, their commission is often shielded from discovery because the acts occur in private. And others may occur frequently, but because they are consensual moral offenses, they represent true victimless crimes that arguably lie beyond the modern criminal regulatory authority of the state.

Sodomy

For centuries, laws have proscribed acts of oral and anal intercourse, generally subsuming these acts under the general term **sodomy**. The term *sodomy* comes from the Biblical story of the destruction of Sodom.[3] Sodomy has not always been considered a crime. For example, sodomy played a large part in the ancient cultural tradition of *Paiderastia*[4] (not to be confused with pedophilia), in which citizens "had the obligation to take as a lover and pupil a younger male and train him in the arts of war and citizenship."[5]

The spread of Christianity in Europe brought revulsion to homosexuality and therefore punished sodomy as an ecclesiastical offense.[6] Sodomy was made a crime against the state at common law in the sixteenth century by Henry VIII.[7] By the Victorian Era, the mass suppression of sexuality of all types led to the criminalization of all acts of sodomy, whether between members of the same or opposite sex.[8] The Puritans brought the sodomy laws with them to the colonies. As the country grew, sodomy laws spread as a part of common law and were in effect in all fifty states.

Early English sodomy laws prohibited only anal sex. But the definition was broadened either by legislation or judicial construction to include both oral sex as well as sexual contact with an animal.[9] Laws against such conduct have not only been designated as sodomy laws, but also as "the crime against nature," "buggery," and "deviate sexual intercourse."[10]

SODOMY INVOLVING PEOPLE

Up until the mid-1960s, sodomy laws facially applied to both same-sex sodomy and opposite-sex sodomy, although the targets of prosecution were usually homosexuals.[11] As society became more open to sexuality through the 1960s and 1970s, a number of states altered their sodomy statutes so heterosexual acts of sodomy would be beyond the reach of the criminal law, officially making sodomy statutes apply only to acts of same-sex sodomy.[12]

In 1961, every US state had a criminal sodomy law.[13] Between 1961 and the US Supreme Court's decision in *Bowers v. Hardwick*[14] upholding the constitutionality of sodomy laws (see Chapter 2), approximately a dozen more states decriminalized sodomy through legislative repeal or through state court judicial action.[15] *Lawrence v. Texas* invalidated the nation's remaining sodomy laws in 2003, provided the acts occurred in private between consenting adults.[16]

The Court in *Lawrence* specially noted that sodomy laws may be enforced in situations "where consent might not easily be refused."[17] This qualification has particular implications for criminal justice professionals and members of the US Armed Forces. *United States v. Marcum* upheld a conviction for sodomy against a military service member who outranked his sexual partner.[18] The *Marcum* court reasoned that although *Lawrence* protects private, consensual sexual activity between adults in most settings, the military setting raises unique concerns that require consideration of contexts such as rank. The *Marcum* court quoted the following Air Force regulations:

> Unduly familiar relationships between members in which one member exercises supervisory or command authority over the other can easily be or become unprofessional. Similarly, as differences in grade increase, even in the absence of a command or supervisory relationship, there may be more risk that the relationship will be, or be perceived to be unprofessional because senior members in military organizations normally exercise authority or some direct or indirect organizational influence over more junior members.
>
> Relationships are unprofessional, whether pursued on or off-duty, when they detract from the authority of superiors or result in, or reasonably create the appearance of, favoritism, misuse of office or position, or the abandonment of organizational goals for personal interests.[19]

The *Marcum* court reasoned that, as a supervising noncommissioned officer, the defendant held "a position of responsibility and command within his unit with respect to his fellow airmen."[20] Because he "supervised and rated" his subordinate in the chain of command, the person with whom he engaged in sexual activity might have coerced or otherwise been in a position "where consent might not easily be refused."[21] As the next case reveals, even when charges of sodomy are not filed explicitly, the reach of the *Marcum* case extends to other charges in the military setting.

UNITED STATES, Appellee,

v.

Livingston T. TIMSUREN, Appellant.

72 M.J. 823 (A.F. Ct. Crim. App. 2013).

The appellant was a junior officer . . . [who] engaged in sexual intercourse with a senior airman and . . . with a different enlisted member. Also . . . , he hosted a promotion party at his off-base residence at which he served copious amounts of alcohol. He invited two Air Force Academy cadets . . . [he was] assigned to oversee . . . during their orientation. During the party, the appellant served alcohol to an underage female cadet and engaged in flirtatious behavior with her. He then persuaded her to kiss him for a brief period, and ultimately, she decided to sleep in the appellant's bed, although no sexual activity occurred.

The Government charged the appellant with dereliction of duty (for providing alcohol to the female cadet and failing to maintain a professional relationship with her), . . . and two specifications of fraternization (for engaging in sexual intercourse with the two enlisted members). [He pled guilty, but appealed his convictions claiming his pleas were entered improvidently because] the military judge improperly failed to explain to him the difference between private, consensual sexual activity that is constitutionally protected and that which is criminally proscribed.

***

In the instant case, the military judge . . . conducted a thorough inquiry into the fraternization specifications, resulting in the appellant's admissions that his actions in having sexual intercourse with the two enlisted members violated the custom of the Air Force that officers shall not fraternize with enlisted members on terms of military equality, that his conduct prejudiced good order and discipline (in part because he supervised enlisted members), and that his conduct was service discrediting.

***

We recognize that *Lawrence* and *Marcum* broadly indicate that a protected liberty interest may be implicated for any private, consensual sexual activity. However, both cases did so in the context of consensual sodomy, not fraternization with an enlisted member. We also recognize that this Court has held that the *Marcum* analysis is applicable to any private, consensual sexual conduct regardless of which UCMJ article the Government employs to charge the conduct. [For example, *United States v. Harvey*[22] . . . involved an act of consensual sodomy that the Government happened to charge [under the article prohibiting conduct unbecoming an officer] instead of the sodomy article, and it involved a litigated specification in which the accused's liberty interest was very much implicated. . . . In fact, this Court held that the conduct was permissible and survived scrutiny under *Marcum*, although we then held . . . that his conduct could nonetheless be proscribed as conduct unbecoming an officer and a gentleman.[23] The instant case is significantly different in that it involves a guilty plea to fraternization, a long-recognized prohibition in the armed forces that has not faced the constitutional challenges that consensual sodomy has. . . .

The appellant's charged misconduct involved private, consensual sexual activity, but the gravamen of the offense was the overly familiar relationship he allowed himself with these enlisted members. Sexual intercourse was merely the means by which this inappropriate relationship completed. . . . The fraternization and inappropriate relationship could just as easily have been consummated through gambling, borrowing and loaning money, or sharing living accommodations. . . .

The appellant's fraternization with two enlisted members is therefore very different from the situations . . . implicated by private, consensual sodomy. Under *Lawrence* and *Marcum*, certain consensual sexual activity may . . . be proscribed while some may be permitted, depending on the facts of the particular situation. Conversely, fraternization requires proof that the member's conduct violated the custom of the service that officers shall not fraternize with enlisted members on terms of military equality, and that the conduct was to the prejudice of good order and discipline in the armed forces or was of a nature to bring discredit upon the armed forces. Fraternizing through sexual conduct does not qualify for constitutional protection in the military context. . . .

Questions

1. The Military Code of Justice (MCJ) provisions criminalizing consensual sodomy were repealed effective in 2014—after the decision in *Timsuren*.[24] In light of this, do you think the outcome in *Timsuren* would be different today? Explain your reasoning.
2. The MCJ provides that "Any commissioned officer, cadet, or midshipman who is convicted of conduct unbecoming an officer and a gentleman shall be punished as a court-martial may direct."[25] Keeping in mind the decision in *Timsuren*, do you think adultery violated this provision?[26] What about public drunkenness while the person was in uniform?[27] How about writing a sexually suggestive letter to a teenager under the age of consent in which an officer asked the teen to send nude photos of herself to him?[28]

BESTIALITY

Bestiality is a crime involving human sexual activity with an animal. Depending on the jurisdiction, bestiality may be its own criminal offense, may be subsumed in the definition of sodomy, or may be prosecuted under statutes that prohibit cruelty to animals. The crime constitutes a misdemeanor in approximately twenty-four states and a felony in about twenty-one states; in the remaining states and the District of Columbia, bestiality is not a criminal offense.[29]

There are important public health reasons for prohibiting such acts, especially preventing the spread of disease. Additionally, an animal cannot grant legally valid consent to engage in sexual activity with a human. Accordingly, acts of bestiality can continue to be criminally prosecuted and punished under sodomy laws or animal cruelty laws without running afoul the central holding of *Lawrence v. Texas*. Indeed, in 2019, the Virginia Court of Appeals upheld the constitutionality of the provision in the state's sodomy law that says, "If any person carnally knows in any manner any brute animal or voluntarily submits to such carnal knowledge, he is guilty" of a low-level felony.[30] The defendant in that case had solicited a deputy sheriff to engage in "bestiality type stuff" and offered to show the deputy cell phone videos of the defendant's girlfriend in engaged in sex acts with a dog.[31] The court emphasized that bestiality "can be considered animal abuse because the sexual molestation of animals by humans may physically injure or kill the animal victim. . . . The [state's] interest in protecting public health also provides a justification for the ban on bestiality."[32]

States differ as to whether bestiality offenders must register as sex offenders. An appellate court in Kansas ruled that a man who had sex with a Rottweiler was required to register as a sex offender,[33] whereas an appellate court in Michigan reached the opposite conclusion in a case involving a man who had multiple convictions for having sex with sheep.[34]

Sex Outside of Marriage

In the late ninth century, Alfred of Wessex codified one of the first Anglo-Saxon Codes in which fornication (sex between unmarried persons) and adultery (sex with someone other than one's spouse) were made finable under civil law. By end of the twelfth century, though, these acts were considered "illicit unions," and therefore had evolved into public wrongs punishable as crimes.[35] After the Norman invasion in 1066, fornication and adultery became ecclesiastical offenses. They remained in the exclusive province of the Church until Statute of Laborers was passed to remedy the labor shortage caused by the Black Death. That law made it a crime to entice, retain, or harbor deserting servants. Gradually, the ability to sue for the taking of a person in whom the "owner" had a property interest came to cover the loss of consortium in a marital relationship, or the loss of one's daughter's virginity to someone other than her husband. Thus, fornication and adultery were not only punishable under canon law, but also gave the father of the fornicating female or the husband of the adulterous wife a civil remedy against the person with whom the wife or daughter was having an affair. In other words, neither adultery nor fornication were common-law crimes, but rather were torts.

When the Puritans settled in North America, they designated both acts as criminal offenses "against morality and chastity."[36] Fornication and adultery eventually became crimes in almost every US jurisdiction. "Most of those statutes were enacted in the 1800s and were vigorously enforced."[37] In 1955, the Model Penal Code recommended that adultery be decriminalized, but not fornication. But as many states adopted variations of the Model Penal Code in 1960s and 1970s, they opted to decriminalize both acts.

"MODERN" FORNICATION LAWS

Prior to the decision in *Lawrence v. Texas*, a number of states maintained statutes that criminalized **fornication**, which is sexual intercourse between unmarried, consenting persons. As originally proscribed, the crime of fornication occurred when an unmarried adult female engaged in consensual sexual intercourse, showing the sexist nature of the offense. Even today, Massachusetts, Virginia, Georgia, Idaho, Mississippi, North Carolina, Utah, and South Carolina still have fornication laws on their books. Prosecutions under these laws are virtually nonexistent. In *Martin v. Ziherl*, the Virginia Supreme Court relied on *Lawrence* when it declared Virginia's fornication law unconstitutional.[38] The Georgia Supreme Court did the same in *In re J.M.*[39]

Several months before *Lawrence* was decided, the Supreme Court of Georgia had invalidated that state's fornication law on state constitutional grounds. That case is notable because the defendant was a minor. He was sixteen years of age and charged with violating the fornication law for having consensual sex with his girlfriend, another sixteen-year-old, after the girl's mother found the boy in her daughter's bed in the wee hours of the morning.[40] Because the case involved two minors, *Lawrence* would not apply.

"MODERN" ADULTERY STATUTES

In the roughly twenty states that continue to criminalize **adultery**,[41] it is usually defined as sexual intercourse between consenting persons during a time when at least one of the participants is married to someone else. It is typically a misdemeanor, but is a felony in some jurisdictions.[42]

In many states, a single act of sexual intercourse outside of the marital relationship is insufficient to warrant criminal sanction. For instance, adultery is defined in South Carolina as having "habitual carnal intercourse" with someone who is married to another person.[43] Similarly, some statutes explicitly state that adultery is only criminal when "open and notorious."[44]

Another common approach to adultery defines the crime by limiting the enforceability of the statute by the criminal justice system. For example, in Arizona "[n]o prosecution for adultery shall be commenced except upon complaint of the husband or wife."[45] A North Dakota court summarized the rationale underlying this approach as follows:

> Laws of this character are evidently enacted for the purpose of protecting the sanctity of the home, and in recognition of the principle that the crime of adultery is a crime peculiarly infringing upon the rights of the innocent parties to the marriage relation, and that if such innocent parties see fit to condone the offense, and from a desire to avoid scandal and humiliation, and to preserve the integrity of the home, and prevent the disgrace of children and relatives, refuse to prosecute, the public is not sufficiently interested or injured to justify the institution of criminal proceedings, as in other cases, by any member of the community.[46]

On the other hand, this approach can provide a legal mechanism for coercing a cheating spouse into accepting certain divorce settlement terms on the threat of criminal prosecution or, even worse, blackmailing an unfaithful spouse with regarding to other criminal activity.

Adultery prosecutions are so uncommon that "when a Wisconsin district attorney actually prosecuted someone for adultery in 1990, the story rated the front page of *The New York Times*."[47] Most prosecutions for adultery occur in military courts when the act is "prejudicial to good order and discipline" or otherwise brings "discredit upon the armed forces."[48] Given the types of harms that are unique to the military setting, compounded by the military interests in preserving honor, challenges to adultery courts martial based on *Lawrence* have been unsuccessful.[49]

Outside the military context, it remains an open question whether adultery laws can survive constitutional scrutiny on the grounds that they serve a legitimate governmental interest in promoting healthy marriages and preserving the integrity of the family. Most contemporary civilian cases discussing adultery within one of two contexts: whether adultery continues to serve as legally adequate provocation for mitigating murder to manslaughter as it did at common law (see Chapter 7); or whether the rules of evidence allow the prosecution to use criminal adultery as evidence of a defendant's prior bad acts to rebut defense arguments concerning the defendant's good reputation. But in 2017, a Kansas man was convicted of both adultery and rape in *Salazar-Moreno v. State*.[50] He successfully appealed his adultery conviction, but not on grounds related to *Lawrence*. Rather, the court reasoned that the verdicts were inconsistent because adultery is a consensual sex crime and rape is premised on a lack of consent.

Bigamy

Polygamy, the practice of having multiple, live spouses at the same time, was an ecclesiastical offense at common law, although it became a statutory crime in 1604.[51] Polygamy was illegal in colonial America and, contrary to some ill-informed beliefs that the practice is legal in Utah (it is not),[52] polygamy has always been illegal in the United States.[53]

Bigamy laws criminalize polygamy. The crime of **bigamy** is typically defined as "the act of marrying while the spouse by a former marriage is still alive and the former marriage is still in force, or claiming to marry a person when already married to another."[54]

In most US jurisdictions, the crime of bigamy requires *scienter*—knowledge that oneself is still legally married to another person or, alternatively, knowledge that the person one purports to marry is still legally married to another person.[55] That requirement means someone is not guilty of bigamy if he or she neither knows nor had reason to know that his or her spouse was already legally married to another person. The *scienter* requirement also means that one is not guilty of bigamy if he or she reasonably believes that his or her own previous marriage was dissolved by death, divorce, or annulment.

Prosecutions for bigamy are infrequent, primarily because few people marry someone while still be married to another person. When the crime occurs, it is usually part of a fraudulent plot to obtain someone's property or as part of some other type of criminal scheme. The other situation that prompts bigamy prosecutions concerns the activities of splinter religious groups that continue the practice polygamy to this day in spite of fact that the mainstream religions from which these offshoots broke away prohibit polygamy. Consider that even though the Church of Jesus Christ of Latter Day Saints officially abandoned the practice in 1890, a breakaway, fundamentalist Mormon sect still practices plural marriage. Bigamy prosecutions of members of these sects often arise from situations like those described in books like *God's Brothel: The Extortion of Sex for Salvation in Contemporary Mormon and Christian Fundamentalist Polygamy*[56] or *Saints Under Siege*,[57] which document how a warped view of religion is used to justify rape, incest, orgies, and violence—even against young girls who are taken as "wives" at remarkably young ages.

In *Reynolds v. United States* (1879), the US Supreme Court ruled that Utah's criminalization of bigamy (a law Utah was required to enact before it was admitted to the Union) was constitutionally permissible in spite of the First Amendment right to the free exercise of religion. *Reynolds* has never been overruled. Moreover, defendants convicted of violating bigamy laws have not been successful in arguing that *Lawrence* changed the legal landscape. For example, in the 2006 case of *State v. Holm*,[58] the Utah Supreme Court upheld the state's bigamy law, reasoning it did not concern the criminal regulation of private sexual activity between consenting adults, but rather the regulation of marriage.

> The people of this State have declared monogamy a beneficial marital form and have also declared polygamous relationships harmful. As the Tenth Circuit stated . . . Utah "is justified, by a compelling interest, in upholding and enforcing its ban on plural marriage to protect the monogamous marriage relationship." The distinction between private, intimate sexual conduct between consenting adults and the public nature of polygamists' attempts to extra-legally redefine

the acceptable parameters of a fundamental social institution like marriage is plain.[59]

Criminal laws against *cohabitation* prohibited unmarried persons from living together. Such a morals offense is invalid under *Lawrence*. In some states, however, the crime of bigamy also includes cohabitating or living with someone other than his or her lawful spouse under circumstance that give the appearance that the cohabitating couple are legally married when, in fact, they are not.[60] Such a law was successfully challenged in 2013 in a civil lawsuit brought by Kody Brown and his four "wives" after they appeared on the TLC television show *Sister Wives*.[61] The plaintiffs lived in a state of cohabitation in which they lived together without getting legally married, although their relationship resembled a marriage. Indeed, they appropriated "the terminology of marriage," though not purporting "to have actually acquired the legal status of marriage."[62] Because they did not actually engage in polygamy, their polyamorous relationship lay beyond the applicability of the *Reynolds* decision. The court found there was no rational basis to prohibit this type of cohabitation. It therefore invalidated the state's bigamy statute as applied to cohabitation, but upheld the constitutionality of the statute's prohibition on actual bigamy.[63]

SEX CRIMES THAT ARE ROUTINELY PROSECUTED

The Court in *Lawrence* was careful to point out that its decision did not restrict the regulation of sexual activity that occurs in public, involves sex for money, involves minors, or is otherwise exploitative.[64] The remainder of this chapter explores sex crimes that fall into these categories.

Incest

Most US jurisdictions define **incest** as either the marriage or sexual intercourse between closely related persons.[65] With the exception of a handful of ancient cultures in Persia, Egypt, Incaic Peru, and Bali that sanctioned the marriage of members of royal families, bans on incest have been present in nearly all societies since at least Biblical times, if not earlier.[66]

"While the ecclesiastical courts of England punished incest as an 'offense against good morals,' at common law incest was not an indictable offense."[67] In the United States, however, incest has been a statutory crime since colonial times and remains so in nearly all states today. The degree of kinship banned by incest statutes varies by jurisdiction. Most states do not permit any coupling of persons who are within a close degree of consanguinity—parents, siblings, aunts, uncles, and grandparents. But states differ on whether sex or marriage between first cousins or former in-laws is permissible.[68]

Although *Lawrence* undercuts moral reasons for criminalizing consensual incest, there are public health reasons to prevent incest, especially to prevent inbreeding, a practice that increases the likelihood of offspring being born with harmful genetic mutations that negatively affect health. Additionally, incest laws are intended to deter coercion, protect the integrity of the family unit, and prevent the significant psychological harm that incest can cause.[69]

The thought of sexual relationships or marriage between closely related relatives produces repugnance and nausea for most people. Given such visceral reactions, it is not surprising that there are few cases dealing with such conduct. Most incest prosecutions concern child molestations committed by a relative.[70] When such acts occur, defendants may be lawfully convicted of both incest and rape/child molestation without violating the Double Jeopardy Clause of the US Constitution since these crimes have distinct elements.[71]

Outside the realm of molestations, incest prosecutions are rare, but they do occur. *Lawrence* is not a bar to such prosecutions. For example, a federal appeals court denied a habeas corpus petition for a stepfather who was imprisoned under Ohio law for having engaged in sexual intercourse with his twenty-two-year-old stepdaughter. The court reasoned that "the stepparent-stepchild relationship is the kind of relationship in which a person might be injured or coerced or where consent might not easily be refused, regardless of age, because of the inherent influence of the stepparent over the stepchild."[72] And in 2020, an appellate court in Virginia upheld a conviction of a defendant who had conditionally pled guilty to charges of both incest and adultery when he cheated on his wife by having sex with his eighteen-year-old stepdaughter. The court rejected the defendant's argument that the statute criminalizing incest was unconstitutional when applied to people over the age of consent who are not related by blood.[73]

Sex Offenses of a Public Nature

Many US states have laws against **lewd and lascivious conduct**, but most statutes define the offense tautologically insofar as they use phrases such as "lewd act" or "lascivious act" or "unnatural act" to define the crime without specifically stating the acts that are prohibited by the law.[74] As a rule, such statutes ban the commission of any act of sexual gratification, either by oneself or with another person, with knowledge or reasonable anticipation that the participants are being viewed by others. Some states, however, have special **public sexual indecency** laws that target sex acts in public place or in public view,[75] or sex acts that occur when "another person is present, and the defendant is reckless about whether such other person, as a reasonable person, would be offended or alarmed by the act."[76]

The lewd and lascivious conduct statutes in some US states include **indecent exposure.**[77] In other states, indecent exposure constitutes a separate criminal offense that is usually defined as the knowing exposure or exhibition of the genitals, anus, or female nipples in a public place or on the private premises of another, or so near thereto as to be seen from such private premises, in a vulgar or indecent manner, or to be naked in public except in any place provided or set apart for that purpose.[78] In the past, indecent exposure laws did not exclude breast-feeding, but today, the laws of nearly all states specifically exempt breast-feeding from the definition of indecent exposure.[79]

Regardless of whether a jurisdiction has separate statutes for these types of offenses or lumps them all together in a single lewdness statute, it is clear that specific intent (i.e., either purpose or knowledge) is not required to violate these laws. As you may recall from *State v. Rocker*[80] in Chapter 4, reckless conduct will suffice. *State ex rel. A.T.* serves as another example.[81] In that case, a fifteen-year-old, while fully clothed, "grabbed ahold of his crotch and shook it up and down" for ten to fifteen seconds while in a 7-Eleven parking lot in view of a woman who had parked her car in the convenience store's lot.[82] The woman was "shocked" and "[v]ery uncomfortable."[83] A plainclothes deputy sheriff witnessed the event and arrested the boy for lewd and lascivious conduct. A juvenile court adjudicated him a delinquent for the act. On appeal the Utah Supreme Court affirmed, reasoning that the boy's actions "conveyed the appearance of masturbation" and that he "should have known his behavior would likely cause affront or alarm to the woman in the parking lot."[84] Accordingly, the court held his acts constituted a "act of lewdness" within the meaning of the state's law prohibiting such conduct. The "You Make the Public Policy Call" feature contained in Box 9.1 considers the question of whether "mooning" constitutes lewd and lascivious conduct.

The Utah lewdness statute includes a provision barring "trespassory voyeurism."[85] Such a provision is aimed at the "Peeping Tom" who trespass on the property of others in order to view inside their homes. Other states have separate laws punishing **voyeurism** as an invasion of privacy. Ohio's Criminal Code, for example, provides that: "No person, for the purpose of sexually arousing or gratifying himself or herself, shall commit trespass or otherwise surreptitiously invade the privacy of another, to spy or eavesdrop on another."[86]

Prostitution

The crime of **prostitution** involves engaging in sexual activity with another person in exchange for some form of compensation.[87] The compensation is usually money, but it could be any other item of economic value, such as drugs or jewelry.[88] The item offered or exchanged for sex, however, need not be particularly valuable. For example, a defendant was convicted of prostitution for offering sex in exchange for a piece of bubble gum.[89]

A BRIEF HISTORICAL OVERVIEW OF PROSTITUTION

Frequently described as "the oldest profession," laws regulating prostitution have existed for millennia. Notably, though, many of these laws recognized prostitution as a legitimate profession and granted specific rights to those who engaged in prostitution.[90] Criminal laws against certain forms of prostitution began to emerge sporadically in Western Europe

BOX 9.1

YOU MAKE THE PUBLIC POLICY CALL

Is Mooning Obscene?

In *Commonwealth v. Quinn*, the defendant was charged with lewdness for pulling down his pants in front of four thirteen-year-old girls "exposing his buttocks along with a pair of red 'thong' underwear."[200] Because he did not expose his genitals, he was not charged with indecent exposure. Although the court ruled that exposure of the genitals was not necessary to support a charge of lewdness, it ruled that the lewdness statute did not provide the defendant "with fair notice that deliberately exposing his thong-clad buttocks may be illegal." The court, therefore, ruled that the statute was unconstitutionally vague as applied to the defendant in that case.

With the *Quinn* decision, the Supreme Judicial Court of Massachusetts judicially defined the contour of the lewdness statute in that case to include "the intentional exposure of genitalia, buttocks, or female breasts to one or more persons."[201] As a result, future vagueness challenges would fail since the court's decision provides notice of what conduct is prohibited (see Chapter 1). Thus, any such exposures after the decision in *Quinn* would constitute lewdness if done in a manner that recklessly disregards a substantial risk of public exposure to others who might be offended by such conduct.

1. Critique the application of lewdness laws to "mooning." Should such activity constitute lewdness?
2. For indecent exposure to constitute criminal conduct under Iowa law, it must be sexually motivated—"to arouse or satisfy the sexual desires of either party."[202] As a result, the Iowa Supreme Court has held that "even deliberate exposure done without a sexual motive, such as streaking, nude protesting or urinating in public" does not violate the state's statute.[203] Would any of these behaviors constitute lewdness in Massachusetts in light of the decision in the *Quinn* case? Explain your reasoning.
3. Refer back to Figure 8.1 in Chapter 8. Do you think outcomes in lewd and lascivious conduct cases might vary in different states depending on the age of consent? Why or why not?

starting in 525 CE.[91] But such laws proliferated in the late fifteenth century when a wave of syphilis spread throughout Europe.

This epidemic significantly changed the European perspective of prostitution. A decree issued in 1495 by Emperor Maximilian of Habsburg declared prostitutes as the main source of syphilis and other venereal diseases. As a consequence, brothels were closed down and other forms of prostitution were outlawed throughout Europe. Henry VIII issued a royal proclamation in 1546 ending England's regulation of prostitution by banning the practice. In 1586, Pope Sixtus V decreed that prostitution was such a sin against nature that Catholics the world over should impose the death penalty on offenders.[92]

In spite of many strict laws against prostitution throughout Europe during the Middle Ages, the practice remained widespread, especially in France.[93] But the Enlightenment brought reforms that replace criminal laws against prostitution with a system of public health regulations designed to prevent the spread of sexually transmitted infections.[94] These regulations, however, were quite harsh on women.

The Contagious Disease Acts of 1868 and 1869 in England, for example, allowed police to arrest women they suspected of being prostitutes and force them to undergo medical examination for venereal diseases. If the tests were positive, the women were hospitalized until they were cured. Notably, though, the men who frequented prostitutes were not subject to arrest, medical examination, and forced hospitalization.[95]

The Victorian Era's repressive stance on sexuality ended social tolerance of prostitution in England and in the United States.[96] Moral crusaders successfully led campaigns to criminalize a wide range of behaviors associated with prostitution, including "night walking, vagrancy, and a variety of improprieties of conduct, such as cross-dressing."[97] By 1925, all US states had enacted laws directly targeting selling sexual services.[98]

CRIMINAL LAWS AGAINST PROSTITUTION

The common law provided that only a woman could be convicted of prostitution.[99] Today, however, prostitution laws apply to sex acts performed by men and women alike.[100] In most US jurisdictions today, any form of sexual activity for hire falls within the statutory prohibition on prostitution. In other words, oral sex, vaginal sex, anal sex, and assisted masturbation all fall within the acts proscribed by prostitution laws in the United States.[101] Under most of these laws, both parties to acts of prostitution (i.e., the "buyer" and the "seller") are guilty of offense, although prosecutions of persons selling sexual services are far more common than of those who purchase or attempt to purchase such services.

In most states, prostitution is either a strict liability offense or a crime of general intent, carrying recklessness or negligence.[102] A handful of US states, however, require specific intent to agree to an act of prostitution—purposefully or knowingly agreeing to any sex act in exchange for compensation.[103] Regardless of what particular level of *mens rea*, if any, is required by a statute, "[i]t is the formation of the agreement, not what happens afterwards, that creates a prima facie prostitution case in the majority of American jurisdictions."[104]

OFFENSES RELATED TO PROSTITUTION

As with other crimes, inchoate liability may affix on anyone who solicits, knowingly facilitates, or purposefully aids or abets the crime of prostitution.[105] These inchoate offenses, however, typically require high levels of *mens rea* (i.e., purpose or knowledge), while, as previously mentioned, the substantive crime of prostitution is typically either a strict liability or general intent crime.[106]

Many states have enacted specialized statutory offenses for crimes related to prostitution. Although the specific definition of these offenses vary from state to state, these law often include **pandering**—forcing, deceiving, decoying, enticing, inducting, or otherwise recruiting someone to become a prostitute; **pimping**—sharing in the earnings of a prostitute; and maintaining a place where prostitution is habitually practiced.[107] Additionally, to prevent prostitution, some jurisdictions have enacted statutes which prohibit **loitering** for the purposes of prostitution, which requires a showing of specific intent (i.e., purpose) to engage in the sale or purchase of sexual services.[108]

DECRIMINALIZATION

Debates about the decriminalization of prostitution are almost as old as the crime itself.[109] Although some people argue that prostitution laws are "victimless crimes" or that they infringe autonomy and privacy rights, legal challenges to prostitution laws, even those decided after *Lawrence*, universally uphold the right of the state to regulate such conduct in the name of public health, morality, and the protection of people from exploitation.[110]

Several counties in Nevada have decriminalized prostitution under a comprehensive set of regulations, as have a number of foreign countries.[111] Other than the notable exception of Nevada, prostitution is considered a misdemeanor in all other US states, although the charge can be elevated to a felony if multiple prostitution charges accumulate over time.[112]

Some people oppose prostitution (and its decriminalization) because it "objectifies, exploits, and ultimately dehumanizes women; others decry it for precipitating social ills, such as the proliferation of communicable diseases, crime, rape" and the prevention of exploitation.[113] Indeed, that last rationale is of particular concern with respect to both domestic and international human trafficking.

HUMAN TRAFFICKING

Human trafficking involves transporting someone into a situation of exploitation, including forced labor, marriage, organ removal, and prostitution. Data on the number of victims is hard to come by because the cases often go undetected, but most estimates range to more than 40 million people world-wide at any given time, at least a quarter of whom are children.[114] *Fortune* magazine declared this modern form of slavery to be of "epidemic" proportions, generating "global profits of about $150 billion a year—$99 billion from sexual exploitation."[115] More than half of the active cases in the United States involve sex trafficking of minors, many of whom were either in the foster care system or were runaways who had been sexually abused.[116]

In 2000, the federal government enacted the Trafficking Victims Protection Act (TVPA).[117] The law established two forms of human trafficking as federal crimes: *sex trafficking*—a commercial sex act induced by force, fraud, or coercion, or in which the person induced to perform such an act has not attained eighteen years of age; and *labor trafficking*—the recruitment, harboring, transportation, provision, or obtaining of a person for labor or services, through the use of force, fraud, or coercion for the purpose of subjection to involuntary servitude, peonage, debt bondage, or slavery. The TVPA also sought to prevent human trafficking and protect both victims and survivors of trafficking.[118]

In 2005, Congress enacted the Trafficking Victims Protection Reauthorization Act (TVPRA)[119] and, three years later, expanded it to explicitly address the relationship between state prostitution enforcement and federal attempts to control human trafficking.[120] One of its key provisions created a "safe harbor" for minors engaged in commercial sex work and adults who has been forced or coerced into prostitution.[121] As critics point out, however, federal laws designed to protect the victims of human trafficking who are forced into prostitution are often at odds with state prostitution laws which, all too often, treat the victims of human trafficking as criminals—especially when they are minors.[122] Some reforms, however, have begun to address these concerns.

PROSTITUTION LAW REFORMS FOR CERTAIN VICTIMS

Human rights activists and the US Department of Justice successfully lobbied all fifty US states to enact legislation similar to the TVPRA, although the scope of state safe harbors for victims of human sex trafficking vary significantly.[123] Most states "provide judicial protections for survivors, establish funding sources for anti-trafficking efforts, coordinate stakeholder efforts, regulate businesses to mitigate the impact of trafficking and educate the public on trafficking issues."[124]

In spite of wide variation, a few reforms have been adopted in a sizable number of states and those numbers grow with each passing year. First, juveniles engaged in prostitution are increasingly viewed as "children incapable of legally consenting to commercial sex acts. Lawmakers are beginning to recognize the legal incongruence between statutory rape laws, which view minors as victims, and prostitution laws that view them as criminal defendants."[125] Thus, roughly twenty states prevent minors from being charged with prostitution; rather, minors engaged in prostitution are directed to social service agencies.[126] But some states either limit their safe harbors to first-time arrests or to particularly young children (while still criminalizing prostitution by older teenagers who are nonetheless under the age of majority).[127] Second, legislatures have statutorily created an affirmative defense to prostitution for those who were coerced or forced into the act.[128] Finally, roughly half of US states now provide post-conviction relief from prostitution convictions via expungement. This, in turn, allows an "exit option" for those who were forced, tricked, or coerced into acts of prostitution, thereby erasing criminal records that could stand in the way of gainful employment.[129]

Obscenity

As briefly summarized in Chapter 2, sexually explicit expression which is indecent, but not obscene, is protected by the First Amendment. Where the line is drawn between indecency and obscenity, though, is not subject to easy explication.

EARLY UNDERSTANDINGS OF OBSCENITY IN THE UNITED STATES

The first real crusade to reshape how the government handled sexually explicit material was prompted by Anthony Comstock. After reading literature that he deemed inappropriate, Comstock found the publisher and had him arrested. Finding reward in his actions, he continued on a mission to eliminate explicit materials and eventually founded New York's YMCA Committee for the Suppression of Vice. Under New York law, this organization was empowered with the rights to search, seize, and arrest. With the financial support of J.P. Morgan and Samuel Colgate, Comstock was able to lobby Congress to enact a statute that prohibited the mailing of obscene materials and anything related to birth control or abortion, which was known as the Anti-Obscenity Act of 1873 or the Comstock Act.[130]

During the Comstock era, many books were banned by classic authors such as Chaucer, Hemingway, Steinbeck, F. Scott Fitzgerald, Daniel Defoe, Voltaire, James Joyce, Walt Whitman, and D. H. Lawrence. Soon thereafter, the Comstock Act was amended to prohibit sending of obscene materials through the mail. Even today, the US Criminal Code still provides as follows:

> Whoever knowingly uses the mails for the mailing, carriage in the mails, or delivery of anything declared . . . to be nonmailable [by virtue of being obscene] . . . shall be fined under this title or imprisoned not more than five years, or both, for the first such offence, and shall be fined under this title or imprisoned not more than ten years, or both, for each such offense thereafter.[131]

At that time in US history, in order to determine whether materials were classified as obscene, and therefore prohibited to be published or mailed, law enforcement generally relied upon the precedent established in *Rosen v. United States*.[132] In that case, the US Supreme Court had decided that indecent materials would be assessed using the test adopted in English in *Regina v. Hinklin*,[133] namely whether the material in question tends "to deprave and corrupt those whose minds are open to such immoral influences, and into whose hands a publication of this sort may fall."[134] As a result, a literary work could be deemed obscene for the *potential effect* of an isolated passage on the most susceptible readers or viewers.

Although the *Hicklin* test became the guiding principle for US courts through the early twentieth century, the judiciary was soon called upon again because of the overly broad language outlined in *Regina v. Hinklin*. The *Hinklin* test met began to meet its demise in *United States v. One Book Entitled "Ulysses."*[135] In ruling that James Joyce's book *Ulysses* was not obscene, a federal district judge rejected the "isolated passages" and "susceptible person" doctrines of the *Hinklin* test because literary works must be judged by their dominant effect on people. Not only did this landmark case mark one of the first times a federal court recognized that obscenity laws may conflict with the First Amendment, but it was also the first case to establish that the conflicting interests underlying obscenity laws and the First Amendment must be considered by examining the materials in question in their entirety, not just on isolated parts.

ROTH AND THE MID-TWENTIETH CENTURY

The period between the late nineteenth century and the mid-twentieth century brought significant changes to how the US population received information. Print journalism, especially in most newspapers, became much more professionalized. Magazine publishing also changed dramatically as a function of the rise of commercial advertising and the availability of four-color printing, resulting in an explosion of magazine options. Starting in the 1920s, other media such as radio and motion pictures also became popular means of communicating news, political analysis, and entertainment. By the 1950s, television emerged as a powerful mode of mass communication. As each of these forms of mass communication developed, they increased the channels through which potentially obscene materials could be disseminated. Concerns over indecent material contributing to social decay were used to justify content-based regulations of free expression which, in turn, prompted the courts—and the US Supreme Court, in particular—to examine restrictions under the First Amendment in ways that were previously unnecessary.[136]

Following the demise of the *Hinklin* test, new parameters for obscenity were established by the US Supreme Court's decision in *Roth v. United States*.[137] Rather than specifically addressing whether the material presented in the case was obscene, the Court opted to tackle whether obscenity in general was "utterance within the area of protect speech and press."[138] Delivering the majority opinion for the Court, Justice Brennan concluded that obscenity was not protected under the First Amendment. In his analysis, Brennan began by asserting that when the First Amendment was ratified, there were forms of speech in various states (such as blasphemy and defamation) that were banned or regulated under state law. Although he believed that "[a]ll ideas having even the slightest redeeming social importance—unorthodox ideas, controversial ideas, [and] even ideas hateful to the prevailing climate of opinion" were protected under the First Amendment, obscenity did not qualify for such protection.[139]

In addition to offering a logical explanation for obscenity law, Justice Brennan also sought to delineate the meaning of obscenity because the First Amendment was primarily concerned with nonobscene sexual matters. He did not equate sex to obscenity or vice versa: "[o]bscene material is material which deals with sex in a manner appealing to prurient interest."[140] Outlining the definition of *prurient interest*, Brennan referred to the Model Penal Code's draft definition of obscenity as embodying "a shameful or morbid interest in nudity, sex, or excretion."[141] Using this definition of obscenity, and incorporating the reasoning in *United States v. One Book Entitled "Ulysses,"* Justice Brennan directed judges to examine "the effect of the book, picture, or publication considered as a whole . . . upon the average person in the community, [asking whether the material offends] the common conscience of the community by present-day standards."[142] But this definition of obscenity caused much confusion in the lower courts.

MILLER AND CURRENT OBSCENITY LAW

Sex and its relationship to obscenity remained highly controversial during the late 1960s and early 1970s. This was due, in large part, to societal concern over an emerging counterculture whose members protested the Vietnam War, questioned the legitimacy of police power, and participated in a number of acts then-considered to be immoral and, in some cases, illegal, such as fornication, vagrancy, and illicit drug use.[143] During this time, the US Supreme Court decided *Miller v. California*,[144] an obscenity case that remains the law to this day.

The appellant in *Miller* had mailed brochures to advertise his sexually explicit illustrated books. The brochures consisted of pictures and drawings that depicted men and women engaging in a variety of sexual activities. One of the recipients of the mailing complained to the police who subsequently arrested him for violating the state's obscenity law. He was convicted and appealed. The Court clarified the holding in *Roth* by setting forth a three-part test for obscenity. Under *Miller*, material is obscene if,

1. the average person, applying contemporary community standards, finds that the work, taken as a whole, appeals to the prurient interest (i.e., a shameful or morbid interest in nudity, sex, or excretion);
2. the work depicts, in a patently offensive way, sexual conduct specifically defined by the applicable state law; and
3. the work, taken as a whole, lacks serious literary, artistic, political, or scientific value.[145]

The first prong of the *Miller* test mirrors the test set forth in *Roth* with one notably distinction. Whereas *Roth* referenced broad, amorphous contemporary societal standards, *Miller* clarified that trial courts are supposed "to rely on knowledge of the standards of the residents of the community to decide whether the work appeals to a prurient interest."[146] Thus, there are no national standards for what constitutes obscenity; rather, local standards govern. In other words, material that may not be considered obscene in New York may be obscene in Mississippi.

In an attempt to more clearly clarify the kinds of material that fall under the second part of the *Miller* test, the Court offered a few examples. By "patently offensive," the Court was referring to "the representation or description of ultimate sexual acts, normal or perverted, actual or stimulated . . . [,] masturbation, excretory functions, and lewd exhibition of the genitals."[147] Thus, even though courts in Georgia determined an R-rated movie starring Jack Nicholson and Candice Bergen was obscene, the US Supreme Court reversed because the film did not include graphic depictions of sexual or excretory functions.[148]

The third and final prong of the *Miller* test refined the portion of *Roth* that required a determination that obscene material be "utterly without redeeming social value."[149] *Miller* clarified this amorphous standard by specifying that "social value" meant "serious literary, artistic, political, or scientific value."[150] By way of example, the *Miller* Court explained that medical books that depict graphic illustrations and descriptions of human anatomy for the purpose of educating physicians would not be considered obscene. But might determinations of what constitutes serious literature or art lie, like beauty, in the eye of the beholder? Consider, for instance, that the manager of an Abercrombie and Fitch store was arrested on obscenity charges for displaying photos of models that included the upper buttocks of a shirtless young man and the partially bare breast of a young woman.[151] Although charges were dropped, the arrest demonstrates the subjective nature of obscenity determinations.

In *Pope v. Illinois*,[152] the US Supreme Court clarified that whether a work possesses "serious literary, artistic, political, or scientific value" is not a question to be decided by contemporary community standards. Community standards only guide the determination of the first prong of the *Miller* test concerning whether the material in question appeals to the prurient interest. Rather, the third prong of *Miller* presents a question that transcends the amount of acceptance a work may have won within a given community. Accordingly, in obscenity cases that go to trial, expert testimony is often necessary to help the trier-of-fact determine if the challenged work has "serious literary, artistic, political, or scientific value." But such testimony is not conclusive, as illustrated by *Luke Records, Inc. v. Navarro*.[153] In that case, the rap group 2 Live Crew released a recording entitled *As Nasty as They Want to Be*. The recording contained both profane and sexually graphic lyrics. It was declared obscene by a Florida judge. The group appealed and won because the prosecution "submitted no evidence to contradict [2 Live Crew's expert] testimony that the work had artistic value."[154]

Possession of Obscene Materials

Even though governmental entities may constitutionally criminalize the production and distribution of obscene materials, the same is not true for possession of obscene materials. In *Stanley v. Georgia*,[155] the US Supreme Court upheld the ability of person to possess obscene materials in the privacy of one's home, reasoning that "[w]hatever the power of the state to control public dissemination of ideas inimical to the public morality, it cannot constitutionally premise legislation on the desirability of controlling a person's private thoughts."[156]

Stanley v. Georgia applies only in the home. Out in the community, recall from Chapter 2 that First Amendment liberties may be curtailed under valid time, place, and manner restrictions. Thus, for example, in *Renton v. Playtime Theatres, Inc.*,[157] the Supreme Court upheld a zoning ordinance that kept adult movie theatres out of residential neighborhoods. The ordinance was aimed, not at the content of the films shown in the theaters, but rather at the "secondary effects"—such as crime and deteriorating property values—that these theaters fostered.[158]

Stanley v. Georgia also does not apply to the possession of child pornography. In *Osborne v. Ohio*,[159] the Court reasoned that because "safeguarding the physical and psychological well-being of a minor" is a compelling government interest, bands on possessing child pornography, even in the privacy of one's own home, "passes muster under the First Amendment."[160]

Protecting Children

As the holding in *Osborne v. Ohio*[161] suggests, protecting children from sexual exploitation historically centered on efforts to eradicate child pornography. With the advent of the internet, however, children face a variety of dangers online. The criminal law may be ill-suited to addressing some of these dangers.

CHILD PORNOGRAPHY

In *New York v. Ferber*,[162] the defendant sold two films to an undercover police officer that depicted underage boys masturbating. The defendant was charged with and convicted of two counts of violating a state law criminalizing the knowingly promotion or distribution of any material depicting sexual performances by children under the age of sixteen. An intermediate appellate court upheld the convictions, but the highest court in New York reversed on the grounds that the statute was "underinclusive because it discriminated against visual portrayals of children engaged in sexual activity by not also prohibiting the distribution of films of other dangerous activity. It was also overbroad because it prohibited the distribution of materials produced outside the State, as well as materials, such as medical books and educational sources."[163] The US Supreme Court reversed.

Although the Court recognized that laws aimed at curbing child pornography may run the risk of suppressing protected expression, the Court made it clear that child pornography is, per se, obscene and, therefore, is entitled to no First Amendment protection. The conclusion rested on several lines of reasoning. First, the state has a compelling interest in safeguarding children by ensuring that their physiological, physical, cognitive, and emotional well-being are not disrupted as they develop into young adults. Second, "[t]he distribution of photographs and films depicting sexual activity by juveniles is intrinsically related to the sexual abuse of children."[164] Third, the production, distribution, and advertisement of child pornography provide an economic motive for the industry to persist. Conversely, outlawing child pornography helps to prevent future sexual exploitation of children. Fourth, children engaging in lewd sexual conduct via live performances or photographs offer no redeeming literary, artistic, political, or scientific value. Lastly, whether the First Amendment protects speech depends on its content. In the case of child pornography, it lacks this protection because "the evil to be restricted so overwhelmingly outweighs the expressive interests, if any, at stake, that no process of case-by-case adjudication is required."[165]

Two years after *Ferber* was decided, Congress passed the Child Protection Act of 1984.[166] It criminalized the production, distribution, or possession of child pornography, regardless of whether the material was obscene under *Miller* or *Ferber*. The Child Protection Act, as amended, defines child pornography as the "visual depiction" of anyone under the age of eighteen engaging in "sexually explicit conduct," which includes "(i) sexual intercourse, including genital-genital, oral-genital, anal-genital, or oral-anal, whether between persons of the same or opposite sex; (ii) bestiality; (iii) masturbation; (iv) sadistic or masochistic abuse; or (v) lascivious exhibition of the genitals or pubic area of any person."[167] In *United States v. Dost*, a federal district court ruled that nude pictures of minors photographed in sexually suggestive poses fell within the "lascivious exhibition" provision and, therefore, constitutes child pornography.[168]

Two years later, the Child Sexual Abuse and Pornography Act of 1986[169] criminalized all advertisements for child pornography. Two years later, Congress enacted the Child Protection and Obscenity Enforcement Act of 1988 to outlaw the use of computers to traffic child pornography.[170] In 1990, not only did *Osborne v. Ohio*[171] reject applying *Stanley* to the possession of child pornography, but also Congress passed the Child Protection Restoration and Penalties Enhancement Act of 1990, making it a federal crime to possess three or more child pornography items.[172]

Congress has enacted a series of other statutes with the intent of protecting children from exploitation, such as the Child Pornography Prevention Act of 1996 (CPPA).[173] It was the first law of the modern era targeting child pornography that was subsequently declared unconstitutional. Prior to the passage of this law, child pornography could only be criminalized if it involved the *actual depiction* of children engaging in sexual conduct. The CPPA sought to extend such laws in the Digital Age by making it illegal to produce or distribute computer-generated and computer-altered sexual images of children. The law attempted to criminalize so-called virtual kiddie porn because even though an actual child was not involved in the production of the offending images, distribution of such material nonetheless encouraged pedophilia.

In *Ashcroft v. Free Speech Coalition*,[174] the US Supreme Court declared the CPPA unconstitutionally overbroad because it banned images that some may consider indecent, but that were not legally obscene, such as books and movies that have teenage sexual activity as a theme. Indeed, the court discussed two Oscar-nominated films, *Traffic* and *American*

Beauty, as examples of films that could run afoul the overbroad provisions of the CPPA because they depicted children engaging in sexual acts.[175]

> The mere tendency of speech to encourage unlawful acts is not a sufficient reason for banning it. . . . The Government has shown no more than a remote connection between speech that might encourage thoughts or impulses and any resulting child abuse. Without a significantly stronger, more direct connection, the Government may not prohibit speech on the ground that it may encourage pedophiles to engage in illegal conduct.[176]

In the wake of that decision, Congress enacted the Prosecutorial Remedies and Other Tools to End the Exploitation of Children Today Act of 2003 (PROTECT Act).[177] The Act prohibits "pandering" (i.e., the knowingly advertising, promoting, or soliciting) material "in a manner that reflects the belief, or that is intended to cause another to believe" that the advertised material is child pornography involving real minors, even if the underlying material does not, in fact, include real minors or is otherwise completely innocuous."[178] The US Supreme Court upheld the constitutionality of the PROTECT Act in *United States v. Williams*.[179] The Court made it clear that it was not overruling *Ashcroft v. Free Speech Coalition*: "Simulated child pornography will be as available as ever, so long as it is offered and sought *as such*, and not as real child pornography."[180] In other words, although computer-generated images of child pornography are protected by the First Amendment, the speech associated with either offering such images to others or seeking such images from others may be criminally proscribed.

INDECENCY ON THE INTERNET

In addition to regulating obscenity, lawmakers have also attempted to regulate "indecent" materials. Some of these regulations constitute valid time, place, and manner restrictions on speech and, therefore, do not run afoul the First Amendment. For example, *Federal Communications Commission v. Pacifica Foundation*[181] upheld regulations banning certain words from being broadcast on the radio so that children and nonconsenting adults would not hear them. But the lengths to which the criminal law may be used to regulate that which may be indecent, but not obscene, are clearly limited. *Reno v. American Civil Liberties Union*, for instance,[182] invalidated on First Amendment grounds portions of the Communications Decency Act (CDA) that prohibited the "knowing sending or displaying of patently offensive messages in a manner that is available to a person under 18 years of age."[183] The Court reasons that the CDA was both and overbroad:

> We are persuaded that the CDA lacks the precision that the First Amendment requires when a statute regulates the content of speech. In order to deny minors access to potentially harmful speech, the CDA effectively suppresses a large amount of speech that adults have a constitutional right to receive and to address to one another. That burden on adult speech is unacceptable if less restrictive

alternatives would be at least as effective in achieving the legitimate purpose that the statute was enacted to serve.[184]

GROOMING ON THE INTERNET

The internet—especially social media sites—can be a dangerous place for children and vulnerable adults. Indeed, sexual predators can use the internet to communicate with potential victims in ways that are designed to prepare the victims for sexual contact—a process referred to as **grooming.**

Grooming is a preparatory process that involves a range of methodical behaviors in which a perpetrator gradually gains a person's trust with the intent of eventually being sexually abusive.[185] Grooming may include "targeting the victim, securing access to and isolating the victim, gaining the victim's trust, and controlling and concealing the relationship."[186]

As you learned in Chapter 8, forcible sexual activity with minors or adults whose cognitive abilities to grant consent are impaired constitutes the crime of rape. Such activity that does not involve the use or threatened use of force may constitutes lesser forms of sexual assault and, in the case of child victims, either child molestation or statutory rape, depending on victim's age. To prevent such victimization, some states have enacted criminal laws targeting sexual grooming behaviors. Keeping in mind what you learned about the First Amendment in Chapter 2 and about inchoate offenses in Chapters 5 and 6, consider the following case.

STATE of Minnesota, Appellant,
v.
Krista Ann MUCCIO, Respondent.
890 N.W.2d 914 (2017).

[A] father reported to law enforcement that he found inappropriate photos on his 15-year-old son's iPad. The photographs depicted a female's bare genitals, a female naked from the neck to below the waist, and a female's buttocks covered by a thong. These photos were sent to the 15-year-old through respondent Krista Muccio's Instagram account via a direct message. At the time, Muccio was 41 years old. In a statement to the police, the 15-year-old said that, after he received these pictures from Muccio, he sent her a picture of his genitals. Additionally, Muccio and the 15-year-old exchanged sexually explicit text messages. In these messages, Muccio and the 15-year-old detailed the sexual acts they wanted to engage in with each other, including fellatio and anal sex.

[T]he State of Minnesota charged Muccio in count one with felony communication with a child describing sexual conduct, in violation of [the state's anti-grooming law]. . . . This statute prohibits "a person 18 years of age or older" from "using the Internet, a computer, . . . or other electronic device capable of electronic data storage or transmission" to "engage in communication with a child or someone the person reasonably believes is a child, relating to or describing sexual conduct." To violate the statute, the adult must act "with the intent to arouse the sexual desire of any person. . . ." A "child" is "a person 15 years of age or younger." "Sexual conduct" is "sexual contact of the individual's primary genital area, sexual penetration . . . , or sexual performance."[187]

* * *

Contrary to Muccio's argument, . . . the statute does not proscribe non-targeted mass electronic communications, such as posting non-targeted social-media posts that a child happens to view. Similarly, Internet social-media posts with a more limited audience, such as a post that can only be viewed by a person's Facebook friends or a message posted on an Internet message board, are not directed at a child simply because the people who could possibly view such a post include children. Instead, for a transmission to be directed at a child, the child must be the object of the adult's attention. In other words, to engage in communication with a child, the adult must take some affirmative act to specifically select or designate the child as a recipient of the transmission.

* * *

First Amendment protections do not extend to speech used "as an integral part of conduct in violation of a valid criminal statute. . . ." Speech is integral to criminal conduct when it "is intended to induce or commence illegal activities," such as "conspiracy, incitement, and solicitation. . . ."

The . . . communications falling within the purview of the statute are part of a process called "grooming." Grooming is a process sexual predators use to shape a child's perspective and lower the child's inhibitions with respect to later criminal sexual acts. . . . As part of the grooming process, the offender typically desensitizes the child to sexual conduct by exposing the child to sexual content. . . . Through the grooming process, the offender increases the likelihood that the child will cooperate with the adult and reduces the likelihood that the child will disclose the adult's wrongful acts. . . . After desensitizing the child to sexual content, the offender typically solicits the child to engage in some type of sexual conduct that may include sexual intercourse, sex trafficking, or child pornography. . . . Although communications made during the grooming process occur before the criminal acts of criminal sexual conduct, sex trafficking, or the creation of child pornography, the adult communicates the sexual content with the purpose of having the child engage in later criminal activity. . . . In this context, the communication is both linked to and designed to facilitate the commission of the later crime. . . . We agree with the State that when grooming is done for the purpose of later using the child in sexual conduct, it resembles solicitation of the child, and . . . such solicitation falls outside First Amendment protections.

* * *

[The court also evaluated whether the communications at issue could be regulated as obscene speech.] Applying the *Miller* standard of obscenity, we conclude that the speech [the statute] proscribes will often be obscene. . . . [It] prohibits communications an adult directs at a child relating to sexual conduct that are made with the intent to arouse sexual desire. Communications of the sort proscribed . . . are likely designed by the adult to arouse the child's sexual desire for the adult, or the adult's sexual desire for the child. Sexual desire between an adult and a child is clearly a "shameful interest in sex. . . ." The statute's intent requirement—mandating the intent to arouse—indicates that many communications falling within its scope will appeal to prurient interests.

The second prong of the *Miller* test . . . is also often met because many of the communications [the anti-grooming law] covers will depict sexual acts in a patently offensive way. As stated above, what is offensive is examined differently when, as in this case, the speech is aimed at children.

Finally, speech subject to [the anti-grooming law] will often meet the final prong of the *Miller* test. . . . Because the communication must be made with the specific intent to arouse . . . , many communications falling within the statute will lack literary, artistic, political, or scientific merit.

The legitimate sweep of [the anti-grooming law] is to protect children from sexual abuse and exploitation and from exposure to harmful sexual material. . . . And because of its specific-intent requirement, . . . the statute does not target broad categories of speech.

Questions

1. One critic of the *Muccio* decision argued that the court got it wrong because the law is a content-based restriction on free speech related to or describing sexual conduct that could infringe on constitutionally protected works. "For example, the law would prohibit sharing songs online, such as Beyoncé's *Drunk in Love* [or] Katy Perry's *I Kissed A Girl*."[188] Look up the lyrics to these songs and then evaluate whether you agree with this critic's assessment that online sharing of these songs with a minor could fall within the reach of Minnesota's anti-grooming law.
2. That same critic argued that it would be better to have such laws omit the *mens rea* requirement of "intent to arouse the sexual desire of any person" and replace it with the "intent to engage in sexual conduct with the child." Do you think that proscribing the "intention to prey on a minor, instead of merely the sexual thoughts inside an individual's head" is a better approach?[189] Why or why not?
3. Should grooming be considered part of a drawn-out solicitation process and punished as the crime of solicitation? Might it even constitute attempted child molestation? Explain your reasoning for your responses to both questions.

SEXTING

Mobile devices with built-in cameras have created a "new frontier for the production and or distribution of child pornography, including self-produced images."[190] Indeed, for a disturbingly large number of teenagers,

> the combination of technology, hormones, and stupidity has led to a practice called "sexting," the cell phone texting of sexually-explicit photos [and videos], often of themselves. What's worse, most of these kids are hitting "send" without realizing that in many states, their actions could violate child pornography laws.[191]

Some states have used their child pornography laws to prosecute **sexting** by adolescents.[192] Under such laws, teenagers may be charged with possession and/or distribution of child pornography if they are caught with explicit images on their cell phone. The irony, of course, is that the same laws that were meant to protect minors from sexual exploitation by adults are now being used to punish adolescents for engaging in what Dr. Peter Cumming asserts is the "modern-day equivalent of playing 'spin the bottle.' "[193]

Most instances of teenage sexting are never brought to the attention of legal authorities. When they are, the cases are typically either handled informally or punished minimally. But as the "Case Study Extra" feature in Box 9.2 illustrates, some cases are prosecuted in ways that resemble traditional child pornography cases. This, in turn, has led some critics to claim that law enforcement or legislatures are "so determined to save teens from themselves . . . [that] they're willing to brand them for life in the process."[194]

Despite the claim that there is no difference between sexted images and child pornography once such material is made available on the internet, a critical aspect of teen sexting demarcates it from "traditional" child pornography. Sexted images are usually self-created by a minor motivated by normal adolescent curiosity and sexual exploration. The lack of any child abuse or exploitation places sexting by teenagers in a qualitatively different position than "lascivious [images] of the genitals or pubic area" that were taken to exploit an adolescent minor, the definition of child pornography under federal law.[195] In light of such a difference, at least 20 states have enacted legislation to address incidents of sexting among minors since 2009.[196] Most of these laws approach the problem in one of two ways, either by explicitly exempting teenagers who sext with each other from being prosecuted under state child pornography laws, or by incorporating so-called Romeo and Juliet provisions into their child pornography laws. The latter approach amends preexisting child pornography laws to include an age-gap provision. Minors who sext with other teenagers within the relevant age-range window are either exempt from prosecution or are punished at a much lower level—such as for a misdemeanor offense, rather than a felony—and are usually exempted from having to register as a sex offender.[197] Some states have supplemented age-gap provisions to add additional legislative deterrents to sexting. For example, in Arizona, minors are provided a defense if they "did not ask for the image,

BOX 9.2

CASE STUDY EXTRA

Should Sexting Between Teenagers Be Prosecuted Under Child Pornography Laws?

While living in Florida, eighteen-year-old Philip Alpert was dating his sixteen-year-old girlfriend.[204] Over the duration of their two-year relationship, she sent him many nude and provocative pictures of herself. Following a fight one night, Alpert made the decision to retaliate by sending the explicit photos of his girlfriend to her friends and family. Unaware of the consequences for this action, Alpert was arrested, charged, and convicted for the distribution of child pornography. As a result, he was mandated to register as a sex offender within the state of Florida and placed on probation for five years. The collateral consequences of his sex offender status and felony conviction were expulsion from college, harsh living restrictions, and employment tribulations because he was perceived as someone who has committed a sex offense against a child victim. Interestingly, while Alpert was charged with the distribution of child pornography, his girlfriend, who created the images, was not punished for its production.

In 2009, the Iowa Supreme Court upheld a felony conviction for knowingly disseminating obscene material to a minor.[205] The case involved eighteen-year-old Jorge Canal, who texted a naked picture of himself to a fourteen-year-old female friend after numerous requests from her; the picture was captioned "I love you." The girl's mother saw the picture and turned it over to the police. Canal was convicted by a jury. He appealed to the Iowa Supreme Court, arguing that the photo was not obscene because the image only appealed to a natural interest in sex rather than a prurient interest in sex. But the court rejected this argument. Canal, therefore, had to register as a sex offender and was placed on probation.

Although the aftermath of the *Alpert* and *Canal* cases may seem somewhat extreme given the circumstances, there are instances when malice or coercion may warrant more severe sanctions. In 2010, for example, nineteen-year-old Anthony Stancl deceived fellow classmates by fictitiously posing as a girl on Facebook and convincing thirty-one males to send him nude pictures of themselves.[206] Stancl then used the photos to blackmail at least seven of his classmates—all of whom were between the ages fifteen to seventeen—into performing sexual acts with him. Stancl had threatened that he would widely distribute the nude images of his victims at school. Once law enforcement was notified, Stancl was arrested and charged with two felony counts of sexual abuse of a child. He was convicted and sentenced to fifteen years in prison.[207] Of course, the Stancl case involved coercive sex, whereas the sexting at issue in the cases of Philip Alpert and Jose Canal did not.

Child advocacy groups warn that sexting is a growing problem with which the United States has yet to come to grips. When sexted pictures are distributed, they can promote harassment, cyberbullying, and potentially lead to victimization at the hands of sexual predators. But even if the activity just causes humiliation, that emotion, in and of itself, can have devastating consequences. Consider the case of Jesse Logan. Jesse, an eighteen-year-old girl living in Cincinnati, had sent a nude picture of herself to her boyfriend while they were dating.[208] After the two broke-up, the photo made its way around her school, causing Jesse to endure name-calling and harassment. Embarrassed, Jesse began skipping classes and it was only then that her parents were made aware of her struggles at school. Jesse went public with her story, appearing on a local television news station in an attempt to warn other teens of the potential consequences of sexting. "I just want to make sure no one else will have to go through this again," she said.[209] But her attempt at public service did not stop the taunting she received at school. Some students even physically assaulted Jesse by throwing things at her. Just two months after her story aired on television, Jesse hanged herself in her bedroom; her cell phone "was in the middle of the floor."[210] Thirteen-year-old Hope Witsell similarly hanged herself after "relentless taunting at her school near Tampa," in September 2009, although her death was not publicly reported for nearly three months.[211]

1. Should teens who sext face child pornography charges? Why or why not?
2. If consensual sexting between teenagers were removed from the reach of child pornography laws, should there be special criminal laws targeting this behavior? How should such laws treat this conduct? What alternatives might there be to criminalizing sexting altogether?

attempted to destroy or delete it, or reported it to a parent or school official, and did not further distribute it."[198] If, however, there is any type of malicious conduct during the act of sexting (e.g., the image was not taken voluntarily), a harsher statutory punishment is authorized to reflect the increase severity of the offense.

Some states have designed diversion programs for adolescent sexters. New Jersey, for instance, gives minors the opportunity to avoid punishment by attending an educational program, provided that they are first-time offenders who were unaware that their actions constituted a crime.[199]

CONCLUSION

Learning Objectives	Summaries
1. Evaluate the ways in which *Lawrence v. Texas* limits laws criminalizing sodomy, fornication, adultery, and bigamy.	*Lawrence v. Texas* limits laws criminalizing private, sexual activity between consenting adults. But sex acts involving minors, commercial sex (i.e., prostitution), or circumstances in which consent might not easily be refused. Thus, private, consensual acts of sodomy (oral or anal sex) or fornication (sex between unmarried persons) by adults may not be criminally regulated under most circumstances. But because acts of adultery (sex between consenting persons during a time when at least one of the participants is married to someone else) and bigamy (having or purporting to marry two or more spouses at the same time) involve the state's interest in preserving marriages, criminal laws against these acts may still be enforceable.
2. Define the crime of incest.	Incest is marriage or sexual intercourse between closely related persons by blood or marriage.
3. Differentiate between the various laws criminalizing sex offenses of a public nature.	Statutes criminalizing lewd and lascivious conduct prohibit act of sexual gratification, either by oneself or with another person, with knowledge or reasonable anticipation that the participants are being viewed by others. Public sexual indecency laws target sex acts in public place or in public view, that occur when another person is present the participant(s) are reckless about whether others would be offended or alarmed by witnessing the act. Indecent exposure involves the knowing exposure or exhibition of the genitals, anus, or female nipples in a public place for indecent purposes.
4. Compare and contrast the crime of prostitution with related crimes that aid or abet the offense.	Prostitution involves engaging in sexual activity with another person in exchange for some form of compensation. Pandering involves forcing, deceiving, or inducting someone to become a prostitute. Pimping concerns the sharing in the earnings of a prostitute. Human trafficking involves transporting someone into a situation of exploitation, including forced labor, marriage, organ removal, and prostitution.
5. Explain the elements of the crime of obscenity.	Material is obscene if the average person, applying contemporary community standards, finds that the work, taken as a whole, appeals to the prurient interest; depicts, in a patently offensive way, sexual conduct specifically defined by the applicable state law; and taken as a whole, lacks serious literary, artistic, political, or scientific value.
6. Discuss the ways in which criminal laws attempt to protect children and teenagers from sexual exploitation.	Unlike pornography involving adults, sexually explicit images of children receive no First Amendment protection. Accordingly, both the production of child pornography and its possession may be criminally punished. This has implications for minors who engage in sexting—the electronic exchange of explicit images. By contrast, merely indecent materials that are not obscene may not be criminally proscribed, but may be regulated in ways to prevent children from accessing them. To prevent child molestation and other forms of child exploitation, some states have enacted anti-grooming laws aimed at punishing communications with a child relating to or describing sexual conduct for the purposes of promoting sexual arousal or sexual victimization.

KEY TERMS

adulteryvoyeurism list:

- adultery
- bestiality
- bigamy
- fornication
- grooming
- human trafficking
- incest
- indecent exposure
- lewd and lascivious conduct
- loitering
- pandering
- pimping
- prostitution
- public sexual indecency
- sexting
- sodomy
- voyeurism

10

Other Crimes Against The Person

Outline

LEARNING OBJECTIVES

1. Compare and contrast the crimes of assault and battery.
2. Explain how the defense of consent operates in cases involving crimes against persons.
3. Define the elements of reckless endangerment.
4. Explain why most US states have enacted domestic violence laws.
5. Differentiate child abuse from child neglect.
6. Discuss the ways in which the crimes of elder abuse and neglect occur.
7. Analyze the similarities and differences between kidnapping and false imprisonment.
8. Discuss how common crimes of unlawful restraint differ from specialized offenses involving child abduction and custodial interference.
9. Describe how criminal law responds to crimes against persons that are proven to be motivated by bias.

INTRODUCTION

The crimes of assault and battery are often confused. Part of this confusion stems from the fact that some US jurisdictions have merged to the definitions of the two crimes into a single criminal offense, following the lead of the Model Penal Code § 211.1. But they were distinct legal concepts at common law and continue to be distinct criminal offenses in some US states today. The key difference between assault and battery is whether the perpetrator actually touched the victim. A battery requires an actual touching, whereas an assault only requires that the victim be in reasonable apprehension of being touched.

Battery

Battery is defined as the unlawful application of force to the person of another resulting in either (1) bodily injury; or (2) an unwanted, offensive touching.[1] As a crime of general intent, battery need not be intentional; reckless conduct (i.e., a subjective awareness of the risk that an injury might occur) suffices for liability.

Simply battery, such a slap across the face, is a misdemeanor in most jurisdictions. In contrast, an *aggravated battery*, which typically constitutes a felony, occurs if a deadly weapon was used, or if serious bodily harm was inflicted on the victim. Some jurisdictions also include the status of the victim—for example, the battery of a child, an elderly person, a judge, or police officer—in their definitions of what will elevate a simple battery to an aggravated one.

Some states have abolished an "unwanted offensive touching" as a result element of battery, opting instead to define the simply as the unlawful application of force to another person result in bodily injury. In such jurisdictions, unwanted offensive touching that do not cause bodily injury would not be criminalized, especially in jurisdictions that adopted the Model Penal Code's *de minimis* provision. Under it, judges are supposed to dismiss *de minimis* infractions if they find that the defendant's conduct:

(1) was within a customary license or tolerance, neither expressly negated by the person whose interest was infringed nor inconsistent with the purpose of the law defining the offense; or
(2) did not actually cause or threaten the harm or evil sought to be prevented by the law defining the offense or did so only to an extent too trivial to warrant the condemnation of conviction; or
(3) presents such other extenuations that it cannot reasonably be regarded as envisaged by the legislature in forbidding the offense.[2]

Normally, police or prosecutorial discretion are typically exercised in a way that screens out *de minimis* violations of law before anyone is formally charged. But in the event charges are filed, a defendant may move to have charged dismissed by a judge if the *de minimis* exception to criminal liability applies. Box 10.1, "Statutory Analysis Exercise," illustrates this point.

Assault at Common Law

Assault is either (1) an attempt to commit a battery; or (2) the intentional creation—other than by mere words—of a reasonable apprehension in the mind of the victim of imminent bodily harm. If there has been an actual touching, the crime is battery, not assault. Unlike battery, which is a general intent crime that can be committed with criminal recklessness, common-law assault requires specific intent. Thus, the prosecution must prove either than the defendant intended to commit a battery, but failed, or that that the defendant intended to create a reasonable apprehension in the mind of the victim of imminent bodily harm.

As with simple battery, *simple assault* is usually a misdemeanor, but it can be raised to the felony of *aggravated assault* if perpetrated using a deadly weapon, or against a particular victim (e.g., a police officer in the line of duty), or if the assault is coupled with the specific intent to do another crime, such as assault with intent to kill, assault with intent to rape, or the like.

Assault and Battery

Often, an assault and battery takes place at the same time. For example, if one creates a reasonable apprehension in the mind of the victim of imminent bodily harm, an assault has been committed. If the person committing the assault then actually hits the victim, a battery has also been committed. But it is possible to commit one without the other. If no actual touching takes place, even if it was one's specific intent to batter another, then only an assault has taken place. In contrast, if one were to sneak up behind his or her victim and hit the victim over the head, a battery has clearly taken place, but since the victim was never placed in reasonable apprehension of imminent bodily harm because the perpetrator snuck up so the victim could not see the batterer approaching, no assault occurred.

Merger of Assault and Battery Under the Model Penal Code

As previously mentioned, the Model Penal Code merged the offenses of assault and battery into a single offense named *assault*. Section 211.1 declares a person is guilty of simple assault, a misdemeanor, if he or she:

(a) attempts to cause or purposely, knowingly or recklessly causes bodily injury to another; or
(b) negligently causes bodily injury to another with a deadly weapon; or
(c) attempts by physical menace to put another in fear of imminent serious bodily injury.

A person commits the felony of aggravated assault if he or she:

(a) attempts to cause serious bodily injury to another, or causes such injury purposely, knowingly or recklessly under circumstances manifesting extreme indifference to the value of human life; or

BOX 10.1

STATUTORY ANALYSIS EXERCISE

Does Grazing Someone's Face Count as an Assault or Battery?

In *State v. Cabana*,[144] the defendant was an incumbent political candidate for reelection to local office. His opponent circulated a political flier critical of him. With the flier in hand, he approached his opponent at a political social function and initiated a confrontation. They engaged in heated argument. While angrily waving the flier, the defendant struck his opponent's chin with the knuckle of his right index finger forcing his opponent's "head back in a jerk, causing her to stagger backward and experience physical pain."[145]

New Jersey is one of the jurisdictions that merged assault and battery into a single offense. Thus, its assault statute includes a provision that a person is guilty of assault if he or she "[a]ttempts to cause or purposely, knowingly or recklessly causes bodily injury to another,"[146] which would constitute a battery at common law and in the states that retain the distinction today. New Jersey law defines bodily injury as "physical pain, illness, or any impairment of physical condition."[147] The state also adopted the Model Penal Code's *de minimis* exception.[148]

In reasoning through what happened, a court noted that

> we have all observed two workers or friends or a parent and child arguing when one may firmly grab the arm of the other to direct action or emphasize a point. As a result, physical pain may occur, but any "bodily injury" caused is not sufficiently serious to fall within the assault statute. Rather, it is an offensive touching. No other conduct is intended by the actor and there is no risk of harm to which society is exposed by this conduct.

1. Analyze whether there was an assault or a *de minimis* offensive touching that was noncriminal by its nature. Put differently, does inadvertent contact with another person while angrily gesturing with one's hands constitute a criminal assault? Explain your reasoning.
2. Paying particular attention to the *mens rea* element for the crime of battery, would your answer change if the case had occurred in a jurisdiction that still follows the common-law approach to battery?
3. In *Watson v. United States*,[149] a husband and wife got into an argument while in the District of Columbia, a jurisdiction that does not recognize the notion of a *de minimis* infraction. At some point during their heated conversation, the wife flipped open her mobile telephone to make a call and the husband deliberately grabbed the phone's flip-top to stop her, accidently breaking it loose. Did a criminal battery occur? Why or why not?

(b) attempts to cause or purposely or knowingly causes bodily injury to another with a deadly weapon.

Thus, drawing on the respective common-law *mens rea* elements of assault and battery, modern assault may be a specific intent crime if it occurs as a result of an attempt (which always requires purpose) or if the completed act was committed either purposefully or knowingly. But assault may also be a general intent crime if bodily injury was caused recklessly or even negligently if a deadly weapon was used. At first blush, the term "deadly weapon" may seem self-evident. But this term of art requires explication.

Assault or Battery with Deadly Weapons

The use of a deadly weapon can raise a simple assault or battery to their aggravated forms, which are typically felonies. A **deadly weapon** is any instrumentality—even one that is not necessarily inherently dangerous—capable of inflicting serious bodily injury or death, depending on how it is used. Consider the following passage from the Tennessee case of *State v. Eaves*:

> A hard-plastic BIC or Papermate pen, as the object was described by the witnesses, is capable, in our view, of causing either "extreme pain" or "obvious disfigurement." Had the victim been struck in the eye, the seriousness of the risk is apparent. Objects other than traditional weapons may, depending on their use, be deadly. The pen, in this case, was used in such a manner. A pillow, a sock, telephone wire, a hairbrush, and a long-handled flashlight have all been held to constitute deadly weapons because of the manner in which they were used. Thus, we hold that the evidence was sufficient to support the conviction for aggravated assault.[3]

The "You Make the Public Policy Call" feature in Box 10.2 asks you to examine which objects qualify as deadly weapons.

Verbal Assaults?

You may have heard the term "verbal assault" before. Because mere words do not technically constitute an assault, that term is a bit of misnomer. That is not to say, however, that mere words cannot subject a speaker to criminal liability. In fact, there are several criminal offenses that punish verbal assaults, provided that they narrowly focused in ways that avoid running afoul the First Amendment. For example, as you learned in Chapter 2, fighting words[4] and speech that is likely to provoke imminent lawlessness[5] receive no First Amendment protection. Such speech may be criminally punished as **terroristic threats** if they are designed to terrorize people with fear of imminent personal injury.[6] Other states have enacted **menacing** statutes that punish "any threat or physical action" that is knowingly made to place or attempt to place another person "in fear of imminent serious bodily injury."[7] Even if no direct threat is made, someone using email or a telephone in a manner that reasonably causes someone else to be "seriously alarmed, annoyed or harassed" may be guilty of **harassment**.[8]

The Defense of Consent

The defense of **consent** traces its history to the Roman law principle of *volenti non fit injuria* ("to a willing person, no injury is done"), which posited that an invited guest could not be considered a trespasser.[9] Early English common law embraced this principle to an extreme in allowing individuals to consent to harm-causing acts.[10] In the 1600s, however, acts that had been considered violations of a particular victim's interests came to be viewed as an affront to the public good as a "disturbance of the society."[11] As a result in this shift, consent lost its status as a legitimate defense to many crimes, including common-law assault and battery.[12] Indeed, in *Matthew v. Ollerton*, the court held that "If I licence a man to beat me, such licence is void" because it disturbed the public peace.[13]

Although more than 315 years old, the rule announced in *Matthew v. Ollerton* that consent of the victim is not a defense to criminal prosecution remains largely intact in the United States today unless the criminal offense is predicated on a lack of consent, such as theft or rape.[14] However, such a blanket statement is not entirely accurate.

> What is called a "fond embrace" when gladly accepted by a sweetheart is called "assault and battery" when forced upon another without consent; and the act of one who grabs another by the ankles and causes him to fall violently to the ground may result in a substantial jail sentence under some circumstances, but receive thunderous applause if it stops a ball carrier on the gridiron.[15]

The Model Penal Code recognizes consent as a criminal defense only if it negates "an element of the offense or precludes the infliction of the harm or evil sought to be prevented by the law defining the offense."[16] The latter clause is generally interpreted as permitting a consent defense to assaults only when the injury is "not serious."[17] Thus, the general rule is that one may consent to a simple assault or battery, since these do not engender serious bodily harms. But one may not consent to an aggravated assault or battery since these involve injuries of a more serious nature. But this distinct is of "limited use . . . for offenses involving bodily harm" since what constitutes a "serious" injury is ill-defined and open to debate, especially in different contexts.[18] Consider, for example, the difference in the way the criminal law treats batteries that occur in sports with those that occur within the context of sex.

CONSENT TO ASSAULT AND BATTERY IN SPORTS

Assaults or batteries that often cause serious physical injuries are part-and-parcel of many contact sports.[19] Under the **voluntary participant rule**, athletes participating in contact sport give effective legal consent to the type of battery attendant to being "checked" in hockey, tackled in football, punched in boxing, or kicked in a variety of martial arts. But

BOX 10.2

YOU MAKE THE PUBLIC POLICY CALL

What Counts as a Deadly Weapon?

In *Lee v. State*,[150] a Florida appellate court ruled that a shoe is not an inherently dangerous or deadly weapon for the purposes of aggravated assault or battery charges. But the court recognized that a shoe can nonetheless be used in a manner that determines whether it falls within this category.

A Texas appellate court ruled that a kitchen knife was not an inherently dangerous or deadly weapon because "kitchen knives were designed for purposes other than inflicting death or serious bodily injury."[151] Thus, whether such a knife is used in a manner capable of causing death or serious bodily injury determines whether it is a "deadly weapon."

Which of the following do you think qualifies as being "inherently dangerous" deadly weapon as opposed to a deadly weapon depending on how it is used?

- An assailant's body[152]
- An automobile[153]
- A cigarette[154]
- A dog[155]
- A flight of stairs[156]
- A lawn chair[157]
- Pepper spray[158]
- An unloaded firearm[159]

this consent "is limited to the ordinary or usual risks and hazards of the sport."[20] In contrast, when athletes grossly exceed the scope of the rules of a game such that they intentionally inflict serious bodily injury, the consent defense does not shield them from criminal liability as the prosecutions in the "Case Study Extra" feature in Box 10.3 illustrate.

CONSENT TO ASSAULT AND BATTERY IN OTHER CONTEXTS

Consent to assault or battery is not limited to the context of sports. For example, religious flagellation has been considered lawful for centuries.[21] A much more common practice, however, involves sexual relations in which the parties mutually agree to engage in some form of violence or restraint that would constitute a crime in a nonconsensual context.[22]

Consensual sexual behaviors that involve some form of violence are often lumped together, perhaps problematically, under the terms "sadomasochism" ("S&M") and/or "bondage and discipline."[23] Regardless of the label applied to behavior involving consensual sex and violence, precisely defining the scope of sadomasochism proves to be a difficult task.[24] Whatever specific behaviors these sexual practices may entail, it is clear that consent is their cornerstone.

Applying the Model Penal Code's "not serious" principle to the context of S&M, it appears that consent constitutes a valid defense to minor assaults/batteries that do not cause serious physical injury, such as spanking. But in the S&M context, courts consistently find "serious harm" in the overwhelming majority of cases even when the injuries are not permanent, seriously debilitating, or harmful enough that they cause a risk of death.[25] For example, criminal liability has been upheld for injuries S&M participants received from being hit with a belt or a riding crop.[26] The hostility toward recognizing consent in this context is often grounded in a belief that the consent given by S&M participants is irrational and, therefore, legally defective. For example, in upholding an "aggravated assault for whipping an apparently willing victim in the course of production of a pornographic movie," the court "dismissed the very possibility of such consent," reasoning that it was a matter of "common knowledge that a normal person in full possession of his mental faculties does not freely consent to the use, upon himself, of force likely to produce great bodily injury."[27] But this logic is easily challenged; it could easily be applied to boxers, mixed-martial artists, so-called extreme fighters, and many other athletes, thereby illustrating the overinclusiveness of the approach.[28]

MAYHEM AND MALICIOUS DISFIGUREMENT

At common law, the crime of battery could be elevated to the more serious crime of **mayhem** if the victim suffered some permanent injury to a part of the body rendering it disabled, disfigured, or useless, such as putting out an eye or cutting off a limb, the tongue, an ear, the nose, and so on. Today, the statutory law of most US states today do not provide for a specific mayhem offense since it is subsumed under the definition of aggravated assault or aggravated battery.[29] But the federal criminal code[30] and a handful of US jurisdictions retain the crime.[31]

Under the federal statute, specific intent to "torture, maim, or disfigure" must be proved as an element of the offense of mayhem.[32] At common law, such specific intent constituted the crime of *aggravated mayhem*, whereas general criminal intent sufficed for mayhem in its nonaggravated form. California maintains this distinction by requiring recklessness for a mayhem conviction[33] and purposeful conduct for an aggravated mayhem conviction, a felony the state punishes with a potential life sentence.[34]

The degree of impairment attendant to mayhem need not be as severe as it was at common law. Thus, in *People v. Newble*,[35] the court upheld a conviction for mayhem based upon the infliction of a three-inch long facial wound and observed, "the modern rationale of the crime [of mayhem] may be said to be the preservation of the natural completeness and normal appearance of the human face and body." Similarly, in *People v. Page*,[36] the court reasoned that "[t]he law of mayhem as it has developed protects the integrity of the

BOX 10.3

CASE STUDY EXTRA

Playing Sports Beyond the Rules of the Game

On March 8, 2004, Vancouver Canuck forward Todd Bertuzzi blind-sided Steve Moore of the Colorado Avalanche with a punch to the side of the head and then a pile-drive to the ice. As a result of Bertuzzi's violent act, Moore suffered three broken vertebrae in his neck and a concussion. . . . Bertuzzi was suspended for the rest of the 2004 National Hockey League season, costing him over $500,000 in salary.[160]

Bertuzzi was also criminally charged, but he negotiated a special plea on a conditional charge that allowed him to escape having a criminal record.[161]

During an NHL hockey game, Boston Bruins' Marty McSorley approached Vancouver Canucks' Donald Brashear from behind, and with a quick two-handed swing of his stick, clubbed Brashear on the side of his face: Brashear suffered a severe concussion and was hospitalized. McSorley was handed a one-year suspension from the NHL and was found guilty of assault with a weapon by a provincial court in British Columbia.[162]

Criminal prosecutions of athletes for assaults or batteries that go far beyond the rules of the game are not limited to hockey. A Canadian court held two athletes liable for punching another in the face during a soccer game, leaving the victim with a broken nose and permanent damage to his facial structure.[163] And in *People v. Freer*,[164] a defensive football player punched a ball carrier while tackling him. When the play ended, the ball carried punched the defensive tackler back. The court said,

> Initially it may be assumed that the very first punch thrown by the complainant in the course of the tackle was consented to by defendant. The act of tackling an opponent in the course of a football game may often involve "contact" that could easily be interpreted to be a "punch." Defendant's response after the pileup to complainant's initial act of "aggression" cannot be mistaken. Clearly, defendant intended to punch complainant. This was not a consented to act.[165]

1. Why do you think the law accepts serious injury as a consequence of certain athletic activities? At least one commentator answered this question by explaining that sports have "social utility which outweighs the harm of the activity to the individual," including physical fitness, recreation, and "an entertainment benefit to society at large."[166] Do you agree with him? Why or why not?
2. Law professor Cheryl Hanna posited a provocative argument as to why the law accepts serious injury as a potential consequence of certain athletic activities: gender roles. She argued that sports reaffirm and reify masculinity while appropriately sublimating masculine impulses in socially acceptable ways.[167] Moreover, because sports occur in a regulated environment—complete with referees—the risks of serious harm are mitigated.[168] What do you make of this explanation for our acceptance of violent injury in the context of sports?

victim's person," and affirmed a mayhem conviction based on the application of permanent tattoos to the victim's breast and abdomen.[37]

The crime of **malicious disfigurement** is closely related to mayhem. In the few jurisdictions that draw a distinction, the elements of mayhem are satisfied if the victim is permanently disabled by the injury, whereas a conviction for malicious disfigurement requires that the defendant not only intended to disfigure the victim, but was successful in causing permanent disfigurement.[38]

RECKLESS ENDANGERMENT

The crime of **reckless endangerment** (referred to as *wanton endangerment* in some jurisdictions) occurs when a person "commits an act that places another in imminent danger of death or serious bodily injury."[39] Such statutes are aimed at deterring the commission of potentially harmful conduct before an injury or death occurs.

Often, conduct constituting an assault or battery overlaps with the conduct that would satisfy the *actus reus* element of reckless endangerment. But unlike with a battery, a person may be properly convicted of reckless endangerment in the absence of any injury or touching. Unlike with assault, no specific intent to cause a particular result is required.

As the name of the crime plainly suggests, reckless endangerment is a general intent crime satisfied by reckless conduct. That is to say that when an individual consciously disregards the risk that his or her actions could cause death or serious bodily injury to another person, the *mens rea* for the offense is satisfied.

As the next case illustrates, in some US states, gross negligence suffices the *mens rea* requirement for this offense. Put differently, when the accused's conduct, when viewed objectively, constitutes a gross departure from the standard of conduct that an ordinary, reasonable, prudent person would have observed because it created a substantial and unjustifiable risk of death or serious injury, then such gross negligence falls within the conduct that reckless endangerment statutes were designed to punish.[40]

Timothy Allen BOYER

v.

STATE of Maryland

666 A.2d 1269 (Md. App. 1995).

* * *

A domestic argument occurred between appellant and his wife, Joni Boyer, over the couple's impending separation and their daughter's custody arrangements. Following the argument, Mrs. Boyer went to a nearby gas station and telephoned the Charles County Sheriff's Department. Officer Ralph Aquaviva met Mrs. Boyer at the gas station, where she showed him a barely visible cut on her hand and informed him that appellant had assaulted her. . . .

Although Mrs. Boyer's injury was minor, Officer Aquaviva and Officer Gary Holt accompanied Mrs. Boyer to the couple's home to investigate the dispute. When they entered the couple's driveway, the officers triggered an alarm system, which signaled their arrival to appellant, who was inside "playing with" his licensed and registered MAC 11, 9-mm machine gun. Upon hearing the alarm, appellant put the gun under the bedsheet and laid down to watch television with his eleven-month old daughter. Mrs. Boyer directed the officers to the bedroom, where they found appellant lying in bed, partially under the bedsheet. Officer Aquaviva testified that he smelled alcohol and noticed that appellant's eyes were bloodshot; however, Officer Aquaviva also testified that the scene was "peaceful and quiet."

The officers refused appellant's request that they leave his home. When questioned by Officer Aquaviva, appellant refused to discuss his wife's assault allegations. During his conversation with appellant, Officer Aquaviva "observed [appellant's] right hand under the covers and . . . felt like [he] was in danger." Consequently, Officer Aquaviva ordered appellant to remove his hand from under the bedsheet, and, when appellant refused, Officer Aquaviva pulled the bedsheet away and discovered the gun, which he seized and handed to Officer Holt, who disengaged it. Officer Aquaviva also testified that appellant's gun safe, located in the couple's bedroom, was open and contained various weapons.

The officers conceded that appellant made no physical contact with the gun in their presence, and they testified that appellant made no aggressive or offensive gestures with the gun. Officer Aquaviva did testify, however, that, when he pulled back the bedsheet, the machine gun was pointed directly at him. The machine gun was loaded, with its "safety" in the "fire" position, its setting on "SMG" (sub-machine gun), and a round of ammunition in the chamber. After appellant's arrest, the officers found a second loaded magazine for the machine gun underneath appellant's pillow.

* * *

Appellant asserts that the evidence was insufficient to support his convictions for reckless endangerment of his daughter, Officer Aquaviva, and Officer Holt. He insists that he engaged in no conduct that rose to the level of "substantial risk of death or serious injury," as contemplated by Maryland's reckless endangerment statute, now codified as MD. ANN. CODE, art. 27 § 120 (1992) (hereinafter "§ 120").

* * *

In the [present] case . . . , the jury convicted appellant of reckless endangerment based on the following evidence: (1) appellant had been drinking and allegedly assaulted his wife; (2) when appellant heard the driveway alarm, he placed, underneath his bedsheet, a loaded, sub-machine gun with the safety off, ready to fire; (3) appellant refused to co-operate with the officers and was visibly agitated while the officers were in his room; (4) appellant's eleven-month old daughter was in bed with appellant, just inches away from the loaded machine gun; (5) when Officer Aquaviva pulled appellant's bedsheet back, the submachine gun was pointed at him; and (6) Officer Aquaviva found a loaded magazine clip underneath appellant's pillow.

* * *

Although appellant may not have had physical contact with the machine gun hidden beneath his bedsheet, it was in his possession and control. Also, the evidence demonstrated that, while the officers were in the bedroom, the machine gun was loaded, pointed at Officer Aquaviva, and its safety was off. Appellant and his eleven-month old daughter were inches away from the gun and appellant had his hand under the sheet, next to the gun. . . . [A]ppellant arguably did not intend to harm the officers or his daughter; however, . . . we hold that, viewing the evidence in a light most favorable to the State, a reasonable trier-of-fact could have reasonably concluded that appellant's conduct, when viewed objectively, was so reckless that "[it] constituted a gross departure from the standard of conduct that a law-abiding person would observe and . . . created the substantial risk that [§ 120] was designed to punish."[41]

Questions

1. The US Supreme Court's decision in *Voisine v. United States*[42] upheld the application of a federal law banning possession of firearms by any person convicted of a misdemeanor interpersonal violence offense.[43] The Court specifically held that even interpersonal violence convictions based on reckless (rather than intentional) conduct fell within the statutory ban on firearm possession. Critique the decision in the *Boyer* case in light of the *Voisine* decision.
2. In *Key v. Commonwealth*,[44] the defendant pointed a gun within two feet of another person's face and asked, "Do you want some of this?" He then fired the gun twice near the victim's feet causing gravel to fly up and strike the victim. In addition to aggravated assault, the defendant was convicted of reckless endangerment. In upholding his conviction, the court held that "pointing of a gun, whether loaded or unloaded (provided there is reason to believe the gun may be loaded) at any person constitutes conduct that 'creates a substantial danger of death or serious physical injury to another person.' "[45] The law in most states is in accord with this proposition because pointing a gun at another person conduct creates a serious risk of death.[46] Do you agree? Why or why not? Does it make a difference if the gun is loaded or not? What about if the safety is engaged?

Just over half the states and the District of Columbia have enacted **Child-Access Prevention (CAP) Laws**, a subtype of reckless endangerment laws that impose criminal liability on parents when a child gains access to a firearm because it was negligently stored.[47]

> The strictest laws impose criminal liability on adults who negligently leave firearms accessible to children when a child may or is likely to gain access to a gun. A larger number impose liability only when children actually gain access to the gun. And other state laws impose liability only if the child uses the gun or carries it to a public place. . . . Some other states simply impose criminal liability when a person intentionally, knowingly and/or recklessly provides firearms to minors.[48]

DOMESTIC VIOLENCE AND INTIMATE-PARTNER VIOLENCE

The terms *domestic violence* and *intimate-partner violence* are often used interchangeably. But a distinction should be made between the two. **Domestic violence** refers physical violence, sexual violence, stalking, and psychological aggression against members of one's household. This can include both romantic partners, family members, and even roommates.[49] In contrast, **intimate-partner violence** (IPV) "describes physical violence, sexual violence, stalking, and psychological aggression (including coercive acts) by a current or former intimate partner."[50] IPV is the preferred term when applied to romantic partners since word "domestic" connotes cohabitation, while IPV recognizes that continued cohabitation is not a necessary condition to describe this public health problem.

Domestic violence occurs across all races, sexual orientations, and socioeconomic groups. The same is true for IPV that can occur between members all of the following groups:

- current spouses (including common-law spouses)
- current nonmarital partners
- dating partners, including first date
- boyfriends/girlfriends
- former marital partners
- divorced spouses
- former common-law spouses
- separated spouses
- former nonmarital partners
- former dates
- former boyfriends/girlfriends

Historically, IPV was not considered a serious issue for the criminal justice system.[51] Instead, IPV was seen primarily as a private, family matter.[52] Participants in the criminal justice system, including police officers, prosecutors, and judges, believed "that the importance of protecting families from interference outweighed the importance of protecting women from abuse."[53] This made it particularly difficult for IPV victims to obtain legal assistance.[54] It was not until the late 1970s that IPV began to become widely recognized as warranting criminal sanction.[55] By the mid-1980s, state legislatures had begun to make significant changes to IPV law due in large part to an influential study commonly referred to as the "Minneapolis Experiment."[56] The Minneapolis Experiment reported that IPV offenders are less likely to recidivate if they are arrested than if they are merely counseled by police or asked to leave the premises where the incident occurred.[57] As a result of this study and other important research, many jurisdictions adopted policies that shifted discretion from law enforcement officers to the judicial system.[58]

IPV make take the form of crimes against property and a wide range of crimes against the person, including simple or aggravated assault and battery, rape and other forms of sexual assault, and homicide. Most states have enacted domestic violence or IPV violence last in their civil domestic relations/family laws or in social services statutes. These laws provide the legal authority for victims of domestic violence or IPV to obtain social services and civil **orders of protection**—court orders, sometimes called "restraining orders," that require someone to refrain from contact with another person. Violations of these orders constitute the crime of contempt of court.

Additionally, roughly forty US states have also created special classes of criminal offenses that specifically address violence between current or former intimate partners.[59] The federal government similarly enacted the Interstate Domestic Violence Act of 1994, a criminal law punishing when someone forces and intimate partner to travel across state lines and commits a crime of violence against that person.[60]

The criminal laws of approximately thirty-six states include children within the class of persons encompassed by their criminal domestic violence statutes and seven states include grandchildren.[61] Unlike between spouses other related persons, the parental privilege to discipline a minor child may be asserted as a defense against a charge under a state's criminal domestic violence statute, subject to certain limitations.[62]

Criminal IPV or domestic violence offenses are often graded differently than their counterparts in other parts of a criminal code. For example, first offenses are often classified as misdemeanors and are handled with an eye toward rehabilitation and reconciliation. They may even be litigated in special courts with diversion programs that include counseling for both victims and offenders.

CHILD ABUSE AND NEGLECT

Child abuse involves the active infliction of injury through physical, sexual, or psychological abuse. In contrast, child neglect involves passive abuse—a failure to live up to one of the duties imposed by law regarding the care of children.

Child Abuse

In common parlance, the term *child abuse* is a broad term that often includes sexual assault or exploitation, severe forms of neglect (i.e., reckless endangerment of a child), and physical abuse. For criminal law purposes, however, child abuse is often narrowly understood to target physical abuse because there are separate laws targeting sexual offenses against children and child neglect. But the same could be said of several crimes against the person, most notably assault and battery, that could be used to prosecute physical abuse. Indeed, child abuse may be treated as any number of crimes, including assault, battery, assault with a dangerous or deadly weapon, aggravated battery of a child, and homicide if death results. Nonetheless, most US jurisdictions have enacted separate criminal **child abuse** statutes that are either better suited to dealing with special problems attendant to child victims, or are graded as more serious crimes than other types of assaults or batteries, and and therefore is generally punished with a more severe sentence. Washington State, for example, enacted a special "homicide by abuse" statute that punishes an abuse-related death as the equivalent of a first-degree murder without the need for the prosecution to prove premeditation or intent to kill.[63]

CORPORAL PUNISHMENT

Parents are given a limited privilege to use a reasonable amount of physical force to discipline their children.[64] Because of this **parental privilege**, a parent intentionally putting a child in reasonable apprehension of imminent bodily harm usually does not constitute criminal assault, and a parent spanking a child generally does not constitute a criminal battery. The privilege to use physical force to discipline a child even extends to those acting *in loco parentis* (in lieu of the parent). Thus, in *Ingraham v. Wright*, the US Supreme Court upheld the use of corporal punishment in schools.[65]

But the privilege to use force to punish a minor child is limited. The force used must be "reasonably believed to be necessary for [the child's] proper control, training, or education."[66] As a rule, spanking falls within the scope of permissible discipline, while burning and cutting clearly do not. But in between lies a range of corporal punishments that fall into a gray area. Is beating a child with a belt child abuse? There is no clear-cut answer to the question since the degree or severity of the beating would matter, as would the location on the child's body that was hit. So long as the child is subjected to discomfort, rather than injury (e.g., lacerations, bruising that lasts for days), the parental privilege likely insulates such discipline from criminal liability.[67]

Child Neglect

Parents and other persons responsible for children have a legal duty to provide the children with food, clothing, shelter, medical care, sanitation, education, and a reasonable physical and moral environment in which to live (i.e., supervision). **Child neglect** is the failure to live up to one of the duties.

Recall from Chapter 7 the case of *Commonwealth v. Twitchell*,[68] in which parents who failed to reasonably provide for their child's medical needs, even when having failed to do so was based upon the tenets of their religion, were subjected to criminal liability for child neglect. The exact same result occurred in *State v. Neumann*,[69] in which parents were held criminally responsible for the death of their daughter because they relied on "prayer treatment," rather than having her diabetes medically treated. In 2013, the Wisconsin Supreme Court upheld the parents' conviction for reckless homicide (involuntary manslaughter).

The *Neumann* case is interesting because Wisconsin is one of several states that have enacted a treatment-through-prayer exception to its child abuse statute. The provision states: "A person is not guilty of an offense under this section solely because he or she provides a child with treatment by spiritual means through prayer alone for healing in accordance with the religious method of healing . . . in lieu of medical or surgical treatment."[70] The Wisconsin Supreme Court reasoned that because the treatment-through-prayer exception was a part of the state's child abuse statutes, it was only available as a defense to child abuse charges, not homicide charges. Indeed, the court relied on the *Twitchell* case as persuasive authority for its decision.

Mandatory Reporting of Child Abuse and Neglect

To help combat child abuse and neglect, all US states have enacted **mandatory reporting laws**[71] that require certain people to report suspected child abuse to law enforcement or an appropriate social services agency. The people obligated by law to report suspected child abuse are referred to as *mandatory reporters*. In most states, this class of people is comprised of those who have frequent interaction with children, such as teachers, social workers, healthcare professionals (including, but not limited to nurses, physicians, and medical examiners), mental health professionals (e.g., counselors and therapists), childcare providers, and law enforcement officers. And in approximately eighteen states, *any* person, regardless of profession, who suspects a child is the victim of abuse or neglect is legally obligated to report their suspicions.

The consequences of failing to report suspected abuse or neglect vary across US jurisdictions. In addition to facing potential civil liability, almost all states impose criminal liability as well.

> In Florida, a mandatory reporter who fails to report as required by law can be charged with a felony. Failure to report is classified as a misdemeanor or a similar charge in 40 States and American Samoa, Guam, and the Virgin Islands. In Arizona and Minnesota, misdemeanors are upgraded to felonies for failure to report more serious situations; while in Connecticut, Illinois, Kentucky, and Guam, second or subsequent violations are classified as felonies.[72]

ELDER ABUSE AND NEGLECT

Elder abuse is a broad term encompassing physical abuse, psychological or verbal abuse, sexual abuse, financial exploitation, and neglect. "Although it has probably existed since antiquity, elder abuse was first described in the medical literature in the 1970s."[73] In 1980, the US House of Representatives issued a report entitled, "Elder Abuse: An Examination of a Hidden Problem."[74] Then, in 1990, the House issued a follow-up report entitled, "Elder Abuse: A Decade of Shame and Inactivity" which estimated that at least 5 percent of elderly persons in the United States—roughly 1.5 million people at that time—were abused each year.[75] As the US population has aged, these estimates have risen.

Because elder abuse can take many forms, it is remarkably complex:

> Physical abuse is violent conduct resulting in pain or bodily injury. Common examples include hitting, sexual molestation, physical or chemical restraints. Psychological abuse is behavior that induces significant mental anguish and may consist of threats to harm, to institutionalize, or to isolate the elder adult. While the effects of physical abuse are usually visible, the effects of psychological abuse may be less obvious; however, psychological abuse can cause a wide range of responses including depression, nervous system disorders, fearfulness, physical illness, and in extreme cases, suicide. Financial abuse or exploitation is theft or conversion of property by the elder's relatives, caregivers, or others; it can range from expropriating small amounts of cash to inducing the elder to sign away bank accounts or other property. Financial exploitation is often accompanied by physical or psychological abuse. Neglect is the failure to fulfill a care-taking obligation necessary to maintain the elder's physical and mental well-being; examples include abandonment and denial of, or failure to provide, food or health-related services. Neglect may be intentional or negligent, resulting from the caretaker's own infirmity or ignorance. It can arise from an overwhelmed or dysfunctional care-giving system, the isolation of the elder, refusal of the elder to accept assistance, or other complex and multi-faceted causes.[76]

The overwhelming majority of elder maltreatment cases involve neglect or financial abuse, most of which is committed by the adult children of elderly victims (or the spouses of those adult children); in contrast, physical abuse accounts for just shy of 16 percent of cases.[77]

In response to the alarming reports of elder abuse, numerous states enacted criminal laws targeting both active abuse and passive neglect of the elderly. But this dichotomy presents a bit of a slippery slope since neglectful behaviors can transform into abuse depending on "the frequency of the mistreatment, as well as its duration, intensity, and severity."[78] Of course, all states have criminal laws that could be used in cases of elder abuse or neglect, including assault, battery, rape and sexual assault, and various types of theft or fraud offenses. Nonetheless, some states enacted specialized elder abuse laws that increase the criminal penalties for violations of these general criminal laws if the victim is over a certain age.

Some states have enacted laws that apply to senior citizens over a certain age, typically sixty[79] or sixty-five.[80] Other states eschew specific ages and use terms such as "dependent adult" or "vulnerable adult." Idaho, for example, defines a vulnerable adult as any person over the age of eighteen "who is unable to protect himself from abuse, neglect or exploitation due to physical or mental impairment which affects the person's judgment or behavior to the extent that he lacks sufficient understanding or capacity to make or communicate or implement decisions regarding his person, funds, property or resources."[81] It is a felony punishable by up to ten years in prison to abuse or neglect a vulnerable adult in Idaho "under circumstances likely to produce great bodily harm or death."[82] Other types of abuse or neglect of a vulnerable adult in Idaho are punished as misdemeanors.[83]

California takes a somewhat novel approach to elder abuse. First, California incorporates both a specific age (65 and older) and the notion of a dependent adult (a vulnerable person age eighteen or older) in its statute. But unlike some other states' elder abuse laws that simply increase penalties for crimes that could be prosecuted as assault, battery, or certain financial crimes,[84] California criminalizes behaviors that would not have been criminally sanctioned prior to the enactment of a specialized statute:

> Any person who knows or reasonably should know that a person is an elder or dependent adult and who, under circumstances or conditions likely to produce great bodily harm or death, willfully causes or permits any elder or dependent adult to suffer, or inflicts thereon unjustifiable physical pain or mental suffering, or having the care or custody of any elder or dependent adult, willfully causes or permits the person or health of the elder or dependent adult to be injured, or willfully causes or permits the elder or dependent adult to be placed in a situation in which his or her person or health is endangered, is punishable by imprisonment in a county jail not exceeding one year, or by a fine not to exceed six thousand dollars ($6,000), or by both that fine and imprisonment, or by imprisonment in the state prison for two, three, or four years.[85]

Prior to the enactment of elder abuse laws, it may not have been possible to hold a caregiver criminally liability for failing to meet the needs of an elderly or vulnerable person unless the conduct rose to the level of reckless endangerment.[86] And although civil law allowed for the voidability of contracts and wills when someone exercised *undue influence*—the exploitation of a relationship or position of power or trust to manipulate or deceptively control a vulnerable person's decision-making, some elder abuse laws now explicitly impose criminal sanctions for such actions, thereby bypassing the need for prosecutors to have to worry about defenses of consent to many theft crimes.[87]

Similarly, in the name of combating sexual abuse of older adults, some states have criminalized consensual sexual conduct that would otherwise be legally permissible. For example, in the state of Washington, it is a crime for a disabled person age sixty or older to engage in consensual sexual activity with someone who provides that person with paid transportation. In Vermont, it is a crime for anyone who works or volunteers at a caregiving facility or program to engage in sexual acts with any person whose ability to care for him or herself is impaired due to "infirmities of aging."[88]

Most US states have enacted mandatory reporting laws for elder abuse akin to those for child abuse and neglect.[89] Most of these laws designate healthcare workers as mandatory reporters; others include "law enforcement personnel, clergy, social workers, lawyers, caretakers, and caretaker facilities."[90] Failure to report suspect elder abuse or neglect is usually punished as a misdemeanor.

ROBBERY

Although most people think of robbery as type of theft because it involves theft from a person using force or threat of force, it is properly classified as a crime against the person. Nonetheless, because some of the elements of robbery involve theft terminology that has not yet been discussed in this book, robbery is addressed with crimes against property in Chapter 11.

UNLAWFUL RESTRAINT OFFENSES

A range of criminal offenses are aimed as *unlawful restraint*—the involuntary detention of another living person. These offenses generally share the same *actus reus* of unlawfully restraining or confining another person. But both the common law and modern criminal statutes differentiate different unlawful restraint offenses based largely on varying levels of *mens rea* and the circumstances attendant to the victim's confinement.

Kidnapping

Unlike other unlawful restraint crimes, **kidnapping** is almost always a specific intent crime concerned with taking and moving another person for nefarious purposes, such as for ransom, for inflicting terror, or for the commission of another crime. Both the involuntary nature of a victim's detention and the reasons underlying it play important roles in determining kidnapping liability.

At early common law, the offense of kidnapping was a misdemeanor that involved the forcible abduction of a person from one country to another.[91] The long-term effects of transporting someone far away from their home was the evil targeted by the crime. It is therefore unsurprising that the transportation of a victim from one place to another remains an important element of the crime to this very day. Over time, the common-law crime of kidnapping evolved into a broader offense with harsher penalties, especially in the early 1900s when kidnappings for ransom became increasingly commonplace.[92] Eventually, the crime came to consist of the following elements:

1. the unlawful confinement of a living person by means of either:
   a) abduction (i.e., some movement of the victim against his or her will); or
   b) concealment of the victim in a secret place without the victim's content;
2. for a substantial period of time;
3. for the purpose of either:
   a) the commission of another crime; or
   b) to inflict bodily injury on or terrorize the victim.

Under the Model Penal Code, a person is guilty of kidnapping if he or she

> unlawfully removes another from his [or her] place of residence or business, or a substantial vicinity from the vicinity where he [or she] is found, or if he [or she] unlawfully confines another for a substantial period in a place of isolation, with any of the following purposes: (a) to hold for ransom or reward, or as a shield or hostage; (b) to facilitate the commission of any flight or felony thereafter; (c) to inflict bodily injury on or to terrorize the victim or another; or (d) to interfere with the performance of any governmental or political function.[93]

LAWFUL VERSUS UNLAWFUL RESTRAINT

Both at common law and today, kidnapping is an offense concerned with *unlawful* restraint—those situations in which the victim is confined against his or her will in the absence of legal authority to confine the person. But when the person restraining another, even forcibly, is permitted to do so under the law—such as when police make an arrest, the state incarcerates someone upon lawful conviction, a parent grounds a child, or by a shopkeeper detains someone upon a reasonable belief that the detainee had stolen from him or her—then the confinement is not unlawful and, therefore, no kidnapping liability attachments to such acts of restraint.

ABDUCTION: TAKING OR CONFINING WITHOUT CONSENT

The first method of satisfying the unlawful confinement element of kidnapping involves an *abduction*—the movement or confinement of a victim against his or her will. The lack of consent by the victim is essential to the crime of kidnapping. Indeed, according to the US Supreme Court, it is the involuntary nature of the taking or confining that constitutes "the very essence of the crime."[94] Such a lack of consent may exist at the time of the initial transportation, or it may surface later if the victim revokes consent to remaining with the perpetrator.[95]

Although kidnapping does not require that the victim protest or resist, consent must be granted voluntarily—as a matter of free will.[96] Thus, is not a defense to kidnapping that the person taken or confined was "passively" gave consent due to unconsciousness, significant intoxication, or mental incapacity.[97]

Kidnapping nearly always involves the unlawful confinement of a person accomplished by force, threats of force, or acts of deception. In some jurisdictions, the prosecution must prove that the defendant used force, threats of force, deception, or some other means of instilling fear.[98] In many of the jurisdictions that require proof of force or threats of force, the movement of a person is considered *forcible* when "it is accomplished through the giving of orders which the victim feels compelled to obey because he or she fears harm or injury from the accused, and such apprehension is not unreasonable under the circumstances."[99]

ASPORTATION

At common law, a kidnapping by abduction was sometimes referred to as kidnapping by *asportation* because it requires some movement of the victim over "some distance" or a "substantial distance." As a result of the distance requirement, forced movement within a structure (such as from one room to another in a house) was legally insufficient to establish a kidnapping.[100]

Over time, the "substantial distance" requirement eased, although courts continued to struggle to delineate distances that were substantial (e.g., 10 to 13 blocks within a city)[101] from those that were insubstantial (e.g., 25 feet from a road to a field; movement around the same premises).[102]

The Model Penal Code is unconcerned with distance when someone is taken from their home or place of employment. But movement of a "substantial vicinity" from where the victim was otherwise found is required when the victim is taken from a location other than his or her home or place of business. Many states have rejected this approach to modern kidnapping. As a result, the offense usually requires no particular minimum distance of removal today; "the distance traversed is immaterial."[103]

CONCEALMENT

Even if the victim had not been moved against his or her will over a sufficient distance to satisfy the asportation requirement of kidnapping, the *actus reus* of the offense could nonetheless be satisfies by proof that the victim was confined in some secret place that made it highly unlikely the victim would ever be found.[104]

Both at common law and under the Model Penal Code, the concealment does not require total isolation in spite of the terms like "secret place" or "place of isolation." Rather, the element of concealment is satisfied when a victim "is prevented from effectively communicating his [or her] situation to others and the accused's intention to keep the victim's predicament secret is made manifest."[105] Thus, for example, confining someone in a car that is driven into an alleyway to avoid passersby on the stress would satisfy this element of the crime,[106] as would confining some "in plain sight" in an automobile kept in constant motion on highways.[107] The commentary to the Model Penal Code opines that even confinement in one's own home may satisfy the concealment element of kidnapping "if the circumstances of detention make discovery or rescue unlikely."[108]

MERGER RULE: LIMITATION ON CONFINEMENTS INCIDENTAL TO OTHER OFFENSES

The overwhelming majority of US jurisdictions do not apply kidnapping statutes to unlawful confinements that are incidental to other criminal offenses. For example, if a sexual assault or robbery victim is restrained at knifepoint during the commission of those crimes, most states consider such restraint as part-and-parcel of the underlying offense. But other states take a different view and hold that even a minimal confinement "that enhances the control of the perpetrator over the victim will constitute asportation required for kidnapping when it is not an inherent part of a separate offense."[109] Consider the following case.

STATE of North Carolina

v.

Raeford Lee MORGAN

645 S.E.2d 93 (N.C. App. 2007).

[Defendants] Raeford Lee Morgan . . . and Daquann Curtis Brunson . . . appeal from judgments entered after a jury found them to be guilty of two counts of first-degree kidnapping and two counts of robbery with a dangerous weapon.

* * *

James Brannon . . . Patsy Brannon . . . were staying at the Extended Stay Hotel in Raleigh, North Carolina on 25 November 2003. Sometime after 8:00 p.m., the victims ordered food from a Steak-Out Restaurant. An employee of Steak-Out delivered the food to their hotel room about forty-five minutes later. The Steak-Out employee failed to deliver two beverages the victims had ordered and reimbursed Mrs. Brannon $2.50 for the missing beverages. Mrs. Brannon placed the money on a counter in the hotel room.

A few minutes later, Mrs. Brannon heard a knock on her hotel room door. She thought the Steak-Out employee had returned to deliver the missing beverages. Mrs. Brannon answered the door. A man pushed the door open and entered the victims' hotel room along with two other men. . . . One man pushed Mrs. Brannon against the wall, slammed her onto the floor, and restrained her with duct tape. Another man pushed Mr. Brannon onto the floor and restrained him with duct tape. Mr. Brannon testified that one of the men had a gun, which looked like a black revolver, and he poked Mr. Brannon in the head with the gun several times.

The three men ransacked the victims' hotel room. The men could not find any money and left the hotel room with $2.50 and the victims' cellular telephones. Mrs. Brannon cut the duct tape off of her and Mr. Brannon's hands and called 9-1-1.

* * *

A person may not be convicted of kidnapping and another felony if the restraint or removal is an inherent and inevitable element of the other felony, such as robbery with a dangerous weapon.[110] Defendant argues the restraint of the victims was an inherent part of the robbery and no separate or independent restraint or removal occurred.

Whether a defendant's restraint or removal of a person during the commission of an armed robbery will support a separate conviction for kidnapping is guided by two factors: (1) whether the person was forcibly removed for any reason other than the commission of the robbery, or (2) whether the restraint or removal exposed the person to a greater danger than was inherent in the other offense.[111]

* * *

In *State v. Love*, this Court considered whether the defendants released the kidnapping victims in a safe place.[112] The defendants in *Love* argued the victims were released at a safe place when they were left bound and gagged in their home by the defendants. The Court considered whether "release" merely requires a relinquishment of dominion or control over a person. The defendants bound each of their four victims to chairs and gagged them. They subsequently bound all four chairs and victims together, checked the bindings of the victims before departure, placed further bindings on the victims, and stated that they would return. The Court in *Love* required "an affirmative action other than the mere departing of a premise."[113]

We find no affirmative or willful action on the part of defendants to "release" the victims. Sufficient evidence was presented of a restraint and removal separate from the armed robbery and defendants' failure to "release" the victims to submit the first-degree kidnapping charge to the jury. This assignment of error is overruled.

Questions

1. If the Brannons had been robbed at gunpoint, but not bound with duct tape, do you think the result in this case would have been different? Explain your reasoning.
2. Had this case occurred in a common-law jurisdiction, the defendants could not have been lawfully convicted of kidnapping. Explain why that is.

TIME AS AN ATTENDANT CIRCUMSTANCE

Common-law kidnapping required that the unlawful confinement (whether by abduction or concealment) last for a "substantial" period of time. In other words, short detentions never qualified. Today, however, this requirement has been abolished in many US jurisdictions. In those states, the prosecution does not need to establish any minimum period of confinement for kidnapping liability.[114] Notably, however, the Model Penal Code retains an attendant circumstance requirement that an unlawful confinement be "for a substantial period" if the confinement was achieved by concealment "in a place of isolation."[115]

MENS REA REQUIREMENT

Kidnapping is generally a specific intent crime. At common law, the defendant must have intended that the unlawful confinement of the victim be for one of two purposes—either the commission of another crime or the inflicting of bodily injury or psychic terror on the victim. The Model Penal Code retained the latter objective, but refined the former such that any criminal objective would not qualify for kidnapping liability. Rather, the criminal intent underlying the unlawful confinement must be either to obtain payment of ransom or reward; to use the person as a hostage or shield; to interfere with the performance of any governmental or political function; to commit a felony; or to effectuate successful flight from the commission of felony.[116] As with most crimes, intent may be inferred from the defendant's conduct, remarks, and the surrounding circumstances. Consider what occurred in *State v. Thompson*.[117]

In that case, the defendant sexually assaulted the victim in a house into which both people had voluntarily entered. After the rape ended, the defendant ordered the victim to lie with him on the floor. She complied. As the two lay naked on the floor, the defendant restrained the victim by wrapping his arms around her waist.[118] When the defendant fell asleep, the victim escaped. He was subsequently convicted of both rape and kidnapping. In affirming the convictions, the court reasoned:

> The defendant argues that there was no evidence presented at trial supporting the conclusion that when he restrained [the victim] on the floor after sexually assaulting her, he did so with the intent to harm her further. We disagree. Construing the evidence in the light most favorable to the state, the jury reasonably could have found that when the defendant forcibly ordered [her] to lie with him on the living room floor, he intended to inflict additional physical injury upon her or violate or sexually abuse her further. . . . Such further restriction of her movements was surely not necessary to consummate his initial assault or sexual assault of her. Instead, by reasonable inference, the defendant imposed such further restraint upon her with other purposes in mind. As she and the defendant were still naked, and he had made it clear to her, by pulling her more tightly to him when she first attempted to get away after he raped her, that he was not yet finished with her, the jury reasonably could have found that he intended to violate her further when he regained his strength.[119]

RESULT REQUIREMENTS

Recall that the common law requires that the perpetrator of a kidnapping must have entertained specific intent to engage in either the commission of another crime or to inflict bodily injury on or terrorize the victim. The Model Penal Code retains these requirements, but also adds other potential outcomes, such as interfering with the performance of any governmental or political function, or holding the victim for ransom, reward, as a shield, or as hostage. Depending on the perpetrator's objectives at the time of the unlawful confinement, proof of causation of result may be required.

If the purpose of a kidnapping is to commit another crime or to obtain a ransom or reward, the crime is complete at the time of the taking or confinement with such intent. The object crime(s) of the kidnapping need not occur. Thus, if the ransom or reward is not paid, or the target offenses are not committed successfully, such facts will not defeat a conviction for kidnapping since the perpetrators intent at the time of the abduction is what is key to liability for the crime.[120]

If the purpose of a kidnapping is not to commit another crime, but rather is to inflict bodily injury on or terrorize the victim, then the state must prove causation of one of these results. For the purposes of kidnapping liability, "bodily injury" results whenever the victim experiences any physical injury upon his or her body, however slight the injury may be.[121] Similarly, for the purposes of a kidnapping conviction, a person is "terrorized" in accordance with the usual dictionary definition of the term, namely "when they are caused to feel terror or anxiety, or they are coerced through threats or violence."[122]

False Imprisonment

If the unlawful confinement element of kidnapping is not satisfied either because the victim was not moved a substantial distance or concealed in a secret place, the *actus reus* of the offense is not satisfied. Alternatively, if specific intent to commit another crime or to inflict bodily injury on or terrorize the victim cannot be proven, then the *mens rea* element of kidnapping is lacking. Either way, without proof of all elements of the crime, then no kidnapping can be found to have occurred even though a victim may have been confined against his or her will. But that does not mean that the perpetrator escapes criminal liability due to the crime of **false imprisonment**.

COMMON-LAW FALSE IMPRISONMENT

The common-law elements for false imprisonment were as follows:

1. the confinement or restraint on the liberty or freedom of movement of another;
2. done with the intent to confine;
3. without the consent of the victim;
4. where the person so confining or restraining had no legal authority to confine or restrain the victim.

As with kidnapping, the confinement or restraint for false imprisonment liability must be unlawful and without the consent of the victim. And as is the case with kidnapping, false imprisonment merges with an underlying crime if the confinement or restraint "was simply a minimal intrusion necessary and integral to other crimes committed against the victim and was not simultaneous or inseparable from these other crimes."[123]

Unlike with kidnapping, however, neither movement nor confinement in a secret place needs to occur. The *actus reus* element is satisfied simply by restraining another person's freedom of movement. The *mens rea* element requires proof that the defendant intended to confine the victim, not any proof that the confinement was used as a means to some other criminal end.

The term "false arrest" is sometime used interchangeably with false imprisonment, but they are technically distinct concepts. False arrest is a tort that occurs when someone is falsely imprisoned by a person who asserts legal authority to confine the person, but it turns out that true legal authority is lacking, such as when a law enforcement officer makes an arrest without probable cause. False arrest may also be a crime in some jurisdictions, but the critical distinction between it and false imprisonment is whether the defendant claims to have confined a person pursuant to the legal authority to do so.

FALSE IMPRISONMENT UNDER THE MODEL PENAL CODE

The Model Penal Code differentiates two types of false imprisonment. The offense constitutes a felony if the defendant knowingly (a) restrains another unlawfully in circumstances exposing him or her to risk of serious bodily injury; or (b) holds another in a condition of involuntary servitude.[124] Without such aggravating factors, the knowing restraint of other person that interferes substantially with his or her liberty constitutes a misdemeanor.[125]

Defenses to Unlawful Restraint Crimes

Most defenses to kidnapping center on the creation of reasonable doubt as to the *actus reus, mens rea,* or any required attendant circumstances or result elements. As with most crimes, defenses that might negate *mens rea* and defenses of excuse may be applicable. Unlike with most criminal offenses, however, because lack of consent of the victim is an element of kidnapping and false imprisonment, the victim's consent may serve as a valid defense to these crimes.

Many kidnapping statutes provide limited defenses of mitigation that allow a perpetrator to receive a lesser punishment if they release a victim unharmed in safe space. Importantly, such actions reduce the grading of the crime (e.g., from a certain level of felony to a lower level of felony), it does serve as complete defense to kidnapping.[126]

CHILD ABDUCTION AND CUSTODIAL INTERFERENCE

Accurate estimates of the number of children who are abducted in the United States each year are difficult to obtain. Although approximately 1.31 million children are estimated to go "missing" each year, caretakers (i.e., parents, legal guardians, babysitters) do not always report a missing child to a law enforcement agency.[127] In fact, only about 797,500 of those children are reported to legal authorities as being missing.[128] Of those, between 91 and 96 percent are either missing for a benign reason, are lost, or are runaways.[129] In contrast, roughly 2 percent of missing children are kidnapped by nonfamily members (many of whom are known to the child); the remainder of childhood abductions are committed by family members at rate approximately 3.5 times as high as those committed by strangers.[130] According to the Polly Klass Foundation, fewer than 100 children (a small fraction of 1 percent) "are kidnapped each year in the stereotypical stranger abductions you hear about in the news."[131] State and federal laws alike seek to address these abductions.

State Laws

The statutory schemes in most US states prevent a parent from being convicted of kidnapping his or her own child because children lack the legal capacity to grant consent to be taken. Rather, when a child is under a certain age (usually fourteen or sixteen, but sometimes up to eighteen years of age), consent must be granted or denied by a parent, guardian, or legal custodian.[132]

In the United States, parents have a fundamental right to the care, custody, and control of their children. "Custody" refers to an assortment of parental rights and responsibilities regarding a child. US law often distinguishes between "physical custody," or residing with a child and providing for a child's daily needs, and "legal custody," or the authority to make significant, long-term decisions affecting a child. Married parents and unmarried mothers enjoy full rights of physical and legal custody by operation of law from a child's birth. Unmarried fathers generally secure full rights of custody by acknowledging or securing an adjudication of paternity. In the absence of a court order to the contrary, parents with rights of custody share their rights equally and co-extensively with his or her co-parent. This equal decision-making responsibility generally means that a parent with rights of legal custody has full and separate authority to make decisions affecting the child without demonstrating the affirmative consent of the child's other parent. Stated another way, for most purposes the law presumes that parents who share legal custody act with the consent of the other. Where parents disagree about a course of action, a parent may seek court intervention to prevent a co-parent from acting.[133]

Thus, in the absence of a court order affecting the custody of a child, either parent or legal guardian is permitted to take exclusive physical possession of a child.[134] This presents a substantial barrier to establishing one of the essential elements of kidnapping—nonconsent—when one a parent (or legal guardian) takes a child.

To avoid the complex legal issues with proving consent issues in a would-be kidnapping case in which a child is taken by a parent or guardian in contravention of a court order establishing certain custody arrangements, all fifty US states and the District of Columbia have enacted special **child abduction/custodial interference** statutes to deal with the situation of a legal custodian engaging in behaviors that would otherwise constitute kidnapping. These laws go by a variety of names, including, child abduction, parental kidnapping, custodial interference, child stealing, and child concealment.[135]

ELEMENTS OF THE CRIME

Child abduction statutes vary significantly from state to state. In general, and unlike with true kidnapping statutes, these laws usually omit elements concerning consent and elements of force, threats of force, or deception. The *actus reus* is usually interfering with lawful custody of a child and the *mens rea* is typically set at recklessness or higher. Arizona's "custodial interference" statute, which requires knowledge at its *mens rea*, exemplifies a typical approach to the crime:

A person commits custodial interference if, knowing or having reason to know that the person has no legal right to do so, the person does one of the following:

1. Takes, entices, or keeps from lawful custody any child, or any person who is incompetent, and who is entrusted by authority of law to the custody of another person or institution.
2. Before the entry of a court order determining custodial rights, takes, entices, or withholds any child from the other parent denying that parent access to any child.
3. If the person is one of two persons who have joint legal custody of a child takes, entices or withholds from physical custody the child from the other custodian.
4. At the expiration of access rights outside this state, intentionally fails or refuses to return or impedes the return of a child to the lawful custodian.[136]

Many states, however, add an attendant circumstance element to their child abduction laws requiring either that the custodial interference last for a statutorily prescribed minimum period of time (e.g., at least twelve hours)[137] or that there be proof that the that defendant intended to interfere with custody indefinitely or for a protracted period of time.[138]

Federal Laws

Congress enacted two federal laws to address child abductions that cross state lines or international borders. The Parental Kidnapping Prevention Act[139] grants full faith and credit to the family law decrees of a state. Moreover, when a noncustodial parent leaves a state with his or her child in violation of a child custody order, the FBI is empowered to seek the parent as a fugitive from justice. The International Parental Kidnapping Crime Act makes it a federal felony offense to remove a child from the United States (or to retain a child outside the United States) "with intent to obstruct the lawful exercise of parental rights," including sole or joint-custody and visitation rights.[140]

Defenses

Federal laws and most state laws targeting custodial interference recognize that a non-custodial person who genuinely cares for the child in question might flee with the child in order to protect the child from physical abuse, sexual abuse, child neglect, or interpersonal violence situations. But in order to avail oneself of such a defense, the parent fleeing with the child must usually notify law enforcement agencies within a specific period of time and then apply for changes in the court-ordered custody agreement to deny the abusive parent of custodial rights.

BIAS-MOTIVATED SENTENCING ENHANCEMENTS

As explained in Chapter 2, the First Amendment to the US Constitution does not permit the punishment of speech, even symbolic speed like flag burning, based on content that some consider to be offensive or even hateful.[141] But when criminal acts like assault and battery are motivated by the victim's perceived race, ethnicity, religion, sexual orientation, national origin, and other such characteristics, **bias-crime laws** may constitutionally enhance the sentence for the underlying crimes.[142] These laws generally subject an offender to more severe penalties than would have been imposed for committing the same crimes in the absence of a hateful motivation.

Hate crime laws are probably misnamed since they rarely require the prosecution to prove that the perpetrator hated or even disliked the victim. Rather, most statutes simply require proof that that one of the listed characteristics was a substantially motivating factor in the decision to commit the crime.[143] Proof of bias often comes from the perpetrator's own statements (including slurs), writings (including on the internet and on social media site), membership in a group that espouses hate, possession of symbols associated with bias, or testimony from witnesses.

CONCLUSION

Learning Objectives	Summaries
1. Compare and contrast the crimes of assault and battery.	Assault is a specific intent crime that can be committed either by purposefully attempting to commit a battery or by purposefully creating a reasonable apprehension in the mind of the victim of imminent bodily harm, other than by mere words. Battery, is a general intent that requires the reckless, unlawful application of force to the person of another that results in either bodily injury or an unwanted, offensive touching.

Learning Objectives	Summaries
2. Explain how the defense of consent operates in cases involving assault and battery.	A person may consent to a simple assault or battery because these do not engender serious bodily harms. But people may not lawfully consent to aggravated assault or batteries that these involve injuries of a more serious nature.
3. Define the elements of reckless endangerment.	Reckless endangerment occurs when someone acting with recklessness or gross negligence places another person in imminent danger of death or serious bodily injury.
4. Explain why most US states have enacted domestic violence laws.	Domestic violence can encompass a wide range of crimes against the person, including simple or aggravated assault and battery, rape and other forms of sexual assault, and even homicide. To prevent reoffending, especially with serious outcomes, domestic violence statutes allow victims to obtain social services and civil orders of protection that require an offender to refrain from contact with the victim.
5. Differentiate child abuse from child neglect.	Child abuse involves the active infliction of injury through physical, sexual, or psychological abuse. Child neglect involves passive abuse—a failure to live up to one of the duties imposed by law regarding the care of children.
6. Discuss the ways in which the crimes of elder abuse and neglect occur.	Elder abuse is a broad term encompassing physical, sexual, psychological, or verbal abuse, financial exploitation, or neglect of a vulnerable adult who is unable to care for himself or herself.
7. Analyze the similarities and differences between kidnapping and false imprisonment.	Kidnapping is a complex crime of unlawful confinement either by abduction or concealment in a secret place for a substantial period of time for the purpose of either the commission of another crime or to inflict bodily injury on or terrorize the victim. False imprisonment does not require the elements of abduction or concealment nor the intent to terrorize or commit another crime. Rather, it requires only the intentional restraining another person's freedom of movement without the victim's consent.
8. Discuss how common crimes of unlawful restraint differ from specialized offenses involving child abduction and custodial interference.	Of course, children can be kidnapped. But the issue of consent can prove difficult if the child willing goes with a noncustodial parent or guardian. To address issues of proof with the complexities of kidnapping, child abduction statutes punish interfering with lawful custody of a child. Reckless interference often suffices, although knowing or purposeful conduct is more common.
9. Describe how criminal law responds to crimes against persons that are proven to be motivated by bias.	When crimes against the person are motivated by the victim's perceived race, ethnicity, religion, sexual orientation, national origin, and other such characteristics, bias-crime laws can subject an offender to more severe penalties than would have been imposed for committing the same crimes in the absence of a hateful motivation.

KEY TERMS

assault
battery
bias-crime laws
child abduction/custodial interference
child abuse
child neglect
Child-Access Prevention (CAP) Laws
consent
deadly weapon
domestic violence
elder abuse
false imprisonment
intimate-partner violence
kidnapping
malicious disfigurement
mandatory reporting laws
mayhem
orders of protection
parental privilege
reckless endangerment
voluntary participant rule

11

Theft, Robbery, and Crimes Against Property

LEARNING OBJECTIVES

1. Compare and contrast larceny, larceny by trick, and false pretenses.
2. Explain what consolidated theft statutes and what common-law offenses are often subsumed in them.
3. Analyze the elements of embezzlement as a distinct crime from other forms of theft.
4. Differentiate the generic term fraud from specific types of fraud crimes.
5. Differentiate the generic term cybercrime from at least two types of specific digital offenses.
6. Compare and contrast the common-law and contemporary approaches to robbery.
7. Analyze the distinction between burglary and criminal trespass.
8. Apply the elements of arson to determine liability under both the common-law and modern arson statutes.
9. Explain the crime of malicious destruction of property.

Outline

INTRODUCTION

Under the Model Penal Code and the statutory law of many US jurisdictions, select offenses involving the stealing of property are covered by broad theft statues.[1] But at common law and under the current criminal laws in roughly one-quarter of US states,[2] there were dozens of different types of thefts. A study of three of these common-law theft crimes—larceny, larceny by trick, and false pretenses—should illustrate why the law has collapsed many of the common-law theft offenses into broad, general theft laws. The chapter then analyzes several other distinct theft offenses that remain on the books in many states.

For pedagogical purposes, this chapter then delves into the crime of robbery after reviewing theft offenses that are truly crimes against property. Recall from Chapter 10 that robbery is properly classified as crime against the person even though it shares many common elements with other theft offenses, because it consists of a larceny using force or threats of force. Perhaps because robbery involves forceable thefts, some states' criminal codes list the offense as crime against property even though there are human victims of violence.[3]

Finally, the chapter concludes with an exploration some of the other most common crimes against property, including burglary, arson, the malicious destruction of property, and criminal trespass.

LARCENY

The common-law crime of **larceny** required proof of the following elements:

1. the taking/caption;
2. and asportation;
3. of tangible personal property;
4. of another who had lawful custody or possession of the property;
5. by trespass (i.e., without consent)
6. with *animus furandi*—the specific intent or purpose to steal.[4]

The elements of common-law larceny involve terms of art that require explanation. Before exploring the specific meanings of these terms, note that the common law differentiated between two types of larceny based solely on the value of the goods stolen. *Petit* or *simple larceny* was a less severe crime, whereas *grand larceny* was punished more severely.

Actus Reus: Taking and Asportation

The *actus reus* of larceny requires the "taking" and "asportation" of the personal property of another person. Each of these terms of art require explanation.

A *taking* (or *caption*) in this context, involves more than the removal of property by voluntary action. Rather, *taking* of another person's personal property may also be accomplished by exercising "dominion and control over the property for a period of time, however temporary, in a manner wholly inconsistent with the owner's continued rights."[5] For example, a person "takes" a vehicle by sitting behind the wheel and starting the engine. Even if the car remains parked—meaning there is no movement of the vehicle whatsoever—the *taking* element of larceny is satisfied since the car is under that person's dominion and control.[6] Moreover, even momentary control over property that is inconsistent with the owner's rights satisfies the taking element for larceny liability.[7] In other words, because no minimum period of time is required to establish a taking, the fact that a person sits in a parked car and turns on the engine for just a few seconds before being caught would nonetheless constitute a taking.[8] But larceny requires more than a taking; the element of an asportation would not be satisfied in this example.

As explained in the discussion of kidnapping in Chapter 10, an *asportation* requires some movement. The term has the same meaning in the context of larceny insofar as the perpetrator must move (i.e., "carry away") the property of another person, however slightly.[9] If one obtained control of another's property but did not actually move or carry away the property, then no larceny would be deemed to have occurred. To return to the prior example of a person taking a vehicle by sitting behind the wheel and starting the engine, the asportation element of larceny would be satisfied only if the perpetrator moved the car.

One of the authoritative cases on this element of larceny is *Harrison v. People*, an 1872 case[10] in which a pickpocket grasped the victim's wallet and lifted it a few inches. The perpetrator was unable to get the wallet all the way out of the victim's because the victim noticed what was transpiring, grabbed his own wallet, and thrust it back down to the bottom of his pocket. The highest court in New York held that a completed larceny had been committed because the defendant took and moved the victim's personal property without consent and with intent to steal. The fact that the wallet was moved only a few inches was irrelevant.

Attendant Circumstances

The crime of larceny has three attendant circumstance elements. The theft must involve (1) tangible personal property, (2) of another person in lawful custody or possession of the property, (3) by trespass.

Tangible personal property consists of the movable items that a person can own. Because personal property only includes things that one can touch, it does not include *real property* (real estate—land or anything affixed to it), intangible property (ideas, patents, trademarks, copyrights, goodwill), or personal services. Thefts of these other types of property were associate with different common-law theft crimes.

Common-law larceny required that personal property must be taken from another person who was *in lawful custody or lawful possession* of the property, regardless of actual ownership.[11] If the person from whom the personal property was taken and carried away did not have lawful custody or possession of the property to begin with (say, for example, that he or she had stolen the property from its rightful owner), then no larceny could be deemed to have taken place at common law. Similarly, if property has been abandoned, then no larceny can be proven since the owner has relinquishes his or her rights to custody and possession of the property.

Lawful possession is a term of art under the law. The term does not necessarily require physically possession of property. Rather, lawful possession involves having a great scope of authority to deal with property. In contrast, someone who does not have broad authority to deal with property would be deemed to have *custody* over that property, not lawful possession. Ordinarily, a low-level employee only has custody of an employer's property, and can therefore commit a larceny of such property. A high-level employee, like a bank manager, on the other hand, typically has greater authority over property entrusted to his or her care and would therefore not be guilty of larceny for taking such property, but rather would be guilty of embezzlement (discussed later).

For larceny liability to attach, the taking and asportation of tangible personal property must be accomplished *by trespass*, meaning without the owner's consent. This should make logical sense since if the owner of property gives permission for another person to take their property, there would obviously be no theft—only a loan, a gift, or a bailment (i.e., a contractual, placement of property with another person who is given mere temporary possession of property, not a large degree of control over it, such as when a car is given to a valet parking attendant).

Mens Rea

The *mens rea* element of common-law larceny required *animus furandi*—intent to steal. Such intent required proof that the defendant intended to permanently deprive the rightful owner of his or her interest in the property. In lieu of such permanent intent to deprive, an intent to create a substantial risk of loss or an intent to sell or pledge the goods to the owner is sufficient to constitute *animus furandi*. Any intent that did not meet these criteria was insufficient to establish *animus furandi*. For example, if the defendant mistakenly believed he or she took his or her own property, there was no larceny. Also, if someone took property under some claim of right, such as to keep the person property of another as repayment for a debt, then there was no larceny, as there was no *animus furandi*.

Similarly, if a person only intended to borrow the personal property of another and then return it later to the person in lawful possession of it, there was no larceny. If believed by a trier-of-fact, the argument that a defendant intended to return property to its rightful owner after "borrowing" it could be a successful defense to larceny. To address this problem, the common law developed related crimes that did not require proof of intent to permanently deprive the rightful owner of his or her interest in the property, such a *criminal deprivation to property* (trespass to chattels) and joyriding.[12]

As with most crimes, there must be a union of *actus reus* and *mens rea*. The timing of the *mens rea* requirement, therefore, was critical; it had to exist at the time the *actus reus* occurred. In other words, *animus furandi* had to exist *at the time of the taking* for a larceny to have taken place. Thus, if one took and carried away the person property of another in lawful possession of that property without his or her consent but did not develop permanent intent to deprive the owner of the property until some later period of time, no larceny took place under the common law.

LARCENY BY TRICK AND FALSE PRETENSES

Larceny is primarily concerned with punishing the unlawful possession of another person's property. Thus, a trespass—a taking without consent—is a critical element of the crime. But sometimes someone in lawful possession of property grants consent for another to take the property in question, but the consent is obtained via deception. The common law developed two related offenses to deal with such situations: larceny by trick and false pretenses.

Assume that a car thief pretended to be a valet parking attendant. Upon getting behind the wheel of a car that was voluntarily relinquished to the thief by the car's owner (under the wrongful assumption that the thief was simply going to park the car), the perpetrator absconds with the vehicle. Because the owner of the car consensually relinquished control of the vehicle to the thief, but that consent was induced by fraud, then the crime was **larceny by trick**, a different theft crime at common law from regular larceny.[13]

The crime involves the same logic as larceny by trick insofar as possession of the property is obtained by deception. But the critical difference has to do with the nature of the property.

Larceny by trick is limited to circumstances in which *possession* of personal property is obtain by fraud. In contrast to possession, the common-law crime of **false pretenses** involves obtaining *title* to property by fraud. Legal title refers to ownership of certain assets or property. Title is often evidenced by the issuance of a formal legal document that serves as proof of the person's ownership. Unlike real estate that is always evidenced by a deed, a certificate of title is rarely issued for most forms of property other than motor vehicles and intangible property, like stock or bond certificates. If someone tricks the rightful owner of property into signing over the title to the property, then the crime of false pretenses occurs.[14]

MODERN THEFT OFFENSES

Modern law has eliminated many of the common-law technicalities of the various forms of larceny. As a result, most states now have consolidated theft statutes that criminalize the unlawful obtaining of goods or services regardless of many of the technicalities required at common law.

Consolidated Theft Statutes

The Model Penal Code eliminated the need for an asportation and, in its place, substituted the "exercise unlawful control." Under the Model Penal Code, a person is guilty of theft if:

1. he or she unlawfully takes or exercises unlawful control over
2. the property
3. of another person
4. with the purpose to deprive him or her of that property.[15]

The Model Penal Code and most modern statutory definitions of theft have expanded the requirement of tangible personal property to include immoveable property, services, and intangibles, such as stock and goodwill. As a result, the distinction between a theft by trespass (without consent) and a theft by trick (in which consent is fraudulently obtained) is a no consequence in most US jurisdictions today.

Similarly, because the Model Penal Code does not require *animus furandi* (in terms of an intent to permanently deprive the owner of property), the "intent to borrow" defense is largely irrelevant for modern theft offenses. As a result, temporary deprivation of property, such as unauthorized use of vehicles (i.e., joyriding), constitute theft today.[16] Consider Colorado's theft statute:

(1) A person commits theft when he or she knowingly obtains, retains, or exercises control over anything of value of another without authorization or by threat or deception; or receives, loans money by pawn or pledge on, or disposes of anything of value or belonging to another that he or she knows or believes to have been stolen, and:
  (a) Intends to deprive the other person permanently of the use or benefit of the thing of value;
  (b) Knowingly uses, conceals, or abandons the thing of value in such manner as to deprive the other person permanently of its use or benefit;
  (c) Uses, conceals, or abandons the thing of value intending that such use, concealment, or abandonment will deprive the other person permanently of its use or benefit;
  (d) Demands any consideration to which he or she is not legally entitled as a condition of restoring the thing of value to the other person; or
  (e) Knowingly retains the thing of value more than seventy-two hours after the agreed-upon time of return in any lease or hire agreement.

(1.5) For the purposes of this section, a thing of value is that of "another" if anyone other than the defendant has a possessory or proprietary interest therein.[17]

Other types of stealing that are covered in broad, modern theft statutes include theft by extortion, receipt of stolen property, and embezzlement.[18] But because some US jurisdictions maintain these three crimes as distinct criminal offenses, their specific elements will be explored in greater detail in this chapter.

Shoplifting and Shopkeepers' Privilege

Shoplifting is a form of theft that usually involves concealing an item in a retail store to avoid having to pay for it. As such, it is a form of pure larceny. But shoplifting can also encompass price-altering or tag-switching in order to avoid ping the full price of something available for retail sale. Although the price-altering form of shoplifting would not have constituted a true larceny at common law, it constitutes theft under modern statutes.

Contrary to popular belief, goods need not be taken from a store for a shoplifting theft to occur. Store employees, including their private security staff, often wait to confront a suspected shoplifter until he or she attempts to leave a store in order to avoid confronting people with insufficient evidence that would not hold-up in court. But the reality is that the crime of shoplifting is complete when "a shopper treats merchandise in a manner inconsistent with the owner's continued rights—and in a manner not in accord with that of a prospective purchaser," such as hiding the items under clothing or in a purse, case, or other bag or container.[19]

The common law granted retail merchants and their employees a limited privilege to detain suspected shoplifters for a reasonable amount of time to investigate whether a theft had occurred. But the so-called **shopkeepers' privilege** applied only if the proprietor or agent had reasonable grounds to believe that the person being detailed had, in fact, committed or attempted to commit some theft from the store. Moreover, the detention had to be conducted in a reasonable manner, meaning that only a reasonable amount of nondeadly force could be used to detail the suspect for the short period of time needed to investigate the situation. Shopkeepers who abided by all of these requirements would have a defense against civil and criminal charges related to false imprisonment. In effect, this doctrine permits shopkeepers to make a citizen's arrest of shoplifters until law enforcement officials can arrive on the scene.[20] The common-law privilege has been codified in some states[21] and continues to be recognized by courts in many US jurisdictions.[22]

Possession of Stolen Property

A person commits the crime of being in **possession of stolen property** when he or she knowingly buys or receives property that was obtained by any manner constituting theft or extortion.[23] The *actus reus* of the offense is being in possession of stolen property. The *mens rea* of the offense is actual or constructive knowledge that the property was stolen. In most jurisdictions, the prosecution must also prove an attendant circumstance, namely that the property was, in fact, stolen.[24]

Many jurisdictions also require additional *mens rea*, namely proof that the defendant intended to deprive the rightful owner of the property.[25] Because of this requirement, intent to return the property to its rightful owner can negate the *mens rea* for the crime.

COMMONWEALTH of Pennsylvania, Appellee,
v.
Joseph M. FOREMAN, Appellant.
797 A.2d 1005 (Pa. Super. Ct. 2002).

* * *

[T]he Pennsylvania State Police . . . executed a search warrant at . . . a motorcycle repair business owned and operated by Appellant. . . . As a result of the search, two stolen motorcycles, thirteen engines from stolen motorcycles, one frame of a stolen motorcycle, and six sets of metal punch stamps were seized. . . . [Punch stamps are devices that can be used to alter identification numbers found on stolen goods. At trial, an expert in forensic toolmark identification testified that] certain of the stamps found . . . had been used to alter the altered serial numbers on the motorcycle engines seized by police from that shop.

* * *

At trial, Appellant's strategy was to admit that the items were stolen, but deny that he knew that they were stolen. Appellant estimated that there were approximately 100,000 motorcycle parts in his shop when the police executed their search warrant and said he had no knowledge that the seized items were stolen. He also denied altering identification numbers on any of the seized goods and stated that he fired Paul Dorward, a former employee who had been stealing from him, prior to the execution of the search warrant. Appellant accused Mr. Dorward of purchasing the metal punch stamps and leaving them behind. . . .

* * *

"[A] permissible inference of guilty knowledge may be drawn from the unexplained possession of recently stolen goods without infringing upon an accused's right of due process or his right against self-incrimination, as well as other circumstances, such as the accused's conduct at the time of arrest."[26] Nonetheless, the mere possession of stolen property is insufficient to prove guilty knowledge, and the Commonwealth must introduce other evidence, which can be either circumstantial or direct, that demonstrates that the defendant knew or had reason to believe that the property was stolen. . . .[27] This additional evidence can include the nature of the goods, the quantity of the goods involved, the lapse of time between possession and theft, and the ease with which the goods can be assimilated into trade channels.[28] Further, whether the property has alterations indicative of being stolen can be used to establish guilty knowledge.[29] Finally, even if the accused offers an explanation for his possession of stolen property, the trier of fact may consider the possession as unexplained if it deems the explanation unsatisfactory.[30]

In the instant case, after Appellant testified that either he or his employees check the vehicle identification numbers and serial numbers on goods purchased for resale, he conceded on cross-examination that serial numbers on at least three engines found in his shop visibly had been altered. Furthermore, with regard to one of the stolen motorcycles seized by police, Appellant could not say where he obtained it and testified that he made no effort to check its identification numbers.

* * *

We find that sufficient circumstantial evidence existed for the trier of fact to conclude that Appellant received stolen goods knowing that they were stolen. This evidence includes: 1) Appellant's admission that he or an employee checked engine serial numbers and some of these numbers visibly were altered on engines found at Appellant's shop; 2) the existence of the six sets of metal stamps on Appellant's business premises; [and] 3) the fact that such a significant number, sixteen, of stolen items were found at Appellant's business. . . .

* * *

Questions

1. *Mens rea*, like any element of a crime, may be established by circumstantial evidence. In this case, the court ruled the circumstantial evidence was sufficient to support the conclusion, beyond a reasonable doubt, that the defendant received stolen goods knowing that they were, in fact, stolen. Evaluate the conclusion based on the facts of the case.
2. Might an argument be made that rather than knowing he was in possession of stolen goods, Foreman was reckless—he just didn't care, so he ran his business with a conscious disregard of the risk that he was in receipt of stolen parts? If so, would that make a difference in his criminal liability? Why or why not?

Fencing

Fencing is closely related to the possession of stolen property. A *fence* is "dealer of stolen goods" who often "serves as the middleman between the thief, whose goal is to quickly convert the goods he steals into cash, and the willing consumer, who is always in search of a discount."[31] Put differently, the crime of fencing occurs when someone conceals, transports, or offers stolen goods for sale.

As with possession of stolen property, the crime of fencing generally requires the actor to have either actual or constructive knowledge that the goods in question were, in fact, stolen.[32] Such dealing in stolen property is often classified as a felony.[33]

Embezzlement

Unlike the abolition of the distinctions between theft by trespass and a theft by trick, the distinction between lawful possession and custody has been maintained in many US jurisdictions through the differentiation of larceny-type thefts from embezzlements, which are largely concerned with thefts that breach the trust associated with fiduciary relationships.[34]

The common-law crime of **embezzlement** required proof of the following elements:

1. the fraudulent conversion;
2. of personal property;
3. of another;
4. by a person in lawful possession of that property.

The second and third elements—the personal property of another—mirror their use in other common-law theft offenses. And recall that *lawful possession* requires more than mere custody of property; it involves either ownership or possession of property that has been entrusted to someone who is given substantial authority to exercise dominion and control over that property. The key element differentiating embezzlement from larceny-type crimes is that of *fraudulent conversion.*

FRAUDULENT CONVERSION

Unlike larceny-type thefts that are concerned with taking another person's property either by trespass or trick, embezzlement is concerned with the fraudulent conversion of property. **Fraudulent conversion** occurs "when a person who has been entrusted with another's property treats the property as his own and uses it for his own purpose."[35] Put differently, fraudulent conversion concerns the intentional misappropriation of property that rightfully came into the defendant's possession.[36]

The "fraudulent" part of *fraudulent conversion* incorporates the *mens rea* of purpose—the specific intent to mishandle the property of another person entrusted to the embezzler.[37] Due to this *mens rea* requirement, embezzlement is not committed if property is converted pursuant to some claim of right (just as common-law larceny did not include property taken pursuant to some claim of right).[38]

BORROWING WITHOUT PERMISSION

Recall that property taken with the intent to borrow did not constitute the crime of larceny at common law because borrowing connotes an intent to return the property, thus negating *animus furandi*. But *animus furandi* is not an element of embezzlement—only the intent to misuse or misappropriate property.[39] Thus, intentionally using another's property in a manner inconsistent with the arrangement by which the defendant had possession of it satisfies both the *actus reus* and *mens rea* for embezzlement liability unless the defendant intended to restore the *exact* same property in the *exact* same condition. If the intent was to restore similar property or substantially identical property in only a similar condition, the common law reasoned that an embezzlement occurred.

MODERN APPROACH EASES THE DISTINCTION BETWEEN POSSESSION AND CUSTODY

Modern embezzlement statutes have eased the formal distinctions between lawful possession and custody. Thus, for example, in *Gwaltney v. Commonwealth*,[40] an appellate court upheld a conviction for embezzlement, rather than for larceny, against an employee who took cash from the teller's drawer at the bank where she had been employed even thought she had only custody of the cash because of the position of trust she had occupied as a bank employee. In jurisdictions that have adopted such an approach, the level of authority exercised over the property is no longer determinative, but rather whether an employee misappropriates property that had been entrusted him or her by virtue of the person's employment.

FRAUD AND RELATED OFFENSES

There are a host of other theft-offenses that are perpetrated through reliance on an actor's fraudulent intent. **Fraud** involves dishonesty calculated to achieve some advantage. Thus, fraudulent intent involves the intentional (i.e., purposeful or knowing) deception or attempted deception of another person in a manner designed to result in financial or personal gain.

The common-law approach to criminal fraud was loose. It clearly involved deception for personal gain, but specific elements remained elusive.[41] The Model Penal Code did little to clarify the elements of criminal fraud, namely because it does not contain any general fraud provision. Instead, variations of fraud, such as fraudulent or defraud, appear as an element of a number of crimes.[42] The federal criminal code similarly does not recognize a district crime of fraud. Rather, the concept of fraud is a part of numerous, specific fraud crimes, such as mail fraud, wire fraud, computer fraud, bank fraud, securities fraud, and health fraud.[43] Federal law does, however, recognize conspiracy to defraud.

Some states mirror the federal system by eschewing a general fraud crime and instead providing a comprehensive statutory schedule against a range of specific fraudulent practices. For example, the criminal code of Georgia contains the following specific provisions, just to name a few:

- Forgery[44]
- Manufacturing, selling, or distributing false identification documents[45]
- Deposit account fraud[46]
- Check, credit card, and ATM card fraud[47]

- Computer fraud[48]
- Fraud associated with the sale or transfer of vehicles[49]
- Identity theft[50]
- And a host of other "fraudulent practices" including depictive business practices, improper solicitation of money, mortgage fraud, and deception related to qualifying for public housing.[51]

Other states have enacted specific fraud statutes that use amorphous language, like this one:

> Any person who, pursuant to a scheme or artifice to defraud, knowingly obtains any benefit by means of false or fraudulent pretenses, representations, promises or material omissions is guilty of a class 2 felony.[52]

Regardless of the approach taken, laws against fraud or fraudulent practices typically require the union of at least two criminal elements. First, the *actus reus* element tends to involve either making a material misrepresentation of fact (i.e., lying) or failing to disclose a material fact (i.e., lying by omission). Second, the *mens rea* element involves some specific fraudulent intent, either through a purposeful or knowing deception. Consider the specific types of fraud-related offenses in Table 11.1.

Table 11.1 Specific Types of Fraudulent Offenses

Offense	Elements
Counterfeiting	Copying or imitating an item without authorization and then passing (or attempting to pass) the copy off as if it were the genuine or original item.
Forgery	Making or altering and writing with apparent legal significance so that it purports to make a false representation with the intent to defraud.
Uttering	Offering as genuine any instrument that may be the subject of a forgery, and therefore is false, with the intent to defraud.
False Impersonation	Assuming another person's character either (1) to make that other person liable for any crime, civil lawsuit, payment of any sum of money, charge, forfeiture, or penalty; or (2) to accrue any benefit as a result of the impersonation.*

* *See, e.g.*, Barkus v. State, 926 P.2d 312 (Okla. Crim. App. 1996).

CYBERCRIME

As many commentators have noted, **cybercrime** is an broad term that can described "any crime that is facilitated or committed using a computer, network, or hardware device."[53]

Between 2005 and 2019, the number of annual data breaches rose from 157 to 1,506.[54] The number of records exposed during these breaches varied from 19.1 million in 2006 to more than 4.6 billion in 2016.[55] Starting in 2018, efforts to stem these digital invasions finally caused a reduction in the number of data breaches, yet the number of people whose personal information was exposed in such breaches nonetheless reached 471.23 million—a record high that same year.[56]

Cybercrime may involve the use computers and related technology to commit theft, extortion, or a range of fraud-related crimes, including theft of credit card or bank information, theft of intellectual property (including piracy of software and audio-visual media), industrial espionage, the fraudulent manipulation of computer records, ransomware (extortion via computer), and identity theft. But cybercrimes may also involve "new" types of activity that are not necessarily aimed at any type of theft, such as:

- tampering with data or networks, including spreading malware, viruses, worms, and spyware;
- perpetrating denial of service attacks (overloading a system with so many requests it cannot operate normally);
- disclosing personal information (including "revenge porn");
- cyberbullying and cyberstalking (harassing or stalking someone online);
- spamming (distributed unsolicited messages);
- hacking (i.e., the deliberate circumvention of computer security systems);
- cracking (the unauthorized access to or modification of computer programs);
- bullying or selling illicit goods online; and
- making, digitally distributing, or possessing child pornography.

Identity Theft

The term **identity theft** is a broad one that encompasses a variety of offenses related to the unauthorized use of another person's identity.[57] The crime typically involves use of some personal identifying information being used to open fraudulent new accounts, ranging from credit cards and utility account to mortgages and auto loans.[58] But the crime can also be committed in seemingly countless other ways, such as filing fake tax returns in order to obtain a fraudulent tax refund; using health insurance information to obtain medical care, prescriptions, or even reimbursements of claims; and giving another person's identity when someone is arrested.[59] Nearly 60 million people in the United States have been the victim of identity theft, with more than 16.7 people being affected annually at a cost of more than $16.8 billion in stolen goods and services.[60]

Both the federal government and most states have enacted criminal laws against identity theft.[61] Oregon law, for example, provides: "A person commits the crime of identity theft if the person, with the intent to deceive or to defraud, obtains, possesses, transfers, creates, utters, or converts to the person's own use the personal identification of another person."[62]

The crime of identity theft varies by jurisdiction, but frequently is defined with minor variations of the following elements:

1. *actus reus*: Transferring, using, or attempting to use the identity of another person (or entity) to commit, aid, or abet any unlawful activity (sometimes limited to felonies and misdemeanor thefts, frauds, or obstruction of justice offenses);
2. attendant circumstance: Without authorization or consent;
3. *mens rea*: With purpose/specific intent to defraud.[63]

Some states require the actual use of the false identity in order to obtaining goods or services. Other jurisdictions go even further by defining the *actus reus* of identity theft as obtaining, recording, or accessing *personally identifying information* (e.g., Social Security, passport, driver's license, and bank account numbers) that would assist in accessing financial resources or other benefits rightfully belonging to another person or entity. Under such an approach, the actual use of the stolen identity is not required.[64]

Identity theft can be a type of cybercrime that is often accomplished by *phishing* schemes that trick people into providing personal information by masquerading as a legitimate entity. Alternatively, *malware* might surreptitiously capture such information. But identities can also be stolen using paper documents—such tax returns, bank statements, and credit card solicitations—that were discarded not shredded (sometimes called *dumpster diving*). Similarly, someone can get close to a victim in a place like a bank or a state motor vehicles office and observe personal information (sometimes called *shoulder surfing*). Thus, identity theft need not always be a form a cybercrime. Box 11.1, You Make the Public Policy Call, explores additional contours of identity theft.

Digital Piracy

Digital piracy concerns the unauthorized stealing, copying, or sharing of a digital work, such as software, movies, books, and music. But because the lawful purchase of such items cost money, they are often the subject of digital theft. Such thefts might take the form of high-tech industrial espionage or major illicit distribution rings of pirated materials. But a tremendous amount of digital piracy takes place in the homes of everyday people.

In the early days of television, a handful of channels were freely available to anyone who could afford a television set and an antenna to receive the wireless signals broadcast locally by network-affiliated stations. By the 1980s, however, cable television revolutionized the delivery of home entertainment. In exchange for fees, people were able to obtain more channels delivered via a coaxial cable to their homes. As cable television industry grew, people tried all sorts of ways to obtain services without paying for them. Given the ways in which some statutes were written at the time to require a "taking" and "asportation," stealing cable services proved difficult to prosecute. This prompted some states to move away from common-law crimes and adopt integrated theft statutes that include the theft of services. Other states responded by enacting "theft of cable television service" laws to specifically criminalize knowingly using any equipment "for the purpose of intercepting or receiving any programming or service" from a cable television system without authorization."[65]

BOX 11.1

YOU MAKE THE PUBLIC POLICY CALL

Synthetic Identity Theft: What Does It Mean to Actually Steal an Identity?

Many cases of identity theft involve the use of real person's Social Security Number and date of birth, but often with a false name and address.[109] But in a variation of the crime sometimes known as *synthetic identity theft*, a person creates a fictitious person and assumes the fake identity with fraudulent intent.

The defendant in *State v. Washington* had been charged and convicted of identity theft.[110] He argued that he had not, in fact, stolen anyone's identity because he made up a fictitious person and obtained credit cards in that person's name which he then used to buy merchandise. The Supreme Court of New Hampshire agree with him, ruling that the language of the state statute in question required that someone pose of an actual, rather than fictitious person. The court reasoned as follows:

> when the legislature intends to refer to a noun and to some fictional representation of that noun, it does so expressly. For example, the legislature has identified robbery as a class B felony when the defendant was either "actually armed with a deadly weapon" or "reasonably appeared to the victim to be armed with a deadly weapon."[111]

In 2009, the US Supreme Court similarly ruled that in a federal identity theft case, the government must prove that a defendant "knew that the 'means of identification' he or she unlawfully transferred, possessed, or used, in fact, belonged to 'another person.' "[112] In that case, in order to secure employment, the defendant had given his employer a false name and birthdate, along with a made-up Social Security number that did not belong to anyone and a counterfeit "green card."

1. Do you agree that identity theft must involve taking an actual person's identity? Explain your reasoning.
2. Since the type of deceptive identity practices involved in the two cases summarized in Box 11.1 do not constitute identity theft, of what crimes, if any, might it be proper for such defendants to be convicted? Why?

Today, home entertainment looks quite different than it did in the 1980s. Everything from computer, tables, and mobile phones to smart appliances are connected to the internet. Using the internet, people can now play games against each other despite the fact that they are separated by thousands of miles. Similarly, people need not go to movie theaters anymore to watch feature films; they can watch them at home whenever they wish. And gone are the days when people need to go to a music store to buy a record, tape, or CD; with the advent of digital music technology, people can listen to whatever they want, whenever they wish. But the internet has opened up new avenues for the electronic theft of copyrighted audiovisual media, from games to movies to music.

Criminal Copyright Infringement

Copyright is a type of intellectual property. Unlike real property (land and buildings) or personal property (tangible things), *intellectual property* "refers to creations of the mind."[66] Patent law protect the creators of inventions. Trademark law protects the commercial use of symbols, names, and images, and copyright law protects grants legal protections to the creators of "original works of authorship fixed in a tangible medium of expression, now known or later developed."[67] These protections include a wide range of works: literature; music; motion pictures, television, and other audiovisual media; and all types of visual and performing arts, including photography, graphic, sculptural work, dramatic, choreographic, and architectural works.[68]

Creators of copyrighted work may sell or their intellectual property interests to others or license them for specific types of distribution. When movies, television, music, and other forms of audiovisual materials are licensed to played in theaters, broadcast on television or the internet, sold on CDs or DVDs, or made available for download or streaming on sites licensed to distribute the works in that manner, the copyright holder typically earns income in the form of royalties to compensate them for their work. But when any copyrighted work is made available outside of the lawfully established distribution chains, violators can be subject both civil and criminal penalties. Contrary to the popular belief that copyright violations are victimless crimes, they are not. Digital piracy of copyrighted music, movies, television, and software costs the US economy "between 230,000 and 560,000 jobs and between $47.5 billion and $115.3 billion in" reduced gross domestic product each year.[69]

In 1997, Congress enacted the No Electronic Theft Act (NET Act),[70] which strengthened federal protection for copyrighted works. The NET Act modified prior copyright laws such that money-making schemes are no longer required for criminal copyright liability. Rather, criminal liability may be imposed for "private financial gain" for the "receipt, or expectation of receipt, of anything of value, including the receipt of other copyrighted works." Note that the word "receipt" is not qualified. Thus, it includes streaming, downloading, peer-to-peer sharing, stream-ripping, and other ways that people might receive copyrighted works.

As a result, the federal criminal copyright statute now provides:

> Any person who willfully infringes a copyright shall be punished . . . if the infringement was committed—
>
> (A) for purposes of commercial advantage or private financial gain;
>
> (B) by the reproduction or distribution, including by electronic means, during any 180-day period, of 1 or more copies or phonorecords of 1 or more copyrighted works, which have a total retail value of more than $1,000; or
>
> (C) by the distribution of a work being prepared for commercial distribution, by making it available on a computer network accessible to members of the public, if such person knew or should have known that the work was intended for commercial distribution.[71]

The use of the term "willfully" should make it clear that the *mens rea* for criminal copyright infringement is purpose. But because this *mens rea* is tied to the *actus reus,* the law applies if someone purposefully infringes a copyright; they need not know the details of the copyright law itself.

The punishments for criminal copyright infringement vary depending on what type of violation occurred. First-time violators of subsection A "shall be imprisoned not more than 5 years, or fined [up to $250,000] or both, *if the offense consists of the reproduction or distribution,* including by electronic means, during any 180-day period, of at least 10 copies or phonorecords, of 1 or more copyrighted works, which have a total retail value of more than $2,500."[72] All other violations of subsection A—meaning those that do not involve the "reproduction or distribution" of copyrighted works or if the numerical and monetary thresholds are not met—are punished as misdemeanors that "shall be imprisoned not more than 1 year, or fined in the amount set forth in this title, or both, in any other case."[73] First-time violators of subsection B "shall be imprisoned not more than 3 years, or fined [up to $250,000], or both, if the offense consists of the reproduction or distribution of 10 or more copies or phonorecords of 1 or more copyrighted works, which have a total retail value of $2,500 or more."[74] And first-time violators of subsection C "shall be imprisoned not more than 3 years, fined under this title, or both."

The distinction in sentencing for subsection A violations is odd, at least today. Regardless of whether the infringement was for purposes of commercial advantage or private financial gain, the punishment depends on whether the work in question was either (1) subject to illegal reproduction or distribution, or (2) otherwise infringed, such as by an unauthored public performance. This distinction may have made sense at the time the law was written, but it has a bizarre effect today in the age of streaming services like Netflix, Hulu, Amazon, and many more services to which people subscribe pay fees to access licensed content on-demand. Streaming is currently considered a public performance; thus, illegal streaming is punishable as a misdemeanor. By contrast, downloading is consider distribution, which is punishable as a felony. This bizarre distinction has been dubbed the "streaming loophole," and Congress is considering changing the law to treat all infringement as felonies.

In 1998, Congress enacted the Digital Millennium Copyright Act (DMCA).[75] It is basically a digital trespass law that provides criminal penalties for willfully circumventing technological measures designed to prevent unauthorized access to copyrighted works, such as scrambling or encoding systems. The DMCA also punishes trafficking in technology that allows such circumvention. Like the NET Act, its provisions apply to people who violate the law either for commercial advantage or for "private financial gain." Its punishments involve fines up to $500,000 and five years of imprisonment for first offenses.

The "Statutory Analysis Exercise" in Box 11.2 asks you to apply these laws explained in this section to two common forms of copyright theft.

BOX 11.2

STATUTORY ANALYSIS EXERCISE

How Should We Punish Those Who Digitally Steal Copyrighted Works?

Three recent federal prosecutions cast some light on how federal law enforcement officers are trying to combat digital piracy.

Federal agents investigated Xbox-scene.com, a website "that hosted online forums dedicated to the discussion of modifying video game consoles by installing 'modification chips' (or 'mod chips') in them so that they could run software for which the consoles were not originally designed."[113] Jeffrey J. Reichert was one of the moderators of the discussion forums hosted on the site. An undercover agent contacted him requesting a modified Nintendo Wii. "Reichert responded to the agent's requests, purchased a Wii, installed a modification chip, and sold the modified Wii to the agent for a $50 profit. When the Wii was tested, it was able to play both legitimate video games and pirated ones."[114]

Business partners Hisham Alshaikhli and Laith Alqaraghuli opened a store in El Cajon, California to sell devices that had been "jailbroken" to allow users to stream movies and television shows with a subscription.[115] These devices were designed to be plugged into a television and load a series of legitimate-looking apps that allow the user to access unauthorized troves of media, and the devices were sold to consumers with sales pitches that explicitly described the illegal purpose of the devices.

Darryl Polo and Luis Villarino, two computer programs based in Las Vegas, ran two illegal streaming sites that offered subscribers access to roughly 118,000 television shows and 11,000 movies—"more content than Netflix, Amazon Prime, Hulu and Vudu."[116] They used software programs to scour the web, locate desired media, and then download that content via torrents. They earned more than $1 million by selling their illegally obtained content to subscribers.

1. For each of these three cases, do you think that the defendants violated the federal criminal copyright law, the DMCA, both, or neither? Explain your reasoning.
2. If these defendants were convicted, how would you sentence them if you were the judge presiding over each of their cases? Why?
3. In light of the laws described in his chapter and cases summarized in this box, what do you think your own criminal liability might be if you were to "jailbreak" an Amazon Fire Stick and then use it to stream copyrighted materials for which you did not pay to access? Why?

ROBBERY

Robbery is a larceny that is committed by force or threat of force against the person from whom the property is being stolen.[76] Because of the use or threatened use of force, robbery combines larceny with an assault or battery.

Common-Law Robbery

The common-law elements of robbery were:

1. a taking and asportation;
2. of the personal property of another;
3. from the other's person or in that person's presence;
4. by force or threats of force to the victim or some person in the victim's presence;
5. with the intent to permanently deprive the victim of the property.[77]

As with the crime of larceny, a robbery requires that the perpetrator take the personal property of another person and carry it away with *animus furandi*—the intent to permanently deprive the victim of the property. For these reasons, larceny is a lesser included offense of robbery. But robbery adds two attendant circumstance requirements that differentiate it from any crime against property.

First, the perpetrator must take the property in question either from a person or in the person's presence. If the person is not physically present to witness the taking and asportation, then the crime is one against property, like larceny, not a crime against the person.

Second, robberies involve the actual use of force that engenders a risk of immediate physical injury, or some form of intimidation that explicitly or implicitly threatens such an injury to either the robbery victim himself or herself, or to someone else in the immediate vicinity. Thus, although robbery involves theft or attempted theft, it is property classified as a crime against the person.[78]

The classic example of a robbery is when an armed person holds a gun or a knife up to a victim and says, "Your money or your life." But neither a deadly weapon nor threats to one's life are necessary to satisfy the force element of the crime of robbery. Indeed, the force used can be slight, but it must be more than what is required to gain control over and move the property.

Carjacking constitutes a specific type of robbery, although it has been designated as a separate criminal offense in some jurisdictions.[79] In contrast, a purse snatching, may or may not constitute a robbery. If no force was used other than that necessary to take the victim's purse, then the crime is one against property, such as larceny or the statutory offense that some states have created for the unarmed and otherwise nonforcible stealing of a purse or a wallet called **sudden snatching**.[80] But if the perpetrator employs more than the force necessary to remove the property from the person, then the theft crime is elevated to a robbery.

Robbery Under the Model Penal Code

Under the Model Penal Code, a robbery occurs when "in the course of committing a theft," a person inflicts or threatens serious bodily injury on or against another person.[81] Under this approach, the technical requirement of an asportation has been abolished; the robbery is complete when the perpetrator takes possession of the property.[82]

Also note that the Model Penal Code requirement of "serious bodily injury" departs from the common-law definition of the crime of robbery. Notably, many states that adopted the Model Penal Code nonetheless retained the common-law approach to this element, thereby rejecting the notion that a robbery must involve the infliction of threatened inflection of serious bodily injury. Thus, so as long as force or the threat of force is used in the course of committing a theft, a defendant may be convicted of robbery, as illustrated by *Messina v. State*.[83] In that case, the victim had left her purse in a shopping cart while she transferring the items she had purchased into the trunk of her case. The defendant came over, grabbed the purse, and ran away. The victim chased him until he made it into his car and closed the door. At that point, she sat on the hood of the defendant's car, thinking that would prevent him from driving away. But he instead started and stopped the car a few times and eventually succeeded in getting her to fall off. The court upheld his robbery conviction not because if of the force he had used to snatch the purse, but rather because of the force he subsequently used once the victim tried to regain possession of her property. Note, however, that resistance of a robbery victim is not an element of the offense. Indeed, because most possessions have little value when compared to the value of one's health or life, robbery victims are well-advised not to resist.

The *Messina* case also illustrates another important principle of the law of robbery. The union of *actus reus* (the taking and asportation) and *mens rea* (intent to steal) must occur simultaneously, but the use of force or intimidation does not have to occur contemporaneously with the taking.[84]

Federal Robbery Statutes

Congress enacted two federal statutes to address forms of robbery that are unique to federal jurisdiction—the Hobbs Act and the Bank Robbery Act. The former is aimed at thefts that occur while goods are being transported across state lines. The definition of robbery in the Hobbs Act mirrors its common-law definition. But the law also criminalizes obtaining another person's property via **extortion**—the inducement of consent "by wrongful use of actual or threatened force, violence, or fear, or under color of official right."[85]

The Bank Robbery Act[86] is aimed at any robbery of a bank, credit union, or savings and loan association because their deposits are federally insured up to a certain amount. The statute not only criminalizes bank robbery, but also "unlawful entry" into a federally insured bank with the intent of robbing it.

CRIMES AGAINST PROPERTY INVOLVING DAMAGE OR TRESPASS

Given the sanctity of property rights under both the common-law tradition, the criminal law has long been used to protect both personal property and real property. That remains true today in light of the dominant political philosophy in Western nations today. Accordingly, all US states not only criminalize the theft or destruction of private property, they also ban certain types of interference with owners; exclusive rights to use and enjoy their property.

Burglary

Upon returning from a vacation to find one's home has been broken into and one's personal possessions have been stolen, people often exclaim, "I've been robbed!" But a burglary, not a robbery, occurred. A **burglary** is a crime against property in which a defendant illegally enters premises with the purpose of committing a felony once inside.

COMMON-LAW BURGLARY

The common-law elements of burglary were as follows:

1. a breaking (*actus reus*)
2. and entering (*actus reus*)
3. of another's dwelling (attendant circumstance)
4. at nighttime (attendant circumstance)
5. with the intent to commit a felony in the structure (*mens rea*).[87]

Each one of these elements had special definitions at common law.

A *breaking* was defined as the creation or enlargement of an opening.[88] Moreover, the creation or enlargement of such an opening had to be accomplished by at least minimal force (although not necessarily violence), fraud, or intimidation.[89] Accordingly, if a person obtained the owner's consent to enter the premise, the entry was not a breaking. Similarly, if one walked through a wide-open door or crawled through a wide-open window, there was no breaking. Without such a breaking, there was no burglary at common law.

Entering was defined as placing any portion of the body into the place being burgled.[90] Alternatively, an entering could be accomplished by using some instrument that was used to commit a crime once inside the dwelling.

A *dwelling* was defined as a structure regularly used for sleeping purposes.[91] Even if such a structure were also regularly used for other purposes, that would not change its character as a dwelling for the purposes of the crime of burglary.

At common law, one could not burglarize one's own dwelling. Actually, ownership was irrelevant. So long as the dwelling was occupied by someone other than the defendant, the dwelling would be deemed that "of another."

The common-law crime of burglary could only be committed at night. Night was typically defined as starting 30 to 60 minutes before sunset and ending 30 to 60 minutes after sunrise, largely because it is difficult to see a person's face during twilight at either sunset or sunrise.[92] Even if all of the other elements of the crime were met, if they occurred during the day, no burglary could be deemed to have occurred at common law.

Finally, the person had to have possessed the intent to commit a felony once inside at the time of entering the dwelling.[93] Note the felony did not have to be a theft related offense; the intend to commit crimes against the person satisfied the *mens rea* requirement. If there was no such intent (e.g., one simply wanted to look around and then leave), then no burglary could be deemed to have occurred at common law. Nor would any intent formed *after* entering the dwelling suffice since the intent to commit a felony had to exist at the time of the breaking and entering. It should also be noted that the intended felony did need not need to be carried out. The intent to commit the felony alone was sufficient under the common law.

MODERN BURGLARY

The Model Penal Code and modern burglary laws have eliminated many of the arcane technicalities required under common law.[94] Most modern burglary statutes no longer require an actual breaking; illegal entry or remaining unlawfully on premises will suffice. No longer must the structure be a dwelling; warehouses and office buildings can thus be burglarized under modern laws. The nighttime requirement has been abolished so that time of day is normally irrelevant to the definition of the crime. Finally, the intent requirement has been modified in many jurisdictions so that the intent to commit any crime, whether a felony or misdemeanor, suffices.

Under both the common-law and modern burglary statutes, the actor's intent is key to the definition of the crime. Without the intent to commit a crime once inside the structure, there is no burglary, but rather the crime of criminal trespass.

Criminal Trespass

A number of theft offenses involve trespass to personal property. But the term *trespass* is actual a broad term that encompasses any unlawful act against the property or rights of another person. In the context of real property, **criminal trespass** is committed in one of two ways.

First, a criminal trespass is committed when someone wrongful intrudes onto the lands or premises of another person. Most statutes require that the actor have actual or constructive knowledge that they are entering someone else land or premises without consent, such as when they enter lands with signs marked "private property" or when they ignore fences, walls, or other enclosures that are clearly designed to prevent unauthorized persons from entering the property. Second, even if someone did not enter premises illegally, the actor trespasses when he or she refuses to leave premises after his or her privilege to be there is revoked. This could occur when someone is told to leave premises and they refuse.

Criminal trespass can constitute a **lesser included offense** of burglary. That term means that a less serious crime contained within a more serious crime. Indeed, the Model Penal Code specifies that a lesser included offense "differs from the offense charged only in the respect that a less serious injury or risk of injury to the same person, property or public interest or a lesser kind of culpability suffices to establish its commission."[95] For example, as explained in Chapter 7, an unintentional killing that is reckless would constitute involuntary manslaughter, whereas an unintentional killing that is so grossly reckless that it manifests an extreme indifferent to human life would constitute the more serious crime of depraved heart murder. Involuntary manslaughter can be a lesser included offense of depraved heart murder because the only difference would be how reckless a jury believes the defendant to have been in causing an unintentional death.[96] The "Case Study Extra" feature in Box 11.3 illustrates explores the concept of lesser included offenses in more detail.

POSSESSION OF BURGLARY TOOLS

In order to prevent burglaries, nearly all states have enacted laws that criminalize the possession of certain tools or devices that are commonly used to break and enter other's premises if such possession coincides with the intent to commit a burglary.[97] Depending upon the jurisdiction, the crime of **possession of burglary tools** would include possession of such items often include crowbars, tension bars, lock picks, screwdrivers, hammers, pliers, master keys, masks, torches, rope (for climbing), explosives, and so on.[98] Interesting, there is scant evidence to suggest that these laws are effective in reducing burglary.[99]

Arson

Most people think of arson as the act of deliberate setting fire to a building. But arson neither requires specific intent nor does it only apply to buildings—at least not anymore.

ARSON AT COMMON LAW

Common-law **arson** was defined by the following four elements:

BOX 11.3

CASE STUDY EXTRA

Double Jeopardy and Crimes Committed in Burglaries Gone Bad

The defendant in *Kinsey v. State*[117] was convicted of convicted of attempted murder, aggravated robbery, and burglary for actions summarized by the Supreme Court of Arkansas as follows:

> Mrs. Elaine Paul . . . testified that the appellant came to her door holding the prescription drugs she had ordered for her husband, Dr. Edgar Paul. She opened the door and appellant came toward her with a gun, backed her to the wall, and told her to hold out her fingers. He inspected her jewelry, commenting that it was "cheap." When Dr. Paul entered the room and told the appellant to get out, the appellant shot Dr. Paul in the right shoulder. Dr. Paul fell to the floor, and Mrs. Paul ran to the back of the house where she pushed an alarm button and called the police. When she returned the appellant had fled, taking only the medicine.[118]

The court affirmed Kinsey's convictions over his arguments that the Double Jeopardy Clause barred these multiple convictions and associated punishments. The court wrote:

> In some instances this argument would have merit, in that one form of aggravated robbery includes the element that the defendant "inflicts or attempts to inflict death or serious injury upon another person" with the purpose of committing a theft. . . . In this case, however, the aggravated robbery and the attempted first degree murder were two different criminal actions with separate victims. The aggravated robbery had already been fully performed when the appellant held Mrs. Paul at gunpoint and examined her jewelry with the purpose of committing a theft. The attempted first degree murder occurred separately when the appellant shot Dr. Paul. Although crimes are committed in the same escapade, they are not part of the same conduct when committed against different persons. . . .
>
> Neither is aggravated robbery a lesser included offense of burglary. Aggravated robbery requires some type of serious force or threat of force used with the purpose of committing a theft, none of which is required to commit burglary. Burglary requires only that the defendant enters or remains unlawfully in an occupiable structure with the purpose of committing any offense punishable by imprisonment. Although aggravated robbery was the punishable offense which the appellant had the purpose of committing, a defendant may be convicted of the burglary for entering the home and the subsequent offense he commits after the entry. The unlawful entry is

an independent and substantive offense with the result that cumulative penalties may be imposed for entering with intent to steal and for stealing.

1. This case demonstrates the difference between burglary and robbery. Neither crime requires the other to occur; neither one is a lesser included offense of the other; but both may occur during the same factual series of events. Which do you think is the more dangerous crime deserving a more severe criminal punishment? Why?
2. From what facts could the court infer Kinsey's intent in satisfaction of the *mens rea* requirement for burglary? For robbery? Do you agree with the court's reasoning on either count? Explain.

1. the malicious (*mens rea*)
2. burning (*actus reus*)
3. of another's dwelling (attendant circumstance).[100]

The *mens rea* requirement encompassed the mental states traditionally associated with malice—either specific intent to burn or reckless disregard of an obvious risk of burning. Accordingly, while specific intent to burn the dwelling of another clearly would have satisfied the elements for arson liability, such specific intent was not required. Acting with a reckless disregard of a substantial and unjustifiable risk of fire would have also sufficed.

Burning was a term of art at common law. It required some damage to the dwelling by fire, as opposed to smoke or water damage. But there was never any requirement that the dwelling be destroyed or even significantly damaged. A "mere charring" was sufficient to impose arson liability.

The use of the term *dwelling* had the same meaning for the crime of arson as it had for the crime of burglary: a place regularly used for sleeping. Interestingly, though, one could not commit an arson of one's own home at common law since the dwelling had to be that of another to qualify as a true arson. When one burned one's own house, it was the common-law crime of **house burning**.

MODERN ARSON

Modern arson statutes have largely eliminated the common-law attendant circumstances of being a dwelling of another. Thus, one can now commit an arson of one's own home, office, or warehouse. Indeed, not only are buildings and vehicles including in most states' arson laws, but some states even include the burning of crops, pastures, and forests in their arson statutes.[101]

Modern laws have modified the *mens rea* for arson. Some states set degrees of arson and the associated punishments depending on the amount of damaged caused.[102] Other states differentiate arson in the first degree, or aggravated arson, when it is done with specific intent (i.e., purpose or knowledge), from arson the second degree, or simple arson, when it is committed recklessly. Still other jurisdictions differentiate the levels of arson based on the type of structure, with an occupied dwelling being the most serious type of arson.[103] But as the following case illustrates, neat categories of *mens rea* are not always easily applied to arson.

Kimberly LAWRENCE

v.

The STATE of Georgia

Supreme Court of Georgia

453 S.E.2d 733 (1995).

Kimberly Lawrence was found guilty of involuntary manslaughter, arson, aggravated battery, felony murder, and cruelty to children.... Lawrence argues that the evidence was insufficient to support the arson conviction. We disagree.

... Kimberly Lawrence awoke when she heard her daughter Tyesha crying for her. Entering the bedroom, she found her four-year-old son, Taiwan, lying bloody and motionless in his bed. Suspecting that her seven-year-old son had stabbed his brother and thinking that she could cover up the cause of the wounds by starting a fire, she turned on the burners on her stove, ignited newspapers and placed the burning papers under a couch. She then left the room, with the fire burning, and went back to bed. She got up again only to see why the fire alarm had not gone off; at this time the fire was out of control and the apartment was engulfed in flames. Her son Taiwan was killed, her daughter Tyesha suffered third-degree burns, lacerations and a punctured lung, and ten units in the apartment complex were destroyed in the fire.

Under § 16-7-60, a person commits first-degree arson when she knowingly damages a dwelling under such circumstances that it is reasonably foreseeable that human life might be endangered. Here, the evidence clearly authorized a jury to find Lawrence guilty of arson.

Lawrence argues that she did not intend to endanger a life. Even if she did not specifically intend to endanger a life, she did, as she admitted, set the fire, and damage apartments in the complex, under circumstances that endangered human life, and "that is all that the statute requires be proved."[104] Lawrence argues further that under *Reinhardt v. State*,[105] arson requires an intent not only to set a fire, but also to damage a building, and that there was insufficient evidence of her intent to damage the building. This argument is meritless. There was evidence from which a jury could determine that Lawrence set the fire to cover up the stabbing of her younger son, an act which necessarily involved damage to the building. Indeed, reviewing the evidence in a light most favorable to the jury's determination of guilt, we conclude that a rational trier of fact could have found Lawrence guilty of all of the crimes for which she was convicted.

* * *

Questions

1. Does the arson statute at issue in *Lawrence* require a higher or lower degree of *mens rea* than the common-law crime of arson required?
2. The *Lawrence* court concluded there was sufficient evidence from which to infer the defendant's intent to both endanger human life and to damage a building. Do you agree? Why or why not?
3. If you were the sentencing judge and had unlimited discretion to sentence the defendant to anything ranging from time served to probation to a maximum of twenty-five years in prison, what sentence would you impose? Why?

Malicious Destruction of Property

Nearly all US states criminalize the malicious destruction of or damage to another person's property. Some jurisdictions refer to the offense as **criminal damage**, while others use **malicious destruction of property**. In some jurisdictions, vandalism is subsumed into this offense,[106] whereas in other states, vandalism is a separate crime.[107]

Punishment for the offense is usually graded based on the value of the property that was destroyed or harmed. For example, property damage of several hundred dollars might be classified as a misdemeanor, whereas differing degrees of felony charges might be applicable to increasing amount of damage, such a low-level felony for damage of $1,000 to $2,000, a higher-level felony for $2,000 to $10,000 worth of damage, and still a higher level of felony classification for damage in excess of $10,000.[108]

CONCLUSION

Learning Objectives	Summaries
1. Compare and contrast larceny, larceny by trick, and false pretenses.	Larceny is the taking and asportation of the personal property of another person in lawful custody or possession of it without consent and with the specific intent to steal. If consent is obtained using deception, then the crime is larceny by trick. If lawful title to property is obtain by fraud, then the crime is false pretenses.

Learning Objectives	Summaries
2. Explain what consolidated theft statutes and what common-law offenses are often subsumed in them.	Consolidated theft statutes abolish the technicalities of common-law theft offenses by defining the crime as the unlawful taking or exercising control over the property of another person with the purpose to deprive him or her of that property. Even though crimes like embezzlement, shoplifting, and possession of stolen property could fall within the broad language of consolidated theft laws, some states still designate those crimes as separate offenses.
3. Analyze the elements of embezzlement as a distinct crime from other forms of theft.	Embezzle involves the fraudulent conversion of another's personal property by someone with lawful possession of that property. It is the misappropriation of property that had been entrusted to someone by virtue of the person's employment that distinguishes embezzlement from other theft crimes.
4. Differentiate the generic term fraud from specific types of fraud crimes.	Fraud refers to deception for financial or personal gain. It serves as *mens rea* requirement for a number of criminal offenses, including forgery, counterfeiting, false impersonation, and a number of fraudulent practices designed to steal money or property using deception.
5. Differentiate the generic term cybercrime from at least two types of specific digital offenses.	Cybercrime is a broad term that can described any crime that is facilitated or committed using a computer, network, or hardware device. Examples include spreading computer viruses or malware, cyberbullying, and hacking.
6. Compare and contrast the common law and contemporary approaches to robbery.	Common-law robbery involves the taking and asportation of the personal property of another from the other's person or in that person's presence by force or threats of force to the victim or some person in the victim's presence with the intent to permanently deprive the victim of the property. Some of these technicalities have been abolished such that robbery is now defined as when a theft occurs by inflicting or threatening another person with bodily injury.
7. Analyze the distinction between burglary and criminal trespass.	Common-law burglary involves breaking and entering another's dwelling at night with the intent to commit a felony in the structure. Modern burglary statutes criminalize the unlawful entry onto premises with the intent to commit a crime once inside.
8. Apply the elements of arson to determine liability under both the common-law and modern arson statutes.	Common-law arson involved the malicious burning of another person's dwelling. The requirement of a dwelling has largely been abolished such that the burning of any structure now qualifies with varying levels of *mens rea* and attendant circumstances being relevant to the grading of modern arson offenses.
9. Explain the crime of malicious destruction of property.	The malicious destruction of or damage to another person's property, when done with recklessness or higher levels of *mens rea*, is criminally punished through most of the United States.

KEY TERMS

arson
burglary
copyright
counterfeiting
criminal damage/malicious destruction of property
criminal trespass
cybercrime
embezzlement
extortion
false impersonation
false pretenses
fencing
forgery
fraud
fraudulent conversion
house burning
identity theft
larceny
larceny by trick
lesser included offense
possession of burglary tools
possession of stolen property
robbery
shopkeepers' privilege
shoplifting
sudden snatching
uttering

12

Public Order Offenses and Crimes Against The State

Outline

LEARNING OBJECTIVES

1. Differentiate the major classes of drug crimes.
2. Compare and contrast the *per se* approach and the impairment approach to the crime of driving under the influence.
3. Explain the elements of disorderly conduct.
4. Analyze the constitutional limits of regulating vagrancy, panhandling, and loitering.
5. Distinguish between treason, sedition, and espionage.
6. Explain the two most common forms of immigration offenses.

INTRODUCTION

A host of criminal offenses, most of which are classified as violations or misdemeanors, aim to maintain public order and the safe operation of society. Criminal traffic offenses, such as criminal speeding (i.e., speeding in excess of twenty or twenty-five miles per hour over the posted limit) are excellent examples of this offense type. Chapter 6 explored some of public order offenses related to the administration of justice. In this chapter, we examine additional public order offenses, include drug crimes, driving under the influence, and various quality of life crimes. This chapter concludes with a brief examination of select crimes against the state.

DRUG OFFENSES

Since the early 1970s, and increasing dramatically in the 1980s, the United States has been waging a "war on drugs."[1] Drug enforcement, interdiction, treatment, and prevention costs the United States more than $50 billion each year, with more than half ($28.88 billion) coming from the federal budget.[2] As a result of enforcement efforts, arrests for drug-related crimes account for the single largest category of arrests made every year. In 2016, 1.57 million people were arrested for drug-related crimes, exceeding the number of arrests for all types of property crime combined (1.35 million).[3] Approximately 8 percent of these arrests were for drug possession charges only, whereas roughly 15 percent were for the sale or manufacture of controlled substances.[4] This volume of arrests over several decades and the corresponding penalties for the underlying drug offenses is the single-greatest contributor to the staggering numbers of people incarcerated in the United States:

> In 1980, federal prisons incarcerated just 4,900 people for drug offenses, representing roughly twenty-five percent of the federal prison population. n172 By 2014, those same prisons held 96,500 people for a drug offense, accounting for 50% of the federal prison population and a 1,869% increase since 1980. . . . The states have seen a similarly dramatic increase in drug offenders in prison. In 1980, state prisons incarcerated roughly 19,000 people for a drug offense, representing 6.5% of states' total prison populations. By 2014, states cumulatively incarcerated roughly 208,000 people for a drug offense—a 995% increase since 1980; drug offenders accounted for 15.3% of states' prison populations in 2014.[5]

The impact of mass incarceration has disproportionately affected people of color, partially due to aggressive enforcement of drug laws in communities with large African American and Hispanic populations. Consider, for example, that although Whites and African

Americans use drugs are roughly the same rates, African Americans are arrested at more than twice the rate of their White counterparts for drug offenses.[6]

Controlled Substances

The term *controlled substance* refers to any substance whose manufacture, use, or possession is regulated by law. Each state classified its own controlled substances laws slightly differently, but at the federal level, the most important law classifying drugs, drug offenses, and penalties is the Comprehensive Drug Abuse Prevention and Control Act of 1970.[7] Title II of that law is known as the Controlled Substance Act (CSA).[8]

The CSA classifies a range of drugs into five different categories known as *schedules*, which are summarized in Table 12.1. Schedule I drugs are the most strictly regulated under the CSA and restrictions ease as schedule numbers increase.

Note that marijuana is classified as a Schedule I substance under the CSA, even though marijuana does, in fact, have known medical uses for treating pain, insomnia, glaucoma, nausea, and a range of other symptoms. These medical uses have led approximately thirty-three states and the District of Columbia to legalize the medical use of marijuana.[9] Yet the federal government has not yet rescheduled marijuana despite medical, criminal justice, and public policy groups advocating for the drug to be reclassified.[10]

Jurisdictional Enforcement

Illicit and prescribed drugs alike are regulated by both state and federal law. Thus, for example, smoking marijuana in a national park could get someone arrested by a federal law enforcement officer triggering case processing in the federal system. But federal prosecutions for drug use or simple possession are exceedingly rare (less than a fraction of 1 percent by some estimates).[11] Most federal prosecutors would decline to pursue simple possession cases so that they can focus on more important drug-related cases, such as those involving the illicit manufacture of drugs or on drug trafficking—the purposeful or knowing possession of controlled substances with the intent to transport or distribute them.[12]

Possession

The state of actual or constructive possession (Chapter 3) of contraband, like a controlled substance, qualifies as an *actus reus* for any crime that bans the possession of an item. All US states have laws criminalizing the **possession of a controlled substance**. Possession laws vary with regard to the types of drugs and the amounts. All states ban the possession of controlled substances like cocaine, methamphetamine, and heroin. But approximately eleven US states have legalized the recreational use of marijuana.[13] These laws limit the amount of the substance that may be possessed, as well setting restricting use to adults twenty-one years of age or older. Even in states that have not legalized the recreational use of marijuana, many states have decreased the penalties for simple possession to be low-level misdemeanors or even civil infractions/violations.[14]

Table 12.1 Federal Schedule of Controlled Substances

Schedule	Definition	Examples
I	Drugs with no currently accepted medical use and a high potential for abuse	Heroin, gamma hydroxybutyric acid (GHB), lysergic acid diethylamide (LSD), marijuana (cannabis), 3,4-methylenedioxymethamphetamine (ecstasy), methaqualone, and peyote
II	Drugs with approved medical uses that have a high potential for abuse, with use potentially leading to severe psychological or physical dependence.	Combination products with less than 15 milligrams of hydrocodone per dosage unit (Vicodin), cocaine, methamphetamine, phencyclidine (PCP), methadone, morphine, hydromorphone (Dilaudid), meperidine (Demerol), oxycodone (OxyContin), fentanyl, Dexedrine, Adderall, and Ritalin
III	Drugs with approved medical uses with a moderate to low potential for physical and psychological dependence.	Products containing less than 90 milligrams of codeine per dosage unit (Tylenol with codeine), ketamine, anabolic steroids, testosterone, and some barbiturates
IV	Drugs with approved medical uses with a low potential for abuse and low risk of dependence.	Xanax, Soma, Darvon, Darvocet, Valium, Ativan, Talwin, Ambien, Tramadol
V	Drugs with approved medical uses with lower potential for abuse than Schedule IV and consist of preparations containing limited quantities of certain narcotics. Schedule V drugs are generally used for antidiarrheal, antitussive, and analgesic purposes.	Cough preparations with less than 200 milligrams of codeine or per 100 milliliters (Robitussin AC), Lomotil, Motofen, Lyrica, Parepectolin

Source: U.S. DEPARTMENT OF JUSTICE, DRUG ENFORCEMENT AGENCY, DRUGS OF ABUSE: A DEA RESOURCE GUIDE 9–10 (2017), https://www.dea.gov/pr/multimedia-library/publications/drug_of_abuse.pdf.

Although two states, Florida and Washington, have some drug possession laws that carry strict liability,[15] the overwhelming number of drug possession laws require knowledge as the *mens rea* for conviction. But this *mens rea* element attaches to the state of knowing possession; in contrast, strict liability typically attaches to the quantity of the drug. Thus, if one knowingly possesses a controlled substance, one need not have any intent regard how much of the drug is actually possessed, even though exceeding a certain amount set by the law of any particular jurisdiction may result in more serious penalties.[16]

The **possession of drug paraphernalia**—equipment that is used to prepare, conceal, or administer illicit drugs—is also criminalized in most US jurisdictions. Examples of such paraphernalia include bongs, rolling papers, syringes, and a variety of pipes using for smoking marijuana, crack cocaine, crystal meth, and other controlled substances.

Simple possession of controlled substances is typically punished on a sliding scale, based on the amount of the substance possessed and the arrestee's prior record. But in most states, being in possession of a statutorily proscribed amount of most drugs creates a presumption that the person intends to sell drugs. **Possession with intent to distribute** and drug dealing are punished more harshly than simple possession for personal use. They generally involve selling illicit drugs on a relatively small scale (compared to drug trafficking), although the severity of the offense and associated punishments typically increase with larger amounts of the drug in question. Similarly, selling drugs in a school zone or to people under a certain age are also punished more severely than other drug dealing. Just as it is with the quantity of a controlled substance possessed, strict liability typically attaches to attendant circumstances that elevate the severity (and associated punishment) of a possession with intent to distribute charge. Thus, not knowing the age of the person to whom a drug is sold or not knowing that one is in a school zone generally has no effect on criminal liability for these sorts of enhancements.[17]

Manufacture and Trafficking of Drugs

Drug manufacturing involves the knowing production of a controlled substance. Although pharmaceutical companies are licensed to create prescription drugs that are controlled substance, private persons are not. Similarly, even in jurisdictions that have legalized either the medical or recreational use of marijuana, only persons licensed to run dispensaries are permitted to grow more than a certain amount of the drug. In contrast, and depending on the laws of the jurisdiction, private persons who grow more than small amount that may be legally permitted to be privately cultivated will be subject to criminal charges.

Drug trafficking laws criminalize the purposeful or knowing importation, transportation, and sale of controlled substances. In contrast to local drug dealing, drug trafficking typically refers to dealing in large quantities of controlled substances, often across jurisdictional borders. As illustrated in Table 12.2, these felony offenses often carry long minimum mandatory prison sentences depending on the drug and quantity

TABLE 12.2 Federal Drug Trafficking Penalties

FEDERAL TRAFFICKING PENALTIES

Drug & Schedule	Quantity	Penalties	Quantity	Penalties
Cocaine (Schedule II)	500–4999 grams mixture	**First Offense:** Not less than 5 years, and not more than 40 years If death or serious injury, not less than 20 or more than life. Fine of not more than $5 million if an individual, $25 million if not an individual. **Second Offense:** Not less than 10 years, and not more than life. If death or serious injury, life imprisonment. Fine of not more than $8 million if an individual, $50 million if not an individual.	5 kgs or more mixture	**First Offense:** Not less than 10 years, and not more than life. If death or serious injury, not less than 20 or more than life. Fine of not more than $10 mil- lion if an individual, $50 million if not an individual. **Second Offense:** Not less than 20 years, and not more than life. If death or serious injury, life imprisonment. Fine of not more than $20 million if an individual, $75 million if not an individual. **2 or More Prior Offenses:** Life imprisonment. Fine of not more than $20 million if an individual, $75 million if not an individual.
Cocaine Base (Schedule II)	28–279 grams mixture		280 grams or more mixture	
Fentanyl (Schedule II)	40–399 grams mixture		400 grams or more mixture	
Fentanyl Analogue (Schedule I)	10–99 grams mixture		100 grams or more mixture	
Heroin (Schedule I)	100–999 grams mixture		1 kg or more mixture	
LSD (Schedule I)	1–9 grams mixture		10 grams or more mixture	
Methamphetamine (Schedule II)	5–49 grams pure or 50–499 grams mixture		50 grams or more pure or 500 grams or more mixture	
PCP (Schedule II)	10–99 grams pure or 100–999 grams mixture		100 gm or more pure or 1 kg or more mixture	

PENALTIES FOR OTHER SCHEDULED CONTROLLED SUBSTANCES

Drug & Schedule	Quantity	Penalties
Other Schedule I & II drugs (and any drug product containing Gamma Hydroxybutyric Acid)	Any amount	**First Offense:** Not more than 20 years If death or serious injury, not less than 20 years, or more than life. Fine $1 million if an individual, $5 million if not an individual. **Second Offense:** Not more than 30 years If death or serious bodily injury, life imprisonment. Fine $2 million if an individual, $10 million if not an individual.
Flunitrazepam (Schedule IV)	1 gram	
Other Schedule III drugs	Any amount	**First Offense:** Not more than 10 years. If death or serious injury, not more than 15 years Fine not more than $500,000 if an individual, $2.5 million if not an individual. **Second Offense:** Not more than 20 years If death or serious injury, not more than 30 years Fine not more than $1 million if an individual, $5 million if not an individual.

Continued

TABLE 12.2 Continued

FEDERAL TRAFFICKING PENALTIES		
All other Schedule IV drugs	Any amount	**First Offense:** Not more than 5 years Fine not more than $250,000 if an individual, $1 million if not an individual.
Flunitrazepam (Schedule IV)	Other than 1 gram or more	**Second Offense:** Not more than 10 years Fine not more than $500,000 if an individual, $2 million if other than an individual.
All Schedule V drugs	Any amount	**First Offense:** Not more than 1 yr. Fine not more than $100,000 if an individual, $250,000 if not an individual. **Second Offense:** Not more than 4 years Fine not more than $200,000 if an individual, $500,000 if not an individual.

FEDERAL TRAFFICKING PENALTIES – MARIJUNA			
Marijuana (Schedule I)	1,000 kg or more marijuana mixture; or 1,000 or more marijuana plants	Not less than 10 years. or more than life. If death or serious bodily injury, not less than 20 years., or more than life. Fine not more than life. Fine not more than $10 million if an individual, $50 million if other than an individual.	Not less than 20 years. or more than life. If death or serious bodily injury, life imprisonment. Fine not more than $20 million if an individual, $75 million if other than an individual.
	100 kg to 999 kg marijuana mixture; or 100 to 999 marijuana plants	Not less than 5 years. or more than 40 years. If death or serious bodily injury, not less than 20 years., or more than life. Fine not more than life. Fine not more than $5 million if an individual, $25 million if other than an individual.	Not less than 10 years. or more than life. If death or serious bodily injury, life imprisonment. Fine not more than $20 million if an individual, $75 million if other than an individual.
	More than 10 kgs hashish; 50 to 99 kg marijuana mixture More than 1 kg of hashish oil; 50 to 99 marijuana plants	Not less than 20 years. If death or serious bodily injury, not less than 20 years., or more than life. Fine $1 million if an individual, $5 million if other than an individual.	Not less than 30 years. If death or serious bodily injury, life imprisonment. Fine $2 million if an individual, $10 million if other than an individual.
	Less than 50 kilograms marijuana (but does not include 50 or more marijuana plants regardless of weight) marijuana plants; 1 to 49 marijuana plants;	Not less than 5 years. Fine not more than $250,000, $1 million if other than an individual	Not less than 10 years. Fine $500,000 if an individual, $2 million if other than individual
Hashish (Schedule I)	10 kg or less		
Hashish Oil (Schedule I)	1 kg or less		

*The minimum sentence for a violation after two or more prior convictions for a felony drug offense have become final is a mandatory term of life imprisonment without release and a fine up to $20 million if an individual and $75 million if other than an individual.

Source: US DEP'T OF JUST., DRUG ENFORCEMENT AGENCY, DRUGS OF ABUSE: A DEA RESOURCE GUIDE: 2020 EDITION 36–37 (2020), https://www.dea.gov/sites/default/files/2020-04/Drugs%20of%20Abuse%202020-Web%20Version-508%20compliant-4-24-20_0.pdf

of it being trafficked. Drug trafficking is of significant concern to criminal justice system actors not only because of the public health implications attendant to large amounts of drugs being available, but also because the business of the drug trade often involves significant violence by gangs, drug cartels, and other crime syndicates.[18] Moreover, proceeds from drug trafficking often fund civil wars, governmental insurrections, and terrorism.[19]

DRIVING UNDER THE INFLUENCE

"Alcohol is a substance that reduces the function of the brain, impairing thinking, reasoning and muscle coordination. All these abilities are essential to operating a vehicle safely."[20] As Table 12.3 reveals, impairment of driving ability occurs with even low-levels of blood-alcohol concentration (BAC), measured in the number of grams (g) of alcohol per 100 milliliters (ml)/1 deciliter (dL) of blood, usually express as a percentage (0.xxg/dL).

Despite the dangers of driving while impaired, each year approximately 10,500 people die in the United States in crashes in which a vehicle was operated by someone impaired by drugs or alcohol—an average of death one every 50 minutes.[21] These deaths constituted 29 percent of the total traffic fatalities in the United States that year.[22] According to the Federal Bureau of Investigation, police make approximately 1 million arrests annually for **driving under the influence** (DUI), accounting for one of the highest counts among specific categories of arrests, along with larceny-type thefts, simple assaults, and drug arrests.[23] As Figure 12.1 illustrates, the total number of DUI-related fatalities has fallen in the past decade, although the number has risen a bit since 2014.

In addition to the toll on human life, between medical and legal costs, lost productivity, insurance administration, and property damage, DUI-related accidents cost roughly $44 billion per year.[24] To address the loss of life and financial costs associated with DUI, laws against driving while impaired were enacted "almost as soon as the automobile itself began to appear on American roads and streets."[25] But driving while impaired was not considered to be a particularly great social problem for most of the twentieth century. When Candy Lightner's daughter was killed by an intoxicated driver in the late 1970s, however, she formed Mothers Against Drunk Driving (MADD) and that organization focused public attention on the problem.[26] Over the course of the 1980s, that group's grass-roots efforts caused impaired driving to become recognized as "a prominent social concern" that shifted criminal justice policy "toward an increased emphasis on deterrence, retribution, and incapacitation . . . the common thread of this social climate [being] harsher punishment of offenders."[27]

Today, we recognize the driving while impaired is a serious problem that goes beyond "drunk driving." Impairment of the ability to drive occurs at levels far below levels of intoxication associated with manifest drunkenness, and impairment also occurs as a result

Table 12.3 Typical Blood Alcohol Effects

Blood Alcohol Concentration (BAC)	Typical Effects	Predictable Effects on Driving
.02%	• Some loss of judgment • Relaxation • Slight body warmth • Altered mood	• Decline in visual functions (rapid tracking of a moving target) • Decline in ability to perform two tasks at the same time (divided attention)
.05%	• Exaggerated behavior • May have loss of small-muscle control (e.g., focusing your eyes) • Impaired judgment • Usually good feeling • Lowered alertness • Release of inhibition	• Reduced coordination • Reduced ability to track moving objects • Difficulty steering • Reduced response to emergency driving situations
.08%	• Muscle coordination becomes poor (e.g., balance, speech, vision, reaction time, and hearing) • Harder to detect danger • Judgment, self-control, reasoning, and memory are impaired	• Decreased concentration • Short-term memory loss • Diminished speed control • Reduced information processing capability (e.g., signal detection, visual search) • Impaired perception
.10%	• Clear deterioration of reaction time and control • Slurred speech, poor coordination, and slowed thinking	• Reduced ability to maintain lane position and brake appropriately
.15%	• Far less muscle control than normal • Vomiting may occur (unless this level is reached slowly or a person has developed a tolerance for alcohol) • Major loss of balance	• Substantial impairment in vehicle control, attention to driving task, and in necessary visual and auditory information processing

Source: US CTRS. FOR DISEASE CONTROL & PREVENTION, EFFECTS OF BLOOD ALCOHOL CONCENTRATION (BAC) (n.d.), https://www.cdc.gov/motorvehiclesafety/pdf/bac-a.pdf.

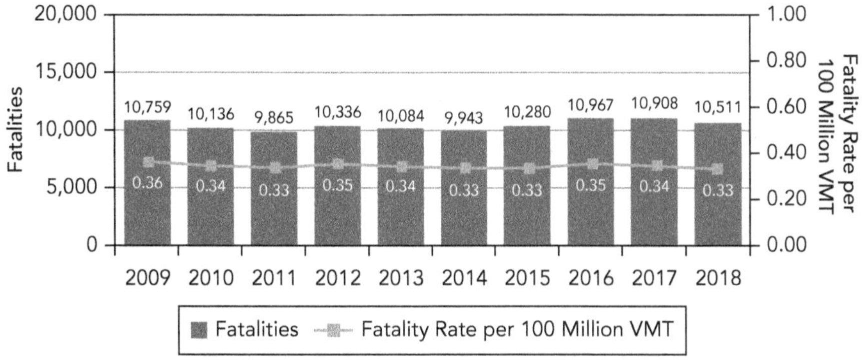

FIGURE 12.1

Fatalities and Fatality Rate per 100 Million Vehicle Miles Traveled

Source: Nat'l Highway Traffic Safety Admin., Traffic Safety Facts 2018 Data: Alcohol-Impaired Driving 2 (2019), https://crashstats.nhtsa.dot.gov/Api/Public/ViewPublication/812864.

of taking both illicit and prescribed drugs. Most criminal laws utilize a dual approach to address the problems associated with impaired driving.

The *Per Se* Approach

All fifty US states and the District of Columbia established a threshold that make it a criminal offense to drive or be in physical control of a motor vehicle with a blood-alcohol concentration (BAC) of 0.08g/dL or higher, although some states set the limit even lower. For example, Utah's BAC limit became 0.05g/dL or higher in December of 2018.[28] In addition, some states have lower BAC cut-off points for persons operating commercial vehicles[29] or for juveniles old enough to be licensed to drive, but not old enough to consume alcohol legally.[30] These laws embody the so-called *per se* approach to DUI by relieving prosecutors of the need to prove impairment in the operation of a vehicle by establishing a BAC limit over which all drivers are conclusively presumed to be incapable of driving safely. Because of the way the body processes alcohol, many states apply per se laws to any operation of a vehicle within a two or three hour window of a blood or breath test.

The Impairment Approach

In addition to *per se* BAC cut-offs, DUI laws prohibit people from operating or being in physical control of a motor vehicle while impaired by any amount of alcohol or drugs—both illicit and prescribed. Under such laws in some states, impairment occurs whenever a substance causes a person to become "incapable of safely operating a vehicle."[31] In other states, like Arizona, driving while impaired "to the slightest degree" is prohibited.[32]

The *Mens Rea* for DUI

In some states, DUI is a strict liability offense. In other states, the defense might technically be a general intent crime, but such laws tend to function as de facto strict liability offenses since getting behind the wheel after having consumed alcohol or drugs is deemed to constitute criminal recklessness.[33]

STATE of Kansas, Appellant,

v.

Brian M. COLLINS, Appellee.

138 P.3d 793 (2006).

After several hours of drinking, Collins and his passenger left a bar at 2 a.m. . . . in his pickup truck. He followed behind a motorcycle driven by his friend Jesse Winsky. Robyn Curtis was riding on the motorcycle with Winsky. When the motorcycle pulled ahead and out of sight, Collins sped up to catch it. Collins' passenger testified that when Collins next saw the motorcycle, it was parked in the roadway with Curtis still seated on board. Winsky had gotten off to urinate nearby. Collins' passenger yelled at Collins to stop. Collins attempted to stop the truck but hit the motorcycle and Curtis was killed.

Collins was charged with involuntary manslaughter while driving under the influence of alcohol. At trial, Collins called an accident reconstruction expert who testified that the accident would have occurred even if Collins had not been intoxicated. In arriving at this opinion, the witness considered the truck's braking ability; the placement of the motorcycle in the road; its location just beyond a curve in the road; the time of the accident; the reaction time of a normal, unimpaired driver; and the stopping distance for the truck being driven at Collins' speed of 55 miles per hour at the time. . . . The jury found Collins guilty of the lesser included offense of driving under the influence of alcohol. . . .

* * *

In [*State v. Creamer*],[34] the intoxicated defendant used his pickup truck to pull a utility trailer. The trailer detached from the pickup and struck another vehicle, resulting in the death of that vehicle's driver and severe injuries to the pregnant passenger. Creamer was charged with involuntary manslaughter while driving under the influence of alcohol. . . . and injury to a pregnant woman while driving under the influence of alcohol. . . . Upon conviction, the issue before this court was . . . whether conviction under these statutes requires proof of specific criminal intent on the part of the defendant. . . .

> We hold the crimes . . . are absolute or strict liability crimes. Accordingly, the only proof required is that the individual was engaged in the driving of a motor vehicle while under the influence of alcohol or drugs, . . . and that the death or injuries occurred during the commission of the act of DUI. There is no requirement that the State prove a specific criminal intent.[35]

This last quoted sentence is most instructive. It points out that these are strict liability crimes in the sense that there is no requirement for specific criminal intent. The court in *Creamer* did not consider the separate issue of causation....

In [*State v. Chastain*],[36] the defendant was charged with involuntary manslaughter... following a collision at an intersection which resulted in the death of Robert Glenn. The State contended Chastain was under the influence of alcohol and driving at a high rate of speed. Chastain contended that Glenn ran a stop sign at the intersection and that this was the cause of the accident and Glenn's death, not Chastain's conduct or condition.

* * *

During deliberations, the jury in *Chastain* asked the trial court whether the fault of each driver is to be considered when interpreting the phrase "unintentionally killed" in the court's instructions. . . . In response, the trial court . . . informed the jury that the issue of the decedent's fault was to be considered along with other evidence to determine whether the defendant's conduct was the direct cause of the decedent's death. The jury convicted *Chastain* of the lesser included offense of driving while under the influence of alcohol....

> While contributory negligence is no defense in a prosecution for a driving offense of involuntary manslaughter or vehicular homicide, it is a circumstance to be considered along with all other evidence to determine whether the defendant's conduct was or was not the proximate cause of the decedent's death. In some instances, a decedent's contributory negligence may have been a substantial factor in his or her death and a superseding cause thereof; it may have intervened between a defendant's conduct and the fatal result so as to be itself the proximate cause.[37]

* * *

Based upon the holdings in *Creamer* and *Chastain*, we conclude that while [involuntary manslaughter while driving under the influence of alcohol is] a strict liability crime in the sense that no showing of specific criminal intent is required, there must be evidence that the conduct of the defendant was the cause of the victim's death. Given the evidence, and Collins' argument, that the sole cause of the accident was Curtis sitting on a stationary motorcycle in the middle of the road at night with no warning for a reasonably prudent, nonintoxicated approaching driver, the district court did not err in instructing the jury on proximate cause....

Questions

1. The *Collins* case makes clear that DUI can be a strict liability offense. Nonetheless, when a DUI leads to an unintentional homicide, causation must still be proven.

Drawing on what you learned in Chapters 4 and 7, conduct your own proximate cause analysis based on the facts of the case. In other words, do you think that Curtis sitting on a stationary motorcycle in the middle of the road at night should be classified as a dependent, intervening cause or an independent, supervening cause? Why?

2. Assume that a driver, after consuming one strong mixed drinks, has a BAC of approximately 0.05 percent. Further assume that his passenger is quite intoxicated and passed out, in the passenger seat, while not wearing a seatbelt. If the driver runs off the road and crashes into a tree and the passenger dies in the accident, should that driver be held responsible for involuntary manslaughter while driving under the influence of alcohol? Put differently, can poor road conditions, like poorly lit roads with sharp turns that are slippery during a night-time rainstorm, be classified as a dependent, intervening cause or an independent, supervening cause? Does the victim's level of intoxication and failure to have worn a seatbelt play any role in determining proximate causation?[38]

Grading

People who operation or physically control a motor vehicle with a BAC over the *per se* limit typically commit a misdemeanor offense that is punishable by a fine, the suspension of a driver's license for three to twelve months, mandatory drug and alcohol education courses, and a hefty insurance surcharge once driving privileges are restored.[39] Increase penalties are provided for higher BAC levels, such a 0.15, 0.20, or 0.25 g/dL, which are sometimes referred to as "extreme DUI" or "super-extreme DUI," depending on the level of BAC.[40] Unsurprisingly, the higher the BAC, the more severe the potential punishment.

Jail sentences are statutorily authorized for first offenses in most states, although most state allow a first-time offender to avoid incarceration. That being said, a handful of states impose a mandatory jail sentence for first-time offenders in an attempt to deter impaired driving.[41] Felony convictions, with associated prison sentences, are authorized for a variety of aggravating factors, including, for instance, repeat violations within a certain number of years, a re-offense while the operator's driver's license was already suspended, or for driving while impaired with a child in the vehicle.[42]

QUALITY OF LIFE CRIMES

There are range of criminal offenses designed to enhance people's quality of life by targeting littering, disorder, and the quiet enjoyment of one's home and neighborhood. Although the First Amendment to the US Constitution guarantees the rights to free speech and peaceable assembly (Chapter 2), the government can regulate the time, place, and manner of the exercise of these rights. When people exercise their First Amendment rights in a manner that violates valid restrictions, they may be charged with a number of public order crimes.

Disturbing the Peace and Disorderly Conduct

The offense of "breach of the peace" has a long history in the common law. The offense was quite broad, often described as "creating a public disturbance or engaging in disorderly conduct, particularly by making an unnecessary or distracting noise."[43] Note the use of the phase "disorderly conduct" in the definition of breach of the peace. *Black's Law Dictionary* defined **disorderly conduct** as "[b]ehavior that tends to disturb the public peace, offend public morals, or undermine public safety."[44] The fact that the definition of each crime refers to the other should give you a strong sense of how closely related these offenses are.

> At common law there was no offense known as disorderly conduct, although the offense of breaching the peace made many public disturbances criminal. In addition, this offense could be based on behavior that might cause another to respond in a violent manner even though the party guilty of the breach of the peace acted quietly or secretly, as when a person challenged someone to a duel. The enactment of statutes making disorderly conduct punishable went beyond the common-law notion of a breach of the peace by including behavior that merely tended to disturb the safety, health, or morals of others or that was intended only to annoy another. Further definitions were added later.[45]

The ways in which states statutorily define these crimes today vary significantly. Following the Model Penal Code,[46] criminal liability for **disturbing the peace** in most US jurisdictions does not depend on whether the conduct was intended to purposefully disturb the peace; one can do so recklessly—meaning with a conscious disregard for whether others will be disturbed, although some states do require higher levels of *mens rea*. Nevada, for example, requires that a "breach of the peace" be "maliciously and willfully committed."[47]

The *actus reus* of the offense also varies considerably. Consider all of the types of conduct covered in Missouri's law:

> A person commits the offense of peace disturbance if he or she:
>
> (1) Unreasonably and knowingly disturbs or alarms another person or persons by:
>   (a) Loud noise; or
>   (b) Offensive language addressed in a face-to-face manner to a specific individual and uttered under circumstances which are likely to produce an immediate violent response from a reasonable recipient; or
>   (c) Threatening to commit a felonious act against any person under circumstances which are likely to cause a reasonable person to fear that such threat may be carried out; or
>   (d) Fighting; or
>   (e) Creating a noxious and offensive odor;
>
> (2) Is in a public place or on private property of another without consent and purposely causes inconvenience to another person or persons by unreasonably and physically obstructing:

(a) Vehicular or pedestrian traffic; or
(b) The free ingress or egress to or from a public or private place.[48]

The "Statutory Analysis Exercise" in Box 12.1 contains New Mexico's disorderly conduct law. Evaluate the situation explained in that box using that state's law and the one quoted in the preceding list from Missouri.

BOX 12.1

STATUTORY ANALYSIS EXERCISE

When Might Certain Childhood Behaviors Constitute Disorderly Conduct?

A police officer in New Mexico was dispatched to a business address in the downtown area of Artesia in response to a call that children were throwing rocks. When the officer arrived at the scene, he "heard little bangs or noise coming from the metal roof like . . . little pellets or BB guns striking the top of the metal roof and . . . hitting the ground."[151] Upon investigation, he found a child playing with plastic gun. Using candy and plastic ammunition, the child was "shooting targets up on the top of the roof."[152] Huerta testified that he then called Child's grandmother and cited Child for firing the BB gun within the city limits and trespass. The officer arrested the child. The child was subsequently adjudicated a delinquent for having engaged in disorderly conduct.

In New Mexico, the crime of disorderly conduct consists of:

A. engaging in violent, abusive, indecent, profane, boisterous, unreasonably loud or otherwise disorderly conduct which tends to disturb the peace; or
B. maliciously disturbing, threatening or, in an insolent manner, intentionally touching any house occupied by any person.[153]

Relevant precedent directs that the statute is to be construed narrowly such that "unless the acts complained of fall clearly within the statute, they are not disorderly."[154] Precedent also established that the offense has two distinct elements: "the conduct and the tendency of that conduct to disturb the peace."[155]

1. Analyze whether the child's conduct constituted the crime of disturbing the peace under New Mexico law.
2. Would your opinion change if this had occurred in a residential neighborhood around 2:00 a.m.?
3. Do you think the result would have been different if the case had occurred in Missouri, rather than New Mexico? Explain your reasoning.

Because boisterous behavior that can disturb the peace is so common when people get drunk, many jurisdictions have laws criminalizing **public intoxication**. Most states operationalize this offense by defining the *actus reus* as being under the influence of alcohol-controlled substances, coupled with an attendant circumstance requirement that the intoxication be in public place. In many, but not all states, the "under the influence" part requires proof that the intoxication was substantial enough to render people out-of-control such that they cannot take care of themselves, are endangered the safety of others or property, or, alternatively, that they are causing a public disturbance.[49]

PROFANITY AND DISORDERLY CONDUCT

The way the Section 1(b) of the Missouri statute is written complies with the First Amendment because the statute limits its applicability to offense language communicated "face-to-face" in ways "likely to produce an immediate violent response from a reasonable recipient." By contrast, a North Carolina that made it a misdemeanor "on any public road or highway and in the hearing of two or more persons, in a loud and boisterous manner, [to] use indecent or profane language" was declared unconstitutional.[50]

A state may not simply criminalize the use of profane or indecent language in public, at least not in the abstract. But shouting profanities which are "intended and plainly likely to provoke violent retaliation and thereby cause a breach of the peace" may be criminally punished without violating the First Amendment.[51] Consider the following case.

Paul Robert COHEN, Appellant,
v.
State of CALIFORNIA.
403 U.S. 15 (1971).

[T]he defendant was observed in the Los Angeles County Courthouse . . . wearing a jacket bearing the words "Fuck the Draft" which were plainly visible. There were women and children present in the corridor. The defendant was arrested. The defendant testified that he wore the jacket knowing that the words were on the jacket as a means of informing the public of the depth of his feelings against the Vietnam War and the draft. [He was convicted of maliciously and willfully disturbing the peace or quiet of any neighborhood or person by offensive conduct and sentenced to 30 days' imprisonment].

* * *

[T]he issue flushed by this case . . . is whether California can excise, as "offensive conduct," one particular scurrilous epithet from the public discourse, either upon the theory of the court below that its use is inherently likely to cause violent reaction or upon a more general assertion that the States, acting as guardians of public morality, may properly remove this offensive word from the public vocabulary.

The rationale of the California court is plainly untenable. At most it reflects an undifferentiated fear or apprehension of disturbance (which) is not enough to overcome the right to freedom of expression. . . . We have been shown no evidence that substantial numbers of citizens are standing ready to strike out physically at whoever may assault their sensibilities with execrations like that uttered by Cohen. There may be some persons about with such lawless and violent proclivities, but that is an insufficient base upon which to erect, consistently with constitutional values, a governmental power to force persons who wish to ventilate their dissident views into avoiding particular forms of expression. The argument amounts to little more than the self-defeating proposition that to avoid physical censorship of one who has not sought to provoke such a response by a hypothetical coterie of the violent and lawless, the States may more appropriately effectuate that censorship themselves. . . .

The constitutional right of free expression is powerful medicine in a society as diverse and populous as ours. It is designed and intended to remove governmental restraints from the arena of public discussion, putting the decision as to what views shall be voiced largely into the hands of each of us, in the hope that use of such freedom will ultimately produce a more capable citizenry and more perfect polity and in the belief that no other approach would comport with the premise of individual dignity and choice upon which our political system rests. . . .

To many, the immediate consequence of this freedom may often appear to be only verbal tumult, discord, and even offensive utterance. These are, however, within established limits, in truth necessary side effects of the broader enduring values which the process of open debate permits us to achieve. That the air may at times seem filled with verbal cacophony is, in this sense not a sign of weakness but of strength. We cannot lose sight of the fact that, in what otherwise might seem a trifling and annoying instance of individual distasteful abuse of a privilege, these fundamental societal values are truly implicated. . . .

Against this perception of the constitutional policies involved, we discern certain more particularized considerations that peculiarly call for reversal of this conviction. First, the principle contended for by the State seems inherently boundless. How is one to distinguish this from any other offensive word? Surely the State has no right to cleanse public debate to the point where it is grammatically palatable to the most squeamish among us. Yet no readily ascertainable general principle exists for stopping short of that result were we to affirm the judgment below. For, while the particular four-letter word being litigated here is perhaps more distasteful than most others of its genre, it is nevertheless often true that one man's vulgarity is another's lyric. Indeed, we think it is largely because governmental officials cannot make principled distinctions in this area that the Constitution leaves matters of taste and style so largely to the individual.

Questions

1. Key to the Court's rationale were the facts that Cohen did not engage disruptive conduct. Indeed, he was quietly walking through the corridors of a courthouse when he was arrested. Do you think the outcome would have been different if he had been running up and down the hallways yelling the same slogan he had on his jacket? Why or why not?
2. What if instead of being in a courthouse, Cohen had been a high school student who wore the same jacket to school? Explain whether you think the outcome in the case should be different under such circumstances.
3. Recalling what you learned in Chapter 2 about symbolic speech, do you think a disturbing the peace charge could be constitutionally upheld against a group of civilians wearing Black Lives Matter buttons if they entered a public convention center while a police conference was taking place? Explain your reasoning.

Despite *Cohen v. California*, it is important to note that just because anti-profanity laws may be applied in an unconstitutional manner, they are still "on the books" in several jurisdictions. Oklahoma, for example, has a law criminalizing "any obscene or lascivious language or word in any public place, or in the presence of females, or in the presence of children under ten (10) years of age."[52] In Michigan, "[a]ny person . . . who shall profanely curse or damn or swear by the name of God, Jesus Christ or the Holy Ghost, shall be guilty of a misdemeanor."[53] Mississippi criminalizes profanely swearing, cursing or using "vulgar and indecent language, or be drunk in any public place, in the presence of two (2) or more persons."[54] If coupled with other conduct that constitutes a breach of the peace or disorderly conduct, or if communicated as "fighting words" in ways that are likely to provoke imminent violence (Chapter 2), these statutes may pass constitutional muster. Otherwise, the fact that others might find profanity offensive does not take remove it from First Amendment protections.[55] Consider, for example, *Brendle v. City of Houston*.[56]

In *Brendle*, a police officer accompanied a customer of a mechanic shop because the customer was having a dispute with the shop's owner. During the discussion, the owner said, "I'm tired of this God d--- police sticking their nose in s--- that doesn't even involve them." The officer warned the owner that if he swore again, he would be arrested. The owner continued to swear and was arrested accordingly. He was convicted of violating the Mississippi anti-profanity statute. On appeal, the court quoted from *Cohen v. California* and reversed the defendant's conviction:

> Even assuming that Brendle used the "f" word in his speech, Brendle's language while vulgar, indecent, and arguably profane, did not rise to the level of "fighting

> words." His language was not "by its very utterance" sufficient to incite an immediate breach of the peace. This is not to say that shouting profanities at a police officer is appropriate or proper behavior in any circumstance. In fact, such conduct may give rise to a situation where an immediate breach of the peace may occur. However, the facts in this case do not support such a situation. Rather the testimony shows that some of the vulgarities used by Brendle were spoken as he turned away from Officer Ford attempting to return to his office. Even further, there was no evidence that Brendle's epithets sought to incite others to prevent his arrest.[57]

PROTESTING VERSUS RIOTING

The First Amendment guarantees the right of the people to peaceably assemble (Chapter 2). Protestors may want to hold a demonstration to gain attention to their cause, and they have a right to, but not whenever they choose. No one has the right to "insist upon a street meeting in the middle of Times Square at the rush hour as a form of freedom of speech."[58] Thus, the time of a demonstration can be prescribed, but not its content.

Protests do not always remain peaceful. In order to prevent protests from turning violent, English common law punished three, tiered offenses:

> The first such offense was unlawful assembly; the second, rout; and the third, riot. Blackstone defines unlawful assembly as an assembly "when three, or more, do assemble themselves together to do an unlawful act. . . ." A rout occurs "where three or more meet to do an unlawful act . . . and make some advances towards it." A riot occurs "where three or more actually do an unlawful act of violence . . . or even do a lawful act . . . in a violent and tumultuous manner."[59]

The crime of rout is rare in the United States today, but most jurisdictions have statutory provisions criminalizing both unlawful assembly and riot.[60] **Unlawful assembly** prohibits a certain number of people or more from gathering either "for the purpose of committing any unlawful act by force" or "with the intent to carry out any purpose in such a manner as will disturb or threaten the public peace."[61] The crime of **riot** occurs when, while participating in an assembly of the minimum number of people specified in a statute, a "person engages in tumultuous and violent conduct in a public place and thereby causes, or creates a substantial risk of causing, damage to property or physical injury to a person."[62] The minimum number of people is typically three, mirroring the common law, but it ranges from a low of two to a higher seven.[63]

Both the *mens rea* and the *actus reus* for the crime of riot vary significantly across the United States. Some states require specific intent, while others require recklessness.[64] A handful of states require the actual use of force or violence as a predicate to riot liability. Iowa, for example, requires a showing of "unlawful force or violence . . . against another person, or causing property damage."[65] Other states premise riot liability on the threat of force or violence, or the threat of tumultuous and violent conduct. Still, given the First Amendment right to peaceably assemble, most state courts narrowly construe their laws on unlawful assembly and riot. For example, the California Supreme Court interpreted the state's "unlawful assembly" law as permitting gatherings unless protestors either engage in violence or if their conduct presents "a clear and present danger of imminent violence."[66] Such an interpretation aligns with the common-law history of the offense.[67]

Some disorderly conduct statutes, like Rhode Island's, include provisions that can be used to curb protests since they proscribe disturbing others "by making loud and unreasonable noise which under the circumstances would disturb a person of average sensibilities" if the disturbance occurs "in a public place or near a private residence that he or she has no right to occupy."[68] In addition to disturbing the peace and disorderly conduct laws, several other criminal laws may come into play during protests to avoid them turning violent, including **failure to disperse** and **inciting a riot.** The statutes from Maine and South Carolina, respectively, illustrate these offenses:

- Under Maine law, failure to disperse is defined as when "6 or more persons are participating in a course of disorderly conduct likely to cause substantial harm or serious inconvenience, annoyance, or alarm, a law enforcement officer may order the participants and others in the immediate vicinity to disperse. . . . A person is guilty of failure to disperse if the person knowingly fails to comply with [such an order]."[69]
- Under South Carolina law, a person may be guilty of either a felony or a misdemeanor, depending on the purpose of incitement, for "instigating, promoting, or aiding" a riot, the provision may "not be construed to prevent the peaceable assembling of persons for lawful purposes of protest or petition."[70]

In *Hess v. Louisiana*, the US Supreme Court overturned a conviction for a defendant who shouted, "[w]e'll take the fucking street later" during a demonstration.[71] Because the statement was not directed to a particular person, the Court reasoned that the words did not constitute an incitement to riot, but rather was protected First Amendment expression. But the Court was careful to point out that lack of imminent, likely illegal actions was an important consideration in the case.[72]

Law professor Tabatha Abu El-Haja observed that despite narrow judicial interpretations of the applicability of unlawful assembly, failure to disperse, and riot laws, police "regularly make arrests for these crimes in situations that could not result in a conviction."[73] She points to arrests made in Ferguson, Missouri, in the wake of police killing of Michael Brown. Specifically, twenty people were arrested for participating in a sit-in at a Quick-Trip gas station and a legal observer from the National Lawyers Guild was also arrested for unlawful assembly. As a result, the right to peaceable assembly may not be as strong in practice as a reading of the First Amendment suggests:

> Forced to navigate a wide array of hurdles to gain permission to be out in public legally and faced with police officers routinely handing out citations, at their discretion, for a variety of minor public order offences, protesters often experience their First Amendment right to peaceably assemble as somewhere between weak and nonexistent.[74]

By way of another example, consider that police arrested thirty-one people from a group of roughly 1,000 protesters who at the state capitol building in Virginia to protest a bill requiring women to have an ultrasound before having an abortion. "The protestors were not violent; the police claimed they were called in because the group was 'getting really large and we didn't want things to get out of hand.'"[75]

FALSE ALARM

When some people think of false alarms, they might think of someone who accidentally triggers a home or car security system. While the sounds from such events undoubtedly disturb the peace, they do so accidentally, not with any criminal intent. By contrast, the crime of **false alarm** involves deliberate action that wrongfully triggers responses from first responders. Not only do such actions typically cause significant commotions, but they take police, fire, and emergency medical personnel away from other calls that may be life threatening. Ohio's statute, which is representative, provides that no one may do any of the following actions:

(1) Initiate or circulate a report or warning of an alleged or impending fire, explosion, crime, or other catastrophe, knowing that the report or warning is false and likely to cause public inconvenience or alarm;
(2) Knowingly cause a false alarm of fire or other emergency to be transmitted to or within any organization, public or private, for dealing with emergencies involving a risk of physical harm to persons or property;
(3) Report to any law enforcement agency an alleged offense or other incident within its concern, knowing that such offense did not occur.[76]

Vagrancy, Panhandling, and Loitering

By some estimates, the Black Death, the deadliest pandemic in history, killed upward of 60 percent of the population of Europe during the late Middle Ages.[77] The plague caused the breakdown of the feudal system in England. The Crown responded by enacting the Statute of Labourers in 1349 and modifying it through 1351. That law was primarily designed to fix wages, control prices of goods, and restrict the movement of people at a time when labor was in short supply.[78] A provision in that law, based on the assumption that unemployed serfs would need to turn to crime in order to survive, made it a crime to be unemployed and exist in a state of idleness.

By the reign of Elizabeth I, another wave of the Black Death resurfaced. "At its height, the disease killed 1,000 people each week in London, a city of 200,000, and left countless children parentless and destitute."[79] Poverty became so rampant in England that Elizabeth worked with Parliament to enact The Poor Relief Act 1601.[80] By harnessing charitable contributions, religious institutions, and new taxes, the law was designed to promote social welfare. It provided for the impotent poor, people who could not work because of age or disability, by placing them into almshouses. Children were placed in orphanages and required to become apprentices to learn skills that would allow them to work. The able-bodied poor were required to work. But the idle poor—those who refused to work, "could be committed to a house of correction; whipped, branded, or put in pillories and stoned; or even put to death."[81] In short, it became illegal to be poor and unemployed. The offense of roaming the streets without any visible means of supporting oneself was dubbed **vagrancy**, whereas **loitering** punished simply spending time idly.[82]

VAGRANCY

American colonies adopted vagrancy and loitering laws modeled on those from Elizabethan England, primary for crime control purposes.[83] Largely as a function of the poor not having the right to counsel until the US Supreme Court's 1963 decision in *Gideon v. Wainwright*,[84] these laws went unchallenged for nearly 200 years.[85] Within a decade of that landmark decision, vagrancy laws were challenged on the basis that they criminalized poverty and homelessness, the US Supreme Court declared them unconstitutional in the 1972 case of *Papachristou v. City of Jacksonville*.[86] But the Court did not totally invalidate such laws; it simply required that they be drafted with more clarity to provide adequate notice to people of what is prohibited without infringing on what is constitutionally protected or simply punishing the status of being homeless. As a result, broad vagrancy laws are largely unenforceable today, although most have been replaced by statutes targeting panhandling and loitering.

PANHANDLING

Panhandling prohibits stopping people on the streets and asking for money or food. Notably, panhandling laws are typically written in a way that targets private begging, but exempts charitable organizations such as churches, the Boy or Girl Scouts, or the Salvation Army. Critics point out that laws targeting panhandling have the effect of criminalizing poverty.[87] Because it represents a lawful type of solicitation in which "one individual asking another individual for help" the activity itself is a constitutionally protected form of speech.[88] Thus, in many cities, panhandling laws regulate the time, place, and manner of panhandling. Some jurisdictions, for instance, ban panhandling near ATMs, parking meters, and restaurants and, among other restrictions, limits the activity to daytime hours.[89] But others have gone even further by banning "aggressive" panhandling, defined in some cities as begging with the intent to intimidate, coerce, or harass another person into giving money or goods.[90] Tennessee even acted a statewide law criminalizing aggressive panhandling if the person soliciting money or goods touches the person being solicited without consent; obstructs the path of a person or vehicle being solicited; by following a person walking away; or makes "any statement, gesture, or other communication that would cause a reasonable person to feel fear of personal harm for refusing a solicitation of a donation."[91] But what actually constitutes aggressive panhandling can be quite subjective, inviting challenges of vagueness (Chapter 1), overbreadth (Chapter 1), and discriminatory enforcement (Chapters 2 and 13). Consider the case in the "Case Study Extra" feature contained in Box 12.2.

LOITERING

Like vagrancy laws, statutes banning simple loitering—hanging around with no apparent purpose—have been repeatedly challenged since the 1960s and are often invalidated on many of the same grounds applicable to vagrancy and panhandling laws, namely vagueness (Chapter 1) and overbreadth (Chapter 1) within the context of the First Amendment, and discriminatory enforcement, which raised Equal Protection Clause concerns (Chapters 2 and 13). They can even be invalidated under the Eighth Amendment's Cruel and Unusual Punishment Clause (Chapter 2) for criminalizing someone's status, as poor or homeless, in the absence of some *actus reus* that indicates criminality.[92]

But even when loitering laws target a specific type of activity, they can still be vague and overbroad. Consider, for example, that New York's highest court invalided its former loitering law which made it an offense to loiter "about any toilet, area, station, station platform, waiting room or other appurtenance of an air or bus terminal" unless the loiterer was able "to give satisfactory explanation of his presence."[93] And "courts are split even as to the constitutionality of loitering statutes based on the Model Penal Code, which provides in part that a person commits a violation if he or she 'loiters or prowls in a place, at a time, or in a manner not usual for law-abiding individuals, under circumstances that warrant alarm for the safety of persons or property in the vicinity.'"[94]

Nonetheless, a carefully crafted loitering law—especially those aimed at curbing specific illegal activity—can survive constitutional scrutiny if they are narrowly tailored to achieve a compelling governmental interest. For example, the Supreme Court of Washington upheld a Tacoma loitering ordinance that made it "unlawful for any person to loiter in or near any thoroughfare, place open to the public, or near any public or private place in a manner and under circumstances manifesting the purpose to engage in drug-related activity."[95] An Ohio court upheld a loitering ordinance providing that no one "shall remain or wander in a public place and repeatedly beckon to, or repeatedly attempt to engage passersby in conversation, or repeatedly stop or attempt to stop motor vehicles, or repeatedly interfere with the free passage of other persons for the purpose of engaging in soliciting or procuring sexual activity for hire."[96] The Supreme Court of Wisconsin did the same with its statewide loitering statute aimed at loitering "in a manner and under circumstances manifesting the purpose of inducing, enticing, soliciting or procuring another to commit an act of prostitution."[97]

BOX 12.2

CASE STUDY EXTRA

Can Nonaggressive Panhandling Trigger Criminal Liability for Pedestrian Interference?

In *City of Spokane v. Marr*,[156] the defendant was charged with two counts of being a public nuisance and two counts of pedestrian interference after police witnessed her approach people in downtown Spokane, Washington and ask for money. She was acquitted on the public nuisance changes, but convicted of two counts of pedestrian interference.

Under the city code in effect at the time, a person commits the misdemeanor offense of pedestrian interference "if, in a public place, he or she intentionally (1) obstructs pedestrian or vehicular traffic, or (2) aggressively solicits."[157] Under the ordinance, to "obstruct pedestrian or vehicular traffic" means to "walk, stand, sit, lie or place an object in such manner as to intentionally block passage by another person or a vehicle, or to require another person or a driver of a vehicle to take evasive action to avoid physical contact."[158] The trial court found that the defendant had obstructed pedestrian traffic, but did not aggressively solicit. She appealed, arguing it was her intent to beg, which is constitutionally protected speech. Any blocking of pedestrian traffic "was merely incidental to the exercise of her constitutionally protected right to beg in a nonaggressive manner."[159]

Ms. Marr's appeal relied on *City of Seattle v. Webster*,[160] which upheld a nearly identical pedestrian interference ordinance against a challenge that it was unconstitutionally overbroad. But the court in *Webster* upheld the ordinance specifically because it did not prohibit "innocent intentional acts which merely consequentially block traffic or cause others to take evasive action," such as trying to obtain signatures on a petition.[161] The court noted that "mere sauntering" is lawful, even walking at a slow pace might cause another person to "take evasive action."[162] Reasoning that begging is a constitutionally protected activity, Mrs. Marr argued it should not be unlawful to incidentally obstruct pedestrian traffic in order to exercise that right. The court agreed.

> The legislative body acknowledged a right to beg that does not rise to the level of "aggressive solicitation," or it would have proscribed begging altogether. By expressly proscribing one type of solicitation, the ordinance implicitly allows other types not otherwise proscribed. . . . Here, the [trial] court specifically found that Ms. Marr did not aggressively panhandle. Therefore, Ms. Marr cannot be found to have violated the ordinance.[163]

1. In this case, the court applied a rule of statutory construction known as *expressio unius est exclusio alterius*—to express one thing implies the exclusion of the other. What do you make of this approach to statutory interpretation?

2. Assume, for the sake of argument, that the court found that even though nonaggressive solicitations were legal, that still did not mean incidental infringements on pedestrian traffic in a city was permissible. What would be the practical effect of such an approach? And what do you think the First Amendment implications of it would be?
3. In *People v. Griswold*, the defendant stood on a sidewalk in Rochester, New York facing traffic and holding a handwritten sign that read: "Homeless. Hungry. Please Help."[164] He did not approach or initiate conversations with any pedestrians, motorists, vehicle passengers, nor did he impede or obstruct any pedestrian or vehicle traffic. He "simply stood silently on the sidewalk with his sign in his hands" but was nonetheless arrested for violating the city's aggressive panhandling statute.[165] A court ultimate determined that the aggressive panhandling ordinance was unconstitutional as applied to the defendant in the case. Do you agree? Why or why not? In light of arrests of people like Mr. Griswold, what do you think of aggressive panhandling laws? Explain.

ANTI-GANG LOITERING

Because loitering statutes targeting prostitution and illicit drug activity may be constitutionally enforceable, some jurisdictions enacted loitering statutes targeting gang activity. Scholars differ on their views of what constitutes a gang, but most "describe them as groups segregated by age and gender—usually comprised of teen and young adult males—that share a group identity, occupy territory, and engage in crime or other disruptive activity."[98] Some gangs are loose networks, while others are highly structured with rules.[99] Most street gangs exist in poor neighborhoods and, accordingly, are disproportionately comprised of people from racial or ethnic minority backgrounds.[100] In their most recent assessment, the FBI and the National Gang Assessment Center report that there are more than 1.4 million gang members in the United States who collectively were responsible for half of all violent crime in most US jurisdictions and upward of 90 percent in select major cities.[101]

Many jurisdictions have enacted laws targeting gang activity. Florida and Kentucky, for example, have special criminal solicitation statutes aimed at curbing gang recruitment.[102] A number of states, like New Jersey and Tennessee, permit local schools to enact dress codes to prevent wearing gang-related apparel at school.[103] The federal government and some states, like California and Illinois, now provide for criminal sentencing enhancements when certain crimes are committed in furtherance of a gang's criminal activities.[104]

Chicago enacted a loitering ordinance to curb gang-related crime. But the city council framed its law far too broadly by criminalizing remaining "in any one place with no apparent purpose." The US Supreme Court invalidated the ordinance in *City of Chicago v. Morales* as unconstitutionally vague.[105] In the wake of the *Morales* decision, courts have invalidated other loitering laws, even those that were targeted curbing gang-related drug activity.[106] In *Johnson v. City of Cincinnati*, for instance, a federal appeals court invalidated a municipal ordinance banning people convicted of drug crimes from entering areas of the city where drug crimes were pervasive.[107] The court determined the ban violated the First Amendment's guarantee of free association since it prevented people from visiting family or even conferring with their lawyers in impoverished neighborhood.

In short, although it is not easy to craft loitering laws that comply with the mandates of the US Constitution, it is possible. Such laws must clearly define the *actus reus* of the offense to target conduct, not status, in ways that are is narrowly tailored to achieve a compelling governmental interest like preventing specific types of crimes. Moreover, the laws should require proof of some harmful purpose contain via a *mens rea* requirement. Consider the ordinance in the "You Make the Public Policy Call" in Box 12.3.

BOX 12.3

YOU MAKE THE PUBLIC POLICY CALL

Can Loitering Laws Be Used to Protect Children?

Illinois law provides that it is "unlawful for a child sex offender to knowingly loiter within 500 feet of a school building or real property comprising any school while persons under the age of [eighteen] are present in the building or on the grounds."[166]

A Peoria police officer was patrolling in the area near an elementary school when he noticed a car parked "partially in" a T-intersection in front of the school. The car was about 15 feet from school property and was facing toward the school. It was a weekday and between 80 to 100 young children were playing in the school yard. The office ran a check on the car's license plates and learned it was registered to a known sex offender. The officer approached the parked car, verified that the driver was the owner defendant, arrested him for violating the child sex offender loitering statute. At trial, the defendant explained he was not loitering, but rather was waiting for a friend who had gone into the school to deliver lunch to her grandchildren. This story proved true; as the officer and defendant were speaking, the defendant's friend returned to the vehicle and confirmed for the officer that defendant had given her a ride to her grandchildren's school so she could drop off lunch for them. She confirmed that she had been inside the school for less than five minutes.

1. Do you think the sex-offender loitering law is constitutional on its face? Or does it suffer from some constitutional infirmity, such as being void for vagueness or overbroad?
2. Assume for the sake of argument, that the sex-offender loitering law is constitutional on its face. Might it nonetheless be unconstitutional as applied to the defendant in the case? To answer that question, be sure to analyze the defendant's actions with regard to the *actus reus*, *mens rea*, and attendant circumstances of the loitering offense.

Firearms

Just as there are limits to the First Amendment freedoms of speech and peaceable assembly, there are also limits to the Second Amendment's right to bear arms (Chapter 2). Thus, states have enacted several public order offenses that limit the purchase or possession of certain types of firearms by all persons,[108] possession of all firearms by select persons (e.g., those adjudicated insane or those convicted of certain enumerated offenses),[109] and the discharge of firearms in certain places.[110] As explained in Chapter 2, most lower court decisions to date have upheld a range of state and local regulations on firearms.

SELECT CRIMES AGAINST THE STATE

Because this book is devoted to common criminal laws, an comprehensive review of crimes against the state is beyond the scope of this book. After all, most law enforcement officers in policing or criminal prosecution will never deal with a case involving treason, sedition, or espionage. Still, despite being rare, because those crimes are important, they are briefly in the final part of this chapter. By contrast, immigration offenses are one of the most common crimes against the state. Accordingly, we will delve into those offenses more deeply.

Treason

Article III, Section 3 of the US Constitution states:

> Treason against the United States, shall consist only in levying War against them, or in adhering to their Enemies, giving them Aid and Comfort. No Person shall be convicted of Treason unless on the Testimony of two Witnesses to the same overt Act, or on Confession in open Court. The Congress shall have power to declare the Punishment of Treason, but no Attainder of Treason shall work Corruption of Blood, or Forfeiture except during the Life of the Person attainted.

While presiding during the treason trial of Aaron Burr, US Chief Justice John Marshall wrote that treason was "the most atrocious offence which can be committed against the political body."[111] Dante "placed traitors in the Ninth and lowest Circle of Hell (far below the murderers of the Seventh Circle)."[112] Perhaps that is why **treason** is the only crime defined by the Constitution. The precise description of this offense reflects awareness by the Framers of the Constitution of the danger that unpopular views might be branded as traitorous.

The Supreme Court interpreted the phrase "levying war" literally when it dismissed treason charged against two of Burr's associations in *Ex parte Bollman & Swarthout* because they conspired to levy war, but did not actually follow through with an "actual assembling of men for the treasonable purpose to constitute a levying of war."[113] Similarly, the Court also narrowly construed the other *actus reus* that can constitute treason in its decision in *Cramer v. United States*.[114] In that case, the defendant had been convicted of treason for helping Nazi soldiers. In reversing his conviction, the Court said:

> Thus, the crime of treason consists of two elements: adherence to the enemy and rendering him aid and comfort. A citizen intellectually or emotionally may

> favor the enemy and harbor sympathies or convictions disloyal to this country's policy or interest, but, so long as he commits no act of aid and comfort to the enemy, there is no treason. On the other hand, a citizen may take actions which do aid and comfort the enemy—making a speech critical of the government or opposing its measures, profiteering, striking in defense plants or essential work, and the hundred other things which impair our cohesion and diminish our strength—but if there is no adherence to the enemy in this, if there is no intent to betray, there is no treason.[115]

Although two witnesses testified that the defendant in the case had met, drank together, and extended in long conversations, there was no proof that the defendant had provided any information, furnished shelter, sustenance, supplies, or even paid for their drinks. Thus, the Court revised his conviction. There were, however, more than a dozen people convicted of treason in connection to the Second World War. But there have been no successful prosecutions for treason in the United States since the early 1950s.[116] Indeed, it is likely because of the highly restrictive nature of the crime of treason that prosecutors tend to favor other types of prosecutions for crimes against the state.

Sedition

Sedition is closely related to treason in that **sedition** involves inciting revolt or violence against a lawful authority with the goal of destroying or overthrowing it. Federal law makes it a crime for two or more people to:

- conspire to overthrow or destroy by force the government of the United States or to level war against them;
- oppose by force the authority of the United States government;
- prevent, hinder, or delay by force the execution of any law of the United States; or
- take, seize, or possess by force any property of the United States contrary to the authority thereof.[117]

It is not enough to merely advocate for the use of force to overthrow the government. That is protected speech under the First Amendment.[118] But planning such actions, such as obtaining weapons or scheme the details of an attack, certainly qualifies.

Sedition laws were used in the South to prosecute those who spoke out against slavery.[119] But since then, prosecutions have been quite rare and "the prosecution rarely prevails."[120] For example, in 1987, a federal jury acquitted fourteen White supremacists despite there being an unusually strong case against them for plotting a series of murders and the destruction of a gas pipeline.[121] That same year, a different federal jury acquitted seven defendants of sedition even though they had previously been convicted of bank robbery and placing bombs in banks and military recruitment offices.[122] And in 2010, nine members of a militia group were prosecuted for plotting an antigovernment uprising by targeting the murders of federal, state, and local law enforcement; they, too, were acquitted.[123]

One of the few successful prosecutions for sedition in the past few decades involved the case again Sheikh Omar Abdel-Rahman and nine others who were convicted of seditious conspiracy in 1995. In the wake of the first World Trade Center bombing in 1993, the group began planning a series of bombings around New York City, including the United Nations Building and several bridges and tunnels connecting the island of Manhattan to surrounding land. A federal appeals court upheld his conviction, reasoning that "the evidence . . . showed beyond a reasonable doubt that he crossed this line. His speeches were not simply the expression of ideas; in some instances they constituted the crime of conspiracy to wage war on the United States . . . and solicitation of attack on the United States military installations . . . ."[124]

Espionage

Shortly after the United States joined the First World War, Congress enacted the Espionage Act. It criminalized the sharing of information intended to disrupt US military interests. Today, the crime of **espionage** is a favorite topic for novelists and script writers. It is common knowledge that the offense involves spying—obtaining secret or confidential information or sharing such information without permission. Today, however, federal law contains a number of provisions aimed at broad range of spying activities:

- 18 U.S.C. § 641 criminalizes sealing government property or records either for one's own use or for use of another person or entity;
- 18 U.S.C. § 973 prohibits gathering, transmitting, or losing information related to national defense "with intent or reason to believe that it is to be used to the injury of the United States or to the advantage of any foreign nation."
- 18 U.S.C. § 974 prohibits gathering or delivering military defense information "with intent or reason to believe that it is to be used to the injury of the United States or to the advantage of a foreign nation."
- 18 U.S.C. §§ 975–977 prohibit photographing, sketching, or otherwise imaging military defense installations without proper authorization, as well as reproducing, selling, publishing, or otherwise distributing such images.
- 18 U.S.C. § 978 prohibits the knowing disclosure of classified information to any unauthorized person, entity, or foreign government, as well as the use of any such information "in any manner prejudicial to the safety or interest of the United States or for the benefit of any foreign government to the detriment of the United States."
- 18 U.S.C. § 979 prohibits any violation of air and space regulations from NASA related to the "protection or security of any laboratory, station, base, or other facility," or any: aircraft, missile, spacecraft, or similar vehicle."
- 50 U.S.C. § 3131 prohibits the intentional disclosure of information that identifies undercover intelligence officers, agents, informants, and sources.

These laws do not differentiate between allies or enemies. Nor do they require that the United States actually be injured.[125]

While many of the most high-profile espionage cases occurred during World War II and the Cold War, the case against Robert Hanssen is a comparably most recent espionage case that caused significant damage to the United States. Hanssen was an FBI counterintelligence agent who received hundreds of thousands of dollars in cash and diamonds from Russia and the former Soviet Union in exchange for US secrets. He disclosed the identifies of dozens of US assets, revealed "top secret" and "codeword" protected documents, and compromised national counterintelligence investigative techniques, sources, methods, and operations.[126] In 2001, he pled guilty to fifteen counts of espionage and was sentenced to life imprisonment without the possibility of parole.[127]

Critics of these espionage laws point out that they lump three different types of violators all together—true spies, like Robert Hanssen, but also whistleblowers and those who leak of governmental secrets. A whistleblower is an "employee who reports employer wrongdoing to a governmental or law-enforcement agency."[128] Whistleblowing is a complex process when one works for the government, especially when the person has access to classified information. A slip-up navigating those complexities could result in someone being charged under the Espionage Act.

Someone who leaks protected information discloses it to anyone who is not entitled to receive it, including the media. No matter what the motivation, a leaker might find himself or herself charged with espionage. Consider the high-profile cases of Edward Snowden and Chelsea Manning. Snowden leaked classified information to the media to reveal the scope of illegal governmental surveillance programs. Despite the fact that he was motivated to show how the US government was violating its own laws, he was charged with espionage. Manning provided thousands of pages of classified military information to Wikileaks. She did so in the hopes of prompting changes in the way the US government handled war by forcing attention on the military's lack of attention to reports of abuse. No one disputes that Snowden and Manning broke the law. But might their motivations differentiate them from true spies like Robert Hanssen?[129]

Immigration Offenses

The US Constitution provides that the federal government has the power to "establish an uniform Rule of Naturalization."[130] As a result, and because "[i]mmigration policy can affect trade, investment, tourism, and diplomatic relations for the entire Nation," the federal government has broad authority over immigration.[131] Thus, although states have a limited role to play in the enforcement of immigration laws, it primarily the responsibility of the federal government to enforce immigration laws via agencies housed in the US Department of Homeland Security, such as the U.S Immigration and Customs Enforcement (ICE), US Customs and Border Protection (CBP), US Citizenship and Immigration Services (USCIS).[132] The US Departments of Justice, Labor, Health and Human Services, and State also have significant roles to play in regulating immigration into the United States.

IMMIGRATION AND CRIME

Immigration has been a hot-button political topic for well over a century.[133] In the mid-1800s though early 1990s, concerns revolved around immigration from Asia (especially

China, Japan, Korea, and the Philippines), Eastern Europe (especially Russia, Greece, and Turkey), and European counties with large Catholic or Orthodox Christian populations (most notably Ireland, Italy and Greece).[134] Today, concern tends to focus on immigration from Latin American and Middle Eastern countries.[135] But the questions are remarkably similar: How much immigration is the right amount? Should the United States prioritize certain groups for legal entry into the country? If so, which ones—people from certain countries? Refugees? Family members of US citizens? Skilled workers in needed sectors of the economy? Those who were brought to the United States illegally as children but have grown up in this country?

Even more controversy attaches to the issue of illegal immigration. Some people fear that undocumented immigrants bring crime, take jobs from native-born families, and strain the economy. Others counter such fears by pointing out immigrants are less likely to commit serious crimes and be incarcerated than native-born people and high rates of immigration are associated with lower rates of violent crime and property crime.[136] This holds true even for immigrants who entered the United States illegally.[137] Scholar attribute this to the fact that immigrants tend to be "self-selected risk takers who leave their homes, families, and languages to move to a new country to improve their and their children's lives. They have good reasons to work hard, defer gratifications, and stay out of trouble."[138] Additionally, because undocumented immigrants pay taxes but are ineligible for many government programs, as a group, they are net economic contributors, meaning they who pay more income, social security, Medicare, and other taxes than they receive in benefits.[139] Nonetheless, because any sovereign nation has the right to control its borders, few people would argue with the fact that Congress should regulate immigration. Although it does so primarily through civil laws, there are a number of criminal laws that are also a part of the complex web of US immigration laws.

Congress has specified categories of aliens who may not be admitted to the United States. Unlawful entry and unlawful reentry into the country are federal offenses. Once here, aliens are required to register with the federal government and to carry proof of status on their person. Failure to do so is a federal misdemeanor. Federal law also authorizes States to deny noncitizens a range of public benefits, and it imposes sanctions on employers who hire unauthorized workers.[140]

Physically being present in the United States without proper authorization is a civil offense punishable by a fine and removal from the country, a process referred to as *deportation*.[141] But criminal offenses related to immigration include bringing in and harboring certain aliens;[142] fraudulently misusing visas, permits, and other documents;[143] failing to report arrival at a designated border crossing and present articles for customs inspection;[144] misusing a passport;[145] and forgery of a passport.[146] But by far, the most commonly criminal violations of immigration law concern illegally entering or reentering the United States.[147] In fact, criminal prosecution of immigration crimes began to increase in 1990 such that by 2010, offenses related to illegal entry into the United States had become the most commonly prosecuted crimes in the US federal court system.[148] By 2016, prosecutions account for more than half of all criminal prosecutions in the federal court system and that proportion increased through 2019.[149]

DEFINING ILLEGAL ENTRY AND REENTRY

Under 8 U.S.C. § 1325, the crime of **illegal entry** is defined as unlawfully entering the United States. It is a misdemeanor offense—punishable by a fine, up to six months in prison, or both. This provision applies to those who knowingly enter the country without proper inspection at a valid port of entry, as well as to those who knowingly make false statements when entering or attempting to enter the country.

Under 8 U.S.C. § 1326, **illegal reentry**— a felony punishable by up to two years in prison—is defined as purposefully and unlawfully reentering, attempting to unlawfully reenter, or being found in the United States after having been deported, ordered removed, or denied admission to the country. It is a specific intent crime that requires proof of intent to enter the country free from official restraint The punishments increase to up to ten years imprisonment if the person has a criminal record consisting of misdemeanors and simple felonies, and up to twenty years for more serious felony offenses.

DEPORTABLE OFFENSES

Even when people enter the United States legally, until such time as they become a naturalized US citizen, they are subject to removal from the country if they commit a **deportable offense**. The list of crimes that constitute deportable offenses is quite long, but it includes the commission, attempted commission, conspiracy to commit, or aiding and abetting the following:

- Crimes of "moral turpitude," such as a wide range of theft and fraud crimes, burglary, arson, malicious destruction of property;
- Crimes against persons, such as murder and voluntary manslaughter; assault with intent to rob, rape, or kill; domestic violence; kidnapping; robbery; nonconsensual sex crimes; lewdness/public sexual indecency; prostitution; possession of child pornography; and contributing to the delinquency of a minor;
- Select public order offenses, such as aggravated DUI; bribery; counterfeiting; obstruction of justice (especially perjury and harboring a fugitive); tax evasion; and trafficking in guns, illicit drugs, humans, or destructive devices.[150]

CONCLUSION

Learning Objectives	Summaries
1. Differentiate the major classes of drug crimes.	Although some states punish drug possession without *mens rea*, most states criminalize the knowing possession of a controlled substance. The same *mens rea* applies to knowing possession of drug paraphernalia. Possession of more than a certain amount gives rise to a more the serious crime of possession with intent to distribute. Severe penalties attach to the illicit manufacture and distribution of controlled substances.

Learning Objectives	Summaries
2. Compare and contrast the *per se* approach and the impairment approach to the crime of driving under the influence.	All states make it a crime to operation a vehicle with more than a certain amount of alcohol in one's system. But even when that *per se* level of intoxication is not met, one may still be guilty of driving under the influence if one's ability to safely operate a vehicle is impaired.
3. Explain the elements of disorderly conduct.	The offense varies significantly, but typically prohibits the intentional or reckless engaging in violent, abusive, threatening, unreasonably loud, or otherwise disorderly conduct which tends to disturb the peace. The extent to which profanity can be regulated under these laws is significantly curtailed by the First Amendment.
4. Analyze the constitutional limits of regulating vagrancy, panhandling, and loitering.	Vagrancy prohibits roaming the streets without any visible means of supporting oneself. Such laws are largely unconstitutional for punishing poverty and homelessness. Panhandling is soliciting money or goods, whereas loitering punishes spending time idly in public place. Because both offenses can infringe on First Amendment liberties, they are unenforceable unless written in ways that target specific types of criminal conduct coupled with proof of some harmful purpose via a *mens rea* requirement.
5. Distinguish between treason, sedition, and espionage.	Treason involves "levying war" against the United States or adherence to an enemy and rendering that aid and comfort. Sedition involves inciting revolt or violence against a lawful authority with the goal of destroying or overthrowing it, typically by conspiring with others to plan an overthrow by force. Espionage is the crime of obtaining secret or confidential information or sharing such information without permission. Particular subtypes of espionage require different levels of *mens rea*, attendant circumstances, and result elements.
6. Explain the two most common forms of immigration offenses.	It is a misdemeanor offense to illegally enter the United States either by failing to submit to a proper inspection at a valid port of entry, or by making false statements when entering or attempting to enter at such an inspection point. It is a felony to reenter the country illegally after having been deported, ordered removed, or denied admission. Even when people enter the United States legally, they are subject to remove if they commit one or more deportable offenses, which include many crimes against persons, crimes against property, and select offenses against public order.

KEY TERMS

deportable offenses
disorderly conduct
disturbing the peace
driving under the influence
espionage
failure to disperse
false alarm
illegal entry
illegal reentry
inciting a riot
loitering
panhandling
possession of a controlled substance
possession of drug paraphernalia
possession with intent to distribut
public intoxication
riot
sedition
treason
unlawful assembly
vagrancy

13

Defenses that Negate or Mitigate *Mens Rea* and Procedural Defenses

LEARNING OBJECTIVES

1. Evaluate the circumstances under which mistakes may constitute a criminal defense.
2. Compare and contrast how the defenses of necessity and duress work.
3. Explain the requirements for a successful defense of intoxication.
4. Discuss the scope of double jeopardy as a criminal defense.

Outline

5. Differentiate the constitutional and statutory bases for speedy trial defenses.

6. Define the elements of the entrapment and outrageous governmental conduct defenses.

7. Explain the primary ways in which someone might be immune from prosecution.

8. Assess the defense of selective prosecution.

INTRODUCTION

As discussed in Chapter 1, the principle of *culpability* generally limits criminal punishment to those who are responsible for their conduct in a morally blameworthy way. Numerous criminal defenses exist which are premised upon a lack of culpability. Defenses of justification and excuse seek to mitigate or even completely negate criminal responsibility on the grounds that relieve or diminish culpability.

> If *A*'s claim is that what he did was fully warranted—he shot *B* to stop *B* from killing other people—*A* offers a justification; if *A* acknowledges that he acted wrongfully but claims he was not to blame—he was too disturbed mentally to be responsible for his behavior—he offers an excuse. . . . [Put differently, in] the one defense, briefly, we accept responsibility but deny that it was bad; in the other, we admit that it was bad but don't accept full, or even any, responsibility. In effect, when we say that a person's behavior was justified, we are saying that she did the right, or at least, a permissible thing. . . . [I]f we say that a person's behavior was excused, we are saying, at the very least, that the behavior in which she engaged is properly deemed impermissible but that due to some internal or external factors beyond her control she is not to be held blameworthy for her actions.[1]

This chapter explores defenses aimed at demonstrating a defendant is not culpable due to reasons that either negate or mitigate the *mens rea* for certain crimes. This chapter also briefly summarizes select procedural defenses that are available to criminal defendants when the government has some culpability for misconduct in the investigation or prosecution of criminal cases. Other defenses of excuse are examined in Chapter 14 and defenses of justification are explored in Chapter 15.

MISTAKE OF LAW

There is an old maxim which states: *ignorantia legis neminem excusat.*[2] Translated from the Latin, it means "ignorance of the law excuses no one," or, in simpler terms, "ignorance of the law is no excuse." The rule was well settled under Ancient Roman law "which was founded on the straightforward (if fictitious) rationale that the law was 'certain and capable of being ascertained.' "[3] The common law maintained this tradition. Even today, while certainly few people actually know the requirements of criminal law, the legal system still presumes, for the most part, that everyone has constructive knowledge of the law since it is generally knowable.

The Rule: Ignorance of the Law Is Not an Excuse

Modern criminal law maintains the tradition from ancient times that everyone has constructive knowledge of the law once it is enacted and either published or otherwise reasonably made available prior to the conduct alleged. In other words, everyone in society is conclusively presumed to know what the law prohibits them from doing or else ignorance "would arrest the administration of justice" and provide a "shield for the guilty."[4] Accordingly, a **mistake of law**—either with regard to the existence of a criminal law or to its meaning—is not a generally not a defense to any crime.[5]

Exceptions to the Rule That Ignorance of the Law Is Not an Excuse

There are limited circumstances under which a mistake of law might qualify as a criminal defense.

If the law has not been made reasonably available, the principle of legality—inextricably tied to due process as explained in Chapter 2, might be violated. Accordingly, the Model Penal Code permits a defense of ignorance of law when the law defining the offense is actually (i.e., subjectively) unknown to the defendant and the law "has not been published or otherwise made available prior to the conduct alleged."[6] Of course, this defense would not apply to any crime published in a jurisdiction's criminal code since such publication is deemed to give constructive knowledge of the existence of all such laws. It may be applicable, in contrast, to local ordinances that are not made reasonably available.

Another exception to the rule that a mistake of law is not a criminal defense concerns a mistaken belief with regard to the existence or meaning of a law that is founded upon an official statement of law. An "official statement" does not include one's erroneous interpretation of a statute or even the bad advice of an attorney or police officer. Rather, the erroneous interpretation of the law relating to the offense has to be made by a high-ranking public servant, a governmental agency, or an official body that is charged with administering, interpreting, or enforcing the law.[7] For example, where "a criminal statute has been held unconstitutional by a court of last resort and then later held constitutional, a person who committed the prohibited act during the interval between the two decisions is not liable" in light of his or her reliance on the official misstatement of law in the first judicial opinion.[8]

The 1965 US Supreme Court case of *Cox v. Louisiana* presents the leading example of the highly unusual facts that must occur for a mistaken reliance on an official misstatement of law to qualify as a criminal defense.[9] In that case, the defendant had been convicted of leading a demonstration near a courthouse. The demonstration took place precisely 101 feet from the courthouse because that was where officials told Cox was the minimum distance the demonstrators needed to keep from the courthouse.[10] In fact, on the day of the demonstration, Cox met the Chief of Police, the county sheriff, and the city's mayor. In the presence of these officials, the police chief assured Cox that the demonstrator could peaceably assemble where they did.[11] Yet Cox and his fellow demonstrators were arrested for demonstrating "near" the courthouse. The Court reversed the convictions on due process grounds, reasoning that Cox was entitled to rely on representations on such high-ranking officials. The result would likely have been different, however, if Cox had sought the advice of his own attorney or a patrolman since neither lawyers nor most law enforcement officers are state officials who are charged with giving official interpretations of law on behalf of a state or any of its political subdivisions.

MISTAKE OF FACT

When a person makes a mistake regarding a factual matter which, if true, would have justified the act or omission which is the subject of a criminal prosecution, he or she may be able to assert the defense known as **mistake of fact** if the mistake negates the *mens rea* of the crime with which the defendant is charged.[12] In other words, if a factual error effectively erases or nullifies the criminal intent component of a crime, the law excuses what might otherwise constitute criminal conduct if the mistake was honest and reasonable.

Honest and Reasonable Mistakes

The requirement that a mistake of fact be an honest mistake is purely subjective. Thus, it requires no more than the defendant to have actually (subjectively) been laboring under some factual error. The second requirement, however, is objective. It requires that the person's honest mistaken belief be objectively reasonable. In other words, the mistake must have been one that the ordinary, reasonable, prudent person could have made if in the defendant's situation. If either of these requirements are not met, then the defense should be unsuccessful. Due to this requirement, this defense may not be invoked for mistakes that were the product of mental illness or intoxication (those situations are covered by other criminal defenses with their own specific requirements). As the following case illustrates, people may differ with regard to the determination of whether a factual error is objectively reasonable.

STATE of New Jersey, Plaintiff-Respondent,
v.
Joseph PELLETERI, Defendant-Appellant.
683 A.2d 555 (N.J. Super. Ct. App. Div. 1996).

[O]ur Legislature proscribed the "knowing" possession of "assault firearms" [defined as a] semi-automatic rifle with a fixed magazine capacity exceeding [fifteen] rounds....

* * *

We need not recount the facts at length. Defendant, an expert marksman who at one point was employed as a firearms instructor, won a Marlin semi-automatic rifle in the late 1980s by placing first in a police combat match. An avid gun collector, defendant placed the weapon in his safe. Defendant claimed that he neither inspected nor used the firearm. When the police recovered the gun from defendant's residence in December 1993, it still had the manufacturer's tags and the owner's manual attached to the trigger guard. The owner's manual indicated that the rifle could hold at least seventeen cartridges. Defendant claimed that he never read the manual. While conceding that he knew the rifle was a semi-automatic weapon, defendant contended that he was unaware that the firearm had a magazine capacity exceeding fifteen rounds.

At trial, defendant advanced the defense[] of mistake of . . . fact. He asserted that he made diligent inquiry respecting whether the guns in his collection constituted "assault firearms" when the 1990 legislation was enacted and obtained the requisite registration for some of his weapons. Defendant testified that he did not register the Marlin rifle because he did not know its fixed capacity exceeded fifteen rounds. The trial judge barred the defense[] . . . on the grounds that the statutory prohibition was clearly written and published, and that knowledge of the specific character of the weapon did not constitute an element of the offense. In response to a question propounded by the jury during its deliberations, the judge charged that defendant could be found guilty if he knowingly possessed the firearm but was unaware that its fixed capacity exceeded fifteen rounds. Defendant was convicted and placed on probation.

* * *

The question squarely presented is whether the State was required to prove that the defendant knew the gun in his possession was an assault firearm. We hold that knowledge of the character of the weapon is not an element of the offense.

N.J.S.A. 2C:39-5f provides in pertinent part that "any person who knowingly has in his possession an assault firearm is guilty of a crime of the third degree." The word "knowingly" thus modifies the phrase "has in his possession." The Code defines "possession" in terms of whether the "possessor knowingly procured or received the thing possessed or was aware of his control [of it] for a sufficient period to have been able to terminate his possession. . . ." The Code provides that "a person acts knowingly with respect to the nature of his conduct . . . if he is aware that his conduct is of that nature. . . ."

We are satisfied that the Legislature intended to proscribe knowing possession, as distinguished from knowledge of the illegal character of the article possessed.[13] In that context, "knowing possession is not to be confused with criminal intent or guilty knowledge. . . ."

We are concerned here with a statute dealing with gun control. . . . This is an area in which "regulations abound and inquiries are likely," and where the overarching purpose is to insure the public safety and protect against acts and threats of violence. . . .[14] When dealing with guns, the citizen acts at his peril. In short, we view the statute as a regulatory measure in the interests of the public safety, premised on the thesis that one would hardly be surprised to learn that possession of such a highly dangerous offensive weapon is proscribed absent the requisite license. Affirmed.

Questions

1. Given Mr. Pelleteri's knowledge of both the statute and of guns, the court had no problem holding that even if he honestly (i.e., subjectively) did not know that the weapon in question required registration since it held more than the statutorily allowed number of rounds, such a belief was not objectively reasonable. Do you agree with this conclusion? Why or why not?
2. Recall from Chapter 9 that the crime of bigamy is typically defined as the marriage of any person who, already having a husband or wife living, marries another person. If a married person remarried under the mistaken belief that his or her spouse is dead (i.e., the spouse thought to be dead is actually alive), under what circumstances might such a person be found guilty of bigamy? Explain. What if that person knew their spouse was alive, but thought they had been divorced in a "quickie-divorce" obtained in Mexico?[15]

Limited to Crimes of Purpose, Knowledge, and Recklessness

Because a mistake of fact can be a defense when it is both honest and reasonable, it can be asserted as a defense to any crime that has purpose, knowledge, or recklessness as its requisite *mens rea*. It cannot, however, be used as a defense to crimes that carry negligence or strict liability. The reason for this is simple. Since mistake of fact can only be used as a defense when it negates *mens rea*, and crimes of strict liability have no concern with the *mens rea* of the defendant, logic dictates that a mistake should be irrelevant. Consider the common-law crime of statutory rape. Even an honest and objectively reasonable mistake as the age of the victim would not bar conviction since statutory rape was (and still is in many jurisdictions) a strict liability crime (see Chapter 8).

But what of crimes of negligence? By definition, being criminally negligent means that one did not act reasonably because he or she failed to perceive some risk that the ordinary, reasonable, prudent person would have perceived if in the defendant's position. Since mistake of fact can only be a defense if it negates *mens rea* when it involves an honest and reasonable mistake, and negligent conduct is per se unreasonable, such mistakes do not constitute a defense to crimes that carry negligence as their requisite *mens rea*.

COMPULSION OF CIRCUMSTANCES DEFENSES

The criminal law recognizes that there are times when someone acts not on his or her free will, but rather due to the necessary circumstances of the moment or the coercion of another. When such situations exist, the law permits a defendant to argue that his or her conduct should either not be punished at all or should mitigated to a less serious charge. Notably, these defenses act as either justifications (the *necessity* defense) or excuses (the *duress* defense) for a defendant having formed *mens rea* under extraordinary circumstances that render it unfair to hold him or her responsible for the unlawful conduct.

Necessity and Duress

There are two defenses that fall within the general ambit of compulsion of circumstances: necessity and duress. These two defenses are so closely related that many courts treat duress and necessity as the same defense today.[16] But a few jurisdictions maintain the common-law distinctions between the two.

The defense of **necessity** (sometimes referred to as the *choice of evils* defense) may be invoked when circumstances beyond the actor's control forces him or her to engage in criminal conduct to avoid a more substantial evil.[17] Technically, the defense of necessity applies in situations in which physical forces beyond the actor's control render illegal conduct the lesser of two evils. Natural disasters (e.g., hurricanes and earthquakes), brake failures, shipwrecks, plane crashes, and the like are all examples of situations that could give rise to a necessity/choice-of-evils defense. In contrast, when unlawful human agency (rather than external physical circumstances) causes an emergency situation, the proper defense is duress. The defense of **duress** excuses criminal conduct when the actor is unlawfully coerced or compelled to do an unlawful act by another person in order to avoid immediate threats of unlawful force against the person (or, in some jurisdictions, the person of another, such as a member of the defendant's family).[18]

Requirements for Asserting a Compulsion of Circumstances Defense

There are three requirements for asserting a compulsion of circumstances defense. First, there must be a bona-fide emergency, which threatened the defendant with serious, imminent harm, arising without fault on the part of actor concerned.[19] The type of harm is usually limited by statute to the imminent use (or threatened imminent use) of unlawful force against the person or the person.[20] Moreover, because the defendant must be free from any fault in giving rise to the emergency situation, the defense is not available when someone purposefully, knowingly, or recklessly places himself or herself in a situation or position in which it was probable that he or she would be subject to an emergency.[21] "The defense is also unavailable if [the defendant] was negligent in placing himself in such a situation, whenever negligence suffices to establish culpability for the offense charged."[22]

Second, there must be a true necessity to commit the crime in order to avoid the harm presented under the emergency situation. In other words, there must be no reasonable or adequate legal alternative to avoid the harm without committing the crime.[23]

Third, the choice to commit the crime must be the lesser of two evils; the harm avoided by committing the crime must be more substantial or more serious than that harm caused by the commission of the crime.[24]

If all three of these criteria are met, a person may assert a compulsion of circumstances defense (either necessity or duress) to any crime other than a homicide offense.[25] For example, assume that a dog is locked in car on a hot summer's day. The dog panics and flails as the temperature rises to potentially fatal levels. If a passerby shatters the car window to rescue the dog, that person would likely be able to assert the defense of necessity to criminal vandalism charges.[26] The "Case Study Extra" feature in Box 13.1 provides an example of how the defense of necessity normally operates.

Necessity and duress are affirmative defenses. Accordingly, if permitted to assert a necessity defense, the defendant typically bears the burden of persuasion to prove that a person of reasonable firmness in his or her situation would have been unable to resist doing what was done in light of the emergency situation.[27] Similarly, if permitted to assert the defense of duress, defendant must prove, usually by a preponderance of the evidence, that the threatened use of force must be of such a nature as to cause a person of "reasonable firmness" to be unable to resist the compulsion to act in light of "well-grounded apprehension of death or serious bodily injury."[28]

Limitations on Compulsion of Circumstances Defenses

There are several important exceptions to the availability of the necessity and duress defenses. First, neither defense may be used to excuse acts of civil disobedience.[29] Hence, one may not engage in disruptive protests of war, abortion, or other socio-political causes.[30]

Second, because the defenses are limited to situations in which the actor is faced with the threat of immediate physical injury, neither may be used to justify actions to avoid economic or business harms.[31]

Third, under the common law and the approach taken by many states today, neither defense can be used to escape criminal liability for homicide offenses.[32] Certainly, the criminal law has long recognized that that select killings are "necessary"—and therefore justifiable—when they occur in war or against those who are unlawful attacking other people (the defenses of self-defense and defense of others are explored in Chapter 15). In contrast, the criminal law does not sanction the taking of an innocent human life, even when it might be argued that doing so was the lesser of two evils. The logic underpinning this limitation to compulsion of circumstances defenses is that no one may choose between himself or herself and the life of another.

One of the leading cases in this area is an English case from 1884, *Regina v. Dudley and Stephens*.[33] In that case, four members of the crew of a yacht, comprised of three adult men and a seventeen-year-old teenage boy, were stranded at sea on a lifeboat after they were forced to abandon ship during a storm. They floated for twenty days, subsisting on rainwater, some canned turnips, and the meat of a turtle they caught. As the situation grew increasingly dire, Dudley proposed to the two adult men that they draw lots to see who might be killed so that the other could subsist by eating the remains of the deceased person. The two men refused. The next day, Dudley proposed that the boy should be killed because he was close to death as a result or starvation and dehydration. Stephens agreed, but the other man did not. Nonetheless, Dudley then killed the boy and all three men at the boy's body and drank his blood for four days, when they were rescued. The men were charged with murdering the boy. A jury returned a "special verdict" reporting that they had concluded two key facts. First, the men would have died prior to being rescued if they had not eaten and drunk from the boy. Second, the boy was so close to death he

BOX 13.1

CASE STUDY EXTRA

What Might Necessitate Driving on a Suspended License?

In *State v. Cole*,[128] the defendant's wife was six months pregnant and had developed pains in her back and stomach. He did not have telephone to call for help and his only neighbor was not at home. The next closest phone was more than a mile and a half away. So even though his driver's license had been suspended, he drove to the phone to call for help. As he was returning to his house, he was stopped by the police for a broken taillight and was arrested for driving under a suspended license.

The judge presiding over Cole's criminal trial refused to allow Cole to argue the defense of necessity. The defendant was convicted. On appeal, the Supreme Court of South Carolina reversed his conviction, holding that the trial court should have allowed Cole to assert the defense of necessity. A jury should have been able to decide whether the three elements of the necessity defense were satisfied since prima facie evidence of all three criteria had been presented. Specifically, first, there appears to have been a bona-fide, emergency situation that not only presented a reasonable apprehension of death or serious bodily harm, but also that had arisen without fault on the part of the defendant. Second, there does not appear to have been any other reasonable alternative, other than committing the crime of driving on a suspended license, that could have avoided potential harm posed by the emergency. Third, driving on a suspended license certainly appears to be the lesser of two evils when juxtaposed against the fact that doing nothing under the circumstance could have meant the death of Cole's wife or her unborn child.

1. Assume that Cole had been permitted to assert a necessity defense. If you were on the jury, would you have voted to convict him of driving on a suspended license, or would you have acquitted him on the basis of the defense of necessity? Explain your reasoning.
2. Cell phones were not widely available at the time this case was decided. But according to the US Census, only 5.2 percent of households were without a landline telephone in 1990.[129] Given that Cole's wife was pregnant, an argument could be made that his failure to have a home telephone line was negligent or reckless. On the other hand, the Coles may not have been able to afford phone service. Do you think their failure to have telephone service should deprive them of the defense of necessity? Why or why not?
3. Assume that someone was stranded in the forest and needed food and shelter. If that person came across a cabin, do you think the defense of necessity should excuse criminal liability for breaking into the cabin and eating whatever food might be found in it? Explain your reasoning.

would have predeceased the men. With these facts in mind, the jury convicted the men of murder. An appellate court affirmed their convictions, noting that they "might possibly have been picked up next day by a passing ship; they might possibly not have been picked up at all; in either case it is obvious that the killing of the boy would have been an unnecessary and profitless act." Moreover, the court reasoned as follows:

> To preserve one's life is generally speaking a duty, but it may be the plainest and the highest duty to sacrifice it. War is full of instances in which it is a man's duty not to live, but to die. The duty, in case of shipwreck, of a captain to his crew, of the crew to the passengers, of soldiers to women and children, . . . these duties impose on men the moral necessity, not of the preservation, but of the sacrifice of their lives for others. . . .
>
> * * *
>
> It is not needful to point out the awful danger of admitting the principle which has been contended for. Who is to be the judge of this sort of necessity? By what measure is the comparative value of lives to be measured? Is it to be strength, or intellect, or what? It is plain that the principle leaves to him who is to profit by it to determine the necessity which will justify him in deliberately taking another's life to save his own.

The defendants were sentenced to death. But the Queen of England thereafter commuted their sentences to six months' imprisonment.[34]

The limitation expressed in *Regina v. Dudley & Stephens* has been repeated in numerous US cases, most famously in *United States v. Holmes*.[35] But the Model Penal Code departed from this approach by not categorically excluding the defense of necessity from applying to certain forms of homicide.[36] Nonetheless, few states have abandoned the common-law bar on the defense in homicide settings.[37] Those that have usually limit its application such that necessity and duress can only mitigate the degree of homicide to a less serious level of criminal liability.[38] Apply the law of compulsion of circumstances in the "You Make the Public Policy Call" feature contained in Box 13.2.

Finally, there are special limitations on the use of a necessity defense within the context of a criminal escape. Suppose, for example, that one were in prison and had been specifically threatened with death, forcible sexual attack, or substantial bodily injury in the immediate future, yet the prison authorities dismissed pleas for help and there was insufficient time to seek the assistance of the courts. Under such circumstances, a prisoner might be allowed to assert the defense of necessity to the crime of escape (or attempted escape) in order to avoid the impending attack. But as a rule, the escape needs to be supported by egregious facts that truly could not be avoided by any viable alternative to

BOX 13.2

YOU MAKE THE PUBLIC POLICY CALL

The Hypothetical Mountaineer Case

Suppose two people are climbing a mountain. The climbers are held together by a rope. At one point, they both slip and slide over a precipice. The rope, still holding them both, becomes dangerously frayed. It clearly will not hold both of them much longer. Both face imminent death if nothing is done. Should the upper climber cut loose the lower climber, letting him fall to his death, and thus enable himself to climb up to safety? By doing so, the one climber will accelerate the death of the other slightly, but also avoid the greater evil, namely, the certain death of both.[130]

The official commentary to the Model Penal Code claims that the mountaineer who eventually cuts the rope "must certainly be granted the defense that he accelerated one death slightly but avoided the only alternative, the certain death of both."[131] The commentary justifies the availability of the defense on utilitarian grounds: "[M]ost persons probably think a net saving of lives is ethically warranted if the choice among lives to be saved is not unfair. Certainly the law should permit such a choice."[132]

1. How do you think the case of the mountaineer should be resolved? Do you think the defense of necessity should be completely unavailable in such circumstances? Or do you think the defense should either completely exonerate the mountaineer who cuts the rope from all criminal liability or, a minimum, reduce the mountaineer's homicide liability from murder to some lessor form of homicide?
2. Compare and contrast how the mountaineer hypothetical might be similar to the situation in which a viable fetus threatens the mother's life.
3. In his article analyzing killing by necessity, John Alan Cohan recounted a story from the Holocaust.

   A group of Jews was hiding from the Nazis. They sought to prevent the Nazis from discovering their hiding place, but a crying baby jeopardized their safety. The group smothered the baby to death in order to prevent the Nazis from discovering their hiding place and killing them all. A rabbi was asked to analyze the facts, and rendered the opinion that the action was permissible "since the baby would have been killed along with all the others if the Nazis had found them." The rabbi added that the action was not required, but permissible (i.e., excusable) and that it would have been an act of holiness not to kill the infant under the circumstances.[133]

   Do you think the killing of the infant meets the requirements of a compulsion of circumstances defense? Explain your reasoning.

escape. Importantly, the person must then immediately surrender to authorities since there is no necessity to remain at large.[39]

INTOXICATION DEFENSES

The criminal law has a relatively short history of permitting those who are intoxicated to assert that their state of intoxication interfered with their ability to form *mens rea*. Until the 1800s, the common law disallowed a defendant from using intoxication as an excuse for any criminal offense.[40] But in the nineteenth century the common-law rule changed; since then, intoxication has been recognized as a limited defense to specific intent crimes.[41] Today, many US jurisdictions still recognize defenses of intoxication,[42] but the success of such defenses, however, is largely dependent on two main factors: (1) whether the intoxication was voluntary or involuntary; and (2) the level of *mens rea* of the crime for which the defense was being asserted.

Voluntary Intoxication

Intoxication is a generic term in the criminal law. It refers not only to a state induced by alcohol, but also by both legal and illicit drugs. When one is voluntarily intoxicated, he or she has introduced a substance into the body which the person either knew or should have known was likely to have intoxicating effects (i.e., "a disturbance of mental or physical capacities").[43] For **voluntary intoxication** to constitute a criminal defense, the intoxication must have been substantial. Thus, how much of the intoxicant was consumed over what period of time is highly relevant.[44] Additional relevant factors include the actor's conduct as perceived by others; results of forensic tests; and, to a lesser extent, the actor's own subjective to recall events.[45]

THE COMMON-LAW APPROACH

Voluntary intoxication could be as a common-law defense in two distinct ways. First, the defendant could assert his or her voluntary intoxication in an attempt to negate the *actus reus* element of a crime. Put differently, the defendant could attempt to prove that he or she was so intoxicated at the time of alleged crime that he or she could not have physically performed the conduct required by the definition of the crime. Second, and much more frequently, evidence of intoxication could be offered to negate *mens rea* of specific intent. In other words, defendants were permitted to assert that they were so intoxicated that they could not have formed specific intent to kill, rape, steal, and so on. When so offered, however, voluntary intoxication was not a complete defense. Rather, voluntary intoxication was used to mitigate a crime of specific intent down to one of general intent.

THE MODEL PENAL CODE APPROACH

The Model Penal Code follows a very similar approach to the common law with respect to voluntary intoxication. It recognizes voluntary intoxication as a defense only to disprove the existence of an element of the offense.[46] Thus, as with the common law, it can be used to show that the defendant was too intoxicated to have performed the conduct element of an offense, thereby disproving *actus reus*. The defense may also be used to negate the *mens rea* elements of any crime of either purpose or knowledge, just as the common law allowed it to be used to disprove specific intent.

The Model Penal Code's handling of the defense when dealing with the *mens rea* level of recklessness is more complex. Recall that recklessness is defined as the conscious disregard of a known risk. If, due to voluntary intoxication, a defendant was not subjectively aware "of a risk of which he would have been aware had he been sober, such unawareness is immaterial."[47] In other words, voluntary intoxication cannot be a defense to crimes of recklessness; in fact, under the Model Penal Code, "an intoxicated person who merely behaved negligently can be punished for a reckless crime."[48]

Fewer than fifteen US states adopted the Model Penal Code's formulation of the intoxication defense with regard to crimes requiring recklessness as their *mens rea*.[49] In other states, voluntary intoxication is either not recognized as a defense to any crime regardless of the crime's requisite level of *mens rea*,[50] or voluntary intoxication may only be used to show that a defendant did not form specific intent (i.e., purpose of knowledge) if required as an element of the crime charged.[51] Although the statutory abolition of the intoxication defense in some states initially raised due process concerns, the US Supreme Court ruled in *Montana v. Egelhoff*[52] that the due process does not require that a criminal defendant be allowed to introduce evidence of intoxication to show that he or she did not entertain the requisite *mens rea* for a given offense. In the wake of *Egelhoff*, several more states followed Montana's lead by abolishing the voluntary intoxication defense.[53]

Given that nonpathological, voluntary intoxication is not a defense to crimes that carry recklessness as their *mens rea*, it should come as no surprise that the defense will not work for those crimes which have negligence as their requisite level of *mens rea*. Intoxicated persons are held to the standard of the ordinary, reasonable, prudent person in a sober state, rendering his or her intoxication irrelevant. And voluntary intoxication is never a defense to crimes of strict liability, since such offenses have no *mens rea* that intoxication could negate.

Involuntary Intoxication

The defense of **involuntary intoxication** is relatively rare, but it was recognized as a complete defense to all crimes at common law and continues to operate in the same fashion today in most US jurisdictions.[54] Section 2.08(4) of the Model Penal Code provides: "Intoxication that (a) is not self-induced or (b) is pathological is an affirmative defense if by reason of such intoxication the actor at the time of his conduct lacks substantial capacity either to appreciate its criminality [wrongfulness] or to conform his conduct to the requirements of law." This definition includes two distinct types of involuntary intoxication.

INTOXICATION THAT IS NOT SELF-INDUCED

Involuntary intoxication includes situations in which a person did not voluntary consume an intoxicant. In other words, if someone neither knew nor had reason to know that he or she ingested an intoxicant, then any resulting intoxication would be involuntary. For example, in one case, the defendant killed someone after consuming what he thought were breath mints, but were actually cocaine tablets.[55] In a similar case, in a police officer was acquitted of having fatally shot someone after having consumed a beer that, unbeknownst to the officer, had been laced with a drug.[56] Intoxication is also considered involuntary if the actor was forced to consume an intoxicant under duress.[57]

Involuntary intoxication is a complete defense, meaning it can result in an acquittal for all types of crimes, regardless of their level of *mens rea*. But it is an affirmative defense that is incredibly difficult to prove. To be successful, the defendant must prove three distinct elements:

1. He or she was intoxicated at the time of the criminal act;
2. The intoxication was involuntarily created; and
3. His or her mental state at the time met the jurisdiction's test for insanity.

Stated differently, involuntary intoxication must render a person temporarily insane in order to negate *mens rea* and thereby excuse criminal liability. Chapter 14 contains detailed information on insanity. For now, however, consider the following case:

THE PEOPLE of the State of California, Respondent,
v.
Walter Stephen SCOTT, Appellant.
146 Cal. App. 3d 823; 194 Cal. Rptr. 633 (1983).

[The defendant attended a family reunion with his brother Charles. Charles witnessed a punch bowl being refilled several times during the party and he also saw his brother drink the punch. At some point, Charles volunteered to go to a store to get more ice. When he left, everyone, appeared to be behaving normally.] However, when he returned the brother noticed that the behavior of the party guests had changed dramatically. He began looking for defendant and while doing so he noticed a number of guests holding cups of punch behaving strangely and in some cases bizarrely. One man, pointing to the floor, stated there was a dog in the room. Several people holding glasses of punch in their hands were vomiting. When [Charles] finally located [his brother], he noticed that defendant's eyes were unusually large and dilated, and that defendant appeared uncoordinated. Defendant also appeared not to recognize his brother. Feeling that something was wrong, the brother took defendant by the hand and led him out of the house and into his car.

On the way home defendant told his brother he could see a big fireball in the sky and that he could see the brother and his in-laws in the flames. Defendant described it as "Hell" and he stated either that they were trying to pull him in there or he was trying to pull them out. At some point during the ride home, defendant stuck his head out of the car window and stated that he felt "good enough to fly home." The brother, who had received some instruction on drug intoxication and had also previously seen people who were on PCP (phencyclidine), believed defendant might be on PCP.

* * *

During an interview with Dr. Robert Summerour, a forensic psychiatrist, defendant stated that at some point during the party he began to see intense colors and heard helicopters and loud sirens. He stated that his body was clumsy, he was sweating, had difficulty talking, and felt as if his heart was beating rapidly. Defendant remembered being led away from the party and into a car by his brother and also his attempt to jump out of the car window during the ride home. . . .

Defendant further told Dr. Summerour that the next day he felt a little more hyperactive than usual but attended church with his family and proceeded through the day without incident. However, when he awakened on Monday morning, August 3, 1981, he felt queasy and decided not to go to work. After taking his children to school, defendant took his mother-in-law, Frances Nichols, with him to purchase some glass to replace broken windows at his house. While inside the store, defendant began to feel the same feelings he had at the party. The clerk "spooked" him because he (the clerk) "looked like he was from Mars." Defendant ran out of the store and into his car, and then imagined he observed a long funeral go by in which he sensed that he was the deceased. Defendant began to drive on the freeway at a high speed.

* * *

Ms. Nichols observed defendant looking over his shoulder frequently, driving fast and making rapid lane changes. While on the freeway, defendant stated to Ms. Nichols the CIA was after him and was following him in an airplane because he was a secret agent. He said he had to get to the police for help. He started calling Ms. Nichols "Baby," an affectionate term that he usually addressed to his wife. Defendant was sweating profusely and repeatedly stated that he was thirsty. Ms. Nichols observed that defendant's eyes were "glassy and weird," that he was talking fast and that he did not seem to be making sense. Finally, when the car overheated and stopped running, defendant jumped out of the car and ran up the off-ramp. Ms. Nichols eventually lost sight of him.

About this time, 13-year-old Robert Briggs was sitting on his motor bike in the driveway of a gas station in Riverside County. Defendant approached him, stated he was a secret agent and demanded the boy give him the motor bike. When Robert refused, defendant hit him on the helmet, knocking him off the bike, and then proceeded to mount the bike. Defendant attempted to kick-start the cycle, but was unsuccessful.

* * *

[Our] Vehicle Code provides in part: "Any person who drives or takes a vehicle not his own, without the consent of the owner thereof, and with intent either permanently or temporarily to deprive the owner thereof of his title to or possession of the vehicle, whether with or without intent to steal the same, . . . is guilty of a public offense. . . ." Conviction under this section requires a finding that the accused had the specific intent to deprive the owner of title to or possession of his vehicle.[58]

[T]o negate the specific intent requirement . . . , defendant asserted . . . involuntary intoxication. He presented the testimony of several witnesses who stated in essence that at the time of the commission of the alleged offenses, defendant was acting irrationally and in a bizarre manner and appeared to be under the influence of something. Defendant also introduced the testimony of three psychiatrists who all stated that, in their opinions, at the time of the incident defendant did not have the mental capacity to form the specific intent to deprive the owners of their vehicles, either temporarily or permanently. . . .

* * *

The evidence establishes that defendant unknowingly and therefore involuntarily ingested some kind of hallucinogen which caused him to act in a bizarre and irrational manner and that, acting under the delusion that he was a secret agent and that he was acting to save his own life or possibly that of the President, defendant attempted to "take" vehicles belonging to others without their consent. The only question is whether or not a crime has been committed. . . .

* * *

Although defendant's mistake of fact was undoubtedly irrational, it was also undoubtedly reasonable under the circumstances, because the circumstances include that the mistake emanated from a delusion caused by defendant's involuntary intoxication resulting from unknowingly ingesting some unspecified hallucinogenic substance.

We conclude therefore that even if the evidence is sufficient to support the trial court's finding that defendant intended to temporarily deprive the owners of possession of their vehicles, defendant's actions . . . were . . . not criminal.

Questions

1. Do you think it makes sense to excuse criminal liability when someone is involuntarily intoxicated? Why or why not? Be sure to include the doctrine of culpability in your answer.
2. What if, before drinking any of the drug-laced punch, Scott had seen other people drink the punch and then start behaving bizarrely? Would his intoxication have been involuntary? Or would have had gained constructive knowledge that the punch was laced, thereby converting his situation into a voluntary intoxication defense?
3. Evaluate Scott's liability if this case had been tried with a voluntary intoxication defense, rather than an involuntary intoxication defense.

PATHOLOGICAL INTOXICATION

Involuntary intoxication also includes instances of **pathological intoxication.** Intoxication is pathological if it is a result of an unforeseeable, grossly excessive reaction to the voluntary ingesting of an intoxicant in light of the amount taken.[59] In other words, even though a person voluntary consumes an intoxicant, if the reaction is unforeseeable and grossly disproportionate to the amount consumed, then such pathological intoxication may be asserted as a defense.

Suppose that someone became highly intoxicated after drinking only a few sips of wine. Historically, the law would treat such a grossly excessive reaction as being pathological, presuming that the reaction was unforeseeable.[60] But to have been unforeseeable, the person could not have known of his or her susceptibility to such a disproportionate reaction.

Pathological intoxication "has been a medical diagnosis since the nineteenth century," although the symptoms and caused of such a disorder were inconsistently described in the early medical literature.[61] Modern medicine is dubious of such mental condition as related to the consumption of alcohol. If fact, the American Psychiatric Association criticized the notion of pathological intoxication as being a remnant of a time before modern understandings of psychiatry:

> The literature on [pathological intoxication] is entirely anecdotal, filled with inconsistencies, and intertwined with comorbid factors that could account for [pathological intoxication]; it contains no clear empirical evidence to support its existence. Numerous scientific studies have failed to reproduce this syndrome in a laboratory setting, and no double-blind, placebo-controlled experiments have been performed that establish the existence of [pathological intoxication].[62]

Perhaps it is unsurprising, therefore, that several states do not recognize pathological intoxication stemming from the voluntary consumption of alcohol.[63]

Pathological intoxication may also be deemed to occur when a patient experiences a state of intoxication as the unforeseeable side-effect of a medically prescribed drug. Note the use of the word "unforeseeable" as opposed to "unforeseen." If the side-effect is one that is warned against on the bottle or in the packaging, then presumably it is not unforeseeable. Following the same logic, if the voluntary consumption of a prescribed drug has a stronger effect than the one anticipated, or if someone took more than the prescribed dosage, that would not render the intoxication pathological and, therefore, involuntary.[64] The "You Make the Public Policy Call" contained in Box 13.3 explores how pathological intoxication might work in real cases.

BOX 13.3

YOU MAKE THE PUBLIC POLICY CALL

Did Their Medicine Made Them Do It?

William Freeman killed his best friend, Donny Hazelwood, by shooting him in the head at a hunting cabin. At his trial, Freeman could not answer why he had shot his best friend, and he was subsequently convicted of murder. Furthermore, Freeman's long-term use of what was supposed to be a very short-term drug, Halcion, was never raised as a defense in his murder trial. Two years later, Freeman's family sued the Upjohn Company, claiming that Freeman had suffered a homicidal reaction to his prescription sleeping pills. The sleeping pills, manufactured solely by Upjohn under the brand name Halcion, were, at the time, the most widely prescribed in the world. Freeman's family alleged that Upjohn failed to warn about Halcion's potentially adverse side effects, including amnesia, aggression, paranoia, and hallucinations. After a five-week civil trial, the jury rendered the nation's first verdict in a Halcion case. The Texas jury determined that Upjohn failed to warn physicians adequately of the potentially violent side effects of Halcion and awarded the Freeman family $1.8 million.[134]

The same year as the Freeman case, fifty-seven-year-old Ilo Grundberg killed her eighty-three-year-old mother. She could not explain why she shot her mother eight times in the head. Untimely, the state dismissed murder charges against Grundberg "after a court-appointed psychiatrist concluded that Grundberg acted involuntarily due to an adverse reaction to Halcion."[135]

1. Do you think these cases fall within the ambit of either the voluntary intoxication defense or the involuntary intoxication defense vis-à-vis a pathological reaction to the drug? Explain your reasoning.
2. What kind of proof should be required before allowing a pathological intoxication criminal defense based on a "my medicine made me do it" argument? Do you think such a defense would be easily abused? Why or why not?

PROCEDURAL DEFENSES

Procedural defenses are technical defenses created under the law for public policy reasons. Factual guilt, criminal culpability, or situational circumstances are irrelevant to these defenses. Rather, procedural defenses are rooted in concern for due process and other forms of procedural justice. At least two procedural defenses are provided for in the US Constitution itself—in the Fifth Amendment's prohibition against double jeopardy and in the Sixth Amendment's guarantee of a speedy trial. The following sections explores both of these defenses, along with some other procedural defenses of note.

Double Jeopardy

The Fifth Amendment to the US Constitution contains a clause that states, "nor shall any person be subject for the same offense to be twice put in jeopardy of life or limb." The US Supreme Court has interpreted the Double Jeopardy Clause as guaranteeing three distinct, albeit related rights: "It protects against a second prosecution for the same offense after acquittal, against a second prosecution for the same offense after conviction, and against multiple punishments for the same offense."[65] The **double jeopardy** defense argues that one of these three rights was violated.

Double jeopardy protections apply to criminal prosecutions for felonies and misdemeanor alike, as well as to juvenile delinquency proceedings, provided that the prosecutions or punishments are for the same offense.[66] Put differently, double jeopardy does not apply to civil actions arising from the same course of conduct for which any criminal prosecution may have occurred.

SAME OFFENSE

A defendant may not be prosecuted more than once for the *same offense*. Under the US Supreme Court's decision in *Blockburger v. United States,* when "the same act or transaction constitutes a violation of two distinct statutory provisions, the test to be applied to determine whether there are two offenses or only one is whether each provision requires proof of an additional fact which the other does not."[67] Under this approach, if two people conspired to rob a bank and then did so, they could both be prosecuted for the inchoate offense of conspiracy in addition to the target crime of bank robbery.[68] But if two crimes share the same elements, such that one is a lesser included offense of the other, then two crimes constitute the same offense for double jeopardy purposes. For example, larceny is a lesser included offense of robbery. If someone were tried for a robbery, double jeopardy would prohibit a subsequent trial for larceny stemming from the same course of events.

WHEN IS SOMEONE IN JEOPARDY?

The protections of the Double Jeopardy Clause only apply after jeopardy attaches in a criminal proceeding. Someone is "in jeopardy" once the jury is impaneled and sworn.[69]

But when a defendant has a bench trial—a trial without a jury in which the judge acts as both the trier of fact and trier of law—jeopardy attaches when the judge begins to hear evidence. Jeopardy attaches to all criminal proceedings, whether felony or misdemeanor, and to juvenile delinquency proceedings, even though juvenile proceedings are technically civil in nature.

EXCEPTIONS TO DOUBLE JEOPARDY

A second trial for the same offense is generally permitted if a mistrial is declared during the first trial because the jury deadlocked, meaning it members could not reach a verdict.[70] Similarly, retrial is generally allowed if a defendant's conviction is overturned on appeal for reasons other than insufficiency of the evidence.[71]

Double jeopardy also does not bar successive trials or punishments by separate sovereigns, a principle affirmed by the US Supreme Court's 2019 decision in *Gamble v. United States*.[72] Thus, if a person's actions violate both state and federal laws, that person may be prosecuted for the state law violations in state court and the federal law violations in federal courts.[73] Similarly, double jeopardy does not bar prosecutions by two different states since each state is its own separate sovereign entity.

By contrast, a state and its municipalities (whether county or local governments) are not separate sovereigns. For example, in *Waller v. Florida*,[74] the defendant was charged and convicted of violating two ordinances enacted by the City of St. Petersburg—one for destruction of city property and the other for breach of the peace. The state subsequently charged him with a theft offense for the same acts that formed the basis of his city ordinance convictions. The US Supreme Court held that double jeopardy prohibited the prosecution under state law for theft because, under the state constitution,

> "[T]he judicial power of the State of Florida is vested in a supreme court . . . and such other courts, including municipal courts . . . as the legislature may from time to time ordain and establish." These provisions . . . demonstrate that the judicial power to try petitioner on the first charges in municipal court springs from the same organic law that created the state court of general jurisdiction in which petitioner was tried and convicted for a felony.[75]

Accordingly, double jeopardy not only bars repeated prosecutions by a state and a municipality in that state, but also by multiple municipalities within the same state.

Speedy Trial

The right to a **speedy trial** is guaranteed by the Sixth Amendment to the US Constitution. Importantly, the right only attaches only once a criminal prosecution has begun and it extends only to those persons who have been officially accused in the course of that prosecution, usually by arrest or indictment.[76]

THE CONSTITUTIONAL RIGHT

In the landmark case of *Barker v. Wingo*, the US Supreme Court explained that the Sixth Amendment's provisions dealing with speedy trials stemmed from the fact that unnecessary delays, whether intentional or a function of negligence, can prejudice an accused person's rights to defend themselves.[77] Thus, when the right is violated, a defendant can seek a complete dismissal of the charges. The Court set forth a four-factor balancing test to guide courts when evaluating claims by defendants that their speedy trial rights have been violated. These factors include:

1. the length of the delay;
2. the reason for the delay;
3. the defendant's assertion of the right; and
4. the prejudice resulting from the delay.

The length of a delay is clearly the "triggering mechanism" for asserting a speedy trial violation.[78] If, after delay, the defendant asserts his or her speedy trial rights, then the question as to whether charges should be dismissed will turn on the answers to the other questions. Consider what the Supreme Court said about the reasons for the delay:

> A deliberate attempt to delay the trial in order to hamper the defense should be weighted heavily against the government. A more neutral reason such as negligence or overcrowded courts should be weighted less heavily but nevertheless should be considered since the ultimate responsibility for such circumstances must rest with the government, rather than with the defendant. Finally, a valid reason, such as a missing witness, should serve to justify appropriate delay.[79]

Finally, courts must look at whether the defendant's case has been hurt in some way as a function of the delay. Certainly, lengthy periods of pretrial detention and the emotional toll of having criminal charges pending both play some role in this factor.[80] But what the courts are really concerned about is whether the ability to fairly litigate one's defense has been materially hampered. "If witnesses die or disappear during a delay, the prejudice is obvious. There is also prejudice if defense witnesses are unable to recall accurately events of the distant past. Loss of memory, however, is not always reflected in the record, because what has been forgotten can rarely be shown."[81]

STATUTORY RIGHTS: STATUTES OF LIMITATIONS

In 1974, Congress enacted the federal Speedy Trial Act.[82] That law established specific time periods in which federal criminal cases need to be commenced and prosecuted. For example, an indictment (or other formal charging mechanism) is supposed to issue within 30 days of arrest and a trial is supposed to be begin within 70 days of formal charges being filed. This law works independently of the Sixth Amendment, although it was clearly aimed at making sure that cases move along in the federal system on a schedule designed to honor speedy trial rights. Nonetheless, there are many reasons for delay that are specifically excluded from the time calculations under the statute that range from the need to handle pretrial motions and to, coordinate prosecutions among defendants in complex cases, to delays caused by the unavailability of the defendant or a key witness.

Each US state has a parallel state speedy trial statute designed to move criminal cases forward in a timely manner. But the limit vary dramatically; some set specific times while others do not. The far more common approach to enforcing the timeliness of prosecutions is via statutes of limitations. A **statute of limitations** requires prosecutors to charge a crime within a specified period of time, such as misdemeanors within a year and felonies with three, five, or seven years. But such statutes are, as their name implies, a statutory, not constitutional, creation. Thus, the limitations period may be abolished either for specific crimes (e.g., murder, child molestation, tax fraud) or even for all crimes (e.g., Wyoming and South Carolina).

Entrapment and Outrageous Governmental Conduct

> Ken is desperately in need of money. He approaches Rocky for a loan. Rocky refuses, but convinces Ken, who has no history of drug use, to join a drug transaction. Ken and Rocky drive to a highway intersection where they meet Willy. Willy gives Ken $300. Willy and Ken agree to meet later that day to complete the transaction. Ken reluctantly accepts a bag containing three grams of cocaine from Rocky. Rocky, Ken and Willy later meet in a parking lot. When Ken gives Willy the bag, he is arrested and charged with dealing in cocaine.[83]

Under these facts, Ken will almost certainly be convicted. But what if Willy were an undercover officer who pressured Rocky to act as a government informant in order to avoid punishment on other charges? These facts occurred in *Kats v. Indiana*.[84] Ken's conviction was ultimately set aside on the grounds of entrapment.

Entrapment "refers to the use of inducements that cause a normally law-abiding person to commit a crime."[85] This judicially created is designed to prevent government officials, especially law enforcement officers, from instigating otherwise innocent people to commit crimes.[86] The defense appears to have been recognized by courts during prohibition as means of keeping police behavior in check.[87]

Procedurally, entrapment is an affirmative defense that must be pled in a timely manner. The defendant must admit to committing the crime and, at minimum, come forward with some evidence that would support proof of the following elements at trial:

1. a governmental agent must have originated the idea to commit the crime in question;
2. that governmental agent must induce, incite, deceive, or otherwise unduly persuade the defendant to commit the crime; and
3. the defendant must not have been predisposed to commit the crime.[88]

At trial, the burden of persuasion varies. In some states, the defendant must prove all elements of entrapment by a preponderance of the evidence.[89] In other states and in the federal system, the defendant must come forward with some evidence of governmental inducement. The burden then shifts to the prosecution to prove, beyond a reasonable doubt, that there was either no inducement or that the defendant was predisposed to commit the crime.[90]

MERE SOLICITATION DOES NOT QUALIFY

Entrapment does not occur when someone is ready to commit a crime and is merely solicited to do so. "Suspected persons can be tested by being offered an opportunity to transgress the law; however, they may not be put under any extraordinary temptation or inducement."[91] Thus, for instance, person seeking to hire a prostitute who solicits an undercover vice officer and is then arrested has not been entrapped. If an undercover officer were to solicit someone who readily agrees to an act of prostitution, that too would not constitute entrapment.[92]

The same principle applies to drug transitions. An undercover law enforcement officer who offers to buy drugs from a dealer does not entrap the person selling the controlled substances.[93] Even elaborate "sting" operations do not constate entrapment, provided that they merely offer people the opportunity to engage in criminal conduct.[94] In short, entrapment requires some conduct—beyond mere solicitation—that constitutes inducement.

INDUCEMENT AND PREDISPOSITION

The type of inducement that a defendant must prove to show entrapment does not necessarily require deceit, such as laying a trap.[95] Rather, the type of inducement can involve any conduct that creates a substantial risk that an otherwise law-abiding citizen would commit an offense, including "fraudulent representations, threats, coercive tactics, harassment, promises of reward."[96] But even less coercive conduct can satisfy the inducement element of entrapment, such as "aggressive persuasion, coercive encouragement, lengthy negotiations, pleading or arguing with the defendant, repeated or persistent solicitation, persuasion, importuning, and playing on sympathy or other emotion."[97]

In practice, establishing inducement is usually not the difficult part of an entrapment defense. Rather, the tricky part concerns the final element. A defendant must show that he or she was not predisposed to commit the crime. That's an uphill battle for someone who did, in fact, commit the offense! Nonetheless, it is possible to do so if they person lacked a prior criminal record for offenses related to the one charged and, most importantly, expressed reluctance to engage in the criminal activity but did so only after some governmental agent pressured the defendant to do so.[98]

United States v. Jacobson is one of the leading entrapment cases ever decided by the US Supreme Court.[99] The defendant in that case ordered magazines through an adult bookstore that contained nude photos of nude preteens and teenagers. He thought that he had ordered nudist magazines and was surprised to see photos of underage minors in them. The minors were not engaged in sexual activity. And, importantly, neither ordering nor receiving such magazines was legal illegal at the time. Shortly thereafter, however, Congress enacted a law making it illegal to receive sexually explicit materials of children through the mail. Government agents found the defendant's name and address in the bookstore's mailing list and then reached out to him over a two-and-half-year period of time "through five fictitious organizations and a bogus pen pal, to explore [his] willingness to break the new law by ordering sexually explicit photographs of children through the mail."[100] He eventually responded to one solicitation and ordered a magazine that depicted teens engaged in sexual activity. He was arrested and convicted of possession of child pornography. The Court overturned his conviction because there was no evidence that the defendant was predisposed to commit the offense. His initial magazine order was legal. His subsequent, illegal order occurred only after "he had already been the target of twenty-six months of repeated mailings and communications from Government agents and fictitious organizations."[101]

THE MODEL PENAL CODE'S REJECTION OF SUBJECTIVE ENTRAPMENT

The Model Penal Code rejected the subjective approach that examines the defendant's character and predisposition to commit crimes.[102] Rather, the Code uses an objective approach to the entrapment defense by asking a court to determine, as a matter of law, whether governmental actors either (1) knowing made "false representations designed to induce the belief that such conduct is not prohibited"; or (2) employed "methods of persuasion or inducement that create a substantial risk that such an offense will be committed by persons other than those who are ready to commit it."[103] Under this approach, which a minority of US jurisdictions use, the inquiry focuses on the governmental conduct, not a defendant's predisposition to commit a criminal offense. In *People v. Wisneski*, for instance, a court determined that a physician had been entrapped when police sent in a woman to pose as a patient who engaged in sexual activity with the physician in order to get him to write her a prescription for narcotics.[104]

The objective approach to entrapment is closely related to the defense of **outrageous government conduct**. This criminal defense posits the "conduct of law enforcement agents is so outrageous that due process principles would absolutely bar the government from invoking judicial processes to obtain a conviction."[105] It is extraordinarily rare for this defense to be successful, though. It generally requires proof of excessive government involvement in the creation of the crime. For example, a court dismissed drug charges against defendants in a case in which police manufactured crack cocaine and then arrested the people who bought the crack from them.[106]

Immunity

There are three types of immunity from criminal prosecution: legislative immunity, diplomatic immunity, and witness immunity, which may come in one of two forms.

First, Article I, Section 6 of the US Constitution states that members of Congress "shall in all cases except treason, felony, and breach of the peace, be privileged from arrest during their attendance at the sessions of their respective houses, and in going to and returning from the same." This type of **legislative immunity** is weak since charges may be held in abeyance against members of Congress until the legislative body adjourns.

Second, nearly every nation on Earth has signed onto the Vienna Convention on Diplomatic Relations.[107] This international treaty provides that all diplomatic officers, such as ambassadors and consuls, their families, have full **diplomatic immunity** from local jurisdiction. That means they are not subject to criminal prosecution or civil lawsuits while abroad. Even the staff of diplomatic agents enjoy varying degrees of immunity.[108] Collectively, diplomatic immunity promotes effective foreign relations and prevents diplomats from political and legal harassment while in host nations. "If American diplomats did not have immunity, they would be at constant risk of detention and prosecution on trumped-up charges, especially in countries where the United States is unpopular or where the government bows to popular pressure."[109] Importantly, diplomatic immunity may be waived by the foreign government of which a diplomat is a citizen.[110] When a diplomat commits a serious crime, the host country may make a formal request to the foreign government to waive diplomatic immunity. If the foreign government refuses, then the diplomat in question can be expelled from the host country.[111]

Finally, the federal and most state governments have enacted statutes that provide for granting immunity to cooperating witnesses under specific circumstances. Witness immunity serves to accommodate the mandates of the Fifth Amendment's privilege against self-incrimination (Chapter 2) while simultaneously allowing the government to a witness to testify in order to prosecute important cases. Witnesses may be grated either transactional immunity or use immunity. Witness **transactional immunity** protects a witness from prosecution for all of the offense related to the witness's cooperating testimony. By contrast, witness **use immunity** (sometimes referred to as "derivative use immunity") only bars the subsequent use of compelled testimony from being used against a witness in subsequent prosecution, but such a prosecution may still go forward using other evidence. As you might imagine, most cooperating witnesses strongly prefer transaction immunity over use immunity.

Selective Prosecution

Prosecutors in the United States are vested with incredibly broad discretion. They have virtually unfettered discretion with regard to whether to charge or decline to prosecute any case.[112] They have similar latitude with regard to whether to offer and accept plea bargains and, if so, under what terms. But the authority to be harsh or lenient can lead to systematic unfairness through discrimination.[113]

In the 1880s, San Francisco ordinance that prohibited operating laundries in wooden buildings without the consent of the board of supervisors. When two Chinese people were convicted of violating the ordinance, they successfully appealed their convictions to the US Supreme Court by showing that the board routinely denied all applications from Chinese applicants but approved nearly all the applications filed by non-Chinese people. Although this landmark case, *Yick Wo v. Hopkins*,[114] never mentions the phrase "selective prosecution," it its credited for recognizing the defense by holding that discriminatory prosecutions violate the guarantee of equal protection (Chapter 2).[115]

Selective prosecution (sometimes referred to as discriminatory prosecution) is premised on the argument that the government is targeting the defendant for impermissible reasons that are not supposed to guide the criminal law or judicial process.[116] In other words, people asserting this defense allege that the enforcement or prosecution of a criminal law is "directed so exclusively against a particular class of persons . . . with a mind so unequal and oppressive" so as to amounts to a denial of equal protection.[117]

In *United States v. Kahn*,[118] the defendants were charged with several crimes stemming from their connections to Islamic terrorist groups, including conspiracy to violate the Neutrality Act, a law enacted in the 1930s in response to the growing threats that eventually led to the Second World War. The Act makes it a federal offense to take plan, facilitate or take part in any "military or naval expedition or enterprise" that might to be carried out against a US ally "with whom the United States is at peace."[119] The defendants were convicted of violating this Act for "training co-conspirators in combat skills through paintball games" and helping them acquire weapons that might be used in Kashmir to fire on people and positions in India.[120] The defendants argued that they were being selectively prosecuted for being "Muslim in a post-9/11 world."[121] In support of this argument, they offered evince that the US government did not prosecute more than twenty members of the Cambodian Freedom Fighters who planned and successfully launched an attack against Cambodia, nor did it prosecute Irish-Catholic Americans who provided money and weapons to the Irish Republican Army who carried out terrorist attacks against England.[122] In rejecting such a defense, a federal appeals court reasoned that "[t]he Executive branch has the right to focus its prosecutorial energies on alleged terrorist groups that present the most direct threat to the United States and its interests."[123]

Claims of selective prosecution are extraordinarily difficult to prove. They require proof that police or prosecutors involved in the particular case are motivated by some impermissible type of discrimination, such as on the case of race, ethnicity, religion, or sex. Neither anecdotal evidence, like that in the *Khan* case, nor statistical proof of discriminatory effect suffice without additional proof of discriminatory purpose.[124] This requires a showing that the government "declined to prosecute similarly-situated suspects" of other races, ethnicities, religions, or sexes for violating the same law.[125] To say this presents defendants with an uphill battle would be an understatement, especially because all of the evidence "to prove such a claim lie in the government's hands."[126] Obtaining that evidence is quite difficult since it requires the defendant to make a strong preliminary showing of discriminatory prosecution before a court will allow discovery (the process of turning over information relating to a legal dispute), yet it is that very process of discovery that may reveal the evidence needed to support such a claim. This catch-22 situation is exacerbated by the fact that courts are rarely swayed by statistical evidence, leaving "defendants with little proof beyond their suspicions of discrimination."[127] As a result, such defenses are rarely pled and succeed even more infrequently.

CONCLUSION

Learning Objectives	Summaries
1. Evaluate the circumstances under which mistakes may constitute a criminal defense.	Ignorance of or a mistake as to the meaning of a law does not give rise as a valid criminal defense unless the law has not been made reasonably available or if the is founded upon an official statement of law. By contrast, an honest and reasonable mistake of fact can serve as a valid criminal defense if the mistake negates the *mens rea* for the crime.
2. Compare and contrast how the defenses of necessity and duress work.	Necessity and duress are both compulsion of circumstance defenses that seek to justify or excuse criminal conduct if there is an emergency which threatens the defendant with serious, imminent harm that the actor bears no fault in facilitating, and harm avoided must be more substantial than that harm caused by the commission of the crime.
3. Explain the requirements for a successful defense of intoxication.	Depending on the jurisdiction, voluntary intoxication may be a partial defense that mitigates specific intent crimes to general intent crimes, provided that the intoxication actually negates purpose or knowledge; it generally cannot be used to excuse crimes that carry recklessness or negligence. By contrast, involuntary intoxication can be complete defense to both specific and general intent crimes if the intoxication negates the *mens rea* of the offense, and if it was either not self-induced or if it rendered the person temporarily insane.
4. Discuss the scope of double jeopardy as a criminal defense.	Double jeopardy protects against a second prosecution for the same offense after acquittal, against a second prosecution for the same offense after conviction, and against multiple punishments for the same offense. It does not apply to mistrials on account of a deadlocked jury; if a conviction was overturned on appeal for any reason other than insufficiency of the evidence; or to prosecutions by separate sovereigns.
5. Differentiate the constitutional and statutory bases for speedy trial defenses.	The Sixth Amendment bars criminal prosecutions that were unnecessarily delayed if there are no good reasons for the delay and if the delay somehow prejudiced the defendant's case. Statutes of limitations, however, established specific time periods in which federal criminal cases need to be commenced and prosecuted.
6. Define the elements of the entrapment and outrageous governmental conduct defenses.	Both defenses are designed to limit governmental author. Entrapment applies when a government actor originates the idea to commit a crime and then induces a defendant to commit it despite the defendant's lack of predisposition to commit the offense. Outrageous government conduct occurs when the conduct of law enforcement agents is so outrageous that due process principles would absolutely bar the government from invoking judicial processes to obtain a conviction.

Learning Objectives	Summaries
7. Explain the primary ways in which someone might be immune from prosecution.	Legislators are temporarily immune from prosecution while in attendance at the sessions of their respective houses, and in going to and returning from the same. Diplomatic are completely immune from all local and civil jurisdiction. Cooperating witnesses may be granted transactional immunity, which protects a witness from prosecution for all of the offenses related to the witness's testimony, or use immunity, which bars the subsequent use of compelled testimony from being used against a witness in subsequent prosecution.
8. Assess the defense of selective prosecution.	Selective prosecution is premised on the argument that the government is targeting the defendant for impermissible reasons, such as race, religion, or sex, that are not supposed to guide the criminal law or judicial process. It is extraordinary difficult to prove since neither anecdotal evidence nor statistical proof of discriminatory effect suffice without additional proof of discriminatory purpose.

KEY TERMS

diplomatic immunity
double jeopardy
duress
entrapment
involuntary intoxication
legislative immunity
mistake of fact
mistake of law
necessity
outrageous government conduct
pathological intoxication
procedural defenses
selective prosecution
speedy trial
statute of limitations
transactional immunity
use immunity
voluntary intoxication

14

Defenses of Excuse

Outline

LEARNING OBJECTIVES

1. Explain how young age can excuse criminal conduct.
2. Compare and contrast competency to stand trial from insanity.
3. Evaluate the different approaches to the insanity defense.
4. Analyze the salient differences between the insanity and diminished capacity defenses.

INTRODUCTION

The doctrine of culpability presumes the mental capacity to commit crime (Chapter 1). If such capacity is lacking, due to reasons like youthful age or mental illness, the criminal law has long recognized a series of defenses which excuse what would otherwise constitute criminal conduct. In this chapter, we explore three of leading defenses of excuse premised on mental incapacity: age, insanity, and diminished capacity.

AGE

The law refers to a person who has not reached the age of majority, usually set at age eighteen, as a *minor* or an *infant*. The defense of **age** or **infancy** refers to someone whose youthful age excuses their criminal liability.

The ecclesiastical and Roman law doctrine of *doli incapax* expressed the belief that a child under the age of seven was "incapable of evil."[1] In the middle ages, England adopted this rationale by establishing a conclusive presumption that of a child under the age of seven could not form *mens rea* and, therefore, lacked the mental capacity to commit a crime.[2] Between the ages of seven and fourteen, the law continued to presume that children could not differentiate right from wrong and, therefore, could not commit a crime, but that presumption was rebuttable.[3] By the time children reached the age of fourteen, the common law presumed them to be both sane and capable of formulating the necessary mental intent to commit of a crime. Evidence to the contrary, however, was admissible to rebut the presumption of capacity in an individual case.[4]

US states take a broad range of approaches to age as a criminal defense. Some adopted the common-law model,[5] while others modified the age at which criminal incapacity was presumed for children.[6] Today, "the application of the infancy defense in the United States is primarily addressed by statute and the age at which the infancy defense applies varies by jurisdiction. Significantly, it is the age at the time of the alleged conduct and not at the time of prosecution that is controlling."[7] Regardless of the age at which the presumption of capacity attaches, jurisdiction over such juvenile offenders usually lies with a juvenile court.[8] Nearly all states, however, allow juveniles to be tried as adults either though judicial, prosecutorial, or statutory waivers to adult court.[9] In some states, the defense of youthful age is irrelevant when a child is charged in the juvenile justice system because adjudication as a delinquent is not the same as being convicted of a crime.[10] In other states, minors may assert a defense that they lacked the capacity to commit a crime because a statutory presumption of juvenile incapacity applies in juvenile proceedings.[11] Consider the following case.

STATE of Washington, Respondent,

v.

Carlos LINARES and Isaac Lee PAM, Appellants.

880 P.2d 550 (Wash. Ct. App. 1994).

* * *

[Linares, age 11, was convicted of burglary for breaking into an elementary school with two other boys and stealing a radio. Pam, also 11, was convicted of malicious mischief for breaking windows on an office building by throwing rocks at them. Washington establishes a statutory presumption of incapacity for children between 8 and 12 years of age that applies in juvenile proceedings. The State has the burden of rebutting the presumption of incapacity by clear and convincing evidence at a hearing to determine a child's capacity to commit a crime.]

At Linares' capacity hearing, Officer Sweeney testified that Linares admitted entering the school and taking a radio. He also testified that Linares made the following statement: "I know what I did is wrong. Those things didn't belong to me. I wasn't supposed to be inside the school." Besides Sweeney's testimony, the court heard testimony from Linares, [a teacher, and a school psychologist. . . . His teacher testified that Linares told her that he] knew what he had done was wrong and that he took responsibility for it. She explained that Linares understands rules, but not the consequences of breaking those rules. She also testified that Linares has learning disabilities and was receiving special education at the time. . . .

[The school psychologist] testified that . . . Linares "has a lot of difficulty processing and getting into long-term memory things." She also testified that, on a comprehension subtest designed to measure a child's understanding of cultural and social information, Linares scored below a 7-year-old level. . . . In her opinion, Linares did not have the capacity to understand the crimes with which he was charged.

* * *

At Pam's capacity hearing, [only the arresting officer testified. He said that Pam had acknowledged his actions were wrong].

* * *

Capacity determinations, by their nature, are fact-specific inquiries and must be determined on a case by case basis. In addition to the nature of the crime, the following factors are relevant in determining whether a child knew the act he or she was committing was wrong: (1) whether the child evinced a desire for secrecy, (2) the child's age, (3) prior conduct similar to that charged, (4) any consequences that attached to that conduct, and (5) acknowledgment that the behavior is wrong and could lead to detention.

We conclude that there was sufficient evidence presented in Linares' case to enable a rational trier of fact to find capacity by clear and convincing evidence. In addition to

Linares' statement to Officer Sweeney, the court considered his statement to [his teacher, as well as her testimony and testimony from] a school psychologist regarding his level of maturity and intellectual development. Although some of these witnesses felt Linares did not understand the legal prohibitions against his acts, none testified that he did not understand that his conduct was wrong. The court was also able to observe Linares' demeanor when he took the stand at the hearing. Linares' conduct during and after the break-in is also highly probative in establishing that he appreciated the wrongfulness of his conduct. The finding of capacity is further supported by the fact that Linares was 11 years old at the time of the incident, the upper end of the age range in which a child is presumed incapable of committing a crime.

The State did not meet its burden in Pam's case. Apart from the fact that Pam was 11 years old at the time of the incident, there was no other evidence presented at the hearing besides his custodial statement on which the court could have based its capacity finding. Pam did not testify at the hearing, and the court did not have an opportunity to observe his demeanor. The court did not hear testimony from any other witness besides [the arresting officer]. Although in his statement to [the officer] following the incident Pam acknowledged that his actions were wrong, that is insufficient evidence from which a rational trier of fact could have concluded that Pam appreciated the wrongfulness of his act at the time it was committed.

Questions

1. There was specific evidence that Linares had problems processing cultural and social information, especially in terms of understanding the consequences of one's actions. The court concluded, however, that in spite of such evidence, the state had introduced sufficient evidence to rebut the statutory presumption of incapacity for a juvenile of Linares's age. Upon what evidence did the court rely? Do you agree with the court's conclusion that it rose to the level of clear and convincing evidence? Explain your reasoning.
2. Neuropsychological research suggests that the common law's approach to the defense of young age was remarkably ahead of its time. Specifically, children process information in the part of the brain associated with primitive impulses, whereas adults process similar information in an area of the brain responsible for impulse control, good judgment, the assessment of present risks and future consequences, and moral decision-making. Importantly, that area of the that is not fully developed until one's mid-20s.[12] In light of such findings, do you think that the defense of infancy should be reinstated in those jurisdictions which have ruled the defense inapplicable to delinquency proceedings in juvenile court? Explain your reasoning.

COMPETENCY TO STAND TRIAL

Competency to stand trial is often confused with insanity. The two doctrines are related insofar as they are both concerned with the mental status of a criminal defendant. But they are quite different in terms of their goals, justifications, and processes.

Competency to stand trial is not a criminal defense. The doctrine is concerned with whether a court should be deprived of jurisdiction over a defendant due to his or her state of mind at the time criminal proceedings occur. In contrast, insanity is concerned with the defendant's state of mind at the time the criminal offense is alleged to have taken place.[13]

Because insanity is an affirmative criminal defense, it must be timely asserted by the defendant, usually through counsel, in order to be used at trial. The defendant cannot spring the defense on the court in the middle of trial. Proper notice must be given by the defense that they intend to pursue an insanity defense.[14] If an insanity plea is not entered in a timely manner, the defense is waived.[15] In contrast, competency to stand trial may be raised at any time in the criminal process, even after conviction, by the defense, the prosecution, or by the court itself.[16]

The prosecution usually bears the burden of persuasion of proving, by a preponderance of the evidence, that a defendant is competent to stand trial.[17] There are, however, some states that have shifted the burden of persuasion to the defense. The Supreme Court specifically approved of this allocation of the burden of persuasion over a due process challenge in *Medina v. California*,[18] although the Court invalidated other states' attempts to require the defendant to prove incompetence by clear and convincing evidence.[19]

A trial court judge must conduct an evidentiary hearing whenever there is evidence before the court that raises a "bona fide doubt" about the defendant's competency.[20] Although a concise rule, what constitutes a "bona fide doubt" is ambiguous, and reasonable people can offer differ with respect to whether such a doubt exists given the facts of any particular case.[21]

According to the Supreme Court's 1960 landmark decision in *Dusky v. United States*, competency to stand trial requires a defendant to possess (1) "a rational as well as factual understanding of the proceedings against him" and (2) "sufficient present ability to consult with his lawyer with a reasonable degree of rational understanding."[22]

If, after clinical evaluation and a hearing, the defendant is found competent, the case proceeds to trial. Such a determination of competency does not prevent the defendant from asserting the insanity defense. The more difficult scenario occurs when a defendant is found to be incompetent. The normal course of events in such a case is for criminal proceedings to be held in abeyance while the defendant undergoes treatment to restore competency, usually on an inpatient basis.[23] If, after a period of evaluation often set by statute, the psychiatric staff feels the defendant can be respired to competency, the defendant will remain for treatment and the government must report to the court on the defendant's progress at regular intervals, often every six months. Assuming the original belief of the psychiatric staff was correct and the defendant is restored to competency, he or she will then face trial.

On the other hand, if the defendant's condition is unchanging and the psychiatric staff does not believe the condition will improve, the defendant may not be held indefinitely. This was not always the case, though. Until the Supreme Court's decision in *Jackson v. Indiana*,[24] defendants found incompetent to stand trial were routinely kept hospitalized indefinitely, often for a period of time that was in excess of the maximum sentence that could have been imposed had they been convicted (a fact especially so for defendants charged with misdemeanors). In some cases, such defendants were kept hospitalized for the remainder of their lives.[25] *Jackson* changed that by holding a defendant committed after a finding of incompetency to stand trial could not "be held more than a reasonable period of time necessary to determine whether there is a substantial probability that he will attain that capacity in the foreseeable future"—not at some distant time.[26] Most research suggests that six months is a sufficient period of time to restore a criminal defendant to competence if restoration appears possible,[27] although many state laws provide up to one, three, or even five years to restore competency.[28] If the treatment being provided to the defendant either does not advance the defendant toward competency, or advances the defendant only marginally without a fair probability that competency will be restored within in the foreseeable future, "then the state must either institute customary civil commitment proceedings to detain the defendant, or release the defendant."[29]

INSANITY

The insanity defense[30] is controversial for many reasons, not the least of which is that the public labors under a series of misperceptions about the defense arising from inaccurate fictional stories or from distortions of a small number of nonrepresentative yet highly publicized real cases.[31] Indeed, the public often view the "allegedly 'popular' insanity defense is nothing more than a 'legalistic slight-of-hand.' "[32] But the insanity defense is raised in fewer than 1 percent of all felony cases, and when invoked, it is successful less than 25 percent of the time.[33]

The public also seems to fear that the insanity defense will be used by defendants who fake mental illnesses in order to escape convictions.[34] Hollywood storylines often exacerbate these concerns, although they are ill-founded. Clinicians on both sides of the criminal dispute agree on clinical diagnoses between 88 percent[35] and 92 percent of the time.[36] Moreover, modern diagnostic instruments and procedures allow clinicians to distinguish those who are truly mentally ill and those who are faking between 92 percent and 95 percent of the time.[37] Thus, when defendants fake mental illness, it is extraordinarily difficult for them to "get away with it."[38]

The Wild Beast Defense

Justice Tracy, a thirteenth-century judge in King Edward's court, first formulated the foundation of a common-law insanity defense when he instructed a jury it should acquit a defendant if they found that he was "a man that is totally deprived of his understanding and memory, and doth not know what he is doing, no more than an infant, than a brute, or a wild beast."[39] His wild beast test "set the standard which would be applied in English courts throughout the eighteenth century."[40] There are few records about how the wild beast test was actually applied, but "commentators of the period consistently spoke of a requirement that the defendant lack understanding of good and evil or be devoid of all reason, and often equated the insane with animals or infants."[41]

The defense evolved significantly in 1800 when James Hadfield, believing he was acting on orders from God, shot King George III.[42] At Hadfield's trial for treason, his defense counsel argued that Hadfield's delusions, stemming from head trauma suffered during battle, caused his actions. Several physicians offered testimony corroborating Hadfield's head trauma claims. The jury acquitted Hadfield because "the prisoner appear[ed] to be under the influence of insanity at the time the act was committed."[43]

The *Hadfield* case represented a departure from the wild beast test in two ways. First, "it rejected the argument that the defendant must be totally deprived of all mental faculty before acquittal."[44] Second, it was the first time that a verdict of not guilty by reasons of insanity (NGBRI) "became a separate verdict of acquittal."[45] However, within a few years of the *Hadfield* decision, English jurisprudence reverted to using Justice Tracy's wild beast test, which did require a near complete deprivation of mental faculties for an acquittal.[46]

The *M'Naghten* Test

In 1843, the *M'Naghten* case[47] set a legal standard for insanity that many US jurisdictions still use today. Daniel M'Naghten was indicted for the first-degree murder of Edward Drummond, the secretary to the English Prime Minister Sir Robert Peel. M'Naghten had intended to kill Peel, but mistook Drummond for him. He wanted to kill the Prime Minister "because the Tories in my city follow and persecute me wherever I go, and have entirely destroyed my peace of mind. They do everything in their power to harass and persecute me; in fact, they wish to murder me."[48]

At M'Naghten's trial, defense attorneys argued that he suffered from paranoid persecutory delusions. To support this defense, M'Naghten was represented by four well-respected barristers and nine prominent medical experts.[49] In contrast, the prosecution put on no experts. The jury found M'Naghten not guilty by reason of insanity. In spite of the fact that M'Naghten was committed to Bedlam, the notorious asylum, where he lived until his death, public outrage over the verdict led the House of Lords to enacted what became known as the ***M'Naghten* rule** for insanity. It provides:

1. A person is not responsible for criminal conduct if, at the time of the offense,

2. the defendant suffered from a mental disease or defect
3. that caused the defendant either:
   a. not to know the nature and quality of the act he or she committed, or
   b. knowing the quality or nature of the act, nonetheless not to know that the act was wrong.[50]

The first element illustrates that the insanity defense is concerned with a defendant's mental state at the time the criminal act is alleged to have taken place. The second element requires that the defendant suffer from a "mental disease or defect," a concept explored later in this chapter. And the third part of the test concerns causation—a link between the mental illness and either *cognitive incapacity*—the inability to know the nature and quality of the act committed, or *moral incapacity*—the inability to know that the act committed was wrong.[51]

The cognitive incapacity part of *M'Naghten* excuses liability when the defendant is incapable of forming *mens rea*. For example, if a man strangled another person believing that he was squeezing the juice out of a lemon, he did not understand the nature and quality of his act.[52] Cognitive incapacity is rare because it requires that a person suffer from a psychotic disorder of such severity that he or she is removed from reality and is unaware of his or her actions. For example, M'Naghten knew the nature and quality of his act. He wanted to kill the Prime Minister and attempted to do so. He was, therefore, not cognitively incapacitated under the first prong of this formulation of the test for insanity.

The second part of the *M'Naghten* rule—the lack of moral capacity to distinguish right from wrong—is usually at the crux of an insanity defense. This part of the insanity test relieves a defendant from criminal liability even if the person formed the requisite *mens rea* (as M'Naghten formed an intent to kill) so long as the actor did not understand that his or her act was wrong.[53]

For years, scholars criticized the *M'Naghten* rule because it only looked at the cognitive and moral aspects of the defendant's actions. The test did not evaluate either the affective and volitional elements of human behavior and, therefore, failed to consider "that mentally ill offenders might be aware that their behavior is wrong, yet nonetheless be emotionally unable to restrain themselves or control their conduct."[54] The *M'Naghten* test was also criticized for its focus on "right" and "wrong," a standard that often requires moral judgments.[55] These problems led to the development of other formulations of the insanity defense.

The *Durham* Rule

The US Court of Appeals for the District of Columbia Circuit formulated a new insanity test in *Durham v. United States*.[56] The court held that "an accused is not criminally responsible if his unlawful act was the product of a mental disease or defect."[57] This finding came to be known as the *Durham* "product test" or the ***Durham* rule**.

Although the *Durham* rule did away with both the cognitive focus and moral judgments embedded in the *M'Naghten* test, it proved to be an unworkable standard. It led to an influx of expert witnesses whose testimony largely narrowed the jury's role as fact-finders.[58] Additionally, the number of criminal acquittals rose dramatically.[59] Some viewed this increase as having replaced insanity as a limited excuse with a rule that excused all mentally ill persons from criminal responsibility, regardless of the type or degree of impairment.[60] The *Durham* rule was eventually overruled by the D.C. Court of Appeals in 1972 in *United States v. Brawner*,[61] which adopted a formulation of the insanity defense based on the Model Penal Code. Today, only New Hampshire uses the *Durham* test for insanity.[62]

The ALI/Model Penal Code Affective Test

The Model Penal Code formulation of the insanity defense is usually referred to as the **ALI/MPC affective test** and provides that "a person is not responsible for criminal conduct if, at the time of such conduct as of a result of a mental disease or defect, [the defendant] lacks the substantial capacity to appreciate the criminality of his conduct or to conform his conduct to the requirements of law."[63] The first two elements of the test are the same as those required under the *M'Naghten* rule. Both look at the defendant's conduct at the time of the offense, and both require a mental disease or defect. However, a slight difference in the ALI/MPC formulation of the insanity defense insofar as it specifically excludes antisocial personality disorder and psychopathy.[64] The principal difference concerns the result elements.

As discussed earlier, the *M'Naghten* rule focused on the cognitive aspects of behavior: did the defendant *know* what he or she was doing, and if so, did the defendant *know* it was wrong? It was an all or nothing standard that required total or near total impairment. The ALI/MPC formulation replaced the *M'Naghten* rule's focus on lacking a pure and almost complete cognitive knowledge of the wrongfulness of one's acts with a less stringent test requiring that the defendant lack the "substantial capacity to appreciate" the wrongfulness of actions. As a result, mental health experts and, ultimately, juries were permitted to "consider the defendant's moral, emotional, and legal awareness of the consequences of his or her behavior... [in recognition that] there are gradations of criminal responsibility and that the defendant need not be totally impaired to be absolved of such responsibility."[65]

Additionally, the MPC test for insanity allowed even those who knew and appreciated that their acts were wrong to claiming insanity because they were unable to abide by the law. This aspect is known as the **irresistible impulse test**. The ALI sought to implement the irresistible impulse test nationwide response to its recognition that the evolving state of behavioral science knowledge clearly acknowledged that one's volition was often impacted by mental illness, especially in the presence of compulsions.

The ALI/MPC formulation of the insanity defense was repeatedly criticized by scholars, lawyers, and psychiatrists for the inclusion of the irresistible impulse test.[66] These critics argued that an irresistible impulse was just an impulse that was not, in fact, resisted. For example, would a criminal defendant have committed the crime if a policeman had been next to him? Because the answer to this hypothetical question in all likelihood would be "no," it suggests that the impulse was not truly irresistible. Moreover, allowing such impairment to qualify as the basis of an excuse is inconsistent "with a criminal justice system premised on free will."[67] Despite of the criticisms, a majority of the states and all but one federal circuit eventually adopted this formulation of the insanity defense.

The Insanity Defense Reform Act of 1984

In the late 1970s, John Hinckley, an obsessed fan of Jodie Foster, made several attempts to woo Foster while she was a first-year student at Yale University.[68] When Foster rebuffed his overtures, Hinckley decided he needed to do something that would make an impression on her-some "historic deed [that would] finally gain her respect and love for him."[69] On March 30, 1981, he carried out his plan by attempting to assassinate then President Ronald Reagan.

At his trial for attempted murder, Hinckley asserted the insanity defense. "After weeks of conflicting testimony by defense and prosecution psychiatrists-testimony that struck some as an affront to common sense, the jury found Hinckley not guilty by reason of insanity."[70] At least for some jurors, the ALI/MPC formulation of the insanity defense determined the outcome of the case. One juror reported feeling "trapped" by the test: "My conscience had me voting one way, but the law would not allow me to vote that way."[71]

Hinckley's insanity acquittal sparked a furor over the defense and focused critical, national attention on it.[72] In the wake of the verdict, the insanity defense underwent sweeping reforms in both the federal system and in many states.[73] After twenty-six different pieces of legislation were introduced in Congress to either abolish or restrict the insanity defense at the federal level, Congress enacted the **Insanity Defense Reform Act of 1984 (IDRA)**.[74] In doing so, Congress codified the federal insanity defense for the first time and legislatively overruled the application of the ALI/MPC insanity test in all federal cases.

A defense based on IDRA will prevail if, "at the time of the commission of the acts constituting the offense, the defendant, as of a result of a severe mental disease or defect, was unable to appreciate the nature and quality or the wrongfulness of his acts. Mental disease or defect does not otherwise constitute a defense."[75] In effect, the IDRA returns the law of insanity to where it was at the time the *M'Naghten* rule was adopted. Like the previous insanity defense formulations, the first element looks at the mental state of the defendant at the time of the commission of the offense and the second element requires a mental disease or defect. But the IDRA added the requirement that the mental disease or defect be "severe." This requirement effectively limited the applicability of the defense to people suffering from psychoses and intellectual disability (formerly mental retardation), thereby eliminating many mental illnesses as predicate mental diseases or defects.

The third element of the IDRA is similar to all prior formulations of the insanity defense insofar as there must be a causal nexus between the mental illness and the crime committed. However, the third element changed the insanity defense as it existed in the federal courts quite significantly in two important ways. First, the result element omitted the volitional aspect of the ALI/MPC insanity defense as expressed in the irresistible impulse test. Thus, an inability to conform one's conduct to the requirements of the law does not qualifies as the basis of an insanity defense under the IDRA. Second, the result element effectively reinstated the *M'Naghten* rule with a slight modification. Instead of requiring a lack of knowledge that one's conduct is wrong to qualify a person as legally insane, the IDRA requires an inability to "appreciate" the wrongfulness of one's conduct. This leaves the door open slightly for some affective component, rather than having to focus exclusively on cognitive incapacity.

The IDRA also made a critical change in how the way the insanity defense is litigated. Prior to the IDRA, the prosecution had to prove, beyond a reasonable doubt, that the defendant was legally sane at the time of a criminal offense. The IDRA shifted the burden by making insanity an affirmative defense in which the defense must prove by clear and convincing evidence that the defendant was insane at the time of the criminal offense.[76] Whether this shift in the burden of proof has had a significant impact on case outcomes is questionable considering the few studies that have failed to demonstrate "any consistent relationship between the imposition of the burden of proof and the acquittal rate."[77]

By 1985, thirty-three states had followed Congress in reevaluating the insanity defense as it applied in their respective jurisdictions.[78] Many states followed IDRA and made insanity an affirmative defense, thereby shifting the burden of persuasion from the prosecution to the defense to prove the defendant's insanity, usually by a preponderance of the evidence.[79] Other states left the burden of persuasion with the government to show the defendant's sanity, but tightened the substantive test for insanity by requiring a severe mental disease or defect or some equivalent.[80] Twelve states replaced the insanity defense with some variant of the "guilty, but mentally ill" verdict (discussed in the next section).[81] And five states abolished the insanity defense and replaced it with a more restrictive *mens rea* approach.[82]

Guilty But Mentally Ill

In August 1975, Michigan was the first US state to supplement its tradition not guilty by reason of insanity (NGBRI) verdict by adding another verdict alternative termed **guilty but mentally ill** (GBMI).[83] Under it, a jury may return a verdict of GBMI if the following three criteria were found beyond a reasonable doubt:

1. The defendant is guilty of an offense;
2. The defendant was mentally ill at the time of the commission of the offense; and
3. The defendant was not legally insane at the time of the commission of the offense.

This verdict was, in effect, a compromise. It allowed juries to acquit those defendants who were clearly insane under a traditional NGBRI verdict while also giving jurors a "middle ground" verdict to convict those who were not clearly insane, but who did suffer from a mental illness at the time of the commission of a criminal offense.

The GBMI verdict received much criticism from scholars.[84] Notably, empirical research demonstrated that the verdict had little if any effect on the NGBI adjudication rate, leading researchers to conclude that the new GBMI verdict "merely substituted a new name for certain defendants who, in the absence of the new statute, probably would have been found guilty."[85] Nonetheless, several states followed Michigan's lead and adopted the GMBI verdict.[86]

One of the primary objectives of the GBMI verdict was to get treatment for those defendants who, although mentally ill, were not so cognitively impaired as to be rendered legally insane. In reality, however, "GBMI prisoners are treated like any other prisoners; they will get extra treatment if they need it, but that's the same treatment [the prison will] give everyone else."[87] In fact, researchers reported that 75 percent of GBMI defendants in Michigan received no psychiatric treatment at all, usually due to financial constraints.[88] But even when treatment is provided, whether it treatment produces effective outcomes is questionable. As the former chair of the parole board in Kentucky stated, "From psychological evaluations and treatment summaries, the Board can detect no differences in treatment or outcome for [inmates adjudicated as GBMI] from those who have been adjudicated as simply 'guilty.' "[89]

Guilty Except Insane

Not all states structured their insanity defense variations along the lines of GBMI. Under Arizona's approach, for instance, a person may be found **guilty except insane** (GEI) if

1. at the time of the commission of the criminal act
2. the person was afflicted with a mental disease or defect of such severity
3. that the person did not know the criminal act was wrong.[90]

Like the IDRA, this approach makes insanity an affirmative defense which the defendant must prove by clear and convincing evidence. Arizona's GEI statute also significantly restricts the mental illness that may qualify as the basis of a GEI plea. The "Statutory Analysis Exercise" in Box 14.1 explores these limitations.[91]

The GEI verdict holds a defendant responsible (i.e., "guilty"), but simultaneously exempts the legally insane from criminal punishment. Arizona's statute returns to the *M'Naghten* rule's concept of defining insanity as not knowing right from wrong. As a result, it the statute suffers from the same criticisms levied against the *M'Naghten* test for this earlier formulation—its exclusive focus on the cognitive aspects of thought and behavior to the exclusion of affective elements.

In Arizona, a defendant found GEI of a crime involving a death or physical injury does not go to a correctional institution, but rather enters the custody of a state-run mental health facility.[92] The person remains confined until it is shown by clear and convincing

BOX 14.1

STATUTORY ANALYSIS EXERCISE

What Qualifies as GEI?

Natalie was detained in a juvenile detention center. While there, she attempted suicide twice. One day, she refused to return to her cell as instructed. Officers responded and tried to forcibly take Natalie back to her cell. Natalie resisted, causing the specialized suicide prevention clothing she was wearing to open, exposing her. That caused one of the officers to let go of her. Natalie responded by charging at and then head-butting the officer, causing the officer to fall against a wall and suffer a concussion. Natalie was charged with aggravated assault for the incident.

At her delinquency proceeding, Natalie argued she was GEI. because, as the Arizona statute provides, she "was afflicted with a mental disease or defect of such severity that the person did not know the criminal act was wrong." An expert testified that Natalie suffered from Bipolar Type I disorder, a severe mood disorder in which people vary from manic episodes to severe depression. On direct examination, he stated that it was "likely that Natalie did not know what she was doing was wrong, nor did she even take that into account at the moment." However, under further examination by the court, he agreed it was equally likely Natalie had reacted angrily to the conditions in which she found herself, including that she had been detained and made to wear suicide prevention clothing referred to as a "turtle suit."

Arizona law states:

> A person may be found guilty except insane if at the time of the commission of the criminal act the person was afflicted with a mental disease or defect of such severity that the person did not know the criminal act was wrong. A mental disease or defect constituting legal insanity is an affirmative defense. Mental disease or defect does not include disorders that result from acute voluntary intoxication or withdrawal from alcohol or drugs, character defects, psychosexual disorders or impulse control disorders. Conditions that do not constitute legal insanity include but are not limited to momentary, temporary conditions arising from the pressure of the circumstances, moral decadence, depravity or passion growing out of anger, jealousy, revenge, hatred or other motives in a person who does not suffer from a mental disease or defect or an abnormality that is manifested only by criminal conduct.[190]

1. Does Natalie suffer from a qualifying mental disease or defect? Why or why not?
2. Apply Arizona GEI statute to Natalie's case. What should the outcome be? Explain your reasoning.

evidence that he or she no longer suffers from the mental disease or defect. However, a conditional release is available if the person is still mentally ill, but the illness is under control and the person poses no danger to his or herself or to others.[93] Additionally, if the person's crime did not involve a death or physical injury, then a court must release the person upon a judicial determination that he or she poses no risk of danger to himself and herself or to others.[94] On the other hand, if there is a risk of dangerousness, then civil commitment proceedings are instituted, and their strict due process supervision requirements must be met.[95]

Abolition of the Insanity Defense: The *Mens Rea* Approach

Five states—Alaska, Idaho, Montana, Utah, and Kansas—have abolished the traditional insanity defense and allow the introduction of mental illness evidence only to show that the level of *mens rea* the state requires was not possessed by the defendant due to his or her mental condition.[96] This is known as the ***mens rea* approach**.

In *State v. Korell*,[97] the Montana Supreme Court rejected a challenge to the constitutionality of abolishing the insanity defense, relying primarily on the US Supreme Court's decision in *Leland v. Oregon*.[98] In *Leland*, the Court upheld an Oregon statute requiring the defendant to prove insanity beyond a reasonable doubt.[99] The *Leland* Court reasoned this was constitutionally permissible because the burden to prove the requisite *mens rea* remained with the prosecution.[100] Relying on this holding, the Montana Supreme Court in *Korell* upheld the abolition of the insanity defense since the state still had to prove the state of mind element of the underlying criminal offense beyond a reasonable doubt.[101] The highest courts of Idaho, Utah, and Kansas all reached similar conclusions,[102] although the Nevada Supreme Court reached the opposite conclusion when it invalidated the state legislature's abolition of the insanity defense on due process grounds.[103]

In 2020, the US Supreme Court decided *Kahler v. Kansas*, which upheld the constitutionality of the *mens rea* approach over a due process challenge, reasoning that "[h]istory shows no deference to *M'Naghten* that could elevate its formula to the level of fundamental principle."[104]

> [A] defendant may introduce any evidence of any mental illness to show that he did not have the intent needed to commit the charged crime. Suppose, for example, that the defendant shot someone dead and goes on trial for murder. He may then offer psychiatric testimony that he did not understand the function of a gun or the consequences of its use—more generally stated, "the nature and quality" of his actions. . . . And a jury crediting that testimony must acquit him. As everyone here agrees, Kansas law thus uses M'Naghten's "cognitive capacity" prong—the inquiry into whether a mentally ill defendant could comprehend what he was doing when he committed a crime. . . . If the defendant had no

> such capacity, he could not form the requisite intent—and thus is not criminally responsible.
>
> [But] Kansas does not recognize any additional way that mental illness can produce an acquittal. Most important for this case, a defendant's moral incapacity cannot exonerate him. . . . Assume, for example, that a defendant killed someone because of an insane delusion that God had ordained the sacrifice. . . . The defendant knew what he was doing (killing another person), but he could not tell moral right from wrong; indeed, he thought the murder morally justified. In many States, that fact would preclude a criminal conviction, although it would almost always lead to commitment in a mental health facility. In Kansas, by contrast, evidence of a mentally ill defendant's moral incapacity—or indeed, of anything except his cognitive inability to form the needed *mens rea*—can play no role in determining guilt . . . [although at] the sentencing phase, a Kansas defendant has wide latitude to raise his mental illness as a reason to judge him not fully culpable and so to lessen his punishment.[105]

This quote illustrates the primary difference between a traditional insanity defense and the *mens rea* approach. Under former, a psychosis responsible for a delusionary belief can excuse the defendant's criminal act because the defendant did not know that what he did was wrong, but that is not true under the *mens rea* approach.[106] The fact that a serious mental illness was responsible for forming the defendant's specific intent to kill is irrelevant for determining guilt, but it would be relevant in sentencing.[107]

What Is a Mental Disease or Defect?

Courts have consistently refused to define the term **mental disease or defect**, instead holding that it constitutes a question of fact to be decided at trial. Courts are guided by the medical categories of mental illnesses as defined by the psychiatric community in the American Psychiatric Association's *Diagnostic and Statistical Manual of Mental Disorders*, currently in its fifth edition (DSM-5).[108]

The DSM-5 contains a cautionary section regarding its use and application in court because the definitions and classifications of disorders in the DSM-5 were "developed to meet the needs of clinicians, public health professionals, and research investigators rather than all of the technical needs of the courts and legal professionals."[109] Nonetheless, court actors often use the DSM when they decide which mental illnesses will qualify as the basis for an insanity plea. However, courts do not rely on medical labels exclusively. "[W]hat definition of 'mental disease or defect' is to be employed by courts enforcing the criminal law is, in the final analysis, a question of legal, moral, and policy—not of medical—judgment."[110] Although the law does not recognize every psychiatric condition in the DSM as a mental disease or defect for insanity defense purposes, without a genuine psychiatric diagnosis, courts rarely allow defendants to plead insanity.

PSYCHOSES

Courts tend to restrict qualifying mental diseases and defects in insanity defense cases to severe conditions that until recently were labeled psychoses, such as schizophrenia, major depressive disorders, and bipolar disorder.[111] These mental illnesses are often "characterized by regressive behavior, inappropriate mood, diminished impulse control," and abnormal thought content, such as delusions and hallucinations.[112] As a result, these disorders significantly impair "a person's ability to think, respond emotionally, remember, communicate, interpret reality, and behave appropriately... so as to interfere grossly with the capacity to meet the ordinary demands of life."[113]

PERSONALITY DISORDERS

According to the DSM, personality disorders represent deeply ingrained and maladaptive patterns of behavior that impair personal relationships or social functioning. Some federal appellate courts have specifically held that personality disorders are not "mental diseases or defects" within the meaning of the insanity defense.[114] Other federal circuit courts have determined that although personality disorders are mental diseases or defects, they are not "severe enough" under the modern federal formulation of the insanity defense to serve as the basis for an insanity defense.[115] At least one federal circuit refused to adopt a rule covering personality disorders as a class of psychiatric diagnoses, considering instead the specific diagnosis on a case-by-case basis.[116]

There is a similar split of authority at the state level regarding whether personality disorders qualify as mental diseases or defects for insanity defense purposes. At least two states, California and Alabama, exclude personality disorders from the definition of mental disease or defect entirely, whereas others exclude only certain types of personality disorders, most notably antisocial personality disorder and psychopathy. All jurisdictions agree, however, that impulse-control disorders like kleptomania, pyromania, and the paraphilias (e.g., pedophilia), do not qualify as mental diseases or defects for insanity defense purposes.[117]

DRUGS, ALCOHOL, AND SETTLED INSANITY

The DSM classifies alcoholism and numerous drug addictions as "substance related disorders." As explained in Chapter 13, involuntary intoxication on drugs or alcohol was a complete defense to a crime at common law and continues to be so in nearly all US jurisdictions today. Voluntary intoxication, however, has never been a complete defense under the criminal law.

Two issues regarding intoxication and insanity that continue to divide US courts. The first is whether an addiction to drugs or alcohol can qualify as a mental disease or defect for the purposes of an insanity defense. The second is whether **settled insanity**—a drug- or alcohol-induced psychosis (when unaccompanied by some other mental illness)—is a qualifying mental disease or defect for an insanity defense. The overwhelming number of US jurisdictions answer both questions in the negative, even though psychiatry recognizes a host of substance abuse disorders as mental illnesses in the DSM. This is even true even for cases involving iatrogenic addictions (i.e., those that resulted from medical treatment).

Alcohol and or drug addiction is not a mental illness for usable in an insanity defense purposes for several reasons, but the primary justification is the voluntariness of the person's addiction. People cannot choose whether to have schizophrenia. But people can choose whether they will drink or take drugs. Biological predispositions to alcoholism and addiction aside, the law takes the view that one should seek treatment for an illness he that one has brought upon oneself, not rather than seeking excuse from the harm he has caused by failing to control his one's own behavior.

What Is Wrong?

What is meant by "wrong" in the insanity defense context of "knowing right from wrong" or "appreciating the wrongfulness" of conduct? The law tends to eschew moral and religious standards in this regard and instead looks to an objective legal standard. Imagine the consequences if a person could argue that killing is not wrong because human sacrifice is considered a sacred act under the tenets of the belief system of a particular religion. For instance, in *State v. Crenshaw*,[118] the defendant killed his wife, delusionally believing that she was having an affair. He claimed he did not know it was "wrong" to kill his wife because, under the tenets of his Muscovite faith, a husband may kill an adulterous wife. The jury and an appellate court rejected this argument, reasoning that "it is society's morals, and not the individual's morals, that are the standard for judging moral wrong under *M'Naghten*."

As the next case indicates, even people with psychotic symptoms may be able to discern right from wrong by societal standards.

Lori BARCROFT, Appellant,

v.

STATE of Indiana, Appellee.

111 N.E.3d 997 (Ind. 2018).

* * *

[The court began by noting the defendant had a normal upbringing and good life until the early 2000s, when her marriage failed and she became depressed.] She sought counseling and underwent periodic mental-health evaluations on an outpatient basis. But other than ADHD, medical records indicate no formal diagnoses of a psychiatric disorder. Still, her cognitive faculties continued to wane. And, in 2007, Barcroft—living then with her son, Jordan Asbury, and his wife Tamia—began to exhibit increasingly odd behavior. According to Asbury, his mother described seeing messages on the refrigerator, she became obsessed with the color of cars, and she often rambled nonsensical codes. This behavior progressively worsened after her father died in 2010.

Concerned with his mother's deteriorating mental health, and fearful for Tamia's life, Asbury confided in Jaman Iseminger, a pastor at the family's church. Pastor Jaman believed Barcroft needed prayers and hospitalization. And he urged Asbury to have his mother leave the home. Indeed, Barcroft moved out sometime in early 2012 to live with her mother.

Two or three months later, . . . Jaman was working in his church office. He had arrived early . . . to meet Jeff Harris, a church volunteer. . . . [A]s Harris was preparing coffee in the church kitchen, he noticed someone walking alongside the building outside, dressed in black clothing and carrying a backpack. [He] went outside to find this person—later identified as Barcroft—peering into a window of the church basement. When he approached her, Barcroft asked if Pastor Jaman was there. Harris reentered the church to find the pastor in his basement office, unaware that Barcroft had followed him into the building. With the pastor in tow, Harris then led the way back to where he had left the visitor. As they ascended the basement stairs, Barcroft stood waiting above at the landing. Harris walked past her, unsuspecting and without comment. Suddenly, a single gunshot shattered the early-morning silence. Harris turned to find Barcroft pointing a gun in his direction, commanding him to "Go. Go."

Harris fled to safety as two more gunshots rang out. From the parking lot, he saw Barcroft run, "crouched down" along the building, and then disappear between two houses across the street. . . . Lisa Walden, another church volunteer, also witnessed Barcroft flee while covering her head with the hood of her black sweatshirt. Moments later, Pastor Jaman emerged from the church . . . [and then died].

The State charged Barcroft with murder. . . . Barcroft invoked the insanity defense and waived her right to a trial by jury. Three mental-health experts testified at Barcroft's bench trial. . . . All three experts concluded that Barcroft was legally insane at the time of the offense and could not appreciate the wrongfulness of her actions. No expert found evidence of feigning or malingering. . . .

Several eyewitnesses also testified at trial: the responding officers, the lead detective, and Harris and Walden. These witnesses—none of whom knew Barcroft prior to the day of the crime—testified only to the defendant's demeanor before, during, and just after the shooting.

The trial court judge found Barcroft GBMI. . . . While acknowledging Barcroft's "complex delusions," the court ultimately concluded that she understood the gravity of her crime. . . .

* * *

Expert opinion . . . is purely advisory, not conclusive. . . . Even when experts are unanimous in their opinion, the factfinder may discredit their testimony—or disregard it altogether—and rely instead on other probative evidence from which to infer the defendant's sanity. . . .

* * *

Barcroft contends that it was contrary to law for the trial court to find her GBMI. . . . [But] ample demeanor evidence supports the trial court's rejection of Barcroft's insanity defense. . . .

First, Barcroft exhibited deliberate, premeditated conduct in the weeks and days leading up to the crime: She asked another member of the church when Pastor Jaman planned to return from a mission trip. She purchased a handgun and waited for a permit. She prepared goodbye letters to members of her family. She packed several rounds of ammunition, a pair of binoculars, and other personal items in her backpack. And she planned to confront the pastor during the early morning hours—before the day's activities had started and to avoid potential witnesses. Barcroft's choice of clothing—black pants and a black, hooded sweatshirt—likewise show a calculated attempt to evade detection or to obscure her identity. . . .

Barcroft's actions during and right after the shooting also suggest a consciousness of guilt. As she spoke with Harris outside the church, she kept her handgun—a.22 caliber pistol—concealed in her front pocket. . . . Even more revealing was her decision to spare Harris's life. Expert testimony suggested that this conduct reflected Barcroft's delusional state, the inference being that a sane person would have shot the eyewitness to avoid criminal implication. But a factfinder could have reasonably come to the opposite conclusion: that Barcroft's decision not to shoot showed an understanding that killing is wrong. . . .

Cloaked by the hood of her sweatshirt, Barcroft then fled from the crime scene and attempted to hide, taking great pains to conceal herself under the foliage of an overgrown lot. She lay motionless in her hiding spot even as police ordered her to surrender, emerging only when an officer threatened to shoot. . . .

Finally, when the detective asked whether Barcroft understood that she "had to be arrested" for her crime, she replied that she had "actually planned on not getting caught." This comment implies a consciousness of guilt. . . .

We thus find the demeanor evidence more than sufficient to support the trial court's rejection of Barcroft's insanity defense.

Questions

1. Just because someone is capable of premeditation does not mean they appreciate the wrongfulness of their conduct. Indeed, delusional defendants often act with premeditation. Does that mean the court got this appeal wrong? Why or why not?
2. Both the defense's experts and independent experts appointed by the court all agreed that the defendant was legally insane. What effect, if any, does that fact have on your own assessment of the defendant's criminal liability?

Consequences of an Insanity Acquittal

A common criticism of the insanity defense is based on the misperception that people found NGBRI go free. Such is not the case; in fact, only about 1 percent of insanity acquittees are immediately released without any conditions.[119] In contrast, between 84 and 95 percent of those found NGBRI are hospitalized, often for very long periods of time.[120] For example, John Hinckley was acquitted and institutionalized via a NGBRI verdict in 1981 and remained incarcerated in St. Elizabeth's Hospital's wing for the criminally insane for thirty-five years. His lengthy post-acquittal confinement is representative, not exceptional.[121]

Most states automatically commit someone found NGBRI for at least a sixty-day period and then place the burden on the person committed to show when they are no longer mentally ill and dangerous. The overwhelming number of people found NGBRI are confined in mental hospitals for years beyond what they would have served in prison had they been criminally convicted. For example, in New York and California, insanity acquittees serve more than double the average length of criminal incarceration.[122]

States differ markedly on how long insanity acquittees may be incarcerated. Some states limit the period of confinement in a mental health facility to no longer than the maximum potential sentence would have been if the defendant had been convicted of the offense.[123] But other states impose an indefinite period of treatment of "one day to life," committing NGBRI acquittees to a mental institution indefinitely, often on the presumption that they remain both mentally ill and dangerous and places until the person proves otherwise.[124]

Notably, once released from treatment, insanity acquittees recidivate at rates far lower than those convicted of criminal offenses upon release from correctional institutions. In contrast to two-year rearrest rates in New York for 42 percent of females and 56 percent males after their release from prison, only 2 percent of females and 14 percent of males were rearrested after their release from psychiatric hospitals.[125] Moreover, the years immediately after release are the salient ones; the risk of rearrest drops by half within two years of release, by two-thirds within five years of release, and approached zero by the tenth year.[126]

Impact of Insanity Defense Changes

Table 14.1 summarizes the various contemporary approaches to the insanity defense.

Does it matter which formulation applies? Most empirical research suggests that changes in the law have had little impact on the overall rate of NGBRI verdicts,[127] although at least one study found that the post-Hinckley statutory changes to the insanity defense in Georgia and New York resulted in fewer defendants entering insanity pleas in both jurisdictions.[128]

The lack of empirical evidence to support the proposition that IDRA and state changes modeled after it have actually had an effect on the incidence and success rates of the insanity defense is not surprising for a few reasons. First, "generally, in the absence of either

Table 14.1 Summary of Insanity Defense Formulations

At the time of the offense,

Formulation	*Predicate*	*Result*
M'Naghten	The defendant suffered from a mental disease or defect	that caused the defendant either not to know the nature and quality of the act he or she committed, or knowing the quality or nature of the act, nonetheless not to know that the act was wrong
Durham	The defendant suffered from a mental disease or defect	that caused the defendant to commit an unlawful act
ALI/MPC	The defendant suffered from a mental disease or defect	that caused the defendant to lack the substantial capacity to appreciate the criminality of his conduct or to conform his conduct to the requirements of law
IDRA	The defendant suffered from a *severe* mental disease or defect	that caused the defendant to be unable to appreciate the nature and quality or the wrongfulness of his acts
GBMI	The defendant was mentally ill	but not legally insane
GEI	The defendant suffered from a *severe* mental disease or defect	that caused the person not to know the criminal act was wrong
Mens rea approach	The defendant suffered from a mental disease or defect	that prevented him or her from forming the *mens rea* required for conviction either because the defendant could not comprehend what he or she was doing when committing the crime

exceptionally persuasive or 'objective' evidence, jurors reject the notion that an alleged mental disorder is severe enough to excuse criminal behavior."[129] Thus, regardless of the actual formulation of the insanity defense, juries tend to view the defense with skepticism.

Second, when faced with evidence of insanity, it appears jurors use their own views or constructs of what insanity is, such as:

> [P]erceptions of the defendant's incapacity, awareness, clarity of thinking, ability to control behavior, capability of evil motive, and whether any other person or persons were at fault for the criminal act . . . Essentially, jurors resort[] to their own common sense definition of insanity, one that seem[s] much more complex than the simplistic conceptualization of the insane person embodied in the major rules.[130]

Finally, jurors bring "their own personal sense of justice" to their insanity defense deliberations including "attitudes about the morality of the insanity defense and the punishment of mentally ill offenders."[131] Perhaps, then, there are crimes so heinous that it offends one's sense of justice to the point where one cannot excuse criminal responsibility even in the face of strong evidence of insanity? Consider the sensational prosecutions of infamous assassins, mass murders, and serial killers like Jack Ruby, John Wayne Gacy, Jeffrey Dahmer, Charles Manson, Colin Ferguson, and John Salvi. All pled insanity; all were convicted. In contrast, Andrea Yates killed her children by drowning them in a bathtub and was found insane after a second trial. The outcome in her case, however, is the exception and not the rule.

DIMINISHED CAPACITY

People who are mentally ill, but not "severely" enough to qualify as legally insane under the IDRA and its state-law counterparts, may nonetheless not be as culpable as those who are not mentally ill. Variations on diminished capacity might be an option for such people.

Unfortunately, there is no standard definition for the doctrine of diminished capacity. The doctrine exists, either statutorily or in case law, in more than half of all US jurisdictions.[132] Although diminished capacity is often referred to as a defense, doing so is somewhat inappropriate because is not a defense per se, but rather deals with the admissibility of evidence concerning the accused's mental state.[133] It is most frequently invoked in first-degree murder cases to negate premeditation.[134]

Although there are clearly "differing views regarding the meaning and application of the diminished capacity concept," the favored view of **diminished capacity** is that it is "a type of evidence . . . admitted to rebut the specific intent required to convict the defendant of the crime charged."[135] In other words, a defendant invoking the diminished capacity doctrine asserts that his or her mental state prevented him or her from forming the requisite *mens rea* for the crime.[136] But the use of diminished capacity evidence to negate the existence of *mens rea* "is not an affirmative defense and does not result in an acquittal unless there is a failure to establish intent for the offense and for all of its lesser-included counterparts."[137] Thus, the burden of persuasion to prove intent remains with the prosecution when a defendant argues diminished capacity;[138] the defendant only needs to create a reasonable doubt with regard to state of mind in order to be acquitted.[139] Accordingly, diminished capacity is not only easier to use, but also is much "more likely to succeed than the insanity defense."[140]

The term *diminished capacity* is often used to encompass the related concept of **diminished responsibility**, but they are distinct. Diminished responsibility is concerned not with capacity to form intent, but rather with punishment.[141] Diminished responsibility allows either a jury or a judge "to mitigate the punishment of a mentally disabled but sane offender in any case where the jury believes that the defendant is less culpable than his normal counterpart who commits the same criminal act."[142] Diminished responsibility has not been embraced by the courts of the United States, but has been in England.[143] However, a number of US jurisdictions, the Model Penal Code, and the Federal Sentencing Guidelines allow for the admission of mental abnormality evidence in sentence mitigation.[144]

Applying Diminished Capacity

Some jurisdictions restrict the use of diminished capacity evidence to specific intent crimes.[145] Other states further limit its use to cases where evidence of diminished capacity might negate the specific intent requirement for murder only.[146] Still other jurisdictions have adopted the Model Penal Code's approach, which allows diminished capacity evidence in any case where the defendant's mental state is at issue.[147] This last approach has been endorsed by the American Bar Association[148] and is the one most frequently followed in US states that recognize diminished capacity.[149] Some states, however, bar all evidence of mental illness for diminished capacity purposes, allowing expert testimony on a defendant's mental state only for insanity defense purposes.[150]

Predicate Mental Disorders

In light of the IDRA and the majority of states that adopted its approach, it is clear that significant cognitive impairment is necessary for an insanity finding in most of the United States today. In contrast, diminished capacity incorporates a significantly broader range of impairment. For example, a learning disability generally does not constitute a "mental disease or defect" for insanity purposes. But if a learning-disabled person strikes someone, but is unable to know that the blow could kill as a result of his or her disability, he or she might be able to assert diminished capacity to negate the *mens rea* of intent to kill if charged a crime.[151] Although personality disorders rarely qualify as mental diseases or defects for insanity defense purposes, certain personality disorders, such as Borderline Personality Disorder, may qualify as a mental disease or defect for a diminished capacity defense in certain states.[152]

Defenses Extending Diminished Capacity

There have been some novel attempts at extending diminished capacity. One of the most notable cases to do so was *People v. White*.[153] The defendant in case, Dan White, had been a member of the San Francisco Board of Supervisors. He resigned his position on the Board, but then sought to be reinstated by San Francisco Mayor George Moscone who was responsible for filling vacancies on the Board. Initially, Moscone had assured White that he would be reappointed, but Moscone changed his mind because one of the other members of the Board of Supervisors, Harvey Milk, opposed White's reappointment. Shortly thereafter, Moscone made arrangements to hold a press conference announcing the appointment of someone else to fill the vacancy created by

White's resignation. But Moscone never had to chance to make the announcement because, less than one hour prior to the time the press conference was scheduled to occur, White repeatedly shot and killed both Mayor Moscone and Supervisor Harvey Milk. He was charged with two counts of murder in the first degree. At White's trial, three psychiatrists and a psychologist testified that White had become clinically depressed. As part of White's depression, he gorged himself on Twinkies and Coca-Cola. But White was hypoglycemic (a low blood-sugar condition). The experts opined that the sugar and caffeine White had ingested caused a brief reactive psychosis that rendered him unable to control his actions. His defense was dubbed the "Twinkie Defense" and it worked; the jury convicted White of manslaughter rather than murder, apparently believing that his capacity was, in fact, diminished because of his hypoglycemic reaction to the sugar and caffeine. The public outrage at the successful extension of diminished capacity in the *White* case eventually led California to statutorily abolish the diminished capacity doctrine in that state.[154]

PTSD AND RELATED DEFENSES

Extreme cases of Posttraumatic Stress Disorder (PTSD) may serve as the qualifying "mental disease or defect" for an insanity defense.[155] Of course, to do so effectively in the overwhelming majority of courts in the United States, the disorder would have to render the defendant unable to substantially appreciate the wrongfulness or criminality of his or her actions. But if the level of impairment does not rise to the level of insanity, the disorder may still be used to support a finding of diminished capacity.

PTSD was first noted in America after the Civil War, though little was known about it then.[156] Subsequent wars, especially the two World Wars (during which time it was often referred to as "shell shock" and "combat fatigue") and the Vietnam War, led to study of the condition.[157] PTSD was recognized as a mental disorder in 1980 by the American Psychiatric Association.[158] The condition originally applied only to veterans of wars who experienced intense "flashbacks" to times of combat during which individuals were known to have violent outbreaks. But PTSD evolved to encompass almost any individual who experienced extreme trauma or violence.[159] Such exposure remains a "necessary, but not sufficient, condition for the development of PTSD."[160] Because PTSD can affect one's perception of reality—including the circumstances in which one finds oneself even in "normal" situations—PTSD can interfere with the formation of *mens rea*, and therefore serve as a predicate for introducing diminished capacity evidence.[161]

Since its acceptance as a genuine medical condition, courts have been more accepting of the PTSD defense than other excuse defenses since it appears to be the very type of disorder diminished capacity is designed to encompass. For example, in *State v. Phipps*,[162] the defendant was a Gulf War veteran. While he was in combat, his wife cheated on him. Within a month of his return home, he learned that his wife was had been living with her boyfriend and that she wanted a divorce. One night, Phipps went to his wife's home, where upon he got into an argument with the boyfriend, who threatened Phipps with a stick. Phipps took the stick and hit the boyfriend repeatedly with it, eventually killing him. At trial, four experts testified that Phipps suffered from major depression and posttraumatic stress disorder. Even the prosecution's expert testified that his impairment was "of a sufficient level to significantly affect his thinking, reasoning, judgment, and emotional well-being."[163] Moreover, his PTSD "may have lessened his threshold or made him more sensitive to defending himself and protecting himself and increased the likelihood of him over-reacting to a real or perceived threat."[164] The trial court judge nonetheless refused to give a jury instruction which would have allowed the jury to consider the evidence of mental disorders in relation to whether Phipps possessed the required *mens rea* for first-degree murder. The appeals court reversed the decision, holding that evidence of the defendant's mental state at the time of the offense is admissible to refute elements of specific intent in first-degree murder cases.[165]

The acceptance of PTSD as a form of diminished capacity has not been universal. Some critics challenge the diagnosis as being overly subjective, largely due to the fact that a PTSD diagnosis is based on patient testimonials and personal observations.[166] Still, there is some research demonstrating a physiological basis for a PTSD diagnosis[167] that permits mental health professionals to testify not only as to whether a defendant has PTSD, but also whether the disorder influenced the defendant's capacity to form the requisite criminal intent at the time of the offense.[168] Moreover, even when it is not available or successful as a criminal defense, evidence of PTSD is admissible in sentencing proceedings to mitigate punishment.[169] Consider that in *Porter v. McCollum*,[170] the US Supreme Court ordered a new sentencing hearing for a veteran with PTSD who had been sentenced to death for killing his former girlfriend and her then-current boyfriend. The Court specifically instructed that resentencing needed to take into account the stress and emotional toll that combat in war had taken on the defendant.[171]

In contrast to people like veterans who experience trauma in combat, those who argue that they have endured cultural trauma which induced a variant of true PTSD are unlikely to find the courts sympathetic to their arguments. For example, psychiatrists William H. Grier and Price M. Cobbs first advanced the notion of Black rage in 1969 when they asserted that African Americans, as an insular racial minority in the United States, have endured years of discrimination starting in colonial days with slavery and continuing to the present.[172] Collectively, these injustices can result in so much "pent-up frustration" and "justifiable paranoia" that it can lead to someone snapping and committing violent acts.[173]

The Black rage defense has been criticized as an invalid extension of other forms of diminished capacity. PTSD, for example, seeks to explain the conduct of a single person which arose in connection with an identifiable, traumatic event that is generally outside the range of usual human experience, such as military combat; violent personal or sexual assault victimization; being kidnapped or taken hostage; being in a terrorist attack or natural disaster; being tortured; and incarceration as a prisoner of war or in a concentration camp.[174] Although there is no doubt that African Americans have endured invidious discrimination, it is questionable whether discrimination in the post-Civil Rights Era qualifies as a trauma of such magnitude that it causes something akin to PTSD.[175] As a result, although this defense resulted in the reversal of a criminal conviction in 1846 and an insanity acquittal in 1971, it a has not been used successfully in contemporary jurisprudence since then.[176]

Finally, being the victim of physical abuse can also cause someone to experience PTSD. But because lashing out at one's abuser often occurs within the context of self-defense or defense of others, these topics are discussed in Chapter 15.

CULTURAL DEFENSES

Absent growing up in an area ravaged by war or similar childhood experiences that expose someone to true trauma, a disadvantaged social background, a toxic social upbringing, or even unique cultural circumstances do not give rise to true PTSD-related defenses. Nonetheless, so-called **cultural defenses** are offered as evidence of diminished responsibility at sentencing, as well as the basis of diminished capacity defenses that are typically aimed at reducing culpability for murder down to manslaughter. For example, some immigrants to the United States from countries that permit honor killings—executions by family members as punishment for behavior that dishonors their families—have argued that the victim's behavior served as provocation for their actions in the heat of passion.[177] Others have argued that cultural traditions of marriage "by capture" (kidnapping and sexual assault as the predicate to valid claim of marriage) mitigate *mens rea* for these crimes,[178] and others have attempted to excuse or mitigate their criminal responsibility for child abuse for using unreasonable force when disciplining children based on their cultural customs that differ significantly from those in the United States.[179] Although these defenses are not formally recognized, they are offered from time to time as diminished capacity variations. More often than not, these attempts are rejected, although there are some examples of cultural defenses that have successfully mitigated or excused criminal culpability.[180]

MEDIA INTOXICATION

There is an extensive body of research linking viewing violent media (television programs, movies, and video games) and subsequent aggressive behavior.[181] Similar research findings have linked the viewing of pornography with both attitudes accepting of violence against women and with the likelihood of sexual aggression, especially for males with predispositions to sexual aggression.[182] Such findings have led to defendants to argue that long-term exposure to such media depictions affected their cognitive, affective, and volitional functioning such that their criminal culpability for acts of violence should be mitigated or excused. Courts have rejected these **media intoxication** arguments in both diminished responsibility and diminished capacity contexts. For example, serial killer Bobby Joe Long unsuccessfully asserted in the sentencing phase of his murder trial that his addiction to violent pornography should have constituted a mitigating factor against the death penalty.[183]

In *Schiro v. Clark*, the defendant "argued that he was a sexual sadist and that his extensive viewing of rape pornography and snuff films rendered him unable to distinguish right from wrong." The defendant produced the testimony of two leading experts on the link between violence and pornography and sought to have it used as evidence of insanity and as a type of intoxication which the applicable state law recognized as a mitigating factor. The defendant was convicted and his subsequent appeals were all denied on the rationale that allowing a criminal defense based on exposure to materials protected by the First Amendment would be incongruous. Similar reasoning resulted in the unsuccessful assertion of an analogous argument using music lyrics in the case of Ronald Ray Howard. The nineteen-year-old defendant killed a police officer and sought to avoid the death penalty by arguing that his addiction to "gangsta rap" was a mitigating factor. The argument was rejected by the jury who sentenced Howard to death.[184]

BEHAVIORAL GENETICS

Unlike the law, which assumes people, as autonomous creatures, exercise free will when engaging in conduct (Chapter 1), behavioral science posits that human behavior is a function of a complex interplay between genes and environmental influences. That is not to say that human behavior is necessarily predetermined; there is no such thing as a "crime gene," for example. Early criminological studies of the link between genes and predetermined behavior have been discredited. Thus, for instance, shoddy research positing that an extra *Y* chromosome (expressed as an "XYY" karotype) created "supermales" genetically predisposed to aggression and violence has been rejected by both science and in courts of law.[185] Nonetheless, there is little doubt that "genes play a vital role in the body's development and physiology, and it is through the body, acting in response to and upon surrounding environments, that behavior manifests itself."[186] In other words, human behavior is influenced by a wide variety of bio-psycho-social causes.

Genetic predispositions have been established to a range of dysfunction—including substance abuse disorders; mental illness; impulsivity, thrill-seeking, and risk-taking; and propensity to aggression and violence.[187] Although the precise mechanisms by which genetic predispositions influence behavior are unknown, science has established strong links between behavior and several important biological factors relevant to criminal behavior, especially neurotransmitter or hormone imbalances, and differences in brain structure and functioning.[188] Evidence of cognitive impairment from behavioral genetics and neuroscience, in particular, is increasingly used to show diminished responsibility in sentencing.[189] But should such evidence also form the basis of a diminished capacity defense? Box 14.2, "You Make the Public Policy Call," asks you to decide.

BOX 14.2

YOU MAKE THE PUBLIC POLICY CALL

Should Your Genes Mitigate Responsibility for Murder?

In what was described as a "bloody rampage," Bradley Waldroup "shot his wife's friend Leslie Bradshaw, eight times, killing her before attempting to kill his wife by chopping her up with a machete." Leading up to the rampage, Waldroup and his wife had been experiencing marital distress. At the time of the incident, Waldroup's wife was dropping off their children at Waldroup's cabin. Waldroup greeted his wife and her friend with a. 22 rifle and demanded that his wife stay to have a discussion. Waldroup then took his wife's keys from her vehicle and threw them into the woods. After a heated exchange, Waldroup opened fire on Mr. Bradshaw and then attempted to kill his wife. Reports indicated that Waldroup had told his children to say goodbye to their mother. The prosecution believed that proving premeditation and deliberation would be a straightforward issue—that is, until the defense introduced evidence of Waldroup's genetic pre-disposition to antisocial behavior. At trial, the court admitted evidence that Waldroup suffered from a genetic polymorphism resulting in low (production of enzymes regulating neurotransmitters) that, when combined with a history of childhood abuse, led to Waldroup's explosive reaction. The end game, of course, was demonstrating that Waldroup's actions were not the product of premeditation and deliberation.[191]

1. Under these circumstances, and drawing on what you learned in Chapter 7, do you think Waldroup should be convicted of first-degree murder or voluntary manslaughter for killing Bradshaw? Why?
2. Critics of diminished capacity defenses rooted in neuroscience and behavioral genetics sometimes argue that such evidence might lead us down a slippery slope toward that allows behavioral determinism—the notion that our genes, brain chemistry, and social environments control our conduct—will undermine traditional notions of criminal responsibility based on the exercise of free will.[192] Evaluate this argument.

CONCLUSION

Learning Objectives	Summaries
1. Explain how young age can excuse criminal conduct.	At common law, children under the age of seven were conclusively presumed incapable of crime. Children between the ages of seven and fourteen were presumed to be incapable of crime, but that that presumption could be rebutted by competent evidence. Children over the age of fourteen were presumed capable of crime, but that presumption was also rebuttable. Most states still follow the approach, although the ages vary by jurisdiction.
2. Compare and contrast competency to stand trial from insanity.	Competency to stand trial concerns a criminal defendant's mental state at the time of trial, whereas insanity concerns the state of mind at the time of an offense. The former is a jurisdictional matter that can be raised by any party at any time, whereas the insanity defense must be timely pled by a defendant. There are also differences in the burden of persuasion that vary by jurisdiction.
3. Evaluate the different approaches to the insanity defense.	All variations of the insanity defense concern the defendant's state of mind at the time of offense as a function of a qualifying mental disease or defect. In most states and the federal system, the defect must be severe (i.e., a serious psychotic disorder) and must have rendered the defendant incapable of knowing the nature and quality of his or her act or, alternatively, from appreciating that those acts were legally wrong. A minority of states have abandoned the latter formulation and allow evidence of mental illness only to the extent that it prevented a defendant from forming *mens rea.*
4. Analyze the salient differences between the insanity and diminished capacity defenses.	Insanity typically serves as a complete defense, whereas evidence of mental illness that do not render someone legally insane may nonetheless be used to show a defendant did not entertain *mens rea* such that their conduct should be excused or mitigated to a lesser crime. Typically, a broader range of mental illnesses qualify for diminished capacity than insanity, although some states refuse to allow any evidence of mental illness to be used outside of disproving that a defendant entertained the requisite *mens rea* for an offense.

KEY TERMS

ALI/MPC affective test (for insanity)
competency to stand trial
diminished capacity
diminished responsibility
Durham rule (for insanity)
guilty but mentally ill
guilty except insane
infancy
Insanity Defense Reform Act (IDRA)
irresistible impulse test (for insanity)
mens rea approach (to insanity)
mental disease or defect
M'Naghten rule (for insanity)
settled insanity

15

Defenses of Justification

LEARNING OBJECTIVES

1. Analyze the elements of a valid self-defense claim using nonlethal force.
2. Analyze the elements of a valid self-defense claim using nonlethal force.
3. Explain when force may be used to defend other persons.
4. Explain when force may be used to defend property.
5. Evaluate the limits the place places on law enforcement officers when using force.
6. Discuss the scope of parental privilege to use force to discipline children.
7. Describe the ways in which the law attempts to accommodate the use of force by victims of abuse.

Outline

INTRODUCTION

Defenses of justification are generally concerned with situations in which a defendant argues that he or she was legally privileged to use force, and therefore committed no wrongdoing. The primary defenses of justification include self-defense, defense of others, and defense of property. There are special privileges for law enforcement officers to use reasonable force in executing their duties. Similarly, parents hold a limited privilege to use reasonable force in disciplining children. Justification principles underlying self-defense merge with some principles of excuse for select defenses to crimes committed by persons against their abusers. This chapter explores all of these defenses.

SELF-DEFENSE

The law of self-defense can be summarized in one sentence: a person is *privileged* to use a *reasonable amount* of physical force against another person when the actor *reasonably believes* that such force is *necessary* for the purpose of protecting against an *imminent attack* upon himself or herself from *unlawful force*.[1] Each of the italicized words and phrases in the preceding sentence, however, are terms of art that must be explained.

What Is a Privilege?

A **privilege** is a particular and unusual benefit, advantage, or immunity conferred a person or limited group beyond those normally conferred on others in society, usually by virtue of their position or occupation. It is not a *right*—which is legally secured claim generally available to all, but rather is something that exempts privilege specific holders either from some form of legally liability, or from the performance of a legally imposed duty or obligation that applied to everyone else. For example, firefighters, emergency medical technicians, and police are all granted a limited privilege to disregard certain driving laws when responding to a call for emergency service within the scope of their public duties. Similarly, parents and legal guardians of children are granted a limited privilege to use a reasonable amount of physical force to discipline children. All human actors are granted a limited privilege to use reasonable amount of force to defend themselves, others, and in some circumstances, even their property.

What Is Unlawful Force?

The use of force in self-defense must be against *unlawful force*, such as a criminal battery. If *lawful force* is being applied, then one has no privilege to act in self-defense.[2] For example, law enforcement officers are privileged to use a reasonable amount of force to make an arrest, so there is no privilege to use force to resist arrest.[3] This is true even if the arrest is unlawful under the law of criminal procedure.[4] The only exception to this rule would be if the physical force used by law enforcement exceeds that allowed by law and, therefore, is unreasonable. In other words, if police officers use *excessive force* when making an arrest, then their use of force is not lawful and the person resisting the excessive force by law enforcement officers may invoke the defense of self-defense.[5] The same would be true for prisoners; inmates may only assert self-defense against excessive force used by correctional officers.[6]

A person who is trespassing on another's property may not use physical force to resist removal because the property owner is privileged to use a reasonable amount of physical force to evict trespassers.[7] But as with police who use excessive force, the trespasser may use force to resist the eviction if threatened with death or serious bodily harm, since that level of force would be unlawful.[8]

A person may not use force in response to mere words, such as abusive language or verbal threats, since even the most insulting language does not involve unlawful force.[9] As the schoolyard rhyme goes, "sticks and stones may break my bones, but words can never hurt me." Thus, verbal provocation alone, without more (such as an assault), will not justify the use of physical force.

The Requirement of Imminent Necessity

The law of self-defense requires that force be *necessary* to defend oneself from the *imminent*, unlawful application of force by another person. If force is not actually necessary, then the actor will not be able to assert self-defense. For example, in some US states, if people know that they can "avoid the necessity of using such force with complete safety by retreating," then they have a legal **duty to retreat** rather than unnecessary use force.[10] Following the lead of the Model Penal Code, some states only impose a duty to retreat in situations involving deadly force.

Additionally, the privilege to use reasonable force in self-defense applies only to *imminent attack*, not threats of future harm.[11] An honest and reasonable mistake as to whether an attack is actually imminent will not deprive the actor of the defense.[12] This caveat to the law of self-defense is of key importance to defenses based on the defendant's history of abuse (discussed later in this chapter).

The Reasonableness Requirement

The law of self-defense requires that the amount of force used must be *reasonable* under the circumstances. Reasonable force is limited to that which is necessary to repel the unlawful attack. And, as a general rule, reasonable force is roughly proportional. Thus, for example, when faced with an imminent attack using nondeadly force, a person would not be permitted to respond with deadly force since deadly force would be an unreasonably excessive response. Similarly, if one uses a reasonable amount of physical, nondeadly force to stop an unlawful attack, he or she must cease using the force once the attacked has been thwarted. Continuing the use force after the attack has been stopped is both unreasonable and unnecessary.

Although proportionality of response is a good rule of thumb, the determination of reasonableness is more complicated. Reasonableness requires a two-part analysis that is comprised both of a subjective and objective standard. The defendant must have honestly believed that he or she was in imminent danger from unlawful force and that it was necessary to respond to this imminent threat by using force. This is purely a subjective standard that simply examines what the defendant thought in his or her own mind.

The other part of the reasonableness test is an objective one. Would the ordinary, reasonable, prudent person in the same circumstances as the defendant have also believed that the use of such force was necessary to protect against the imminent application of unlawful force? If the answer to this question is "yes," then the defendant acted reasonably; if the answer is "no," then the defendant acted unreasonably. Given this standard, it should be evident that the defendant is not deprived of the defense just because he or she was honestly and reasonably mistaken. Presuming such a mistake, then the criteria for invoking self-defense are satisfied because the defendant acted honestly (subjectively) and reasonably (objectively).

The level of objectivity to be applied when assessing the reasonableness of the defendant's actions has been the subject of debate for many years. No US jurisdiction uses a purely subjective standard, but states disagree whether to apply a purely objective approach or some modified standard that considers the unique character of the defendant, such as his or her age, intelligence, level of education, or past experiences. The difference between these approaches is explored later in this chapter in case of *People v. Goetz.*[13]

Provocation: The Initial Aggressor Limitation

A major exception to the availability of the defense of self-defense concerns those who are at fault in provoking the emergency situation against which he or she feels it necessary to defend using physical force. Such a person is called the **initial aggressor**. The initial aggressor may not use force if he or she wrongfully caused the confrontation unless one of two situations arise.

An initial aggressor may use force to defend himself or herself if he or she withdrew from the encounter, thereby effectively ending the confrontation.[14] If the other person still pursues the initial aggressor after such a withdrawal, then the other person is viewed as the "new" aggressor, and the initial aggressor is free to defend himself or herself against the attacks of the other. It should be noted that actual withdrawal by the initial aggressor is not necessary, since it cannot always be accomplished. If the initial aggressor clearly communicates to the other his or her intent to withdraw from the encounter, that will be sufficient.

The other major situation in which the initial aggressor exception will not apply is when other person responds in a grossly disproportionate manner to the force used by the initial aggressor. For example, if the initial aggressor slaps the other person across the face, and then the other person takes out a baseball bat and assaults the initial aggressor, the response is grossly disproportionate to the provocation of the initial aggressor. The other person has therefore exceeded the scope of his or her privilege to act in self-defense since the response was unreasonable, making this grossly disproportionate response unlawful. Under such circumstances, the initial aggressor is free to defend himself or herself.[15]

Special Rules Limiting the Use of Deadly Force in Self-Defense

The general rules governing self-defense apply to the use of deadly force. But when deadly force is an issue, there are additional rules. At common law, deadly force could only be used when the actor reasonably perceived it necessary to defend against the imminent use of deadly force. The Model Penal Code expanded the ability to use deadly force to defend against not only death, but also serious bodily harm, kidnapping, and/or rape.[16] Some states have added additional crimes to the list justifying deadly force, such as arson of an occupied dwelling, robbery, or burglary of an occupied dwelling.[17]

Some jurisdictions impose a **duty to warn** before using deadly force, such as "Stop or I'll shoot!" But even where such warnings are required, there are times when giving the warning might mean the difference between having the opportunity to act in self-defense or being deprived of that opportunity. Thus, in warning jurisdictions, the requirement to give a warning is excused if it would be useless or in vain.

The Model Penal Code and a minority of US jurisdictions require a person to retreat if they can do so in complete safety before using deadly force in self-defense.[18] The rationale underlying the duty to retreat is that the law should not sanction taking a life unless it is necessary to do so. But if retreat to safety is not a viable possibility, then an actor may use deadly force in self-defense, presuming the other criteria for self-defense are met.

Exceptions to the Usual Requirements for Self-Defense

There are three exceptions to the usual requirements of self-defense that, depending upon the jurisdiction, may excuse the duty to warn, the duty to retreat, and even the duty to respond with a reasonable amount of force.

CASTLE DOCTRINE

Premised upon the notion that one's home is one's castle, the **castle doctrine** specifies that no one has a legal duty to retreat from his or her own home before using deadly force in self-defense, provided he or she was not the initial aggressor. The castle doctrine has been extended in some states to offices and other places of business.[19]

The common-law approach to the castle doctrine simply excused the duty to retreat from one's home before using deadly force in self-defense, but it did not exempt the actor from the other aspects of the law of self-defense. Thus, for example, there still needed to be a reasonable belief that deadly force was necessary to defend oneself from the imminent attack involving potentially deadly force. But most US states have taken a broader approach to the castle doctrine. The most widespread approach allows the lawful occupant of a dwelling

> to use deadly force whenever the occupant reasonably believes that the intruder intends to commit a "felony" therein. Under many such statutes, any "felony" or "crime" in or upon the dwelling house in which the defender is located is sufficient. Other statutes require that the intruder be committing one or more listed felonies, almost always including burglary or theft.[20]

The Model Penal Code sanctions an expansive view of the castle doctrine by permitting the use of deadly force—without any duty to retreat—when one's home is threatened.[21] Under this approach—one that differs from the common law rather substantially, "there is 'no requirement that the homeowner be in danger, or even apprehension, of receiving any physical harm' from the home invasion; it is enough that his interest in real property is threatened."[22] Although several states follow this approach, some states have gone even further. Georgia, for example, expanded the castle doctrine to apply to one's car.[23] At least two states—Colorado and Oklahoma—have gone even further by adopting so-called "make my day" laws, based on the dialogue in the Dirty Harry movie, *Sudden Impact.*

MAKE MY DAY LAWS

Make my day laws[24] not only excuse any duty to retreat from one's home before using deadly force, but also excuse the requirement that the amount of force used be reasonable under the circumstances.[25] These laws create a statutory presumption that an actor entertained reasonable fear of imminent peril of death or great bodily harm when someone unlawfully enters their home. The "Statutory Analysis Exercise" in Box 15.1 illustrates such a law.

Most US jurisdictions have rejected the "make my day" approach to the use of deadly force in self-defense. Instead, most states require that the use of deadly force must always be reasonable, even in one's home when the castle doctrine excuses a duty to retreat. Of course, as previously discussed, reasonableness is a relative term. Moreover, the reasonableness of one's actions are further blurred by the fact that roughly thirty-five states have enacted "stand your ground" laws.

STAND YOUR GROUND LAWS

In 2005, Florida was the first state to enact a **stand your ground** (SYG) law.[26] Based on model legislation drafted by the National Rifle Association (NRA), Florida's SYG law altered traditional duty to retreat.[27] Prior to the adoption of a SYG law in Florida, the state followed the traditional common-law formulation of self-defense by providing that "a

BOX 15.1

STATUTORY ANALYSIS EXERCISE

Shoot First and Ask Questions Later?

In 2012, Zoey Ripple got drunk one night and stumbled into the home of Timothy Justice and Doreen Orion at approximately 3:00 a.m. Tim and Doreen were asleep in bed. They had shut off the lights and closed the blinds but left one side of their bedroom French door open for ventilation. They awoke to find an intruder had come in through the sliding screen door, carrying what looked to them like a flashlight. They shouted at the person to leave and warned they had a gun. The intruder kept coming. Justice fired one shot toward the light, striking a Zoey Ripple in the hip. Ripple told a detective she thought she was at a friend's house and was confused by all the shouting and yelling.[120]

Colorado law provides,

* * *

> (2) [A]ny occupant of a dwelling is justified in using any degree of physical force, including deadly physical force, against another person when that other person has made an unlawful entry into the dwelling, and when the occupant has a reasonable belief that such other person has committed a crime in the dwelling in addition to the uninvited entry, or is committing or intends to commit a crime against a person or property in addition to the uninvited entry, and when the occupant reasonably believes that such other person might use any physical force, no matter how slight, against any occupant.
>
> (3) Any occupant of a dwelling using physical force, including deadly physical force, in accordance with the provisions of subsection (2) of this section shall be immune from criminal prosecution for the use of such force.

1. When Ripple's entered the Justice's home, she was "armed with a cellphone."[121] Under Colorado law, should Timothy Justice be charged with any criminal offense? If so, which crime(s)? If not, why not?
2. Assume, for this question, that Colorado still followed the common-law tradition that deadly force may only be used when the actor reasonably perceives it necessary to defend against deadly force. Further assume that that the common-law duty to warn applies, but so does the common-law castle doctrine. Do you think the outcome of the case would be different? Explain your reasoning.
3. Evaluate the wisdom of "make my day" laws. Are they good public policy? Why or why not?

person may not resort to deadly force without first using every reasonable means within his or her power to avoid the danger, including retreat," unless the castle doctrine applied.[28] But the SYG law changed that. Indeed, the prefatory language in the bill adopting the SYG law explained that "no person or victim of crime should be required to surrender his or her personal safety to a criminal, nor should a person or victim be required to needlessly retreat in the face of intrusion or attack."[29] With this rationale made explicit, the statute provides, in relevant part:

A person who is not engaged in an unlawful activity and who is attacked in any other place where he or she has a right to be has no duty to retreat and has the right to stand his or her ground and meet force with force, including deadly force if he or she reasonably believes it is necessary to do so to prevent death or great bodily harm to himself or herself or another or to prevent the commission of a forcible felony.[30]

Within two years of Florida adopting its SYG law, twenty-one other states had adopted similar laws abolishing any duty to retreat before using deadly force in self-defense, nine of which specifically included language stating that one may "stand his or her ground."[31] That number had risen to thirty-five states by 2017, although the scope of these laws varies in different jurisdictions. Thus, only fifteen states maintain the common-law duty to retreat.[32]

SYG laws permit the use of deadly force, without first retreating, when someone reasonably believes such force is necessary to prevent imminent death or bodily injury. Additionally, the laws provide significant procedural protections to homicide defendants alleging self-defense. First, the laws presume that persons using deadly force against others in their own dwelling, place of business, or motor vehicle have a reasonable belief that this force was necessary to prevent unlawful entry or to compel the unlawful intruder to leave. This places an additional burden of proof on the prosecution to disprove a presumption that the individual was acting reasonably. Second, if an individual reasonably uses deadly force in self-defense when he is in an area where he is lawfully permitted to be and not engaged in an unlawful activity, he will receive legal protection. This legal protection comes in the form of either a decision by police not to arrest the individual or a decision by prosecutors not to press criminal charges, thus granting the individual immunity from prosecution.[33]

Some state SYG laws, like Florida's, provide additional procedural protections to someone who stands his or her ground beyond creating a statutory presumption of reasonableness under certain circumstances. For example,

> Florida's statute provides defendants with an opportunity to request an "immunity hearing" prior to trial, during which the district court judge must consider whether the facts of the case prove by a preponderance of the evidence that the defendant is justified in his actions under the Stand Your Ground law. If the court

finds this burden has been met, the defendant will be granted immunity, and the trial will be dismissed with all relevant charges dropped. Unlike traditional self-defense laws, which allow the use of self-defense as an affirmative defense for manslaughter or murder, Florida's law permits criminal defendants that claim self-defense to avoid trial and prosecution entirely.[34]

Imperfect Self-Defense

What if a defendant makes a subjectively honest, but objectively unreasonable mistake regarding the use of force in self-defense? The common law and the Model Penal Code answer this question differently.

At common law, the defendant who made a subjectively honest, but objectively unreasonable mistake about the need to use force in self-defense would be deprived of the defense in its entirety unless charged with a homicide. Such a mistake that resulted in the death of another was called **imperfect self-defense**. It reduced a charge of murder to manslaughter, as explained in Chapter 7. If the victim survived, however, imperfect self-defense led to a curious outcome as explored in the Case Study Extra presented in Box 15.2.

The Model Penal Code provides that someone who did not make an honest and reasonable mistake acted with at least criminal negligence. The Code would therefore hold such a defendant liable for any number of crimes that have criminal negligence as their requisite *mens rea*. In the case of an honest, but unreasonable mistake that results in the death of another human being, this likely would result in a conviction for criminally negligent homicide in those jurisdictions that recognize this level of homicide. If the defendant was grossly negligent (e.g., using a deadly weapon), then a conviction for manslaughter may even be appropriate (Chapter 7).

Modified Objective Test to Determine Reasonableness

Most US jurisdictions do not use a purely objective standard—that of the ordinary, reasonable, prudent person—when determining the reasonableness of a defendant's use of deadly force. Rather, most states use a modified objective standard that asks the trier-of-fact, usually a jury, to assess the reasonableness of the defendant's actions from the defendant's perspective. This involves not only an examination of all of the facts and circumstances surround the incident itself, but also consideration of how a reasonable person would have reacted in the same situation if they were the same size, gender, intelligence, and educational level of the defendant and had undergone the same prior experiences as the defendant, as the following case illustrates.[35]

BOX 15.2

CASE STUDY EXTRA

A Curious Outcome When an Imperfect Self-Defense Victim Survives

In late August of 2006, Kasey Guyton lived with his mother. While he was taking his son out to eat, the two were in an accident with a van driven by Adam Saldivar. Both Saldivar and his passenger, Edner Flores, yelled at Guyton to pull over. Guyton and Salidvar exited their vehicles and began to argue. Guyton told Salidvar that he had insurance and that Saldivar should call the police.

While they were arguing, Flores got out of the van and started yelling at Guyton. Flores told Guyton that he caused the accident and pulled a black gun out from his shirt. Flores told defendant that either defendant would pay or Flores would take his car. Flores repeated that statement a second time.

Saldivar and Flores got back into the van but told defendant that the encounter was not over. Saldivar drove off. Guyton took his son to his mother's house and parked his car. He took his gun from his car and began to walk home. As he was walking, he saw Saldivar's van approaching and feared the van would hit him, so he walked south, and when he was near a tree, he saw Flores reach down with his right arm. As Flores put his arm back up, Guyton fired his gun at the van. Guyton testified that he thought Flores was going to shoot him. After he shot into the van, he ran to his car and drove to his girlfriend's house, where he spent the night and left his gun.[122] Salidvar died from a gunshot wound to the head; Flores was superficially injured.

Guyton was charged with the first-degree murder of Saldivar and the attempted first-degree murder of Flores. Guyton argued that he acted in self-defense. Then jury found that although he honestly (subjectively) believed he was acting in self-defense, that belief was not objectively reasonable. Jurors therefore convicted him of a lessor form of homicide. Under Illinois law, however, imperfect self-defense can mitigate a completed homicide, but not an attempted one. As a result, Guyton's shooting at Flores resulted in conviction for attempted first-degree murder, a more serious criminal charge for which Guyton received twice the prison sentence length than he received for killing Saldivar.

1. Do you think Guyton's actions were both subjectively honest and objectively reasonable? Or do you agree with the jury that it was objectively unreasonable for Guyton to shoot at the van under the circumstances? Explain your reasoning.
2. Guyton's "single act of shooting led to penalties that were dramatically disproportionate to the harm done to the victims."[123] Critique this outcome.

The PEOPLE of the State of New York, Appellant,

v.

Bernhard GOETZ, Respondent.

497 N.E.2d 41 (N.Y. 1986).

* * *

Troy Canty, Darryl Cabey, James Ramseur, and Barry Allen boarded an IRT express subway train in The Bronx and headed south toward lower Manhattan. The four youths rode together in the rear portion of the seventh car of the train. Two of the four, Ramseur and Cabey, had screwdrivers inside their coats, which they said were to be used to break into the coin boxes of video machines.

Defendant Bernhard Goetz boarded this subway train at 14th Street in Manhattan and sat down on a bench towards the rear section of the same car occupied by the four youths. Goetz was carrying an unlicensed .38 caliber pistol loaded with five rounds of ammunition in a waistband holster. . . .

It appears from the evidence before the Grand Jury that Canty approached Goetz, possibly with Allen beside him, and stated "give me five dollars." Neither Canty nor any of the other youths displayed a weapon. Goetz responded by standing up, pulling out his handgun and firing four shots in rapid succession. The first shot hit Canty in the chest; the second struck Allen in the back; the third went through Ramseur's arm and into his left side; the fourth was fired at Cabey, who apparently was then standing in the corner of the car, but missed, deflecting instead off of a wall of the conductor's cab. After Goetz briefly surveyed the scene around him, he fired another shot at Cabey, who then was sitting on the end bench of the car. The bullet entered the rear of Cabey's side and severed his spinal cord.

* * *

[Nine days later, Goetz surrendered. He admitted] that he had been illegally carrying a handgun in New York City for three years. He stated that he had first purchased a gun in 1981 after he had been injured in a mugging. Goetz also revealed that twice between 1981 and 1984 he had successfully warded off assailants simply by displaying the pistol.

According to Goetz's statement, the first contact he had with the four youths came when Canty, sitting or lying on the bench across from him, asked "how are you," to which he replied "fine." Shortly thereafter, Canty, followed by one of the other youths, walked over to the defendant and stood to his left, while the other two youths remained to his right, in the corner of the subway car. Canty then said "give me five dollars." Goetz stated that he knew from the smile on Canty's face that they wanted to "play with me." Although he was certain that none of the youths had a gun, he had a fear, based on prior experiences, of being "maimed."

Goetz then established "a pattern of fire," deciding specifically to fire from left to right. His stated intention at that point was to "murder [the four youths], to hurt them, to make them suffer as much as possible. . . ." Goetz recalled that the first two he shot "tried to run through the crowd [but] they had nowhere to run." Goetz then turned to his right to "go after the other two." One of these two "tried to run through the wall of the train, but . . . he had nowhere to go." The other youth (Cabey) "tried pretending that he wasn't with [the others]" by standing still, holding on to one of the subway hand straps, and not looking at Goetz. Goetz nonetheless fired his fourth shot at him. He then ran back to the first two youths to make sure they had been "taken care of." Seeing that they had both been shot, he spun back to check on the latter two. Goetz noticed that the youth who had been standing still was now sitting on a bench and seemed unhurt. As Goetz told the police, "I said '[y]ou seem to be all right, here's another,' " and he then fired the shot which severed Cabey's spinal cord. Goetz added that "if I was a little more under self-control . . . I would have put the barrel against his forehead and fired." He also admitted that "if I had had more [bullets], I would have shot them again, and again, and again."

***

Penal statutes in New York have long codified the right recognized at common law to use deadly physical force, under appropriate circumstances, in self-defense. . . . These provisions have never required that an actor's belief as to the intention of another person to inflict serious injury be correct in order for the use of deadly force to be justified, but they have uniformly required that the belief comport with an objective notion of reasonableness. . . .

***

Goetz . . . argues that the introduction of an objective element will preclude a jury from considering factors such as the prior experiences of a given actor and thus, require it to make a determination of "reasonableness" without regard to the actual circumstances of a particular incident. This argument, however, falsely presupposes that an objective standard means that the background and other relevant characteristics of a particular actor must be ignored. To the contrary, we have frequently noted that a determination of reasonableness must be based on the "circumstances" facing a defendant or his "situation. . . ." Such terms encompass more than the physical movements of the potential assailant. As just discussed, these terms include any relevant knowledge the defendant had about that person. They also necessarily bring in the physical attributes of all persons involved, including the defendant. Furthermore, the defendant's circumstances encompass any prior experiences he had which could provide a reasonable basis for a belief that another person's intentions were to injure or rob him or that the use of deadly force was necessary under the circumstances.

Accordingly, a jury should be instructed to consider this type of evidence in weighing the defendant's actions.

Questions

1. *Goetz* suggests that prior victimization may provide someone with special expertise in assessing a situation that the ordinary, reasonable, prudent person would not have. Do you agree? Why? What are the benefits and drawbacks of allowing such prior experiences to be considered by a jury?
2. Do you think jurors are capable of putting themselves in the shoes of a defendant who has had experiences that the typical juror has not had? Why or why not?
3. The limbic system controls the flight/fight response when one perceives oneself to be in danger. The response is not under voluntary control. Given that the flight/fight response can be a directing force for a substantial period of time, is it reasonable to expect that people can rationally assess when they are out of danger and withdraw from acting in self-defense accordingly? Explain your response.

DEFENSE OF OTHERS

One may act to defend another person in much the same way one may act in self-defense.[36] Thus, a person is privileged to use a reasonable amount of physical force against another person when the actor reasonably believes that such force is necessary to protect another person against the imminent application of unlawful force.

Sometimes, defending another person unfolds in a manner that can deprive an actor of the usual benefits of a mistaken belief about the use of force. Consider, for example, if someone comes to the aid of another person, reasonably believing it necessary to defend the third party, but it turns out that the person had no right to act in self-defense, perhaps because he or she was the initial aggressor, was a trespasser, or was unlawfully resisting arrest. Even if the actor coming to the aid of such a person makes an honest and reasonable mistake, the law will generally not permit the actor to assert defense of others. This is called the **mistaken intervener rule**, also referred to as the *alter-ego rule*. Under this approach, the intervener acts at his or her own risk when stepping into the shoes of the person being defended because the mistaken intervener holds only whatever privilege to act in defense of the other person as the third party possesses to act in self-defense.

The mistaken intervenor rule is designed to discourage people coming to the rescue of others without knowing all of the facts. Consider the case of *People v. Young*,[37]in which two plain-clothes police officers witnesses an argument occurring between a motorist and pedestrian (in his late teens) in the middle of a midtown Manhattan street and intervened. One of the officers attempted to move the pedestrian out of the street so that traffic could pass, but the teenager resisted the officer's efforts. The officer identified himself and then tried to arrest the teen for disorderly conduct. The pedestrian resisted and, in doing so, physically assaulted and injured the officers. The defendant in the case, however, observed the two men (whom he had no reason to know were police officers in civilian clothing) scuffling with the pedestrian and, believing the teen to need help, pulled one of the officers off the teenager. The court upheld assault charges against the mistaken intervenor, even though he acted in good faith, because the defendant became the alter ego of the teenage pedestrian who had no privilege to use force to resist a lawful arrest.

The New York State Assembly legislatively overruled the *Young* case by adopting the Model Penal Code approach to the mistaken intervener situation. Under this approach, the actor is excused for mistakenly intervening if he or she reasonably believed it necessary to prevent unlawful harm to the third party. This approach parallels the Model Penal Code's approach to the mistake of fact defense. Few states, however, adopted this approach. The majority of states have retained the common law's approach to discourage the rescue of others for precisely the type of reasons that occurred in the *Young* case.

DEFENSE OF PROPERTY

One may use of a reasonable amount of *nondeadly* force to prevent imminent, unlawful interference with one's property. Accordingly, nondeadly force may be used to prevent or terminate: (1) an unlawful entry or other trespass onto one's land; or (2) the unlawful carrying away of tangible, movable property in the actor's lawful possession.[38] The privilege to use nondeadly force in defense of property applies only after the property owner:

> first requests the person against whom such force is used to desist from his interference with the property, unless the actor believes that: (1) such request would be useless; or (2) it would be dangerous to himself or another person to make the request; or (3) substantial harm will be done to the physical condition of the property that is sought to be protected before the request can effectively be made.[39]

In contrast, deadly force can generally not be used solely to defend personal property. The rationale underlying this prohibition is that life should be valued more than property or possessions. That means the law deems mechanical devices to be per se unreasonable to defend property because of the risk they pose to innocent persons, such as children who unwittingly trespass on property; public servants such as firefighters, police, and first-aid workers; and public utility workers. Thus, for example, *People v. Ceballos* upheld a conviction for assault with deadly weapon against a defendant who had set up a spring gun to prevent the burglarizing of a garage where the defendant sometimes slept.[40] Because he was not present when the gun shot the boy who was attempting to break into the garage, the actions were unreasonable as a matter of law. And in *Katko v. Briney*, two homeowners were held liable for civil damages for injuries caused to a trespasser who set off a spring gun set as a trap in an abandoned house.[41]

Keep in mind that the rule against using deadly force to defend property has only limited applicability if an intruder enters one's home and the homeowner is present at the time of a break-in. As previously explained, then contemporary variations on the Castle Doctrine, such as "make my day" and "stand your ground" laws may operate to change the scope of legally permissible force.[42]

USE OF FORCE BY LAW ENFORCEMENT

Law enforcement officers are privileged to use force in self-defense under the same rules which govern private persons. They are also privileged to use force in defense of others without being subject to the mistaken intervener rule since it is their job to protect others. Accordingly, if the police make an honest and reasonable mistake by defending someone who had no privilege to act in self-defense, they will not be subjected to criminal liability. Unlike private citizens, however, in light of their law enforcement duties, police and correctional officers are privileged to use force to make an arrest or prevent an escape from custody. There are limits, however, on their ability to do so. Before exploring the limitation on the use of force by law enforcement, it is important to note that under the US Supreme Court's decision in *Graham v. Connor,* claims of excessive force course of an arrest, investigatory stop, or other seizure of a nonincarcerated person are properly analyzed under the Fourth Amendment's "objective reasonableness" standard, rather than under a substantive due process standard (see Chapter 2).[43] Thus, reasonableness of any use of force by law enforcement officials is judged "from the perspective of a reasonable officer on the scene, rather than with 20/20 vision of hindsight."[44] This approach grants police a significant benefit of the doubt when it comes to their use of force in recognition of fact that they "are often forced to make split-second judgments—in circumstances that are tense, uncertain, and rapidly evolving—about the amount of force that is necessary in a particular situation."[45]

Nondeadly Force

The Fourth Amendment of the US Constitution protects people against "unreasonable searches and seizures." Because an arrest is a "seizure" of a person, the Fourth Amendment limits the circumstances under which law enforcement officials may make an arrest. Specifically, a person may not be lawfully arrested unless, under the facts and circumstances known to law enforcement, there is probable cause to believe that the person to be arrested has committed or is committing a criminal offense.[46]

When a suspect submits to the authority of law enforcement and offers no resistance, officers may not use any force to make such an arrest other than the minor levels of physical force needed to apply handcuffs and escort the arrestee to a police vehicle or station.[47] If, however, the person resists arrest, then law enforcement officers are permitted to use force to subdue a suspect and make an arrest.[48]

A law enforcement officer's privilege to use force to arrest someone depends on the degree of force used and the context in which it is used. The basic rule covering the use of force while making an arrest is that law enforcement personnel may use whatever force is reasonably necessary to make the arrest, but may not use excessive force.[49] Determining what constitutes excessive force, however, always require an examination of the totality of the circumstances to determine the reasonableness of the actions of the police.

Deadly Force

Unlike ordinary citizens, law enforcement officers, by the nature of their public safety duties, are empowered to use deadly force to stop a fleeing suspect under limited circumstances. As the following case illustrates, the use of deadly by police is justified when there is probable cause (thereby making it "reasonable") to believe that a fleeing felon poses some sort of danger. Either the felon must be dangerous, or the felony must be dangerous. Accordingly, police may not use deadly force to apprehend a fleeing suspect of a misdemeanor, or to stop a suspected felon who poses no immediate threat of death or serious bodily harm.

An honest and reasonable mistake about the need to use deadly force will not subject a law enforcement officer to criminal liability. Thus, even if a police officer uses deadly force on someone who did not commit a crime, the officer will be excused if he or she acted reasonably when making the assessment.

State of TENNESSEE, Appellant,
v.
Cleamtee GARNER, et al.
471 U.S. 1 (1985).

* * *

Memphis Police Officers Elton Hymon and Leslie Wright were dispatched to answer a "prowler inside call." Upon arriving at the scene, they saw a woman standing on her porch and gesturing toward the adjacent house. She told them she had heard glass breaking and that "they" or "someone" was breaking in next door. While Wright radioed the dispatcher to say that they were on the scene, Hymon went behind the house. He heard a door slam and saw someone run across the backyard. The fleeing suspect, who was appellee-respondent's decedent, Edward Garner, stopped at a 6-feet-high chain link fence at the edge of the yard. With the aid of a flashlight, Hymon was able to see Garner's face and hands. He saw no sign of a weapon, and, though not certain, was "reasonably sure" and "figured" that Garner was unarmed. He thought Garner was 17 or 18 years old and about 5'5" or 5'7" tall.

While Garner was crouched at the base of the fence, Hymon called out "police, halt" and took a few steps toward him. Garner then began to climb over the fence. Convinced that if Garner made it over the fence he would elude capture, Hymon shot him. The bullet hit Garner in the back of the head. Garner was taken by ambulance to a hospital, where he died on the operating table. Ten dollars and a purse taken from the house were found on his body.

In using deadly force to prevent the escape, Hymon was acting under the authority of a Tennessee statute and pursuant to Police Department policy. The statute provides that "[i]f, after notice of the intention to arrest the defendant, he either flee or forcibly resist, the officer may use all the necessary means to effect the arrest."[50] The Department policy was slightly more restrictive than the statute, but still allowed the use of deadly force in cases of burglary....

Garner's father then brought this action ... seeking damages ... for asserted violations of Garner's constitutional rights....

* * *

Whenever an officer restrains the freedom of a person to walk away, he has seized that person.[51] While it is not always clear just when minimal police interference becomes a seizure,[52] there can be no question that apprehension by the use of deadly force is a seizure subject to the reasonableness requirement of the Fourth Amendment.... [R]easonableness depends on not only when a seizure is made, but also how it is carried out.[53]

* * *

The use of deadly force to prevent the escape of all felony suspects, whatever the circumstances, is constitutionally unreasonable. It is not better that all felony suspects die than that they escape. Where the suspect poses no immediate threat to the officer and no threat to others, the harm resulting from failing to apprehend him does not justify the use of deadly force to do so....

[However, where] the officer has probable cause to believe that the suspect poses a threat of serious physical harm, either to the officer or to others, it is not constitutionally unreasonable to prevent escape by using deadly force. Thus, if the suspect threatens the officer with a weapon or there is probable cause to believe that he has committed a crime involving the infliction or threatened infliction of serious physical harm, deadly force may be used if necessary to prevent escape, and if, where feasible, some warning has been given ...

It is insisted that the Fourth Amendment must be construed in light of the common-law rule, which allowed the use of whatever force was necessary to effect the arrest of a fleeing felon, though not a misdemeanant.... [But] the common-law rule ... arose at a time when virtually all felonies were punishable by death.... Courts have also justified the common-law rule by emphasizing the relative dangerousness of felons.[54]

Neither of these justifications makes sense today. Almost all crimes formerly punishable by death no longer are or can be.[55] And while in earlier times "the gulf between the felonies and the minor offenses was broad and deep," today the distinction is minor and often arbitrary.[56] Many crimes classified as misdemeanors, or nonexistent, at common law are now felonies. . . .

[Also, the] common-law rule developed at a time when weapons were rudimentary. Deadly force could be inflicted almost solely in a hand-to-hand struggle during which, necessarily, the safety of the arresting officer was at risk. Handguns were not carried by police officers until the latter half of the last century. . . . Only then did it become possible to use deadly force from a distance as a means of apprehension. . . .

* * *

Officer Hymon could not reasonably have believed that Garner—young, slight, and unarmed—posed any threat. Indeed, Hymon never attempted to justify his actions on any basis other than the need to prevent an escape. . . . [T]he fact that Garner was a suspected burglar could not, without regard to the other circumstances, automatically justify the use of deadly force. Hymon did not have probable cause to believe that Garner, whom he correctly believed to be unarmed, posed any physical danger to himself or others.

The dissent argues that the shooting was justified by the fact that Officer Hymon had probable cause to believe that Garner had committed a nighttime burglary. While we agree that burglary is a serious crime, we cannot agree that it is so dangerous as automatically to justify the use of deadly force. The FBI classifies burglary as a "property" rather than a "violent" crime.[57] Although the armed burglar would present a different situation, the fact that an unarmed suspect has broken into a dwelling at night does not automatically mean he is physically dangerous. This case demonstrates as much. . . .[58]

* * *

Justice O'Connor, Dissenting:

* * *

The clarity of hindsight cannot provide the standard for judging the reasonableness of police decisions made in uncertain and often dangerous circumstances. . . . Because burglary is a serious and dangerous felony, the public interest in the prevention and detection of the crime is of compelling importance. Where a police officer has probable cause to arrest a suspected burglar, the use of deadly force as a last resort might well be the only means of apprehending the suspect. With respect to a particular burglary, subsequent investigation simply cannot represent a substitute for immediate apprehension of the criminal suspect at the scene.

* * *

Questions

1. The dissent points out that expecting a police officer to make split-second determinations of reasonableness and dangerousness in the haste of the moment when tensions are running high may or may not seem objectively reasonable when viewed in hindsight by a judge or jury. Do you agree? Why or why not?

2. The *Garner* case involved a burglary, clearly one of the more difficult crimes to assess the dangerousness of the perpetrator. When the felony itself is an inherently dangerous one, this case would allow the police to use deadly force to apprehend a fleeing suspect. Which felonies do you think should qualify? Which ones should not?

The "You Make the Public Policy Call" feature contained in Box 15.3 asks you to apply the Garner case to high-speed vehicle chases.

The Use of Force by Correctional Personnel

The reasonableness standard that governs excessive force under the Fourth Amendment generally does not apply to convicted persons serving correctional sentences. Rather, inmates' right to be free from excessive force is governed by the Eighth Amendment ban on cruel and unusual punishment. In *Whitley v. Albers*,[59] the Court empowered correctional officials to use force in a good-faith effort to maintain or restore discipline. Only force that is applied maliciously and sadistically for the very purpose of causing harm is constitutionally impermissible. In deciding whether force was used in a good-faith effort to maintain or restore discipline, the Court suggested several factors that should be examined in each case, including the need for the force, the relationship between the need and the actual amount of force used, the extent of the injury inflicted, the extent of the threat to the safety of the staff and inmates, and any efforts made to temper the severity of the force used.[60] A few years later in *Hudson v. McMillian*,[61] the Court clarified that the standards set forth in *Whitley v. Albers* were not limited to cases in which correctional officials were trying to quell a prison riot; the standard expressed in *Whitley v. Albers* also apply to "lesser disruptions" in correctional institutions.

The US Supreme Court has not yet addressed the use of deadly force to prevent a prison escape. Several federal courts of appeal have done so. Applying *Whitley v. Albers*, most of these courts have upheld the use of deadly force to stop an inmate from escaping.[62]

Forcible Bodily Searches for Evidence

In *Schmerber v. California*,[63] the US Supreme Court held that police may use reasonable force to subdue a suspect and take a blood sample without the suspect's consent to gather evidence of driving under the influence (DUI). Three points were key to the Court's rationale. First, it determined that the process had been a reasonable one performed in a reasonable manner since blood was taken from a person arrested for drunk driving by a physician in a hospital environment according to accepted medical practices. Second, there was a clear indication in advance that the evidence sought would be found; specifically, the arrestee had glassy, bloodshot eyes and the smell of alcohol emanated from his breath. Finally, there were exigent circumstances and hence insufficient time to obtain a

BOX 15.3

YOU MAKE THE PUBLIC POLICY CALL

Applying *Garner* to High-Speed Chases

In *Scott v. Harris*,[124] a Georgia county deputy clocked a vehicle traveling at 73 miles per hour on a road with a 55-mile-per-hour speed limit. The deputy activated his blue flashing lights, but the driver sped away, initiating a chase down a two-lane road at speeds exceeding 85 miles per hour. Six minutes and nearly 10 miles after the chase had begun, the deputy terminated the high-speed chase by employing a "Precision Intervention Technique"—a maneuver which, by applying the deputy's push bumper to the rear of the suspect's vehicle, is designed to cause the fleeing vehicle to spin to a stop. The maneuver caused the driver to lose control of his vehicle, which left the roadway, ran down an embankment, overturned, and crashed. The driver was badly injured and was rendered a quadriplegic.

The driver filed a civil lawsuit alleging that the officer's actions constituted excessive force and, therefore, violated the Fourth Amendment to the US Constitution. In ruling in favor of the sheriff's deputy, the US Supreme Court decided that because the car chase that the driver initiated posed a substantial and immediate risk of serious physical injury to others, the deputy's attempt to terminate the chase by forcing the suspect off the road was reasonable. The Court reasoned that because the suspect intentionally placed himself and the public in danger by unlawfully engaging in reckless, high-speed flight, the deputy acted reasonably in forcing the suspect's car off the road even though doing so placed the fleeing motorist at risk of serious injury or death. In so deciding, the Court rejected the driver's argument that safety could have been assured if the police simply ceased their pursuit.

1. How is the situation in *Scott* like the one in *Garner*? How is it different?
2. Do you concur with the Court's conclusion in *Scott v. Harris*, or do you think that *Garner* required the deputy to allow the suspect to flee in light of the fact that the underlying offense was speeding? Explain your reasoning.

warrant before the percentage of alcohol in the blood diminished. When there is time to obtain a warrant, however, the Court's decision in *Missouri v. McNeely* requires law enforcement officers to obtain one.[64]

In contrast to *Schmerber*, the New Jersey Supreme Court ruled in *State v. Ravotto*[65] that the police used excessive force in subduing a DUI suspect for the withdrawal of a blood sample because the suspect had expressed a fear of needles and had offered to take a breath test. The case illustrates the importance of the totality of the circumstances in determining the overall reasonableness of the use of force by law enforcement officials.

Although the routine blood test in *Schmerber* was upheld, more invasive procedures may be constitutionally unreasonable. (And, although beyond the scope of this text, the ability to obtain a search warrant prior to medical personnel retrieving blood from a suspect is an important part of the calculus.)[66] For example, in *Rochin v. California*, the Supreme Court refused to sanction the act of pumping an arrestee's stomach in a hospital environment as part of a search for pills believed to be drugs. "This is conduct that shocks the conscience. Illegally breaking into the privacy of the petitioner, the struggle to open his mouth and remove what was there, the forcible extraction of his stomach's contents—this course of proceeding by agents of government to obtain evidence is bound to offend even hardened sensibilities."[67] Similarly, in *Winston v. Lee*,[68] the Court prohibited the surgical removal under general anesthesia of a bullet from the suspect's chest area.

USE OF FORCE IN DISCIPLINING CHILDREN

The common law permitted parents, or those acting *in loco parentis* (in place of parents), to use a reasonable amount of force to discipline a child. This use of force is sometimes referred to as **parental privilege**. The *in loco parentis* doctrine permitted teachers to corporally punish their students at common law. Today, most US states have statutorily banned corporal punishment in schools, although in the states that have not done so, teachers "may impose reasonable, but not excessive force to discipline a child" if permitted to do so under the rules and regulations of a particular school board or district.[69]

Cases involving claims of parental privilege tend to focus on one or two questions. First, was the actor privileged to use force to discipline a child? And second, if so, was the amount of force used reasonable? The next case illustrates both lines of inquiry.

Jason McREYNOLDS, Appellant-Defendant,

v.

STATE of Indiana, Appellee-Plaintiff.

901 N.E.2d 1149 (Ind. App. 2009).

* * *

McReynolds lived in Yavonne Wasson's home. In exchange for a place to stay, McReynolds agreed to babysit Wasson's two children, ten-year-old A. R. and seven-year-old M. R., while she was at work. He also provided the children with transportation to and from school and helped them with homework. McReynolds generally asked Wasson's permission before disciplining the children.

In October of 2006, M. R. was exhibiting some behavioral problems. He was wetting his pants and lying about his homework. Wasson had progressively disciplined M. R., starting with withdrawing privileges and progressing to spanking with a belt. On October

11, 2006, M. R. lied to Wasson about his homework, and she "spanked him three times lightly." That evening, as Wasson was saying goodnight to M. R., he told her that he had been hearing voices. During the night, M. R. began banging his head against the wall or the floor. Wasson went into his room to investigate, and M. R. told her that the voices were telling him to bang his head.

On October 12, 2006, Wasson went to work. There, she scheduled an evaluation for M. R. at Deaconess Cross Pointe, a psychiatric hospital, for 3:00 p.m. that day. McReynolds took A. R. to school, but decided not to take M. R. because he had marks on his face from banging his head. Instead, McReynolds decided to take M. R. to work with him. McReynolds told M. R. to get ready to leave and asked him if he needed to use the restroom. M. R. said no, and then subsequently wet his pants. McReynolds asked him why he lied, and M. R. said that "he didn't know, he didn't care." McReynolds used a belt and a wooden clothes hanger with metal prongs to spank M.R. at least five times. According to M. R., McReynolds spanked him because he lied.

Later, at Deaconess Cross Pointe, Wasson saw blood on the back of M. R.'s shirt, and when she pulled it up, she discovered severe bruising and bleeding on M. R.'s buttocks. An ambulance was called, and M. R. was transported to Deaconess Gateway Hospital. M. R. was treated with antibiotics and pain medication through intravenous therapy and remained in the hospital for at least two days. A week later, his injuries still required bandages.

On October 17, 2006, the State charged McReynolds with battery resulting in serious bodily injury to a person less than fourteen years of age, a class B felony. On July 1, 2008, a jury found McReynolds guilty of class D felony battery to a person less than fourteen years of age, a lesser included offense. The trial court sentenced McReynolds to eighteen months in the Department of Correction.

On appeal, McReynolds argues that the evidence is insufficient to support his conviction . . . [because IND. CODE § 35-41-3-1 provides that] . . . "[a] parent is privileged to apply such reasonable force or to impose such reasonable confinement upon his [or her] child as he [or she] reasonably believes to be necessary for its proper control, training, or education."[70]

* * *

[O]ur review of the record leads us to conclude that McReynolds was not a person *in loco parentis*. McReynolds was neither a stepparent nor romantically involved with M. R.'s mother. He did not act as a father figure, nor did he have the responsibilities of a father or stepfather. He did not make parenting decisions on his own or even in conjunction with Wasson. McReynolds acknowledged that he "didn't really ask questions" about Wasson's parental decisions. In short, McReynolds was a babysitter. He drove the children to school and helped them with their homework. When necessary, he asked Wasson's permission to discipline the children, although he did not do so on this occasion. At all times, McReynolds was subject to Wasson's direction. Given the circumstances present here, we conclude that McReynolds was not a person *in loco parentis*, and therefore the parental privilege defense is not available to him.

Even if we were to conclude that McReynolds was entitled to assert the parental privilege defense, we would conclude that his use of force was unreasonable. In determining whether force or confinement is reasonable for the control, training, or education of a child, the following factors are to be considered:

(a) whether the actor is a parent;
(b) the age, sex, and physical and mental condition of the child;
(c) the nature of his offense and his apparent motive;
(d) the influence of his example upon other children of the same family or group;
(e) whether the force or confinement is reasonably necessary and appropriate to compel obedience to a proper command;
(f) whether it is disproportionate to the offense, unnecessarily degrading, or likely to cause serious or permanent harm.[71]

However, this list is not exhaustive, and "not all of the listed factors may be relevant or applicable in every case."[72]

In this case, we need . . . only observe that a seven-year-old child wet his pants and was disciplined such that he received open wounds on his buttocks that required two days of hospitalization. Clearly, the force was disproportionate to the offense, unnecessarily degrading, and could even result in permanent scarring and long-term emotional trauma. Accordingly, we affirm McReynolds's conviction for class D felony battery.

Questions

1. If McReynolds had been romantically involved with M. R.'s mother, would that have changed the outcome? Perhaps more importantly, should it? In other words, why is there something special about being a parental figure that creates a privilege to use force to discipline a child?
2. Even if McReynolds had been the child's parent or someone legally acting *in loco parentis*, the court concluded that the type of injuries inflicted on the child were so severe that they exceeded the scope of the parental privilege to use force to discipline a child. Do you agree? Why or why not?
3. Are there behaviors in which a child might engage that you think would justify the level of force used in the *McReynolds* case? Where do you think the line should be drawn between a reasonable amount of force (constituting lawful discipline under the parental privilege doctrine) and an unreasonable or excessive amount of force (constituting criminal battery and, perhaps felony child abuse)? Explain your reasoning.

USE OF FORCE BY ABUSE VICTIMS

Dr. Lenore Walker first coined the term **Battered Women's Syndrome** (BWS) in her 1979 book, *The Battered Woman*.[73] In it, Walker put forth a theory that attempted to explain why abused women stayed in abusive relationships, and what finally triggers them to strike back.

Walker posited that BWS develops as a result of exposure to a three-phase **cycle of violence** (Figure 15.1) that typifies abusive relationships.[74] The first phase is called the "tension-building phase," which is characterized by arguments and ever-increasing tensions and may include minor acts of violence, such as slapping. Eventually, however, there is an event that triggers the second phase, which Walker called the "acute battering incident." During this phase, the abuser explodes in a fit of rage and batters the victim. Walker hypothesized that the acute battering incident causes the abuser to feel and express remorse, apologize profusely, and engage in loving, caring, and helpful behaviors to promote reconciliation. In spite of the abuser's promises that it will "never happen again," the cycle inevitably repeats itself.

Walker also offered an explanation as to why the cycle repeats itself, borrowing from behavioral psychology's notion of **learned helplessness**.[75] Martin Seligman conducted experiments on dogs during which time the animals were placed in harnesses and were electrically shocked at random intervals. At first, the dogs tried to escape, but given that

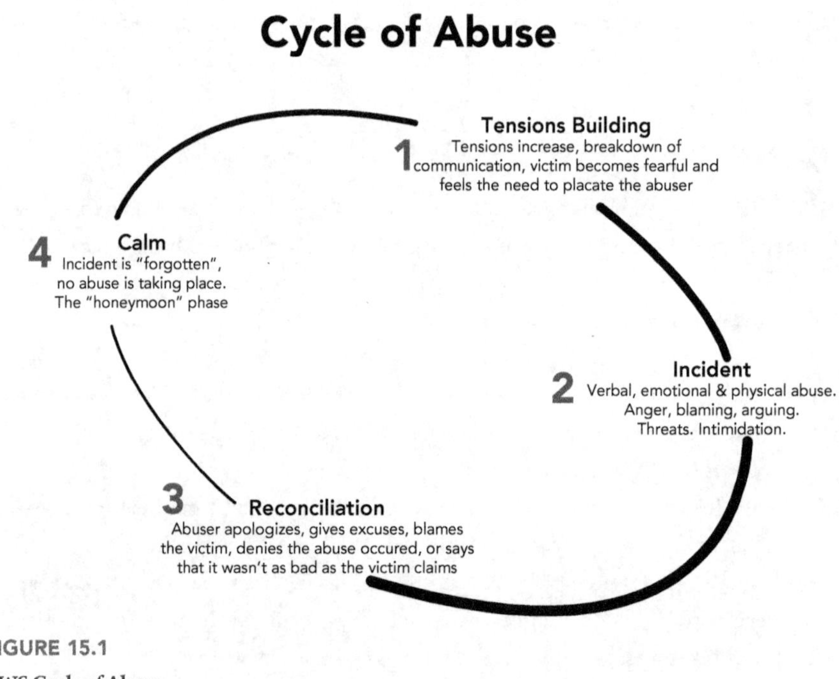

FIGURE 15.1
BWS Cycle of Abuse

the physical restraints in which they were placed made it impossible, the dogs eventually stopped escape attempts. In other words, the dogs eventually accepted the fact that they were helpless to prevent the shocks. More importantly, after the dogs passively acquiesced to the shocks without resistance, Seligman gave the dogs an opportunity to escape, but the dogs failed to avail themselves of the opportunity.

Walker used the theory of learned helplessness to explain why battered women do not leave abusive relationships, building on the work of other researchers who had attempted to show how learned helplessness develops in humans.[76] According to Walker, a woman stays for a number of psycho-social reasons. She may have old-fashioned notions that "a woman's proper place is in the home."[77] She may be economically dependent on the abuser. They may have children and the woman may not want to separate them from their father. The stigma that attaches to a woman who leaves the family without her children undoubtedly also acts as a further deterrent to moving out. Some women may even perceive the battering cycle as normal, especially if they grew up in a violent household. Even when battered women want to leave, they are typically unwilling to reach out and confide in their friends, family, or the police, either out of shame and humiliation, fear of reprisal by their husband, or the feeling they will not be believed. But one of the most important factors for Walker in a woman's decision to stay with her abuser is the loving and caring behavior the batterer exhibits during the reconciliation phase. For Walker, the abuser's contrite behavior acts as a "positive reinforcement for [the victim] remaining in the relationship."[78]

The combination of these factors leads a victim of abuse to feel powerless to leave. Moreover, as she stays and tries to prevent the cycle of violence from repeating, she learns that it is not really within her power to control the abuser's feelings and temper. Her repeated failures to prevent tension from building up to an acute battering incident mirrors the learning of the dogs in Seligman's research. The repeated, failed attempts "to control the violence would, over time, produce learned helplessness and depression as the repeated batterings, like electrical shocks, [would] diminish the woman's motivation to respond."[79]

According to Walker, the cycle of violence tends to worsen as time passes. Not only may acute battering incidents become more frequent, but also they may become more severe. Eventually, however, the woman endures "so much frustration, despair, and isolation that her perceptions of violence are altered. The woman may violently strike back against the batterer in an effort to free herself from the cycle of abuse that she may believe ultimately will lead to her death."[80] But such striking back could lead to of criminal charges, often for serious crimes such as aggravated assault or homicide. If the elements of the traditional defense of self-defense appear to be missing, BWS evidence may become the foundation of the abuse victim's defense.

Before turning to the specifics of how criminal law responded to BWS, it should be noted that Walker's research has been criticized as "little more than a patchwork of pseudo-scientific methods employed to confirm a hypothesis that its author and participating researchers never seriously doubted."[81] Alternatives, especially those that challenge the notion of learned helplessness in abuse victims, have become far more accepted. For example, Edward Gondolf and Ellen Fisher proposed *survivor theory* as an alternative to learned helplessness.[82] Based on a study of more than 6,600 victims, they reported that many victims of domestic violence make "extremely assertive efforts to stop the violence."[83] Survivor theory "now dominates our understanding of the reactions of women to intimate terrorism. The core idea is that battered women respond to severe abuse with innovative coping strategies and active help-seeking."[84] Still, there can be no doubt that Walker's work had a significant impact on the law.

The Battered Woman's Syndrome Defense

Whether there is actually a Battered Woman's Syndrome Defense (BWSD) is actually a matter of some controversy. "The defense of battered women who kill their mates is slowly developing a distinct style or technique called the abused spouse defense," which is a hybrid of "the more familiar and established defenses of self-defense and diminished capacity."[85] Others insist it is not a defense in and of itself, but rather a psychological theory offered in support of a theory of self-defense or imperfect self-defense.[86]

The purpose of offering evidence of BWS is to fill a gap left by the law of self-defense and by the PTSD. BWSD is most frequently used in courts to explain the behavior of women who turn on their abusers and, in turn, to reduce their criminal responsibility.[87] BWSD is similar to PTSD in that the defendant's prior history or experience triggers a violent response. Battered women were frequently unable to assert PTSD, however, because they could not fulfill all of the diagnostic requirements of PTSD.[88]

Recall that self-defense permits the use of force only when *necessary* to prevent an *imminent* attack from unlawful force.[89] As such, when a battered woman uses force to defend herself from such an unlawful, imminent attack, she may assert self-defense. But in many cases, battered women act against their abusers when they do not appear to be imminent danger and, therefore, are not acting within the technical requirements of the law of self-defense.[90] Alternatively, battered women may use deadly force when the law recognizes the ability only to combat nondeadly physical force with nondeadly physical force.[91] BWS evidence can help to explain why a woman might reasonably believe, in light of her history of abuse, her life was in danger, even though to the lay person, she was not facing what objectively looked like a threat of imminent, unlawful force.[92]

States differ widely on how BWS evidence might be used to explain a woman's belief that force was necessary to prevent and "imminent" attack. In *People v. Stewart*, a leading case decided in 1988, the Kansas Supreme Court held that self-defense may not be used to excuse a homicide committed by a battered wife where there is no evidence of a deadly threat or imminent danger contemporaneous with the killing.[93] But other states disagree. For example, in *State v. Gallegos*,[94] an appellate court in New Mexico allowed BSW evidence in a case in which a woman shot and stabbed her abusive husband while he was lying in bed. The court ruled she had presented "substantial evidence of imminent danger" because her husband had raped her and threatened to kill her.[95] She was, therefore, entitled to a self-defense jury instruction, reasoning that to "require the battered person to await a blatant, deadly assault before she can act in defense of herself would not only ignore unpleasant reality, but would amount to sentencing her to 'murder by installment.'"[96] And in the 2017 case of *Porter v. State*, the highest court in Maryland stressed that BWS evidence is also important to support a defendant's claim of imperfect self-defense because it "can explain to the jury how a woman might actually fear imminent danger during a break between violent episodes."[97] The court emphasized that a claim of imperfect self-defense does not permit an acquittal when an abused women kills her abusive husband under objectively unreasonable circumstances, but it does permit "her to make her case to the jury that she only committed manslaughter."[98] That ruling was particularly notable because the court allowed an imperfect self-defense claim when the defendant had hired a third party to killer her husband.

A woman claiming imperfect self-defense must present evidence that she feared imminent or immediate danger at the time of the killing—she does not have to show that she acted spontaneously. The means by which a woman takes defensive action against her abuser does not affect whether she actually believed she was in imminent danger at the time of the killing. A woman who recruits help in taking defensive action does not forfeit her right to claim imperfect self-defense by doing so.[99] Applying this logic, the court in *Porter* vacated the defendant's conspiracy conviction as well, reasoning that "imperfect self-defense negates the element of malice in homicide offenses and their inchoate forms."[100]

Prior to the rise of the BWS defense, female abuse victims who could not use assert the defense of self-defense were left with no real defense other than insanity.[101] As discussed in Chapter 14, because insanity is an expensive defense that is unsuccessful in the overwhelming number of cases in which it is asserted, the defense offered insufficient protection for the victims of violent abuse.

More broadly, insanity defenses used in these circumstances played into misogynistic stereotypes and ignored the realities of women who live with domestic violence. As Robbin S. Ogle and Susan Jacobs write, psychosis theory "reflects our history of stereotypes about women and a belief that femininity makes crime impossible, thus any woman committing a crime must be crazy to go so far outside her social role." Insanity defenses failed to acknowledge that women who kill their abusers can do so in response to rational, competent fear.[102]

Interestingly, the use of BWS evidence has not been confined to cases where an abused woman strikes out against her abuser. Where the state of mind of the defendant at the time of the crime is at issue, BWS evidence can be offered to show that the defendant did not possess the required mental state—a diminished capacity argument in its purest form.[103]

For example, the family court in *In re Glenn G.* relieved a mother of liability for child abuse after evidence of BWS was offered.[104] The mother, however, was still held liable for child neglect, a strict liability offense under New York law. In *United States v. Marenghi*, the defendant offered BWS evidence to show she lacked the intent necessary for a conviction on possession and distribution of controlled substances.[105] The *Marenghi* court reasoned that the evidence was not being offered as a defense to the charges themselves, but rather as part of an attempt to show that the defendant's capacity was diminished in such a way that she did not entertain the requisite *mens rea*.

As previously noted, Walker's research suffered from serious methodological flaws. In fact, the research fails to demonstrate that most abused women experience the cycle of violence as explained by Walker, or that abused women learn they are helpless to prevent it.[106] Indeed, proponents of the much more widely accepted survivor theory have criticized the notion of a "syndrome" and advocated for a model that examines the actual experiences of a particular abuse victim.[107] Consequently, some courts have excluded BWS evidence as unreliable.[108]

Nonetheless, many courts continue to embrace expert testimony on the effects of battering.[109] Today, however, rather than focusing on BWS, many forensic psychological experts have updated their approach to such testimony, focusing on:

(1) The cumulative history of violence and abuse experienced by the victim in the relationship at issue, including, where relevant, the nature and extent of violence or abuse in a specific episode;
(2) The psychological reactions of the battered woman to the batterer's violence;
(3) The strategies used (or not used) by the battered woman in response to prior violence and abuse, and the consequences of (or the expectations that arise from) those strategies; and
(4) The contextual factors that influenced both the battered woman's strategies for responding to prior violence, and her psychological reactions to that violence.[110]

Regardless of the reasons underlying the continued acceptance of expert testimony to explain the psychological effects of abuse victimization, it is clear that many states continue to allow such evidence under certain circumstances, although few go as far as Maryland did in the *Porter* case.[111] For example, the Louisiana Supreme Court's 2018 decision in *State v. Curley* set aside a murder conviction on the grounds that a lawyer had rendered ineffective assistance of counsel for failing to present expert testimony in the context of a claim of self-defense by a battered woman.[112]

Other Abuse Victims

Some jurisdictions have extended defenses based on the psychological effects of battering in gender-neutral ways. But terms such as "battered person's syndrome" can mask the fact that juries tend to be very skeptical of any such syndrome evidence offered by victims of interpersonal violence abuse other than from women against their abusive husbands. Consider the 1984 case of *Jahnke v. State*.[113] Jahnke was sixteen years old. He waited with a loaded shotgun in his home for his parents to return from dinner. When his father walked in, Jahnke shot him. The evidence showed that the father has physically and psychologically abused Jahnke for most of his life. Jahnke unsuccessfully attempted to assert a "battered person syndrome" defense. On appeal, the Wyoming Supreme Court upheld his conviction, with one judge stating it was a "textbook case of first-degree murder."[114]

Some courts have embraced a broader understanding of abuse since *Jahnke*. For example, several states, including Arizona, Minnesota, New Jersey, Ohio, and Oklahoma, have ruled that expert testimony about the psychological effects of battering against a child is admissible to the same extent as testimony against a woman.[115]

Battering evidence was similarly met with hostility when used by abused husbands and abused partners in a same-sex relationship.[116] Although several states, including Florida, Maryland, Missouri, and South Carolina, have adopted gender-neutral legislation concerning "battered spouse syndrome,"[117] that has not changed the fact that juries often struggle to understand intimate partner victimization against men and same-sex partners.[118]

In the case of heterosexual male survivors, both society and the legal justice system find it difficult to view the man as the weaker party in the relationship. Although the power dynamics and physical size discrepancies can be just as unequal in homosexual relationships as in heterosexual relationships, and there are legitimate instances of men being abused by their female partners, many jurors automatically view the situation as one of mutual battering.[119]

CONCLUSION

Learning Objectives	Summaries
1. Analyze the elements of a valid self-defense claim using nonlethal force.	A person is privileged to use a reasonable amount of physical force against another person when the actor reasonably believes that such force is necessary for the purpose of protecting against an imminent attack upon himself or herself from unlawful force. Force may not be used in response to lawful force, such as when police make an arrest, people defend against initial aggressors, and when property owners evict trespassers.
2. Analyze the elements of a valid self-defense claim using nonlethal force.	A person is privileged to use deadly force against another person when the actor reasonably believes that such force is necessary to protect against an unlawful, imminent attack upon himself or herself from deadly force or to stop select types of serious criminal victimization. In some jurisdictions a warning must be given first unless it would be futile. Similarly, in some jurisdictions, one must retreat if one can do so in complete safety. But in jurisdictions that have expansive castle doctrines, "make my day" laws, or "stand your ground" laws, statutory presumptions ease the common law's restrictions on the use of deadly force in self-defense.

Learning Objectives	Summaries
3. Explain when force may be used to defend other persons.	One may act to defend another person in much the same way one may act in self-defense, but honest and reasonable mistakes will not justify or excuse those who mistakenly intervene to defend someone who lacked the privilege to defend himself or herself.
4. Explain when force may be used to defend property.	One may use of a reasonable amount of nondeadly force to prevent imminent, unlawful interference with one's property. Accordingly, nondeadly force may be used to prevent or terminate: (1) an unlawful entry or other trespass onto one's land; or (2) the unlawful carrying away of tangible, movable property in the actor's lawful possession.
5. Evaluate the limits the place places on law enforcement officers when using force.	Law enforcement officers are privileged to use force in self-defense under the same rules which govern private persons. They are also privileged to use force in defense of others without being subject to the mistaken intervener rule. They may also use a reasonable amount of force to effect an arrest. Deadly force, however, may not be used to stop a feeling suspect there is probable cause to believe that the person committed a dangerous felony or otherwise poses some sort of danger.
6. Discuss the scope of parental privilege to use force to discipline children.	Parents, or those acting *in loco parentis*, are privileged to use a reasonable amount of force to discipline a child.
7. Describe the ways in which the law attempts to accommodate the use of force by victims of abuse.	Evidence of battering victimization may be used to show PTSD as part of an insanity or diminished capacity defense. Under the modified objective standard for self-defense claims, many states also allow evidence of battering victimization to show the reasonableness of someone's use of force in self-defense under circumstances in which a purely objective approach would render such a defense ineffective.

KEY TERMS

Battered Women's Syndrome
castle doctrine
cycle of violence
duty to retreat
duty to warn
imperfect self-defense
initial aggressor
learned helplessness
make my day laws
mistaken intervener rule
parental privilege
privilege
stand your ground laws

Notes

PREFACE

1. L. H. LaRue, *How to Read a Law School Casebook, in* GUIDE TO THE STUDY OF LAW: AN INTRODUCTION (2nd ed. 2001), at § 2.02.
2. M. H. Sam Jacobson, The *Curse of Tradition in the Law School Classroom: What Casebook Professors Can Learn from Those Professors Who Teach Legal Writing,* 61 MERCER L. REV. 899, 908–11 (2010); *see also* Arthur D. Austin, *Is the Casebook Method Obsolete?,* 6 WILLIAM & MARY L. REV. 15 (1965).
3. Jacobson, *supra* note 2, at 909.
4. *See generally* Stephen S. Owen, Henry F. Fradella, Tod W. Burke, & Jerry Joplin, *Conceptualizing Justice: Revising the Introductory Criminal Justice Course,* 17 J. CRIM. JUST. EDUC. 3 (2006); Stephen S. Owen & Tod W. Burke, *Criminal Justice as a Liberal Arts Discipline,* 3 LIBERALARTSONLINE (Feb. 21, 2003), http://www.liberalarts.wabash.edu/lao-3-3-criminal-justice-liber/.
5. *See* FRANK MORN, ACADEMIC POLITICS AND THE HISTORY OF CRIMINAL JUSTICE EDUCATION (1995).
6. *Id.; see also, e.g.,* Donna C. Hale, *Criminal Justice Education: Traditions in Transition,* 15 JUST. Q. 385 (1998).
7. Otwin Marenin & John Worrall, *Criminal Justice: Portrait of a Discipline in Process,* 26 J. CRIM. JUST. 465, 465 (1998).
8. *See, e.g.,* MICHAEL S. ROTH, BEYOND THE UNIVERSITY: WHY LIBERAL EDUCATION MATTERS (2014); FAREED ZAKARIA, IN DEFENSE OF A LIBERAL EDUCATION (2015); *see also* Mark I. McNutt, *There Is Value in Liberal Arts Education, Employers Say,* U.S. NEWS & WORLD REPORT (Sept. 22, 2014), http://www.usnews.com/news/college-of-tomorrow/articles/2014/09/22/there-is-value-in-liberal-arts-education-employers-say; Jessica Kleiman, *Why Getting A Liberal Arts College Education Is Not A Mistake,* FORBES (Apr. 28, 2014), http://www.forbes.com/sites/work-in-progress/2014/04/28/why-getting-a-liberal-arts-college-education-is-not-a-mistake/#44ab82c1a206.
9. David H. Bayley, *The Emptiness of Curricular Reform,* 2 J. CRIM. JUST. EDUC. 193, 196 (1991).

CHAPTER 1

1. CHARLES MCCAGHY, DEVIANT BEHAVIOR 2–3 (McMillian, 1976).
2. Paul W. Tappan, *Who is the Criminal?,* 12 AM. SOCIOLOGICAL REV. 96, 100 (1947).
3. JOHN OGDEN CURRA, THE RELATIVITY OF DEVIANCE (1999).
4. Durganand Sinha, *Culture as the Target and Culture as the Source: A Review of Cross-Cultural Psychology in Asia,* 8 PSYCHOL. & DEVELOPING SOCIETIES 83 (1996).
5. DONALD BLACK, SOCIOLOGICAL JUSTICE 4 (1989) (citing EDWARD ALSWORTH ROSS, SOCIAL CONTROL: A SURVEY OF THE FOUNDATIONS OF ORDER (1901)).
6. Myrna Dawson, *Intimacy and Violence: Exploring the Role of Victim–Defendant Relationship in Criminal Law,* 96 J. CRIM. L. & CRIMINOLOGY 1417, 1435 (2006).
7. PETER CONRAD & JOSEPH W. SCHNEIDER, DEVIANCE AND MEDICALIZATION: FROM BADNESS TO SICKNESS 7 (2d ed. 1992).
8. *Id.* at 140; 177.
9. *See generally* STEPHEN S. OWEN, HENRY F. FRADELLA, TOD W. BURKE, & JERRY JOPLIN, THE FOUNDATIONS OF CRIMINAL JUSTICE (2nd ed. 2015)
10. DONALD BLACK, THE BEHAVIOR OF LAW (1976).
11. CONRAD & SCHNEIDER, *supra* note 7, at 32.
12. JUSTICE POLICY INSTITUTE, SUBSTANCE ABUSE TREATMENT AND PUBLIC SAFETY (Jan. 2008), http://www.justicepolicy.org/images/upload/08_01_REP_DrugTx_AC-PS.pdf.

13. STEVEN VAGO, LAW AND SOCIETY 8 (10th ed. 2012).
14. *Id.* (citing MAX WEBER, LAW IN ECONOMY AND SOCIETY 5 (Max Rheinstein & Edwahard Shils eds. & trans., 1954)).
15. F. James Davis, *Law as a Type of Social Control*, *in* SOCIETY AND THE LAW: NEW MEANINGS FOR AN OLD PROFESSION 39–63 (F. James Davis et al. eds., 1962).
16. *Id.*
17. *See generally* LIEF H. CARTER & THOMAS F. BURKE, REASON IN LAW 12–13 (8th ed. 2010).
18. MARTHA T. ROTH, HARRY A. HOFFNER, JR., & PIOTR MICHALOWSKI, LAW COLLECTIONS FROM MESOPOTAMIA AND ASIA MINOR (2d ed. 1997).
19. *Id.* at 13–23.
20. *Id.* at 71–143.
21. ROTH ET AL., *supra* note 18, at 121.
22. Albert M. Rosenblatt, *The Law's Evolution: Long Night's Journey into Day*, 24 CARDOZO L. REV. 2119, 2127 (2003).
23. Morris J. Fish, *An Eye for an Eye: Proportionality as a Moral Principle of Punishment*, 28 OXFORD J. LEGAL STUDIES 57, 61 (2008).
24. Rosenblatt, *supra* note 22, at 2129.
25. DOUGLAS M. MACDOWELL, THE LAW IN CLASSICAL ATHENS (1978).
26. GEORGE MILLER CALHOUN, THE GROWTH OF CRIMINAL LAW IN ANCIENT GREECE 11, 16, 66, 70, 85, 11, & 131 (1927).
27. David Cohen, *Crime, Punishment, and the Rule of Law in Classical Athens*, *in* THE CAMBRIDGE COMPANION TO ANCIENT GREEK LAW 211 (Michael Gagarin & David Cohen eds., 2005).
28. *See* OLIVIA F. ROBINSON, CRIMINAL LAW OF ANCIENT ROME (1990).
29. James Lindgren, *Why the Ancients May Not Have Needed a System of Criminal Law*, 76 B.U. L. REV. 29, 39 (1996).
30. *Id.* at 50–51.
31. *Id.* at 2135.
32. Rosenblatt, *supra* note 22, at 2135–36.
33. Rosenblatt, *supra* note 22, at 2137–38.
34. *Id.* at 2138; *see also* J. C. HOLT, GEORGE GARNETT, & JOHN HUDSON, MAGNA CARTA (3d ed. 2015).
35. HOLT ET AL., *supra* note 34, at 39–41.
36. *See* MATTHEW HALE, THE HISTORY OF THE COMMON LAW OF ENGLAND (C. M. Gray ed., 1971)(1713).
37. *See* MARKUS DIRK DUBBER, AN INTRODUCTION TO THE MODEL PENAL CODE (2d ed. 2015).
38. GRESHAM M. SYKES, THE SOCIETY OF CAPTIVES: A STUDY OF A MAXIMUM SECURITY PRISON (1958).
39. H. L. A. HART, PUNISHMENT AND RESPONSIBILITY: ESSAYS IN THE PHILOSOPHY OF LAW 4–5 (1968).
40. JEREMY BENTHAM, THE PRINCIPLES OF MORALS AND LEGISLATION (Prometheus 1988) (1789); Cesare Beccaria, *On Crimes and Punishments*, in ON CRIMES AND PUNISHMENTS, AND OTHER WRITINGS 1 (Richard Bellamy, ed., Richard Davies & Virginia Cox, trans., 1995)(1764).
41. Jock Young, *Thinking Seriously About Crime: Some Models of Criminology*, *in* CRIME AND SOCIETY: READINGS IN HISTORY AND THEORY 257 (Mike Fitzgerald, Gregor McLennan & Jennie Pawson eds., 1981).
42. RICHARD KRAUT, SOCRATES AND THE STATE 91–114 (1984).
43. THOMAS HOBBES, LEVIATHAN (1909 ed.) (1651), http://oll.libertyfund.org/titles/hobbes-leviathan-1909-ed; JOHN LOCKE, SECOND TREATISE OF GOVERNMENT (C.B. McPherson ed. 1980) (1690), https://www.gutenberg.org/files/7370/7370-h/7370-h.htm.
44. Edward A. Harris, *From Social Contract to Hypothetical Agreement: Consent and the Obligation to Obey the Law*, 92 COLUM. L. REV. 651, 657 (1992) (citing THOMAS HOBBES, LEVIATHAN 63–66 (I, 13), 105 (II, 20) (J.M. Dent & Sons Ltd. 1914) (1651); John Locke, *The Second Treatise of Government: An Essay Concerning the True Original, Extent, and End of Civil Government*, *in* TWO TREATISES OF GOVERNMENT, 265, 315, 330–51 (§§ 73, 95–126) (Peter Laslett ed. 1988) (3d ed. 1698)).

45. April L. Cherry, *Social Contract Theory, Welfare Reform, Race, and the Male Sex-Right*, 75 OR. L. REV. 1037, 1045 (1996)(quoting THOMAS HOBBES, LEVIATHAN *in* INTRODUCTION TO THOMAS HOBBES 183 (C. B. MacPherson, ed. 1981)(1651)).
46. BECCARIA, *supra* note 40, at 9.
47. *Id.* at 8–10.
48. *E.g.*, EDWARD ALSWORTH ROSS, SOCIAL CONTROL: A SURVEY OF THE FOUNDATIONS OF ORDER (1901).
49. *See* JOHANNES ANDENAES, PUNISHMENT AND DETERRENCE (1974).
50. John Locke, *An Essay Concerning the True Original Extent and End of Civil Government*, *in* SOCIAL AND POLITICAL PHILOSOPHY 169 (John Somerville & Ronald E. Santoni eds., 1963) (1689).
51. *See, e.g.*, ELLSWORTH L. FERSCH, THINKING ABOUT LAW AND ETHICS: ANSWERS TO FREQUENTLY ASKED QUESTIONS WITH CASE EXAMPLES (2007).
52. THOMAS AQUINAS, SUMMA THEOLOGICA (2d rev. ed. 1920) (c. 1485), http://www.newadvent.org/summa/index.html.
53. Daniel S. Nagin, *Criminal Deterrence Research at the Outset of the Twenty-First Century*, *in* 23 CRIME AND JUSTICE: A REVIEW OF RESEARCH 1 (Michael Tonry ed., 1998); Robert Apel & Daniel S. Nagin, *General Deterrence: A Review of Recent Evidence*, *in* CRIME AND PUBLIC POLICY 411 (James Q. Wilson & Joan Petersilia eds., 2011).
54. *See, e.g.*, BURRHUS FREDERIC SKINNER, THE BEHAVIOR OF ORGANISMS (1938); John B. Watson & R. Rayner, *Conditioned Emotional Reactions*, 3 J. EXPERIMENTAL PSYCHOL. 1 (1920).
55. *See, e.g.*, C. Ray Jeffery, *Biological and Neuropsychiatric Approaches to Criminal Behavior*, *in* VARIETIES OF CRIMINOLOGY: READINGS FROM A DYNAMIC DISCIPLINE 15 (Gregg Barak ed., 1994).
56. HERBERT PACKER, THE LIMITS OF THE CRIMINAL SANCTION 53 (1968).
57. Robert Martinson, *What Works? Questions and Answers about Prison Reform*, 35 PUB. INTEREST 22, 25 (1974).
58. Robert Martinson, *New Findings, New Views: A Note of Caution Regarding Sentencing Reform*, 7 HOFSTRA L. REV. 243 (1979).
59. *See* Francis T. Cullen, *The Twelve People Who Saved Rehabilitation: How the Science of Criminology Made a Difference*, 43 CRIMINOLOGY 1 (2005).
60. *Id.*; *see also* Mark W. Lipsey & Francis T. Cullen, *The Effectiveness of Correctional Rehabilitation: A Review of Systematic Reviews*, 3 ANN. REV. L. & SOC. SCI. 297 (2007).
61. *See* Francis T. Cullen, Bonnie S. Fisher, & Brandon K. Applegate, *Public Opinion About Punishment and Corrections*, 27 CRIME & JUST. 1 (2000).
62. *E.g.*, Nathaniel J. Pallone & James J. Hennessy, *To Punish or To Treat: Substance Abuse within the Context of Oscillating Attitudes Toward Correctional Rehabilitation*, 37 J. OFFENDER REHABILITATION 1 (2003).
63. *See, e.g.*, Michael Mitchell & Michael Leachman, *Changing Priorities: State Criminal Justice Reforms and Investments in Education*, Center on Budget and Policy Priorities (Oct. 28, 2014), http://www.cbpp.org/research/changing-priorities-state-criminal-justice-reforms-and-investments-in-education#_ftn46.
64. Daniel McGillis, *National Institute of Justice Program Focus: Resolving Community Conflict: The Dispute Settlement Center of Durham, North Carolina* 3 (1998), https://www.ncjrs.gov/pdffiles/172203.pdf.
65. *Id.* at 13.
66. LOCKE, supra note 43; Rogers M. Smith, *The Constitution and Autonomy*, 60 TEX. L. REV. 175, 176–80 (1982).
67. Bruce J. Winick, *On Autonomy: Legal and Psychological Perspectives*, 37 VILL. L. REV. 1705, 1708 (1992); *see also* JOHN STUART MILL, ON LIBERTY (C. Shields ed., 1956).
68. ISAIAH BERLIN, FOUR ESSAYS ON LIBERTY 124 (1969).
69. THE DECLARATION OF INDEPENDENCE para. 2 (U.S. 1776).
70. *See generally* HILARY BOK, FREEDOM AND RESPONSIBILITY (1998).
71. MILL, *supra* note 67, at 97.
72. Henry M. Hart, Jr., *The Aims of the Criminal Law*, 23 L. & CONTEMP. PROBS. 401 (1958).

73. Ellen Byers, *Mentally Ill Criminal Offenders and the Strict Liability Effect: Is There Hope for a Just Jurisprudence in an Era of Responsibility/consequences Talk?*, 57 ARK. L. REV. 447, 492 (2004).
74. *See* Stuart P. Green, *Why It's a Crime to Tear the Tag Off a Mattress: Over-Criminalization and the Moral Content of Regulatory Offenses*, 46 EMORY L.J. 1533, 1577 (1997).
75. Margaret Shaw, *Criminal Enforcement of Environmental Laws: Relevancy of the Public Welfare Doctrine in Determining Culpability*, 27 NEW ENG. J. ON CRIM. & CIV. CONFINEMENT 337, 345 (2001).
76. Morissette v. United States, 342 U.S. 246, 254–56 (1952).
77. *Id.* at 247.
78. *Id.* at 254–56.
79. *Id.* at 260.
80. *Id.* at 261–63.
81. *Id.*
82. *Id.* at 350–52.
83. Beazell v. Ohio, 269 U.S. 167, 169–70 (1925).
84. United States v. Culbert, 435 U.S. 371, 373–74 (1978).
85. United States v. Brown, 333 U.S. 18, 25–26 (1948).
86. Paul H. Robinson, *Fair Notice and Fair Adjudication: Two Kinds of Legality*, 154 U. PA. L. REV. 335, 345 (2005).
87. *Id.* at 356.
88. Zwicker v. Koota, 389 U.S. 241, 250 (1972).
89. Timbs v. Indiana, 139 S. Ct. 682 (2019).
90. 217 U.S. 349 (1910).
91. 445 U.S. 263 (1980); *Id.* at 274.
92. Wilkerson v. Utah, 99 U.S. 130 (1879).
93. *Id.* at 135–36.
94. 428 U.S. 153, 592 (1976).
95. 433 U.S. 584, 592 (1977).
96. Steven Grossman, *Proportionality in Non-Capital Sentencing: The Supreme Court's Tortured Approach to Cruel and Unusual Punishment*, 84 KY. L.J. 107, 113 (1995).
97. 454 U.S. 370 (1982).
98. Grossman, *supra* note 96, at 141.
99. 463 U.S. 277 (1983).
100. *Id.* at 291–92.
101. *Id.* at 294.
102. *Id.* at 292–94.
103. Grossman, *supra* note 96, at 141.
104. 501 U.S. 957 (1991).
105. *See* WYO. STAT. § 35-7-1031(c) (1988); W. VA. CODE § 60A-4-401(c) (1989).
106. 539 U.S. 11 (2003).
107. *Id.* at 32; *see also* Lockyer v. Andrade, 538 U.S. 63 (2003).
108. *See* LA. STAT. ANN. § 14:42 (West 1997 & Supp. 1998).
109. *Id.*
110. 534 U.S. 551, 560 (2005).
111. Weems v. United States, 217 U.S. 349, 367 (1910).
112. *Atkins*, 536 U.S. at 311.
113. Trop v. Dulles, 356 U.S. 86, 101 (1958).
114. 433 U.S. 584 (1977).
115. 458 U.S. 782 (1982).
116. *See, e.g.*, Tison v. Arizona, 481 U.S. 137 (1987).

117. DOUGLAS HUSAK, OVERCRIMINALIZATION: THE LIMITS OF THE CRIMINAL LAW (2008); Erik Luna, *Overcriminalization: The Politics of Crime*, 54 AM. U. L. REV. 703 (2005).
118. *See, e.g.*, Paul Rosenzweig, *Over-criminalization: An Agenda for Change*, 54 AM. U. L. REV. 809 (2005).
119. *See, e.g.*, HUSAK, *supra* note 118.
120. *Id.* at 735.
121. *See* RAY SURETTE, THE MEDIA, CRIME, AND CRIMINAL JUSTICE: IMAGES AND REALITIES (4th ed. 2011).
122. STANLEY COHEN, FOLK DEVILS AND MORAL PANICS: THE CREATION OF THE MODS AND ROCKERS 9 (2nd ed. 1972).
123. *E.g.*, Lisa L. Sample & Constance Kadleck, *Sex Offender Laws: Legislators' Accounts of the Need for Policy*, 19 CRIM. JUST. POL'Y REV. 40 (2008).
124. *See, e.g.*, Arielle Goldhammer, *A Case Against Consensual Crimes: Why the Law Should Stay out of Pocketbooks, Bedrooms, and Medicine Cabinets*, 41 BRANDEIS L.J. 237 (2002).
125. *See, e.g.*, Jeffrie G. Murphy, *Legal Moralism and Liberalism*, 37 ARIZ. L. REV. 73 (1995).
126. *See* HERBERT L. A. HART, LAW, LIBERTY AND MORALITY (1963).
127. PATRICK DEVLIN, THE ENFORCEMENT OF MORALS 7–14 (1965).
128. *Id.*
129. *See* Bernard E. Harcourt, *The Collapse of the Harm Principle*, 90 J. CRIM. L. & CRIMINOLOGY 109 (1999).
130. *See generally*, Kent Greenawalt, LEGAL ENFORCEMENT OF MORALITY, 85 J. CRIM. L. & CRIMINOLOGY 710, 715, 722–25 (1995).
131. Lisa Moore, *Sticking It to the Scofflaw*, 142 U.S. NEWS & WORLD REPORT 47 (Mar. 18, 2007).

CHAPTER 2

1. *Rights*, BLACK'S LAW DICTIONARY (11th ed. 2019)).
2. Palko v. Connecticut, 302 U.S. 319, 325 (1937).
3. *See* Loving v. Virginia, 388 U.S. 1 (1967); Obergefell v. Hodges, 135 S. Ct. 2071 (2015); Griswold v. Connecticut, 381 U.S. 479 (1965).
4. Engel v. Vitale, 370 U.S. 421 (1962); Lee v. Weisman, 505 U.S. 577 (1992); Santa Fe Ind. Sch. Dist. v. Doe, 530 U.S. 290 (2000); Abington School District v. Schempp, 374 U.S. 203 (1963); Wallace v. Jaffree, 472 U.S. 38 (1985).
5. Everson v. Board of Education, 330 U.S. 1, 16 (1947).
6. 403 U.S. 602, 612–13 (1971).
7. *Everson*, 330 U.S. at 16.
8. Stone v. Graham, 449 U.S. 39 (1980).
9. Rosenberger v. Rector and Visitors of the University of Virginia, 515 U.S. 819 (1995).
10. Church of Lukumi Babalu Aye v. City of Hialeah, 508 U.S. 520, 525 (1993).
11. Reynolds v. United States, 98 U.S. 145 (1878).
12. For discussions of the accommodations that may need to be made to honor people's free exercise of religion rights, see Kara Loewentheil, *When Free Exercise Is a Burden: Protecting "Third Parties" in Religious Accommodation Law*, 62 DRAKE L. REV. 433 (2014); Ira C. Lupu, *Hobby Lobby and the Dubious Enterprise of Religious Exemptions*, 38 HARV. J. L. & GENDER 35 (2015).
13. Tinker v. Des Moines Independent Community School District, 393 U.S. 503 (1969); Thornhill v. Alabama, 310 U.S. 88 (1940); Texas v. Johnson, 491 U.S. 397 (1989).
14. Virginia v. Black, 538 U.S. 343 (2003); R.A.V. v. City of St. Paul, 505 U.S. 377 (1992).
15. *See, e.g.*, Hague v. CIO, 307 U.S. 496 (1939); Cox v. New Hampshire, 312 U.S. 569 (1941); Kunz v. New York, 340 U.S. 290 (1951); Niemotko v. Maryland, 340 U.S. 268 (1951).
16. 391 U.S. 367 (1968).
17. WISC. CRIM. CODE § 947.01.
18. Ira P. Robbins, *Digitus Impudicus: The Middle Finger and the Law*, 41 U.C. DAVIS L. REV. 1403 (2008).
19. Gooding v. Wilson, 405 U.S. 518 (1972); Hess v. Indiana, 414 U.S. 105 (1973).
20. Cox v. Louisiana, 379 U.S. 536, 554 (1965).

21. 432 U.S. 43 (1977).
22. *See also, e.g.*, Shuttlesworth v. City of Birmingham, 394 U.S. 147 (1969); Carroll v. President & Comm'rs of Princess Anne, 393 U.S. 175 (1968).
23. 487 U.S. 474 (1988).
24. *Id.* at 447.
25. *Id.* at 482–84.
26. Lloyd Corp. v. Tanner, 407 U.S. 551 (1972); Madsen v. Women's Health Center, 512 U.S. 753 (1994).
27. *See* New York Times Co. v. Sullivan, 376 U.S. 254 (1964).
28. Schenck v. United States, 249 U.S. 47, 52 (1919).
29. *Id.*
30. 274 U.S. 357 (1927).
31. *Id.* at 371.
32. 395 U.S. 444 (1969).
33. *Id.* at 445.
34. *Id.* at 449.
35. *See, e.g.*, 18 U.S.C. § 2102; N.C. GEN. STAT. § 14–288.2.
36. 315 U.S. 568 (1942).
37. *Id.* at 574.
38. *E.g.*, N.J.S.A. 2C:12-3(a); GA. CODE. ANN. § 16-11-37(a).
39. *See* 18 U.S.C. 871 (a); Watts v. United States, 394 U.S. 705 (1969).
40. *See, e.g.*, 18 U.S.C. § 876 (setting punishment for threats sent by US mail at up to 20 years of incarceration).
41. *See, e.g.*, ARIZ. REV. STAT. § 13–2921.
42. *See, e.g.*, R.A.V. v. City of St. Paul, 505 U.S. 377 (1992).
43. 718 N.E.2d 333 (Ill.App. 1999).
44. *Id.* at 339.
45. *See, e.g.*, Reno v. American Civil Liberties Union, 521 U.S. 844 (1997).
46. FCC v. Pacifica Foundation, 438 U.S. 726 (1978).
47. Hall v. Marion School Dist. No. 2, 31 F.3d 183 (4th Cir. 1994).
48. Nebraska Press Ass'n v. Stuart, 427 U.S. 539 (1976).
49. New York Times Co. v. United States, 403 U.S. 713 (1971).
50. 539 U.S. 19 (2003).
51. District of Columbia v. Heller, 554 U.S. 570, 577 (2008).
52. McDonald v. Chicago, 561 U.S. 742 (2010).
53. *Heller*, 554 U.S. at 630.
54. *Id.* at 626.
55. *See* Nelson Lund, *Second Amendment Standards of Review in a* Heller *World*, 39 FORDHAM URB. L.J. 1617 (2012); Lawrence Rosenthal, *The Limits of Second Amendment Originalism and the Constitutional Case for Gun Control*, 92 WASH. U.L. REV. 1187 (2015).
56. Roberts v. Maine, 48 F.3d 1287, 1291 (1st Cir. 1995).
57. JOHN THIBAUT & LAURENS WALKER, PROCEDURAL JUSTICE: A PSYCHOLOGICAL ANALYSIS (1975); TOM R. TYLER, WHY PEOPLE OBEY THE LAW (2006).
58. *See, e.g.*, JOHN N. FERDICO, HENRY F. FRADELLA, & CHRISTOPHER D. TOTTEN, CRIMINAL PROCEDURE FOR THE CRIMINAL JUSTICE PROFESSIONAL (12th ed. 2015).
59. Murray's Lessee v. Hoboken Land and Improvement Co. 59 U.S. (18 How.) 272, 276 (1856).
60. *See* Chicago & G.T. Ry. v. Wellman, 143 U.S. 339, 344 (1892); Mississippi R.R. Comm'n v. Mobile & Ohio R.R., 244 U.S. 388, 391 (1917); Missouri Pacific Ry. v. Nebraska, 217 U.S. 196 (1910); Nashville, C. & St. L. Ry. v. Walters, 294 U.S. 405, 415 (1935); Loving v. Virginia, 388 U.S. 1 (1967); Obergefell v. Hodges, 135 S. Ct. 2071 (2015); Cruzan v. Director, Missouri Department of Health, 497 U.S. 261 (1990).
61. HERBERT L. PACKER, THE LIMITS OF THE CRIMINAL SANCTION (1968).
62. Plyler v. Doe, 457 U.S. 202, 216 (1982).

63. Truax v. Corrigan, 257 U.S. 312, 331 (1921).
64. 347 U.S. 497, 499 (1954).
65. *See, e.g.*, Brown v. Board of Education, 347 U.S. 483 (1954).
66. Plyler v. Doe, 457 U.S. 202, 215–21 (1982).
67. 514 U.S. 334 (1995).
68. *Id.* at 348.
69. *Id.* at 352.
70. *Id.* at 357.
71. United States v. Carolene Prods. Co., 304 U.S. 144 (1938).
72. Marcy Strauss, *Reevaluating Suspect Classifications*, 35 SEATTLE U.L. REV. 135, 138–40 (2011); *see also* Darren Lenard Hutchinson, *"Unexplainable on Grounds Other than Race": The Inversion of Privilege and Subordination in Equal Protection Jurisprudence*, 2003 U. ILL. L. REV. 615, 636 (2003).
73. *See, e.g.*, San Antonio Independent School District v. Rodriguez, 411 U.S. 1, 28 (1973).
74. *Id.*
75. *Id.; see also* Graham v. Richardson, 403 U.S. 365 (1971).
76. Frontiero v. Richardson, 411 U.S. 677 (1973).
77. *See* Cleburne v. Cleburne Living Center, Inc., 473 U.S. 432 (1985).
78. Perry v. Schwarzenegger, 704 F. Supp. 2d 921, 995 (N.D. Cal. 2010).
79. *See* Marcia Pearce Burgdorf & Robert Burgdorf, Jr., *A History of Unequal Treatment: The Qualifications of Handicapped Persons as a "Suspect Class" Under the Equal Protection Clause*, 15 SANTA CLARA L. REV. 855, 908 (1975).
80. *E.g.*, Brown v. Board of Educ., 347 U.S. 483 (1954); *E.g.*, Reitman v. Mulkey, 387 U.S. 369 (1967). Even purely private acts of discrimination can violate of the Equal Protection Clause if they are customarily enforced throughout the state. Shelley v. Kraemer, 334 U.S. 1 (1948) (holding that courts cannot enforce discriminatory racial covenants on the transfer of real estate).
81. 429 U.S. 190 (1976).
82. *Id.* at 200–01.
83. Parham v. Hughes, 441 U.S. 347, 354 (1979).
84. Rinaldi v. Yeager, 384 U.S. 305, 309 (1966).
85. Weinberger v. Wiesenfeld, 420 U.S. 636, 653 (1975).
86. United States v. O'Brien, 91 U.S. 367, 383–84 (1968); Palmer v. Thompson, 403 U.S. 217, 224 (1971).
87. In 1976, approximately one million fifteen- to nineteen-year-olds became pregnant, one-tenth of all women in that age group. Two-thirds of the pregnancies were illegitimate. Illegitimacy rates for teenagers (births per 1,000 unmarried females ages 14 to 19) increased 75 percent for fourteen- to seventeen-year-olds between 1961 and 1974 and 33 percent for eighteen- to nineteen-year-olds. ALAN GUTTMACHER INSTITUTE, 11 MILLION TEENAGERS 10, 13 (1976); C. CHILMAN, ADOLESCENT SEXUALITY IN A CHANGING AMERICAN SOCIETY 195 (NIH Pub. No. 80-1426, 1980)[footnote #3 in original case].
88. The risk of maternal death is 60 percent higher for a teenager under the age of fifteen than for a women in her early twenties. The risk is 13 percent higher for fifteen- to nineteen-year-olds. The statistics further show that most teenage mothers drop out of school and face a bleak economic future. *See, e.g.*, 11 MILLION TEENAGERS, *supra* [note 88], at 23, 25; Bennett & Bardon, *The Effects of a School Program on Teenager Mothers and Their Children*, 47 AM. J. ORTHOPSYCHIATRY 671 (1977); Phipps-Yonas, *Teenage Pregnancy and Motherhood*, 50 Am. J. ORTHOPSYCHIATRY 403, 414 (1980)[footnote #4 in original case].
89. This is because teenagers are disproportionately likely to seek abortions. CENTER FOR DISEASE CONTROL, ABORTION SURVEILLANCE 1976, 22–24 (1978). In 1978, for example, teenagers in California had approximately 54,000 abortions and 53,800 live births. CALIFORNIA CENTER FOR HEALTH STATISTICS, REPRODUCTIVE HEALTH STATUS OF CALIFORNIA TEENAGE WOMEN 1, 23 (Mar.1980) [footnote #5 in original case].
90. Gerald Gunther, *Foreword: In Search of Evolving Doctrine on a Changing Court: A Model for a Newer Equal Protection*, 86 HARV. L. REV. 1, 8 (1971).

91. Raphael Holoszyc-Pimentel, *Note: Reconciling Rational-Basis Review: When Does Rational Basis Bite?*, 90 N.Y.U.L. REV. 2070, 2071 (2015); *see also* Strauss, *supra* note 73, at 136, n.8.
92. 478 U.S. 186 (1986).
93. *Bowers*, 478 U.S. at 188.
94. *Id.* at 190.
95. Griswold v. Connecticut, 381 U.S. 479 (1965).
96. Eisenstadt v. Baird, 405 U.S. 438 (1972).
97. Roe v. Wade, 410 U.S. 113 (1973).
98. *Bowers*, 478 U.S. at 190–91.
99. *Id.* at 191–95.
100. *Id.* at 196.
101. *Id.* at 196.
102. *E.g.*, The Harvard Law Review, Note, *Right to Privacy and Consensual Sodomy:* Bowers v. Hardwick, 100 HARV. L. REV. 210 (1986); Anne B. Goldstein, *History, Homosexuality, and Political Values: Searching for the Hidden Determinants of* Bowers v. Hardwick, 97 YALE L.J. 1073 (1988).
103. B. J. Williamson, *The Constitutional Privacy Doctrine After* Bowers v. Hardwick: *Rethinking the Second Death of Substantive Due Process*, 62 S. CAL. L. REV. 1297 (1989).
104. Harvard Law Review, *supra* note 103, at 218–19.
105. *Bowers*, 478 U.S. at 190.
106. Planned Parenthood of Southeastern Pa. v. Casey, 505 U. S. 833, 850 (1992).
107. *Id.*
108. Romer v. Evans, 517 U.S. 620 (1996).
109. *Id.* at 624.
110. *Id.* at 634.
111. *Casey*, 505 U.S. at 847.
112. Plyler v. Doe, 457 U.S. at 239 (Powell, J., concurring).
113. 555 U.S. 415 (2009).
114. *E.g.*, Kachalsky v. Cty. of Westchester, 701 F.3d 81 (2d Cir. 2012); Norman v. State, 215 So. 3d 18 (Fla.), *cert. denied*, 215 So. 3d 18 (2017).
115. *E.g.*, State v. Christian, 307 P.3d 429 (Or. 2013); Williams v. State, 10 A.3d 1167 (Md. 2011).
116. *E.g.*, Horsley v. Trame, 808 F.3d 1126 (7th Cir. 2015); Nat'l Rifle Ass'n v. McCraw, 719 F.3d 338 (5th Cir. 2013).
117. *E.g.*, United States v. Masciandaro, 638 F.3d 458 (4th Cir. 2011) (national parks); United States v. Giraitis, 127 F. Supp. 3d 1 (D.R.I. 2015) (court facilities); GeorgiaCarry.Org, Inc. v. Georgia, 764 F. Supp. 2d 1306 (M.D. Ga. 2011), aff'd, 687 F.3d 1244 (11th Cir. 2012) (place of worship); Digiacinto v. Rector & Visitors of George Mason Univ., 704 S.E.2d 365 (Va. 2011) (college campuses); S.B. v. Seymour Cmty. Sch., 97 N.E.3d 288 (Ind. Ct. App. 2018) (schools).
118. *E.g.*, Kelly v. Riley, 733 S.E.2d 194 (N.C. Ct. App. 2012).
119. *E.g.*, United States v. Cox, 906 F.3d 1170 (10th Cir. 2018).
120. *E.g.*, United States v. Bartley, 400 F. Supp. 3d 1066 (D. Idaho 2019), or adjudicated to be a danger to themselves or others due to mental illness, e.g., Hope v. State, 133 A.3d 519 (Conn 2016); Redington v. Indiana, 992 N.E.2d 823 (Ind. Ct. App. 2013).
121. *E.g.*, Silvester v. Harris, 843 F.3d 816 (9th Cir. 2016).
122. 830 P.2d 435 (Alaska App. 1992).

CHAPTER 3

1. *See, e.g.*, William David Gross, *The Unfortunate Faith: A Solution to the Unwarranted Reliance upon Eyewitness Testimony*, 5 TEX. WESLEYAN L. REV. 307, 313 (1999) (citing SIEGFRIED L. SPORER ET AL., PSYCHOLOGICAL ISSUES IN EYEWITNESS IDENTIFICATION, 3 (1966)); BARRY SCHECK, PETER NEUFELD, & JIM DWYER, ACTUAL INNOCENCE: FIVE DAYS TO EXECUTION, AND OTHER DISPATCHES FROM THE WRONGLY

CONVICTED (2000); Aldert Vrij, *Psychological Factors in Eyewitness Testimony, in* PSYCHOLOGY AND LAW: TRUTHFULNESS, ACCURACY, AND CREDIBILITY 105–19 (Amina Memon, Alder Vrij, & Ray Bull eds., 1998); C. RONALD HUFF, ARYE RATTNER, & EDWARD SAGARIN, CONVICTED BUT INNOCENT: WRONGFUL CONVICTION AND PUBLIC POLICY, 66, 83–104 (1996); Arye Rattner, *Convicted But Innocent: Wrongful Conviction and the Criminal Justice System*, 12 LAW & HUM. BEHAV. 283, 287–91 (1988).

2. JOHN HENRY WIGMORE, EVIDENCE IN TRIALS AT COMMON LAW §§ 2485–2488, at 283–93 (James H. Chadbourn rev. 1981).
3. *Id.*
4. *Id.* § 2487.
5. *Id.* at §§ 2485–86.
6. *See* Terry v. Ohio, 392 U.S. 1 (1968); *see also* MICHAEL D. WHITE & HENRY F. FRADELLA, STOP AND FRISK: THE USE AND ABUSE OF A CONTROVERSIAL POLICE TACTIC (2016).
7. *See, e.g.*, Illinois v. Gates, 462 U.S. 213 (1983); *see also, e.g.*, Drey Cooley, *Clearly Erroneous Review Is Clearly Erroneous: Reinterpreting* Illinois V. Gates *and Advocating De Novo Review for a Magistrate's Determination of Probable Cause in Applications for Search Warrants*, 55 DRAKE L. REV. 85 (2006).
8. *See, e.g.*, Mattias Luukkonen, *Knock, Knock. What's Inevitably There? An Analysis of the Applicability of the Doctrine of Inevitable Discovery to Knock and Announce Violations*, 35 MCGEORGE L. REV. 153 (2004); Eugene L. Shapiro, *Active Pursuit, Inevitable Discovery, and the Federal Circuits: the Search for Manageable Limitations upon an Expansive Doctrine*, 39 GONZ. L. REV. 295 (2003–2004).
9. *See* New York Times Co. v. Sullivan, 376 U.S. 254, 285–86 (1964); *see also* ANTHONY LEWIS, MAKE NO LAW: THE SULLIVAN CASE AND THE FIRST AMENDMENT 159 (1991).
10. In re Winship, 397 U.S. 358 (1970).
11. Victor v. Nebraska, 511 U.S. 1, 13–14 (1994).
12. *Id.* at 18.
13. Federal Judicial Center, Pattern Criminal Jury Instructions, at 17–18 (instruction 21).
14. *See, e.g.*, McCullough v. State, 657 P.2d 1157 (Nev. 1983).
15. MODEL PENAL CODE § 2.01(1) (1962).
16. Morissette v. United States, 342 U.S. 246 (1952); Michael M. v. Superior Court of Sonoma County, 450 U.S. 464 (1981).
17. *See generally* Kevin W. Saunders, *Voluntary Acts and the Criminal Law: Justifying Culpability Based on the Existence of Volition*, 49 U. PITT. L. REV. 443 (1988).
18. *Id.* at 467–69; *see also* MODEL PENAL CODE § 2.01(1) (1962).
19. Saunders, *supra* note 17, at 445–56; *see also* Jeffrie G. Murphy, *Involuntary Acts and Criminal Liability*, 81 ETHICS 332 (1971).
20. *See* MODEL PENAL CODE § 2.01(2) (1962).
21. Saunders, *supra* note 17, at 447 (citing Greenfield v. Commonwealth, 204 S.E.2d 414 (Va. 1974) (conviction affirmed despite black-out claim when defendant was a drug user); State v. Utter, 479 P.2d 946 (Wash. 1971)).
22. *See* Mike Horn, Note: *A Rude Awakening: What to Do with the Sleepwalking Defense?*, 46 B.C. L. REV. 149 (2004).
23. MODEL PENAL CODE § § 2.01(1).
24. *See generally* A.P. Simester, *On the So-called Requirement for Voluntary Action*, 1 BUFF. CRIM. L. REV. 403 (1998).
25. *See* Melody J. Stewart, *How Making the Failure to Assist Illegal Fails to Assist: An Observation of Expanding Criminal Omission Liability*, 25 AM. J. CRIM. L. 385, 395 (1998).
26. *See id.*
27. *Id.* (citing OHIO REV. CODE ANN. § 2151.421(A)(1)(a), (b) (Anderson Supp. 1997); *see also, e.g.*, CAL. PENAL CODE § 11166(a) (West 1992); NEB. REV. STAT. § 28–711 (1995).
28. *See* Marcia M. Ziegler, *Nonfeasance and the Duty to Assist: the American Seinfeld Syndrome*, 104 DICK. L. REV. 525 (2000).

29. MINN. STAT. ANN. § 604A.01 (West 1994); VT. STAT. ANN. tit. 12, § 519 (Supp. 1994); R.I. GEN. LAWS § 11-56-1 (1984); WIS. STAT. § 940.34. (West Supp. 1999).
30. MASS. GEN. LAWS ANN. ch. 268, § 40 (West 1983). *See also* HAW. REV. STAT. ANN. § 663–1.6(a) (1984).
31. *See id.* at 527; *see also* Damien Schiff, *Samaritans: Good, Bad and Ugly: A Comparative Law Analysis*, 11 ROGER WILLIAMS U. L. REV. 77 (2005).
32. *See, e.g.*, OHIO REV. CODE ANN. § 2921.23 (Banks-Baldwin 1997); WASH. REV. CODE ANN. § 9A.76.030 (West 1988).
33. *See* Schiff, *supra* note 31, at 109; Stewart, *supra* note 25, at 388 n.9; *see also* Note, *Good Samaritans and Liability for Medical Malpractice*, 64 COLUM. L. REV. 1301 (1964).
34. *See* Jessica R. Givelber, *Imposing Duties on Witnesses to Child Sexual Abuse: A Futile Response to Bystander Indifference*, 67 FORDHAM L. REV. 3169, 3176 (1999).
35. Stewart, *supra* note 25, at 369.
36. *See id.*
37. *See id.*
38. *See id.*
39. *See id.* at 396.
40. *See id.*
41. *See id.*
42. In re Adoption of Webb, 544 P.2d 130 (Wash. App. 1975).
43. *See, e.g.*, Cornell v. State, 32 So.2d 610 (Fla. 1947).
44. JOSEPH GOLDSTEIN, ANNA FREUD, & ALBERT SOLNIT, BEYOND THE BEST INTEREST OF THE CHILD 18 (1973).
45. Marcus D. Dubber, *Policing Possession: The War on Crime and the End of Criminal Law*, 91 J. CRIM. L. & CRIMINOLOGY 829, 857 (2001) (collecting odd possession laws).
46. *See* J. Paul McCutcheon, *Knowledge and the Actus Reus of Possession Offences*, 32 IRISH JURIST (N.S.) 119, 120 (1997)(citing R v. Dugdale (1853) 1 El & BI 435).
47. *Id.*
48. 167 A.D.3d 412 (N.Y. App. Div. 2008).
49. *Id.* at 412.
50. Paul McCutcheon, *supra* note 46, at 121.
51. MODEL PENAL CODE § 2.01(4) (1962).
52. *See, e.g.*, United States v. Culpepper, 834 F.2d 879, 881 (10th Cir. 1987).
53. Martin v. State, 17 So. 2d 427 (Ala. Ct. App. 1944).
54. *Id.* at 427 (citing ALA. CODE 14–120 (1940)).
55. *Id.*
56. *Id.*
57. People v. Galesto, 232 P.3d 650 (Cal. 2010).
58. *Id.* at 652.
59. *Id.* at 654.
60. *Id.*
61. *Id.*
62. *Id.* at 655.
63. Tingley v. Brown, 380 So. 2d 1289 (Fla. 1980) (applying FLA. STAT.§ 370.14 (1977), codified as amended at FLA. STAT. § 379.367 (2018)).
64. *Id.* at 1291.
65. State v. Flaherty, 400 A.2d 363 (Me. 1979).
66. *Id.* at 366.
67. *Id.* at 367.
68. Williams v. State, 110 So.3d 59 (Fl. Ct. App. 2013).
69. *Id.* at 62.

70. *Id.* at 63–65.
71. State v. Holland, 975 So. 2d 595 (Fla. Dist. Ct. App. 2008).
72. *Id.* at 598.

CHAPTER 4

1. Benjamin Levin, *Mens Rea Reform and Its Discontents*, 109 J. CRIM. L. & CRIMINOLOGY 491, 493 (2019).
2. *E.g.*, CAL. PENAL CODE § 141 (criminalizing the manipulation of digital images or video recordings with the "specific intent" to either implicate an innocent person in a crime or to exonerate a guilty person); VA. CODE § 18.2-164 (making it a crime to "maliciously" damage a telephone line, wire, cable, pole, or tower).
3. *See* Jeremy M. Miller, *Mens Rea Quagmire: The Conscience or Consciousness of the Criminal Law?*, 29 W. ST. U. L. REV. 21, 32 (2001).
4. Hicks v. Commonwealth, 9 S.E. 1024 (Va. 1889); Uhl's Case, 6 Grat. (47 Va.) 706 (1849).
5. State v. Fleck, 810 N.W.2d 303, 310–12 (Minn. 2012) (citing 1 WAYNE R. LAFAVE, SUBSTANTIVE CRIMINAL LAW § 5.2(e) (2d ed. 2003)).
6. *See* Miller, *supra* note 3, at 32.
7. State v. Rocker, 475 P.2d 684 (Haw. 1970).
8. *Id.* at 691.
9. State v. Peery, 28 N.W.2d 851 (Minn. 1947).
10. State v. Stevenson, 656 N.W.2d 235 (Minn. 2003).
11. *Id.* at 241.
12. State v. Jama, 923 N.W.2d 632 (Minn. 2019).
13. *See* Martin R. Gardner, *The Mens Rea Enigma: Observations on the Role of Motive in the Criminal Law Past and Present*, 1993 UTAH L. REV. 635 (1993).
14. *Id.* at 671.
15. Bowler v. United States, 480 A.2d 678, 687 (D.C. 1984).
16. People v. Fennell, 677 N.W.2d 66 (2004).
17. People v. Iehl, 299 N.W.2d 46 (1980).
18. *See* Gardner, *supra* note 13, at 682 (quoting Ronald L. Gainer, *The Culpability Provisions of the Model Penal Code*, 19 RUTGERS L.J. 575, 575 (1988)).
19. *Id.* (citing MODEL PENAL CODE § 2.02).
20. *See* MODEL PENAL CODE § 2.02(8) (Official Draft 1985) (defining acting "knowingly" as acting with "awareness" of engaging in the conduct under the defined circumstances of the offense and to be "practically certain" that such conduct will result in any proscribed result. *Id.* § 2.02(2)(a)).
21. 455 So.2d 511 (Fla. App. 1984).
22. *Id.* at 511.
23. United States v. Jewell, 532 F.2d 697, 700 (9th Cir.), *cert. denied*, 426 U.S. 951 (1976).
24. *See* MODEL PENAL CODE § 2.02(3). ("When the culpability sufficient to establish a material element of an offense is not prescribed by law, such element is established if a person acts purposefully, knowingly, or recklessly with respect thereto.")
25. 1 MODEL PENAL CODE AND COMMENTARIES § 2.02, at 237, 241 (Official Draft and Revised Comments 1985).
26. *See* Gardner, *supra* note 13, at 671.
27. For an excellent discussion of the confusing levels of culpability that have been deemed "reckless," "grossly reckless," and "grossly negligent," see Kenneth W. Simons, *Rethinking Mental States*, 72 B.U. L. REV. 463 (1992); Edwin H. Byrd, III, Comment, *Reflections on Willful, Wanton, Reckless and Gross Negligence*, 48 LA. L. REV. 1383, 1383 (1988).
28. Simons, *supra* note 27, at 483 n.70; *see also* State v. Dixon, 186 S.E. 531 (S.C. 1936) ("[t]here can be no question that it is the established rule . . . that one who causes the death of another by the negligent use of a deadly . . . instrumentality may be convicted of involuntary manslaughter").
29. *See* MODEL PENAL CODE § 2.02(2)(d).

30. *See* Leslie Yalof Garfield, *More Principled Approach to Criminalizing Negligence: A Prescription for the Legislature*, 65 TENN. L. REV. 875, 890 (1998
31. 651 A.2d 931 (N.H. 1994).
32. *See* Catherine L. Carpenter, *On Statutory Rape, Strict Liability, and the Public Welfare Offense Model*, 53 AM. U. L. REV. 313, 316 (2003).REFC ("The notion of strict liability has generally been considered an anathema in the criminal law—after all, every first year law student can repeat this mantra: criminal culpability requires an *actus reus* and a *mens rea*.")
33. *See* MODEL PENAL CODE §§ 1.04(5), 2.05 (Official Draft 1985).
34. Carpenter, *supra* note 32, at 316.
35. Morissette v. United States, 342 U.S. 246 (1952).
36. Elonis v. United States, 135 S. Ct. 2001 (2015).
37. *Id.* at 2005.
38. *Id.* at 2004 (citing 18 U.S.C. § 875(c)).
39. *Morissette*, 342 U.S. at 263.
40. *Id.* at 2009 (quoting Staples v. United States, 511 U.S. 600, 608, n.3 (1994)).
41. *Id.* at 2011 (internal citations omitted).
42. Carpenter, *supra* note 32, at 323.
43. *Id.* at 327.
44. Commonwealth v. Olshefski, 64 Pa. D. & C. 343 (Pa. Quar. Sess. 1948).
45. People v. Stuart, 302 P.2d 5 (Cal. 1956).
46. *See* REFO:JARTFrancis B. Sayre, *Public Welfare Offenses*, 33 COLUM. L. REV. 55, 72–75; Jerome Hall, *Prolegomena to a Science of Criminal Law*, 89 U. PA. L. REV. & AM. L. REG. 549, 563–69 (1941).
47. People v. Penny, 285 P.2d 926, 936 (Cal. 1955).
48. *See* MORELAND, LAW OF HOMICIDE 186–87, 244 (citing 1 HALE, PLEAS OF THE CROWN (1778 ed.)).
49. Carpenter, *supra* note 32, at 332.
50. *See* Louis Henkin, *Morals and the Constitution: The Sin of Obscenity*, 63 COLUM. L. REV. 391, 407–11 (1963) (exploring the religious roots of morals legislation); *see also* PATRICK DEVLIN, THE ENFORCEMENT OF MORALS 25 (1965).
51. Carpenter, *supra* note 32, at 334–36 (internal citations omitted).
52. *See* Henry F. Fradella & Kenneth Grundy, *The Criminal Regulation of Sex: The Limits of Morality and Consent*, *in* SEX, LAW, AND (IN)JUSTICE 183 (Henry F. Fradella & Jennifer Sumner eds., 2016).
53. *See id.*; *see also* Carpenter, *supra* note 32, at 344 n. 176.
54. *See* MODEL PENAL CODE § 2.02.
55. *See, e.g.*, United States v. McDonald, 991 F.2d 866, 868 (D.C. Cir. 1993).
56. United States v. Feola, 420 U.S. 671 (1975).
57. *Id.* at 674–75.
58. *Id.* at 685.
59. *See, e.g.*, Eli Lederman, *Models for Imposing Corporate Criminal Liability: from Adaptation and Imitation toward Aggregation and the Search for Self-identity*, 4 BUFF. CRIM. L. REV. 641 (2000).
60. James Herbie DiFonzo, *Parental Responsibility for Juvenile Crime*, 80 OR. L. REV. 1, 65 (2001).
61. *See, e.g.*, Michael John James Kuzmich, *In Vino Mortuus: Fraternal Hazing and Alcohol-Related Deaths*, 31 MCGEORGE L. REV. 1087 (2007).
62. *See id.* at 1122.
63. *See id.*
64. *See id.* at 1122.
65. *See id.* at 1122–23.
66. *See id.* at 1123–25.
67. Nate Schweber, *Closer Eye on Campus Drinking*, N.Y. TIMES (Sept. 23, 2007), http://www.nytimes.com/2007/09/23/nyregion/nyregionspecial2/23Rrider.html.

68. Tony J Hagen, *Settlement Announced in Rider Hazing Death*, TRENTON TIMES (Sept. 24, 2009), http://www.nj.com/mercer/index.ssf/2009/09/settlement_announced_in_rider.html.
69. *See* Anthony M. Dillof, *Transferred Intent: an Inquiry into the Nature of Criminal Culpability*, 1 BUFF. CRIM. L. REV. 501 (1998).
70. *See* MODEL PENAL CODE § 2.03(2) (requiring that intent be transferred only where the harm caused is to a "different person or different property" from that intended).
71. 447 S.E.2d 852 (S.C. 1994).
72. *See* MODEL PENAL CODE § 2.03.
73. *Id.* at § 2.03(a)(1) ("an antecedent but for which the result in question should not have occurred"). For an in-depth examination of the shortcomings of the traditional "but for" test for causation-in-fact, see Lawrence Crocker, *A Retributive Theory of Criminal Causation*, 1994 J. CONTEMP. LEGAL ISSUES 65 (1994).
74. *See* Arthur Leavens, *A Causation Approach to Criminal Omissions*, 76 CAL. L. REV. 547, 566 (1988).
75. *See* Laura Schiesl Goodwin, *Causation in California Homicide*, 36 LOY. L.A. L. REV. 1453, 1459 (2003).
76. *See id.*
77. *See id.* at 1460.
78. LA. REV. STAT. § 14:40.2(A) (2000).
79. LA. REV. STAT. § 14:40.2(C)(1).
80. State v. Terrio, NO. 19-K-90, 2019 WL 1285288 (La. Ct. App. Mar. 20, 2019).
81. 658 A.2d 22 (Vt. 1995).
82. *Cf.* Wiener v. Gamma Phi Chapter of Alpha Tau Omega Fraternity, 485 P.2d 18 (Or. 1971).
83. Huston v. Konieczny, 556 N.E.2d 505 (Ohio 1990).
84. Kelly v. Gwinnell, 476 A.2d 1219 (N.J. 1984).
85. Commonwealth v. Koczwara, 155 A.2d 825 (Pa. 1959), *cert. denied*, 363 U.S. 848 (1960).
86. Stephenson v. State, 179 N.E. 633 (Ind. 1932).

CHAPTER 5

1. *See* MODEL PENAL CODE art. 5 commentary at 293–94 (Proposed Official Draft 1985).
2. Ira P. Robbins, *Double Inchoate Crimes*, 26 HARV. J. ON LEGIS. 1 (1989).
3. Robbins, *supra* note 2, at 7–9 (internal citations omitted).
4. PUBLILIUS SYRUS, SENTENTIAE 104–05 (J. Wight Duff & Arnold M. Duff trans., c. 43 BCE).
5. *See generally* Paul H. Robinson, *Imputed Criminal Liability*, 93 YALE L.J. 609 (1984); Sanford Kadish, *Complicity, Cause and Blame: A Study in the Interpretation of Doctrine*, 73 CAL. L. REV. 323 (1985).
6. Robbins, *supra* note 2, at 29; *see also* MODEL PENAL CODE § 5.02(1); MODEL PENAL CODE § 5.02 explanatory note at 365; *id.* commentary at 368–69 (Proposed Official Draft 1985).
7. Robbins, *supra* note 2, at 30.
8. *Id.*; *see also* MODEL PENAL CODE § 5.02(1); 18 U.S.C. § 373.
9. Robbins, *supra* note 2, at 30.
10. *Id.* at 30–31.
11. *Id.* at 30.
12. *Id.* at 32 (citing State v. Avery, 7 Conn. 266, 270–71 (1828); Commonwealth v. Flagg, 135 Mass. 545, 549 (1883); State v. Hampton, 186 S.E. 251, 252 (N.C. 1936); State v. Blechman, 50 A.2d 152, 153–54 (N.J. 1946); Regina v. Gregory, 10 Cox Crim. Cas. 459, 461–62 (1867)).
13. *Id.* at 33; *see also* MODEL PENAL CODE § 5.02(1).
14. *Id.* at 32 (citing COLO. REV. STAT. § 18-2-301 (1986); GA. CODE ANN. § 16-4-7 (1988); IOWA CODE ANN. § 705.1 (West 1979) (also aggravated misdemeanors); LA. REV. STAT. ANN. § 14:28 (West 1986); ME. REV. STAT. ANN. tit. 17-A, § 153 (1983) (only crimes with maximum penalties exceeding five years); VA. CODE ANN. § 18.2-29 (1988).
15. *Id.* (citing ALASKA STAT. § 11.31.110; ARK. STAT. ANN. § 5-3-301; ILL. ANN. STAT. ch. 38, para. 8-1; KY. REV. STAT. ANN. § 506.030; N.H. REV. STAT. ANN. § 629:2).

16. *Id.* (citing CAL. PENAL CODE §§ 653f, 653l, 1203.046; MICH. COMP. LAWS ANN. § 750.157(b); NEV. REV. STAT. § 199.500; VT. STAT. ANN. tit. 13, § 7).
17. 18 U.S.C. § 373(a).
18. *See* MODEL PENAL CODE § 5.02(3).
19. Evan Tsen Lee, *Cancelling Crime*, 30 CONN. L. REV. 117, 119–20 (1997) (citing MODEL PENAL CODE § 5.02(3)).
20. *See, e.g.*, ARIZ. REV. STAT. § 13-1005(B) (1989).
21. MODEL PENAL CODE § 2.06(3).
22. *See, e.g.*, Grace E. Mueller, Note: *The Mens Rea of Accomplice Liability*, 61 S. CAL. L. REV. 2169, 2186–87 (1988).
23. *E.g.*, ARIZ. REV. STAT. ANN. § 13-1004.
24. *E.g.*, N.Y. PENAL LAW § 115.00.
25. E.g., N.J. STAT. ANN. § 2C:2- 6(c)(1).
26. *See, e.g.*, The National Commission on Reform of Federal Criminal Laws, Final Report of the National Commission on Reform of Federal Criminal Laws: A Proposed New Federal Criminal Code (Title 18, United States Code § 1002 (1971).
27. Robbins, *supra* note 2, at 11.
28. *Id.* at 12 (internal citations omitted).
29. *Id.* at 10.
30. 114 S.E. 504 (Va. 1922).
31. *See* MODEL PENAL CODE § 5.04(1).
32. 474 N.E.2d 538 (Mass. 1985).
33. *Dunne*, 474 N.E.2d at 545 (internal citations omitted).
34. Robert H. Skilton, *The Requisite Act in a Criminal Attempt*, 3 U. PITT. L. REV. 308, 309–10 (1937).
35. Robbins, *supra* note 2, at 13.
36. *Id.* at 16 n.47 (citing MODEL PENAL CODE § 5.01 commentary at 321–24 (Proposed Official Draft 1985)).
37. OR. REV. STAT. § 161.405(1); State v. Walters, 804 P.2d 1164, 1167 (Or.), *cert. denied*, 501 U.S. 1209 (1991).
38. *Walters*, 804 P.2d at 1167.
39. *Id.* at 1167–68.
40. *Id.*
41. United States v. Manley, 632 F.2d 978, 987–88 (2d Cir. 1980), *cert. denied*, 449 U.S. 1112 (1981).
42. *Id.*
43. *E.g.*, State v. Daniel B., 201 A.3d 989, 1007 (Conn. 2019) (quoting State v. Schleifer, 121 A. 805, 807 (1923)).
44. MODEL PENAL CODE, cmt. [6](b)(vii), at 346, n.214 (Proposed Official Draft 1985) (quoting GLANVILLE WILLIAMS, CRIMINAL LAW: THE GENERAL PART 616 (2d ed. 1961)).
45. Audrey Rogers, *New Technology, Old Defenses: Internet Sting Operations and Attempt Liability*, 38 U. RICH. L. REV. 477, 493 (2004).
46. *See, e.g.*, ALA. CODE § 13A-4-2 (1982); ALASKA STAT. § 11.31.100 (1989); ARIZ. REV. STAT. ANN. § 13-1001 (1989); COLO. REV. STAT. ANN. § 18-2-101 (West 1990); CONN. GEN. STAT. ANN. § 53a-49 (West 1985); GA. CODE ANN. § 16-4-4 (1992); HAW. REV. STAT. § 705- 501 (1985); ILL. ANN. STAT. ch. 720, para. 5/8-4 (Smith-Hurd 1993); IND. CODE ANN. § 35-41-5-1 (Burns 1985); KAN. STAT. ANN. § 21-3301 (1988); ME. REV. STAT. ANN. tit. 17-A, § 152 (West 1983); MO. STAT. § 564.011 (Vernon 1979); MONT. CODE ANN. § 45-4-103 (1991); N.Y. PENAL LAW § 110.10 (McKinney 1992); N.D. CENT. CODE § 12.1-06-01 (1985); OHIO REV. CODE ANN. § 2923.02 (Anderson 1993); OR. REV. STAT. § 161.425 (1990); 18 PA. CONS. STAT. ANN. § 901 (1983); TENN. CODE ANN. § 39-12-101 (1991); WASH. REV. CODE ANN. § 9A.28.020 (West 1988).
47. *See* MODEL PENAL CODE § 5.01.
48. Rogers, *supra* note 45, at 495.
49. Kyle S. Brodie, *The Obviously Impossible Attempt: A Proposed Revision to the Model Penal Code*, 15 N. ILL. U. L. REV. 237, 238 (1995).

50. *Id.* at 241.
51. *See, e.g.*, Edwin R. Keedy, *Criminal Attempts at Common Law*, 102 U. PA. L. REV. 464, 473 (1954).
52. *See, e.g.*, Daniel G. Moriarty, *Extending the Defense of Renunciation*, 62 TEMP. L. REV. 1, 5 (1989) (citing MODEL PENAL CODE AND COMMENTARIES § 5.01 comment at 359–60 (Official Draft 1962 and Revised Comments 1985)).
53. *See* MODEL PENAL CODE § 5.01(4).
54. Moriarty, *supra* note 52, at 14–32.
55. MODEL PENAL CODE § 5.01(4).
56. *Id.*
57. 804 P.2d 1208 (Or. Ct. App. 1991).
58. 2 LAFAVE, SUBSTANTIVE CRIMINAL LAW 12, § 6.1 (1986).
59. MODEL PENAL CODE § 5.02(2).
60. State v. Daniel B., 201 A.3d 989 (Conn. 2019).
61. *Id.* at 992.
62. *Id.*
63. CONN. GEN. STAT. § 53a-49(a)(2) & (b).
64. State v. O'Neil, 782 A.2d 209 (2001), *aff'd*, 811 A.2d 1288 (Conn. 2003).
65. State v. Molasky, 765 S.W.2d 597, 602 (Mo. 1989).
66. People v. Thousand, 631 N.W.2d 694 (Mich. 2001).
67. MICH. COMP. LAWS ANN. § 750.157b (2020).
68. MICH. COMP. LAWS ANN. § 750.92 (2020).
69. *Thousand*, 631 N.W.2d at 699 (quoting JOSHUA DRESSLER, UNDERSTANDING CRIMINAL LAW (1st ed.), § 27.07[D][3][a], at 353–54).

CHAPTER 6

1. *See generally* Paul H. Robinson, *Imputed Criminal Liability*, 93 YALE L.J. 609 (1984); Sanford Kadish, *Complicity, Cause and Blame: A Study in the Interpretation of Doctrine*, 73 CAL. L. REV. 323 (1985).
2. Sanford Kadish, *Complicity, Cause and Blame: A Study in the Interpretation of Doctrine*, 73 CAL. L. REV. 323, 336–68 (1985).
3. *See* 18 U.S.C. § 2(a).
4. Adam Harris Kurland, *To "Aid, Abet, Counsel, Command, Induce, or Procure the Commission of an Offense": A Critique of Federal Aiding and Abetting Principles*, 57 S.C. L. REV. 85, 90–91 (2005).
5. Commonwealth v. Rega, 933 A.2d 997, 1015 (Pa. 2007).
6. *See, e.g.*, MODEL PENAL CODE §§ 2.06(6)(a) and (b).
7. Queen v. Tyrell, 1 Q.B. 710 (1894).
8. *See* Grace E. Mueller, Note: *The Mens Rea of Accomplice Liability*, 61 S. CAL. L. REV. 2169, 2169–70 (1988).
9. *See id.* at 2017 (citing Hicks v. United States, 150 U.S. 442, 449–50 (1893)).
10. 150 U.S. 442 (1893).
11. *Id.* at 445–46.
12. *Id.* at 447.
13. *Id.* at 448.
14. *Id.* at 450.
15. *Id.* at 448.
16. *Id.* at 449.
17. *Id.* at 449.
18. *See* Michael S. Moore, Causing, *Aiding, and the Superfluity of Accomplice Liability*, 156 U. PA. L. REV. 395 (2007); Sanford H. Kadish, *Reckless Complicity*, 87 J. CRIM. L. & CRIMINOLOGY 369 (1997).
19. State v. Hinkley, 325 P.2d 889 (Wash. 1958).
20. *See* Kadish, *supra* note 2, at 385–86.
21. People v. Abbott, 445 N.Y.S.2d 344 (1981).

22. *Id.* at 346–47 (internal quotations and citations omitted).
23. Moore, *supra* note 18, at 438.
24. *See* MODEL PENAL CODE §§ 2.06 & 5.01(3).
25. *See* 22 C.J.S. CRIMINAL LAW § 175 (2016 Supp.).
26. *See* Jimmie E. Tinsley, *Withdrawal from or Abandonment of Criminal Enterprise*, 8 AM. JUR. PROOF OF FACTS 2d 231 (2007).
27. *See, e.g.*, Karnes v. State, 252 S.W. 1 (Ark. 1923).
28. MODEL PENAL CODE § 2.06(6)(c)(i)-(ii).
29. *E.g.*, Skelly v. United States, 76 F.2d 483 (10th Cir. 1935); United States v. Brenson, 104 F.3d 1267 (11th Cir. 1997), *cert. denied*, 522 U.S. 884 (1997).
30. Leo Gerard Smith, Note, *Family Member Exemption for Accessory After-the-Fact*, 20 J. FAM. L. 105, 107–09 (1981).
31. WILLIAM BLACKSTONE, 4 COMMENTARIES *38–39. ("But a feme-covert cannot become an accessory by the receipt or concealment of her husband; for she is presumed to act under his coercion, and therefore she is not bound, neither ought she, to discover her lord.")
32. *See* Dan Markel, Jennifer M. Collins, & Ethan J. Leib, *Criminal Justice and the Challenge of Family Ties*, 2007 U. ILL. L. REV. 1147 (2007).
33. *Id.* at 1158–59. "The states that provide exemptions for family members are Florida, Illinois, Indiana, Iowa, Kentucky, Massachusetts, Nevada, New Mexico, North Carolina, Rhode Island, Vermont, Virginia, West Virginia, and Wisconsin." *Id.* at 1159, n. 47; *see, e.g.*, MASS. GEN. LAWS ANN. ch. 274, § 4.
34. Markel et al., *supra* note 32, at 1159, n. 49. ("These states are Arkansas, New Jersey, Washington, and Wyoming.")
35. *See* MODEL PENAL CODE and Commentaries § 2.06, cmt. 1 (1985).
36. Jeremy McLaughlin & Joshua M. Nahum, *Obstruction of Justice*, 44 AM. CRIM. L. REV. 793, 794 (2007).
37. MODEL PENAL CODE § 242.1.
38. *E.g.*, N.J. STAT. ANN. § 2C:29-3 (2020).
39. MODEL PENAL CODE § 242.3.
40. *See, e.g.*, IOWA CODE ANN. § 703.3.
41. *See, e.g.*, WASH. REV. CODE ANN. § 9A.76.070.
42. *See, e.g.*, N.J.S.A. § 2C:29-3.
43. Commonwealth v. Neckerauer, 617 A.2d 1281 (Pa. Super. Ct. 1992).
44. State v. D'Addario, 482 A.2d 961 (N.J. 1984).
45. MODEL PENAL CODE § 242.3(5).
46. *Neckerauer*, 617 A.2d at 1286 (citing MODEL PENAL CODE and Commentary § 242.3(5) (1983)).
47. People v. Meissner, 812 N.W.2d 37, 47 (Mich. Ct. App. 2011) (quoting People v. Thomas, 475 N.W.2d 288 (1991)).
48. *Id.* (quoting People v. Tower, 320, 544 N.W.2d 752, 754 (Mich. Ct. App. 1996) (internal alterations omitted)).
49. *Id.* (quoting People v. Somma, 333 N.W.2d 117, 119 (Mich. Ct. App. 1983) (internal alterations omitted)).
50. MICH. COMP. LAWS ANN. § 750.122.
51. MICH. COMP. LAWS ANN. § 750.505.
52. *E.g.*, 18 U.S.C. §§ 1510, 1511.
53. 21 U.S.C. §§ 853(e), 853(p).
54. U.S. SENTENCING GUIDELINES MANUAL § 3C1.1 cmt. 3–4.
55. For a detailed explanation of the many different ways that courts have defined and interpreted various forms of obstruction of justice, see Annotation, *What Constitutes Offense of Obstructing or Resisting Officer*, 48 A.L.R. 746 (Supp. 2008); and John F. Decker, *The Varying Parameters of Obstruction of Justice in American Criminal Law*, 65 LA. L. REV. 49 (2004).
56. *See* MODEL PENAL CODE § 241.1(1); *see also* 18 U.S.C. §§ 1501–21.
57. *See* MODEL PENAL CODE § 241.2.

58. *See* U.S. SENTENCING GUIDELINES MANUAL § 3C1.1.
59. *See* MODEL PENAL CODE § 241.3(1).
60. United States v. Dunnigan, 507 U.S. 87, 94 (1993).
61. Arthur Andersen, LLP v. United States, 544 U.S. 696, 706 (2005).
62. *Dunnigan*, 507 U.S. at 87.
63. U.S. SENTENCING GUIDELINES MANUAL § 3C1.1.
64. *Dunnigan*, 507 U.S. at 93–98.
65. *See* United States v. Booker, 543 U.S. 220, 239–40 (2005). ("Applying *Blakely* to the Guidelines would invalidate a sentence that relied on such an enhancement if the resulting sentence [were] outside the range authorized by the jury verdict. Nevertheless, there are many situations in which the district judge might find that the enhancement is warranted, yet still sentence the defendant within the range authorized by the jury. . . . Thus, while the reach of *Dunnigan* may be limited, we need not overrule it.")
66. *See* MODEL PENAL CODE § 241.6.
67. *Id.*
68. *See* MODEL PENAL CODE § 241.7.
69. *See* MODEL PENAL CODE § 241.8.
70. MODEL PENAL CODE § 242.2.
71. *See, e.g.,* ARIZ. REV. STAT. § 13-1105(A)(2) (2019).
72. MODEL PENAL CODE § 242.6(1).
73. MODEL PENAL CODE § 242.6(2).
74. *Id.*
75. *See* MODEL PENAL CODE § 5.03.
76. *See* 16 AM. JUR. 2D *Conspiracy* § 2 (2009) (citing State v. Kaakimaka, 933 P.2d 617 (Haw. 1997)).
77. *Id.* (citing State v. DiBella, 254 A.2d 477 (Conn. 1968)); *see also* Mitchell v. State 767 A.2d 844 (Md. 2001).
78. *Id.*; *see also* Hicks v. United States, 150 U.S. 442 (1893).
79. United States v. Jimenez-Recio, 537 U.S. 270, 274–75 (2003) (quoting Salinas v. United States, 522 U.S. 52, 65 (1997); Callanan v. United States, 364 U.S. 587, 593–94 (1961)).
80. United States v. Hemphill, 514 F.3d 1350, 1362 (D.C. Cir. 2008).
81. State v. Euceda-Valle, 641 S.E.2d 858, 864 (N.C. App. 2007).
82. MODEL PENAL CODE §5.03 (1985).
83. MODEL PENAL CODE § 5.03.
84. *See, e.g.,* Christine L. Chinni, *Criminal Law--Whose Head Is in the Sand? Problems with the Use of the Ostrich Instruction in Conspiracy Cases*, 13 W. NEW ENG. L. REV. 35, 41 (1991) (citing Fridman, *Mens Rea in Conspiracy*, 19 MOD. L. REV. 276 (1956); Albert J. Harno, *Intent in Criminal Conspiracy*, 89 U. PA. L. REV. 624 (1941)).
85. Blumenthal v. United States, 332 U.S. 539, 557 (1947).
86. United States v. Dazey, 403 F.3d 1147, 1159 (10th Cir. 2005).
87. Caminetti v. United States, 242 U.S. 470 (1917).
88. *See* 16 AM. JUR. 2d *Conspiracy* § 44 (2009).
89. *See, e.g.,* Arthur L. Alarcon, *Suspect Evidence: Admissibility of Co-Conspirator Statements and Uncorroborated Accomplice Testimony*, 25 LOY. L.A. L. REV. 953, 960 (1992).
90. *See* 16 AM. JUR. 2d *Conspiracy* § 44 (2009).
91. For a more in-depth discussion of hearsay, see Daniel B. Shanes, *Confronting Testimonial Hearsay: Understanding the New Confrontation Clause*, 40 LOY. U. CHI. L.J. 879 (2009).
92. Bourjaily v. United States, 483 U.S. 171 (1987); *see also* 16 AM. JUR. 2d *Conspiracy* § 45 (2009).
93. *See* Krulewitch v. United States, 336 U.S. 440 (1949).
94. Heather J. Sigler, *Federal Criminal Conspiracy*, 46 AM. CRIM. L. REV. 589, 598 (2009) (citing United States v. Nascimento, 491 F.3d 25, 48–49 (1st Cir. 2007) (quoting United States v. Snow, 462 F.3d 55, 68 (2d Cir. 2006); United States v. Samaria, 239 F.3d 228, 235 (2d Cir. 2001)).
95. MODEL PENAL CODE § 2.02 (1985).

96. People v. Lauria, 251 Cal. App. 2d 471, 59 Cal. Rptr. 628 (1967).
97. United States v. Falcone, 311 U.S. 205 (1940).
98. Direct Sales Co. v. United States, 319 U.S. 703 (1943).
99. Regina v. Thomas, 2 All Eng. 181 (1957) (upholding conviction when the defendant rented a room to a prostitute at a grossly inflated rent for the purpose of carrying on her business).
100. People v. McLaughlin, 245 P.2d 1076 (Cal. App. 1952) (upholding conviction of the suppliers of horse-racing information by wire for conspiracy to promote bookmaking, when it had been established that wire-service information had no other use than to supply information needed by bookmakers to conduct illegal gambling operations).
101. Jessica A. Kozlov-Davis, *A Hybrid Approach to the Use of Deliberate Ignorance in Conspiracy Cases*, 100 MICH. L. REV. 473, 479–80 (2001).
102. WHARTON'S CRIMINAL LAW § 681 (1996).
103. United States v. Shabani, 513 U.S. 10 (1994).
104. *See* MODEL PENAL CODE § 5.03(5).
105. *See, e.g.*, 18 U.S.C. § 371 (2010).
106. *See* Gebardi v. United States, 287 U.S. 112 (1932).
107. United States v. Brenson, 104 F.3d 1267 (11th Cir. 1997).
108. Sigler, *supra* note 99, at 595 (citing United States v. Nascimento, 491 F.3d 25, 48–49 (1st Cir. 2007).
109. Braverman v. United States, 317 U.S. 49 (1942).
110. *See* FED. R. EVID. 801(d)(2)(E); Bourjaily v. United States, 483 U.S. 171 (1987).
111. Kotteakos v. United States, 328 U.S. 750 (1946).
112. Model Penal Code § 2.06.
113. United States v. Kissel, 218 U.S. 601, 608 (1910).
114. 16 AM. JUR. 2D *Conspiracy* § 4 (2016).
115. MD. CODE CRIM. LAW § 1-202.
116. R.I. GEN. LAWS 1956 § 11-1-6.
117. MODEL PENAL CODE § 5.03(1).
118. MODEL PENAL CODE § 5.03(6).
119. See Young v. States, 908 So.2d 819 (Miss. Ct. App. 2005) (upholding conviction).
120. WEST'S FLA. STAT. ANN. § 777.03 (2020).
121. United States v. Fuchs, 467 F.3d 889 (5th Cir. 2006).
122. *Id.* at 908–09.

CHAPTER 7

1. BLACK'S LAW DICTIONARY 346 (7th ed. 1999); ROLLIN M. PERKINS & ROLAND N. BOYCE, CRIMINAL LAW 140 (3d ed. 1982).
2. 40 AM. JUR. 2D *Homicide* § 4 (Supp. 2008).
3. *Id.* (citing Golden v. State, 629 So. 2d 109 (Fla. 1993)).
4. Kirsten Rabe Smolensky, *Defining Life from the Perspective of Death: An Introduction to the Forced Symmetry Approach*, 2006 U. CHI. LEGAL F. 41, 46 (citing *Time of Death: Medicolegal Considerations* §2, 16 AM JUR PROOF OF FACTS 2d 87, 96 (1978)).
5. *Id.* at 45 (citing Bryan J. Jennett, *Medical Definitions of Death*, 3 ENCYCLOPEDIA OF FORENSIC AND LEGAL MEDICINE 230, 231 (2005)).
6. *Brain Death*, THE AMERICAN HERITAGE STEADMAN'S MEDICAL DICTIONARY (2016), *available online at* http://medical-dictionary.thefreedictionary.com.
7. Smolensky, *supra* note 4, at 49–50 (citing BARRY R. FURROW ET AL., BIOETHICS: HEALTH CARE LAW AND ETHICS 207 (2001)); *see also, e.g.*, People v Eulo, 472 N.E.2d 286 (N.Y. App. Ct. 1994).
8. Rogers v. Tennessee, 532 U.S. 451 (2001); 4 W. BLACKSTONE, COMMENTARIES ON THE LAWS OF ENGLAND 197–98 (1769); EDWARD COKE, THE THIRD PART OF THE INSTITUTES OF THE LAWS OF ENGLAND 55 (1644).

9. 40 AM. JUR. 2D HOMICIDE § 13 (Supp. 2008).
10. *Rogers*, 532 U.S. at 462.
11. State v. Rogers, 992 S.W.2d 393, 397–98 (Tenn. 1999), *aff'd* 532 U.S. 451 (2001).
12. *Rogers*, 532 U.S. at 463.
13. *See* MODEL PENAL CODE § 210.1.
14. 40 AM. JUR. 2D HOMICIDE § 13 (Supp. 2008); *see also, e.g.*, Ex parte Key, 890 So. 2d 1056 (Ala. 2003); People v. Rehman, 396 P.2d 913 (Cal. 1964), *cert. denied*, 379 U.S. 930 (1964); United States v. Jackson, 528 A.2d 1211 (D.C. 1987); State v. Dailey, 134 N.E. 481 (Ind. 1922); State v. Moore, 199 So. 661 (La. 1940); Larson v. State, 437 S.W.2d 67 (Mo. 1969); State v. Keerl, 75 P. 362 (Mont. 1904)).
15. CAL. PENAL CODE § 194 (1969).
16. CAL. PENAL CODE § 194 (1996).
17. Commonwealth v. Casanova, 708 N.E.2d 86 (Mass. 1999).
18. *Id.* at 89.
19. *Id.*
20. Smolensky, *supra* note 4, at 57.
21. *Id.* at 58.
22. "The states include: Alabama, Alaska, Arizona, Arkansas, California, Colorado, Florida, Georgia, Idaho, Illinois, Indiana, Iowa, Kansas, Kentucky, Louisiana, Maine, Maryland, Massachusetts, Michigan, Minnesota, Mississippi, Nebraska, Nevada, North Carolina, North Dakota, Ohio, Oklahoma, Pennsylvania, Rhode Island, South Carolina, South Dakota, Tennessee, Texas, Utah, Virginia, Washington, West Virginia and Wisconsin." National Conference of State Legislatures, *Fetal Homicide* (Mar. 2015), *available online at* http://www.ncsl.org/research/health/fetal-homicide-state-laws.aspx.
23. Alabama, Arizona, Georgia, Idaho, Illinois, Kansas, Kentucky, Louisiana, Minnesota, Mississippi, Nebraska., North Carolina, North Dakota, Ohio, Oklahoma, Pennsylvania, South Carolina, South Dakota, Tennessee, Texas, Utah, and Wisconsin. National Conference of State Legislatures, *supra* note 22.
24. *See generally*, Henry F. Fradella, *Why Judges Should Admit Expert Testimony on the Unreliability of Eyewitness Identifications*, 2 FED. CTS. L. REV. 1 (2007).
25. *See* WERNER SPITZ & DANIEL SPITZ, SPITZ AND FISHER'S MEDICOLEGAL INVESTIGATION OF DEATH 811 (4th ed. 2006).
26. *See generally* RICHARD SAFERSTEIN, CRIMINALISTICS: AN INTRODUCTION TO FORENSIC SCIENCE (11th ed. 2014).
27. Catherine M. Guthrie, *The CSI Effect: Legitimate Concern or Popular Myth?*, 41–Aug. PROSECUTOR 14 (2007).
28. *See, e.g.*, Michael Mann, *The "CSI Effect": Better Jurors Through Television and Science?*, 24 BUFF. PUB. INT. L.J. 211, (2005–2006).
29. *Id.* at 211–12.
30. 40A AM. JUR. 2D HOMICIDE § 274.
31. Francis Paul Greene, Comment, *I Ain't Got No Body: The Moral Uncertainty of Bodiless Murder Jurisprudence in New York after* People v. Bierenbaum, 71 FORDHAM L. REV. 2863, 2874 (2003).
32. 40A AM. JUR. 2D HOMICIDE § 274 (Supp. 2008).
33. People v. Lipskey, 443 N.E.2d 925 (N.Y. 1982).
34. *See, e.g.*, 18 U.S.C. § 1111(a).
35. WILLIAM BLACKSTONE, 4 COMMENTARIES ON THE LAWS OF ENGLAND 195 (1769).
36. *Id.* at 199.
37. 40 AM. JUR. 2D HOMICIDE § 37.
38. Alan C. Michaels, *Acceptance: The Missing Mental State*, 71 S. CAL. L. REV. 953, 1003 (1998).
39. 40 AM. JUR. 2D HOMICIDE § 38.
40. John C. Duffy, Note, *Reality Check: How Practical Circumstances Affect the Interpretation of Depraved Indifference Murder*, 57 DUKE L.J. 425 (2007).
41. 40 AM. JUR. 2D HOMICIDE § 38; *see also, e.g.*, Canipe v. Commonwealth, 491 S.E.2d 747 (Va. App. 1997).

42. MODEL PENAL CODE § 210.1.
43. 40 AM. JUR. 2D HOMICIDE § 45.
44. *Id.* (citing People v. Porter, 659 N.E.2d 915 (Ill. 1995)); *see also* People v. Lewis, 139 Cal. App. 4th 874, 44 Cal. Rptr. 3d 403 (4th Dist. 2006).
45. *Id.* (citing State v. McNeill, 485 S.E.2d 284 (N.C. 1997), *cert. denied*, 522 U.S. 1053 (1998)).
46. MODEL PENAL CODE § 210.2(1)(b); *see, e.g.*, State v. Robinson, 934 P.2d 38 (Kan. 1997).
47. KY. REV. STAT. § 507.020, Commentary; MODEL PENAL CODE, § 201.2, cmt. 2.
48. *See* Commonwealth v. Malone, 47 A.2d 445 (Pa. 1946).
49. *See* United States v. Flemming, 739 F.2d 945 (4th Cir. 1984) (upholding depraved heart murder conviction for driver with a.315% B.A.C.).
50. 40 AM. JUR. 2D HOMICIDE §§ 38–39.
51. *Id.* at § 39.
52. *Id.* at § 41.
53. N.Y. PENAL LAW § 125.27 (2020).
54. 40 AM. JUR. 2D HOMICIDE § 44.
55. Commonwealth v. Kosilek, 668 N.E.2d 808 (Mass. 1996).
56. Leyva v. State, 233 A.2d 498, 500 (Md. App. 1967).
57. People v. Anderson, 447 P.2d 942 (Cal. 1968).
58. David Crump, *Murder, Pennsylvania Style': Comparing Traditional American Homicide Law to the Statutes of Model Penal Code Jurisdictions*, 109 W. VA. L. REV. 257, 266 (2007).
59. *Anderson*, 447 P.2d at 949.
60. Crump, *supra* note 58, at 267 (quoting *Anderson*, 447 P.2d at 952); *see also* People v. Tafoya, 164 P.3d 590, 611–12 (Cal. 2007) (internal citations omitted); Woods v. State, 733 So. 2d 980 (Fla. 1999).
61. State v. Sokolowski, 522 S.E.2d 65, 70 (N.C. 1999).
62. *See also* State v. Keough, 18 S.W.3d 175 (Tenn. 2000).
63. *E.g.*, Carmichael v. State, 12 S.W.3d 225 (Ark. 2000).
64. *E.g.*, MODEL PENAL CODE § 210.2(1)(b).
65. Campbell v. State, 227 So.2d 873 (Fla. 1969).
66. LAFAVE, SUBSTANTIVE CRIMINAL LAW, § 7.5 (1986).
67. *See* Commonwealth v. Dellelo, 209 N.E.2d 303 (1965).
68. *See* Guyora Binder, *The Origins of American Felony Murder Rules*, 57 STAN. L. REV. 59, 197–89 (2004).
69. *See id.* at 198–99.
70. *See id.* at 173.
71. 40 AM. JUR. 2d *Homicide* § 135 (2009); *see also* State v. Kirkpatrick, 184 P.3d 247 (Kan. 2008); Redcross v. State, 121 A.2d 1154 (Md. App. 1998).
72. 40 AM. JUR. 2d *Homicide* § 56 (2009); *see also, e.g.* State v. Johnson, 476 S.E.2d 681 (S.C. 1996).
73. 40 AM. JUR. 2d *Homicide* § 48 (2009); *see also, e.g.*, Commonwealth v. Burgess, 879 N.E.2d 63 (Mass. 2008).
74. *E.g.*, Turner v. State, 708 So. 2d 232 (Ala. Crim. App. 1997).
75. State v. Cooley, 342 S.C. 63, 536 S.E.2d 666 (S.C. 2000); Speake v. State, 610 So. 2d 1238 (Ala. Crim. App. 1992).
76. 40 AM. JUR. 2d *Homicide* §§ 49, 53 (2009); *see also, e.g.*, State v. Engelhardt, 119 P.3d 1148 (Kan. 2005).
77. *E.g.*, State v. Byrd, 474 S.E.2d 430 (S.C. 1996).
78. 40 AM. JUR. 2d *Homicide* §§ 60 (2009); *see also, e.g.*, State v. Pittman, S.E.2d 144 (S.C. 2007), *cert. denied*, 128 S. Ct. 1872 (2008); Commonwealth v. Colon, 866 N.E.2d 412 (Mass.), *cert. denied*, 128 S. Ct. 810 (2007).
79. MODEL PENAL CODE § 210.3(1)(a) (2001).
80. People v. Ross, 34 A.D.3d 1124, 1126 (N.Y. App. Div. 2006).
81. Stuart M. Kirschner, Thomas R. Litwack, & Gary J. Galperin, *The Defense of Extreme Emotional Disturbance*, 10 PSYCHOL. PUB. POL'Y & L. 102, 104 (2004).
82. *Id.*

83. *See, e.g.*, ARK. CODE ANN. § 5-4-605(1) (2009); CONN. GEN. STAT. §§53a-54a to 53a-55 (2008); DEL. CODE ANN. tit. 11, § 641 (2009); HAW. REV. STAT. § 707-702 (2009); N.Y. PENAL LAW § 125.20(2) (McKinney 2006); OR. REV. STAT. §§163.118(1)(b), 163.135(1) (2009).
84. People v. White, 590 N.E.2d 236, 237 (N.Y. 1992).
85. *See, e.g.*, DeLuca v. Lord, 77 F.3d 578, 585 (2d Cir. 1996).
86. Donald A. Dripps, *Rehabilitating Bentham's Theory of Excuses*, 42 TEX. TECH L. REV. 383, 400 (2009).
87. *E.g.*, Cynthia Lee, *The Gay Panic Defense*, 42 U.C. DAVIS L. REV. 471 (2008) [hereinafter, "Lee, Gay Panic"]; Cynthia Lee, *Cultural Convergence: Interest Convergence Theory Meets the Cultural Defense*, 49 ARIZ. L. REV. 911 (2007); Victoria Nourse, *Passion's Progress: Modern Law Reform and the Provocation Defense*, 106 YALE L.J. 1331 (1997); *see also* Caroline Forell, *Gender Equality, Social Values and Provocation Law in the United States, Canada and Australia*, 14 AM. U. J. GENDER SOC. POL'Y & L. 27, 42 (2006) (criticizing the EED approach as being "solicitous of male rage and jealousy").
88. Nourse, *supra* note 87, at 1332–49.
89. *Id.* at 1363 (citing People v. Martinez, 591 A.2d 155 (Conn. App. Ct. 1991); People v. Wood, 568 N.Y.S.2d 651 (App. Div. 1991)); *see also* State v. Little, 462 A.2d 117, 118 (N.H. 1983).
90. Kirschner et al., *supra* note 81, at 118–19.
91. *Id.* at 118.
92. *Id.*
93. Cynthia Lee & P. Kwan, *The Trans Panic Defense: Masculinity, Heteronormativity, and the Murder of Transgender Women*, 66 HASTINGS L.J. 77 (2013).
94. MODEL PENAL CODE § 210.3(1)(a) (2001); 40 AM. JUR. 2d *Homicide* § 61(2009).
95. 617 N.E.2d 609 (Mass. 1993).
96. *Id.* at 612.
97. Commonwealth v. Gallison, 421 N.E.2d 757, 761 (Mass. 1981).
98. *Twitchell*, 617 N.E.2d at 612 (citing MASS. GEN. LAWS. c. 273, § 1 (1992 ed.)).
99. *Id.* at 618–20.
100. 55 N.E.2d 902 (Mass. 1944).
101. *E.g.*, People v. Robertson, 95 P.3d 872 (Cal. 2004); Pagotto v. State, 732 A.2d 920 (Md. App. 1999).
102. *E.g.*, Berry v. State, 698 So.2d 225 (Ala. Cr. App. 1996); People v. Searle, 164 P. 819 (Cal. App. 1917).
103. *See* 40 AM. JUR. 2d *Homicide* § 90 (2009).
104. *E.g.*, State v. Campbell, 245 S.W.3d 331 (Tenn. 2008).
105. 40 AM. JUR. 2d *Homicide* § 86 (2009).
106. James J. Dietrich, *Problems and Charging Choices in Prosecuting Vehicular Fatalities*, 31-FEB Prosecutor 32, 32 (1997).
107. *Id.* at 33.
108. *See* Andrew Ashwort, *A Change of Normative Position: Determining the Contours of Culpability in Criminal Law*, 11 NEW CRIM. L. REV. 232 (2008).
109. People v. Stuart, 302 P.2d 5 (Cal. 1956).
110. *Id.*
111. *See* Shelly A. Cassity, *To Die or Not to Die: the History and Future of Assisted Suicide Laws in the U.S.*, 11 J. L. & FAM. STUD. 467 (2009) (citing Maria T. CeloCruz, *Aid-in-Dying: Should We Decriminalize Physician-Assisted Suicide and Physician-Committed Euthanasia?*, 18 AM. J.L. & MED. 369, 373–77 (1992)).
112. Vera Bergelson, *Victims and Perpetrators: an Argument for Comparative Liability in Criminal Law*, 8 BUFF. CRIM. L. REV. 385 (2005) (citing 2 WAYNE R. LAFAVE, SUBSTANTIVE CRIMINAL LAW §15.6, 543 n.3 (2d ed. 2003).
113. *Id.* (citing Wackwitz v. Roy, 418 S.E.2d 861, 864 (Va. 1992); Clift v. Narragansett Television L.P., 688 A.2d 805, 808 (R.I. 1996); Burnett v. People, 68 N.E. 505, 509–11 (Ill. 1903)).
114. *See* Cruzan v. Director of Missouri Dept. of Health, 497 U.S. 261 (1990).
115. Cassity, *supra* note 111, at 473 (citing OR. REV. STAT. §127.800 (2009)).
116. *Id.* at 474 (citing WASH. REV. CODE ANN. §70.245 (2009)).

117. *See, e.g.*, D.C. LAW 21-182 (2017); CAL. HEALTH & SAFETY CODE § 1.85 (2016); VT. STAT. ANN. tit. 18, § 5281 (2013).
118. Baxter v. Montana, 224 P.3d 1211 (Mt. 2009).
119. 527 N.W. 2d 714 (1994), *cert. denied*, 514 U.S. 1083 (1995).
120. Washington v. Glucksberg 521 U.S. 702 (1997)
121. Vacco v. Quill 521 U.S. 793 (1997).
122. Paul H. Robinson & Markus D. Dubber, *The American Model Penal Code: A Brief Overview*, 10 NEW CRIM. L. REV. 319, 340 (2007).
123. MODEL PENAL CODE § 210.1(1).
124. MODEL PENAL CODE § 210.2(1).
125. MODEL PENAL CODE § 210.3(1).
126. MODEL PENAL CODE § 210.4(1).
127. MODEL PENAL CODE § 210.2(1)(b).
128. DEL. CODE ANN. tit. 11, § 335 (2020).
129. State v. Leniart, 215 A.3d 1104 (Conn. 2019).
130. *Id.* at 1111.
131. *Id.* at 1112.
132. *Id.* at 1126.
133. For a fascinating story about how modern forensic science solved one of the most notorious of bodiless homicide cases—the Connecticut Woodchipper case—see ARTHUR HERZOG, THE WOODCHIPPER MURDER (1989).
134. 44 Cal. App. 4th 38, 51 Cal. Rptr. 2d 185 (1996).
135. MINN. STAT. § 609.185.
136. MINN. STAT. § 609.19.
137. MINN. STAT. § 609.195.
138. State v. Coleman, No. A19-0708, 2020 Minn. App. LEXIS 113 (Minn. Ct. App. Apr. 27, 2020).
139. State v. Foresta, No. A14-2146, 2016 WL 207698 (Minn. Ct. App. Jan. 19, 2016).
140. State v. Williams, No. A19-0639m 2020 Minn. App. Unpub. LEXIS 251 (Minn. Ct. App. Mar. 30, 2020).
141. State v. Petersen, 910 N.W.2d 1 (Minn. 2018).
142. State v. Thomas, 590 N.W.2d 755 (Minn. 1999).

CHAPTER 8

1. JENNIFER L. TRUMAN, & LYNN LANGTON, CRIMINAL VICTIMIZATION, 2014 (2015), http://www.bjs.gov/content/pub/pdf/cv14.pdf.
2. Matthew J. Breiding et al., *Prevalence and Characteristics of Sexual Violence, Stalking, and Intimate Partner Violence Victimization — National Intimate Partner and Sexual Violence Survey, United States, 2011*, 63 SURVEILLANCE SUMMARIES 1 (2014), http://www.cdc.gov/mmwr/preview/mmwrhtml/ss6308a1.htm.
3. MIKEL L. WALTERS, JIERU CHEN & MATTHEW J. BREIDING, THE NATIONAL INTIMATE PARTNER AND SEXUAL VIOLENCE SURVEY (NISVS): 2010 FINDINGS ON VICTIMIZATION BY SEXUAL ORIENTATION 10 (2013), https://www.cdc.gov/violenceprevention/pdf/nisvs_sofindings.pdf.
4. *Id.* at 11.
5. SANDY E. JAMES ET AL., THE REPORT OF THE 2015 U.S. TRANSGENDER SURVEY (2016), https://www.transequality.org/sites/default/files/docs/USTS-Full-Report-FINAL.PDF.
6. CANDACE KRUTTSCHNITT, WILLIAM D. KALSBEEK, & CAROL C. HOUSE, ESTIMATING THE INCIDENCE OF RAPE AND SEXUAL ASSAULT (2014); *see also* Corey Rayburn Yung, *How to Lie with Rape Statistics: America's Hidden Rape Crises*, 99 IOWA L. REV. 1197 (2014).
7. KRUTTSCHNITT ET AL., *supra* note 6, at 15 (internal citations omitted).
8. JAMES ET AL., *supra* note 5, *passim*.
9. WILLIAM BLACKSTONE, COMMENTARIES ON THE LAWS OF ENGLAND 210 (1769).

10. Meredith J. Duncan, *Sex Crimes and Sexual Miscues: The Need for a Clearer Line between Forcible Rape and Nonconsensual Sex*, 42 WAKE FOREST L. REV. 1087, 1093 (2007); *see also* Henry F. Fradella & Kegan Brown, *Withdrawal of Consent Post-Penetration: Redefining the Law of Rape*, 41 CRIM. L. BULL. 3 (2005) (citing Stacy Futter & Walter R. Mebane, Jr., *The Effects of Rape Law Reform on Rape Case Processing*, 16 BERKELEY WOMEN'S L.J. 72, 74 (2001)).
11. Fradella & Brown, *supra* note 10, at 4.
12. MATTHEW HALE, HISTORY OF THE PLEAS OF THE CROWN 628 (1778).
13. Fradella & Brown, *supra* note 10, at 4; Jill Elaine Hasday, *Contest and Consent: A Legal History of Marital Rape*, 88 CAL. L. REV. 1373 (2000).
14. *See, e.g.*, MODEL PENAL CODE § 213.1(1)(a)-(d) (1962) (requiring a penetration against the will of the female).
15. *See, e.g.*, State v. Montgomery, 974 P.2d 904 (Wash App. 1999).
16. *See, e.g.*, People v. Wallace, 189 P.3d 911 (Cal. 2008), *as modified by* 2008 Cal. LEXIS 12312 (Oct. 22, 2008), *cert. denied*, 556 U.S. 1223 (2009).
17. *See* JOSHUA DRESSLER, UNDERSTANDING CRIMINAL LAW (4th ed. 2006).
18. Vivian Berger, *Man's Trial, Woman's Tribulation: Rape Cases in the Courtroom*, 77 COLUM. L. REV. 1 (1977).
19. HALE, *supra* note 12, at 635.
20. Moran v. People, 25 Mich. 356 (1872); *see also* Bruce A. MacFarlane, *Historical Development of the Offence of Rape* (1993), http://www.canadiancriminallaw.com/articles/articles%20pdf/Historical_Development_of_the_Offence_of_Rape.pdf (originally published in 100 YEARS OF THE CRIMINAL CODE IN CANADA; ESSAYS COMMEMORATING THE CENTENARY OF THE CANADIAN CRIMINAL CODE (Josiah Wood & Richard C. C. Peck eds., 1993)).
21. MacFarlane, *supra* note 20, at 19.
22. *Id.* at 18–19 (quoting Bishop, *in* THE CRIMINAL CODE OF CANADA 275–76 (James Crankshaw ed., 1902)).
23. *Id.* at 19.
24. *Id.* at 20.
25. MODEL PENAL CODE § 213.1 cmt. (1980), at 305.
26. Brown v. State, 106 N.W. 536 (Wis. 1906).
27. *Id.* at 537.
28. *Id.* at 538.
29. Susan Estrich, *Rape*, 95 YALE L.J. 1087, 1090 (1986).
30. Berger, *supra* note 18, at 8.
31. Ronald J. Berger, Patricia Searles, & W. Lawrence Neuman, *The Dimensions of Rape Reform Legislation*, 22 LAW & SOC'Y REV. 329 (1988).
32. MODEL PENAL CODE § 213.1.
33. *Sexual Assault and Related Offenses*, AM. L. INST., https://www.ali.org/projects/show/sexual-assault-and-related-offenses/ (last visited July 3, 2020).
34. Julie Horney & Cassia C. Spohn, *Rape Law Reform and Instrumental Change in Six Urban Jurisdictions*, 25 LAW & SOC'Y REV. 117 (1991).
35. *See* GA. CODE ANN. § 16-6-1 (retaining the common-law definition of rape).
36. *See, e.g.*, ALASKA STAT. § 11.41.410(a)(1); ARIZ. REV. STAT. ANN. § 13-1406(A).
37. Fradella & Brown, *supra* note 10, at 5 (citing CASSIA SPOHN & JULIE HORNEY, RAPE LAW REFORM: A GRASSROOTS REVOLUTION AND ITS IMPACT 22 (1992)).
38. SPOHN & HORNEY, *supra* note 37, at 22; Hasday, *supra* note 13, at 1375.
39. *See* Bennett Capers, *Real Rape Too*, 99 CAL. L. REV. 1259 (2011).
40. *See* Michelle J. Anderson, *Marital Immunity, Intimate Relationships, and Improper Inferences: A New Law on Sexual Offenses by Intimates*, 54 HASTINGS L.J. 1465 (2003); Jessica Klarfeld, *Striking Disconnect: Marital Rape Law's Failure to Keep Up with Domestic Violence Law*, 48 AM. CRIM. L. REV. 1819 (2011).
41. Hasday, *supra* note 13, at 1375.
42. *Id.*

43. David P. Bryden, *Forum on the Law of Rape: Redefining Rape*, 3 BUFF. CRIM. L. REV. 317, 357 (2000).
44. Fradella & Brown, *supra* note 10, at 6 (citing ALA. CODE § 13A-6-60(8); DEL. CODE ANN. tit. 11, § 761(h)(1); IDAHO CODE § 18-6101; LA. REV. STAT. ANN. § 14.42.1(A)(1); WASH. REV. CODE § 9A.44.010(6)); *see also* John F. Decker & Peter G. Baroni, *"No" Still Means "Yes": The Failure of the "Non-consent" Reform Movement in American Rape and Sexual Assault Law*, 101 J. CRIM. L. & CRIMINOLOGY 1081 (2011).
45. Fradella & Brown, *supra* note 10, at 7 (citing IOWA CODE ANN. § 709.5; MINN. STAT. ANN. § 609.347(2); MONT. CODE ANN. § 45-5-511(5); N.J. STAT. ANN. § 2C:14-5(a); OHIO REV. CODE ANN. § 2907.02(c); R.I. GEN. LAWS § 11-37-12; VT. STAT. ANN. tit. 13, § 3254(1); VA. CODE ANN. § 18.2-67.6).
46. *See* MODEL PENAL CODE § 213.1(1); *see also, e.g.*, Commonwealth v. Sherry, 437 N.E.2d 224 (Mass. 1982), *overruled on other grounds*, Commonwealth v. King, 834 N.E.2d 1175 (Mass. 2005).
47. Angela Christene Artherton, *"Raped, But Not by a Rapist": The Arkansas Rape Statute Provides No Legal Recourse to Some Victims*, 65 ARK. L. REV. 317 (2012).
48. Fradella & Brown, *supra* note 10, at 7 (citing Bryden, *supra* note 43, at 358–59).
49. Horney & Spohn, *supra* note 34, at 139.
50. *Id.* at 372.
51. Fradella & Brown, *supra* note 10, at 8 (citing In re M.T.S., 609 A.2d 1266 (1992)).
52. *Id.* at 8 (quoting Kit Kinports, *Rape and Force: The Forgotten Mens Rea*, 4 BUFF. CRIM. L.R. 755, 757 (2001)).
53. Director of Public Prosecutions v. Morgan, 1976 App. Cas. 182, 205, 2 W.L.R. 913, 2 All E.R. 347 (H.L.1975).
54. *See* Patricia J. Falk, *Rape by Drugs: A Statutory Overview and Proposals for Reform*, 44 ARIZ. L. REV. 131 (2002).
55. MODEL PENAL CODE § 213.1(1)(b).
56. *E.g.*, People v. Ramirez, 143 Cal. App. 4th 1512, 50 Cal. Rptr. 3d 110 (2006).
57. MINN. STAT. § 609.341, subd. 7 (2020) (emphasis added).
58. State v. Khalil, 956 N.W.2d 627, 630 (Minn. 2014) (describing the factual circumstances as "an experience no person should ever have to endure").
59. *See* Ben A. McJunkin, *Deconstructing Rape by Fraud*, 28 COLUM. J. GENDER & L. 1 (2014).
60. Margo Kaplan, *Rethinking HIV-Exposure Laws*, 87 IND. L.J. 1517 (2012).
61. Ari Ezra Waldman, *Exceptions: The Criminal Law's Illogical Approach to HIV-Related Aggravated Assaults*, 18 VIR. J. SOC. POL'Y & L. 550 (2011).
62. State v. Smith, 554 A.2d 713 (Conn. 1989).
63. *See* Duncan, *supra* note 10, at 1094–95.
64. *See* Berger, *supra* note 18, at 12–32.
65. *See* LEROY G. SCHULTZ, RAPE VICTIMOLOGY (1975).
66. *See* Leigh Bienen, *Rape Reform Legislation in the United States: A Look at Some Practical Effects*, 8 VICTIMOLOGY 139, 139 (1983).
67. Heather D. Flowe, Ebbe B. Ebbesen, & Anila Putcha-Bhagavatula, *Rape Shield Laws and Sexual Behavior Evidence: Effects of Consent Level and Women's Sexual History on Rape Allegations*, 31 LAW & HUM. BEHAV. 159, 160 (2007) (citing FED. R. EVID. 412).
68. *Id.* (citing MIL. R. EVID. 412).
69. *Id.*
70. *Id.*
71. *Id.* (citing Michelle J. Anderson, *From Chastity Requirement to Sexuality License: Sexual Consent and a New Rape Shield Law*, 70 GEO. WASH. L. REV. 51 (2002)).
72. *E.g.*, Miller v. State, 779 P.2d 87 (Nev. 1989).
73. *See* Olden v. Kentucky, 488 U.S. 227 (1988).
74. Fradella & Brown, *supra* note 10, at 20; *see also* Kinports, *supra* note 52, at 761.
75. Fradella & Brown, *supra* note 10, at 20.
76. Fradella & Brown, *supra* note 10, at 20.
77. *See* Kinports, *supra* note 52, at 774.

78. Reynolds v. State, 664 P.2d 621 (Alaska Ct. App. 1983).
79. Confusingly, however, the court repeatedly used the word "recklessly" even though a "should have known" standard connotes the *mens rea* of negligence.
80. Kinports, *supra* note 52, at 782–83 (quoting State v. Reed, 479 A.2d 1291, 1296 (Me. 1984)).
81. *Id.* at 758.
82. People v. Williams, 614 N.E.2d 730, 736 (N.Y. 1993).
83. *In re* John Z, 60 P.3d 183 (Cal. 2003).
84. *Id.* at 185.
85. People v. Roundtree, 77 Cal. App. 4th 846, 851 (2000).
86. State v. Flynn, 329 P.3d 429 (Kan. 2014).
87. *John Z.*, 60 P.3d at 190.
88. *See also, e.g., Flynn*, 329 P.3d at 438; State v. Baby, 946 A.2d 463 (Md. 2008).
89. TENN. CODE § 39-13-502 (2020).
90. TENN. CODE § 39-13-503 (2020).
91. *See, e.g.*, KIMBERLY A. LONSWAY & JOANNE ARCHAMBAULT, VICTIM IMPACT: HOW VICTIMS ARE AFFECTED BY SEXUAL ASSAULT AND HOW LAW ENFORCEMENT CAN RESPOND (2019), https://www.evawintl.org/Library/DocumentLibraryHandler.ashx?id=656.
92. Morgan Namian, *Hypermasculine Police and Vulnerable Victims: The Detrimental Impact of Police Ideologies on the Rape Reporting Process*, 40 WOMEN'S RTS. L. REP. 80, 119–20 (2018).
93. *Id.* at 121–22 (internal citations and quotations omitted).
94. Pub. L. 103–322, 108 Stat. 1902 (1994) (codified as amended at 18 U.S.C. §§ 2247–66 & 34 U.S.C §§ 10441 *et seq.*).
95. Leslie D. Robinson, *It Is What it Is: Legal Recognition of Acquaintance Rape*, 6 AVE MARIA L. REV. 627, 644 (2008).
96. *Id.*; *see also* Andrea A. Curcio, *The Georgia Roundtable Discussion Model: Another Way to Approach Reforming Rape Laws*, 20 GA. ST. U. L. REV. 565, 573 (2004).
97. Curcio, *supra* note 96, at 573–74.
98. *E.g.*, ALASKA STAT. §§ 11.41.410 (a)(1).
99. *E.g.*, FLA. STAT. ANN. § 794.001 .
100. *E.g.*, ALASKA STAT. §§ 11.41.400 (a)(1) .
101. UNIF. CODE MIL. JUST. art. 120(e) (2005).
102. *See, e.g.*, Damon Mitchell et al., *Effects of Offender Motivation, Victim Gender, and Participant Gender on Perceptions of Rape Victims and Offenders*, 24 J. INTERPERSONAL VIOLENCE 1564 (2009).
103. For a fascinating discourse on the problems associated with proving "sexual gratification" in cases in which heterosexual boys engage in acts of sexual violence, see Patricia Wencelblat, Note, *Boys Will Be Boys? An Analysis of Male-on-male Heterosexual Sexual Violence*, 38 COLUM. J.L. & SOC. PROBS. 37 (2004).
104. ARIZ. REV. STAT. §§ 13-1401 & 13-1404.
105. S.D. STAT. § 22-22-1.
106. ARIZ. REV. STAT. §§ 13-1405 & 13-1410.
107. ARIZ. REV. STAT. § 13-705.
108. IND. CODE § 35-42-4-3.
109. *Id.*
110. Catherine L. Carpenter, *On Statutory Rape, Strict Liability, and the Public Welfare Offense Model*, 53 AM. U. L. REV. 313, 334 n.122 (2003).
111. Rita Eidson, *The Constitutionality of Statutory Rape Laws*, 27 UCLA L. REV. 757 (1980)(quoting 3 Edw. 1, c.13).
112. Michelle Oberman, *Turning Girls into Women: Re-Evaluating Modern Statutory Rape Law*, 8 DEPAUL J. HEALTH CARE L. 109 (2004–2005).
113. Carpenter, *supra* note 110, at 339–40.
114. Oberman, *supra* note 112, at 120.

115. *Id.*
116. 450 U.S. 464 (1981).
117. Carpenter, *supra* note 110, at 335.
118. Colorado, Illinois, Louisiana, Missouri, Nebraska, New Mexico, New York, and Texas. *See* Oberman, *supra* note 112, at 119.
119. Arizona, California, Delaware, Florida, Idaho, North Dakota, Oregon, Tennessee, Utah, Virginia, Wisconsin, and Wyoming. See Oberman, *supra* note 112, at 119.
120. MODEL PENAL CODE § 213.3(1)(a).
121. N.J. STAT. ANN. § 2C:14-2.
122. *See, e.g.*, ARK. CODE §§ 5-14-103, 5-14-125, & 5-14-126.
123. Michael M. v. Superior Court of Sonoma County, California, 450 U.S. 464 (1981).
124. Carpenter, *supra* note 110, at 338.
125. *Id.* at 342–43.
126. *Id.* at 343; *see, e.g.*, ALASKA STAT. § 11.41.445(b); KY. REV. STAT. ANN. § 510.030.
127. *See, e.g.*, MINN. STAT. ANN. § 609.342; MONT. CODE ANN. § 45-5-502(5)(b).
128. *E.g.*, WASH. REV. CODE ANN. 9A.44.030.
129. People v. Paz, 80 Cal. App.4th 293, 95 Cal. Rptr.2d 166 (2000).
130. *Id.* at 295 (quoting People v. Olsen, 685 P.2d 52, 58 (Cal. 1984)).
131. Kay L. Levine, *Women as Perpetrators of Crime: No Penis, No Problem*, 33 FORDHAM URB. L.J. 357 (2006).
132. Katherine Dollar et al., *Influence of Gender Roles on Perceptions of Teacher/Adolescent Student Sexual Relations*, 50 SEX ROLES 91, 387 (2004); Jodi A. Quas et al., *Effects of Victim, Defendant, and Juror Gender on Decisions in Child Sexual Assault Cases*, 32 J. APPLIED SOC. PSYCHOL. 1993, 2011 (2002); Sylvia Broussard et al., *Undergraduate Students' Perceptions of Child Sexual Abuse: The Impact of Victim Sex, Perpetrator Sex, Respondent Sex, and Victim Response*, 6 J. FAM. VIOLENCE 267, 269–72 (1991).
133. Broussard et al., *supra* note 132, at 275.
134. 900 N.E. 2d 834 (Mass. 2009).
135. Ryan White Comprehensive AIDS Resources Emergency Act, Pub. L. No. 101-381, 104 Stat. 576 (1990), *codified as amended at* 42 U.S.C. §§ 300ff (2016).
136. Robert C. Gallo & Luc Montagnier, *The Discovery of HIV as the Cause of AIDS*, 349 NEW ENG. J. MED. 2283 (2003).
137. U.S. Centers for Disease Control and Prevention. *HIV and AIDS–United States, 1981–2000*, 50 MORBIDITY & MORTALITY WEEKLY REPT. 430 (June 1, 2001), http://www.cdc.gov/mmwr/preview/mmwrhtml/mm5021a2.htm.
138. U.S. Centers for Disease Control and Prevention, *HIV-Specific Criminal Law* (2014), http://www.cdc.gov/hiv/policies/law/states/exposure.html, at ¶ 1.
139. *Id.* at 1000.
140. Margo Kaplan, *Rethinking HIV-Exposure Crimes*, 87 IND. L.J. 1517, 1519 (2012).
141. *E.g.*, FLA. STAT. § 384.24 (2020); IDAHO CODE § 39-608(3)(a) (2020).
142. ALA. CODE § 22-11A-21(c) (2020).
143. E.g., NEB. REV. STAT. § 28-934; TENN. CODE ANN. § 39-13-109.
144. *E.g.*, ALA. CODE § 22-11A-21(c); CAL. HEALTH & SAFETY CODE § 120291(a); N.J. STAT. ANN. § 2C:34-5.
145. J. Stan Lehman et al., *Prevalence and Public Health Implications of State Laws that Criminalize Potential HIV Exposure in the United States*, 18 AIDS BEHAV. 997, 1000 (2014).
146. *Id.* at 1001; *see also* COLO. REV. STAT. § 18-7-205.7 (2015).
147. Lehman et al., *supra* note 145, at 1003.
148. *Id.* at 998.
149. *Id.* at 1001.
150. *See* Leslie E. Wolf & Richard Vezina, *Crime and Punishment: Is There a Role for Criminal Law in HIV Prevention Policy?*, 25 WHITTIER L. REV. 821 (2004).

151. For an example of the language courts used with regard to HIV being a terminal disease, see State v. Hinkhouse, 912 P.2d 921 (Ore. App. 1996).
152. *See, e.g.*, Dallas Swendemana, Barbara L. Ingramb, & Mary Jane Rotheram-Borus, *Common Elements in Self-Management of HIV and Other Chronic Illnesses: An Integrative Framework*, 21 AIDS CARE 1321 (2009).
153. *See, e.g.*, Carol L. Galletly & Stephen D. Pinkerton, *Preventing HIV Transmission Via HIV Exposure Laws: Applying Logic and Mathematical Modeling to Compare Statutory Approaches to Penalizing Undisclosed Exposure to HIV*, 36 J. L. & MED. ETHICS 577 (2008); Carol L. Galletly et al., *New Jersey's HIV Exposure Law and HIV-Related Attitudes, Beliefs, and Sexual and Seropositive Status Disclosure Behaviors of Persons Living with HIV*, 102 AM. J. PUB. HEALTH 2135 (2012); Keith J. Horvath, Richard Weinmeyer, & Simon Rosser, *Should It Be Illegal for HIV-Positive Persons to Have Unprotected Sex Without Disclosure? An Examination of Attitudes Among US Men Who Have Sex with Men and the Impact of State Law*, 22 AIDS CARE 1221 (2010).
154. Lehman et al., *supra* note 145, at 999.
155. *E.g.*, Isabel Grant, *Rethinking Risk: The Relevance of Condoms and Viral Load in HIV Nondisclosure Prosecutions*, 54 MCGILL L.J. 389 (2009); Ari Ezra Waldman, *Exceptions: The Criminal Law's Illogical Approach to HIV-Related Aggravated Assaults*, 18 VIR. J. SOC. POL'Y & L. 550 (2011).
156. Waldman, *supra* note 155, at 605.
157. State v. Keene, 629 N.W.2d 360, 365 (Iowa 2001).
158. IOWA CODE §§ 709D.2–D.3 (2020).
159. Diana Ginn, *Can Failure to Disclose HIV Positivity to Sexual Partners Vitiate Consent?*: R. v. Cuerrier, 12 CANADIAN J. WOMEN & L. 235 (2000).
160. Jed Rubenfeld, *The Riddle of Rape-by-Deception and the Myth of Sexual Autonomy*, 122 YALE L.J. 1372 (2013).
161. State v. Neatherlin, 154 P.3d 703 (N.M. Ct. App. 2007); *cf.* Boyer v. Belleque, 659 F.3d 957, 968 (9th Cir. 2011).
162. N.J. STAT. ANN. § 2C:7-1-1.
163. *See* State v. Timmendequas, 773 A.2d 18, 23 (N.J. 2001).
164. *E.g.*, Smith v. Doe, 538 U.S. 84 (2003); State v. McCuin, 808 P.2d 332 (Az. Ct. App. 1991).
165. *See generally* Wayne A. Logan, *Criminal Justice Federalism and National Sex Offender Policy*, 6 OHIO ST. J. CRIM. L. 51 (2008).
166. Pam Lychner Sexual Offender Tracking and Identification Act of 1996, Pub. L. No. 104-236, 110 Stat. 3093 (codified at 42 U.S.C. § 14072 (2006)).
167. Protection of Children from Sexual Predators Act of 1998, Pub. L. No. 105-314, § 102(2), 112 Stat. 2974, 2975-76 (1998) (codified at U.S.C. § 14071 and scattered section of 18, 28 & 42 U.S.C.).
168. Prosecutorial Remedies and Other Tools to End the Exploitation of Children Today [PROTECT] Act, Pub. L. No. 108-21, 117 Stat. 650 (2003).
169. Pub. L. No. 109-248, 120 Stat. 587 (2006).
170. Logan, *supra* note 165, at 74 (quoting 42 U.S.C. § 16901 (2006)).
171. KAN. STAT. ANN. § 59-29a01 *et seq.* (1994).
172. Kansas v. Hendricks, 521 U.S. 346 (1997).
173. Kansas v. Crane, 534 U.S. 407 (2002).
174. Director of Public Prosecutions v. Morgan, 1976 App. Cas. 182, 205, 2 W.L.R. 913, 2 All E.R. 347 (H.L.1975).
175. MASS. GEN. LAWS ch. 265 § 22 (2020).
176. Commonwealth v. Grant, 464 N.E.2d 33, 36 (Mass. 1984).
177. Commonwealth v. Lopez, 745 N.E.2d 961 (Mass. 2001).
178. State v. Garron, 827 A.2d 243, 249 (N.J. 2003).
179. *Id.* at 259.
180. James B. Johnston, *How the Confrontation Clause Defeated the Rape Shield Statute: Acquaintance Rape, the Consent Defense, and the New Jersey Supreme Court's Ruling in* State v. Garron, 14 SO. CAL. REV. L. & WOMEN'S STUDIES 197, 198 (2005).

181. *See, e.g.*, Sydney Janzen, *Amending Rape Shield Laws: Outdated Statutes Fail to Protect Victims on Social Media*, 48 J. MARSHALL L. REV. 1087 (2015).
182. Manisha Krishnan, *How Rape Victims' Social-Media Feeds Are Being Used Against Them in Court*, VICE (Aug. 17, 2016), https://www.vice.com/en_us/article/7bmbp4/how-rape-complainants-are-having-their-social-media-feeds-used-against-them-in-court, at para. 2.
183. *Id.* at para. 4.

CHAPTER 9

1. Lawrence v. Texas, 539 U.S. 558 (2003).
2. *Id.* at 578.
3. Genesis 19:1–29.
4. HAVELOCK ELLIS, THE PSYCHOLOGY OF SEX: A MANUAL FOR STUDENTS (Emerson 1964) (1933); BYRNE R. S. FONT, HOMOPHOBIA: A HISTORY (2000).
5. KENNETH DOVER, GREEK HOMOSEXUALITY 19 (1978).
6. Arthur E. Brooks, Doe *and* Dronenburg: *Sodomy Statutes are Constitutional*, 26 WM. & MARY L. REV. 645, 648 (1985).
7. 25 Hen. VIII, c. 6 (1533), *repealed by* 9 Geo. 4, c. 31 (1828).
8. Brooks, *supra* note 6, at 648.
9. Debra McCloskey Barnhart, Commonwealth v. Bonadio: *Voluntary Deviate Sexual Intercourse —a Comparative Analysis*, 43 U. PITT. L. REV. 253 (1981).
10. *Id.* at. 254.
11. William N. Eskridge, *Law and the Construction of the Closet: American Regulation of Same-Sex Intimacy 1880–1946*, 82 IOWA L. REV. 1007 (1997).
12. *Id.* at 141; *see also* Henry F. Fradella, *Legal, Moral, and Social Reasons for Decriminalizing Sodomy*, 18 J. CONTEMP. CRIM. JUST. 279 (2002).
13. David A. Catania, *The Universal Declaration of Human Rights and Sodomy Laws: A Federal Common Law Right to Privacy for Homosexuals Based on Customary International Law*, 31 AM. CRIM. L. REV. 289 (1994).
14. Bowers v. Hardwick, 478 U.S. 186 (1986).
15. Henry F. Fradella, Lawrence v. Texas: *Genuine or Illusory Progress for Gay Rights in America*, 39 CRIM. L. BULL. 597 (2003).
16. 539 U.S. 558, 567 (2003).
17. *Lawrence*, 539 U.S. at 578.
18. 60 M.J. 198 (C.A.A.F. 2004).
19. *Id.* at 207.
20. *Id.* at 208.
21. *Id.*
22. 67 M.J. 758, 761 (A.F. Ct. Crim. App. 2009), *rev. denied*, 68 M.J. 489 (C.A.A.F. 2010).
23. *Id.* at 762.
24. Pub. L. 113–66, Div. A, Title XVII, § 1707(a), 127 Stat. 961 (2013) (repealing 10 U.S.C. § 925 Art. 125 (1956)).
25. 10 U.S.C. § 933 Art. 133 (2020).
26. United States v. Czekala, 38 M.J. 566 (A.C.M.R. 1993), *reconsideration denied, review granted in part* 40 M.J. 310 (1994), *aff'd* 42 M.J. 168, *cert. denied*, 516 U.S. 954 (1995) (upholding conduct unbecoming charge).
27. United States v. Schumacher, 11 M.J. 612 (A.C.M.R. 1981) (upholding conduct unbecoming charge).
28. United States v. Hartwig, 39 M.J. 125 (C.M.A. 1994) (upholding conduct unbecoming charge).
29. Rebecca F. Wisch, *Table of State Animal Sexual Assault Laws* (2017), https://www.animallaw.info/topic/table-state-animal-sexual-assault-laws.
30. VA. CODE ANN. § 18.2-361 (2020).
31. Warren v. Commonwealth, 69 822 S.E.2d 395 (Va. Ct. App. 2019).
32. *Id.* at 402.

33. State v. Coman, 214 P.3d 1198 (Kan. Ct. App. 2009).
34. People v. Haynes, 760 N.W.2d 283 (Mich. App. 2008).
35. *Id.* at 203.
36. Jeremy D. Weinstein, *Adultery, Law, and the State: A History*, 38 HASTINGS L.J. 195, 212 (1986).
37. JoAnne Sweeny, *Undead Statutes: The Rise, Fall, and Continuing Uses of Adultery and Fornication Criminal Laws*, 46 LOYOLA U. CHI. L.J. 127, 130 (2014).
38. 607 S.E.2d 367 (Va. 2005).
39. 575 S.E.2d 441 (2003).
40. *In re* J.M., 575 S.E.2d 441 (Ga. 2003).
41. Henry F. Fradella & Kenneth Grundy, *The Criminal Regulation of Sex: the Limits of Morality and Consent, in* SEX, SEXUALITY, LAW, AND (IN)JUSTICE 183, 200 (Henry F. Fradella & J. Sumner eds. 2016).
42. Sweeny, *supra* note 40, at 148–51.
43. S.D. CODIFIED LAWS §16-15-70.
44. ILL. COMP. STAT. 5/11-35.
45. ARIZ. REV. STAT. § 13-1408(B).
46. State v. Wesie, 118 N.W. 20, 21 (N.D. 1908).
47. Katherine Annuschat, *An Affair to Remember: The State of the Crime of Adultery in the Military*, 47 SAN DIEGO L. REV. 1161, 1164, n. 21 (2010).
48. *Id.* at 1177.
49. United States v. Orellana, 62 M.J. 595 (2005).
50. Salazar-Moreno v. State, No. 115,031, 2017 WL 383433 (Kan. Ct. App. Jan. 27, 2017).
51. Shayna M. Sigman, *Everything Lawyers Know about Polygamy Is Wrong*, 16 CORNELL J.L. & PUB. POL'Y 101, 125 (2006).
52. *See* Reynolds v. United States, 98 U.S. 145 (1878).
53. *See* Paul Finkelman, *The Ten Commandments on the Courthouse Lawn and Elsewhere*, 73 FORDHAM L. REV. 1477, 1507 (2005).
54. 11 AM. JUR. 2d *Bigamy* § 1 (2009) (citing Wilson v. State, 184 P. 603 (Okla. 1919)).
55. *E.g.*, 720 ILL. COMP. STAT. 5/11-45; MINN. REV. STAT. 609.355).
56. ANDREA MOORE-EMMETT, GOD'S BROTHEL: THE EXTORTION OF SEX FOR SALVATION IN CONTEMPORARY MORMON AND CHRISTIAN FUNDAMENTALIST POLYGAMY (2004).
57. STUART A. WRIGHT & JAMES T. RICHARDSON, SAINTS UNDER SIEGE: THE TEXAS STATE RAID ON THE FUNDAMENTALIST LATTER DAY SAINTS (2011).
58. State v. Holm, 137 P.3d 726 (Utah 2006), *cert. denied*, 549 U.S. 1252 (2007).
59. *Id.* at 743–45; *see also* State v. Fischer, 199 P.3d 663 (Ariz. Ct. App. 2008).
60. *E.g.*, TEX. PENAL. CODE § 205.014; UTAH CODE ANN. § 76-7-101.
61. Brown v. Buhman, 947 F. Supp. 2d 1170 (D. Utah 2013).
62. *Id.* at 1197–98.
63. *Id.* at 1190.
64. Lawrence v. Texas, 539 U.S. 558, 578 (2003).
65. MODEL PENAL CODE § 230.2 (2007).
66. Terry L. Turnipseed, *Scalia's Ship of Revulsion Has Sailed: Will Lawrence Protect Adults Who Adopt Lovers to Help Ensure Their Inheritance from Incest Prosecution?*, 32 HAMLINE L. REV. 115–16 (2009) (citing Note, *Inbred Obscurity: Improving Incest Laws in the Shadow of the "Sexual Family,"* 119 HARV. L. REV. 2464, 2464 (2006)).
67. Naomi Cahn, *Accidental Incest: Drawing the Line —or the Curtain? —for Reproductive Technology*, 32 HARV. J. L. & GENDER 59, 116 (2009)(citing State v. Rogers, 133 S.E.2d 1, 2 (N.C. 1963)).
68. Note, *supra* note 69, at 2470.
69. *See* J. Kelly Strader, Lawrence's *Criminal Law*, 16 BERKELEY J. CRIM. L. 41 (2011).
70. *See generally* Alison Adams, *Seen But Not Heard: Child Sexual Abuse, Incest, and the Law in the United States*, 11 J. L. & FAM. STUD. 543 (2009).

71. *See, e.g.*, Douglas v. State, 327 P.3d 492 (Nev. 2014); Johnson v. Commonwealth, 292 S.W.3d 889 (Ky. 2009).
72. Lowe v. Swanson, 663 F.3d 258, 264 (6th Cir. 2011).
73. Ferguson v. Commonwealth, 838 S.E.2d 75 (Va. Ct. App. 2020).
74. *E.g.*, FLA. STAT. ANN. § 800.02; NEV. REV. STAT. § 201.210; VT. STAT. ANN. § 2601.
75. *E.g.*, ARK. CODE ANN. § 5-14-111.
76. ARIZ. REV. STAT. § 13-1403(A).
77. *E.g.*, KAN. STAT. ANN. § 21-3508(1); *see also* N.J. STAT. ANN. § 2C:14-4; N.Y. PENAL LAW 245.00
78. *E.g.*, FLA. STAT. ANN. § 800.03; NEV. REV. STAT. § 201.220.
79. *E.g.*, FLA. STAT. ANN. § 800.02; REV. CODE WASH. 9A.88.010.
80. 475 P.2d 684 (Haw. 1970).
81. 34 P.3d 228 (Utah 2001).
82. *Id.* at 230.
83. *Id.*
84. *Id.* at 232.
85. UT. CODE ANN. § 76-9-702(d).
86. OHIO REV. CODE ANN. § 2907.08(A).
87. *See* 63C AM. JUR. 2d *Prostitution* § 1 (2009); *see also, e.g.*, FLA. STAT. 796.01.
88. *E.g.*, Muse v. United States, 522 A.2d 888 (D.C. 1987) (gold necklace offered in exchange for sexual acts).
89. State v. Henderson, 2007 WL 2897806 (Ohio Ct. App. 2d Dist. Montgomery County 2007).
90. *See* NILS JOHAN RINGDAL, LOVE FOR SALE: A WORLD HISTORY OF PROSTITUTION (2004); WILLIAM W. SANGER, THE HISTORY OF PROSTITUTION: ITS EXTENT, CAUSES, AND EFFECTS THROUGHOUT THE WORLD (2013)(1858).
91. Sanger, *supra* note 94, at 92–93; Elisabeth Jandro, *The Regulation of Sex Work and Sex Workers*, *in* SEX, SEXUALITY, LAW, AND (IN)JUSTICE 216 (Henry F. Fradella & Jennifer Sumner eds., 2016).
92. Jandro, *supra* note 95, at 220–21 (internal citations omitted).
93. *Id.* at 221.
94. *Id.*
95. *Id.*
96. *Id.*
97. *Id.*
98. *Id.*
99. *E.g.*, State v. Stoyell, 54 Me. 24, 27 (1866).
100. *See* 63C AM. JUR. 2d *Prostitution* § 1 (2009).
101. Jandro, *supra* note 95, at 233.
102. *See* Amanda Peters, *Modern Prostitution Legal Reform & the Return of Volitional Consent*, 3 VA. J. CRIM. L. 1 (2015) *see also* Glegola v. State, 871 P.2d 950, 952 (Nev. 1994).
103. *E.g.*, California v. Dell, 283 Cal. Rptr. 361, 371 (Cal. Ct. App. 1991).
104. Peters, *supra* note 106, at 7.
105. *See* 63C AM. JUR. 2d *Prostitution* §§ 8, 9 (2009).
106. *Id.*at § 3.
107. *Id.* at §§ 15–17.
108. *Id.* at § 12.
109. *See* Ronald Weitzer, *Legalizing Prostitution: Morality Politics in Western Australia*, 49 BRIT. J. CRIMINOLOGY 88 (2009).
110. *E.g.*, State v. Romano, 155 P.3d 1102 (Haw. 2007).
111. *See* NEV. REV. STAT. §§ 244.345 & 201.354; *see also* Weitzer, *supra* note 113, at 88–89.
112. Jandro, *supra* note 95, at 232.
113. *See* Zachary David Streit, *Birds of an Illegal Feather: Prostitution and Paid Pornography Should Be Criminalized Together*, 5 CARDOZO PUB. L. POL'Y, & ETHICS J. 729, 729–30 (2007).

114. INT'L LABOUR ORG. & WALK FREE FOUND., GLOBAL ESTIMATES OF MODERN SLAVERY (2017), http://www.ilo.org/wcmsp5/groups/public/---dgreports/---dcomm/documents/publication/wcms_575479.pdf.
115. Jaclyn Gallucci, Human Trafficking Is an Epidemic in the U.S. It's Also Big Business, Fortune (Apr. 14, 2019), https://fortune.com/2019/04/14/human-sex-trafficking-us-slavery/.
116. *See 2018 U.S. National Human Trafficking Hotline Statistics*, POLARIS PROJECT (2020), https://polarisproject.org/2018-us-national-human-trafficking-hotline-statistics/.
117. Pub. L. No. 106-386, § 103, 114 Stat. 1464, 1469 (Oct. 28, 2000) (codified as amended at 22 U.S.C. §§ 7101 et seq. and in scattered sections of 8, 18, & 22 of the U.S. Code).
118. *See* Shelly George, *The Strong Arm of the Law Is Weak: How the Trafficking Victims Protection Act Fails to Assist Effectively Victims of the Sex Trade*, 45 CREIGHTON L. REV. 563 (2012).
119. Pub. L. No. 109-164, § 201, 119 Stat. 3558, 3567-69 (2006) (codified as amended at 42 U.S.C. § 14044)).
120. William Wilberforce Trafficking Victims Protection Reauthorization Act of 2008, Pub. L. No. 110-457, § 225, 122 Stat. 5044, 5072 (codified as amended at 22 U.S.C.A. § 7101 (West 2009)).
121. 22 U.S.C. §§ 7102(8); 7105(b)(1)(A).
122. *See, e.g.*, Moira Heiges, *From the Inside Out: Reforming State and Local Prostitution Enforcement to Combat Sex Trafficking in the United States and Abroad*, 94 MINN. L. REV. 428 (2009); Elizabeth Kaigh, *Whores and Other Sex Slaves: Why the Equation of Prostitution with Sex Trafficking in the William Wilberforce Reauthorization Act of 2008 Promotes Gender Discrimination*, 12 SCHOLAR 139 (2009).
123. Nat'l Conf. State Legislatures, *Human Trafficking Overview* (July 7, 2020), https://www.ncsl.org/research/civil-and-criminal-justice/human-trafficking.aspx.; *compare, e.g.*, COLO. REV. STAT. § 19-1-306 *with* CONN. GEN. STAT. § 53a-82.
124. *Id.*
125. Peters, *supra* note 106, at 14.
126. *Id.* at 15.
127. *E.g.*, 720 ILL. COMP. STAT. 5/11-14; MINN. STAT. § 609.093 (1)(a)(1).
128. *E.g.*, GA. CODE. § 16-3-6(a)(3) & (b); IOWA CODE §§ 710A.3 & 725.1; MINN. STAT. § 609.325(4).
129. Peters, *supra* note 106, at 23–24.
130. Comstock Act of 1873, ch. 258, 17 Stat. 598 (1873), *current version codified as amended at* 18 U.S.C. §§ 1416-62 (2016) and 19 U.S.C. § 1305 (2016).
131. 18 U.S.C. § 1461.
132. Rosen v. United States, 161 U.S. 29 (1896).
133. Regina v. Hinklin, L.R.3 Q.B. 360 (1868).
134. *Id.*at 371.
135. United States v. One Book Entitled "Ulysses" by James Joyce, 5 F. Supp. 182 (S.D.N.Y. 1933), *aff'd* 72 F.2d 705 (2d Cir. 1934).
136. *See* DON R. PEMBER & CLAY CALBERT, MASS MEDIA LAW (17th ed. 2011).
137. Roth v. United States, 354 U.S. 476 (1957).
138. *Id.* at 481.
139. *Id.* at 484.
140. *Id.* at 487.
141. *Id.* at 488.
142. *Id.* at 490.
143. *See* J. ROBERT LILLY, FRANCIS T. CULLEN, & RICHARD A. BALL, CRIMINOLOGICAL THEORY: CONTEXT AND CONSEQUENCES (2010).
144. Miller v. California, 413 U.S. 15 (1973).
145. *Id.* at 74.
146. PEMBER & CALVERT, *supra* note 140, at 475.
147. *Miller*, 413 U.S. at 25.
148. Jenkins v. Georgia, 418 U.S. 153 (1974).

149. *Miller*, 413 U.S. at 21, 22.
150. *Id.* at 26.
151. *See* Steve Stone, *Virginia Beach Police Seize Photos from Abercrombie Store*, VIRGINIAN-PILOT (Feb. 3, 2008), http://pilotonline.com/news/virginia-beach-police-seize-photos-from-abercrombie-store/article_02112c17-3d3d-5870-8fa2-313d65fa76d9.html.
152. Pope v. Illinois, 481 U.S. 497 (1987).
153. Luke Records, Inc. v. Navarro, 960 F.2d 134 (11th Cir.), *cert. denied*, 506 U.S. 1022 (1992).
154. *Id.* at 138.
155. Stanley v. Georgia, 394 U.S. 557 (1969).
156. *Id.*at 566.
157. 475 U.S. 41 (1986).
158. *Id.* at 49 (internal quotations and citations omitted).
159. Osborne v. Ohio, 495 U.S. 103 (1990).
160. *Id.* at 109.
161. *Id.*
162. New York v. Ferber, 458 U.S. 747 (1982).
163. *Id.*at 752.
164. *Id.* at 759.
165. *Id.* at 763–64.
166. Child Protection Act of 1984, Pub. L. No. 98-292, 98 Stat. 204 (1984), *codified as amended* at 18 U.S.C. §§ 2251-2255 (2016).
167. 18 U.S.C. § 2256(2)(A).
168. United States v. Dost, 636 F. Supp. 828 (S.D. Cal. 1986).
169. Child Sexual Abuse and Pornography Act of 1986, Pub. L. No. 99-628, § 2, 100 Stat. 3510 (1986), *codified as amended* at 18 U.S.C. § 2251 (2016).
170. Child Protection and Obscenity Enforcement Act of 1988, Pub. L. No. 100-690, § 7501, 102 Stat. 4485 (1988) (codified as amended at 18 U.S.C. §§ 2251A-2252 (2016)).
171. Osborne v. Ohio, 495 U.S. 103 (1990).
172. Child Protection Restoration and Penalties Enhancement Act of 1990, Pub. L. No. 101-647, §§ 301, 323, 104 Stat. 4816 (1990) (codified as amended at 18 U.S.C. § 2252(a)(4)(B) (2016)).
173. Child Pornography Prevention Act of 1996, Pub. L. No. 104-208, 110 Stat. 3009-26 to 3009-31 (1996), *codified as amended at* 18 U.S.C. § 2251 *et seq.* (2000), *declared unconstitutional by* Ashcroft v. Free Speech Coalition, 535 U.S. 234 (2002).
174. *Ashcroft*, 535 U.S. at 234.
175. *Id.* at 247–48.
176. *Id.* at 253–54.
177. Prosecutorial Remedies and Other Tools to End the Exploitation of Children Today Act of 2003 (PROTECT Act), Pub. L. 108–21, 117 Stat. 650 (2003) (codified at scatters sections of the U.S. Code).
178. PEMBER & CALVERT, *supra* note 140, at 481.
179. United States v. Williams, 553 U.S. 285 (2008).
180. *Id.* at 303.
181. 438 U.S. 726 (1978).
182. 521 U.S. 844 (1997).
183. 47 U. S. C. § 223(d) (Supp. 1997), *declared unconstitutional by* Reno v. ACLU, 521 U.S. at 874–77.
184. *Reno*, 521 U.S. at 874.
185. *E.g.*, Daniel Pollack, *Understanding Sexual Grooming in Child Abuse Cases*, AM. BAR ASS'N (Nov. 1. 2015), https://www.americanbar.org/groups/public_interest/child_law/resources/child_law_practiceonline/child_law_practice/vol-34/november-2015/understanding-sexual-grooming-in-child-abuse-cases/.

186. *Id.*; *see also* Georgia M. Winters & Elizabeth L. Jeglic, *Stages of Sexual Grooming: Recognizing Potentially Predatory Behaviors of Child Molesters*, 38 DEVIANT BEHAV. 724 (2017).
187. MINN. STAT. § 609.352 (2020) (internal citations and alterations omitted).
188. Kelsey K. Chetosky, *Minnesota v. Muccio: The Constitutionality of Minnesota's Sexual Grooming Law*, 114 NW. U. L. REV. ONLINE 1, 16 (2019).
189. *Id.* at 20.
190. Mary Graw Leary, *Self-Produced Child Pornography: The Appropriate Societal Response to Juvenile Self-Sexual Exploitation*, 15 VA. J. SOC. POL'Y L. 1, 24 (2007).
191. *To Deal with "Sexting," XXXtra Discretion Is Advised*, USA TODAY (May 5, 2009), at 10A.
192. *See* Henry F. Fradella & Marcus A. Galeste, *Sexting: The Misguided Penal Social Control of Teenage Sexual Behavior in the Digital Age*, 47 CRIM. L. BULL. 438 (2011).
193. *Id.* at 443.
194. Sally Kalson, *Sexting . . . and Other Stupid Teen Tricks*, PITTSBURGH POST-GAZETTE (Mar. 29, 2009), http://www.post-gazette.com/opinion/sally-kalson/2009/03/29/Sexting-and-other-stupid-teen-tricks/stories/200903290190.
195. 18 U.S.C. § 2256(2)(A).
196. Sameer Hinduja & Justin W. Patchin, *State Sexting Laws: A Brief Review of State Sexting and Revenge Porn Laws and Policies* (2015), http://cyberbullying.org/state-sexting-laws.pdf.
197. *Id.*
198. Jordan J. Szymialis, *Sexting: A Response to Prosecuting Those Growing Up with a Growing Trend*, 44 IND. L. REV. 301, 320 (2010); *see also* ARIZ. REV. STAT. § 8-309.
199. N.J. STAT. ANN. § 2A:4A-71.1.
200. 789 N.E.2d 138, 141 (Mass. 2003).
201. *Id.* at 146.
202. IOWA CODE § 709.9(1)(a) (2020).
203. State v. Isaac, 756 N.W.2d 817 (Iowa 2008).
204. *See, e.g.*, Deborah Feyerick & Sheila Steffen, *"Sexting" Lands Teen on Sex Offender List*, CNN.COM (Apr. 8, 2009), http://www.cnn.com/2009/CRIME/04/07/sexting.busts/index.html#cnnSTCText.
205. State v. Canal, 773 N.W. 2d 528 (Iowa 2009).
206. Mike Johnson & Jacqui Seibel, *New Berlin Teen Accused of Using Facebook for Sexual Blackmail*, MILWAUKEE J. SENTINEL (Feb. 5, 2009), http://www.jsonline.com/news/waukesha/39124037.html.
207. Laurel Walker, *Stancl Gets 15 Years in Prison in Facebook Coercion Case*, MILWAUKEE J. SENTINEL (Feb. 24, 2010), http://www.jsonline.com/news/waukesha/85252392.html.
208. Mike Celizic, *Her Teen Committed Suicide Over "Sexting,"* TODAY: PARENTS (Mar. 6, 2009), http://www.today.com/parents/her-teen-committed-suicide-over-sexting-2D80555048.
209. *Id.* at ¶ 2.
210. *Id.* at ¶ 17.
211. Dena Cassella, *Sexting is Common Among Young People, Survey Says*, DIGITAL TRENDS (Dec. 2, 2009), at ¶ 21, http://www.digitaltrends.com/home/sexting-is-common-among-young-people-survey-says.

CHAPTER 10

1. 6 AM. JUR. 2D *Assault and Battery* § 2 (2016).
2. MODEL PENAL CODE § 2.12.
3. State v. Eaves, 959 S.W.2d 601 (Tenn. Crim. App. 1997) (internal citations omitted).
4. Chaplinsky v. New Hampshire, 315 U.S. 568 (1942).
5. Brandenburg v. Ohio, 395 U.S. 444 (1969).
6. *E.g.*, N.J. STAT. ANN. 2C:12-3(a); GA. CODE. ANN. § 16-11-37(a).
7. COLO. REV. STAT. § 18-3-206 (2020).
8. *See, e.g.*, ARIZ. REV. STAT. § 13–2921.

9. Terence Ingman, *A History of the Defence of Volenti Non Fit Injuria*, 26 JURID. REV. 1, 1–2 (1981); Randolf v. de Richmond, Y.B. 33 Edw. 1 (1305).
10. Vera Bergelson, *The Right to Be Hurt: Testing the Boundaries of Consent*, 75 GEO. WASH. L. REV. 165, 172 (2007).
11. *Id.*
12. *Id.* at 172–73.
13. *Id.* (quoting Matthew v. Ollerton, (1692) 90 Eng. Rep. 438, 438 (K.B.)).
14. *Id.* at 173; *see also* MODEL PENAL CODE § 2.11(2). Approximately 13 states explicitly recognize a general defense of consent; the reaming U.S. jurisdictions do not. Bergelson, *supra* note 10, at 174 n. 55 (statutory citations omitted).
15. Bergelson, *supra* note 10, at 173–74.
16. MODEL PENAL CODE § 2.11(2).
17. MODEL PENAL CODE § 2.11(2)(a).
18. Bergelson, *supra* note 10, at 174.
19. *See* Cheryl Hanna, *Sex is Not a Sport: Consent and Violence in Criminal Law*, 42 B.C. L. REV. 239 (2001).
20. State v. Shelley, 929 P.2d 489, 490 (Wash. Ct. App. 1997); *see also* Charles Harary, *Aggressive Play or Criminal Assault? An In-Depth Look at Sports Violence and Criminal Liability*, 25 COLUM. J.L. & ARTS 197, 211 (2002); Benjamin C. Thompson, *Personal Foul . . . 15 Years In Jail: Sports' Problem with Excessive Violence and the Severe Punishment Solution*, 76 UMKC L. REV. 769 (2008).
21. Bergelson, *supra* note 10, at 180.
22. Consider that nearly half of Americans engage in activities such as using a blindfold during sex, having been tied up or restrained during sex, or having been spanked as part of sex. JUNE M. REINISCH & RUTH BEASLEY, KINSEY INSTITUTE NEW REPORT ON SEX: WHAT YOU MUST KNOW TO BE SEXUALLY LITERATE 162 (Debra Kent ed., 1990); Marty Klein, *Poll*, PLAYBOY, Nov. 1998, at 81.
23. *See generally* CHARLES MOSER & PEGGY J. KLEINPLATZ, SADOMASOCHISM: POWERFUL PLEASURES (2006).
24. Kelly Egan, Comment, *Morality-Based Legislation is Alive and Well: Why the Law Permits Consent to Body Modification But Not Sadomasochistic Sex*, 70 ALB. L. REV. 1615, 1616 (2007)(internal citations omitted).
25. Bergelson, *supra* note 10, at 177.
26. Bergelson, *supra* note 10, at 177 (citing State v. Collier, 372 N.W.2d 303, 304 (Iowa Ct. App. 1985); Commonwealth v. Appleby, 402 N.E.2d 1051, 1054 (Mass. 1980)).
27. Bergelson, *supra* note 10, at 185 (quoting People v. Samuels, 58 Cal. Rptr. 439, 447 (Ct. App. 1967)).
28. *See, e.g.*, People v. Fitzsimmons, 34 N.Y.S. 1102 (1895).
29. *E.g.*, State v. Woods, 594 A.2d 481 (Conn. App. 1991).
30. 18 U.S.C. § 114.
31. *E.g.*, CAL. PENAL CODE § 203; D.C. CODE § 22–3202; MASS. GEN. L. ch. 265, § 14.
32. 18 U.S.C. § 114.
33. CAL. PENAL CODE § 203; *see also* D.C. CODE § 22–3202; MASS. GEN. L. ch. 265, § 14.
34. CAL. PENAL CODE § 205.
35. People v. Newble, 120 Cal. App. 3d 444, 451 (Cal. App. 1981).
36. People v. Page, 104 Cal. App. 3d 569, 578 (1980).
37. People v. Keenan, 227 Cal. App. 3d 26, 34 (1991).
38. D.C. CODE § 22–3202.
39. 6 AM JUR 2d, *Assault and Battery* § 21 (2016).
40. *See, e.g.*, Boyer v. Maryland, 666 A.2d 1269 (Md. 1995).
41. *Id.* at 139.
42. Voisine v. United States, 136 S. Ct. 2272 (2016).
43. *See* 18 U.S.C. § 922(g)(9).
44. Key v. Commonwealth, 840 S.W.2d 827 (Ky. Ct. App. 1992).
45. *Id.* (citing KY. REV. STAT. § 508.060).
46. *E.g.*, People v. Tuck, 660 N.E.2d 1137 (N.Y. 1995).

47. James E. Fleming & Linda C. McClain, *Has the Constitution Fostered a Pathological Rights Culture? The Right to Bear Arms: Ordered Gun Liberty: Rights with Responsibilities and Regulation*, 94 B.U.L. REV. 849, 877–78 (2014).
48. *Id.*
49. *E.g.*, ALA. CODE §§ 15-10-3; 13A-11-8; IDAHO CODE § 18–918.
50. CENTER FOR DISEASE CONTROL AND PREVENTION, INJURY PREVENTION & CONTROL: VIOLENCE PREVENTION: INTIMATE PARTNER VIOLENCE: DEFINITIONS ¶ 1 (2016), https://www.cdc.gov/violenceprevention/intimatepartnerviolence/definitions.html.
51. *See* Edna Erez, *Intimacy, Violence, and the Police*, 39 HUM. REL. 265 (1986).
52. *See* Sally F. Goldfarb, *Reconceiving Civil Protection Orders for Domestic Violence: Can Law Help End the Abuse Without Ending the Relationship?*, 29 CARDOZO L. REV. 1487, 1495–96 (2008).
53. *Id.* at 1495; *see also* Ida M. Johnson, *Victims' Perceptions of Police Response to Domestic Violence Incidents*, 35 J. CRIM. JUST. 498, 498 (2007).
54. *See* Joan E. Crowley, Robert T. Sigler & Ida M. Johnson, *Variations Across Agency Types in Perceptions of Seriousness of Family Abuse*, 18 J. CRIM. JUST. 519, 526 (1990)(reporting that social service and criminal justice professionals view domestic violence more as grounds for divorce than as a basis for criminal responsibility).
55. *See* Johnson, *supra* note 53, at 498.
56. *See* Nancy Egan, *The Police Response to Spouse Abuse: A Selective, Annotated Bibliography*, 91 L. LIBR. J. 499, 502–03 (1999).
57. Lawrence W. Sherman & Richard A. Berk, *The Specific Deterrent Effects of Arrest for Domestic Assault*, 49 AM. SOC. REV. 261, 267 (1984).
58. *See, e.g.*, Douglas L. Yearwood, *Judicial Dispositions of Ex-Parte and Domestic Violence Protection Order Hearings: A Comparative Analysis of Victim Requests and Court Authorized Relief*, 20 J. FAM. VIOLENCE 161 (2005); Joanne Belknap et al., *Factors Related to Domestic Violence Court Dispositions in a Large Urban Area: The Role of Victim/Witness Reluctance and Other Variables* (2000), http://www.ncjrs.gov/pdffiles1/nij/grants/184112.pdf.
59. *E.g.*, IND. CODE § 35-42-2-1.3; NEV. REV. STAT. § 200.485;
60. Interstate Domestic Violence Act, Pub. L. 103–322, title IV, § 40221(a), 108 Stat. 1926 (Sept. 13, 1994) (codified as amended at 18 U.S.C. § 2261).
61. *See generally* Child Welfare Information Gateway, *Definitions of Domestic Violence* (2013).
62. *See, e.g.*, Hamilton ex rel. Lethem v. Lethem, 270 P.3d 1024 (Haw. 2012).
63. REV. CODE WASH. § 9A.32.055.
64. 1 W. BLACKSTONE, *Commentaries* *134.
65. Ingraham vs. Wright, 430 U.S. 651 (1977).
66. *Id.* at 661.
67. *E.g.*, CAL. WELF. & INST. CODE § 300(a); GA. CODE. ANN. §§ 19-7-5, 19-15-1.
68. Commonwealth v. Twitchell, 617 N.E.2d 609 (Mass. 1993).
69. State v. Neumann, 832 N.W.2d 560 (Wis. 2013).
70. WIS. STAT. § 948.03(6); *see also, e.g.*, ORE. REV. STAT. § 163.206.
71. Child Welfare Information Gateway, *Mandatory Reporters of Child Abuse and Neglect* (2016), https://www.childwelfare.gov/topics/systemwide/laws-policies/statutes/manda/.
72. Child Welfare Information Gateway, *Penalties for Failure to Report and False Reporting of Child Abuse and Neglect* 2 (2016), https://www.childwelfare.gov/pubPDFs/report.pdf.
73. Mark S. Lachs & Karl A. Pillemer, *Elder Abuse*, 373 NEW ENG. J. MED. 1947, 1947 (2015).
74. Subcomm. on Health & Long-Term Care of the House Select Comm. on Aging, 97th Cong., *Elder Abuse: An Examination of a Hidden Problem* (1981).
75. Subcomm. on Health & Long-Term Care of the House Select Comm. on Aging, 101st Cong., *Elder Abuse: A Decade of Shame and Inaction* (1990).
76. *Id.* at 597–600 (internal citations omitted).

77. National Center on Elder Abuse, *What We Do: Research: Statistics/Data* (2016), https://ncea.acl.gov/whatwedo/research/statistics.html; *see also* Janey C. Peterson, et al., *Financial Exploitation of Older Adults: A Population-Based Prevalence Study*, 29 J. GEN. INTERNAL MED. 1615 (2014).
78. Seymour Moskowitz, *Contemporary Legal Developments in Elder Abuse and Neglect*, 36 LOY. L.A. L. REV. 589, 597 (2003).
79. *E.g.*, NEV. REV. STAT. § 200.5099.
80. *E.g.*, GA. CODE ANN. § 30-5-8(a).
81. IDAHO CODE ANN. § 18-1505(4)(e); *see also, e.g.*, NEB. REV. STAT. § 28–386; OKLA. STAT. tit. 21, § 843.3; MD. CODE ANN., CRIM. LAW § 3–604; S.C. CODE ANN. § 16-3-1050.
82. IDAHO CODE ANN. § 18-1505(1).
83. IDAHO CODE ANN. § 18-1505(2).
84. *See, e.g.*, N.Y. PENAL LAW §§ 260.31(3), 260.32.
85. CAL. PENAL CODE § 368(b)(1).
86. *See* Nina A. Kohn, *Elder (In)Justice: A Critique of the Criminalization of Elder Abuse*, 49 AM. CRIM. L. REV. 1, 9–10 (citing N.H. REV. STAT. § 631:8; N.Y. PENAL LAW §§ 260.32, .34 W. VA. CODE § 61-2-29).
87. *Id.* at 10–11 (citing, *inter alia*, GA. CODE ANN. § 30-5-3; 720 ILL. COMP. STAT. ANN. 5/17-56(a), (c); MONT. CODE ANN. § 52-3-803(a)(3); VT. STAT. ANN. tit. 13, § 1380(a)).
88. *Id.*at 11–12 (citing, *intêr alia*, VT. STAT. ANN. tit. 13, § 1379(a); WASH. REV. CODE § 9A.44.100(1)(f)).
89. *See* Jennifer Beth Glick, *Protecting and Respecting Our Elders: Revising Mandatory Elder Abuse Reporting Statutes to Increase Efficacy and Preserve Autonomy*, 12 VA. J. SOC. POL'Y & L. 714 (2005).
90. *Id.* at 721–22.
91. John L. Diamond, *Kidnapping: A Modern Definition*, 13 AMER. J. CRIM. L. 1, 2–3 (1985); 4 W. BLACKSTONE, COMMENTARIES ON THE LAWS OF ENGLAND (1769) p. 219.
92. *Id.* (citing NOTE, *A Rationale of the Law of Kidnapping*, 53 COLUM. L. REV. 540 (1953)).
93. MODEL PENAL CODE § 212.1.
94. Chatwin v. United States, 326 U.S. 455, 464 (1946).
95. United States v. Epstein, 91 F. Supp. 3d 573 (D.N.J. 2015).
96. People v. Sattiewhite, 328 P.3d 1, 26 (Cal. 2014).
97. *Id.*
98. *See, e.g.*, People v. Majors, 92 P.3d 360 (Cal. 2004); State v. Bell, S.E.2d 439 (N.C. App. 2012).
99. People v. Hovarter, 189 P.3d 300 (Cal. 2008).
100. *See, e.g.*, *Adams*, 192 N.W.2d at 21 (Mich. App. 1971), *rev'd*, 205 N.W.2d 415 (Mich. 1973).
101. Diamond, *supra* note 91, at 12.
102. *Id.*
103. *See* State v. German, 133 So. 3d 179, 192 (La. Ct. App.), *writ denied*, 152 So. 3d 897 (La. 2014).
104. *See, e.g.*, People v. Adams, 192 N.W.2d 19 (Mich. App. 1971), *rev'd*, 205 N.W.2d 415 (Mich. 1973); People v. Daniels, 459 P.2d 225 (Cal. 1969).
105. State v. Johnson, 549 S.W.2d 627, 632 (Mo. App. 1977).
106. *Id.*; People v. Reeves, 897 N.E.2d 298 (Ill. Appl. 2008).
107. People v. Bishop, 114 N.E.2d 566 (Ill. 1953).
108. MODEL PENAL CODE § 212.1, cmt. 3; *see also* Commonwealth v. Rushing, 99 A.3d 416 (Pa. 2014).
109. Turner v. State, 769 S.E.2d 785, 789–90 (Ga. App. 2015).
110. State v. Irwin, 282 S.E.2d 439, 446 (N.C. 1981).
111. State v. McNeil, 574 S.E.2d 145, 148–49 (N.C. App. 2002), *appeal dismissed and disc. rev. denied*, 578 S.E.2d 323 (N.C. 2003).
112. State v. Love, 630 S.E.2d 234, 242 (N.C. App.), *disc. rev. denied*, 636 S.E.2d 192 (N.C. 2006).
113. *Id.*; State v. Anderson, 640 S.E.2d 797 (N.C. App. 2007).
114. *See* State v. Thompson, 76 A.3d 273 (Conn. App. 2013), *cert. denied*, 81 A.3d 1182 (Conn. 2013).
115. MODEL PENAL CODE § 212.1.
116. MODEL PENAL CODE § 212.1.

117. Thompson, 76 A.3d at 273.
118. *Id.* at 278.
119. *Id.* at 279–81.
120. People v. McCurdy, 331 P.3d 265 (Cal. 2014), *cert. denied*, 135 S. Ct. 1560 (2015).
121. Kinsey v. State, 757 S.E.2d 217 (Ga. App. 2014).
122. State v. Harrell, 357 S.W.3d 256, 258 (Mo. Ct. App. 2012).
123. People v. Kruppenbacher, 917 N.Y.S.2d 405, 408 (3d Dep't 2011).
124. MODEL PENAL CODE § 212.2.
125. MODEL PENAL CODE § 212.3.
126. *E.g.*, Butcher v. State, 454 S.W.3d 13 (Tex. Crim. App. 2015); Rathbun v. State, 257 P.3d 29 (Wyo. 2011).
127. ANDREA J. SEDLAK ET AL., NISMART-2: NATIONAL INCIDENT STUDIES OF MISSING, ABDUCTED, RUNAWAY, AND THROWAWAY CHILDREN 3 (2002).
128. *Id.* at 6.
129. *Id.*
130. *Id.*
131. Polly Klaas Foundation, *National Child Kidnapping Facts* (last visited Dec. 30, 2016), http://www.pollyklaas.org/about/national-child-kidnapping.html?referrer=http://www.pollyklaas.org/about/casemanagement.html.
132. *See, e.g.*, State v. Bates, 927 So. 2d 417 (La. Ct. App. 2005).
133. Lisa Vollendorf Martin, *Reconsidering Dual Consent*, 82 UMKC L. REV. 705, 710–12 (2014).
134. *E.g.*, Wilborn v. Superior Court of Humboldt County, 337 P.2d 65 (Cal. 1959); Anderson v. Cramlet, 789 F.2d 840 (10th Cir. 1986) (applying Colorado law).
135. PATRICIA M. HOFF, FAMILY ABDUCTION: PREVENTION AND RESPONSE 62 (6th ed. 2008).
136. ARIZ. REV. STAT. § 13–1302(A).
137. *E.g.*, WIS. STAT. § 948.31; *see also* State v. Ziegler, 816 N.W.2d 238 (Wisc. 2012).
138. People v. Garcia, 998 N.Y.S.2d 605 (N.Y.C. Crim. Ct. 2014).
139. Parental Kidnapping Prevention Act, Pub. L. 96–611, 94 Stat. 3566 (Dec. 28, 1980), (codified as amended 18 U.S.C. § 1073 (2016)).
140. International Parental Kidnapping Crime Act, Pub. L. 103–773, 707 Stat. 1998 (Dec.2, 1993) (codified as amended 18 U.S.C. § 1204 (2016)).
141. *See* R.A.V. v. City of St. Paul, 505 U.S. 377 (1992); Texas v. Johnson, 491 U.S. 397 (1989); *cf.* Wisconsin v. Mitchell, 508 U.S. 476 (1993).
142. *See* 18 U.S.C. § 249.
143. *See, e.g.*, N.Y. PENAL LAW § 485.05.
144. 716 A.2d 576 (N.J. Super. Ct. 1997).
145. *Id.* at 578.
146. N.J. STAT. ANN. § 2C:12–1(1).
147. N.J. STAT. ANN. § 2C:11–1(a).
148. N.J. STAT. ANN. § 2C:2–11.
149. Watson v. United States, 979 A.2d 1254 (D.C. 2009).
150. Lee v. State, 100 So. 3d 1183 (Fla. Dist. Ct. App. 2012).
151. Alvarado v. State, 317 S.W.3d 749, 750 (Tex. Ct. App. 2010).
152. *Compare, e.g.*, People v. Aguilar, 945 P.2d 1204 (Cal. 1997) (punching and kicking with bare hands and feet), *with* Lucero v. State, 14 P.3d 920 (Wyo. 2000) (kicking with steel-toed boots).
153. *See, e.g.*, Reynolds v. State, 508 S.E.2d 674 (Ga. App. 1998).
154. *See, e.g.*, United States v. Peneaux, 432 F.3d 882 (8th Cir. 2005), *cert. denied*, 549 U.S. 828 (2006).
155. *See, e.g.*, Morris v. State, 722 So. 2d 849 (Fla. Dist. Ct. App. 1998).
156. *See, e.g.*, People v. Warren, 949 N.Y.S.2d 496 (App. Div. 2012).
157. *See, e.g.*, State v. Mills, 726 S.E.2d 926 (N.C. Ct. App. 2012).
158. *See, e.g.*, State v. Harris, 966 So. 2d 773 (La. Ct. App. 2007), *writ denied*, 978 So. 2d 304 (La. 2008).

159. *Compare, e.g.*, State v. Carlson, 828 P.2d 30 (Wash. Ct. App. 1992), *with* State v. Gregory, 501 P.2d 387 (Ariz. 1972).
160. Clete Samson, *No Time Like the Present: Why Recent Events Should Spur Congress to Enact a Sports Violence Act*, 37 ARIZ. ST. L.J. 949, 950–51 (2005).
161. *Id.* at 951.
162. Harary, *supra* note 20, at 198.
163. Regina v. Vargas, 1999 W.C.B.J. LEXIS 8210 (Ont. Ct. Gen. Div. Mar. 1, 1999).
164. People v. Freer, 381 N.Y.S.2d 976 (Dist. Ct. 1976).
165. *Id.* at 978.
166. Robert A. Beattey, Jr., *The Great Bathhouse Bugaboo: A Practitioner's Inquiry Into the Criminal and Public Health Policy of Gay Bathhouses*, 12 MICH. ST. U. J. MED. & L. 341, 343 (2008).
167. Hanna, *supra* note 19, at 249–56.
168. *Id.*

CHAPTER 11

1. MODEL PENAL CODE § 223.1; *see also, e.g.*, N.J. STAT. ANN. § 2C:20-2 (2020); 18 PA. CONS. STAT. ANN. § 3902 (2020).
2. *See* STUART P. GREEN, THIRTEEN WAYS TO STEAL A BICYCLE: THEFT LAW IN THE INFORMATION AGE 27 (2012).
3. *E.g.*, COLO. REV. STA. ANN. 18-4-403 (2020).
4. BLACK'S LAW DICTIONARY (10th ed. 2014).
5. *E.g.*, People v. Zombo, 813 N.Y.S.2d 624, 626 (Sup. Ct. App. Div. 2006).
6. *E.g.*, Rattray v. Brown, 261 F. Supp. 2d 149, 155 (E.D.N.Y. 2003) (applying New York law by citing People v. Alamo, 315 N.E.2d 446 (N.Y. 1974)).
7. *E.g.*, Mauldin v. State, 376 So. 2d 788, (Ala. Crim. App. 1979), *writ denied*, 376 So. 2d 793 (Ala. 1979);
8. *E.g.*, People v. Hardy, 43 N.E.3d 734 (N.Y. 2015).
9. *E.g.*, People v. Williams, 305 P.3d 1241 (Cal. 2013).
10. *E.g.*, Harrison v. People, 50 N.Y. 518 (1872).
11. *E.g.*, Amaechi v. State, 702 S.E.2d 680 (Ga. App. 2010).
12. MODEL PENAL CODE § 223.9.
13. *See,e.g.*, Bell v. United States, 462 U.S. 356 (1983); State v. Sabins, 127 N.W.2d 107 (Iowa 1964).
14. *See, e.g.*, People v. Malach, 507 N.W.2d 834 (Mich. App. 1993); Davies v. Commonwealth, 423 S.E.2d 839 (Va. App. 1992).
15. MODEL PENAL CODE § 223.1 to 223.9
16. *Id.* at § 223.9.
17. COLO. REV. STAT. ANN. § 18-4-401 (2020).
18. *Id.*; 50 AM. JUR. 2D, *Larceny* § 2 (2017).
19. People v. Yagudayev, 937 N.Y.S.2d 279 (Sup. Ct. App. Div. 2012).
20. *See* Ira P. Robbins, *Vilifying the Vigilante: A Narrowed Scope of Citizen's Arrest*, 25 CORNELL J. L. & PUB. POL'Y 557 (2016).
21. *Id.* at 585 (citing ALA. CODE § 15-10-14(a); IND. CODE § 35-33-6-2(a)(1)(A)).
22. *Id.* (citing State v. Santiago, 217 P.3d 89 (N.M. 2009); State v. Garcia, 193 P.3d 181 (Wash. Ct. App. 2008).
23. *E.g.*, CAL. PENAL CODE § 496(a).
24. *E.g.*, People v. Land, 35 Cal. Rptr. 2d 544 (Cal. App. 1994).
25. *E.g.*, Wertheimer v. State, 169 N.E. 40 (Ind. 1930); Parish v. Commonwealth, 145 S.E.2d 192 (Va. 1965).
26. Commonwealth v. Williams, 362 A.2d 244, 248–49 (Pa. 1976) (citations omitted).
27. Commonwealth v. Matthews, 632 A.2d 570, 571 (Pa. Super. 1993).
28. *Williams*, 362 A.2d at 249 n.7.
29. *Id.*
30. *Id.*

31. Dean Lanter, *"In the Business" of Fencing: Making Sense of Federal Sentencing Enhancements for Dealers in Stolen Goods*, 77 TEX. L. REV. 1485, 1485–86 (1999).
32. *E.g.*, FLA. STAT. § 812.019(1).
33. *E.g.*, FLA. STAT. §§ 812.019(1)-(2).
34. 26 AM. JUR. 2D *Embezzlement* § 1 (2017).
35. State v. Curry, 52 P.3d 974, 977 (N.M. 2002).
36. In re Newpower, 233 F.3d 922 (6th Cir. 2000) (applying Michigan law).
37. *E.g.*, State v. Cochrane, 6 P.2d 489 (Idaho 1931).
38. MODEL PENAL CODE § 223.1(3); *see also, e.g.*, State v. Torzeski, 54 N.W.2d 879 (N.D. 1952).
39. State v. Morris, 576 S.E.2d 391 (N.C. App. 2003); Webb v. Superior Court, 202 Cal. App. 3d 872, 248 Cal. Rptr. 911 (5th Dist. 1988).
40. 452 S.E.2d 687 (Va. App. 1995).
41. *Id.* at 1089.
42. Ellen S. Podgor, *Criminal Fraud*, 48 AM. U.L. REV. 729, 746–47. (1999).
43. *Id.*
44. GA. CODE §§ 16-9-1, 16-9-2.
45. GA. CODE § 16-9-4.
46. GA. CODE § 16-9-20.
47. GA. CODE §§ 16-9-21, 16-9-30 to 16-9-39.
48. GA. CODE §§ 16-9-90 to 16-9-109.1; 16-9-150 to 16-9-157.
49. GA. CODE §§ 16-9-110 to 16-9-111.
50. GA. CODE §§ 16-9-120 to 16-9-132.
51. GA. CODE §§ 16-9-50 to 16-9-61.
52. ARIZ. REV. STAT. § 13-2310.
53. Fernando M. Pinguelo & Bradford W. Muller, *Virtual Crimes, Real Damages: a Primer on Cybercrimes in the United States and Efforts to Combat Cybercriminals*, 16 VA. J.L. & TECH. 116 (2011), at ¶ 3 (quoting Sarah Gordon & Richard Ford, *On the Definition and Classification of Cybercrime*, 2 J. COMPUTER VIROLOGY 13, 14 (2006)).
54. *Annual Number of Data Breaches and Exposed Records in the United States from 2005 to 1st half of 2020 (in millions)*, STATISTICA (2020), https://www.statista.com/statistics/273550/data-breaches-recorded-in-the-united-states-by-number-of-breaches-and-records-exposed/.
55. *Id.*; *Data Breaches*, PRIVACY RTS. CLEARINGHOUSE, https://privacyrights.org/data-breaches (last visited Feb. 8, 2021).
56. Statistica, *supra* note 55.
57. *See* 50 AM. JUR. 2D, *Larceny*, § 63.
58. *See* Fed. Trade Comm'n, *Consumer Information: Identity Theft*, https://www.consumer.ftc.gov/articles/0005-identity-theft.
59. *Id.*; Fed. Trade Comm'n, *Consumer Information: Medical Identity Theft*, https://www.consumer.ftc.gov/articles/0171-medical-identity-theft.
60. Al Pascual, Kyle Marchini, & Sarah Miller, 2018 Identity Fraud: Fraud Enters a New Era of Complexity. Pleasanton, CA: Javelin Strategy & Research.
61. *See, e.g.*, 18 U.S.C. §§ 1028, 1028A; Ore. Rev. Stat. § 165.800 (2019).
62. ORE. REV. STAT. § 165.800(1) (2019).
63. *See, e.g.*, MASS. GEN. LAWS ch. 266 § 37E (2019).
64. *See, e.g.*, N.H. REV. STAT. § 638:26 (2019).
65. *E.g.*, N.C. GEN. STAT § 14-118.5 (1984).
66. *What Is Intellectual Property?*, WORLD INTELL. PROP. ORG., https://www.wipo.int/about-ip/en/ (last visited Dec. 16, 2021).
67. 17 U.S.C. § 102.
68. *Id.*

69. David Blackburn et al., NERA Economic Consulting, *Impacts of Digital Piracy on the U.S. Economy*, U.S. CHAMBER OF COMMERCE GLOBAL INNOVATION POL'Y CNTR. (2019), https://www.theglobalipcenter.com/wp-content/uploads/2019/06/Digital-Video-Piracy.pdf, at ii, 14.
70. No Electronic Theft (NET) Act, Pub. L. No. 105-147, 111 Stat. 2678 (1997) (codified as amended at 17 U.S.C. § 101 *et seq.*).
71. 17 U.S.C. § 506(a)(1).
72. 18 U.S.C. § 2319(b)(1).
73. 18 U.S.C. § 2319(b)(3).
74. 18 U.S.C. § 2319(c)(1).
75. Pub. L. No. 105-304, tit. I, § 104, 112 Stat. 2876 (1998) (as codified at 17 U.S.C. § 109).
76. Thomas v. State, 737 A.2d 622 (Md. App. 1999).
77. 67 AM. JUR. 2d *Robbery* § 2 (2017 (citing Price v. Com, 722 S.E.2d 653 (Va. App. 2012)).
78. *See, e.g.*, Tunstull v. Commonwealth, 337 S.W.3d 576 (Ky. 2011).
79. *E.g.*, CAL. PENAL CODE § 215; N.J. STAT. § 2C:15-2.
80. Robinson v. State, 692 So. 2d 883 (Fla. 1997).
81. MODEL PENAL CODE § 222.1(1).
82. *See, e.g.*, State v. Valdez, 977 P.2d 242 (Kan. 1999), *abrogated on other grounds by* State v. James, 79 P.3d 169 (Kan. 2003); McDowell v. State, 813 So. 2d 694 (Miss. 2002).
83. 728 So. 2d 818 (Fla. App. 1999).
84. *See also, e.g.*, State v. Davis, 111 So. 3d 100 (La. App. 2012).
85. 18 U.S.C. § 1951(b)(2).
86. Bank Robbery Act, Pub. L. No. 772, 62 Stat. 796 (Jun. 25, 1948) (codified as amended at 18 U.S.C. § 2113).
87. Helen A. Anderson, *From the Thief in the Night to the Guest Who Stayed Too Long: The Evolution of Burglary in the Shadow of the Common Law*, 45 IND. L. REV. 629 (2012) (quoting SIR EDWARD COKE, THE THIRD PART OF THE INSTITUTES OF THE LAWS OF ENGLAND 63 (1809) (1644).
88. *E.g.*, Finney v. Com., 671 S.E.2d 169 (Va. 2009).
89. State v. Goodman, 322 S.E.2d 408 (N.C. App. 1984).
90. *E.g.*, State v. Mahoe, 972 P.2d 287 (Haw. 1998).
91. *E.g.*, Johns v. Commonwealth, 675 S.E.2d 211 (Va. App. 2009).
92. *See* Minturn T. Wright III, *Statutory Burglary—The Magic of Four Walls and a Roof*, 100 U. PA. L. REV. 411, 417 (1951).
93. *Id.* at 420; Anderson, *supra* note 88, at 637.
94. MODEL PENAL CODE § 221.1.
95. MODEL PENAL CODE § 1.07(4)(c).
96. *See, e.g.*, Michael H. Hoffheimer, *The Rise and Fall of Lesser Included Offenses*, 36 RUTGERS L.J. 351 (2005).
97. Paul A. Clark, *Do Statutes Criminalizing Possession of Burglary Tools Reduce Crime?* 42 CAPITAL U. L. REV. 803 (2014).
98. *E.g.*, ARIZ. REV. STAT. § 13-1505; CAL. PENAL CODE § 466.
99. *See* Clark, *supra* note 98, at 859–60.
100. *See, e.g.*, Paul Sadler, Jr., *The Crime of Arson*, 41 J. CRIM. L. & CRIMINOLOGY 290 (1950–1951).
101. *See, e.g.*, MONT. CODE § 45-6-103.
102. *See, e.g.*, N.M. STAT. § 30-17-5.
103. *See, e.g.*, IDAHO STAT. § 18-802; KY. REV. STAT. §§ 513.020–513.060.
104. Sweet v. State, 382 S.E.2d 376 (Ga. 1989).
105. Reinhardt v. State, 428 S.E.2d 333 (Ga. 1993).
106. *E.g.*, MD. CODE, CRIM. LAW § 6-301.
107. *E.g.*, MASS. GEN. LAWS c. 266 § 126A.
108. *See, e.g.*, MICH. PENAL CODE § 750.377a.

109. Chris Jay Hoofnagle, *Identity Theft: Making the Known Unknowns Known*, 21 HARV. J.L. & TECH. 97, 98 n.6 (2007).
110. 136 A.3d 916 (N.H. 2016).
111. *Id.* at 919 (internal quotations and citation omitted).
112. Flores-Figueroa v. United States, 556 U.S. 646, 647 (2009).
113. United States v. Reichert, 747 F.3d 445, 448 (6th Cir. 2014).
114. *Id.*
115. Kristina Davis, *Illicit Streaming Devices Bring Piracy to the Mass Market — and It's Terrifying Hollywood*, SAN DIEGO UNION-TRIB. (Nov. 3, 2019), https://www.sandiegouniontribune.com/news/courts/story/2019-11-03/illicit-streaming-devices-bring-piracy-to-the-mass-market-and-its-terrifying-hollywood.
116. Dalvin Brown, *FBI Breaks Up 2 Illegal Streaming Sites*, USA TODAY (Dec. 15, 2019), https://www.usatoday.com/story/tech/2019/12/15/istreamitall-jetflix-operators-busted-illegal-streaming/2658505001/.
117. 716 S.W.2d 188 (Ark. 1986).
118. *Id.* at 189.

CHAPTER 12

1. Don Stemen, *Beyond the War: The Evolving Nature of the U.S. Approach to Drugs*, 11 HARV. L. & POL'Y REV. ONLINE 375 (23017); *see generally* JOHANN HARI, CHASING THE SCREAM (2015); DRUG WAR FACTS (Douglas A. McVay ed., 2018), http://drugwarfacts.org.
2. Economics, *in* DRUG WAR FACTS, *supra* note 1, http://drugwarfacts.org/chapter/economics.
3. FBI, 2016 CRIME IN THE UNITED STATES (2017), at Table 18, https://ucr.fbi.gov/crime-in-the-u.s/2016/crime-in-the-u.s.-2016/topic-pages/tables/table-18.
4. Crime, Arrests, and Law Enforcement, *in* DRUG WAR FACTS, *supra* note 1, http://drugwarfacts.org/chapter/crime_arrests.
5. Stemen, *supra* note 1, at 400.
6. Stemen, *supra* note 1, at 401.
7. Pub. L. No. 91-513, 84 Stat. 1236 (codified as amended in scattered sections of 21 U.S.C.).
8. 21 U.S.C. § 811 *et seq.*
9. NAT'L CONF. OF STATE LEGIS., STATE MEDICAL MARIJUANA LAWS (2019), http://www.ncsl.org/research/health/state-medical-marijuana-laws.aspx
10. *E.g.*, David R. Katner, *Up in Smoke: Removing Marijuana from Schedule I*, 27 B.U. PUB. INT. L.J. 167 (2018).
11. *See, e.g.*, Susan R. Klein & Ingrid B. Grobey, *Overfederalization of Criminal Law: It's a Myth*, 28 CRIM. JUST. 23, 24–26 (2013).
12. *Id.*
13. NAT'L CONF. OF STATE LEGIS., MARIJUANA OVERVIEW: LEGALIZATION (2019), http://www.ncsl.org/research/civil-and-criminal-justice/marijuana-overview.aspx.
14. *Id.*; *see also* Stemen, *supra* note 1, at 403–07.
15. *See, e.g.*, Marc B. Hernandez, Note, *Guilt Without Mens Rea: How Florida's Elimination of Mens Rea for Drug Possession is Constitutional*, 66 FLA. L. REV. 1697 (2015).
16. *See, e.g.*, Darryl K. Brown, *Federal Mens Rea Interpretation and the Limits of Culpability's Relevance*, 75 LAW & CONTEMP. PROBS. 109, 127–29 (2012).
17. *Id.*
18. *See, e.g.*, BRUCE M. BAGLEY & JONATHAN D. ROSEN, DRUG TRAFFICKING, ORGANIZED CRIME, AND VIOLENCE IN THE AMERICAS TODAY (2015).
19. *See, e.g.*, PHIL WILLIAMS ET AL., DRUG TRAFFICKING, VIOLENCE, AND INSTABILITY (2012).
20. Nat'l Highway Traffic Safety Admin., *Drunk Driving*, https://www.nhtsa.gov/risky-driving/drunk-driving (last visited July 16, 2020).
21. Nat'l Highway Traffic Safety Admin., *Traffic Safety Facts 2018 Data: Alcohol-Impaired Driving* (2019), https://crashstats.nhtsa.dot.gov/Api/Public/ViewPublication/812864.
22. *Id.* at 1.

23. FBI, 2018 CRIME IN THE UNITED STATES: UNIFORM CRIME REPORTS tbl. 29 (2019), https://ucr.fbi.gov/crime-in-the-u.s/2018/crime-in-the-u.s.-2018/topic-pages/tables/table-29.
24. *Id.* at 3.
25. H. LAWRENCE ROSS, CONFRONTING DRUNK DRIVING: SOCIAL POLICY FOR SAVING LIVES ix (1992).
26. John D. McCarthy et al., *The Founding Social Movement Organizations: Local Citizens' Groups Opposing Drunken Driving, in* ECOLOGICAL MODELS OF ORGANIZATIONS 71 (Glenn R. Carroll ed., 1988).
27. Brandon K. Applegate et al., *Determinate of Public Punitiveness Toward Drunk Driving: A Factorial Survey Approach*, 13 JUST. Q. 57, 57–58 (1996).
28. UTAH CODE § 41-6a-501(1)(a).
29. *E.g.*, ARIZ. REV. STAT. § 28-1381(A)(4).
30. *E.g.*, ARIZ. REV. STAT. § 4-244.34.
31. UTAH CODE § 41-6a-501(1)(b).
32. ARIZ. REV. STAT. § 28-1381(A)(1).
33. Monte Kuligowski, *Rethinking DUI Law in Virginia*, 42 U. RICH. L. REV. 107 (2007).
34. 996 P.2d 339 (Kan. Ct. App. 2000).
35. *Creamer*, 996 P.2d at 344.
36. 960 P.2d 756 (Kan. 1998).
37. *Chastain*, 960 P.2d at 762.
38. *See* State v. Kelly, No. 114,563, 2017 WL 1295354 (Kan. Ct. App. Apr. 7, 2017) (upholding conviction over a challenge that a proximate cause instruction based on road conditions should have been given to a jury).
39. Governors Highway Safety Ass'n, *Alcohol-Impaired Driving laws by State* (2018), https://www.ghsa.org/sites/default/files/2018-04/DrunkDrivingLaws_040418_0.pdf [hereinafter "GHSA"].
40. ARIZ. REV. STAT. §§ 28-1382(A)(1)-(2).
41. GHSA, *supra* note 43; *see also* Henry F. Fradella, *Minimum Mandatory Sentences: Arizona's Ineffective Tool for the Social Control of DUI*, 11 CRIM. JUST. POL'Y REV. 113 (2000).
42. *E.g.*, ARIZ. REV. STAT. §§ 28-1383(A)(1)-(4).
43. *Breach of the Peace*, BLACK'S LAW DICTIONARY (11th ed. 2019).
44. *Disorderly Conduct*, BLACK'S LAW DICTIONARY (11th ed. 2019).
45. Francis Barry McCarthy, *Vagrancy and Disorderly Conduct, in* 4 ENCYCLOPEDIA OF CRIME AND JUSTICE 1589, 1589 (Sanford H. Kadish ed., 1983).
46. MODEL PENAL CODE § 250.2.
47. NEV. REV. STAT. § 203.010.
48. MO. REV. STAT. § 574.010.
49. FLA. STAT. § 856.011; *see also* ALA. CODE § 13A-11-10.
50. State v. Elabanjo, No. 09 CRS 54172 (Orange Cnty. Super. Ct. Jan. 5, 2011).
51. Gooding v. Wilson, 405 U.S. 518 (1972); Hess v. Indiana, 414 U.S. 105 (1973).
52. OKLA. ST. tit. 21 § 906.
53. MICH. COMP. LAWS § 750.103.
54. MISS. CODE ANN. § 97-29-47.
55. Leonard v. Robinson, 477 F.3d 347 (6th Cir. 2007) (limiting Michigan's anti-profanity law)
56. 759 So.2d 1274 (Miss. Ct. App. 2000).
57. *Brendle*, 759 So. 2d at 1284.
58. Cox v. Louisiana, 379 U.S. 536, 554 (1965).
59. Margot E. Kaminski, *Incitement to Riot in the Age of Flash Mobs*, 81 U. CIN. L. REV. 1, 7 (2012) (quoting WILLIAM BLACKSTONE, LAWS OF ENGLAND 146–48 (1769)).
60. *Id.* at 15.
61. MINN. STAT. ANN. § 609.705 (2020).
62. ALASKA STAT. § 11.61.100.
63. Kaminski, *supra* note 65, at 17–18.
64. *Id.* at 25–26.

65. IOWA CODE § 723.1.
66. In re Brown, 510 P.2d 1017, 1025 (Cal. 1973).
67. *See* Schlamp v. State, 891 A.2d 327, 330–33 (Md. 2006) (holding that violence against persons or property is an essential element of the common-law crime of riot).
68. R.I. GEN. LAWS § 11-45-1.
69. ME. REV. STAT. tit. 17-A, § 502.
70. S.C. CODE ANN. § 16-5-130 (2011).
71. 414 U.S. 105, 109 (1973).
72. *Id.* at 108–09.
73. Tabatha Abu El-Haj, *Defining Peaceably: Policing the Line Between Constitutionally Protected Protest and Unlawful Assembly*, 80 MO. L. REV. 961, 973 (2015).
74. *Id.* at 963.
75. Kaminski, *supra* note 65, at 7 (quoting Cassie Murdoch, *Things Get Ugly in Virginia as Riot Police Crack Down on Pro-Choice Protesters*, JEZEBEL (Mar. 5 2012), http://jezebel.com/5890406/things-get-ugly-in-virginia-as-riot-police-crack-down-on-pro-choice-protesters).
76. OHIO REV. CODE § 2917.32.
77. SUZANNE AUSTIN ALCHON, A PEST IN THE LAND: NEW WORLD EPIDEMICS IN A GLOBAL PERSPECTIVE (2003).
78. 23 Edw. 3, c. 1 (1349); 25 Edw. 3, c. 1 (1350).
79. Russell Fowler, *Defying Poverty and Fear Elizabeth I and the Poor Law of 1601*, TENN. B.J. (July/Aug. 2020), at 28, 29.
80. 43 Eliz. 1 c. 2 (1601).
81. WILLIAM TRATTNER, FROM POOR LAW TO WELFARE STATE 11 (1994).
82. 3 JAMES F. STEPHEN, A HISTORY OF THE CRIMINAL LAW OF ENGLAND 267 (1883); Joel D. Berg, *The Troubled Constitutionality of Antigang Loitering Laws*, 69 CHI.-KENT L. REV. 461, 463 (1993).
83. Vanessa Wheeler, *Discrimination Lurking on the Books: Examining the Constitutionality of the Minneapolis Lurking Ordinance*, 26 LAW & INEQ. 467, 469 (2008).
84. 372 U.S. 335, 339–40 (1963).
85. Wheeler, *supra* note 92, at 469–70.
86. 405 U.S. 156 (1972).
87. Drew Sena, *A Constitutional Critique on the Criminalization of Panhandling in Washington State*, 41 SEATTLE U. L. REV. 287, 288 (2017).
88. *Id.; see also* United States v. Kokinda, 497 U.S. 720, 725 (1990).
89. CINCINNATI CITY ORDINANCE 910-12 (2011).
90. Sena, *supra* note 96, at 288.
91. TENN. CODE ANN. § 39-17-313.
92. Farber v. Rochford, 407 F. Supp. 529, 533 (N.D. Ill. 1975).
93. People v. Bright, 520 N.E.2d 1355, 1360 (N.Y. 1988).
94. Wheeler, *supra* note 92, at 474–75 (comparing Fields v. City of Omaha, 810 F.2d 830 (8th Cir. 1987) (invalidating a loitering law based on the MPC for vagueness), *with* State v. Ecker, 311 So. 2d 104 (Fla. 1975) (upholding a loitering law based on the MPC)).
95. City of Tacoma v. Luvene, 827 P.2d 1374, 1379 (1992).
96. City of Cleveland v. Howard, 532 N.E.2d 1325, 1326 (Ohio Mun. Ct. 1987).
97. City of Milwaukee v. Wilson, 291 N.W.2d 452, 455 (1980).
98. Kim Strosnider, *Anti-Gang Ordinances After* City of Chicago v. Morales*: The Intersection of Race, Vagueness Doctrine, and Equal Protection in the Criminal Law*, 39 AM. CRIM. L. REV. 101, 105 (2002).
99. G. DAVID CURRY & SCOTT H. DECKER, CONFRONTING GANGS 78 (1998).
100. Adrienne Freng & Terrance J. Taylor, *Race and Ethnicity: What Are Their Roles in Gang Membership?*, *in* CHANGING COURSE: PREVENTING GANG MEMBERSHIP 135 (Thomas R. Simon et al. eds., 2013).

101. NAT'L GANG INTELLIGENCE CTR., FBI, 2011 NATIONAL GANG THREAT ASSESSMENT: EMERGING TRENDS 9 (2011), http:// www.fbi.gov/stats-services/publications/2011-national-gang-threat-assessment/2011-national-gang-threat-assessment-emerging-trends
102. FLA. STAT. ANN. § 874.05; KY. REV. STAT. ANN. § 506.140.
103. N.J. REV. STAT. § 18A:11-9; TENN. CODE ANN. § 49-6-4215.
104. *E.g.*, 18 U.S.C. § 521; CAL. PENAL CODE § 186.22; 730 ILL. COMP. STAT. 5/5-5-3.2.
105. 527 U.S. 41 (1999).
106. *E.g.*, Johnson v. Athens-Clarke County, 529 S.E.2d 613, 616–17 (Ga. 2000).
107. 119 F. Supp. 2d 735 (S.D. Ohio 2000).
108. *E.g.*, CAL. PENAL CODE §§ 16350, 16790, 16890, 30500-31115; CONN. GEN. STAT. § 53-202a *et seq.*
109. *E.g.*, WASH. REV. CODE 9.41.040.
110. *E.g.*, CONN. GEN. STAT. § 53-203.
111. United States v. Burr, 25 F. Cas. 2, 13 (C.C.D. Va. 1807).
112. J. Richard Broughton, *Constitutional Discourse and the Rhetoric of Treason*, 47 HASTINGS CONST. L.Q. 303, 310 (2020).
113. 8 U.S. (4 Cranch) 75, 126 (1807).
114. 325 U.S. 1 (1945).
115. *Id.* at 29.
116. Erin Creegan, *National Security Crime*, 3 HARV. NAT'L. SEC. J. 373, 379 (2012).
117. 18 U.S.C. § 2384.
118. *See* United States v. Rahman, 189 F.3d 88 (2d Cir. 1999).
119. Jeff Barge, *Sedition Prosecutions Rarely Successful; Government Tries to Beat the Odds in Trial of Blind Cleric's Followers*, ABA J. (Oct. 1994), at 16.
120. *Id.*
121. *Id.*
122. *Id.*
123. Nick Bunkley, *U.S. Judge in Michigan Acquits Militia Members of Sedition*, N.Y. TIMES (Mar. 27, 2012), https://www.nytimes.com/2012/03/28/us/hutaree-militia-members-acquitted-of-sedition.html.
124. United States v. Rahman, 189 F.3d 88, 117 (2d Cir. 1999).
125. United States v. Rosenberg, 195 F.2d 583 (2d Cir. 1952).
126. FBI, *Famous Cases and Criminals: Robert Hanssen*, https://www.fbi.gov/history/famous-cases/robert-hanssen (last visited July 17, 2020).
127. *Id.*
128. *Whistleblower*, BLACK'S LAW DICTIONARY (11th ed. 2019).
129. *See* Lindsay B. Barnes, Comment, *The Changing Face of Espionage: Modern Times Call for Amending the Espionage Act*, 46 MCGEORGE L. REV. 511, 513 (2014).
130. U.S. CONST. art. I, § 8, cl. 4.
131. Arizona v. United States, 567 U.S. 387, 395 (2012).
132. *Id.* at 397.
133. Jessica T. Simes & Mary C. Waters, *The Politics of Immigration and Crime*, *in* THE OXFORD HANDBOOK OF ETHNICITY, CRIME, AND IMMIGRATION 459–60 (Sandra M. Bucerius & Michael Tonry eds., 2014).
134. Julia G. Young, *Making America 1920 Again? Nativism and US Immigration, Past and Present*, 5 J. MIGRATION & HUM. SEC. S37, S41 (2017).
135. *Id.* at S46–S47.
136. Simes & Waters, *supra* note 142, at 457–83; *see also* Graham C. Ousey & Charis E. Kubrin, *Immigration and Crime: Assessing a Contentious Issue*, 1 ANN. REV. CRIMINOLOGY 1 (2017).
137. *See, e.g.*, Michelangelo Landgrave & Alex Nowrasteh, *Incarcerated Immigrants in 2016: Their Numbers, Demographics, and Countries of Origin* (Cato Institute Immigr. Res. & Pol'y Brief #7, June 4, 2018), https://object.cato.org/sites/cato.org/files/pubs/pdf/irpb7.pdf; Michael T. Light & Ty Miller, *Does Undocumented Immigration Increase Violent Crime?*, 56 CRIMINOLOGY 370 (2018).

138. Michael Tonry, *Race, Ethnicity, Crime, and Immigration*, *in* THE OXFORD HANDBOOK OF ETHNICITY, CRIME, AND IMMIGRATION 2 (Sandra M. Bucerius & Michael Tonry eds., 2014).
139. *See, e.g.*, Roy Germano, *Unauthorized Immigrants Paid $100 Billion Into Social Security Over Last Decade*, VICE NEWS (Aug. 4, 2014), https://news.vice.com/en_us/article/zm5k8j/unauthorized-immigrants-paid-100-billion-into-social-security-over-last-decade; *see also* Judith Gans, Immigrants in Arizona: Fiscal and Economic Impacts (2008), http://udallcenter.arizona.edu/immigration/publications/impactofimmigrants08.pdf.
140. Arizona v. United States, 567 U.S. 387, 395–96 (internal citations omitted).
141. *Id.*
142. 8 U.S.C. § 1324.
143. 18 U.S.C. § 1546.
144. 19 U.S.C. § 1459.
145. 18 U.S.C. § 1544.
146. 18 U.S.C. § 1543.
147. 18 U.S.C. § 1544.
148. AM. CIV LIBERTIES UNION, OPERATION STREAMLINE ISSUE BRIEF (2019), https://www.aclu.org/sites/default/files/field_document/15_12_14_aclu_1325_1326_recommendations_final2.pdf.
149. Transactional Records Access Clearinghouse, *Prosecutions for February 2019* (Mar. 27, 2019), https://trac.syr.edu/tracreports/bulletins/overall/monthlyfeb19/fil/.
150. 8 U.S.C. § 1227; U.S. Dep't of State, Foreign Affairs Manual, 9 FAM 302.3 (2018).
151. State v. Jesus B., No. 34,558, 2016 WL 7326535 (N.M. Ct. App. Nov. 21, 2016).
152. *Id.* at *1.
153. N.M. STAT. ANN. § 30-20-1 (2020).
154. State v. Correa, 222 P.3d 1, 4 (N.M. 2009) (overturning conviction on the basis that the "child's acts were not clearly of the kind that would tend to disturb the peace").
155. *Id.* at 7.
156. 120 P.3d 652 (Wash. Ct. App. 2005).
157. Former Spokane Municipal Code 10.10.025 (1994).
158. *Id.*
159. *Marr*, 120 P.3d at 653.
160. 802 P.2d 1333 (Wash. 1990).
161. *Id.* at 1338.
162. *Id.*
163. *Marr*, 120 P.3d at 654.
164. 821 N.Y.S.2d 394 (2006).
165. *Id.* at 397.
166. 720 ILL. COMP. STAT. 5/11-9.3 (2020).

CHAPTER 13

1. Terry L. Price, *Faultless Mistake of Fact: Justification or Excuse?*, 12 CRIM. JUST. ETHICS 14, ¶¶ 4–5 (1993).
2. *See* Edwin R. Keedy, *Ignorance and Mistake in the Criminal Law*, 22 HARV. L. REV. 75, 76 n.1 (1908).
3. Sharon L. Davies, *The Jurisprudence of Willfulness: An Evolving Theory of Excusable Ignorance*, 48 DUKE L.J. 341, 350 (1998).
4. *Id.* at 356 (quoting 1 WAYNE R. LAFAVE & AUSTIN W. SCOTT, JR., SUBSTANTIVE CRIMINAL LAW § 5.1, at 586 (1986)).
5. MODEL PENAL CODE § 2.04(1)-(3).
6. MODEL PENAL CODE § 2.04(3)(a).
7. 21 AM. JUR. 2d *Criminal Law* § 138 (2016).
8. *Id.*
9. 379 U.S. 559 (1965).

10. *Id.* at 568.
11. *Id.* at 570–71.
12. MODEL PENAL CODE § 2.04(1)(a).
13. *Cf.* State v. Labato, 80 A.2d 617 (N.J. 1951).
14. State v. Hatch, 313 A.2d 797 (N.J. 1973).
15. *See, e.g.*, State v. DeMao, 118 A.2d 1 (N.J. 1955).
16. *See* 1 W. LAFAVE & A. SCOTT, SUBSTANTIVE CRIMINAL LAW § 5.4 (1986).
17. MODEL PENAL CODE § 3.02(1)(a).
18. *See, e.g.*, State v. Matson, 921 P.2d 790 (Kan. 1996).
19. *See* 21 AM. JUR. 2d *Criminal Law* § 140 (2016).
20. *Id.*; *see also* MODEL PENAL CODE § 2.09(1).
21. *See* MODEL PENAL CODE § 2.09(2); *see also, e.g.*, United States v. Paul, 110 F.3d 869 (2d Cir. 1997).
22. MODEL PENAL CODE §§ 2.09(2), 3.02(2).
23. 21 AM. JUR. 2d *Criminal Law* §§ 140, 146.
24. MODEL PENAL CODE § 3.02(1)(a).
25. *See, e.g.*, People v. Trippet, 56 Cal. App. 4th 1532, 66 Cal. Rptr. 2d 559 (1997).
26. *See, e.g.*, Jenni James, *When Is Rescue Necessary? Applying the Necessity Defense to the Rescue of Animals*, 7 STAN. J. ANIMAL L. & POL'Y 1 (2014).
27. 21 AM. JUR. 2d *Criminal Law* § 141.
28. 21 Am. Jur. 2d *Criminal Law* § 142 (2009).
29. 21 AM. JUR. 2d *Criminal Law* § 141 (2009); *see also* United States v. Schoon, 971 F.2d 193 (9th Cir. 1991).
30. For an interesting article on how the defense could be used in the civil disobedience context, see Steven M. Bauer & Peter J. Eckerstrom, *The State Made Me Do It: The Applicability for the Necessity Defense to Civil Disobedience*, 39 STAN. L. REV. 1173 (1987).
31. *See* People v. Buena Vista Mines, Inc., 60 Cal. App. 4th 1198, 71 Cal. Rptr. 2d 101 (1998).
32. *See* Michael H. Hoffheimer, *Codifying Necessity: Legislative Resistance To Enacting Choice-of-Evils Defenses to Criminal Liability*, 82 TUL. L. REV. 191 (2007).
33. 14 Q.B.D. 273 (1884).
34. For an in-depth exploration of the various philosophical arguments concerning the defense of necessity as it relates to homicide, read Lon L. Fuller's classic fictional appellate decision in *The Case of the Speluncean Explorers*, 62 HARV. L. REV. 616 (1949).
35. United States v. Holmes, 26 F. Cas. 360 (C.C.E.D. Pa. 1842).
36. *See* Hoffheimer, *supra* note 32, at 222–24.
37. *See, e.g.*, MO. ANN. STAT. §563.026; KY. REV. STAT. ANN. § 503.030; *see also* R.I. Recreation Ctr., Inc. v. Aetna Cas. & Sur. Co., 177 F.2d 603, 605 (1st Cir. 1949).
38. Hoffheimer, *supra* note 32, at 237–42 (citing, *inter alia*, WIS. STAT. ANN. § 939.47).
39. *See* People v. Lovercamp, 43 Cal. App 3d. 823 (1974); United States v. Bailey, 444 U.S. 394 (1980); United States v. Lopez, 622 F. Supp. 1083 (1987).
40. *See* R.U. Singh, *History of the Defence of Drunkenness in English Criminal Law*, 49 LAW. Q. REV. 528, 530 (1933); *see also* Reniger v. Fogossa, 75 Eng. Rep. 1 (K.B. 1551).
41. *See* Meghan Paulk Ingle, *Law on the Rocks: The Intoxication Defenses Are Being Eighty-Sixed*, 55 VAND. L. REV. 607 (2002).
42. *Id.* at 613–14.
43. MODEL PENAL CODE § 2.08(5)(a).
44. *See, e.g.*, State v. R.T., 983 A.2d 1177 (N.J. Super. App. Div. 2009).
45. *See id.*
46. MODEL PENAL CODE § 2.08(1).
47. MODEL PENAL CODE § 2.08(2).
48. Ingle, *supra* note 41, at 620 n.78.

49. *See* ALA. CODE § 13A-3-2(b); CONN. GEN. STAT. ANN. § 53a-7; KY. REV. STAT. § 501.080; MAINE REV. STAT. ANN. tit. 17A, § 37; N.H. REV. STAT. § 626:4; N.J. STAT. ANN. § 2C:2-8; N.Y. PENAL LAW § 15.25; N.D. CENT. CODE ANN. § 12.1-04-02; ORE. REV. STAT. § 161.125; TENN. CODE ANN. § 39-11-503; UTAH CODE ANN. § 76-2-306; WIS. STAT. ANN. § 939.42(2).
50. *E.g.*, MONT. CODE ANN. § 45-2-203; IDAHO CODE ANN. § 18-116; ILL. COMP. STAT. ANN. ch. 38, § 6-3; IND. CODE ANN. § 35-41-3-5(b); MO. ANN. STAT. § 562.076.; PA. CONS. STAT. ANN. § 308; TEX. PENAL CODE § 8-04.
51. *E.g.*, CAL. PENAL CODE § 22 (b); CO. REV. STAT. ANN. § 18-1-804; LA. REV. STAT. ANN. § 14:15; MINN. STAT. ANN. § 609.075.
52. Montana v. Egelhoff, 518 U.S. 37 (1996).
53. Ingle, *supra* note 41, at 615 n.49.
54. 21 AM. JUR. 2d *Criminal Law* § 151 (2009); *see also, e.g.*, Shawn Marie Boyne & Gary C. Mitchell, *Death in the Desert: A New Look at the Involuntary Intoxication Defense in New Mexico*, 32 N.M. L. REV. 243 (2002).
55. People v. Penman, 110 N.E. 894 (Ill. 1915).
56. *See* Robert Boyd Goldstein, *The Mickey Finn Defense: Involuntary Intoxication and Insanity*, 20 BULL. AM. ACAD. PSYCHIATRY LAW 27, 28 (1992).
57. Heard v. State, 887 S.W.2d 94 (Tex. App. 1994); Burrows v. State, 297 P. 1029 (Ariz. 1931); McCook v. State, 17 S.E. 1019 (Ga. 1893).
58. People v. Johnson, 191 Cal. App. 2d 694, 699 (1961); In re Robert V. 132 Cal. App. 3d 815, 821 (1982).
59. MODEL PENAL CODE §§ 2.08(4)-(5).
60. *See* Tim Feulner, Note, *The Minotaur Defense: The Myth of the Pathological Intoxication Defense*, 49 AM. CRIM. L. REV. 1969 (2012).
61. *Id.* at 1971.
62. Harold C. Urschel, III & George E. Woody, *Alcohol Idiosyncratic Intoxication: A Review of the Data Supporting Its Existence*, *in* AM. PSYCHIATRIC ASS'N, 1 DIAGNOSTIC AND STATISTICAL MANUAL OF MENTAL DISORDERS (DSM-IV) SOURCEBOOK 126 (Thomas A. Widiger et al. eds., 1994).
63. *See* Feulner, *supra* note 60, at 1990–92; *see also* Downing v. Commonwealth, 496 S.E.2d 164 (Va. App. 1998).
64. *E.g.*, State v. Sette, 611 A.2d 1129 (N.J. Super. App. Div. 1992).
65. Justices of Boston Municipal Court v. Lydon, 466 U.S. 294, 306–07 (1984).
66. Hudson v. United States, 522 U.S. 93, 99 (1997).
67. 284 U.S. 299 (1932).
68. *See* United States v. Felix, 503 U.S. 378 (1992).
69. Martinez v. Illinois, 134 S. Ct. 2070, 2074 (2014).
70. Blueford v. Arkansas, 566 U.S. 599 (2012).
71. Burks v. United States, 437 U.S. 1 (1978); United States v. Tateo, 377 U.S. 463 (1964).
72. 139 S. Ct. 1960 (2019).
73. Heath v. Alabama, 474 U.S. 82 (1985).
74. Waller v. Florida, 397 U.S. 387 (1970).
75. *Id.* at 393.
76. United States v. Marion, 404 U.S. 307 (1971).
77. Barker v. Wingo, 407 U.S. 514 (1972).
78. *Id.* at 530.
79. *Id.* at 531.
80. *Id.* at 532.
81. *Id.*
82. 18 U.S.C. §§ 3161–74.
83. Anthony M. Dillof, *Unraveling Unlawful Entrapment*, 94 J. CRIM. L. & CRIMINOLOGY 827, 829 (2004).
84. 559 N.E.2d 348 (Ind. Ct. App. 1990).
85. Wroblewska v. Holder, 656 F.3d 473, 478 (7th Cir. 2011)

86. Dillof, *supra* note 83, at 831.
87. KENNETH M. MURCHISON, FEDERAL CRIMINAL LAW DOCTRINE: THE FORGOTTEN INFLUENCE OF NATIONAL PROHIBITION 42–46 (1994).
88. *E.g.*, Graham v. State, 700 S.E.2d 863 (Ga. Ct. App. 2010).
89. *E.g.*, State v. Hammeren, 655 N.W.2d 707 (N.D. 2003); People v. Pierce, 725 N.W.2d 691 (Mich. Ct. App. 2006); State v. Riccardi, 665 A.2d 793 (N.J. Super. App. Div. 1995).
90. *E.g.*, United States v. Kussmaul, 987 F.2d 345 (6th Cir. 1993); Griesemer v. State, 26 N.E.3d 606 (Ind. 2015); People v. Placek, 704 N.E.2d 393 (Ill. 1998).
91. Nelson v. State, 245 P.3d 282, 286 (Wyo. 2010).
92. *E.g.*, People v. Rollova, 508 N.Y.S.2d 653 (N.Y. App. Div. 1986).
93. *E.g.*, People v. Collins, 234 N.W.2d 531 (Mich. Ct. App. 1975).
94. United States v. Gamache, 156 F.3d 1 (1st Cir. 1998).
95. *Id.*
96. United States v. Cortes, 757 F.3d 850, 858 (9th Cir. 2014).
97. Commonwealth v. Madigan, 871 N.E.2d 478, 483 (Mass. 2007).
98. *Id.* at 858 (quoting United States v. Busby, 780 F.2d 804, 807 (9th Cir.1986)).
99. 503 U.S. 540 (1992).
100. *Id.* at 543.
101. *Id.* at 550.
102. MODEL PENAL CODE § 2.13.
103. *Id.*
104. 292 N.W.2d 196 (Mich. Ct. App. 1980).
105. United States v. Russell, 411 U. S. 423, 431–32 (1973).
106. Metcalf v. State, 635 So. 2d 11 (Fla. 1994).
107. U.S. DEP'T OF STATE, DIPLOMATIC AND CONSULAR IMMUNITY: GUIDANCE FOR LAW ENFORCEMENT AND JUDICIAL AUTHORITIES (2019), https://www.state.gov/wp-content/uploads/2019/07/2018-DipConImm_v5_Web.pdf, at 3.
108. *Id.* at 7–9.
109. John Bellinger, *The Importance of Diplomatic Immunity*, LAWFARE (July 18, 2013), https://www.lawfareblog.com/importance-diplomatic-immunity.
110. U.S. DEP'T OF STATE, *supra* note 107, at 21–22.
111. *Id.*
112. Bordenkircher v. Hayes, 434 U.S. 357, 364 (1978); *see also* Robert H. Jackson, *The Federal Prosecutor*, 31 J. CRIM. L. & CRIMINOLOGY 3, 3 (1940).
113. McCleskey v. Kemp, 481 U.S. 279, 312 (1987).
114. 118 U.S. 356 (1886).
115. *See, e.g.*, Yelina Kvurt, *Selective Prosecution In Russia-Myth or Reality?*, 15 CARDOZO J. INT'L & COMP. L. 127, 142 (2007).
116. Bordenkircher v. Hayes, 434 U.S. 357 (1978).
117. United States v. Armstrong, 517 U.S. 456 (1996).
118. 461 F.3d 477 (4th Cir. 2006).
119. 18 U.S.C. § 960.
120. *Khan*, 461 F.3d at 489.
121. Thomas P. McCarty, United States v. Khan, 461 F.3d 477 (4th Cir. 2006): *Discovering Whether "Similarly Situated" Individuals and the Selective Prosecution Defense Still Exist*, 87 NEB. L. REV. 538, 554 (2008).
122. *Id.* at 554–55.
123. *Khan*, 461 F.3d at 498.
124. Oyler v. Boles, 68 U.S. 448, 456 (1962).
125. *Id.* at 458.

126. James Babikian, *Cleaving the Gordian Knot: Implicit Bias, Selective Prosecution, & Charging Guidelines*, 42 AM. J. CRIM. L. 139, 152 (2015).
127. *Id.*
128. State v. Cole, 403 S.E.2d 117 (S.C. 1991).
129. U.S. Census Bureau, *Historical Cense of House Tables: Telephones*, https://www.census.gov/hhes/www/housing/census/historic/phone.html.
130. John Alan Cohan, *Homicide by Necessity*, 10 CHAP. L. REV. 119, 134 (2006).
131. MODEL PENAL CODE § 3.02 cmt. 3, at 15.
132. *Id.*
133. *Id.* at 137.
134. Todd Paul Myers, *Halcion Made Me Do It: New Liability and a New Defense —Fear and Loathing in the Halcion Paper Chase*, 62 U. CIN. L. REV. 603, 603–04 (1993).
135. *Id.* at 612.

CHAPTER 14

1. Barbara Kaban & James Orlando, *Revitalizing the Infancy Defense in the Contemporary Juvenile Court*, 60 RUTGERS L. REV. 33, 35 (2007).
2. *Id.* at 35–37.
3. *Id.*
4. 21 AM. JUR. 2d *Criminal Law* § 34 (2016).
5. *E.g.*, MASS. ANN. LAWS ch. 119, §§ 52–54.
6. *E.g.*, MINN. STAT ANN. § 609.055(1).
7. Kathryn White, *A Chance for Redemption: Revising the "Persecutor Bar" and "Material Support Bar" in the Case of Child Soldiers*, 43 VAND. J. TRANSNAT'L L. 191, 212 (2010).
8. *See* Kaban & Orlando, *supra* note 1, at 37, 41–47.
9. *Id.* at 45–47.
10. *Id.* at 55; In re Tyvonne, 558 A.2d 661 (Conn. 1989).
11. In re Devon, 584 A.2d 1287 (Md. Ct. Spec. App. 1991).
12. Kaban & Orlando, *supra* note 1, at 48.
13. *See generally* Stephanie M. Herseth, *Competency to Stand Trial*, 84 GEO. L.J. 1066, 1076 n.1418 (1996).
14. FED. R. CRIM. PRO. 12.2(a).
15. *Id.*; Bakic v. United States, 971 F. Supp. 697, 700 (N.D.N.Y. 1997); People v. Low, 732 P.2d 622 (Colo. 1987).
16. Bruce J. Winick, *Criminal Law: Reforming Incompetency to Stand Trial and Plead Guilty: A Restated Proposal and a Response to Professor Bonnie*, 85 J. CRIM. L. & CRIMINOLOGY 571, 572 (1995); *see also* Pate v. Robinson, 383 U.S. 375 (1966).
17. 18 U.S.C. § 4241(d); *see also* United States v. Teague, 956 F.2d 1427, 1431 n.10 (7th Cir. 1992).
18. Medina v. California, 505 U.S. 437, 452 (1992).
19. Cooper v. Oklahoma, 517 U.S. 348, 369 (1996).
20. *Pate*, 383 U.S. at 378; *Medina*, 505 U.S. at 452.
21. *E.g.*, Blazak v. Ricketts, 1 F.3d 891 (9th Cir. 1993).
22. Dusky v. *United States*, 362 U.S. 402, 402 (1960); *see also Medina*, 505 U.S. at 452.
23. Winick, *supra* note 16, at 572.
24. Jackson v. Indiana, 406 U.S. 715 (1972).
25. *E.g.*, James J. Gobert, *Competency to Stand Trial: A Pre-and-Post* Jackson *Analysis*, 40 TENN. L. REV. 659, 660 (1973).
26. *Jackson*, 406 U.S. at 738.
27. Debra A. Pinals, *Where Two Roads Meet: Restoration of Competence to Stand Trial From a Clinical Perspective*, 31 NEW ENG. J. CRIM. & CIV. CONFINEMENT 81 (2005).
28. Nicholas Rosina, *How "Reasonable" Has Become Unreasonable: A Proposal for Rewriting the Lasting Legacy of* Jackson v. Indiana, 89 WASH. U.L. REV. 673 (2012).

29. Winick, *supra* note 16, at 580.
30. The section is adapted from Henry F. Fradella, *From Insanity to Beyond Diminished Capacity: Mental Illness and Criminal Excuse in the Post-*Clark *Era*, 18 U. FLA. J.L. & PUB. POL'Y 7 (2007).
31. *See* Tarika Daftary-Kapur et al., *Measuring Knowledge of the Insanity Defense. Scale Construction and Validation*, 29 BEHAV. SCI. & L. 40 (2011).
32. Michael L. Perlin, *"The Borderline Which Separated You From Me": The Insanity Defense, the Authoritarian Spirit, the Fear of Faking, and the Culture of Punishment*, 82 IOWA L. REV. 1375, 1403 (1997)(internal citations omitted).
33. *Id.* at 1404; Stuart M Kirschner & Gary J. Galperin, *Psychiatric Defenses in New York County: Pleas and Results*, 29 J. AM. ACAD. PSYCHIATRY & L. 194, 198–200 (2001); Jeffrey S. Janofsky et al., *Defendants Pleading Insanity: An Analysis of Outcome*, 17 BULL. AM. ACAD. PSYCHIATRY & L. 203, 205 (1989); Eric Silver et al., *Demythologizing Inaccurate Perceptions of the Insanity Defense*, 18 LAW & HUM. BEHAV. 63 (1994).
34. Perlin, *supra* note 32, at 1404.
35. *Id.* at 1405.
36. *Id.*; *cf.* Daniel C. Murrie & Janet I Warren, *Clinician Variation in Rates of Legal Sanity Opinions: Implications for Self-Monitoring*, 36 PROF. PSYCHOL., RES., & PRAC. 519–24 (2005).
37. Perlin, *supra* note 32, at 1405 (citing David Schretlen & Hal Arkowitz, *A Psychological Test Battery to Detect Prison Inmates Who Fake Insanity or Mental Retardation*, 8 BEHAV. SCI. & L. 75, 75 (1990)).
38. *See also* Karen Franklin, *Malingering as a Dichotomous Variable: Case Report on an Insanity Defendant*, 8 J. FORENSIC PSYCHOL. PRAC. 95 (2008).
39. Michael L. Perlin, *Unpacking the Myths: The Symbolism Mythology of Insanity Defense Jurisprudence*, 40 CASE W. RES. L. REV. 599, 632 (1990)(citing Rex v. Arnold, Y.B. 10 Geo. 1 (1724)).
40. Anne C. Gresham, *The Insanity Plea: A Futile Defense for Serial Killers*, 17 LAW & PSYCHOL. REV. 193, 194 (1993).
41. Christopher Slobogin, *An End to Insanity: Recasting the Role of Mental Disability in Criminal Cases*, 86 VA. L. REV. 1199, 1208 (2000).
42. *See* Gerald Robin, *The Evolution of the Insanity Defense*, 13 J. CONTEMP. CRIM. JUST. 224, 226 (1997).
43. *Id.* at 226.
44. Gresham, *supra* note 41, at 194.
45. Robin, *supra* note 44, at 226.
46. *See* RITA JAMES SIMON, THE JURY AND THE DEFENSE OF INSANITY (1967).
47. M'Naghten, 8 Eng. Rep. 718 (H.L. 1843).
48. RICHARD MORAN, KNOWING RIGHT FROM WRONG: THE INSANITY DEFENSE OF DANIEL M'NAGHTEN 90 (1981).
49. *Id.*
50. *Id.* at 722.
51. *See* Clark v. Arizona, 548 U.S. 735, 747–48 (2006).
52. Marc Rosen, *Insanity Denied: Abolition of the Insanity Defense in Kansas*, 8 KAN. J.L. & PUB. POL'Y 253, 261 (1999).
53. *See id.* at 261–62.
54. Robin, *supra* note 44, at 227.
55. Robin, *supra* note 44, at 228.
56. Durham v. United States. 214 F.2d 862 (D.C. Cir. 1954), *overruled by* United States v. Brawner, 471 F.2d 969, 981 (D.C. Cir. 1972).
57. 214 F.2d at 874–75.
58. Robin, *supra* note 44, at 228.
59. SIMON, *supra* note 48, at 203.
60. *See* Herbert Wechsler, *The Criteria of Criminal Responsibility*, 22 U. CHI. L. REV. 367 (1955).
61. United States v. Brawner, 471 F.2d 969 (D.C. Cir. 1972).
62. N.H. REV. STAT. § 628:2 (2014); State v. Abbott, 503 A.2d 791 (N.H. 1985).

63. MODEL PENAL CODE § 4.01(1).
64. *See* ROBERT SCHUG & HENRY F. FRADELLA, MENTAL ILLNESS AND CRIME 386–90, 407–31 (2015).
65. Robin, *supra* note 44, at 230.
66. *See, e.g.*, Stephen J. Morse, *Culpability and Control*, 142 U. PA. L. REV. 1587, 1600 (1994); AM. BAR ASS'N, CRIMINAL JUSTICE MENTAL HEALTH STANDARDS, standard 7-6.1, at 329–32 (1984); AMERICAN PSYCHIATRIC ASS'N, STATEMENT ON THE INSANITY DEFENSE 12 (1982).
67. Christopher Slobogin, *The Interactionist Alternative to the Insanity Defense: Reflections on the Exculpatory Scope of Mental Illness in the Wake of the Andrea Yates Trial*, 30 AM. J. CRIM. L. 315, 320 (2003).
68. PETER W. LOW, JR. ET AL., THE TRIAL OF JOHN W. HINCKLEY, JR.: A CASE STUDY IN THE INSANITY DEFENSE 23–24 (1986).
69. *Id.* at 32.
70. Robin, *supra* note 44, at 231.
71. *Id.*
72. George L. Blau & Richard A. Pasewark, *Statutory Changes and the Insanity Defense: Seeking the Perfect Insane Person*, 18 LAW & PSYCHOL. REV. 69 (1994).
73. Lisa J. Callahan et al., *Insanity Defense Reform in the United States—post-Hinckley*, 11 MENTAL & PHYSICAL DISABILITY L. REP. 54 (1987).
74. Insanity Defense Reform Act of 1989, Pub. L. No. 91-190, 98 Stat. 1837 (1984) (codified as amended at 18 U.S.C. § 17).
75. *Id.*
76. *Id.*
77. Renee Melançon, Note, *Arizona's Insane Response to Insanity*, 40 ARIZ. L. REV. 287, 297 (1998).
78. Callahan et al., *supra* note 75, at 54–56.
79. *Id.*
80. *Id.*
81. *Id.*
82. ALASKA STAT. §§ 12.47.010; IDAHO CODE ANN. § 18–207; KAN. STAT. ANN. § 22–3220; MONT. CODE ANN. §§ 46-14-101, 102, 103; UTAH CODE ANN. § 76-2-305.
83. MICH. COMP. LAWS § 768.36(1).
84. See Christopher Slobogin, *The Guilty But Mentally Ill Verdict: An Idea Whose Time Should Not Have Come*, 53 GEO. WASH. L. REV. 494 (1985).
85. Gare A. Smith & James A. Hall, *Evaluating Michigan's Guilty But Mentally Ill Verdict: An Empirical Study*, 16 U. MICH. J.L. REFORM 77, 80 (1982).
86. *E.g.*, DEL. CODE ANN. tit. 11, §§ 401(b), 408; GA. CODE ANN. § 17-7-131; ILL. COM. STAT. ANN. ch. 720, act. 5, tit. II, art. 6; IND. CODE § 35-36-2-3; KY. REV. STAT. ANN. § 504.120; MONT. CODE ANN. § 46-14-312; N.M. STAT. ANN. § 31-9-3; 18 PA. CONS. STAT. § 314 (1983); S.C. CODE ANN. § 17-24-20 (1993); S.D. CODIFIED LAWS ANN. § 23A-26-14 (1988).
87. Smith & Hall, *supra* note 87, at 106.
88. *Id.*
89. EDITH GREEN & KIRK HEILBRUN, WRIGHTSMAN'S PSYCHOLOGY AND THE LEGAL SYSTEM 220 (7th ed. 2011).
90. *See* ARIZ. REV. STAT. ANN. § 13-502.
91. *Id.*
92. ARIZ. REV. STAT. ANN. § 13-3994.
93. *Id.*
94. *Id.*
95. *See* SCHUG & FRADELLA, *supra* note 66, at 470–90.
96. *See* sources cited *supra* note 84.
97. State v. Korell, 690 P.2d 992, 994 (Mont. 1984).
98. Leland v. Oregon, 343 U.S. 790 (1952).

99. *Id.* at 798–99.
100. *Id.* at 799; *see also In Re Winship*, 397 U.S. 358, 368 (1970).
101. *Korell*, 690 P.2d at 994.
102. *See* State v. Searcy, 798 P.2d 914 (Idaho 1990); State v. Bethel, 66 P.3d 840 (Kan. 2003); State v. Herrera, 895 P.2d 359 (Utah 1995).
103. Finger v. State, 27 P.3d 66 (Nev. 2001).
104. 140 S. Ct. 1021, 1035 (2020).
105. *Id.* at 1025–26.
106. *See* Andrew J. Demko, Note, *Abraham's Deific Defense: Problems with Insanity, Faith, and Knowing Right from Wrong*, 80 NOTRE DAME L. REV. 1961 (2005); Grant H. Morris & Ansar Haroun, *"God Told Me to Kill": Religion or Delusion?*, 38 SAN DIEGO L. REV. 973 (2001).
107. *E.g.*, UTAH CODE ANN. § 76-2-305(1)(b) (2006).
108. *E.g.*, United States v. Cantu, 12 F.3d 1506, 1509, n.1 (9th Cir. 1993); United States v. Johnson, 979 F.2d 396, 401 (6th Cir. 1992).
109. AM. PSYCHIATRIC ASS'N, DIAGNOSTIC AND STATISTICAL MANUAL OF MENTAL DISORDERS 25 (5th ed. 2013) [hereinafter "DSM-5"].
110. United States v. Murdoch, 98 F.3d 472, 478 (9th Cir. 1996), *cert. denied*, 521 U.S. 1122 (1997).
111. Bruce Winick, *Ambiguities in the Legal Meaning and Significance of Mental Illness*, 1 PSYCH. PUB. POL'Y & L. 534, 558–59 (1995).
112. *Id.* at 558 n.102.
113. *Id.* at 558.
114. *See* United States v. Bilyk, 29 F.3d 459 (8th Cir. 1994); United States v. Prescott, 920 F.2d 139, 146 (2d Cir. 1990).
115. *See* United States v. Salava, 978 F.2d 320, 323 (7th Cir. 1992); United States v. Shlater, 85 F.3d 1251 (7th Cir. 1996).
116. United States v. Murdoch, 98 F.3d 472, 478 (9th Cir. 1996), *cert. denied*, 521 U.S. 1122 (1997)
117. *Id.* at 573–74.
118. 659 P.2d 488 (Wash. 1983).
119. Silver et al., *supra* note 33.
120. *Id.*
121. *See* Douglas Mossman, *Is Prosecution "Medically Appropriate"?*, 31 NEW ENG. J. ON CRIM. & CIV. CONFINEMENT 15, 57–58 n.188 (2005).
122. Grant H. Morris, *Placed in Purgatory: Conditional Release of Insanity Acquittees*, 39 ARIZ. L. REV. 1061, 1063 (1997).
123. Maura Caffrey, *A New Approach to Insanity Acquittee Recidivism: Redefining the Class of Truly Responsible Recidivists*, 154 U. PA. L. REV. 399, 423 n.127 (2005).
124. *E.g.*, Jones v. United States, 463 U.S. 354 (1983).
125. Richard Miraglia & Donna Hall, *The Effect of Length of Hospitalization on Re-Arrest Among Insanity Plea Acquittees*, 39 J. AM. ACAD. PSYCHIATRY & L. 524 (2011).
126. *Id.*
127. Randy Borum & Solomon M. Fulero, *Empirical Research on the Insanity Defense and Attempted Reforms: Evidence Toward Informed Policy*, 23 LAW & HUM. BEHAV. 375 (1999).
128. HENRY J. STEADMAN ET AL., BEFORE AND AFTER HINCKLEY: EVALUATING INSANITY DEFENSE REFORM 38 (1993).
129. Perlin, *supra* note 40, at 721; Steadman et al., *supra* note 131, at 44.
130. Blau & Pasewark, *supra* note 74, at 85.
131. GREENE & HEILBRUN, *supra* note 91, at 212.
132. Lucy Noble Inman, *Mental Impairment and Mens Rea: North Carolina Recognizes the Diminished Capacity Defense in* State v. Shank *and* State v. Rose, 67 N.C. L. REV. 1293, 1308–09 (1989).

133. *See* Stephen J. Morse, *Undiminished Confusion in Diminished Capacity*, 75 J. CRIM. L. & CRIMINOLOGY 1, 44 (1984).
134. Inman, *supra* note 135, at 1293.
135. Chesney E. Falk, *Comment, Criminal Law — State v. Phipps: The Tennessee Court of Criminal Appeals Accepts "Diminished Capacity" Evidence to Negate Mens Rea*, 26 U. MEM. L. REV. 373, 383 (1995).
136. Inman, *supra* note 135, at 1298.
137. State v. Phipps, 883 S.W.2d 138, 143 (Tenn. Crim. App. 1994).
138. *Phipps*, 883 S.W.2d at 143.
139. *Id.*; J. Thomas Sullivan, *The Culpability, or Mens Rea, "Defense" in Arkansas*, 53 ARK. L. REV. 805, 816 (2000).
140. Inman, *supra* note 135, at 1299.
141. *E.g.*, Stephen J. Morse, *Diminished Rationality, Diminished Responsibility*, 1 OHIO ST. J. CRIM. L. 289 (2003).
142. Jonas Robitscher & Andrew Ky Haynes, *In Defense of the Insanity Defense*, 31 EMORY L.J. 9, 26 n.66 (1982).
143. Jennifer Kunk Compton, Note, *Expert Witness Testimony and the Diminished Capacity Defense*, 20 AM. J. TRIAL ADVOC. 381, 386–87 (1997).
144. MODEL PENAL CODE § 210.6(4)(g); U.S. SENTENCING GUIDELINES MANUAL 5K2.13 (1998); *see also* Deborah E. Dezelan, *Departures from the Federal Sentencing Guidelines after* Koon v. United States: *More Discretion, Less Direction*, 72 NOTRE DAME L. REV. 1679, 1688–89 (1997).
145. Inman, *supra* note 135, at 1309.
146. *Id.*
147. *E.g.*, COLO. REV. STAT. § 18-1-803.
148. AM. BAR ASS'N, STANDARDS FOR CRIMINAL JUSTICE, CRIMINAL JUSTICE MENTAL HEALTH STANDARDS § 7-6.2 (1984).
149. Compton, *supra* note 146, at 388.
150. Clark v. Arizona, 548 U.S. 735 (2006).
151. *See* State v. Breakiron, 532 A.2d 199 (N.J. 1987).
152. State v. Galloway, 628 A.2d 735 (N.J. 1993).
153. People v. White, 117 Cal. App.3d 270, 172 Cal. Rptr. 612 (1981).
154. Inman, *supra* note 135, at 1309 (citing CAL. PENAL CODE § 28(a)-(b) (1988)).
155. Debra D. Burke & Mary Anne Nixon, *Post-Traumatic Stress Disorder and the Death Penalty*, 38 HOW. L.J. 183 (1994)/
156. Michael J. Davidson, Note, *Post-Traumatic Stress Disorder: A Controversial Defense for Veterans of a Controversial War*, 29 WM. & MARY L. REV. 415, 417–18 (1988).
157. *Id.*
158. Eric H. Marcus, *Post-Traumatic Stress Disorder: Facts and Myths*, 32 TRAUMA 49 (1990).
159. *See* Edgar Garcia-Rill & Erica Beecher-Monas, *Gatekeeping Stress: The Science and Admissibility of Post-Traumatic Stress Disorder*, 24 U. ARK. L. REV. 9 (2001).
160. Patricia J. Falk, *Novel Theories of Criminal Defense Based Upon the Toxicity of the Social Environment: Urban Psychosis, Television Intoxication, and Black Rage*, 74 N.C. L. REV. 731, 761 (1996).
161. Davidson, *supra* note 159, at 422.
162. 883 S.W.2d 138 (Tenn. Crim. App. 1994).
163. *Id.* at 141.
164. *Id.*
165. *Id.* at 149.
166. *E.g.*, Roger K. Pittman & Scott P. Orr, *Psychophysiologic Testing for Post-Traumatic Stress Disorder: Forensic Psychiatric Application*, 21 BULL. AM. ACAD. PSYCHIATRY L. 37, 39 (1993).
167. *E.g.*, Jonathan E. Sherin & Charles B. Nemeroff, *Post-Traumatic Stress Disorder: the Neurobiological Impact of Psychological Trauma*, 13 DIALOGUES IN CLIN. NEUROSCI. 263 (2011).
168. *See* Thomas L. Hafemeister & Nicole A. Stockey, *Last Stand? The Criminal Responsibility of War Veterans Returning from Iraq and Afghanistan with Posttraumatic Stress Disorder*, 85 IND. L.J. 87, 107–32 (2010).

169. *See* Michael L. Perlin, *I Expected It to Happen/I Knew He'd Lost Control": The Impact of PTSD on Criminal Sentencing After the Promulgation of DSM-5*, 2015 UTAH L. REV. 881 (2015).
170. 558 U.S. 30 (2009).
171. *Id.* at 44.
172. WILLIAM H. GRIER & PRICE M. COBBS, BLACK RAGE (1968).
173. Kimberly M. Copp, Note, *Black Rage: The Illegitimacy of a Criminal Defense*, 29 J. MARSHALL L. REV. 205, 229 (1995).
174. DSM-5, *supra* note 111, at 265–75.
175. Copp, *supra* note 176, at 233–34.
176. *See* PAUL HARRIS, BLACK RAGE CONFRONTS THE LAW 9, 19, 30–36, 86–111 (1997).
177. *See* John Alan Cohan, *Honor Killings and the Cultural Defense*, 40 CAL. W. INT'L L.J. 177 (2010).
178. *Id.* at 234–35.
179. *See* R. Lee Strasburger, Jr., *The Best Interests of the Child?: The Cultural Defense as Justification for Child Abuse*, 25 PACE INT'L L. REV. 161 (2013).
180. Cohan, *supra* note 180, at 232–39.
181. Falk, *supra* note 163, at 758–81; Christopher R. Engelhardt et al., *This Is Your Brain on Violent Video Games: Neural Desensitization to Violence Predicts Increased Aggression Following Violent Video Game Exposure*, 47 J. EXPERIMENTAL SOC. PSYCHOL. 1033 (2011).
182. *E.g.*, Gert Hald & Neil Malamuth, *Experimental Effects of Exposure to Pornography: The Moderating Effect of Personality and Mediating Effect of Sexual Arousal*, 44 ARCH. SEXUAL BEHAV. 99 (2015).
183. Long v. State, 517 So. 2d 664 (Fla. 1987), *cert. denied*, 486 U.S. 1017 (1988); Long v. State, 610 So. 2d 1276 (Fla. 1992).
184. Fradella, *supra* note 30, at 68–69 (citing Schiro v. Clark, 963 F.2d 962 (7th Cir. 1992), *aff'd*, 510 U.S. 222 (1994)).
185. Tufik Y. Shayeb, *Behavioral Genetics & Criminal Culpability: Addressing the Problem of Free Will in the Context of the Modern American Justice System*, 19 UDC-DCSL L. REV. 1, 44–46 (2016).
186. Deborah W. Denno, *Courts' Increasing Consideration of Behavioral Genetics Evidence in Criminal Cases: Results of a Longitudinal Study*, 2011 MICH. ST. L. REV. 967, 971–72 (2011).
187. *See generally* CATHERINE BAKER, BEHAVIORAL GENETICS (2004), https://www.aaas.org/page/behavioral-genetics-publications.
188. *Id.*; Laura A. Baker et al., *Behavioral Genetics: The Science of Antisocial Behavior*, 69 LAW & CONTEMP. PROBL. 7 (2008).
189. Denno, *supra* note 189, *passim*.
190. ARIZ. REV. STAT. § 13–502(A).
191. Shayeb, *supra* note 188, at 46–47.
192. *E.g.*, Nita A. Farahany & James E. Coleman Jr., *Genetics, Neuroscience and Criminal Responsibility*, *in* THE IMPACT OF BEHAVIORAL SCIENCES ON CRIMINAL LAW 183 (Nita Farahany ed., 2009).

CHAPTER 15

1. *See* MODEL PENAL CODE § 3.04(1).
2. MODEL PENAL CODE § 3.04(2)(a)(i).
3. *See generally* JOHN N. FERDICO ET AL., CRIMINAL PROCEDURE FOR THE CRIMINAL JUSTICE PROFESSIONAL (12th ed. 2015).
4. *See id.* at 259–71.
5. 6 AM. JUR. 2d *Assault and Battery* § 56 (2010).
6. *Id.*
7. 6 AM. JUR. 2d *Assault and Battery* § 57 (2010).
8. *See, e.g.*, State v. Southworth, 52 P.3d 987 (N.M. Ct. App. 2002).
9. 6 AM. JUR. 2d *Assault and Battery* § 50 (2010).
10. *See* State v. Basting, 572 N.W.2d 281 (Minn. 1997).

11. 6 AM. JUR. 2d *Assault and Battery* § 50 (2010).
12. 6 AM. JUR. 2d *Assault and Battery* § 51 (2010).
13. People v. Goetz, 497 N.E.2d 41 (N.Y. 1986).
14. 6 AM. JUR. 2d *Assault and Battery* § 55 (2010).
15. *Id.*
16. MODEL PENAL CODE § 3.04(2)(b).
17. *E.g.*, COLO. REV. STAT. 18-1-704(2)(c) (2003).
18. MODEL PENAL CODE § 3.04(2)(b)(ii).
19. *E.g.*, Westbrook v. State, 722 So. 2d 788 (Ala. Crim. App. 1998).
20. Stuart P. Green, *Castles and Carjackers: Proportionality and the Use of Deadly Force in Defense of Dwellings and Vehicles*, 1999 U. ILL. L. REV. 1, 14–15 (1999).
21. MODEL PENAL CODE § 3.06(3)(d)(i).
22. Justin F. Marceau, *Killing for Your Dog*, 83 GEO. WASH. L. REV. 943, 986–87 (2015).
23. GA. CODE ANN. § 16-3-24.1.
24. COLO. REV. STAT. 18-1-704(2)(b); 21 OKL. ST. ANN. § 1289.25.
25. *See* State v. Anderson, 972 P.2d 32 (Okla. Ct. Crim. App. 1998).
26. Ben Montgomery & Colleen Jenkins, *Five Years Since Florida Enacted "Stand-Your-Ground" Law, Justifiable Homicides Are Up*, TAMPA BAY TIMES (Oct. 15, 2010), http://www.tampabay.com/news/publicsafety/crime/five-years-since-florida-enacted-stand-your-ground-law-justifiable/1128317.
27. Tamara Rice Lave, *Shoot to Kill: A Critical Look at Stand Your Ground Laws*, 67 U. MIAMI L. REV. 827 (2013).
28. Berrios v. State, 781 So. 2d 455, 457 (Fla. Dist. Ct. App. 2001).
29. FLA. STAT. ANN. § 776.013(3).
30. *Id.*
31. Alexis M. Haddox, *The Ohio Castle Doctrine: Shielding Criminals with a Presumption of Self-Defense*, 41 CAP. U. L. REV. 1105 (2013).
32. Giffords L. Cntr. to Prevent Gun Violence, *Stand Your Ground Laws* (2017), http://lawcenter.giffords.org/gun-laws/policy-areas/guns-in-public/stand-your-ground-laws; AM. BAR ASS'N, FINAL REPORT AND RECOMMENDATIONS FROM THE NATIONAL TASK FORCE ON STAND YOUR GROUND LAWS (2015), http://www.americanbar.org/content/dam/aba/images/diversity/SYG_Report_Book.pdf.
33. Sara L. Ochs, *Can Louisiana's Self-Defense Law Stand Its Ground?: Improving the Stand Your Ground Law in the Murder Capital of America*, 59 LOYOLA L. REV. 673 (2013).
34. *Id.* at 686–87.
35. 6 AM. JUR. 2d *Assault and Battery* § 51 (2010).
36. MODEL PENAL CODE § 3.05(1).
37. 183 N.E.2d 319 (N.Y. 1962).
38. MODEL PENAL CODE § 3.06(1)(a).
39. MODEL PENAL CODE § 3.06(3)(a).
40. 526 P.2d 241 (Cal. 1974).
41. 183 N.W.2d 657 (Iowa 1971).
42. MODEL PENAL CODE § 3.06(3)(d)(i) similarly allows for deadly force to be used to protect one's real property (i.e., land) against someone who is trying to "dispossess" a homeowner of his or her dwelling other than under a legal claim of right to its possession.
43. 490 U.S. 386 (1989).
44. *Id.* at 396.
45. *Id.* at 397.
46. Brinegar v. United States, 338 U.S. 160, 175–76 (1949).
47. *See, e.g.*, Couden v. Duffy, 446 F.3d 483 (3d Cir. 2006).
48. MODEL PENAL CODE § 3.07(1).
49. *E.g.*, Papineau v. Parmley, 465 F.3d 46 (2d Cir. 2006); Smith v. District of Columbia, 882 A.2d 778 (D.C. 2005).

50. TENN. CODE ANN. § 40-7-108 (1982).
51. United States v. Brignoni-Ponce, 422 U.S. 873, 878 (1975).
52. *See* United States v. Mendenhall, 446 U.S. 544 (1980).
53. United States v. Ortiz, 422 U.S. 891, 895 (1975); Terry v. Ohio, 392 U.S. 1, 28–29 (1968).
54. *See, e.g.*, Schumann v. McGinn, 240 N.W.2d 525, 533 (1976).
55. *See, e.g.*, Enmund v. Florida, 458 U.S. 782 (1982); Coker v. Georgia, 433 U.S. 584 (1977).
56. *Carroll*, 267 U.S. at 158.
57. *See* FBI, UNIFORM CRIME REPORTS, CRIME IN THE UNITED STATES 1 (1984).
58. *See also* Solem v. Helm, 463 U.S. 277, 296–97, nn. 22 & 23 (1983).
59. 475 U.S. 312 (1986).
60. *Id.* at 321.
61. 503 U.S. 1 (1992).
62. Kinney v. Indiana Youth Center, 950 F.2d 462 (7th Cir. 1991).
63. 384 U.S. 757 (1966).
64. Missouri v. McNeely, 133 S. Ct. 1552 (2013).
65. 777 A.2d 301 (N.J. 2001).
66. Missouri v. McNeely, M569 U.S. 141 (2013).
67. 342 U.S. 165, 172 (1952).
68. 470 U.S. 753 (1985).
69. Ingraham v. Wright, 430 U.S. 651, 661 (1977).
70. Willis v. State, 888 N.E.2d 177, 182 (Ind. 2008).
71. *Willis*, 888 N.E.2d at 182.
72. *Id.*
73. LENORE E. WALKER, THE BATTERED WOMAN (1979) [hereinafter Walker I]. Walker's original theory was based on her clinical observations of abused women, not on empirical research. Walker's second book followed in 1984, offering empirical data in support of her theory. *See* LENORE E. WALKER, THE BATTERED WOMAN SYNDROME (1984)[hereinafter Walker II].
74. WALKER II, *supra* note 73, at 95–96.
75. *See* Martin E.P. Seligman, et al., *Alleviation of Learned Helplessness in the Dog*, 73 J. ABNORMAL PSYCHOL. 256 (1968).
76. MARTIN E.P. SELIGMAN, HELPLESSNESS: ON DEPRESSION, DEVELOPMENT, AND DEATH(1975); Lyn Y. Abramson et al., *Learned Helplessness in Humans: Critique and Reformulation*, 87 J. ABNORMAL PSYCHOL. 49, 50 (1978).
77. WALKER II, *supra* note 73, at 31, 33–34.
78. *Id.* at 96.
79. *Id.* at 87.
80. Tosha Yvette Foster, Note, *From Fear to Rage: Black Rage as a Natural Progression from and Functional Equivalent of Battered Woman Syndrome*, 38 WM. & MARY L. REV. 1851, 1859 (1997).
81. David L. Faigman & Amy J. Wright, *The Battered Woman Syndrome in the Age of Science*, 39 ARIZ. L. REV. 67, 68 (1997).
82. EDWARD W. GONDOLF & ELLEN R. FISHER: BATTERED WOMEN AS SURVIVORS: AN ALTERNATIVE TO TREATING LEARNED HELPLESSNESS (1988).
83. EDWARD W. GONDOLF & ELLEN R. FISHER: BATTERED WOMEN AS SURVIVORS: AN ALTERNATIVE TO TREATING LEARNED HELPLESSNES 4, 87–88 (1988)
84. MICHAEL P. JOHNSON, A TYPOLOGY OF DOMESTIC VIOLENCE: INTIMATE TERRORISM, VIOLENT RESISTANCE, AND SITUATIONAL COUPLE VIOLENCE 49 (2008).
85. Elizabeth Vaughn & Maureen L. Moore, *The Battered Spouse Defense in Kentucky*, 10 N. KY. L. REV. 399, 399 (1983).
86. Roberta K. Thyfault, Comment, *Self-Defense: Battered Woman Syndrome on Trial*, 20 CAL. W. L. REV. 485, 495 (1984).

87. *See generally* John W. Roberts, *Between the Heat of Passion and Cold Blood: Battered Woman's Syndrome As an Excuse for Self-defense in Non-confrontational Homicide*, 27 LAW & PSYCHOL. REV. 135, 136–37 (2003).
88. Mary Ann Dutton, *Understanding Women's Responses to Domestic Violence: A Redefinition of Battered Woman Syndrome*, 21 HOFSTRA L. REV. 1191, 1199–1200 (1993); Brett C. Trowbridge, *The Admissibility of Expert Testimony in Washington on Post Traumatic Stress Disorder and Related Trauma Syndromes: Avoiding the Battle of the Experts by Restoring the Use of Objective Psychological Testimony in the Courtroom*, 27 SEATTLE U. L. REV. 453, 517–18 (2003).
89. Jane Campbell Moriarty, *"While Dangers Gather": The Bush Preemption Doctrine, Battered Women, Imminence, and Anticipatory Self-Defense*, 30 N.Y.U. REV. L. & SOC. CHANGE 1, 20 (2006).
90. *E.g.*, Trowbridge, *supra* note 88, at 495; Joshua Dressler, *Battered Women and Sleeping Abusers: Some Reflections*, 3 OHIO ST. J. CRIM. L. 457 (2006).
91. Moriarty, *supra* note 89, at 20; *see also* Faigman & Wright, *supra* note 81, at 81.
92. State v. Kelly, 478 A.2d 364, 377 (N.J. 1984); Ibn-Tamas v. United States, 407 A.2d 626, 634 (D.C. 1979).
93. State v. Stewart, 763 P.2d 572 (Kan. 1988); *see also* State v. Norman, 324 N.C. 253, 378 S.E.2d 8, 12 (N.C. 1989); Commonwealth v. Grove, 363 Pa. Super. 328, 526 A.2d 369, 373 (Pa. Super. Ct. 1987).
94. State v. Gallegos, 719 P.2d 1268 (N.M. App. 1986).
95. *Id.* at 1273.
96. *Id.* at 1271.
97. 166 A.3d 1044, 1059 (Md. 2017).
98. *Id.* at 1060.
99. *Id.* at 1061–62. *But see* People v. Yaklich, 833 P.2d 758, 763 (Colo. App. 1991); State v. Anderson, 785 S.W.2d 596, 600 (Mo. Ct. App. 1990); State v. Leaphart, 673 S.W.2d 870, 873 (Tenn. Crim. App. 1983).
100. *Id.* at 164 (citing Christian v. State, 951 A.2d 832 (2008)).
101. ELIZABETH BOCHNAK, WOMEN'S SELF-DEFENSE CASES: THEORY AND PRACTICE 29 (1981); CYNTHIA GILLESPIE, JUSTIFIABLE HOMICIDE: BATTERED WOMEN, SELF-DEFENSE, AND THE LAW 76 (1989).
102. Cara Cookson, *Confronting Our Fear: Legislating Beyond Battered Woman Syndrome and the Law of Self-defense in Vermont*, 34 VT. L. REV. 415, 421 (2009) (quoting ROBBIN S. OGLE & SUSAN JACOBS, SELF-DEFENSE AND BATTERED WOMEN WHO KILL 51 (2002)).
103. Faigman & Wright, *supra* note 81, at 95.
104. In re Glenn G., 587 N.Y.S.2d 464 (Fam. Ct. 1992), *aff'd*, 630 N.Y.S.2d 348 (N.Y. App. Div.), *leave to app. denied*, 662 N.E.2d 791 (N.Y. 1995).
105. United States v. Marenghi, 893 F. Supp. 85, 90 (D. Me. 1995).
106. *E.g.*, OLA W. BARNETT & ALYEE D. LAVOLETTE, IT COULD HAPPEN TO ANYONE: WHY BATTERED WOMEN STAY 105–07 (1993); Regina A. Schuller & Neil Vidmar, *Battered Woman Syndrome Evidence in the Courtroom: A Review of the Literature*, 16 LAW & HUM. BEHAV. 273, 280 (1992).
107. *E.g.*, Mary Ann Dutton, *Understanding Women's Responses to Domestic Violence: A Redefinition of Battered Woman Syndrome*, 21 HOFSTRA L. REV. 1191, 1196 (1993).
108. *See, e.g.*, Hill v. State, 507 So. 2d 554, 555 (Ala. Crim. App. 1986); Buhrle v. State, 627 P.2d 1374, 1377 (Wyo. 1981).
109. *See, e.g.*, United States v. Brown, 891 F. Supp. 1501 (D. Kan. 1995).
110. Dutton, *supra* note 107, at 1202.
111. *See* People v. Aris, 264 Cal. Rptr. 167 (Ct. App. 1989); Knock v. Knock, 621 A.2d 267 (Conn. 1993); Ibn-Tamas v. United States, 407 A.2d 626 (D.C. 1979); Hawthorne v. State, 408 So. 2d 801 (Fla. Ct. App. 1982); Smith v. State, 277 S.E.2d 678 (Ga. 1981); People v. Minnis, 455 N.E.2d 209 (Ill. App. Ct. 1983); State v. Green, 652 P.2d 697 (Kan. 1982); State v. Anaya, 438 A.2d 892 (Me. 1981); State v. Hennum, 441 N.W.2d 793 (Minn. 1989); State v. Kelly, 478 A.2d 364 (N.J. 1984); State v. Gallegos, 719 P.2d 1268 (N.M. 1986); State v. Leidholm, 334 N.W.2d 811 (N.D. 1983); Commonwealth v. Stonehouse, 555 A.2d 772 (Pa. 1989); State v. Wilkins, 407 S.E.2d 670 (S.C. 1991); State v. Furlough, 797 S.W.2d 631 (Tenn. 1990); Fielder v. State, 756 S.W.2d 309 (Tex. 1988); State v. Allery, 682 P.2d 312 (Wash. 1984).
112. State v. Curley, 250 So. 3d 236 (La. 2018).

113. 382 P.2d 991 (Wyo. 1984).
114. *Id.* at 1040.
115. In re Appeal in Maricopa County, 182 Ariz. 60, 893 P.2d 60 (Ariz. Ct. App. 1994); State v. MacLennan, 702 N.W.2d 219 (Minn. 2005); State v. Nemeth, 694 N.E.2d 1332 (Ohio 1998); Perryman v. State, 990 P.2d 900 (Okla. Crim. App. 1999).
116. *See* Denise Bricker, *Fatal Defense: An Analysis of Battered Woman's Syndrome Expert Testimony for Gay Men and Lesbians Who Kill Abusive Partners*, 58 BROOK. L. REV. 1379 (1993).
117. FLA. R. CRIM. P. 3.201; MD. CODE ANN., *Cts & Jud. Proc.* § 10–916; MO. ANN. STAT. § 563.033; S.C. CODE ANN. § 17-23-170.
118. Ruthann Robinson, *Lavender Bruises: Intra-Lesbian Violence, Law and Lesbian Legal Theory*, 20 GOLDEN GATE U. L. REV. 567, 574 (2010).
119. *Annual Review Article: Domestic Violence*, 19 GEO. J. GENDER & L. 266, 248 (2018).
120. David Olinger, *Colorado Gun Laws Afford Rights to Those Shooting in Self-Defense*, DENVER POST (July 29, 2013), http://www.denverpost.com/2013/07/29/colorado-gun-laws-afford-rights-to-those-shooting-in-self-defense/.
121. *Id.*
122. People v. Guyton, 30 N.E.3d 1062, 1068–69 (Ill. App. 2014).
123. Christopher Kopacz & Elena Penick, *The Double-Edge Sword of Victim Survival: Imperfect Self Defense*, 29 CHI. BAR ASS'N RECORD 32, 34 (2015).
124. 550 U.S. 372 (2007).

Case Index

Subject Index

Tables are indicated by *t* following the page number